THE COASTS OF

BOHEMIA

THE COASTS OF

BOHEMIA

A CZECH HISTORY

Derek Sayer

Translations from the Czech by Alena Sayer

PRINCETON UNIVERSITY PRESS · PRINCETON, NEW JERSEY

COPYRIGHT © 1998 BY PRINCETON UNIVERSITY PRESS

PUBLISHED BY PRINCETON UNIVERSITY PRESS, 41 WILLIAM STREET,

PRINCETON, NEW JERSEY 08540

IN THE UNITED KINGDOM: PRINCETON UNIVERSITY PRESS,

CHICHESTER, WEST SUSSEX

SIXTH PRINTING, AND FIRST PAPERBACK PRINTING, 2000

PAPERBACK ISBN 0-691-05052-X

THE LIBRARY OF CONGRESS HAS CATALOGED THE CLOTH EDITION OF THIS BOOK AS FOLLOWS

SAYER, DEREK.

THE COASTS OF BOHEMIA : A CZECH HISTORY / DEREK SAYER ;

TRANSLATIONS FROM THE CZECH BY ALENA SAYER.

P.   CM.

INCLUDES BIBLIOGRAPHICAL REFERENCES AND INDEX.

ISBN 0-691-05760-5 (CLOTH : ALK. PAPER)

1. BOHEMIA (CZECH REPUBLIC)—HISTORY.   2. CZECH REPUBLIC–HISTORY.

I. TITLE.

DB2063.S28   1998

943.71—DC21   97-41418

THIS BOOK HAS BEEN COMPOSED IN BERKELEY BOOK

THE PAPER USED IN THIS PUBLICATION

MEETS THE MINIMUM REQUIREMENTS OF

ANSI/NISO Z39.48-1992 (R1997)

(*PERMANENCE OF PAPER*)

HTTP://PUP.PRINCETON.EDU

PRINTED IN THE UNITED STATES OF AMERICA

9   10

ISBN-13: 978-0-691-05052-2 (pbk.)

ISBN-10: 0-691-05052-X (pbk.)

LADISLAVU BORŮVKOVI

který s českým národem žil, prožil a přežil,

1914-1996

CONTENTS

MAPS AND ILLUSTRATIONS

Maps

Illustrations

ACKNOWLEDGMENTS

Without funding from the Social Sciences and Humanities Research Council of Canada and a period of study leave from the University of Alberta that enabled me to spend eighteen months researching in Prague in 1991–93, this book would never have got off the ground. I also owe thanks to the University of Alberta for awarding me a McCalla Research Professorship in 1994–95 which substantially freed up time for writing, and to its Central Research Fund for financing a second trip to Prague during that year. Earlier versions of some passages in this book have appeared in articles in *METU Studies in Development* (Ankara) and *Past and Present*, and a longer version of the introduction was delivered and subsequently published as the 1997 Kaspar Naegele Memorial Lecture at the University of British Columbia, Vancouver.

I also have more personal debts to acknowledge. When I arrived in Prague in 1991, Professor Jiří Musil put the facilities of the Sociological Institute of the (then) Czechoslovak Academy of Sciences at my disposal and did all he could to facilitate my access to other institutions. Another generous host in those early months was František (Fanda) Smutný, of the Institute of Physics of the Czechoslovak Academy of Sciences. He helped us settle in, gave me a guided tour of Vyšehrad Cemetery, and best of all, took me to hear Smetana's *Má vlast* in Obecní dům on the opening night of the Prague Spring Festival, so that, in his words, I could "relive our nineteenth century." We argued frequently about Czech history. I wish he were still alive to read this book, and we could argue some more. Later, I worked mostly in the library of the Museum of the City of Prague. Jan Jungmann provided me with copies of many historic photographs from the museum's archive, some of which are reproduced in this book. My greatest debt at the City Museum is to *paní* Věra Beňová. A superbly informative guide to her rich collections, she also kept me amply plied with coffee and conversation, patiently putting up with my less than perfect Czech. After I returned to Canada, she responded to my many requests for photocopies, catalogues, and newly published books, often, I suspect, on her own time. I have learned much through her knowledge, but I will always remember her best for her unfailing kindness.

I met with similar consideration from many other librarians, curators, and archivists in Prague: *paní* Černá at the National Library; *paní* Marcela Hojdová at the Scientific Information Division of the National Gallery; Dr. Kybalová, Director of the Jewish Museum; and staff at the Museum of Arts and Crafts, the National Museum, the Institute for the Theory and History of Literature, the Graphic Art Collection of the National Gallery, and elsewhere. At the National Literature Museum a kind gentleman gave me an advance viewing of an exhibition on Karel Čapek and PEN, since otherwise, having to fly back to Canada the next day, I would miss it, which would be a pity. John Wall of the Bodleian Library, Oxford, drew my attention to several box-files of unsorted Czech exhibition catalogues which he had safeguarded after 1968, fearing they might otherwise disappear from history. I am equally grateful to the owners and staff of numerous Prague secondhand bookstores, notably Jiří Lukas at the Antikvariát u Prašné brány on Celetná ulice, who contrived to find me Lamač and Padrta's long-sold-out *Osma a Skupina* and the first two volumes of Karel Teige's *Selected Writings*, no mean feat since most copies of the second of these had been pulped in 1969.

Another who supplied me with valuable materials, among them the collections *Avantgarda* and *Poetismus* and several volumes of *Tvorba*, was my late friend Anna Rossová. Part-Czech, part-Hungarian, part-Jewish, Anna spent her childhood colonizing Podkarpatská Rus, her adolescence in wartime Hungary where she somehow managed to evade the transports. As a young woman she was one of those burning communists Milan Kundera so eloquently writes about, filled with zeal to make the awful Europe she had grown up in a better place. In the fifties she was an editor for the State Publishing House for Political Literature and later Odeon, with responsibility, among other things, for the collected works of Egon Erwin Kisch. Finding herself on the wrong side in 1968, she made the mistake of describing the invasion as a tragedy for Czechoslovak-Soviet relations and duly lost her party card. It *was* a tragedy for her because she *was* a communist. Yet she persisted in referring to the island in the Vltava opposite the National Theater, which had been renamed Slav Island before she was born, by its old Habsburg name of Sophia's Island. Anna welcomed the Velvet Revolution of 1989 with decidedly mixed feelings. She lamented the Americanization of her beloved Prague. But she welcomed us unreservedly. One of her stories that has made its way into this book is that of the National Artist Max Švabinský, his famous portrait of Julius Fučík, and a van-load of French burgundy.

My daughter Miranda will always remember Zdenička, her first teacher at the Troja *mateřská školka*. A father of one of Natasha's school friends in Troja, whom I knew only by his first name of Ota, one day brought me yellowing forty-year-old copies of *Rudé právo* on the Slánský trial saved by his mother because, he said, he wanted the story to be told. Blanka Kuttmannová was a good friend, poking gentle fun at my struggles with Czech (*není žádná blbka!*). Our neighbor in the villa on Povltavská, whom I shall always think of as *paní Hájková* but was permitted, after a year or so as *pan profesor*, to call Marie, was and is the very soul of kindness. On my second trip to Prague in 1994, she had good Czech beer ready for my arrival, fed me good Czech food, and generally was a good *česká maminka*. When I found myself writing at greater length than I had originally planned about the inescapable Zdeněk Nejedlý, she immediately sent me his six-volume *History of Hussite*

Song and other writings, lugging the heavy package—she is over seventy now—by tram to the post office.

In Ostrava our friends Marie (Miki) and Ivan Voráček and their children Bob and Hanička have gone in search of newly published books for us on numerous occasions. Miki's and my long-running conversation on homes and homelands will, I suspect, never come to a conclusion. My wife's parents Ladislav and Lenka Borůvka and brother Jan have facilitated this project in ways too various and multiple to enumerate. It is not just the regular, invaluable flow of books, magazines, catalogues, and newspapers across the Atlantic, without which this book would have been very much the poorer. The last time I saw—or will ever see—my father-in-law, we had a long discussion about F. X. Šalda's article "The Age of Iron and Fire." By then *tata* was over eighty.

Gerald Aylmer, Nanci Langford, and Yoke-Sum Wong were kind enough to read and comment on earlier drafts of this book. I hope Gerald will be reassured by my attempts to provide more by way of socioeconomic background than in the version he first read. Yoke-Sum will recognize her suggestions for the introduction. My old friend Gavin Williams thought up the subtitle. My editor at Princeton University Press, Mary Murrell, has been unreservedly supportive of this project throughout, even when I delivered a manuscript totally different from the book on Prague I was under contract to write (and still hope to turn to next). Don Cooper and Louise Asselstine of the Department of Art and Design at the University of Alberta shot most of the photographs from which the illustrations were prepared. I must thank Ron Whistance-Smith too, for orienting me to the changing coasts of Bohemia in his aptly named William C. Wonders map room.

Finally to Alena. My wife is as responsible for the research on which this book is based as I am. She trawled Prague libraries and bookstores daily for eighteen months. Much of what I comment on here she turned up. In Prague and then back in Canada, she read and worked with the huge archive we had accumulated. A lot of what is in these pages, large and small, originated with her, ideas and interpretations as much as details and facts. She saved me more often than I care to recall from the kind of presumptions and errors, linguistic and otherwise, that foreigners are prone to make. She scrupulously checked all references and citations, a huge task. All translations from Czech sources in this book, except for passages taken from works previously published in English and cited in that form, are hers. Part of her would have preferred not to have spent the last six years of our lives immersed in so personal a past at all. But the other part, like Ota in Troja, wanted the story to be told.

Coronado, Alberta
July 1997

A NOTE ON CZECH PRONUNCIATION

Since there are many Czech names in this book, some indication as to how to pronounce them may be helpful. Written Czech is mostly phonetic, and (unlike in English) letters are pronounced consistently in the same way wherever they occur. Diacritical marks either lengthen the vowel (as in a, á) or change the sound altogether (as in c, č). Stress is usually on the first syllable of a word.

The following is a rough guide: other letters are sounded more or less as they are in English.

a is between the a in bat and the u in but
á is like the a in car
c is like the ts in bats
č is like the ch in church
ď is like the d in dune
e is like the e in end
é is like the ea in pear
ě is like the ye in yet
ch (treated as a single letter) is like the ch in the Scottish loch
i is like the i in bit
í is like the ee in beet
j is like the y in yet, *never* like the English j as in jet
ň is like the ni in onion
q is pronounced kv
r is rolled, as in Scottish English
ř has no English equivalent; it sounds like a combination of a rolled r and the sound ž, as in the name of the composer Antonín Dvořák
š is like the sh in ship
ť is like the t in tune
u is like the oo in foot
ú and ů are like the oo in moon
w is pronounced like an English v
y is identical in sound to i
ý is identical in sound to í
ž is like the s in leisure

When followed by i or í, the letters d, n, and t are pronounced like ď, ň, and ť.

The dipthong ou combines the Czech o and u in sequence, sounding something like the oa combination in boat, *not* like the ou in round or ounce.

As a rule, all letters in Czech are sounded separately (an exception is the j in *jsem*, meaning "I am," which is seldom vocalized). The name Palacký is thus pronounced Pal-ats-kee, *not* Pal-a-kee.

THE COASTS OF

BOHEMIA

Identity. 1. The quality or condition of being the same in substance, composition, nature, properties, or in particular qualities under consideration; absolute or essential sameness; oneness. 2. The sameness of a person or thing at all times or in all circumstances; the condition or fact that a person or thing is itself and not something else; individuality, personality.

The Oxford English Dictionary

In our country everything is forever being remade: beliefs, buildings and street names. Sometimes the progress of time is concealed and at others feigned, so long as nothing remains as real and truthful testimony.

Ivan Klíma, *Love and Garbage*

BEARINGS

T HOU ART perfect then our ship hath touched upon the deserts of Bohemia?" asks Antigonus in act 3, scene 3, of William Shakespeare's *The Winter's Tale* (1609–10).[1] Czechs are inclined to see Shakespeare's furnishing of their country with a coastline as a typical example of foreigners' ignorance of their land, which was to reach its shameful nadir in British Prime Minister Neville Chamberlain's description of Czechoslovakia in 1938 as "a faraway country" inhabited by quarreling peoples "of whom we know nothing."[2] Such flights of geographic fancy can rankle with those unlucky enough to have to suffer their consequences; Chamberlain was distancing the Czech lands from the known world in order to justify his acquiescence in Adolf Hitler's carving them up. Shakespeare, however, was probably doing no more than signaling that the second part of his fable was set in an imagined Arcadia, a realm of youth and innocence located at the opposite moral pole from the world-weariness, sophistication, and decadence of the equally fictionalized Sicilian court in which the play begins. The title *The Winter's Tale*, according to the editors of *The Oxford Shakespeare*, would have "prepared his audiences for a tale of romantic improbability, one to be wondered at rather than believed."[3]

Later, Bohemia acquired rather different, if no less romantic connotations in Western European languages. The Bohemia of Puccini's opera *La Bohème*, which premiered in Turin in 1896, is an unheated Parisian garret in the Latin Quarter around the year 1830, where live a poet, a painter, a philosopher, and a musician who defy poverty for the sake of art and buck proprieties for the love of seamstresses and shopgirls. *The Oxford English Dictionary* gives the first meaning of "Bohemian" as "an inhabitant of Bohemia," a name that comes from the German [*Böhmen*] rather than the Czech word [*Čechy*] for this land. The German expression "*Das sind mir böhmische Dörfer*" translates, roughly, as "It's all Greek to me." Czechs would convey the same sentiment with the expression "*Je to pro mě španělská vesnice*," signifying incomprehensibility by Spanish rather than Bohemian hamlets. The nineteenth-century extension of the sense of Bohemian to mean "a gypsy of society . . . despising conventionalities generally," first introduced into English by Thackeray, derives from an earlier use of the word, which was already current in French in the fifteenth century and had certainly entered English by the seventeenth. The *Dictionary* gives the second meaning of Bohemian as "a gypsy." Apparently when gypsies first entered western Europe—to be politically correct, we should call them by their own name of the Rom, but it is as gypsies that they were known then and for centuries after—"they were thought to have come from Bohemia, or perhaps actually entered the West through that country." One of the characters in Walter Scott's *Quentin* (1823) says of himself: "I am a Zingaro, a Bohemian, an Egyptian, or whatever the Europeans . . . may choose to call me; but I have no country."[4]

In his celebrated cubist poem "Zone" (1912), a work alive with immediacies and simultaneities, Guillaume Apollinaire too situates Bohemia somewhere beyond the Europe where modernity happens, identifying its capital city by the agates in Saint Vitus's Cathedral and the long climb up to Hradčany Castle rather than the bellowing buses, billboards, and pretty stenographers on their way to and from work with which he conjures up contemporary Paris. It is not that early twentieth-century Prague was short of trams, typists, or hoardings plastered with posters. Photographs of the Old Town Square taken then make it appear very much more modern than it does now. The renaissance sgraffiti on the House at the Minute, where Franz Kafka lived briefly as a child, had not yet been exposed, the facade on the House at the Stone Bell was prosaically baroque rather than spectacularly medieval, the neo-Gothic wing of the Old Town Hall, erected in the 1840s, was still standing. Tramlines cut through what is today a cobbled pedestrian precinct. In a competition for remodeling the Old Town Hall held in 1909, the architect Josef Gočár thought nothing of submitting a plan in which the medieval buildings would be dwarfed by a glittering skyscraper.[5] Gočár's nearby department store "At the Black Mother of God," a cubist masterpiece that sits cheek by jowl with the baroque palaces and burgher townhouses of Celetná ulice,[6] was completed in the same year as Apollinaire's "Zone" was published. But it is not these novelties that seized the poet's imagination. He dissociates Bohemia from European time as emphatically as Walter Scott severs it from European space, freezing Prague as a place where "the hands on the clock in the Jewish Quarter run backward."[7] It is an ironic choice of metaphor. By 1912 the Jewish Town Hall, on which this clock is situated, was one of the very few medieval buildings in the old ghetto to have survived the "slum clearance" of the previous two decades, a frenzied auto-da-fé fueled equally by the rationalities of modernist planning and the rapacities of capitalist speculation.

The Bohemia of these quotations—that from Neville Chamberlain included—evidently belongs on the same map as Atlantis, El Dorado, and King Solomon's mines. Its location is not that of the medieval kingdom of Bohemia, an old European state centered on the Czech lands of Bohemia and Moravia, which survived as a legal fiction until 1918 as part of the Austro-Hungarian monarchy and has since formed the heartland of a procession of polities with varying borders, populations, and ideological facades: the Czechoslovak Republic, Czecho-Slovakia, the Protectorate of Bohemia and Moravia, the Czechoslovak Republic (restored), the Czechoslovak Socialist Republic, the Czechoslovak Federal Republic, and latterly the Czech Repub-

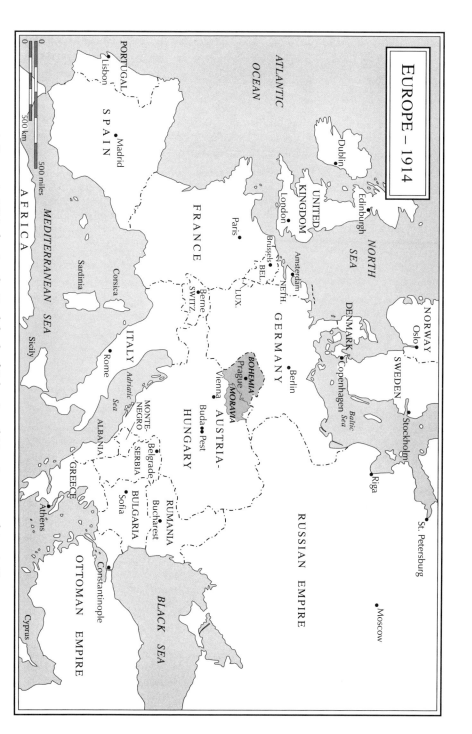

i. Europe in 1914, showing the Czech lands of Bohemia and Moravia as part of Austria-Hungary

lic. Its time is not that of European history, and in particular, of European modernity. But since there *is* a real Bohemia, and the real and the imaginary have a habit of getting hopelessly intertwined, it is worth taking stock of where, for some centuries, Bohemia has been situated in Western imaginations. Not only has it been pastoralized, as with Shakespeare, and romanticized, as by Puccini, Apollinaire, and countless others. It has also been Orientalized, translated to that timeless East where they have plentiful mysteries and abundant antiquities and altogether lack histories. Walter Scott semantically equates Bohemian and Egyptian (of which the word "gypsy" is a corruption, Romanies having been mistakenly assumed to have originated in Egypt), and does not count Bohemians as "Europeans" at all. *The Oxford English Dictionary* does not go quite this far. It does, however, place Bohemia firmly outside the bounds of "the West," wherever that may be. Chamberlain is less specific in his conceptual geography; but faraway is faraway. Prague is clearly closer in his mind to Isfahan or Samarkand than it is to the Paris of Monsieur Daladier, the Rome of Signor Mussolini, or the Berlin of Herr Hitler.

The iron curtain which bisected the old continent after 1945 powerfully reinforced this extrusion of Bohemia from "Europe," "the West," and "modernity"—from both sides. In some ways, indeed, Bohemia may have been less remote to English speakers in Shakespeare's time than it has become since. In the fifteenth century, *The Oxford English Dictionary* tells us, one meaning of the word "Bohemian" was "a follower of John Huss [Jan Hus], a Bohemian Protestant." John Foxe's *Acts and Monuments of the English Martyrs* (1563), which Queen Elizabeth I caused to be placed beside the pulpit in every parish church in her realm, devotes a long chapter to Hus. It situates him in the straight line of Protestant descent from John Wyclif to Martin Luther and gives an informed and informative account of his trial and burning as a heretic in 1415 at the hands of the Council of Konstanz.[8] In 1626, three years after *The Winter's Tale* was printed in Shakespeare's first folio, the renowned English cartographer John Speed published an accurate and very beautiful map of "Bohemia, Newly Described," bordered by colored engravings of Prague, "the court of the Emperor," and native inhabitants, grouped by sex and estate, in representative costume. It shows neither deserts nor a seashore.[9] It was an engraving by the Czech artist and onetime drawing instructor of the future English king Charles II, Václav Hollar (1607–77), one of a long series of his London views, that allowed Shakespeare's Globe Theatre to be rebuilt on its original Southwark site on the south bank of the Thames in the 1990s.

The slogan on which Civic Forum won the first postcommunist Czech elections in 1990 was, rather poignantly, "Back into Europe!" What this might mean only time will tell. But it is probably safe to say that Bohemia remains, for the English-speaking world, a faraway country. What we do know, for the most part, are its romantic improbabilities. We are familiar with Prague's Wenceslas Square, because CNN has brought us images of hundreds of candles flickering beneath Saint Václav's statue in November 1989 and the unforgettably sentimental sight of Alexander Dubček and Václav Havel embracing on the Melantrich balcony to the roars of the thousands below. Those of us of a certain age will recall the "Prague Spring" of 1968— and as likely as not associate it, in a haze of nostalgia, with *les evénements* in Paris that year when students took to the streets with the slogan "Be realists, demand the impossible!", with anti–Vietnam War demonstrations and the police riot at the Democratic National Convention in Chicago, with Country Joe and the Fish and Sergeant Pepper's Lonely Hearts Club Band. Today's Bohemia is a fairy-tale land where velvet revolutions sweep philosopher-playwrights into Kafkan castles, leaving not a pane of glass shattered in their wake. Prague, as described not so long ago in *The New York Times Magazine*, is "the Left Bank of the nineties." If so—and there are so many young Americans in Prague these days that they have their own English-language newspaper, *The Prague Post*—this only confirms that Bohemia is less "back in Europe" than a continuing projection of the Western imagination. Having wandered the world, the figurative Bohemia has finally superimposed itself upon its literal archetype, to the bemusement and sometimes the annoyance of the indigenous populace. A generation ago, Americans of a similar age and inclination would have been hitting the hippie trail to Kathmandu.

Of course, there is a specialized academic literature in English on Czech history and culture. But it is scarcely plentiful—we have an abundance of scholarly histories of Paris or Vienna but nothing remotely comparable on Prague—and its impact is for the most part confined within the professional ghetto of "Slavic Studies." It is esoteric knowledge, walled away behind impenetrable languages and unfathomable cultures, like other Orientalisms. It is therefore not thought an affront to the canons of scholarship that a recent 760-page biography of Franz Kafka, the most famous of all modern Bohemians (in Western eyes), should cite not a single source in Czech, even though Kafka himself was fluent in Czech and lived virtually his whole life in a city that was by then around 94 percent Czech-speaking.[10] It is acceptable for the Museum of Modern Art in New York to stage what it calls a "comprehensive" retrospective show on "Dada, Surrealism, and Their Heritage," whose extensive catalogue contains not one reference to Prague or the Czechoslovak Surrealist Group in its text, its very detailed chronology, or its bibliography.[11] It happens that one of the first surrealist exhibitions to be staged anywhere in the world outside France took place in 1932 in Prague. Entitled "Poesie 1932," the show was organized by the Czech art society SVU Mánes and contained 155 exhibits. On sale were paintings and sculptures by Hans Arp, Salvador Dalí, Max Ernst, Alberto Giacometti, Georgio De Chirico, Paul Klee, André Masson, Joan Miró, Wolfgang Paalen, and Yves Tanguy, alongside a group of "negro sculptures" and the works of Czech artists of whom, nowadays, few in "the West" have heard: Šíma, Muzika, Wachsmann, Makovský, Toyen, Štyrský.[12]

A collection of texts entitled *The Tradition of Constructivism*, first published by Viking Press of New York in 1974 and issued in paperback in 1990 in a series entitled Documents of Twentieth-Century Art, is unusual in that side by side with writings by El Lissitzky and Theo van Doesburg it does include a single Czech contribution, the editorial from the first issue of the Prague avant-garde magazine *Disk* (1923).[13] One of *Disk*'s editors is said to have been a Kurt Seifert; in fact, it was the poet Jaroslav Seifert, who sixty years later won the Nobel Prize in literature. The proclamation is headed "*Obraz*" (Picture). Beneath the title is the single word "Štyrský," which clearly puzzled the translator. A footnote informs us that "this is the adjectival form of Štyrsko, a region in North Bohemia under the Austro-Hungarian Empire," without giving us the faintest clue as to why the name of such a region should pop up at the head of this modernist manifesto. A Dadaist gesture, we might think. But it is simply the name of the painter Jindřich Štyrský, the author of the proclamation, an artist of whose existence, evidently, neither the translator nor the editor of the collection had an inkling.

"I hate pictures as I do the snobs who buy them out of a longing for individuality," Štyrský says, "so that between four walls of their aesthetic furniture they can sigh before them in armchairs (á la Matisse!)." A picture should be "a living advertisement and project of a new life, a product of life, ALL THE REST IS KITSCH!" Štyrský, who lived in Paris from 1925 to 1928, participated in the 1925 international exhibition "*L'art aujourd'hui*" and went on to have two independent Parisian shows of his work (together with that of his compatriot Toyen) in 1926 and 1927; the French surrealist poet Philippe Soupault supplied a foreword to the catalogue for the latter.[14] Both Štyrský and Toyen were later represented in what is perhaps the most famous of all surrealist shows, the International Exposition of Surrealism at the Galerie Beaux-Arts in Paris of January and February 1938.[15] As for the irrelevant Štýrsko, as it is correctly spelled in Czech, with an accented long ý—or in English, Styria—we are once again in the realm of flexible geographies. Austro-Hungarian imperial maps place this dukedom and Habsburg crown land nowhere near north Bohemia but some hundreds of kilometers south, straddling what is today the border between Austria and Slovenia, the most northerly successor state to what we have become accustomed to call the former Yugoslavia. But there can be few Czech émigrés who have not had that embarrassing conversation which runs:

"Where do you come from?"
"Czechoslovakia."
"Oh, Yugoslavia. I've been there."

What is at issue here is more than simply ignorance. It is a question, rather, of the vantage points from which knowledge is constructed. Yes, we "know" Alfons Mucha—though how many of us think of him as a Frenchman?—and Leoš Janáček, Franz Kafka and (maybe) Jaroslav Hašek, Miloš Forman and Milan Kundera. But our knowledge of them is uncontexted. Or more accurately, it is recontexted in a landscape whose features are familiar to *us*. Mucha is situated with reference to the English Arts and Crafts Movement and the Vienna Secession, not to his Czech forebears Josef Mánes and Mikoláš Aleš, and his art remains visible at all only for that decade or so in which he was illuminated by the brilliant electric lights of the 1900 Paris World Exhibition. The name of Václav Havel brings to mind other modern secular saints like Mahatma Gandhi and Martin Luther King, not a Prague dynasty of urban developers and film moguls, one of the richest families in prewar Czechoslovakia. Bohemia and its inhabitants are at best tangential to the central narratives of "Europe," "the West," and "modernity," and when of necessity they do flit in and out of the picture, it is seldom as themselves. Mostly, as with Jindřich Štyrský and the Czech surrealists, they are simply not there at all. These absences are corrosive. It is not just that *other* people's histories are dislocated and deranged. Their displacement from (or misplacement within) the wider stories of which they were always a part—those of art nouveau, surrealism, or constructivism, for example—equally dislocates and deranges what we like to think of as *our* history.

None of this would be in the least remarkable—it is the routine fate of small nations—were it not for the fact that in point of geography, Bohemia lies about as close to the center of Europe as it is possible to get. The country has never had a coastline, though Přemysl Otakar II tried valiantly to provide it with one in the thirteenth century on the Adriatic. The Czech lands are irredeemably landlocked, uncomfortably wedged between Germany to the north and west, Poland to the northeast, Slovakia (which for a thousand years until 1918 was part of the Kingdom of Hungary) and beyond that various Russias to the east, and Austria to the south. Over the centuries— not least in the twentieth century—their borders have been fought over, breached, blurred, and redrawn many times. As the crow flies from London or Paris, Bohemia is not a faraway country. Neville Chamberlain could have driven to Prague from his meeting with Herr Hitler in Munich in less than a day, had he had the slightest interest in Czech views on what was being discussed. Geographically speaking, Bohemia is not part of "Eastern Europe," though that is where, since 1945, it has been firmly lodged in the cartographies of the Western mind. Prague lies on roughly the same longitude as Berlin. It is situated somewhat to the west of Vienna, that city of Mozart and Beethoven, Freud and Mahler, Wittgenstein and Loos, Klimt and Schiele, pillars of modern Western culture all.[16] It is closer to London than is Rome, and nearer to Dublin than to Moscow. But geography is not what matters

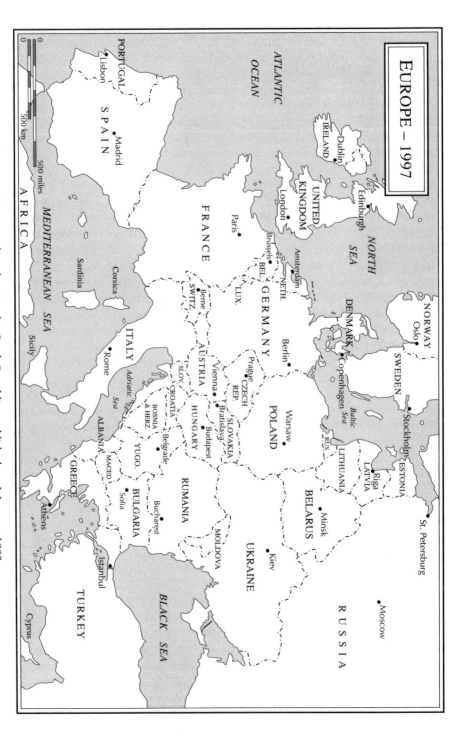

ii: Europe today, showing the Czech Republic established on 1 January 1993

EUROPE – 1997

ATLANTIC
OCEAN

PORTUGAL
Lisbon

S P A I N
Madrid

AFRICA

MEDITERRANEAN SEA

Sardinia

Corsica

Sicily

IRELAND
Dublin

UNITED
KINGDOM
London

Edinburgh

NORTH
SEA

FRANCE
Paris

Brussels
BEL.
NETH.
Amsterdam
LUX.
SWITZ.
Berne

GERMANY

ITALY
Rome

Adriatic
Sea

AUSTRIA
Vienna

SLOV.
CROATIA
BOSNIA
& HERZ.
Belgrade
ALBANIA

Prague
CZECH
REP.
Bratislava
SLOVAKIA
Budapest
HUNGARY

MACED.
YUGO.
GREECE
Athens

NORWAY
Oslo

SWEDEN

Stockholm

DENMARK
Copenhagen

Baltic
Sea

Berlin

POLAND
Warsaw

ESTONIA
Riga
LATVIA
LITHUANIA
RUS.

BELARUS
Minsk

UKRAINE
Kiev

RUMANIA
Bucharest

MOLDOVA

BULGARIA
Sofia

Istanbul

TURKEY

Cyprus

BLACK SEA

St. Petersburg

R U S S I A

Moscow

0
500 km
0
500 miles

here. What has transposed this most centrally located piece of the European continent to its imaginary margins, where it can function as a somewhat bizarrely floating signifier, is its modern history.

Walking along Smetana Embankment in Prague in the spring of 1990, it occurred to me that a Copernican turn on this history might be fruitful. The location is not irrelevant: suffice it to say, for the moment, that in the course of the twentieth century the embankment has been successively named after Emperor Francis I of Austria, Czechoslovakia's first president Tomáš Masaryk, Nazi Reichsprotektor Reinhard Heydrich, and (the communists finding the memory of Masaryk unacceptable) the nineteenth-century Czech "national" composer Bedřich Smetana. What if, I thought, we were to shift perspective; to take the real Bohemia as a vantage point from which to interrogate those historical processes that had so reordered the modern world that the geographic center of Europe had somehow been shunted off to the periphery of European consciousness? It requires an imaginative leap to reconcile the "historic" Prague of the guidebooks, haunted by the ghosts of Rabbi Löw's Golem and Rudolf II's alchemists, with *any* notions of the modern. But the guidebooks seldom conduct us around the grimy nineteenth-century working-class tenements of Žižkov or the unutterably drab communist-period *paneláky*—so called from the reinforced concrete panels out of which these apartment blocks are fabricated—which surround the city. Nor do their suggested itineraries usually include the shooting range in Kobylisy where Nazi occupiers disposed of Czechs by the hundreds, even though it is a national memorial, or the quaintly named *domeček* (little house), where a few years later communist torturers made tomato puree out of male genitalia, which is tucked away behind the exquisite Italianate Loreta Church in Hradčany.[17]

Consider. In the fifteenth century Jan Hus's Bohemia was the cradle of the Protestant Reformation; a hundred years before Martin Luther nailed his Ninety-five Theses to the doors of Wittenberg Cathedral, the Czech polity was already being made into a national and nationalist community of the godly, stoutly defended by Jan Žižka's peasant armies. Two centuries later the Thirty Years' War, which molded the state system with which Europe entered the modern era, began with a defenestration from Prague Castle in 1618. A major casualty of that conflict, seventeenth- and eighteenth-century Bohemia suffered the full rigors of the Counter-Reformation. The Czech lands became a laboratory of techniques for the production of disciplined subjects, from the showy art of the baroque to the *Index Bohemicorum librorum prohibitorum*. In the nineteenth century, as elsewhere in Europe, that identity of peoples and polities took a more secular turn. In the Czech "national rebirth"—and the concurrent transformation of Bohemia's German-speakers and Jewish communities into "national minorities"—we have a classic case of the (re)invention of the "imagined political community" of the modern nation. Central to that rebirth was the multiple identification of the nation with "the people," a word compendiously made flesh by historians, ethnographers, encyclopedists, poets, novelists, painters, composers, and others. Czech communists were in their turn to recycle this discourse of the popular for their own purposes a century later. The Czech national rebirth also prefigured another archetypally modern experience, albeit one that is more often conceptualized in terms of encounters between a monolithic Europe and a generic Other, the mutually self-defining confrontation of colonizer and colonized.

The Kingdom of Bohemia was reborn in 1918 out of the futile carnage of the war to end wars in the renovated guise of the Czechoslovak Republic. Between the wars Czechoslovakia was the most easterly liberal democracy in Europe, and its diplomatic and cultural orientation was decidedly to the West. Czech political and cultural elites gazed mainly toward Paris. Others looked to both Berlin and Moscow; this was a fractured society and a fragile polity, riven by eminently modern fault lines of class and ethnicity. The first republic ignominiously perished at Munich, a name that has since become one of the master symbols of our age. Six months later, the Czech lands became the first place in Europe (I am discounting *Anschluss* Austria) to be invaded and occupied by the Wehrmacht. Eighty thousand Czech and Moravian Jews perished in the Holocaust. Prague's Jewish Museum, founded by Zionists in 1911, was turned on Hitler's personal orders into an "exotic museum of an extinct race." By the war's end it had accumulated the world's largest collection of Jewish religious artifacts outside Israel, the dates of their acquisition coinciding with those of their owners' transportation. In May 1945 Prague was the site of the last serious European fighting of World War II. The clock whose symbolic possibilities had so struck Apollinaire thirty-three years earlier serves the novelist Arnošt Lustig as a more ambivalent metaphor in his story "Clock Like a Windmill." An assortment of Czechs shelter in the cellars of the Jewish Town Hall as the Prague Uprising rages above and around them. Lustig ends: "[They] were thinking that there would be a new beginning, yet it was actually quite otherwise. . . . At that moment, the German cannon was aimed precisely at the tower which housed the clock that turned backward."[18]

Ancient and modern scores were swiftly settled in the brutal ethnic cleansing that followed the war. Three million "Germans"—as they had by this time unambiguously become—amounting to almost one-third of Bohemia's prewar population, were summarily expelled from the country, and the memory of their presence was wiped from Czech maps. The Communist party won the elections of 1946, consolidated its hold on power by a coup d'état two years later, and refashioned Tomáš Masaryk's Czechoslovakia into a westerly outlier of the Soviet imperium. Communism brought its own gamut of modernities, of a sort we would not be able to access in the monuments, the architecture, or the art exhibitions of New York, Paris, or London:

Klement Gottwald's heroic Stalinism, Alexander Dubček's "socialism with a human face," the long dreary years of Gustáv Husák's "normalization." An endless Vichy, normalization produced a rich, if mostly illegal, literature informed by other commonplaces of the modern world—collaborations, disappearances, exile—that often escape Westerners' gaze. I, at least, would want to temper contemporary academic usages of Gramsci's overworked concept of hegemony with Václav Havel's brilliant phenomenology of the knowing complicity of "living in lies."[19] Havel himself, of course, became almost as potent a symbol of the annus mirabilis 1989 as the fall of the Berlin Wall; that he lost the Nobel Peace Prize to Mikhail Gorbachev is the kind of irony their history has taught Czechs to appreciate. Hailed in Washington as the "end of history," 1989 had less tidy outcomes in the untidy center of Europe. The Velvet Revolution was shortly followed by a velvet divorce, in which a country whose life span was pretty much coincident with the short twentieth century broke apart into its component, and thoroughly modern ethnicities.

It should be apparent even from this bald résumé that Bohemia is barren territory for grand narratives. Seen from the outside, Czech history is little more than an incoherent series of lurching discontinuities. To many (like Friedrich Engels, writing in Karl Marx's newspaper the *Neue Rheinische Zeitung* in 1849)[20] it does not appear to be a *history* at all, because it has no clear trajectory, and as importantly, it lacks an unambiguous and unified subject. Bohemia slips into a narrative no-man's-land, where it becomes a passive victim of its unfortunate situation between opposed political and cultural worlds: Catholic and Protestant, German and Slav, capitalist and communist, democratic and totalitarian. Czechs appear on the European landscape only at those moments of "crisis" when their lands become a theater of conflict between others: 1620, 1938, 1968, 1989. From the perspective of Bohemia itself, however, what emerges as most problematic are *our* uninterrogated assumptions of the boundedness of these worlds-in-conflict and the stability of the identities they confer on their imaginary subjects. In Prague, I am constantly reminded of the ironic legend on the pedestal of the broken colossus chanced upon by Shelley's traveler in an antique land: "My name is Ozymandias, king of kings: Look on my works, ye Mighty, and despair!"—which I find, I might say, a comfortingly hopeful sentiment.[21] In the repeated undoings of the artifacts of power, evident here in everything from banknotes and postage stamps to monuments and street names, power is revealed as a precarious and fragile artifact itself. Jan Nepomucký, a saint fabricated by the Vatican in the eighteenth century in the interests of erasing the memory of Hus and Žižka, is co-opted by nationalists in the nineteenth as a patron saint of the Czech language. The Deutsches Kasino, once the proud bastion of German Prague society, is reborn after World War II as The Slav House and serves for a time as the headquarters of the Central Committee of the Communist party. Currently Prague City Council is seeking foreign investors to renovate it. The communists' own Palace of Culture at Vyšehrad, according to popular belief the most expensive palace in a city that abounds in them, after 1989 becomes a venue for trade fairs and erotic entertainments.

Czech history cannot be reduced to an orderly procession of presidents or a triumphal march from sea to shining sea. It is richer and more complicated than that, full of inversions and erasures, miscegenations and ironies. And that, for me, is what makes it so interesting—even, dare I say it, so emblematic. It constantly forces us to rethink what we understand by a history in the first place, and to confront the question of just how much forgetting is always entailed in the production of memory. There is coherence in Czech history, but it is not the coherence of a logical argument. Nobody who knows the Czech lands could for a moment doubt the reality, the tenacity, the rootedness in place and past of Czech identity. But the continuity of this identity exists in, and only in, its perpetual salvagings and reconstructions in the face of repeated disruptions and discontinuities. The imagination of community and invention of tradition never ends; it is a ceaseless labor of bricolage. Bohemia confounds the neat oppositions and orderly sequences upon which our histories and geographies of the modern depend. This is a world of Czech national awakeners whose mother tongue is German, of urban modernities dressed up in timeless peasant costumes, of Jews who are Germans in one decennial census and Czechs in the next and who are gassed, regardless, a few decades later, of communist futures watched over by the resurrected shades of the nationalist past. Once Czech history is granted its integrity, in short, it is the facile abstractions that have effaced it, turning Bohemia into an incoherent other—"Europe," "the West," "modernity"—that come into question. They begin to look positively childish. Manifest destiny dissolves into historical contingency, which is plain as the light of day here, on the fringes of European consciousness, at the center of the European continent.

The maps on which Bohemia has become terra incognita are the cadasters of power. For all but twenty years between the battle of the White Mountain in 1620 and the Velvet Revolution of 1989, the Czech lands have been an appendage of Vienna, Berlin, or Moscow. But provinciality is in the eye of the beholder. In reality Bohemia has been a frontier zone, over which the armies of competing European modernities—Reformation and Counter-Reformation, empire and nation, fascism and democracy, capitalism and communism—have repeatedly rolled back and forth. All have left their imprint on its society and culture; Prague is a pentimento of different ways of being modern, European, and, fitfully, Western. Such a history, I submit, is *central* to the understanding of anything we might want to call the modern world. From the vantage point of London, or Paris, or New York—or, not so very long ago, Moscow—it is possible to identify history with progress, to ascribe to it providence, directionality, and meaning. It is possible to write modernity in the singular, and to prattle about "the end of history." Such fables are believable precisely so long as the Bohemias of this world are forgotten. Their dislocation is the condition of our coherence. Viewed from Bohemia itself, the modern condition looks somewhat different. It is a chiaroscuro of beauties and terrors, whose colors are invariably more vibrant, and whose depths are very much darker, than our anemic narratives of progress are apt to acknowledge. Modernity was never either singular or simple. It was *always* a "postmodern" polyphony, in which the fragile stabilities of location and identity rested on the uncertain vicissitudes of power.

This book is about Czechs and their Czechness; a little nation, by their own estimate, of scant consequence in the councils of the great. It is a history, it might be said, of attempts to equip Bohemia with cultural coastlines to make up for those that nature forgot. It is sometimes romantically improbable, often to be wondered at, occasionally beyond belief. But it is not a winter's tale. Nor is it set in a faraway country. It is a story of the troubled heart of modern Europe and the people who have the good or bad fortune to live at that treacherous crossroads of possibilities. I take my leave of that story in an indefinite future perfect of socialism, circa 1960. Some may feel cheated of a happy ending, especially when for once history seems actually to have provided one. But histories that terminate in the present almost inevitably suggest that the present is the terminus of history, and this is the more true when that present is overshadowed by events of the perceived magnitude of those of 1989. Today, the state of Czechoslovakia can all too easily appear an artificial hybrid, communism an aberrant diversion on the long national pilgrimage from Hus to Havel. Yet in their time both were as authentic incarnations of Czech identity as today's NATO- and EU-bound Czech Republic. If there is a point in writing history, it is to confront what has been remembered with what has been forgotten. Better, I thought, to end this book in a previous moment of equally confident resolution (the Jews were dead, the Germans expelled, the class enemies crushed), a moment of seamless totality stretching into an endless future, which now feels an epoch away, even if it was only the day before yesterday.

ONE

THE COMPANY OF OUR GREAT MINDS

A Great Artist and a Great Czech

FEW ARTISTS so obviously evoke a period and a place as Alphonse Mucha. The period is the fin de siècle, the place Paris. "The poster that launched an epoch,"[1] Mucha's rush order for Sarah Bernhardt in the play *Gismonda*, appeared on Paris billboards on New Year's Day 1895. "Gismonda" not only represented a radical departure in poster design with its elongated shape, subdued pastel colors, and Byzantine decorative elements, it was also unlike anything Mucha himself had ever done before. The poster was an overnight sensation and made its author a celebrity. During the next few years Mucha produced most of the works for which he is best known today, and which in their aim of an affordable everyday art, as much as in their style, did much to define *l'art nouveau*. His output was prodigious. There were many more posters, including "La Dame aux Camélias" and "Medée" for Miss Bernhardt; his famous advertisements for Job cigarette papers, Perfecta cycles, Moët et Chandon champagne, and Lefèvre-Util biscuits; decorative panels with comely young ladies impersonating stars, seasons, flowers, and muses; jewelry and bronzes; illustrated books, magazine covers, calendars, and postcards; and the *Documents décoratifs*, a compendium of designs for everything from cutlery to carpets. Mucha's triumphant Paris exhibition at the Salon des Cent in 1897, at which 448 separate items were shown, was reprised in Prague, Munich, Brussels, London, and New York, and he was commissioned by the Austrian government to decorate the Bosnia-Herzegovina pavillion for the 1900 Paris World Exhibition. The new art was known by various names in different countries: art nouveau, Jugendstil, Secession. In Paris itself, it was often referred to simply as *"le style Mucha."*

Yet to locate Alfons Maria Mucha—to give his name its proper spelling—within the frame of reference suggested by the words "Paris 1900" is in a way utterly to misplace him. He himself fervently believed he belonged somewhere else. Though he lived for many years in Paris, he was not French. In 1897, incensed by press speculations as to his origins (one newspaper report had Sarah Bernhardt plucking him out of a Hungarian gypsy camp where he beguiled her with his violin playing and singing under the light of a full moon),[2] he asked Miss Bernhardt to write to the editor of *La France* putting the record straight. Monsieur Mucha, she said, was "a Czech from Moravia not only by birth and origin, but also by feeling, by conviction and by patriotism."[3] Much as he may seem to personify art nouveau, Mucha had ambivalent relationships toward it, detesting, for instance, the Vienna Secession. As a Czech patriot, what he disliked about the Secession was what he described as its "Germanic" character. His own art, by contrast, he regarded as enduringly "Slavonic."[4] He also became increasingly uneasy with what he saw as the triviality of the decorative work upon which his fame rested. His celebrity, and the genre of work that had produced it, was as much a source of guilt to him as it was of pleasure.

In 1900 Mucha visited the Balkans to research his Bosnia-Herzegovina pavillion for the World Exhibition. According to his own account, the trip was a flash of revelation. He returned to Paris "amazed. What I had been looking for so hard all this time I found among the Balkan Slavs . . . Once again I was doing historical painting, but this time not about Germany[5] but a brotherly Slav nation. Describing the glorious and tragic events in its history I thought of the joys and sorrows of my own country and of all the Slavs." In a letter to a friend he tells what follows:

> It was midnight, and there I was all alone in my studio in the rue du Val-de-Grâce among my pictures, posters and panels. I became very excited. I saw my work adorning the salons of the highest society or flattering people of the great world with smiling and ennobled portraits. I saw the books full of legendary scenes, floral garlands and drawings glorifying the beauty and tenderness of women. This was what my time, my precious time, was being spent on, when my nation [národ] was left to quench its thirst on ditch water. And in my spirit I saw myself sinfully misappropriating what belonged to my people [lid]. It was midnight and, as I stood there looking at all these things, I swore a solemn promise that the remainder of my life would be filled exclusively with work for the nation.[6]

Over the next decade Mucha gradually disentangled himself from Paris and the seductions of "the great world." In the years after 1904 he spent much of his time in the United States, where he hoped to make enough money painting portraits of rich Americans to finance his "work for the nation." His efforts at portraiture were not especially successful; according to his son and biographer Jiří, this was not a medium in which he was much at home.[7] But eventually he found a sponsor for his dream of painting a "Slav Epic," the American diplomat and millionaire Charles R. Crane, a good friend of future Czechoslovak president Tomáš Garrigue Masaryk (1850–1937). Armed with Crane's commission Mucha resettled in Bohemia in 1910. With this, to all intents and purposes, he dropped out of the history of modern art.[8]

This, however, says more about the vantage points from which art histories are usually written than it does about Alfons Mucha. Back home, he continued to create for almost thirty more years. He decorated the Mayoral Hall in Prague's Obecní dům (Municipal House) and gave Saint Vitus's Cathedral in Hradčany (Prague Castle) one of its most glorious stained-glass windows. When his beloved Czechoslovakia became independent from Austria-Hungary in 1918, it was Mucha who provided the infant state with its first postage stamps and banknotes. He even offered suggestions for its police uniforms. He created posters for Czech societies and causes, like the national festivals of the patriotic gymnastic society Sokol and the 1928 celebrations for the tenth anniversary of the Czechoslovak Republic. He designed scenery for theater productions, among them Bedřich Smetana's *Libuše*, an opera composed specifically for solemn national occasions, at the National Theater. Above all, he spent eighteen years working on the *Slovanská epopej* (Slav Epic), twenty monumental canvases on themes from Czech and Slavonic history which he ceremonially handed over to the city of Prague on 1 September 1928. These huge paintings (each measures at least six by four meters) form the most extensive historical cycle in modern Czech art. They have seldom been exhibited outside Mucha's homeland; but when, in 1921, five of them were shown at the Art Institute in Chicago and the Brooklyn Museum in New York, American critics were lavish in their praises, one writing to Mucha that he considered "the *Slovanská epopej* as the greatest work of its type since the beginning of the sixteenth century in Italy."[9] The paintings were compared, favorably, with Puvis de Chavannes's frescoes for the Panthéon in Paris. Whatever their artistic merits, their high seriousness of subject matter and religiosity of feeling make a sharp contrast with the "women and flowers" of Mucha's Paris period. There can be no doubt that in his own eyes the *Slovanská epopej* was Alfons Mucha's masterwork, and the creation for which, above all else, he would have wished to have been remembered.

When Mucha was buried, it was not only as "a great artist," but "a great Czech."[10] His funeral took place on 19 July 1939 at Vyšehrad Cemetery in Prague. It is a significant location. A rocky outcrop above the River Vltava just south of the city's historic boundaries, Vyšehrad was believed to be the seat of the first Czech rulers more than a millennium before. Here Princess Libuše, the mythical heroine of Smetana's opera, had prophesied the glories of the future city of Prague. In the later nineteenth century Vyšehrad's churchyard had been turned into a national cemetery. Mucha was laid to rest in the Slavín, a burial vault inscribed with the legend "Although dead, they still speak to us" erected in 1889–1893 as a monument for great Czech creative artists.[11] The painter and graphic artist Max Švabinský (1873–1962), a man whose art is as rooted in the late nineteenth century as Mucha's own, delivered the valedictory oration on behalf of the Czech Academy of Arts and Sciences. He closed with these words:

> Maestro!
> You have brought to an end a great work and are departing to eternal sleep. The Czech nation and Prague are burying you in the most sacred place, in Vyšehrad,

1. Alfons Mucha seated in front of canvases from his *Slovanská epopej* at the exhibition of the first eleven paintings from the cycle in the Klementinum, Prague, in 1919.

in the most noble place, in the Slavín. In Vyšehrad, seat of the Princess Libuše, you will talk with Bedřich Smetana, with Antonín Dvořák, with the great Miko-láš Aleš, with Jaroslav Vrchlický, with Josef Myslbek, with the young Jan Štursa and with the whole company of our great minds. You will look at Hradčany and Saint Vitus's Cathedral. Dark autumn clouds will scud above your head and winter will cover Slavín with ermine snow; but spring will come again, the meadows and woods will flower in the Czech land, in Vyšehrad the lilac will bloom and the honeysuckle will bloom on Aleš's grave. In Vyšehrad nightingales will sing. Rest sweetly in eternal peace! The Czech nation has never forgotten its great sons and never will forget them. Let it be so![12]

A tradition is being invoked here; and it is not that in which we are accustomed to place Alfons Mucha. We are a long way from Paris and the belle époque, in a faraway country, among people of whom we know nothing.

The End of Culture

What Neville Chamberlain actually said in his infamous broadcast of 27 September 1938 justifying the Munich Agreement was: "How horrible, fantastic, incredible it is that we should be digging trenches and trying on gasmasks here because of a quarrel in a far away country between people of whom we know nothing."[13] As a consequence of that misconceived attempt to secure "peace for our time,"[14] Czechoslovakia [*Československo*] was forced to relinquish around a third of its territory and population to Adolf Hitler's Third Reich. Six months later, on 15 March 1939, what remained of the country was dismembered. The Czech lands [*české země*] of Bohemia [*Čechy*] and Moravia [*Morava*] were invaded by German armies and turned into a "Reichsprotektorat." Slovakia [*Slovensko*], which had seceded from the Czechoslovak Republic the day before, became a nominally independent Axis state; Sub-Carpathian Ruthenia [*Podkarpatská Rus*], to its east, was occupied by Hungary. In Prague, Alfons Mucha was among the first to be arrested by the Gestapo. Although he was soon released, his health rapidly deteriorated thereafter. By then he was seventy-eight. The occupation authorities forbade him a public funeral. The crowd assembled at Vyšehrad, and Max Švabinský spun his meteorological metaphors, in defiance of a ban on "all demonstrations and public speeches."[15]

That the Germans would not countenance a public funeral for Mucha was not altogether surprising. As on many previous occasions in Prague over the preceding eighty years,[16] in 1938–9 deaths of individuals became moments for affirming the vitality of the collectivity for which they came to stand. On Christmas Day 1938—before the German invasion, but after Munich had effectively put an end to Czechoslovak democracy—the writer and playwright Karel Čapek (1890–1938) died at the untimely age of forty-eight. Though the cause of his death was registered as pneumonia, many Czechs believed it to be a heart broken by the Munich capitulation. With reason. Čapek had no truck with pan-Slav mysticism, but his patriotism was no less heartfelt than Mucha's. It was also a kind of patriotism singularly vulnerable to the betrayal that, for Czechs, Munich represented. Čapek saw himself as "a national citizen of the world" (to quote his own approving description of his great nineteenth-century predecessor, the writer and journalist Jan Neruda),[17] and celebrated his faraway country as "the spiritual and intellectual crossroad of Europe."[18] Founder and long-time president of the Czech branch of the international PEN club, his many publications included *Letters from England* and a loving anthology of modern French poetry from Baudelaire to Soupault in his own Czech translations. In his afterword to the second edition of 1936—the date matters, given the darkening clouds in neighboring Germany—Čapek explained that most of the translations dated from 1916, "thus in the middle of the war; and they came into being really under the pressure of the war, as a literary act of solidarity and spiritual alliance with the nation which was then bleeding before Verdun for the cause which was also the cause of our heart and of our faith. . . ." Two years later, Daladier and Chamberlain abruptly shattered all such identifications. Milena Jesenská—who is best known in the West as the recipient, twenty years earlier, of Franz Kafka's *Letters to Milena*—wrote: "He did not fight. He did not wrestle. He did not struggle. He just stopped breathing and he just stopped living. If you like, you believe that he died of bronchitis and pneumonia."[19]

Čapek's close friend Ferdinand Peroutka (1895–1978) has recorded the writer's immediate reaction to the Munich calamity: "Karel Čapek sat among us and monotonously repeated: 'How is it possible, that treaties are not kept; it is the end of culture.' He had sweat on his forehead. Through his whole adult life he had humbly served democracy and humanism. Now—for some time—arrived the victory of that which in his books he had variously styled the Robots, the Newts, the White Disease. . . . It was a dark evening when he died, and many other dark evenings were to come. Dear friend, we are not yet at the end of the journey."[20] This was written on Boxing Day 1953, in exile in America, where Peroutka had fled after the communist coup in Czechoslovakia in February 1948. Peroutka himself was a major figure in Czech journalism between the wars, editing the literary-political reviews *Tribuna* (*The Tribune*, 1919–24) and *Přítomnost* (*The Present*, 1924–39), as well as regularly contributing to the newspaper *Lidové noviny* (*People's News*), of which Karel Čapek had been an editor from 1921. Among his longer books and essays are an iconoclastic critique of the nineteenth-century mythologies of Czech identity that had so inspired Alfons Mucha, *What We Are Like* [*Jací jsme*, 1924],[21] and a massively detailed four-volume history of the early years of the Czechoslovak Republic, *The Building of a State* [*Budování státu*, 1933–38].[22] Peroutka spent the years 1939–45 in Dachau and Buchenwald. He, too, was to be laid to rest among "the whole company of our great minds"—eventually. His ashes were shipped back to Vyšehrad from New York, where he died in 1978, only after the Velvet Revolution of 1989.

Political circumstances in the winter of 1938–9 being what they were, neither the National Museum nor the National Theater would have anything to do with organizing Karel Čapek's funeral. The museum offered the excuse that there was insufficient coal to heat the ceremonial hall normally used for such occasions, the Pantheon. The theater, where so many of Čapek's plays had been performed during the previous two decades, declined to fly a black flag in honor of his memory.[23] A burial in "the most sacred place" was arranged anyway. Continuity was affirmed in the teeth of the reality that would deny it, the travails of the present transcended by the perspective of ages.

Čapek became another link in the great chain of national being, a conduit between the dead, the living, and the unborn. The poet Josef Hora (1891–1945) pointedly rhapsodized over the Czechness [češství] of Čapek's work, the way in which Čapek used Czech "with reverence and understanding for the fact that the native language is a sacred instrument hallowed by tradition and leading us to a new life."[24] An affectionate diminutization, which is possible in Czech in a way it is not in English—it sounds mawkish in literal translation—attended Čapek's induction into the national pantheon. "He has a small and narrow little grave [hrobeček]," reported one journalist, "a step away from where Mikoláš Aleš, Božena Němcová and Jan Neruda are sleeping. You have ascended with them into eternity, their youngest little brother [bratříček nejmladší]."[25] The most famous Czech writer of his generation is addressed here in the familiar verbal form [vystoupil jsi], that used with family, close friends, children, animals, lovers, and God. This is a language of intimacy, familial and familiar, far removed from the usual pomposities of official ceremonial. In other contexts, Czechs might use the word "hrobeček" (from hrob, grave) for the last resting place of a child or a family pet.

Čapek himself would have felt at home in this world of diminutives. He was, after all, the author of the Czech children's classic Dášenka: The Life of a Puppy,[26] as well as of those probing dystopias for which, in the West, he is better known.[27] That he troubled to write for Czech children as well as for the National Theater says much not only about Karel Čapek himself, but also about his culture. Modern Czech writers have had a different relationship to their people (rather than, as we might say, to their public) than that usually found in Anglo-Saxon countries. Czech novelists, poets, and playwrights enjoy great public esteem, even veneration. In his time, Karel Čapek was a household name. But with this comes a responsibility, above all to speak for, to, and in the language of the collectivity that writers are privileged to represent. They are expected to write for the newspapers, to assume moral leadership in moments of national crisis, to host public discussions of their work in bookstores; to remain visibly and accessibly a part of the community that has elevated them. This is one reason why an émigré Czech author like Milan Kundera, whatever his celebrity on the world literary stage, has remained a problematic figure in his homeland. He took himself out of this national circle of intimacy in which, in his own words, "everything and everyone (critics, historians, compatriots as well as foreigners) hooks the art onto the great national family portrait photo and will not let it get away."[28] Alfons Mucha clearly felt its emotional tug when he saw himself misappropriating talents that properly belonged to his people, and unlike with Kundera, it eventually brought him home. As for Karel Čapek, he refused the option of exile in 1938, even though his long and very vocal hostility to fascism put him in obvious personal danger.

Faithful We Shall Remain

Still more poignant, in a different way, was the funeral of Karel Hynek Má-cha, two months before Mucha's; and not just because this "poet of spring and youth"[29] was a few days short of his twenty-sixth birthday when he died. Over a quarter of a million people saw Mácha to his grave. The ceremonies took place during the "time of love" with which Mácha's name is indelibly associated, though the weather that weekend was cold and gray. Draped in a Czech flag, Mácha's remains lay in state in the Pantheon of the National Museum all day on 6 May. Thousands of people streamed past his coffin. Among the official mourners were mayor of Prague Otakar Klapka and the Protectorate's titular "State President" Emil Hácha (1872–1945), no mean poet himself,[30] who (according to newspaper reports) stood before Mácha's catafalque "in deep emotion" for nearly twenty minutes. At five o'clock, ac-companied by a guard of honor of students, the coffin was carried from the Pantheon to the hearse, drawn by two white horses and accompanied by mounted guards, which was to take Mácha to Vyšehrad. Long before that thick crowds had begun to line the streets of the procession route. Their silence broken only by the tolling of Prague's many church bells, they stood bareheaded as "the poet of the nation went . . . through the city, through his city, living more than he ever lived, and the nation paid tribute to its great minstrel."[31] Many people carried Czech flags. Prague buildings were fes-tooned with them as far as the distant suburbs.

Mácha's burial took place on the next day, a Sunday. "Perhaps half Prague" made its way to Vyšehrad, and those who were able brought with them a bouquet of spring flowers. The grave was strewn with white narcissi, red carnations, and blue lilac—the national colors of the defunct Czechoslovak Republic. Again Mácha had a guard of students with drawn rapiers and young girls in white dresses. In the morning there was a funeral mass at-tended by prominent politicians, scientists, and artists. Throughout the ser-vice an unending stream of nameless mourners filed in and out of the church. Monsignor Bohumil Stašek, canon of Vyšehrad, promised before God, the Czech patron saints, and the living poets of the land to remain faithful to Mácha's legacy. "*Věrni zůstaneme*"—"Faithful we shall remain"—was the promise that President Edvard Beneš, now exiled in England, had uttered over the coffin of Czechoslovakia's founder Tomáš Garrigue Masaryk two years before.[32] The origins of the phrase lie in a fifteenth-century Hussite chorale. The same words had formed the title of a petition by over three hundred leading Czech artists and intellectuals in May 1938 calling upon their government to defend Czechoslovak sovereignty against German threats, which was signed in the following weeks by more than a million of their fellow citizens. The service ended with the Lord's Prayer and the "sweetest song of the Czech land," "*Kde domov můj?*" (Where is my home?). Written by Josef Kajetán Tyl (words) and František Škroup (music) for their operetta *Fidlovačka* (*The Shoemakers' Guild Festival*), first performed at the Stavovské divadlo (Estates Theater) in Prague on 21 December 1834, "*Kde domov můj?*" went on to become a favorite Czech patriotic anthem during the nineteenth century. Together with the Slovak song "*Nad Tatrou sa blýska*" (Lightning is flashing over Mount Tatra) it had been the official national hymn of independent Czechoslovakia.[33]

The students stood guard over Mácha's plain oak coffin until the appointed hour of burial. At three o'clock, to the sound of the great bell in the tower of the Church of Saint Peter and Saint Paul, the girls in white led the procession from the church to the neighboring cemetery. Three of them bore a lyre of flowers. On the steps of the Slavín the Prague Teachers' Choir sang a chorale, and the actor Václav Vydra read from Mácha's most famous poem *Máj* (*May*); it is this that begins with the couplet "It was late evening—the first of May— evening May—it was the time of love."[34] It was with other, no less familiar lines from *Máj* that former Czechoslovak army general Rudolf Medek began his farewell oration: "Ah, the beautiful land, the beloved land, my cradle and my grave, my mother, the only land, the land given to me as my birthright, the broad land, the only land."[35] Every Czech would know this passage; apart from anything else, it is reckoned the most beautiful paradigm of poetic alliteration in the Czech language. The passage occurs twice in the poem. Though Medek chose to omit the last five words of the stanza where it is dramatically recalled, his hearers would have known them: "*krev syna teče po ní*," the blood of her son flows over her. Mácha was describing a young man's execution. Just as Mácha's *Máj* is immortal, Medek went on, so is his nation. He concluded his valediction with the words of Bedřich Smetana's Princess Libuše: "My dear Czech nation will not perish!" The coffin was then hoisted onto the shoulders of eight "living followers of the living legacy of the poet," among them František Halas, Josef Hora, Vladimír Holan, and Jaroslav Seifert—the same Jaroslav Seifert (1901–86) who forty-five years later was to become the first Czech to be awarded the Nobel Prize for literature. As they lowered Mácha into his grave "*Kde domov můj?*" was sung once again. With this the ceremonies officially ended. But throughout the evening the streams of unknown mourners kept flowing, until the open grave was filled almost to the brim with May flowers.

What makes these events so poignant is what was oddest about them. Karel Hynek Mácha, the founder of modern Czech poetry, died over a hundred years before, in 1836. He was originally buried in Litoměřice, a town only fifty kilometers northwest of Prague that lay in the *pohraničí* (borderlands) lost to Germany at Munich; the term Sudetenland [*Sudety*] is one generally disliked by Czechs as a name for this region. On 1 October 1938,

2. Karel Hynek Mácha's burial in Vyšehrad Cemetery, Prague, May 1939.

two days after the Czechoslovak government had reluctantly accepted the Munich ultimatum, the governor of the National Bank suggested in a ministerial council that the poet's body be speedily exhumed. A cemetery attendant in Litoměřice by the name of Knobloch filled a paper sack, and the soldiers of an artillery regiment under the command of a Lieutenant Šetek took it to Prague.[36] On 10 October the Wehrmacht moved into the abandoned *pohraničí*. Mácha's remains were holy relics. The intensity of emotion which they inspired can only be explained by the importance of what they signified. They were totems of a national identity.

Karel Čapek would have understood. His last play, The Mother [*Matka*], written in 1938, is prefaced by the following author's note:

This play, the idea for which the author was given by his wife, the subject matter by the age in which we are living, and the final inspiration by a picture of a widow kneeling on one of today's battlefields, will perhaps pass muster without any introduction to explain its meaning more fully. As regards the actual stage setting, however, the author is anxious that the dead who group themselves around the mother in his play should not be regarded as ghosts, but as living people, capable of friendliness and attachment, taking their places in a completely natural manner within the family circle which was their former home. They are just the same as when alive, for they continue to live in their mother's thoughts. They are dead only inasmuch as she can no longer embrace them and they make slightly less noise than we who are alive.[37]

TWO

MATERIALS OF MEMORY

The Crown of Saint Wenceslas

A CENTURY BEFORE these events, Czechs appear to have been much less sure of who they were. This uncertainty is acknowledged in an unlikely source, the 1871 Report of the Prague Statistical Commission. Trying to explain discrepancies between 1851 and 1869 census figures relating to the respective numbers of Czechs and Germans in the population of the city—German numbers, they thought, had been greatly overstated in the earlier census—the authors remark that in 1851 attempts to investigate nationality [národnost] were "premature" because "a clear consciousness of national identity among the majority of Austro-Hungarian nations was, so to speak, still in diapers."[1] This is probably correct. But the image of infancy is misleading. Ambivalence about nationality did not stem from the fact that mid-nineteenth-century Bohemia was only just beginning to emerge from a world conceptually bounded by sacral communities and dynastic realms, as we might be tempted to assume.[2] In the Czech case, a sense of national community is not something unique to modernity. In order to make any sense at all of the nineteenth and twentieth centuries, something needs to be said here about earlier Czech history—not simply to provide background or context,[3] but also because that history itself, in the guise of a recovered memory, was to become a crucial ingredient in (and in some respects a serious problem for) the very clear "consciousness of national identity" that did crystallize among Czechs in the later nineteenth century. Traditions may be invented, nations may be imagined communities.[4] But neither, as a rule, is simply conjured up out of nothing.

Slavonic tribes first settled in the Czech lands, a region previously inhabited by a Celtic people known to the Romans as the Boii (whence the name Bohemia), in perhaps the sixth century A.D. Their mythical leader [Praotec, forefather] was called Čech; it is from him, supposedly, that the Czechs' names for both themselves [Čech] and their land [Čechy] derive. Little is known of Czech history before the ninth century. From Western sources we learn that the Frankish merchant Sámo, an otherwise shadowy figure, ruled over a short-lived confederation sometime in the first half of the seventh century. But the first Western Slavonic state worthy of the name, Great Moravia [Velká Morava], a title coined by the Byzantine emperor Constantine Porphyrogenitus, dates from the early ninth century. It took in Moravia and

Western Slovakia, but not Bohemia. Great Moravia's most significant historical legacy was the introduction of Christianity, and with it a written Slavonic
liturgical language, to the region. At the request of the Moravian prince
Rastislav (846–870), Byzantine emperor Michael III dispatched the missionary brothers Cyril and Methodius northward in 863. Speaking a Slavonic
tongue (the Greeks had previously proselytized among southern Slavs) and
equipped with translated liturgical texts, they rapidly made converts and
ordained indigenous priests. Methodius also made forays into neighboring
Bohemia; among those he baptized were Prince Bořivoj and his wife Ludmila. In 880 Pope John VIII made Methodius the first archbishop of the
Moravian church.[5] The distinctive Slavic character of the early Czech church
did not last long; after Methodius's death in 885 Pope Steven V forbade
further use of the Slavonic liturgy. Great Moravia itself collapsed in the face
of invading Magyars in or around the year 906, an event that had two important long-term consequences for Czech history. Slovakia was severed from
the Czech lands, a division that was to last for over a thousand years; and the
center of gravity of Czech power was definitively shifted westward, from
Moravia to Bohemia.

Prince Bořivoj (d. 894?), whom Methodius converted, is the first historically documented lord of Bohemia. He was a scion of the indigenous Přemyslid dynasty, which originated, according to legend, in the marriage of
Princess Libuše, whom we met in the speeches at Mucha's and Mácha's funerals, to the plowman Přemysl. The Czechs chose Libuše, the wisest of the
equally mythical chieftain Krok's three daughters, to lead them after her father's death; but they also insisted, after she had failed to resolve an inheritance dispute between two feuding brothers, that she take a male consort. A
historically less dubious (if no less mythologized) figure among the early
Přemyslid rulers is Václav, "Good King Wenceslas" of the English Christmas
carol. Murdered by his brother and successor Boleslav I at a mass in Stará
Boleslav in 929 (or possibly 935), Václav was soon beatified as a patron saint
of the Czech land. So was his grandmother, Bořivoj's wife Ludmila. Another
victim of Přemyslid family intrigue, Ludmila too had been murdered, allegedly on the orders of Václav's mother Drahomíra because of disputes over
the young prince's upbringing. Whether or not it was Ludmila's doing, Václav
himself seems to have been both well-educated—unusually among aristocrats of the age, he could read and write—and genuinely pious. It was he
who built the earliest church of Saint Vitus on Hradčany.

Prague was detached from the archdiocese of Regensburg and made an
independent bishopric in 973. Its first incumbent was a Saxon monk, Dětmar (Thietmar). A Jewish trader, Ibrahim Ibn Jakub, who visited the city
eight years earlier, gives some flavor of its life at the time. He described a
town "built of stone and lime, a city that through trade is the richest of all.
From Krakow Russians and Slavs come there with goods, and from the lands

of the Turks Mohammedans and Jews come to the people of Prague, Turks with goods and current coin, and they take away from them slaves, tin, and all manner of furs. . . . Their land is the best of the northern lands and the richest in food."[6] Dětmar's successor Vojtěch (Saint Adalbert) became Prague's first Czech bishop in 982. Ten years later, with the aid of Benedictine monks from Monte Cassino in Italy, he founded the oldest monastery in the Czech lands at Břevnov, now in Prague. Vojtěch spent much of his time as Czech bishop in exile; his reforming Benedictine ideas—which included ending the lucrative trade in Christian slaves—proved less than popular in what was still a semiheathen land. As importantly, he came from the eastern-Bohemian Slavníkovci clan, who were by this time the Přemyslids' only serious remaining rivals for power. Boleslav II (967–999) had all the bishop's close kin murdered en masse at Libice in 995, finally securing undisputed Přemyslid supremacy in the state. On Vojtěch's own death two years later as a missionary in East Prussia, it was another Boleslav, the Polish monarch Boleslav the Valiant, who ransomed the martyr's body for its weight in gold. Vojtěch was duly proclaimed a saint. In the year 1000, in the presence of the emperor, his remains were ceremonially installed in the Polish capital of Gniezdno and a cathedral begun to house them. The Czech martyr became a patron of the Polish church, which partly as a result of his prestige gained its own archbishopric, a see whose first occupant was Vojtěch's half brother Radim. It was only four decades later that the saint was reclaimed for his native land. In 1039 Břetislav I invaded Poland and had Vojtěch's relics brought back to Prague. They were reburied in Hradčany, where they have rested ever since.

The Přemyslid dynasty remained on the Bohemian throne for over four centuries—a remarkable record of continuity, even if one punctuated by frequent internecine strife. Their realm reached its territorial zenith under Přemysl Otakar II (1253–78), whose marital acquisitions and military conquests stretched south through Austria, Styria, and Carinthia to the shores of the Adriatic. Following Otakar's defeat and death at the hands of Rudolf of Habsburg in 1278, Moravia was occupied for five years by Rudolf, Bohemia plundered by Otto of Brandenburg, and all the southern territories lost. These years of occupation were later to furnish Bedřich Smetana with the subject of his first opera *The Brandenburgers in Bohemia* [*Braniboři v Čechách*, 1863]. Despite such vicissitudes of fortune—scarcely unusual ones in medieval Europe—under the Přemyslids the Czech lands were welded into a coherent polity. Václav and Boleslav I had recognized the Saxon emperors Henry I and Otto I as their suzerains, and the Kingdom of Bohemia eventually crystallized into what was, in effect, an administratively sovereign state within the Holy Roman Empire. Emperors first granted royal title to Vratislav II in 1085 and Vladislav II in 1158. From Přemysl Otakar I (in 1198) this honor was made perpetual, and the kings of Bohemia were numbered among the seven electors of the empire. Among the privileges royalty conveyed was the right to appoint the bishop of Prague and (after the Golden Sicilian Bull of 1212) the bishop of Olomouc in Moravia.

The Přemyslid kingdom was impressively unified by the standards of the time; indeed, one might draw some intriguing parallels with another "prematurely" centralized polity on the margins of Romanized Europe, and a state that was also "precocious" in its development of a national awareness, medieval England.[7] The Přemyslids exercised jurisdiction over all within their realm, including (to 1221) the clergy, were able to extract taxes from all free citizens, and governed the country through castellani appointed by royal command rather than through a hereditary nobility. Only from the thirteenth century, when land began to be granted with office, does a truly feudal aristocracy begin to emerge. It was likewise kings, from Přemysl Otakar II onward, who took the initiative in establishing towns. Fatefully, as it later turned out, they peopled them largely with German craftsmen and merchants, seeking to fast-track economic development through large-scale colonization. There is evidence of Czech resentment at Germans' growing presence and power in the state from an early date. The chronicle of František Pražský, written in the 1340s, records that in 1315 Czech lords complained to Jan Lucemburský of "these foreigners who are in the kingdom" who "accumulate money by legal as well as illegal means, appropriate it for themselves, and carry it away from your kingdom." Germans own castles and estates, yet fail even to try to keep the peace on the highways. Were the king instead to bestow domains "on us, who are born in the kingdom and who are prepared to serve you," the nobles suggest, "through us would come peace, king and kingdom would prosper, and the money, which is being drained away, would remain here."[8] It was an ominous precedent.

The pinnacle of Bohemia's medieval glory came not under the Přemyslids—the male line died out with Václav III in 1306—but under a prince of the house of Luxembourg, Charles IV, who succeeded his father, Jan Lucemburský, as Czech king in 1346. Charles IV [Karel IV.] is known to Czechs as "Father of the Homeland" [*Otec vlasti*], a title conferred on him at his Prague funeral in 1378. He is the only Czech ever to have been elected Holy Roman Emperor, if Czech he can be reckoned. Nowadays he features prominently on the currency of the Czech Republic, gracing the hundred-crown bill and keeping company with such icons of Czechness as the seventeenth-century Protestant pedagogue Jan Amos Komenský and the nineteenth-century historian František Palacký and novelist Božena Němcová. Charles's mother was a Přemyslid princess, Eliška, youngest daughter of Václav II, and he himself was born in Prague. He was originally christened Václav after the Czech patron. But he had spent the last eleven years abroad when he arrived in the Czech lands in 1333, aged seventeen, to take up the office of Margrave of Moravia; Jan Lucemburský (1310–46) was an absentee king. In Charles's own words, "We found that several years earlier our mother had died. . . .

And so when we arrived in Bohemia, we found neither father, nor mother, nor brother, nor sisters, nor anyone known to us. Also we had completely forgotten the Czech language, but later again we learned it, so that we spoke and understood it like every other Czech. By God's grace we were able to speak, write and read not only Czech, but also French, Italian, German and Latin, such that we had equal command of all these languages."[9] Later he endeavored to impose the same multilingualism on all future imperial electors, his Golden Bull of 1356 requiring their sons to learn not only German, but also Italian and Czech, from the age of seven. Whether his motives were political or patriotic, Charles was assiduous in claiming and cultivating his Czech heritage.

One facet of this was his nurturing of the memory of his saintly predecessor and original namesake Václav. When Charles rebuilt Hradčany, which on his arrival in 1333 he had discovered "so devastated, ruined, and broken, that since the time of King [Přemysl] Otakar II it had completely tumbled to the ground,"[10] the castle complex was dominated by his magnificent new Saint Vitus's Cathedral, the third on the site. The cathedral's foundation stone was laid by Charles, his father the then king, and his brother Jan on 21 November 1344. Though it is consecrated for Saint Vitus, the heart of the building is the tomb and lusciously ornate chapel of the native Saint Václav, with its walls of jasper, amethyst, and chalcedony. According to the chronicler Beneš Krabice z Weitmile, Charles wished Václav to have a tomb unrivaled in the world, and he girded the saint's skull with pure gold.[11] Nowhere was Charles's "particular pious respect toward his chief protector and helper,"[12] and toward the Přemyslid past more generally, better displayed than at his coronation. Characteristically, Charles drew up the plans for the occasion himself:

On the coronation eve the ceremonies begin with a procession to Vyšehrad— followed by vespers in Saint Vitus's Cathedral. . . . The coronation begins with the ceremony of awakening and dressing of the king—there follows a procession from the king's bedchamber to the church, where there is first of all a sermon— then the king's promise, that he will serve God, defend the Church and the kingdom—then the promise of all those present, that they will obey the king— then a litany beseeching the aid of the saints, above all the patron saints of the land—then prayers of blessing—then holy mass, up to the evangelium—then procession with holy oil, which two abbots bring from the Saint Václav Chapel— then the anointing of the king's head, breast, shoulders, and arms by the archbishop—then the coronation robes . . . will be put on over the tunic, in which the king entered the cathedral—then anointing of the king's hands—then prayers before blessing and handing over of the insignia: the coronation cape, sword, bracelets, ring, scepter, orb, and crown—then the coronation—then the blessing—then enthronement of the king—then the ceremonial oath of homage, at which the chapter choirboys sing the Te Deum in Latin, and the congregation sings *Hospodine, pomiluj ny* in Czech—and to conclude, the king's promise: justice and peace to Church and subjects.[13]

The echoes of a specifically Czech past here are manifest, sustained, and deliberate.

Vyšehrad, by this time, had not been a royal seat for two centuries, since Soběslav I (1125–40). Charles was engaged in a very conscious revivalism. The song "*Hospodine, pomiluj ny*" (Lord, have mercy on us), a Slavonic version of the Kyrie Eleison, is the oldest known hymn in Czech. If it is indeed this song that is referred to in the first Czech chronicle, that of the Prague monk Kosmas, written around the years 1119–25, it was already being sung four centuries before Charles's coronation at the enthronement of Bishop Dětmar in 973.[14] Of note, too, is the crown itself, the symbolic centerpiece of the whole ceremony. Fashioned to Charles's own specifications, it is modeled not only on the French royal crown but also on the crowns of the Přemyslids. Weighing almost 2.5 kilograms, it is made of twenty-two-carat gold and decorated with twenty pearls and ninety-six precious stones; six of its nineteen sapphires are among the ten largest in the world. It has been known ever since as Saint Václav's crown, for reasons Beneš Krabice z Weitmile explains: "The king then gifted the crown, with which he was himself crowned, to Saint Václav, so that on specific days it would be placed on Václav's head in Prague Cathedral, and he laid down that all Czech kings, his heirs, should be crowned with this crown and should use it only on the day of their coronation and lodge it the same day for the night in the Prague sacristy. This was under threat of excommunication, which would be pronounced by the pope."[15]

In Charles's time the Bohemian kingdom reached the summit of its medieval power and prosperity. The Luxembourgs' acquisitions included Cheb (Eger) on the western marches of Bohemia, and Lusatia and Silesia, now parts of Germany and Poland, to the north. For a time (1373–1415) Prague's sway even extended over Brandenburg, and Berlin fell under Bohemian rule. Lusatia was to remain part of the lands of the Bohemian crown until 1635, Silesia until 1742, when it was finally lost to Prussia by empress of Austria Maria Theresa. Charles also strengthened the constitutional position of the Kingdom of Bohemia within the Holy Roman Empire, ending its formal status as an imperial fief, revoking Czechs' right of appeal to imperial courts in legal disputes, and making the Bohemian king preeminent among the lay imperial electors. He took Prague for his imperial capital, and it blossomed into one of medieval Europe's foremost commercial and cultural centers. During his reign it had perhaps forty thousand inhabitants, a population peak it was seldom to attain again before the mid–eighteenth century. The king-emperor did much to give the city the dimensions it kept into the nineteenth century and some of the landmarks it retains to the present day.

He founded Prague's New Town [Nové město], a masterpiece of rational urban planning with its spacious boulevards and squares, in 1348. Karlovo náměstí (Charles Square), as it has since become, was and is the largest city square in Europe. From 1354, Charles had the Bohemian and imperial crown jewels and saints' relics publicly displayed there once a year. He renovated Vyšehrad. He built the 520-meter-long stone bridge over the River Vltava which today bears his name, Charles Bridge [Karlův most], as well as the so-called Hunger Wall—a job-creation project for the unemployed—on Petřín Hill, and the Emmaus Abbey. Founded in 1347, this Benedictine cloister, with papal permission, revived the Old Slavonic liturgy. Three years earlier Charles had already taken advantage of his intimacy with Pope Clement VI (who had been his boyhood tutor in Paris) to have Prague finally elevated to an archbishopric. It was also Charles who in 1348 established in "our *metropolitan* and most charming city of Prague" the oldest university in central Europe. He did this, in his own words, "in order that *faithful subjects of our kingdom*, who ceaselessly hunger for the fruits of knowledge, should not be forced to beg for foreign help . . . [and] seek out alien nations or plead for the satisfaction of their longings in unknown lands."[16]

Against All

Although the Hussite Wars that erupted forty years after Charles's death did much to undo his accomplishments, their memory was to be no less inspirational in the nineteenth and twentieth centuries than the Přemyslid beginnings and Caroline golden age of the medieval Bohemian state. The religious and national tensions that were to tear the kingdom apart built up through the reign of Charles's son and successor, Václav IV (1378–1419). Charles's own attempts to clean up the Czech church, which suffered from all the usual medieval corruptions, were no doubt themselves a contributing factor; he had personally encouraged evangelical preaching throughout the kingdom, in the countryside as well as the towns. He invited to Prague Konrad of Waldhauser, who thundered in the Týn Cathedral on the Old Town Square against simony, frauds with holy relics, and monastic sale of burial plots.

The greatest homegrown preacher of Charles's reign—and a subject, later, of Alfons Mucha's *Slovanská epopej*—was the Moravian Jan Milíč z Kroměříže (d. 1374). Though of humble origins, Milíč became a member of Charles's chancellery and a Prague canon before in 1362 he gave up all his estates and offices in order "in complete poverty to serve Christ and his gospel."[17] He warned of the imminent coming of the Apocalypse and forcefully reminded his congregations of the base equality of all, from king to serf, before the Last Judgment. Twice he was summoned before the pope to answer accusations of heresy. Among those whom Milíč influenced in the next generation were Matěj z Janova (c. 1350–94) and Tomáš Štítný ze Štítného (c. 1333–c.

1409). The quiet and scholarly Prague canon Matěj criticized the cult of saints and their relics, and anticipated the Hussites in his advocacy of communion in both kinds (*sub utraque specie*; i.e., with both bread and wine) for laity as well as priests. Tomáš Štítný was a southern Bohemian squire who sought to popularize Milíč's ideas. His métier was not theology but books of practical moral education, and he was no rebel. But he was a layman writing about religious affairs, and he wrote, moreover, in Czech. Both, from the point of view of the Church, were threatening transgressions. Around the same time, in the 1370s to 1380s, the Bible was first translated into the Czech vernacular.[18]

Jan Hus himself was born around 1370 in Husinec in southern Bohemia. He studied at Prague university, becoming a master of arts in 1396 and lecturing there from 1398, the same year he was ordained a priest. From 1402 he began to preach in Prague's Bethlehem Chapel, a church in the Old Town [*Staré město*] founded in 1391 expressly for the delivery of sermons in Czech. Hus rapidly gained a large popular audience for his attacks on the vices and abuses of the Church. A follower of the English reformer John Wyclif, he enunciated many tenets of what was to become the Protestant Reformation a century before Luther. Wyclifism was a bone of contention in the university from the 1380s, and the theological conflict soon turned into a national one, dividing Germans and Czechs on the faculty. In 1403, under a German rector, the university banned all Wyclif's books as heretical, a stance reiterated by Archbishop Zbyněk z Hazmburka in 1408. The following year Václav IV's Kutná Hora decree gave the Czechs a majority in the university's government, and Hus himself became its rector. Many German professors and students left Prague in protest, to found new universities at Leipzig and Erfurt. In 1410 the archbishop publicly burned Wyclif's works and pronounced an anathema on Hus, who continued preaching at Bethlehem regardless and organized a public defense of Wyclif at the university. The Papal Curia itself now excommunicated Hus as a heretic. Undeterred, he began to preach in 1412 against the sale of papal indulgences. When the Bethlehem Chapel was threatened by Prague Germans in the autumn of that year, Hus fled the city for southern Bohemia. Here he continued to preach and write, evidently to good effect, since the region subsequently became a bastion of the Hussite movement. Beside penning religious tracts, he found the time to reform Czech spelling; it was he who introduced diacritical marks into the written language.

In 1414 Hus was summoned to answer charges of heresy before the Council of Konstanz. Trusting to the safe conduct issued him by Václav's brother Emperor Zikmund (Sigismund), king of Hungary, he complied. On his arrival in Konstanz he was swiftly imprisoned. When he refused to recant before the council, he was burned at the stake on 6 July 1415. His ashes were scraped from the ground and thrown into the Rhine, so that nothing of him should get back to Bohemia. It was a superfluous gesture. The Czech nobility had already condemned Hus's arrest; now they assembled in Prague and sent a blistering protest to Konstanz. They defended Hus as "a good, just and Christian man," who "faithfully preached God's law of the Old and New Testaments." As significantly, they portrayed Hus's immolation as a *national* insult. There were 452 seals attached to the letter, including those of the highest officials in Bohemia and Moravia. The council is accused, repeatedly, of "bringing into disgrace and humiliation our kingdom and margravate." The Czechs remind the prelates that "in times when almost every kingdom of the world often wavered and supported schism in the Church and papal pretenders, our most Christian Czech Kingdom and Moravian Margravate always stood solid as a rock and never ceased to adhere to the Holy Roman Church, giving her unblemished and sincere obedience ever since we first accepted the Christian faith of Our Lord Jesus Christ." As to those "of whatever estate, rank, elevation, station, or order" who allege that "fallacies and heresies run wild in the said kingdom and margravate," "each and every such person is lying through his teeth like the worst villain and traitor of the said kingdom and margravate, like our worst enemy, and is himself the most harmful heretic, filled with all evil and unrighteousness, nay the son of the devil, who is a liar and the father of lies." The only one excepted from this equation of heresy and treason—for the time being—is Emperor Zikmund, "whom we believe and hope is innocent."[19]

The following May another Czech, Master Jeroným Pražský, was burned at Konstanz. Prague university issued its own "Testimonial on Hus and Jeroným,"[20] which provoked the council to order it to be closed indefinitely. This order was ignored, and in March 1417 the university publicly declared itself for communion in both kinds.[21] Though communion in both kinds was not, in fact, part of Jan Hus's own teaching (it came from Jakoubek ze Stříbra, but Hus accepted it in Konstanz), the chalice became the symbol of the Hussite movement. Between 1416 and 1419 papal loyalists were expelled from churches in Prague and elsewhere and replaced by Hussites, and Church lands began to be seized and monasteries suppressed. For a time, Václav IV protected the reformers, but under threat of an imperial invasion in 1419 he ordered the return of all parishes to their former incumbents. Hussite priests continued to administer communion in both kinds to swelling congregations in the open air, and tempers rose. On 30 July 1419 the Hussite revolution, as it was rapidly becoming, turned violent with the so-called first defenestration of Prague, when a crowd fired up by the radical preacher Jan Želivský stormed the Town Hall of the New Town and threw its councillors from the windows. Two weeks later Václav IV died of a heart attack. Over the next three days, Prague mobs attacked monasteries, churches, and the houses of German burghers, many of whom fled the city.

Václav's legal successor as Czech king was his brother, none other than

Emperor Zikmund. Refusing a negotiated settlement with the Hussite nobility, Zikmund obtained papal backing for a crusade against the heretical kingdom. The Czech nobles assembled in Prague Castle in April 1420 and issued a proclamation to all Czechs and Moravians. Their appeal was directed as much to patriotism as religion. It reviled Zikmund as "a great and brutal enemy of the Czech kingdom and language," whose intention is "nothing other than to ignominiously and brutally weed out and obliterate the Czech kingdom and crown and especially the Czech language." The nobles set out their demands as follows: "First, communion of the body and blood of the Lord under both kinds for all lay people. Second, proper and free preaching of the word of God. Third, that priests would be such living examples to us as the Lord Christ commanded and his Apostles and after them the holy fathers instituted. And fourth, the common weal of the kingdom and our Czech language and the cleansing of the kingdom and the Czech language from evil and false rumor."[22]

The first three of these demands, together with another, that clergy be punishable in lay courts for mortal sins, came to form the Four Articles of Prague,[23] which were agreed later that summer as a minimum program acceptable to all the various factions among the Hussite reformers.

In June 1420 Zikmund arrived with a large army and occupied Hradčany. It is at this point that events take an unprecedented turn. Led by the one-eyed Jan Žižka z Trocnova (c. 1360–1424), an impoverished squire [zeman] from southern Bohemia, an army of Hussite peasants had arrived in Prague in May from Tábor, a commune established a few months earlier in expectation of the Second Coming. The Táborites rejected all ecclesiastical authority save that of the Bible; they were also, at least at the beginning, proponents of radical social equality, requiring all adherents to pool their private property. They were soon reinforced by troops from other Hussite strongholds: Slaný, Louny, and Žatec. Žižka's peasants soundly defeated Zikmund's imperial crusaders at Vítkov Hill, which commands the eastern approaches to the city, on 14 July 1420. Two weeks later the Old Town Council seized the property of all those who had fled the city in the turmoils, most of them Germans, and redistributed it among Hussite Czechs. Zikmund, meantime, had himself crowned king of Bohemia in Saint Vitus's. But his army was beaten again at Pankrác trying to relieve Vyšehrad in November, and Praguers promptly laid waste the former royal seat. Zikmund abandoned his kingdom to the Hussites.

Over the next fourteen years four more foreign crusades were repulsed by Žižka, who died unexpectedly in October 1424, and his successor the warrior-priest Prokop Holý. The Hussites' victories were won by peasant infantries, using weapons adapted in many cases from farm implements, and disciplined by a shared and fervent faith; they struck sheer terror as they marched into battle singing "Ye who are the soldiers of God" [Ktož sú boží *bojovníci*]. Such heroic images of Czech unity "against all" [*proti všem*][24] were to be recalled in the nineteenth century as a source of national pride. At the time, however, things were considerably more confused. When not fighting off Zikmund, Czechs were savaging one another. Though the Czech Diet repudiated Zikmund as king in 1421, no agreed or willing successor was found (the Polish Jagellons were approached but were unwilling to defy the pope), and no other effective form of national governance emerged. Power devolved to the local nobility, the cities—especially Prague—and above all the Hussite military communes, of which the most important were Tábor itself, and Oreb in eastern Bohemia. The country was devastated by their activities; Church lands were seized, monasteries sacked, Germans slaughtered or expelled, and defiant towns and villages reduced to rubble. In the face of such persuasion Plzeň (Pilsen) in western Bohemia was the last major town to declare itself for the Articles of Prague, in 1421.

The Hussites also split among themselves. The broadest division was between so-called Utraquists (from *sub utraque specie*), who were satisfied with the Four Articles, and Táborites and other radicals, whose puritanical zeal extended among other things to proscribing dancing and plays as mortal sins. The Táborites celebrated mass in Czech, in extreme simplicity and without ecclesiastical vestments, and encouraged even women and children to read the Bible for themselves, distrusting the pride of the learned. There was a manifest class dimension to this conflict, even if it has often been exaggerated in the cardboard cutouts of communist historiography. But Jan Žižka had no scruples about expelling the still more radical Adamites from Tábor in 1421. The Christian anarchism of Petr Chelčický (c. 1390–c. 1460)—another subject of Mucha's *Slovanská epopej*—also fell on deaf ears; not only did he reject all earthly authority, he also held it wrong for Christians to kill. Conflicts between Utraquists and radicals in Prague culminated in the impromptu execution of Jan Želivský, whose sermons had sparked the defenestration of 1419, together with nine of his followers on the steps of the Old Town Hall in 1422.

After the rout of yet another crusade at Domažlice near the Bavarian border in 1431, the Papacy abandoned force for diplomacy and found willing enough partners to negotiate among the Prague Utraquists. The Hussite cause gained an important moral victory when the council agreed to debate issues of theology with the Czechs and decide them on the basis of Scripture and the practice of the early Church alone. Thus reassured, a Czech delegation led by the Utraquist leader Jan Rokycana (1390s-1471) and Prokop Holý departed for Basle in 1433. The Four Articles were accepted as a basis of settlement by the Church, though with limitations on all of them except communion in both kinds. The Táborite and Orebite fraternities were unwilling to accept this compromise. Combining now with the rump of the Czech Catholics, the Utraquists defeated the radicals at the fratricidal battle of Lipany in 1434. Prokop Holý was one of those killed. With this, the road to settlement was open. The Hussite Church was accepted back into the Roman fold and permitted, as a unique privilege, to celebrate communion in both kinds; Jan Rokycana was recognized by Zikmund as archbishop of Prague (though his appointment was never formally ratified by the Vatican); and Czech aristocrats got to keep the estates they had seized from the Church. On 14 August 1436 Zikmund was ceremonially welcomed at Jihlava as Czech king, and the Compacts of Basle were solemnly proclaimed as the basis for reconciliation. The following year Jan Roháč z Dubé, the leader of the last armed resistance to Zikmund's return, was publicly executed along with fifty-six of his followers in Prague.

One does not have to be a Marxist to detect a social content within these religious wrappings. Though he repeatedly insists that these were medieval, religious struggles, even Josef Pekař (1870–1937), the most conservative of Czech historians, freely concedes that "powerful social and economic influences acted in concert on the development of the [Hussite] movement." He emphasizes the vanguard role of the towns, above all Prague, and within them "the struggle of Czech artisan strata against richer German old-established families, who controlled city governance; during the revolution these families were expelled or slaughtered and their property divided among Czechs." In Bohemia in particular (Moravia was less affected) the revolution culminated in a "Czechization of the burgher estate." Pekař also stresses the interest of the Czech aristocracy, and in particular of the straitened minor nobility, in expropriation of Church lands—more than a third of the realm at the time—and royal estates. The peasants, he says, had no direct economic interest in revolution, unless it were the hope of greater freedom, in which they were to be disappointed; they flocked to Tábor out of religious enthusiasm.[25] But we have seen the radically leveling messages of the preachers who inspired them, from Milíč through Želivský to Chelčický. In thus "explaining" events by their putative material causes, however, we have not entirely dispensed with their cultural significance.

The Compacts of Basle and return of Zikmund did not end the religious strife in Bohemia, which got mixed up with issues of succession after Zikmund's death in 1437. In 1458, the Czech Diet elected as king of Bohemia the Utraquist leader Jiří z Poděbrad (1420–71), who had been regent of the kingdom during Ladislav Pohrobek's minority since 1453. "The Hussite King" Jiří was the first Czech to sit on the Bohemian throne since the Přemyslids, over 150 years earlier. Though the emperor grudgingly recognized him, the Papal Curia would not. Pius II repudiated the Compacts of Basle in 1462, and his successor Paul II excommunicated Jiří z Poděbrad as a heretic in 1466 and proclaimed another holy war. This time the cudgels were taken up by both the Bohemian Catholic nobles of the League of Zelená Hora, and

Mathyas Corvinus of Hungary, who invaded (and was duly defeated) in 1468.

The following year there appeared a "Call to Arms in Defense of the Truth," addressed "to all faithful Czechs and Moravians, genuine lovers of God's truth and disciples of your own Czech language." Issued in the name of representatives "from various regions of the Czech and Moravian land, in number some three thousand, who want in the name of God to see through this truth and this Czech language against all enemies of the Czech language," it portrayed the issues at stake in the conflict that had by now racked Bohemia for more than half a century thus: "Having in mind above all God's glory and the preservation of his holy truth and the calming of this Czech and Moravian land, we understand that the pope, who should protect and defend that holy truth to his death, to the contrary wants, as a disobedient servant of his Lord, to destroy that holy truth and moreover to destroy, wipe out, and utterly suppress the Czech language, merely to preserve his pride, his avarice, and the rest of his vices. . . . He inflames and incites all the nations and languages of the surrounding lands against us."[26] It is a remarkable passage; but one quite typical of its time and place. Virtually all Hussite manifestos since 1420 had struck the same notes. It is evidently medieval in its Christian preoccupations and frame of reference; its fundamentalist certainty is alien, even repellent, to modern sensibilities. But it is no less evidently, and rather disconcertingly, modern—or what we are accustomed, at any rate, to think of as modern—in its identification of truth and virtue with a land, a people, and their language. The Hussites imagined their sacral community in unmistakably national terms and attributed sanctity less to Latin than to their native Czech.

All this happened without the aid of the printing press; the first known book printed in the Czech lands, Guido de Columna's *Trojan Chronicle*, appeared in Plzeň in 1468. But it is perhaps worth recording that when print capitalism did arrive in Bohemia, it too came predominantly in the Czech vernacular. Of forty-four books known to have been printed in Bohemia before 1500, thirty-nine were in Czech. Over the next hundred years some 4,400 books were printed in the Czech lands. Many were of course religious, among them the magnificent Czech Protestant *Bible kralická* of 1579–94. But there were also vernacular histories, geographies, medical works, moral homilies, and (perhaps most tellingly) cookbooks and manuals of household economy. Melantrich, the earliest Czech publishing house (as distinct from individual printer), employed eleven people in 1577. In its thirty-year existence it published at least 223 books—111 of them in Czech, 75 in Latin, and only 3 in German.[27] Pope Pius II, who as papal legate Enea Silvio de Piccolomini visited Bohemia and subsequently wrote *Historia Bohemica* (1458; first published in Czech in 1510 as *Kronika česká*), was one who appreciated the importance to Czechs of their native tongue. Writing to Ladislav Pohrobek after his coronation in 1453, the pope suggests that the Czechs will not let their new boy-king go "until he masters Czech and—beer-drinking."[28]

Three Hundred Years We Suffered

However potent it may have been in later memory, the Hussite period seriously weakened the Bohemian kingdom both economically and politically. Jiří z Poděbrad was the last Czech to wear Saint Václav's crown. At his death in 1471 no domestic candidate could be agreed upon to succeed him, and the Czech Diet turned instead for a king to the Polish Jagellonský royal family. The Jagellons were absentee monarchs, and the country was effectively ruled during their tenure by the Czech nobility. In 1526 the Diet elected a Habsburg, Ferdinand I, brother of Holy Roman Emperor Charles V, to the Bohemian throne. Though thoroughly comprehensible in the circumstances of the time—one of them being the Turkish thrust into central Europe—this proved to be a fateful choice. Ferdinand immediately set about consolidating royal power. He bypassed the Land diets, establishing a Privy Council to handle domestic and foreign policy and a Vienna-based Court Chamber to oversee the royal finances. In 1528 he curbed the autonomy of Prague and other cities, and dissolved the district diets that had been the traditional forums of the lower nobility. The Schmalkaldic War of 1546–47 sparked a revolt by Protestant Czech nobles and most of the royal cities. Ferdinand took advantage of its defeat to subordinate city administrations to appointed royal officials, bring all city and district courts under the jurisdiction of a new Court of Appeal in Prague, and make the convocation and agendas of all future diets the sole prerogative of the crown. He also had the Czech Diet give up its traditional right to elect the king (though it kept the right to "accept" him) and recognize the Habsburg succession as hereditary. Thereafter, the Czech lands were gradually, but inexorably, incorporated into what eventually became the Austrian Empire.

This absorption did not take place without conflict. Czech nobles and burghers came increasingly to resent the Habsburgs' erosion of their traditional power and privileges. Under the new dynasty there was also a renewal of German influence and settlement in Bohemia, stirring up old national animosities. Rudolf II (1576–1611), who was also Holy Roman Emperor, made Prague his imperial capital like Charles IV had before him. He beautified the city, amassed a stupendous art collection, and embellished his court with some of Europe's leading intellectuals, among them Tycho de Brahe (who is buried in the Týn Cathedral) and Johannes Kepler; but this was a glitter that had precious little of Czechness in it. As in the fifteenth century, the ultimate flash point became religion. The ideas of the German Reformation fell on fertile Hussite soil, and by the beginning of the seventeenth century the large majority of Czechs were probably Protestant. Certainly most Czech nobles and burghers were, but under Rudolf and Matyáš (1611–19) the most important offices in what was now a far more centralized kingdom were held by Roman Catholics. The old Utraquist religious compromise had long since broken down. The Utraquist Church itself split into so-called Old and New Utraquists during Ferdinand's reign, and the New Utraquists were for all practical purposes Lutherans. Under this pressure the Old Utraquists gravitated more and more toward Catholicism.[29] The Catholic Church itself during this period was no longer the corrupt and decadent body the Hussites had defied two centuries earlier, but the cleansed and militant champion of the Counter-Reformation. In 1562 Jesuits established their own college in Prague, the Klementinum, which successfully vied with the Utraquist-controlled university for academic prestige. It was given full university status in 1616.

Meanwhile a distinctively Czech Protestant denomination, the Jednota bratrská (Union of Brethren), was gaining in both converts and influence. Though it was never numerically preponderant among Czech Protestants, the Jednota's intellectual impact was considerable both at the time and—equally important here—on later historical memory. Tomáš Masaryk, among others, was to see the moral heritage of the Brethren as lying at the very heart of Czech identity. The Jednota bratrská first coalesced in the mid–fifteenth century out of the fragments of Hussite radicalism, and the Brethren were much influenced in their early phase by the ideas of Petr Chelčický. They definitively broke with both the Catholic and the Utraquist Churches by establishing their own priesthood, with elected bishops, in 1468. They always put greater emphasis on Christian practice than on theology, and veered doctrinally between Lutheranism in the first half of the sixteenth century and Calvinism in the second without ever subscribing fully to either. Nevertheless they enjoyed generally warm relations with Protestants abroad. Luther himself parted with the Brethren's bishop Jan Augusta in Wittenberg in 1542 with the words: "Let you be the Apostles of the Czechs, and I with mine will be the Apostles of the Germans."[30] One aspect of the Jednota's conception of the Christian life that aroused particular ire at the time was the role it permitted women in Church affairs. When in the autumn of 1507 the Moravian noblewoman Marta z Boskovic had the temerity to write to Vladislav II protesting his proscription of the Brethren, her letter provoked the Catholic scholar Bohuslav Hasištejnský z Lobkovic, citing Saint Paul's well-known injunction to women to remain silent in the Church, to spluttering fury: "Perhaps this sex is so protected by the laws of the devil that virtually no heresy in God's Church can spread without them. . . . These women followed our Marta, although it would be better if after the example of the ancient Marta [i.e., the biblical Martha] she were to have her hands full with serving and kept to spinning and weaving."[31]

Jednota bratrská was persecuted with varying degrees of vigor from the time of Jiří z Poděbrad—who wanted a unified Utraquist hegemony—onward, and Vladislav II's Saint James's Mandate of 1502, which closed the Brethren's churches and banned their writings, was several times renewed through the sixteenth century. They thrived nonetheless. From an originally plebeian, otherworldly sect rooted among peasants and craftsmen, the Brethren broadened their appeal both to burghers and to nobles, who since they controlled benefices could often provide support and protection. This expansion was helped by the Brethren's abandonment at the end of the fifteenth century of prohibitions, deriving from Chelčický's teaching, on members holding worldly office, serving in the military, and engaging in business. Certain employments, like juggling or painting, remained forbidden, while office-holding and trade were deemed dangerous to salvation and thus deserving of particular moral scrutiny. The hardest times for the Brethren came under Ferdinand I after 1547, when many of them were driven into exile in Poland, Prussia, and Moravia, which subsequently became a Jednota stronghold. It was in Moravia, in Alfons Mucha's hometown of Ivančice, that they printed the *Bible kralická*, another event the artist—of whose profession the subjects of his picture would certainly not have approved—sought to immortalize in his *Slovanská epopej*. The great late-nineteenth-century national(ist) encyclopedia *Ottův slovník naučný* (*Otto's Encyclopedia*, 28 volumes, 1888–1909) considers this vernacular Bible, which was directly translated from the Greek and Hebrew rather than Latin, to be "the most notable Czech literary work of the Middle Ages from the linguistic point of view, an inexhaustible treasury of the Czech language."[32]

There are obvious parallels to be drawn between the situation in the Czech lands in the first two decades of the seventeenth century and that which had prevailed two hundred years earlier, on the eve of the Hussite Wars. These resemblances were to permit the two to be rhetorically assimilated in later nationalist discourses as comparable episodes in an age-old story of Czech struggles for freedom. In both cases there was a similarly explosive admixture of religious commitment and political resentment, which fused in hostility to an external imperial power. The differences, however, are at least as significant. To begin with, the division between Protestants and Catholics in seventeenth-century Bohemia did not coincide with that between Czechs and Germans. Some of the foremost Czech aristocrats, among them members of the Šternberk and Lobkovic families, remained staunchly Catholic; it was the actions of Rudolf's and Matyáš's Supreme Chancellor Zdeněk z Lobkovic that did much to provoke the eventual revolt. Some leaders of the Protestant nobility, on the other hand, like Counts Thurn, Schlick, and Mansfeld, were German. Most of the German-speaking population in the Czech borderlands were by this time Lutherans. Equally importantly, the Kingdom of Bohemia had for practical purposes already lost its independence, and its internal struggles could not be isolated from the religious and political conflicts engulfing Europe as a whole. It was no longer either in representation or in reality a matter of Czechs "against all." Bohemia was a pawn in a Continental game. Where the Hussite Wars had been integrally and obviously national, the conflicts of the seventeenth century were only secondarily so. Their result, nonetheless, was to jeopardize the very existence of a Czech nation.

Dissension came to a head in the Rising of the Czech Estates, which triggered the Thirty Years' War. Appropriately enough, the rebellion began with a second defenestration of Prague, 199 years after the first. On 21 May 1618 Protestant nobles convened a General Diet, and two days later a mob turfed three Catholic imperial officials (who survived the experience) from the windows of Prague Castle. In August of the next year a General Diet of all the lands of the Czech kingdom formally repudiated the Habsburg succession and offered the throne to Frederick, the protestant elector of the Palatinate, son-in-law of King James I of England and VI of Scotland. Frederick was crowned and moved into Hradčany on 4 November 1619. The "Winter King" reigned for just a year and four days. Despite some initial military successes, the rebellion was decisively crushed by the troops of Emperor Ferdinand II (1619–37), Matyáš's legitimate Habsburg successor, at the battle of Bílá hora—the White Mountain—on the western outskirts of Prague on 8 November 1620. Frederick and his court immediately fled the city, leaving it defenseless before Ferdinand's army. Bílá hora settled the fate of the Kingdom of Bohemia for the next three centuries; it was without any doubt the most cataclysmic event in modern Czech history.

Ferdinand's revenge was swift, brutal, and overwhelming. On Monday 21 June 1621, between five and nine in the morning, twenty-seven Czech aristocrats and burghers were publicly executed in Prague's Old Town Square, Staroměstské náměstí. The executioner dealt with Jan Jesenský (Jessenius), the rector of Prague University, particularly cruelly; his tongue was cut out and nailed to the block before he was beheaded.[33] The heads of twelve of the executed were displayed on the tower of Charles Bridge for ten years until, during the brief occupation of Prague by a Saxon Protestant army in 1631, they were ceremonially buried in the Týn Cathedral. Literal was followed by social decapitation: the indigenous Protestant nobility, burgher estate, and intelligentsia were to all intents and purposes destroyed. The estates of Protestant lords were confiscated on a grand scale, and gifted or sold cheaply to Catholic loyalists. Over three-quarters of the land in the kingdom, Church and crown estates excepted, changed hands in the 1620s.[34] Out of this a largely new—and often foreign—aristocracy emerged, even if some of the biggest beneficiaries, like Albrecht z Valdštejna, creator of the Valdštejn (Waldstein) Palace in Prague, were Czechs.

Non-Catholic priests were banished from Bohemia, and the laity forbidden communion in both kinds, in 1621; in 1624 an imperial patent declared Catholicism to be the sole permitted religion in the kingdom; and three years later Protestant nobles and burghers were given the choice of reversion to Catholicism or banishment. Ferdinand's Re-Catholicization Patent of 31 July 1627 began with a reminder of happier days:

Dear faithful!

It is known throughout the world and within the land that our hereditary Czech kingdom almost never and in no other time enjoyed greater prosperity or elevation than during the life and government of our late highly esteemed ancestor, Emperor Charles IV of blessed and glorious memory. Out of the special fatherly care and love that he had for your forefathers and dear homeland, Charles entirely prudently and well foresaw that religious divergence and disparity in one kingdom and land would be an impossible basis for establishing or safeguarding true lasting peace or true sincere allegiance either to authority, or even among subjects themselves. That is also why he promulgated in the Czech kingdom a law and statutes and bound all his spiritual and lay officials and councils to keep these laws everywhere and always in view and to attend to them with the greatest of diligence, so that outside the holy, apostolic, and only Christian Roman religion (which had endured unassailed ever since the kingdom was first led out of paganism into the Christian faith) no other faith, nor tempting, heretical, and malignant fallacies, bands [roty], or sects, would be introduced or permitted.

Regrettably, it is also well enough known and clear as day that after his blissful death, during the time of the late King Václav [IV], perhaps because of a certain negligence every possible kind of fallacy and heresy sneaked into this our hereditary kingdom, whereupon disorders, quarrels, and wickedness set in among subjects themselves. . . . [This state of affairs] renewed itself repeatedly under almost all subsequent kings. . . .

Up to the time when Almighty God by his divine blessing gave us victory before Prague over our rebels, enemies, and opponents we set out to do nothing greater or more comprehensive than truly to follow the renowned and glorious, worthy example of the blissful Emperor Charles IV (who was in his time reckoned the Father of the Homeland and proved himself such by his deed) . . . in order that now our hereditary Czech kingdom could once again attain the prosperity it enjoyed in the time of our ancestor of glorious memory the late Emperor Charles IV.[35]

Memory was being mobilized here the better to serve forgetting. In the language of a later age, all Ferdinand wanted was normalization, a return, after an unfortunate interval of alien disorders—two centuries of them, in this case—to a path of virtue charted very much earlier, which corresponded to what was asserted to be the nation's own essential character.

In the event, a fifth of Czech and Moravian nobles (185 families) and almost a quarter of the country's burghers chose their faith over their homeland; Prague alone lost around 120 Protestant burgher families, a twentieth of its inhabitants.[36] By the end of the Thirty Years' War in 1648, fighting and emigration between them had reduced Bohemia's population by perhaps as much as a half, and its economy was in ruins. The confiscations and banishments not only decisively tilted the religious balance of power in the kingdom but also wholly reshaped its class structure. In the mid–sixteenth century the combined landholdings of the lesser nobility [stav rytířský] were reckoned to exceed those of the greater [stav panský]. A hundred years later the páni owned 60 percent of the land and the rytíři only 10 percent, while the burghers were so impoverished that they contributed only 13 percent of Bohemia's total tax revenues.[37] It is scarcely surprising that on these foundations the condition of the rural population was to be greatly degraded in the following decades, with ever more onerous labor services eventually provoking the Peasant Revolt of 1680. The uprising was ruthlessly suppressed by the imperial army with a torrent of exemplary executions.

The political fallout of Bílá hora for the Bohemian kingdom was no less ruinous. Augmentation of royal power and integration of the Czech lands into an empire ruled from Vienna, which had been progressing de facto since 1526, was now regularized. When after seven years of absolutist rule the Land constitution was "renewed" in 1627, the Czech Chancellery (which had moved lastingly to Vienna in 1624) had its powers considerably strengthened, while those of the Bohemian Diet were as severely curtailed. The Diet retained the right to grant taxes, but was forbidden to deliberate on matters other than those put before it by the king, and lost all capacity to initiate legislation except (after 1640) in relatively minor matters. It also acquired a clerical first estate, made up of the archbishop and prelates who held freehold tenures, something without precedent in Czech history. Its burgher estate was reduced to practical insignificance; the burghers' collective vote had the same weight as that of each individual in the higher estates. Another important power the Diet lost to the crown was that of regulating residence in the kingdom, which meant that foreigners could freely buy up estates without Czech permission or hindrance. Decisions of Czech courts could now be appealed to the king-emperor—a reversal of the situation that had obtained ever since Charles IV—and the German language gained equal status with Czech, a position it had never previously enjoyed, in the functioning of state bodies. Although the kingdom itself legally remained an independent state linked to Vienna only by the person of the monarch, the Diet lost the residual right it had retained after 1547 to "assent to" each new sovereign. The Habsburg succession was declared hereditary "by sword and by spindle" [po meči i po přeslici; i.e., on both the male and female side].[38] Given the powers that now resided in the crown, this enshrined the effective loss of Czech sovereignty to Vienna in stone. A similar constitution was promulgated for Moravia the following year.

But perhaps the most significant long-term consequences of Bílá hora were cultural. Among the Protestant émigrés were many of Bohemia's leading intellectuals of the day. Most eminent were the historian Pavel Stránský (1583–1657) and the renowned humanist pedagogue Jan Amos Komenský (Comenius, 1592–1670), who was to become in exile the Brethren's last bishop. Komenský's beautifully titled and most famous book, *The Labyrinth of the World and the Paradise of the Heart* [*Labyrint světa a ráj srdce*], was written, in Czech, in "this but too turbulent time, full of disquietude,"[39] in Brandýs nad Orlicí in 1623. It was first printed abroad in 1631; it did not appear in Bohemia until 1782, and was again suppressed by the censor in 1820. In its form *The Labyrinth of the World* resembles John Bunyan's later *Pilgrim's Progress*. The first part of the book, in Komenský's own words, "depicts the follies and inanities of the world, showing how mainly and with great labor it busies itself with worthless things, and how these things at last end wretchedly, either in laughter or in tears. The second describes, partly as through a veil, and partly openly the true and firm felicity of the sons of God; for they are indeed happy who, turning their backs on the world and all worldly things, adhere, and indeed inhere, to God."[40] In the previous three years of war Komenský had successively lost his house, his library, his wife, and his children. He abandoned Bohemia in 1628 and wandered thereafter through Poland, England, Germany, Sweden, and Hungary before finally settling in Holland. He died in Amsterdam in 1670, and is buried in Naarden; Alfons Mucha painted his last days there in the *Slovanská epopej*. Near the end of his life Komenský sadly reflected: "I never had it in mind to write, let alone publish, anything in Latin. I only sought to be useful to my nation and write some books in the native language; this desire came to me in my youth and has never deserted me through all these fifty years; only external circumstances led me to other things."[41] Stránský's *The Czech State*, written in Latin, first came out in Leiden in Holland in 1634. It too was not to be published in Bohemia until over 150 years later, in 1792–1803, in German translation, or in Czech until a full hundred years after that, in 1893.[42] The same fate befell most other works of the emigration. Not for the last time in Czech history, a "Bohemia of the soul" parted ways with the corporeal Bohemia, and as is inevitable in such partings, the two soon lost touch.[43]

Back home, the written word was meanwhile ruthlessly controlled. Prague university was put under Jesuit administration in 1620 and eventually merged with the Klementinum in 1653 to form the Karl-Ferdinand University. Its rectors oversaw all schools in Bohemia and ran an efficient censorship that lasted in its full vigor until Joseph II's reforms in the 1780s. The Jesuit Antonín Koniáš (1691–1760), whose "Index of Prohibited or Dangerous and Suspicious Books," a lengthy local elaboration of the Papal Index, came to provide the main censors' manual in the eighteenth century, boasted of burning upward of thirty thousand books during a thirty-year career traveling through Bohemia and preaching up to five times daily.[44] Prominent among these anathematized readings was that great treasure-house of the Czech language, the *Bible kralická*. Along with the Brethren it had gone, as Czechs say, "over the hills" [*za kopečky*]; it had ceased to be part of the living culture of Bohemia itself. Simply and brutally, "[Koniáš's] *Key* either entirely or at least in part condemned almost all Czech writings from the years 1414–1620, and ordered all Czech exile literature, that is Hussite, Brethren, Lutheran, Calvinist, and Pietist books either to be utterly 'rooted out' or else rectified."[45] *All* Czech books published in Bohemia between 1414 and 1635, according to Rule 21 of the *Index Bohemicorum librorum prohibitorum*, contained heresies.[46] In its consequences this amounted to far more than a merely religious purge. Much that had thus far defined Czech history, and made Czechs who they were, could not be spoken of. The very language itself had acquired the taint of heresy.

The fate of the historian Bohuslav Balbín z Vorličné (1621–88), the leading figure of a generation of Catholic would-be Czech patriots of the later seventeenth century, is instructive. Balbín was a Czech Jesuit priest, trained at the Klementinum. He sought to be loyal equally to his homeland and its old-new religion, and was one of those involved in producing the so-called Saint Václav Bible [*Svatováclavská bible*, 1677–1715], a vernacular replacement for the *Bible kralická*, purged of heresies and errors. His *Miscellanea historica Regni Bohemiae* expresses itself in uncompromising terms about "those, whom it would be possible to number among the names of the learned, if heresy did not overtake and corrupt all the good aspects of their minds and scholarship"; names, in the case of Jan Hus and Jeroným Pražský, he "shrink[s] from pronouncing," for "they are properly to be execrated as Godless."[47] His *Epitome historica Rerum Bohemicarum*, a commentary on Czech history from the beginnings of Christianization to 1526, follows official orthodoxy in glorifying the era of that devout son of the Church, Charles IV. Nevertheless, publication of the *Epitome* was held up for eight years by Bohemia's governor Ignác Bořita z Martinic, the son of one of those defenestrated in Prague in 1618. Among other things Balbín had made the mistake of citing Pavel Stránský's *The Czech State*. What later became Balbín's most famous work, *A Defense of the Slavonic Language, in Particular Czech*, was not permitted to be published at all until 1775 (in Latin; a Czech translation had to wait until 1869). Balbín ends the book with an impassioned prayer to Saint Václav. Its most resonant line is taken from the second-oldest song in the Czech language, the Saint Václav chorale, whose first three verses had been written down by Beneš Krabice z Weitmile three hundred years earlier. The words Balbín borrows are *"Nedej zahynouti nám i budoucím!"*—"Do not let us or our descendants perish!"[48] It is scarcely surprising that under such circumstances Czech intellectual life withered, and not even the most impeccably Catholic patriotism could flourish. This was a climate in which even Pope Pius II's *Historia Bohemica* of 1458 found itself in the Index.[49] Taken together, the destruction of Bohemia's indigenous Protestant elites, absorption of the Catholic rump of its upper classes into a Viennese hegemony, and systematic policing of the written word combined to produce something little short of cultural genocide. No less significant than the multifarious obstacles thrown up by the censorship is the fact that Balbín was already writing all of these works, including his defense of Czech, in Latin. As the seventeenth century wore on into the eighteenth, the number of books of any quality written in Czech grew fewer and fewer.

By the later eighteenth century the overwhelming majority of Czechs, from nobility to peasants, were once again Roman Catholics. Lusatia and most of Silesia were gone, and Bohemia and Moravia had been Habsburg possessions since time out of mind. Prague was little more than a provincial backwater. The upper classes, whether in origin Czech or foreign, had little organic connection to the Czech past, and oriented themselves mainly to Vienna. Like much of the urban population, they spoke German. Many town dwellers, particularly in the capital, were German incomers; Czech-speakers preponderated in Prague only among the lower classes.[50] For the most part Czech had ceased to be a language of either learning or (higher) administration; the rich Czech literary heritage of the past had been mostly erased or forgotten. Where it was kept alive, ironically enough, it was Catholic priests who were mainly to be thanked. Bohemia's sociolinguistic splits were reproduced in the Church; while the episcopal hierarchy was German-speaking, most ordinary parish priests were the sons of Czech peasants. Contrary to some later assertions, the Czech language as such was by no means close to death. But it had retreated to the fields, the stables, and the kitchens. It was a badge not of nationality but of ignorance, the rude tongue of the common folk. Language no longer unified or divided nations, as it had for the Hussites, but merely social classes. It was as a *written* language that Czech so catastrophically declined after Bílá hora. The most characteristic cultural monuments of seventeenth- and eighteenth-century Bohemia are visual rather than literary. The art of the baroque is a feast that appeals to the eye, not the intellect; its architecture is an architecture of sensuous power, designed to impress and intimidate. All those resplendent baroque palaces, churches, and burgher mansions that do so much to define Prague as "the magical metropolis of old Europe" (as André Breton once called it) are testaments to the destruction of the Hussite and Protestant Bohemia on whose ruins they were erected; and a goodly proportion of them were designed by foreigners rather than Czechs.

The magnitude, the complexity, and the savage ironies of the transformation of Bohemian society and Czech identity that took place during the seventeenth and eighteenth centuries is well illustrated in the popular cult of Saint Jan Nepomucký (John of Nepomuk), whose statue inaugurated the stone procession of saints on Charles Bridge in 1683. Indeed, that march of

3. Charles Bridge and Staré město, around 1870. The domed building at center right is the Jesuit Klementinum, the twin-spired church at center left is the Týn Cathedral. To the right of the cathedral is the tower of the Old Town Hall on Staroměstské náměstí.

baroque statues across the once unadorned medieval bridge, which has come to symbolize "historic Prague" for the millions of tourists who now cross it every year, is itself as good a symbol for this transformation as any; like many places in Prague, this beauty has its own peculiar sadness. Legend had it that Jan Nepomucký was thrown from the bridge into the Vltava by Václav IV three centuries earlier, in 1393, after holding his tongue under torture and refusing to reveal the secrets of the confessional. The confession in which the king was so interested was reputedly that of his queen. Seeking a figure to displace Hus in popular memory, the Jesuits encouraged the Nepomucký cult. When the martyr's body was exhumed from its grave on 15 April 1719, his tongue was of course found miraculously intact in his skull. Jan was duly canonized in 1729. From 1771, a Jan Nepomucký festival took place in Prague every May 16. Thousands of Czech-speaking peasants annually flocked to the now "Germanized" city. Describing the scene, the nineteenth-century patriotic poet Boleslav Jablonský (1813–81) puts the following words in the mouths of these simple pilgrims: "Saint Jan, you who know the value of the tongue [*jazyk*], protect for us our golden jewel, protect for us our language [*jazyk*]."[51] What Jan Jesenský might have made of Jablonský's lingual conceit is anybody's guess. A Jesuitic fabrication—even the Vatican finally stripped Nepomucký, who was actually a composite of two four-teenth-century personages, of his sainthood in 1963—had come to watch over the vestiges of the nation of Hus, Žižka, and Komenský.

Had there been no medieval Bohemian state, there might very possibly have been no modern Czech nation either. But this modern nation is not so much rooted in that medieval experience as retrospectively reconstructed out of it. Bílá hora fractured Czech history and identity; the links to the past were severed.

THREE

REBIRTH

The Count's National Theater

TWO HUNDRED YEARS after the second defenestration of Prague, on 15 April 1818, Supreme Burgrave Count František z Kolovrat (1778–1861), Bohemia's highest state official, proclaimed the establishment of a National Museum in the city. Needless to say, Kolovrat's proclamation makes no mention of the anniversary of the Rising of the Czech Estates. But it is by no means devoid of historical reminiscences. It begins by recalling the high state of learning in Bohemia under Charles IV and "his first chancellor the pious and learned Archbishop Arnošt [of Pardubice]," and its revival, "after the storms of the fifteenth and the second half of the sixteenth centuries," during the "golden age" of Emperor Rudolf II. Now that the danger to the homeland from the Napoleonic Wars is passed, Kolovrat continues, the time is again ripe for encouragement of the arts and sciences. Despite several notable recent accomplishments in this area, much remains to be done. "There is not yet any complete comprehensive history of Czech literature, no complete record of Czech antiquities (*monumenta bohemica*), which is extremely important for teaching the history of the homeland [*vlastenská historie*], no complete documentation on natural phenomena in the Czech land . . . no geological portrait of this geologically most important land." The proposed museum aims to fill these gaps. It is intended "to contain everything belonging to the national literature and national production, as well as to survey everything brought about anywhere in the homeland by natural or human agency."

To this end, the collections will be ordered in seven divisions: (1) "A collection of national papers or documents"; (2) "Descriptions or illustrations of all antiquities, tombs, inscriptions, sculptures, . . . bas-reliefs, etc., in the Czech land"; (3) "As complete as possible a collection of coats of arms, seals, and coins of the land, or prints thereof"; (4) "A collection of maps and plans pertaining to geography and statistics, and to the oldest mining in Bohemia"; (5) "A complete natural cabinet, or collection of natural objects . . . with particular reference to the homeland, so that apart from a universal collection of minerals and fossils it will assemble a particular topographical-geological collection from all sixteen districts of the Czech land, and besides a general herbarium it will also bring together particularly Czech flora with their Czech herbal names, similarly with four-legged animals, birds, fish, earthworms, etc."; (6) "A library, encompassing Bohemica in the broadest sense, as well as the so-called incontrovertible knowledges (*scienses exactes*). To the former belong every kind of books and manuscripts written in the Czech language, produced or published by Czechs, or pertaining to Bohemia; to the latter everything belonging to the realm of mathematics and physics, both the core works, and domestic and foreign teaching aids and journals pertaining to these sciences"; and (7) "A crafts hall, in which will be exhibited manufactured and artistic works and discoveries, or exemplars (models) thereof."[1]

The idea of establishing such a museum had been Count Kašpar Šternberk's, and together with Count František Klebelsberk, who drew up its first draft proposal, and Count Kolovrat himself, Šternberk did the fund-raising, assembling of exhibits, and petitioning for imperial permission that brought about its eventual realization. The museum's initial collections and financial endowments were all provided by Czech nobles. Its foundation was the crowning glory of that movement among a section of the Bohemian aristocracy that Czech historians call "land patriotism." The same sentiment, and the same aristocratic circles, had earlier been responsible for setting up the Royal Society of Bohemia in 1784 [*Česká společnost nauk*, from 1790 *Královská česká společnost nauk*], the Patriotic-Economic Society of the Czech Kingdom [*Vlastenecko-hospodářská společnost v Království českém*] in 1788, and the Society of Patriotic Friends of Art [*Společnost vlasteneckých přátel umění*] in 1796. More recent patriotic accomplishments, which were also noted with approval in Count Kolovrat's proclamation, were the establishment of the Prague Polytechnic, which was the first technical institute of higher education in the Austrian Empire, by the Bohemian Estates in 1806, and the founding of the Prague Musical Conservatory, one of the oldest in Europe, in 1811.

The Royal Society had evolved out of a Private Learned Society [*Soukromá učená společnost*] founded in 1774 by Count František Josef Kinský and Knight Ignác Born, a geologist who edited its *Abhandlungen* (*Transactions*), the first volume of which came out the following year. The Society of Patriotic Friends of Art, which provided Bohemia with its earliest art gallery in the Černín Palace in 1796—the gallery moved to the Šternberk Palace in 1814—and set up Prague's Academy of Fine Arts [*Akademie výtvarných umění*] in 1799, had similarly aristocratic origins. This club was started by eight noblemen, among them Kolovrat himself, Kašpar Šternberk's cousin František, and members of the Černín, Lobkovic, and Clam-Gallas families. The earliest meetings of the Private Learned Society may have been held in the home of another leading nobleman of the day, Count František Antonín Nostic-Rieneck (1725–94).[2] As supreme burgrave, Nostic (or Nostitz, as he would himself have spelled the name) built the first public theater in Bohemia on what has been known since 1870 as the Fruit Market [*Ovocný trh*] but was then called Königsgasse, in the Old Town. It was an equally patriotic gesture. Nostic christened the splendid edifice, which opened in 1783, the Count's National Theater [*Gräfliches Nationaltheater, Hraběcí Národní divadlo*] and proudly emblazoned the Latin motto "*Patriae et musis*"—To the Fatherland and the Muses—across the portico.

But what is meant by "national" here, and in all of this patriotic bustle, is very far from straightforward. Nor was it either unambiguous or uncontentious at the time. The proclamation of the founding of the National Museum has since been reproduced countless times as a key text of what Czechs call their *národní obrození*, a term that is usually translated into English as "national revival" but is perhaps more forcefully rendered as "national rebirth."[3] Invariably this text is reprinted in the Czech translation by Josef Jungmann, which appeared ten days after Kolovrat's announcement in a supplement to the Prague newspaper *Kramérius's Imperial and Royal Homeland News* [*Kramériusovy c. k. vlastenské noviny*]. It is Jungmann's translation that has been quoted here; it was in this form, after all, that the establishment of the museum was to enter Czech consciousness and remain in Czech memory. But the proclamation was originally written and published in German; and there are some interesting discrepancies between the German text and its Czech metamorphosis.

Klebelsberk's original draft proposal to establish a museum had indeed carried the title "*Aphorismen zum Entwurf des Plans eines National Museums für Böhmen*," but "after long reflection" the name of the museum was changed.[4] In the actual proclamation the museum is called a *Vaterländisches Museum*, that is, a Museum of the Homeland, which would translate into Czech as *Museum vlasti* (or *Vlastenské museum*,[5] as it was described in its founding articles of 1821). Jungmann instead consistently renders *Vaterländisches Museum* as *Národní české museum*, the National Czech Museum. If we compare Jungmann's description of its collections with that given in the Articles of the Society of the Homeland Museum in Bohemia [*Společnost Vlastenského musea v Čechách*] of 1821—which were this time originally written in Czech—we find similar divergences. The first division of the museum's collection, according to Jungmann, is to contain "national" [*národní*] documents. The Articles, by contrast, say it will contain "a collection of documents pertaining to the homeland" [*sbírka vlastenských písem*]. Where Jungmann describes the sixth division, the library, as containing books or manuscripts "produced or published by Czechs," the Articles speak of works "written by Czechs, or published in Bohemia."[6] Kolovrat's original German proclamation likewise had "books and manuscripts written in the Czech language, written by a Bohemian, or published in Bohemia."[7] Jungmann added a postscript to his translation, from which we may infer that these were no mere slips of the pen. The museum's "chief aim," he informs his readers, "is the preservation of the [Czech] language, the preservation of the Czech nation."[8] The proclamation says no such thing. Jungmann's shift of emphasis is made easier by the fact that in Czech the adjective "*český*" can mean either Bohemian (thus Český Krumlov is the town of Krumlov in Bohemia, Moravský Krumlov the town of Krumlov in Moravia) or Czech (as in *české země*, the Czech lands of Bohemia and Moravia). Semantic quibbles, perhaps; but these are quibbles in which much of the Czech nineteenth century is prefigured.

The sense in which Jungmann construes the nation, as being made up of Czech-speakers, is plainly rather different from that in which Count Nostic described his theater as national. When it was not offering newly fashionable Italian opera—Mozart's *Don Giovanni* had its world premiere there in 1787, after *The Marriage of Figaro* had played to great acclaim the year before—Nostic's theater performed almost entirely in German. Things altered after 1798, when the building was purchased by the Bohemian Estates and renamed the Estates Theater [*Stavovské divadlo*]; to the extent that matinee productions in Czech were staged on Sunday afternoons.[9] The Stavovské's most celebrated musical director during its early years was the German composer Carl Maria von Weber. Similarly, and notwithstanding the stipulation in its Articles that "all members of the museum should understand Czech, and the secretary read and write Czech nimbly,"[10] the working language of the National Museum in its early days remained German. The Royal Society too published its *Abhandlungen* in German, even if the great Slavic philologist and historian Abbé Josef Dobrovský (1753–1829) delivered a renowned address on its behalf during Leopold II's visit to the society on the occasion of his Prague coronation in 1791, in which he took the opportunity to plead the case for the civil rights of the Czech language, citing among other things the historical precedent of Charles IV's Golden Bull.[11] Dobrovský was also careful to spend most of his speech expressing the eternal loyalty and devotion of the empire's "Slavonic nations" to the Austrian royal house.

Count František Josef Kinský (1739–1805), cofounder with Ignác Born of the Royal Society, published what was later remembered as one of the earliest of many "defenses" of the Czech language in 1773. In his words, "As a good descendant of Slavs I have inherited the prejudice that if the mother tongue of a Frenchman is French and of a German, German, then for a Czech the mother tongue must also be Czech."[12] He nevertheless wrote the book in German. Josef Dobrovský's pathbreaking *History of Czech Language and Literature*, the first large-scale modern scholarly work to tackle this topic, also made its appearance in 1792 as *Geschichte der böhmischen Sprache und Literatur*. Kinský's father, Count František Ferdinand, had been both governor of Bohemia and supreme Czech court chancellor; František Josef Kinský himself was a distinguished soldier who rose to the highest rank in the imperial army, founded and directed the Military Academy in Vienna's New Town, and is buried at his own request in its cemetery. Count Kolovrat went on to become imperial minister of the interior in 1826 and the empire's first prime minister in 1848. In none of these instances was there any perceived contra-diction between Bohemian patriotic sentiment and its expression in the German language, or, come to that, loyalty to the house of Habsburg. Nor, conversely, was Bohemia—or in the case of Count Nostic's "national" theater, the nation—conceptualized solely in terms of Czechness. What were later to be recalled as milestones on the long march of the Czech national rebirth were, in fact, the product of a set of sentiments diametrically opposed to any narrowly ethnic or linguistic nationalism.

Land patriotism, as Josef Hanuš nicely puts it in his classic history of the early years of the National Museum, was "the patriotism of our aristocracy, who were of a Czech disposition and laid claim to Czech historical traditions—[they were] Palacký's 'in blood and heart faithful Czechs'—but who spoke and for the most part also read and wrote only German and French."[13] Manifestly, these nobles were indifferent neither to Czech history, knowledge of which they did much to help revive, nor to the plight of the Czech language in the present, whether they themselves spoke it or not. But these formed part of their patriotic attachment, rather than its sum. The object of their loyalty was the Bohemian homeland [*česká vlast*], precisely the patria, rather than the Czech nation [*český národ*], as that community was already being imagined by Jungmann. The clearest indication of this, perhaps, is provided by just what the museum set out to assemble and display. The *land* is what gives coherence to the otherwise unintelligible collection of coats of arms, old coins, manuscripts, discoveries, maps, plants, minerals, and fossils; it is the territorial and political space of the Kingdom of Bohemia that orders this disparate medley of objects, rather than the narrative space of a national history whose subject is a people. It is not insignificant that Klebelsberk's original draft proposal did not envisage the museum as containing anything like so heavily historical a component as it eventually turned out to have; the influence of Dobrovský and other historically minded scholars in the Royal Society probably tipped the scales.[14] The Bohemia represented here is not—yet—coextensive with Jungmann's Czech nation. But it was undoubtedly this Bohemia that Count Nostic sought to elevate with his "national" theater. How else do we resolve what the standard communist-period *History of the Czech Theater* presents as the "paradox" that "the first representative stage of the Bohemian Kingdom was erected as a German national theater?"[15] It is paradoxical only in the light of subsequent conceptions of the "natural" relations between nations, lands, and languages.

One who during these years explicitly did address such questions was the mathematician, philosopher, and theologian Bernard Bolzano (1781–1848). At first sight, Bolzano appears an eccentric and idiosyncratic voice, a sympathetic and engaging man, perhaps, but a figure marginal to the main currents of modern Czech history. By comparison with many of his intellectual contemporaries and successors he gets scant attention in the historical textbooks, whether Czech or foreign. If they are discussed at all, his ideas on nationality are usually dismissed, with the arrogant certainty of hindsight, as out of touch with the drift of the times; "mere utopia," as one modern Czech anthology of writings from the *obrození* puts it.[16] Bolzano fits awkwardly into the story of progressive national "awakening" charted by Czech nationalist and communist historiographies alike (albeit with a different cast of heroes and villains). But the question arises as to whether this marginality is not perhaps an artifact of the standpoints from which these histories are written. For Bolzano was clearly considered worthy of attention by his contemporaries, whatever historians may have made or not made of his significance later.

Born of an Italian immigrant father and a Czech mother in Prague in 1781, Bolzano was no Germanized aristocrat; his father was a petty trader, and he grew up in modest circumstances. His intellectual distinction and virtuosity were apparent early on. He was ordained a priest, obtained his doctorate in philosophy, and applied for (and was offered) teaching posts in both mathematics and religion all in the same year, 1805, at the age of twenty-four. He accepted a position lecturing in religion at Prague university. His lectures were strikingly original in their synthesis of a deep Catholic faith and an equally passionate enlightenment rationalism, and he quickly became the idol of his students. He soon attracted wider notice, and as rapidly made powerful enemies. He also inspired strong loyalties. He long enjoyed the support and protection of the director of philosophy at the university, who was several times dean of its Theological Faculty and became university rector in 1812, Milo Jan Nepomucký Grün, abbot of the Strahov monastery.

After Grün died in 1816, his successor as director of philosophy František Wilhelm twice gave negative reports on Bolzano to the Court Commission. Bolzano's lectures came under suspicion both in Vienna and at the Vatican. Pope Pius VII was informed that in Prague "the preaching is all of mere morality, of dogmas and miracles there is not a word."[17] There were investigations, called for by Emperor Francis II (1792–1835) himself. Though neither the Faculty of Theology of Vienna University nor the Court Commission could find anything in Bolzano's writing that was contrary either to the teachings of the Church or to the censorship laws, he was stripped of his post (by Supreme Burgrave Kolovrat) in 1820. The pretext—a totally fraudulent one—was his alleged involvement in a "secret society" established by his pupil Michal Josef Fesl, a professor at the seminary in Litoměřice. Earlier, playing on his Italian ancestry, Bolzano's opponents had fatuously accused him of membership in anti-imperial secret societies in Italy. After his dismissal from the university Bolzano devoted himself largely to his beloved mathematics, to which he made important contributions in the field of cal-

4. Charles Bridge, Hradčany and Malá strana, 1856. Hradčany Castle, with Saint Vitus's Cathedral at its center, dominates the skyline. The twin towers at the extreme left of the photograph are those of Strahov Abbey on Petřín Hill.

culus. Fesl was less fortunate. He was imprisoned for four years and then interned in Styria; only in 1832 was he permitted to reside in Vienna, and he was never again allowed to return to Bohemia.

Bolzano's reflections on what was to become "the national question" exhibit exactly that combination of Christian virtue and limpid argument for which he was justly famed. In "On Love for the Homeland," he begins, characteristically, by asking a basic question: "What land should each individual consider as his homeland, and how far should its borders extend?" His answer is both unsentimental and unhistoricist; we are in an entirely different world from that of Jungmann (or, come to that, Herder). "The land, in which you live, is your true homeland," says Bolzano, and this land may or may not be the land in which you were born. Though "your parents and grandparents may have lived since time immemorial" in one land, "still more important are the benefits which you have accepted in another." As regards the borders of the homeland, he concludes that "[the homeland] extends as far as the state extends of whom we are the subjects by law." Recognizing that "ordinarily, the borders of the homeland [vlast] do not coincide with an individual land [*země*] and nation [*národ*]," he inveighs against sectarian nationalisms, urging his students to "love and embrace one another as children of a single shared homeland!"[18] He is equally unromantic in his attitude toward language; when set beside later orthodoxies of the centrality of the Czech language to Czech identity, whose echoes we caught at Karel Čapek's funeral, Bolzano's coolly rationalist view of the matter is sheer blasphemy. "The greatest hurdle in the way of unanimity in our homeland," he asserts in "On the Condition of the Two Nationalities in Bohemia" (1816), "is *linguistic difference*. He who could completely do away with this, he who could bring it about that all the inhabitants of our homeland spoke only one language, would become the greatest benefactor of our nation; just as he who could introduce a single speech for the whole world would be the greatest benefactor of the human race."[19] He rejoices in, rather than laments, the ever-diminishing count of languages and dialects in Europe.

This might be dismissed as abstract moralizing, were it not for the fact that Bolzano combines it with a sharply critical awareness of Bohemian social and linguistic realities. He accepts that an Esperanto world is not about to spring magically into being. He is no advocate of the Germanization of Bohemia in the interests of efficient communication either. In the selfsame lecture, he argues that obstacles to national unity derive less from linguistic differences in themselves, unfortunate as they might be, than from their social stratification into advantage and disadvantage. The real problem, he says, is the "*inequality, which exists in character, in mentality, and in level of education between the two nationalities in our land*." This difference between Czechs and Germans is not innate; it is the result of "the inequality of their fates."[20] Here he is unsparing in his criticisms:

> Although allusion to these matters is very risky, I do not intend to keep silent about them. . . . The greatest misfortune of our nation is that the parts from which it is composed were not joined together into one voluntarily but for the most part by external force, and that up to the present day the one part prospers to the detriment of the other and vaunts itself over it! That the memory of wrongs and injustices perpetrated on grandfathers is preserved even by grandsons is understandable; and the more so, when their results last up till now, nay when new iniquities are always being heaped on top of the old. And this is really the case. Or perhaps Germans and those who affiliate to them are not still given precedence in a thousand kinds of very important matters? Is not all higher education here taught in the German language? Was not the German language elevated as the language of state [*jazyk úřední*], in which all public business is transacted? . . . But still more: are not the great and noble in the land, all the rich and the great owners in the nation either born Germans or complete foreigners, or such people as count themselves as Germans, since they long ago set aside the Czech language and Czech ways? Does not the Czech-speaking part of

the population live in a pitiful state of poverty and oppression? Furthermore, and to add insult to injury, was not the governance over these people handed over to persons who are Germans or at least align themselves with them? Persons who, not knowing the language of the people, cannot judge their complaints and suits, their requests and petitions; persons who also have no sympathy for the people, do not reckon them as equals to themselves and therefore do not treat them in a fatherly way, but lord it over them and suck their blood exactly like those Egyptian officials did their serfs? Who that has lived in our homeland . . . would not confirm the truth of what I have said? Who then can be surprised that there is no unity among our people? That Czechs and Germans willingly associate together in nothing? But that they hold one another in mutual contempt, shun one another, hate one another? Certainly there is nothing to be surprised at here, my friends.[21]

One can see why the authorities thought Bolzano dangerous.

What may be surprising, at least to anyone who expects history to go in straight lines, is the conclusions Bolzano draws from all this. They are very different from Josef Jungmann's: "Who knows what we could be or what we could become, if we had handled these inequalities between the two nationalities of which we are composed more wisely in the past, or if we began to do so now? Who knows, what could be made out of us, if we extended our hands in friendship instead of living in hostility and discord? If we made common those virtues, which each part of us has? If little by little we suppressed all the flaws? If we strove to merge both nationalities [obě národnosti] into one, so that in the end they would form one nation [jeden národ]?"[22] The issue is not whether these dreams were realizable in the circumstances of the time; such questions are of their nature unanswerable. In the context of this inquiry, the interest of Bolzano's essays is twofold.

First, he acknowledges—and in no uncertain terms—the reality of the differences that were subsequently to be ordered into a vocabulary of national identities and oppositions. Bohemia's distinctions of language were also palpable distinctions of station, of opportunity, of power. Plentiful grist was there for future nationalist mills; the fabric of the modern Czech nation was not woven out of air. But second, Bolzano regards nationality as something that is made out of, rather than simply given in, these differences. He does not see it as innate, inevitable, or immutable. For him a nation is a political community that can be imagined into existence in various ways, even if the realization of what is imagined is always constrained by the detritus of the past. Notwithstanding the dismal litany of German crimes against Czech-speakers which he recites, an act which in 1816 must have taken considerable courage, he is still capable of envisaging a synthesis of these "nationalities," out of which a new "nation" will emerge. The indeterminacy of reference of these terms throughout these texts is itself very revealing. Sometimes Bolzano uses the word "*národ*" (nation) to refer to Czech-speakers and German-speakers separately, sometimes to both together (as in "the greatest misfortune of our nation is that the parts from which it is composed were not joined together into one voluntarily"). It is this presumption that national communities can be molded in accordance with the dictates of reason and the precepts of Christianity that makes Bolzano appear, in retrospect, so hopelessly utopian. But that, surely, is just the point. What is historically most revealing in Bolzano's essays is exactly that which has led to his marginalization in later historiography as having been out of step with the future. His "utopianism" is the clearest possible indication we could have that in early nineteenth-century Bohemia nationality had not yet become thoroughly embedded in being, was not yet a self-evident ground of personal identity. Even for an intelligent patriot well versed in Czech history and very much alive to Czech oppressions, what constituted the nation remained an uncertain and open field of possibilities. Within a few decades, to most inhabitants of Bohemia, such thoughts would have seemed well-nigh incomprehensible—if not quite the ravings of a madman, then at best the naive fancies of a child.

Enlightenment

The National Museum, the art gallery in the Šternberk palace, the Bohemian Royal Society, and the rest of these institutions were not the early manifestations of a Czech national rebirth. Many of them were hijacked for that project later, and their foundation retrospectively appropriated for nationalist genealogies, but that is a different matter. They were the product of a particular historical moment and a particular constellation of interests.

Aristocratic patronage of the sciences, arts, and technology in Bohemia—another expression of which was the organization of mainland Europe's first industrial exhibition in conjunction with Leopold II's Prague coronation in 1791—was of a piece with a wider Continental spirit of "enlightenment" in the later eighteenth century. Czech aristocrats had formed an Economic Society [*Hospodářská společnost*], which established a school for officials working in the economic sphere and promoted improved methods of sheep breeding, beekeeping, and hop growing, as early as 1769. Consideration of how Bohemia or the nation was represented in the National Museum should not lead us to overlook what was at least as important to its founders, the prominence they gave to the exact sciences (geography, statistics, geology, botany, physics, mathematics) in the plans for its displays and library, and the attention they planned to pay to the industrial and applied arts. The same was true of the Royal Society. Its prime mover in the early days, Ignác Born (1742–1791), was a geologist of European renown, whose collection of minerals was eventually purchased by the British Museum in London. Enlightened aristocrats also fostered historical scholarship, especially by patronage of individuals. Josef Dobrovský was a tutor in Count Nostic's household from 1776 to 1787, while "Father of the Nation" František Palacký, the greatest of nineteenth-century Czech historians, was to begin his career in Prague as an archivist for the Šternberk family. But this scholarship, as epitomized by Gelasius Dobner (1719–90) and above all by Dobrovský himself, was animated by this same ethos of scientific enlightenment. Its objective was certainly not, as Palacký would formulate it later, to awaken the nation by giving it a mirror in which to recognize itself.

Dobner and Dobrovský had some major disagreements, most famously in the 1780s over the existence or otherwise of Saint Jan Nepomucký.[23] But what is significant is the terrain on which they argued, that of primary sources and their proper interpretation. These men studied history in order to rid it of myth; like their natural scientist counterparts they sought to shed light where there had been darkness, to elevate history from mere storytelling into the realm of "incontrovertible knowledges." This is why the collection of as complete a collection as possible of *authentic* documents (and other physical artifacts of the past) for the museum became so important. Through philological and other criticism these could be authoritatively dated, and later accretions and embellishments peeled away to reveal the bare facts of history. Dobrovský first gained notoriety by showing that the so-called Prague Fragment of the Gospel of Saint Mark, brought to Prague from Italy by Charles IV in 1355 and believed to have been written in the apostle's own hand, in fact dated from the sixth century. In so doing he was secularizing (and thus profaning) a holy, not to say a patriotic relic—treating it forensically, as mere objective evidence.[24] Dobner did something similar in his celebrated critical edition (in Latin, 1762–82) of what Palacký later called "the almost too universally known" Václav Hájek z Libočan's *Kronika česká* (*Czech Chronicle*, 1541), a beloved account of Bohemian history that had held sway for over two centuries and been used as a source by Stránský and Balbín among many others.[25] Hájek's chronicle had escaped the post–Bílá hora conflagration of Czech literature because of its firm Catholicism and resolutely negative presentation of the Hussite era. That, like the image of Jan Nepomucký, Hájek's "portrait of the former power and glory of the Czech state" may have "sustained in the people national feeling and love for the Czech language and the native land during the hardest times"[26] did not in the least deter Dobner from clinically dissecting its multiple flaws. But nor was he impelled by a desire to rehabilitate Jan Žižka and Prokop Holý, as his nineteenth-century successors would be.

It is bizarre, but perhaps not strange, that such demystifying activities should have cleared the ground for later nationalist mythmaking, and that Dobner and Dobrovský should have found themselves posthumously conscripted as its intellectual forefathers. This corpus of documents, and the facticity they were seen to embody, was what above all lent authority to the new chronicles of the national odyssey produced in the nineteenth century by Palacký (who hails Dobner's critical edition of Hájek as "a work of immortal merit for Czech history")[27] and others. Invocation of ancient documents to legitimate modern narratives of nationality soon ceased to be a merely intellectual enterprise. The "Deduction of the Legal Continuity of the Constitutional Rights and Freedoms of the Czech Estates," which the Bohemian Diet, advised by Palacký, sent Ferdinand V in May 1847 in the hope of clawing back some of both, begins with a long and learned history lesson. "As far as *the historical sources, documents of the land and laws* extend," it argues, "these show above all that constitutional monarchy with an Estates constitution has governed continuously in Bohemia up to the present day."[28]

The perverse apotheosis of this identification of truth with the physical body of the document is perhaps an authentically twentieth-century fetishism, admirably exemplified in the gigantic All-State Exhibition of Archival Documents that was held at Prague Castle in 1958 under the title "From the Heroic Past Toward the Victory of Socialism." The first exhibit is the Prague Fragment of the Gospel of Saint Mark, now properly assigned to the sixth century and described as "the oldest written object in our territory." The accompanying commentary has all the requisite patina of critical science: the Fragment is represented "rather as evidence of the long-standing predilection for collecting cultural chattels, than as testimony to the oldest period in our history."[29] But why, then, is it not included in the section of the show dealing with Charles IV, who first made it part of Czech history in 1355? It is instead grouped with a series of other documents, some contemporary with what they depict, but most, like Kosmas's twelfth-century chronicle, dating from much later, under the rubric "Written Memorials from the Era of the Foundation of Our State." This visual arrangement belies what is written in the commentary, substantiating instead the narrative of antiquity and continuity of national aspiration of the exhibition's title. Why *exhibit* documents at all? As texts they would be meaningless to most visitors. As signs, however, they are instantly legible. They function exactly as did the Prague Fragment before Dobrovský got his hands on it. From evidence to be used in a scientific quest for knowledge they have been turned back into tangible presences of truth, relics of the past that physically validate the narratives that re-present it. History has come full circle.

Dobner was being described by the end of the nineteenth century in *Ottův slovník naučný* as "the first and mighty awakener of the Czech nation."[30] Dobrovský proved a somewhat more difficult figure to incorporate into the genealogies of national rebirth, if only because the skeptical spirit that characterized his work had led him into open conflict in his later years with self-proclaimed Czech patriots of the younger generation. Jungmann at one point angrily declared that Dobrovský was not a true Czech but "a Slavicizing German."[31] Palacký's own biography of Dobrovský (1833) insists that he "always avowed himself to be a Czech and named Czech as his one and only mother tongue," despite the facts—recounted in the preceding paragraph of Palacký's account—that Dobrovský was born (of Czech parents) in Hungary, raised in an entirely German milieu, and only learned Czech later as a gymnasium student in Německý Brod. But Palacký is honest enough to acknowledge that "despite all his love for this language, [Dobrovský] wrote so little in it because he had long abandoned hope for the revival of a Czech national literature and was also later always of the opinion that at best it might evolve only as a general popular literature."[32] At the same time, Dobrovský's own *History of Czech Language and Literature* (in which a similar pessimism for the future of Czech is expressed),[33] and his *Detailed Grammar of the Czech Language* (1809) and two-volume *Czech-German Dictionary* (1802, 1821), were clearly, in retrospect, key moments in just such a revival. Without Dobrovský's efforts, the written language might not have been restored in its "classical" form at all. The literature since is littered with attempts to square this circle. Zdeněk Nejedlý's Ptolemaic contortions are not untypical:

As far as Dobrovský's *Czech national feeling* [češství] goes, it resounds from his works differently than in the works of other writers of the Enlightenment . . . even if externally his work differs little or not at all from theirs. . . . In Dobrovský, underneath the enlightenment surface there truly beat quite another heart. He still did not have enough faith in the new brilliant future of the Czech nation, but he had deep anxiety and grief over its fall. And from this was also born a new consciousness of duty toward the nation, which made him, contrary to all external foreignness, the first great national awakener [národní buditel].[34]

The more pressing and local stimulus to land patriotism in late eighteenth-century Bohemia, and in particular to its patronage of historical research, was political. Overshadowing the period is the state-making ambition of Empress Maria Theresa (1740–80) and her energetic son Joseph II (co-ruler with his mother from 1765, emperor from 1780 to 1790). In 1749 Maria Theresa disbanded the hitherto separate Czech and Austrian Court Chancelleries and replaced them with a unified Office of Internal and Financial Affairs; the name Czech and Austrian Court Chancellery was restored in 1763, but it remained a single authority that continued to cover both Austria and the Czech lands. In Prague the Vice Regent's Office was abolished and replaced by a new administrative organ, known after 1763 as the Gubernium, which was subordinated to the Court Chancellery in Vienna. In 1751 district officials became paid civil servants appointed directly from Vienna rather than dignitaries of the Estates, and their sphere of authority grew markedly. District boundaries were concurrently redrawn on bureaucratic rather than historical principles. The legal system was similarly rationalized:

judicial and executive organs were more clearly separated, and a Supreme Court established in Vienna covering, once again, both Austria and the Czech lands. The effect of these measures was obviously to shift power upward and outward, and away, in particular, from the Czech Estates. Other manifestations of this centralization included the introduction of regular censuses of the population from 1753, which after 1770 were linked to military conscription, the formation of a customs union between Austria and the Czech lands in 1775, and the Corvée [*Robotní*] Patent of the same year, which regulated (and often lightened) peasant labor services on nobles' estates. Schools, which until then had been in Church or community hands, also became objects of state supervision. From 1774 a universal system of elementary [*triviální*] schools was instituted for each parish, together with secondary [*hlavní*] schools in larger centers and higher [*normální*] schools in Prague and Brno that provided teachers' training. Attendance at elementary schools was (in theory at least) made compulsory for all children after 1805.

With Joseph II's accession in 1780 further reforms came thick and fast. Many were directly aimed at the secular power of the Catholic Church. Joseph disbanded the religious commission of the Counter-Reformation; he proclaimed religious toleration for Lutherans, Calvinists, Greek Orthodox Christians, and Jews; he closed down half the monasteries and convents in the Austrian portion of the empire, especially those that did not provide medical or educational services; he removed the Church's jurisdiction over marriage; and he extended state control over the content of teaching in theology faculties. Catholicism retained its privileged place as the only "public" religion, a distinction that was symbolically expressed by the requirement that non-Catholic "houses of prayer" should have "no bells, spires, or entrances from the street, which would equate them with churches"; but the Toleration Patent of 1781 nevertheless removed the whole apparatus of civil discrimination against Protestants that had been in place in the Czech lands since Bílá hora. They were now permitted to own landed property, practice trades, become burghers, obtain academic degrees, and hold public office.[35] Pope Pius VI personally traveled to Vienna in 1782 in an effort to dissuade the emperor from pursuing so radical a course any further, to little avail.

Hard on the heels of the Toleration Patent, Joseph abolished personal serfdom [*nevolnictví*], though not the labor services [*robota*] tied to servile land tenure [*poddanství*], which were to endure until 1848. Peasants could now marry, learn trades, acquire education, and leave their lordship and reside elsewhere in the kingdom without permission of their lord.[36] Another law of the same year limited the criminal jurisdiction of the lordship over its tenants, and made it possible for tenants to sue their seigneurs. A wider reform of the Criminal Code abolished medieval punishments like branding, public whipping, and "barbaric" methods of execution, and outlawed torture as a judicial instrument. Standardization of the civil law throughout the Austrian half of the empire, which had begun under Maria Theresa, continued under Joseph and was to culminate in the General Civil Code of 1811. This among other things created a uniform state citizenship. Joseph continued his mother's rationalization of administrative and legal institutions, sweeping away remaining vestiges of land, district, and municipal autonomy in these areas. He created a universal register of agricultural land, which included both lords' and peasants' tenancies with a view to taxing both equitably; the survey took four years (1785–89) and resulted in some three million acres in Bohemia being taxed for the first time. By the Tax Patent of 1789 peasants would be allowed to keep 70 percent of their yields, with a further 12 percent going to the state, leaving only 18 percent to cover all obligations to the parish and the lordship, the *robota* included; with this the burden of servile obligations on peasants fell by as much as two-thirds. This particular law was repealed, under strong pressure from the nobility, within months of Joseph's death in 1790. He also considerably liberalized the censorship, abolishing the Index of forbidden books in 1782.

At the same time—and entirely consistently with the modernizing, Erastian thrust of the rest of these reforms—Joseph made German the sole official language of state organs and of higher education. Prague university officially switched from Latin to German when the curriculum was reformed in 1784. The Prague and Brno normal schools and upper grades of the secondary schools set up by Maria Theresa had already been functioning in German for a decade; knowledge of German was also made a requirement for entry into Bohemia's Latin gymnasia in 1780, a measure Dobrovský saw at the time as a near-fatal blow to any hopes of reviving Czech as an educated language.[37] As obstacles to Jewish property ownership and entry to professions and higher education were (somewhat) relaxed, it was forbidden to keep synagogue or business records any longer in Hebrew or Yiddish, and Jews were required to take German family and personal names.[38] It would be erroneous and anachronistic to see in any of this a deliberate program of "Germanization," understood in ethnic or cultural terms, as it has often subsequently been represented. Joseph's objective was efficiency pure and simple. He wanted a uniform language of administration throughout his empire and an up-to-date language of education, appropriate in particular to mastery of the natural sciences, in its schools. In the case of the Jews, he wished to integrate them into civil society on terms that would make them loyal Austrian subjects. Nevertheless such a language policy was to be enormously consequential in the longer term. Taken together, the Josephine reforms opened up a wide range of new social opportunities. They also—for the first time—*systematically* structured these opportunities in a way that disadvantaged non-German speakers, while creating conditions under which (for a time) consciousness of disadvantage could be openly expressed. Though not all the specifics of Joseph's reforms survived him, this Janus-faced legacy, of emancipation from the old constraints of the Counter-Reformation only to face the new disablements of "Germanization," marked the first half of the nineteenth century. Modern Czech nationalism eventually found its support in classes that were simultaneously liberated and thwarted by this contradictory imperative. Here as elsewhere, it was modernization that made nationality a freshly salient issue.

The more immediate response to Theresian and Josephine innovations, however, came from very much more conservative quarters of Bohemian society. Confronted by angry aristocratic protests against Joseph's riding roughshod over "Land rights" from Hungary to the Austrian Netherlands, his brother and successor Leopold II (1790–92) asked diets in 1790 to submit a list of desiderata for imperial and royal consideration. The Bohemian Estates called among other things for abolition of Joseph's tax reforms and the restoration of seigneurial powers over peasants and of Church supervision over schools. On the constitutional front they asked Leopold "above all to confirm the Estates in all those rights, prerogatives, and privileges which were recognized by Emperor Ferdinand II," adding that certain "clauses and limitations" of the 1627 constitution, comprehensible in the circumstances of the time but now "unnecessary, unfitting or humiliating," be "wholly rescinded, revoked, and nullified."[39] In particular they sought a guarantee that the constitution would not be changed thereafter without their own consent, a guarantee Leopold was not prepared to give. They also requested that Czech be reintroduced to the gymnasia, and Latin to the university.

These positions were, in the strictest sense of the word, reactionary; the Estates wished the clock to be set back. History was being invoked in the interest of restoring institutions of aristocratic privilege and Catholic supremacy which the reforms of the previous forty years had comprehensively eroded. The Czech language was likewise mobilized in these *Dezideria* more as a historic symbol of Bohemian political distinction from Austria than as a modern means of communication; the Estates themselves, by this date, were deliberating in German. Language was an issue on which Leopold was prepared to make equally symbolic concessions. Czech was ostentatiously used in his coronation ceremonies in 1791, and while in Prague he took the opportunity to attend not only the ceremonial meeting of the Royal Society at which Josef Dobrovský gave his celebrated address but also a theatrical performance in Czech. The following year a chair of Czech language and literature was established with imperial blessing at Prague university. Its first occupant was the historian František Martin Pelcl (1734–1801), who had distinguished himself by publishing Balbín's *Defense of the Slavonic Language* in 1775. He went on to produce a *New Czech Chronicle* [*Nová kronika česká*, 1791–95] of his own, which was most notable for the fact that it was actually written in Czech.

Less often remarked in the later literature—though Dobrovský thought it important enough to mention in his *History*[40]—but no less indicative of the complexities of the Czech "rebirth," is the fact that a Czech chair had already existed at Prague university for several years before Pelcl's appointment. Two chairs of pastoral theology had quietly been set up in 1778, one German, one Czech; increasingly dethroned by an aggressively modernizing state, the Church had belatedly recognized that if it were to shepherd its flock, it would henceforth have to speak in tongues they understood. The first Czech professor of pastoral theology, Jiljí Chládek (1743–1806), not only wrote manuals of his trade in the vernacular for his students, he produced a little book with the title *The Briefest of Lessons in How to Speak and Write Well in Czech* in 1795. He was an inveterate foe of Voltaire, Helvétius, and all other such apostles of enlightenment.[41] Another similar chair was established, also in 1778, in Olomouc in Moravia. Foremost among those developing an interest in Czech history and language in late eighteenth- and early nineteenth-century Bohemia were the descendants of the carpetbagging beneficiaries of Bílá hora themselves—the greater nobility and the Catholic Church. The *obrození* had multiple and tangled roots.

Home Cooking

By no means all of Joseph II's innovations outlasted him. The administrations of Francis II and Ferdinand V (1835–48) were conspicuous more for their despotism than their enlightenment. Voltaire and Rousseau had by now taken on more sinister connotations; the guillotined French queen Marie Antoinette had after all been Joseph and Leopold's sister. The centralized bureaucratic institutions left by Joseph and his mother proved admirably adapted to the task of policing in post-Napoleonic Europe, and Metternich's censors were no less assiduous than the Jesuits had been. Nevertheless in the Czech lands the outwardly quiet "pre-March" decades that preceded the revolution of 1848 were years in which the intellectual foundations of modern Czech nationalism were laid. They were also years in which the *obrození* remained almost entirely an affair of intellectuals alone. The contemporary witticism that if a certain ceiling in Prague collapsed, so would all hopes of a Czech revival, had more than a touch of truth in it. The activities of these national "awakeners" [*buditelé*], as they have since become known, were cultural rather than overtly political. But nations are cultural constructs. At the time they were writing it is probably fair to say that the early Czech *buditelé* were representative of nobody but themselves—unless it be the interests of the patriotic aristocrats who subsidized much of their work. But their labors created the wherewithal with which to *think* modern Czech nationhood. They developed a vocabulary of national identity that was to be mobilized to enormous effect later in the century, under conditions very different from those in which they themselves were writing. What began as mere words was ultimately made flesh. The consequences have haunted Czech history ever since.

The awakeners' first and most fundamental preoccupation was the revival of the Czech language itself. Literary Czech (*spisovná čeština*, as distinct from *hovorová čeština*, spoken Czech) was gradually formalized and stabilized through dictionaries, grammars, and orthographic reforms; it was popularized by increasing use in newspapers, calendars, songbooks, theater, and other media; and it was reclaimed, slowly and painstakingly, as a vehicle of both literary and scientific expression. The Thám brothers, Karel (1763–1816) and Václav (1765–c. 1816), were not untypical of Czech linguistic patriots of the time in the range of their activities. Karel Thám published the first *Defense of the Czech Language* to be written in Czech in 1783, compiled a number of Czech grammars (in both Czech and German) and dictionaries, translated among others Shakespeare (*Macbeth*) and Schiller into Czech, and gave lessons on the Czech language at Prague's Academic Gymnasium from 1803. Václav Thám was an actor who played a major part in setting up the first modern—and modest—Czech-language theaters in Prague, the Bouda (the Shack, 1786–89) and its successor the Divadlo U Hybernů (1789–1802). He translated plays from French and German, and wrote over fifty plays of his own, among them the first original Czech dramatic work to be staged in modern times, *Břetislav and Jitka*, which premiered at Count Nostic's Theater on 10 January 1786. Most of his works are now lost. He also published the first modern anthology of Czech poetry [*Básně v řeči vázané*, 2 vols., 1785], containing both old and new works, in order, in his own words, "to make known the still-surviving fragments from our Czech minstrels; then to show that, just as in other languages, everything can be poetically expressed and sung in our mother tongue; and lastly to acquaint the reader with many people who are striving by all kinds of efforts both to propagate the Czech language and to foster a more cultivated poetry within it."[42]

Dictionaries, grammars, and textbooks of Czech began to appear with increasing frequency from the 1780s. Karel Thám's *German-Czech Dictionary* came out in 1788; he followed it up with several more, notably the *Up-to-Date Complete Czech-German Dictionary* of 1807–8. František Jan Tomsa (1753–1814), an early advocate of modernizing Czech spelling and of using the Roman rather than the Gothic script for the printed language, published a *Czech Grammar* in 1782, a *Small German-Czech Dictionary* in 1789, and a large *Czech-German-Latin Dictionary* in 1791. Tomsa was a close collaborator of Dobrovský's, and an effective popular interpreter of his ideas. Of Dobrovský's own *Grammar* and *Dictionary* we have already spoken; it was undoubtedly his scholarship that most reconnected modern written Czech to its classical heritage. But it was Josef Jungmann, the translator of Count Kolovrat's proclamation of the establishment of the National Museum, who was to take the project of reviving the written Czech language furthest, albeit in directions that were little to the taste of Dobrovský himself. Jungmann approached the language as a patriot first and a scholar second. His overriding concern was to develop Czech as a living organism, capable of serving the needs of contemporary educated communication, and he had few scruples about comprehensibly overhauling it in the service of that end.

Jungmann (1773–1847) was the sixth of ten children of a country shoemaker. Intended by his mother for the priesthood, he was educated in middle school in Beroun, then through gymnasium and university in Prague. In 1799 he took up a position as a teacher at the gymnasium in Litoměřice, where he worked until 1815. He offered courses in Czech to his pupils, the first person to do so in any high school in the Czech lands. From 1806 he did the same for students at the Litoměřice seminary. The significance of such activities for the formation of an educated Czech elite should not be underestimated; this was still a small world, in which many of these boys and young men would themselves go on to become teachers. In the fall of 1815 Jungmann moved to Prague's Old Town Gymnasium, where he spent the rest of his career. In 1834 he became the school's director [*Praefect*]. The leading light of the city's small circle of patriotic intellectuals, he was elected to the Bohemian Royal Society in 1834. Prague university twice chose him as honorary dean of the Philosophy Faculty (1828, 1839) and once as rector (1840), a position in which he succeeded his brother Antonín, who was a professor in the Medical Faculty. He eventually received official imperial recognition for his work; he was elected to the Vienna Academy of Sciences in 1847 and was awarded the Order of Leopold the same year.

Whatever distaste Jungmann's romantic brand of nationalism may have aroused in some later commentators (notably Tomáš Masaryk), it can scarcely be denied that his practical contributions to the development of modern written Czech—whether or not they met with the approval of linguistic purists—were enormous. While still in Litoměřice, he translated among others Schiller, Chateaubriand, Goethe, Gray's "Elegy," and most famously Milton's entire *Paradise Lost* [*Ztracený ráj*, 1811] into Czech, considerably extending the vocabulary of the written language and more than adequately demonstrating its potential as a vehicle of poetic expression. He was to continue translating throughout his life; one example was Johann Gottfried von Herder's famous chapter on the Slavs, which like Herder's thought in general had a significant impact on early Czech nationalists. The interesting thing about what Jungmann chose to translate is its sheer eclecticism. His choices were dictated less by the content of works than by the possibilities their rendition into Czech offered for extending the communicative range of his own language. His *Slovesnost* (*Poetics: A Collection of Examples, with a Short Treatise on Style*) of 1820 was the first modern Czech reader and textbook in literary theory. It too enriched the lexicon, establishing the basic Czech vocabulary of literary criticism. The word "*slovesnost*" itself, not untypically of Jungmann, comes from the Russian.

Jungmann compiled the *Poetics* in response to a Court Commission decree of 1816, whose instigator was Bolzano's protector Abbot Milo Jan Nepomucký Grün, which permitted partial instruction in Czech in the schools (although this was to be watered down later). This nicely demonstrates an unexpected result of Habsburg centralization. To produce an educated German-speaking class adequate to staff the burgeoning bureaucracy throughout the empire, local vernaculars often perforce had to be used, just as had happened earlier in the Church. Czech was already being employed as a medium of instruction in the Military Academy in Vienna from 1752, the Vienna Polytechnic from 1754, and Vienna University from 1775, where a chair of Czech language and literature was established that year. The 1775 *Allgemeine Schulordnung für die deutschen Normal-, Haupt- und Trivialschulen*, on the face of it as eloquent an example of Germanizing standardization as we could find, had to be published two years later in Bohemia as *Všeobecný školní řád pro německé normální, hlavní a triviální školy* in order to be implemented under Czech conditions at all. There were to be more textbooks in Czech published during the decade of the archcentralist Joseph II's reign than in the whole preceding 150 years.[43]

In 1825 Jungmann published his *History of Czech Literature or Systematic Survey of Czech Writings, with a Short History of the Nation, Education and Language*. This was the first modern history of Czech literature to be written in Czech, covering more than 1,500 writers and 5,428 individual works. The second edition (of 1849, which was completed by the historian V. V. Tomek) extended this count to 7,466 works.[44] Jungmann was mapping the terrain of written Czech culture, and giving impressive testimony as to its compass. He crowned his career with a 120,000-entry, five-volume *Czech-German Dictionary* (1834–39), by far the largest such work yet to have been produced. It had taken him over thirty years to compile. His preface begins with the observation "A dictionary of the national language belongs among the first necessities of the educated individual" and goes on to review the history of lexicography in France, England, Russia, Germany, Italy, and elsewhere. Jungmann then turns to conditions in his native Bohemia:

> If then to these nations, whose mother tongue lives and reigns in all regards and whose educated individuals, having gone through the domestic and public institutions of education, bring with them into civic life a living and rich vocabulary of their natural language, the general national vocabulary is still seen to matter so much: what is to be said of the dear Czech nation, whose efforts are almost entirely devoted to familiarizing itself with other languages, whose natural tongue is left merely to the home and the will and efforts of each individual; the

nation whose educated people, with a few exceptions, became the poorer in their mother tongue, even if they needed it no less in office and civic life, the longer they stayed in the institutions of learning, the more and the harder they educated their spirit through various arts? Can they, I beg of you, desiring or having to read and write Czech, do without a more thorough national dictionary?[45]

Jungmann was equally active in helping provide outlets for others who wrote in their "natural tongue." Together with Jan Svatopluk Presl (1791–1849) and the physiologist Jan Evangelista Purkyně (1787–1869), he founded the first Czech scientific periodical, *Krok*, in 1821. Ten years later, with František Palacký, he organized a fund for supporting publication of Czech scholarly and scientific literature, the Matice česká. It was the Matice česká that brought out his *Czech-German Dictionary*. Jungmann's collaborator in *Krok*, Jan Svatopluk Presl, was coauthor with his brother Karel Bořivoj Presl (1794–1852), custodian of the National Museum's zoological and botanical collections from 1822, of the monumental *Czech Flora* [*Flora Čechica*, 1819]. Between them the Presl brothers did much to systematize modern Czech botanical and zoological terminology, largely in the pages of *Krok* itself. The word "*krok*" means a step or stride, but Krok was also, and not coincidentally, the name of the mythical Princess Libuše's father.

An original Czech literature was also beginning to reemerge by the early nineteenth century. Ten years after Václav Thám's poetic anthology, Antonín Jaromír Puchmajer (1769–1820) published the first modern almanac of entirely contemporary Czech verse, his *Selected Poems and Songs* of 1795. Further volumes under the title *New Poetry* followed in 1797, 1798, 1802, and 1814. Among Puchmajer's own poetic efforts are "An Ode to Jan Žižka z Trocnova" and "An Ode to the Czech Language." A theology student at the time he published his first almanac, Puchmajer was ordained a priest in 1796. He was a close friend of Dobrovský's, to whom he gave considerable assistance on his dictionary. Two more enduring literary names from the early nineteenth century are František Ladislav Čelakovský (1799–1852) and Josef Kajetán Tyl (1808–56). Čelakovský, who was long supported by an annual pension from another member of the Kinský family, Prince Rudolf (1802–36), translated among others Herder, Scott, and Pushkin into Czech and for a time edited *The Prague News* [*Pražské noviny*]. He is best remembered as the author of two collections of poems with the titles *An Echo of Russian Songs* [*Ohlas písní ruských*, 1829] and *An Echo of Czech Songs* [*Ohlas písní českých*, 1839]. We encountered Tyl earlier as the lyricist of "the sweetest song of the Czech land," the future national anthem "*Kde domov můj?*" He was a tireless propagator of Czech theater and the first editor of one of the oldest of Czech magazines, *Květy české* (*Czech Blossoms*, originally entitled *Jindy a nyní*, *Then and Now*, 1833), which has survived under the title *Květy* to the present day. Tyl's own copious writings include the novellas *The Last*

Czech [*Poslední Čech*], *The Love of a Patriot* [*Láska vlastencova*], and *The Love of a Patriotess* [*Láska vlastenky*], as well as many plays, among them *Jan Hus*, which opened in Prague to great enthusiasm on Boxing Day 1848.

In the critical judgment of posterity the undoubted pinnacle of early nineteenth-century Czech literature was Karel Hynek Mácha's *Máj* (1836). But it says much about the period that this great romantic epic should have received a frosty reception from Mácha's patriotic contemporaries, including both Tyl and Čelakovský, who reckoned it insufficiently "national" in its form and content. Čelakovský's attempt to ground the revived national culture in what was already being conceived as a pure folk art untainted by urban and upper-class "Germanization" was more representative of nationalist sentiment of the day. Mácha himself, it should be said, also contributed to this genre, writing a number of poems under the title *"Ohlas písní národních"* (An Echo of National Songs), ten of which were published in *Květy české* in 1834–35.[46] Čelakovský was a pioneering collector of folk songs, proverbs, and sayings. His *Slav National Songs* [*Slovanské národní písně*], which came out in three volumes between 1822 and 1827, was the first such anthology of its type in Bohemia. It was followed by *Popular Proverbs of the Slav Nation* [*Mudrosloví národa slovanského*] in 1852. We might note the conjunction of "Slav" [*slovanský*] and "nation" [*národ*] here, both words being in the singular. It is a further sign of the indeterminacy at this date of the boundaries of Czech nationality, to set beside those drawn from Bolzano earlier; though in this case the complicating factor is the newly discovered linguistic kinsfolk dwelling outside the borders of *země* and *vlast*, rather than the familiar linguistic strangers who had lived for centuries within it.

A slightly later cartographer of the landscape of the popular was Palacký's protégé Karel Jaromír Erben (1811–70), the secretary of the National Museum from 1846, Prague's first official city archivist from 1851, and a much-loved poet in his own right. His solitary book of verses, *Kytice z pověstí národních* [*A Bouquet from National Legends*, 1853], ranks with Mácha's *Máj* and Božena Němcová's novel *Babička* (*Grandma*, 1855) as one of the few truly enduring classics of the literature of the *obrození*. Like many *buditelé*, Erben's culturally awakening activities were many-sided. He republished several chronicles and other historical texts, among them Tomáš Štítný's *Six Little Books on General Christian Matters* and, most important, *Selected Czech Writings of Master Jan Hus*; but he also, like Jungmann and the Presl brothers, devoted much effort to developing a specialized modern Czech technical vocabulary, in his case in the field of law. In 1849 he was appointed official translator of laws into Czech and was summoned to Vienna with the renowned Slavicist Pavel Josef Šafařík and others to sit on a special commission for stabilizing the legal terminology of Slavonic languages. Erben's ethnographic interests were lifelong. In the 1840s he published his two-volume collection *National Songs in Bohemia* [*Písně národní v Čechách*, 1842, 1845], and in 1861 his *Slav Reader* [*Slovanská čítanka*], an anthology of one hundred folk tales and legends narrated in their original dialects. His thematically organized *Popular Czech Songs and Nursery Rhymes* [*Prostonárodní české písně a říkadla*, 1862–64] contained over 2,200 texts.[47] It lovingly reconstructs, through their songs, the lives of Czech country people from cradle to grave, and is a masterpiece of nineteenth-century ethnographic scholarship. František Sušil did the same for Moravia [*Moravské národní písně*, 1835]. This discovery of "the people" [*lid*] was to become central to modern imaginings of Czech identity, as we shall see. *Fidlovačka*, the Singspiel for which Josef Kajetán Tyl wrote "*Kde domov můj?*," is from this point of view a thoroughly appropriate source for the national anthem. It takes its title and setting from the annual Shoemakers' Guild festival in what was then the little village of Nusle, just outside Prague.

In his *History of Czech Language and Literature*, Josef Dobrovský had reckoned Czech to be a language spoken by "perhaps six million Austrian subjects in Bohemia, Moravia, Silesia and Upper Hungary." Elsewhere in the book he breaks down "the Slavonic language" [*slovanská řeč*] into five main "dialects" [*nářečí*], Russian, Polish, Illyrian, Croatian, and Czech, and includes Moravian [*moravština*], Silesian [*slezština*], and the Slovak spoken in Upper Hungary [*slovenština*] as part of Czech.[48] This linguistic space did not coincide with political boundaries. It is a curious but instructive fact that some of the most renowned *buditelé* were not by later reckoning Czechs. The poet and apostle of "Slav reciprocity" [*slovanská vzájemnost*] Jan Kollár (1793–1852) was a Slovak. Educated at the evangelical lyceum in Pressburg (now Bratislava) and the University of Jena, he spent most of his adult life ministering to a poor Slovak Lutheran parish in Budapest before taking up a chair in Slavic antiquities at the University of Vienna in 1849. His great pan-Slavist cycle *Slávy dcera* (*Sláva's Daughter*, 1824) is nevertheless counted as a seminal work of Czech literature, and Tomáš Masaryk (for one) rated Kollár's contribution to the Czech national awakening well above that of Jungmann.[49] Kollár, too, collected folk songs [*Národnie spievanky*, 1834–35].

Kollár's friend and contemporary Pavel Josef Šafařík (1795–1861) was another Slovak who helped make Slavism into a significant strand in modern Czech identity. The son of an evangelical pastor, Šafařík was like Kollár a Jena alumnus, and like Jungmann a gymnasium teacher. He moved to Prague in 1833 at Palacký's invitation, where he was supported by a pension put together by various patriots, among them Prince Rudolf Kinský. Later he became the custodian (1841) and then director (1848) of Prague university library, and in 1848–49 he briefly held the university's newly created chair in Slavonic studies before it was suppressed in the reaction that followed the revolution of 1848. Šafařík's major work is a reconstruction of the ancient history of the Slav peoples, *Slovanské starožitnosti* (*Slav Antiquities*), published by Matice česká in 1836–37. František Palacký himself, though born in Moravia, had strong Slovak (or perhaps we should say Upper Hungarian) connections; he was another graduate of Pressburg's evangelical lyceum, and moved to Prague only in 1823. These three men who made so central a contribution to modern Czech self-consciousness were in fact doubly marginal to Bohemian society as it had been shaped by the turn of the nineteenth century. Not only did they hail from Slovakia, they were also all Protestants.

Palacký (1798–1876) is by common consent the greatest of the *buditelé*, and is known to Czechs as the "Father of the Nation" [*Otec národa*]. From the point of view of articulating a national Czech identity, his *History of the Czech Nation in Bohemia and Moravia* is undoubtedly the single most influential work of the nineteenth century. Its first three volumes were published by Matice česká—in German—between 1836 and 1842. Palacký was not, however, without precursors. Czech history was gradually reassessed and variously reappropriated in the pre-March period. Of formerly forbidden works that resurfaced at the end of the eighteenth century, Balbín's *Defense of the Slavonic Language*, Stránský's *The Czech State*, and Komenský's *Labyrinth of the World* have already been mentioned. František Faustin Procházka (1749–1809), sometime censor and overseer of all gymnasia in Bohemia, published several medieval Czech texts in 1786–87 in editions intended for a popular readership, among them the chronicles of Přibík Pulkava and of "Dalimil,"[50] which dates from the early fourteenth century. The earliest known rhyming chronicle written in Czech, Dalimil had last been published in Prague in 1620. It is noteworthy among other things for its strident hostility to Germans and Germanization.

These years also saw a cautious rehabilitation of Hus and the Hussites. The four-volume *Portraits of Learned Men and Artists of Bohemia and Moravia*, which Pelcl, Born, and Mikuláš Adaukt Voigt began to issue in Latin and German in 1774, included entries on both Hus and Jeroným Pražský. Hus himself was portrayed as a good Catholic, albeit one whose "stubborn smugness" in the rectitude of his own ideas "brought about evils." He is sharply set apart from "Hussite immorality."[51] Kašpar Royko published a four-volume history of the Council of Konstanz, whose first volume was translated into Czech in 1785; it condemns the council and defends Hus. In 1789–90 Augustin Zitte's two-volume German biography of Hus represented the martyr not only as a good Catholic but also as a defender of Czech sovereignty against an overmighty Papacy. Dobrovský himself contributed to rethinking the Hussite period, both in his *History of Czech Language and Literature*, where he sees the combination of the Hussites' own anti-German nationalism and the isolation of Bohemia during the Hussite Wars as having encouraged the development of written Czech,[52] and in his short history of the Adamites and Pikarts of 1788. František Martin Pelcl's *Concise History of the Czechs* (written in German, 1774), deplores the violence of the Hussite revolution— as did Dobrovský, who talks of the Táborites' "brutal spirit"[53]—but nonetheless reclaims its authors for the Czech nation. "Perhaps enthusiasm for the homeland," Pelcl writes in the preface, "has often led me to too great an admiration for the deeds of our heroes; all the same, should not a Czech be proud of the heroism of his Žižka or Prokop? They were of course unfortunate Hussites, but they still believed in Christ, honored his Holy Mother and Saint Václav, why, Žižka even used to have mass read to him daily in camp."[5][4] Pelcl went on to republish various Hussite texts, among them the famous hymn "Ye who are the soldiers of God." There is a subtle but crucial transformation going on here. The religious issues that had led to the obliteration of Hussite memories for more than a century and a half—and that had, at least in their own eyes, motivated both the Hussites and their opponents—were slowly, but inexorably, becoming secondary to the fact that Hus, Žižka, and Prokop Holý were memorable *Czechs*. The past was being nationalized, and the Czech nation in turn identified through (among other things) this reordering of historical significances and symbols.

For all this—and taken together it is quite a lot—before the mid-nineteenth century the Czech *obrození* had very little detectable social impact, and no effect whatsoever on the structures of political power. It was as yet only weakly institutionalized, and nowhere was this clearer than in the world of the printed word. The Czech press and periodical literature was still in its infancy. It is true that a twice-weekly Czech-language newspaper, eventually called *Pražské poštovské noviny* [*The Prague Post*], had been published by successive generations of the Rosenmüller family since 1719. Reports of the demise of written Czech in the eighteenth century are sometimes exaggerated. But perhaps not overly so; the paper finally expired in 1772, a famine year, when in the case of one issue only four copies out of a total print run of one hundred were sold.[55] There was then a gap of ten years before any Czech-language paper appeared at all. The *Post* was revived in 1782 and sold to Jan Ferdinand Schönfeld, who appointed Václav Matěj Kramérius as its editor in 1786. Three years later Kramérius started his own paper, *Kramérius's Imperial and Royal Homeland News* [*Kramériusovy c. k. vlastenské noviny*], as it was called from 1791, which survived after his death under the editorship of his son Václav Rodimil Kramérius and František Bohumil Tomsa (1793–1857, nephew of František Jan) to 1825. These were to be the only Czech newspapers before 1848. The *Post* was bought by the Haas publishing house in 1824 and renamed *Pražské noviny* [*The Prague News*], and successively edited by Josef Linda, Čelakovský and—most famously—Karel Havlíček Borovský. Kramérius's *Homeland News* reportedly sometimes had as many as 1,400 subscribers.[56] In 1808, the *Homeland News* had a print run of 650, Schönfeld's *Post* a print run of 300, and the German-language *Prager Oberpostamts-Zeitung* a print run of 1,400.[57] To put these figures in some sort of perspective, Prague had a population of around 77,000 people in 1800.

These numbers are of little use as an indication of the relative strengths of the Czech and German languages among the newspaper-reading public, since German newspapers were widely available in Prague from Brno, Opava, Pressburg, and Vienna. But they do show both the growth of the Czech reading public during this period (these combined totals were ten times the circulation of all Prague newspapers in the first half of the eighteenth century) and its still very modest extent. This remained a precarious environment for Czech-language newspapers and periodicals, and although a fair number of the latter were started during these years, few survived for very long. Of the periodicals, *Krok* and *Květy české* have been discussed already. The oldest Czech historical journal, which survives to the present day, was started by Palacký and others in 1827 as the *Časopis Českého musea* (*Journal of the Czech Museum*). Other ventures included the first Czech literary magazine *Hlasatel český* (the *Czech Herald*), of which there were four annual volumes (1806–08, 1818); *Čechoslav*, subtitled "A National Magazine for Czechs and Moravians," which produced five volumes under the editorships of Václav Rodimil Kramérius and František Bohumil Tomsa between 1820 and 1825; and Josef Linda's *Zvěstovatel* (the *Courier*, 1820–24). Tyl's *Pražský posel* (the *Prague Messenger*) produced just one volume in 1846. Šafařík's *Světozor* (*Worldwatch*), "The cheapest illustrated publication for the broadening of knowledge for Czechs, Moravians, and Slovaks," was not much more successful. It expired after two volumes in 1834–35. *Krok* itself only managed four irregular volumes between 1821 and 1840.

Václav Matěj Kramérius (1753–1808), the publisher and editor of the *Homeland News*, was himself a notable *buditel*. A close friend of Dobrovský's and an ardent supporter of Joseph II's reforms, he was an indefatigable publicist. In 1784 he published Augustin Zippe's *Das Buch Joseph* in Czech translation, and he initially welcomed the French Revolution. To the disgust of communist historians, for whom such sentiments are not those that progressive *buditelé* were supposed to have, his later pamphlets include the 1793 *Most Grievous News of the Unfortunate Louis XVI, King of France*, and *A Relevant Description of the Cruel Death that Marie Antoinette, Queen of France, Had to Suffer*. The Girondins' declaration of war on Austria the year before was evidently offensive to Kramérius's patriotic sentiments. He also tried his hand at poetry (according to *Ottův slovník naučný* "with decidedly modest success"),[58] publishing a little volume in Prague in 1788 with the engaging title *New Czech Songs for the Beautiful Female Sex* [*Noví čeští zpěvové pro krásné pohlaví ženské*].

Apart from his newspaper, Kramérius's most sterling service to the *obrození* lay in his founding of the first modern Czech publishing house, Česká expedice, in 1790. For the most part it did not deal in serious literature or high culture, which is perhaps why it survived. It is also why, at this date, Kramérius may well have made a far more important practical contribution to the revival of written Czech than many of his more culturally elevated con-

5. Staré město from Malá strana, 1856. The bare hills in the distance are where the suburbs of Vinohrady and Žižkov would soon be built.

temporaries. His products actually penetrated the countryside and small towns where most Czech-speakers then lived. Among his greatest successes were the *New Toleration Calendars* he put out annually from 1787–98, which apart from listing Catholic and Evangelical festivals side by side, the places and times of markets, and so forth, provided a wealth of useful civic information enlivened by educational fables, items of home economics, and snippets of geography. The books published by Česká expedice were likewise aimed at a popular audience: romances set in far-off times and exotic places; travelogues; lowbrow works of history and geography; and uplifting writings for youth, boasting titles like *Merry and Sad Tales of Innocent Children, A Mirror of Nobility for Czech Youth*, and *The New Aesop*. In all Kramérius published perhaps eighty-four books.[59]

The only other Czech publisher of any consequence before 1848 was the firm of Jan Hostivít Pospíšil (1785–1868) in Hradec Králové. It, too, largely targeted the popular market, but it also published among others Čelakovský, and a five-language edition of Komenský's *Orbis pictus* in 1833. Magdaléna Dobromila Rettigová's *Home Cookery, or, A Treatise on Meat Meals for Daughters of Bohemia and Moravia* (1826), to the Czech kitchen what Mrs. Beeton was to the nineteenth-century English or *The Joy of Cooking* to the twentieth-century American, was one Pospíšil success story. Her *A Treatise on Veal* and *A Cup of Coffee and All That Is Sweet* followed in 1843. Rettigová (1785–1845) was a passionate *buditelka*[60] who organized Czech reading circles for women and girls and penned a considerable body of indifferent prose, poetry, and drama for their awakening. *A Little Garland for Patriotic Daughters* [*Věneček pro dcery vlastenecké*, 1825] is the title of one of her collections. Alois Jirásek was later to write a play about her life. The literary historian Arne Novák was less enchanted, complaining in 1905 of how for Rettigová "the whole universe swims in a fog of kitchen steam, the menu becomes the scale of values, a table of gargantuan proportions is shown as the noble goal of women's strivings," and characterizing the lady herself as "a female philistine who found the world as comfortable and philistine as she imagined it in her petty soul."[61] *Ottův slovník naučný* exhibits a touch of the same masculine disdain, judging Rettigová's "patriotic activities" to be "more worthwhile and more important" than her culinary tracts.[62] But the way to the nation's heart, in this case, is much more likely to have been through its stomach. Like Kramérius's calendars and pulp fiction, Rettigová's cookbooks were actually read.

One measure of just how limited, at the time, was the wider social impact of all this revivalist activity is the fate of Čelakovský's *An Echo of Russian Songs*, a work subsequently canonized as a foundational text of the *obrození*. Čelakovský had to bear all the costs of its printing himself, and over half the edition of five hundred copies remained unsold in a crate several years later.[63] The world of the *buditelé* was a small one: small enough for the same few men and their sons—and occasional women—to be writing dictionaries, translating, editing magazines, boosting Czech theater; small enough for many of them to be patronized by the same enlightened band of patriotic nobles; small enough for most of them to know one another personally. Even by the middle of the nineteenth century there were few tangible results of three generations of "awakening." Despite the individual efforts of a Josef Jungmann or a Karel Thám, not a single high school in Bohemia was teaching in Czech before the 1850s (and most were not to do so before the 1860s). Czech theater still led an itinerant existence, never staying long in one building, and periodically jockeying for space at the Stavovské divadlo. Palacký and his circle did succeed in taking over direction of the Royal Society and the National Museum in the 1820s, a position they used among other things to establish the Matice česká. But the Matice was so chronically underfunded that in its first decade it managed to publish a mere six books, two of which were hagiographic pamphlets in honor of Francis I and Ferdinand I. By 1840 there were 2,257 donors to the fund, of whom 1,735 had given less than fifty florins. In a revealing contrast, the Heritage of Saint Jan Nepomucký [*Dědictví svatojanské*], a Catholic foundation devoted to publishing cheap Bibles, catechisms, and other literature in Czech which was founded two years before the Matice in 1829, rapidly sold over twenty thousand memberships in the Czech lands at between ten and forty florins apiece— which again underlines the Catholic contribution to the *obrození*.[64] True, the Church was mightier than the Matice. Even so, this is eloquent testimony to the vast gulf that still lay between the *buditelé* and the nation they were so busily representing, in all the various senses of that word.

Things were to change dramatically in the second half of the century. Dictionaries, grammars, folk songs, almanacs, operas, ethnographies, histories, cookbooks; priests, poets, professors, and playwrights; it is, at first sight, an arcane set of weapons and a somewhat unlikely corps of revolutionaries.[65] But power does not always come out of the barrel of a gun.

FOUR

MIRRORS OF IDENTITY

A Burghers' Banquet

A DESCRIPTION of the events leading up to the foundation of the Prague Měšťanská beseda (Burghers' Club) was read to its members at its first semiannual general meeting of 26 April 1846, and it was formally agreed that this account should be entered in the society's minute book. Entitled "Equality and Concord!" it begins thus:

> The sentiment of nationality, which was reawakened in the nations of mid-Europe after the wars of our time, woke up us Czechs too, albeit as the last ones, and civic life began—at first among modest enough numbers of learned practitioners of sciences and arts and the clergy. Thence it was transferred into the heart and core of the nation—the middle class [stav měšťanský]. After so many storms, catastrophies, and great difficulties, which ordinarily would have had as their consequence if not the death of many great and powerful nations, then at the least a complete overthrow of their life and nationhood [národnost], and this first of all in their capital cities, our ancient and glorious Prague remained in her original Slavic guise. The erstwhile mother of lofty ideas and brilliant deeds of the Czech nation opened her womb again after two hundred years of sleep to the results of contemporary learning, again she accepted the newborn child of Czech nationality to her bosom, in order to multiply the new family, to nurture it for fulfillment of civic virtues, cultivation of the arts, science, and industry, [and] powerful support for Church and throne.[1]

This is a far sharper appreciation of the sociology of nineteenth-century Czech nationalism than that which is found in many subsequent histories. There is no abstract "nation" awakening here. The chronology, trajectory, and social basis of the revival are grasped with unerring accuracy, and Czech nationality is quite explicitly conceived of as "a newborn child." The "sentiment of nationality," at this date, is also not something that is seen as being in conflict with the Catholic Church or the Habsburg state. There is no reason to take the expression of loyalties to "Church and throne" voiced here at anything other than its face value. These men were very far from being revolutionaries, at least in the political sense of that word.

Moves to establish the Měšťanská beseda had begun in 1844. A petition signed by more than ninety Prague burghers was submitted to the Land authorities, and permission for the formation of the society was granted by the Prague city authority, the *magistrát*, in August 1845. Thirty-one of the signatories met on 12 October and elected an eleven-man committee. They were Messrs. [*pánové*] František Pštross, burgher representative and leather manufacturer; Kašpar Slavík, resident burgher; Josef Frič, land advocate and resident burgher; Prokop Richter, resident burgher and jeweler; Jan Slavík, resident burgher and miller; František Ditrich, resident burgher and timber merchant; Petr Faster, victualler; Bedřich Franzl, resident burgher and miller; Jan Rypota, resident burgher and master builder; Matěj Mišák, manufacturer of playing cards; and Jan Schwertner, resident burgher and "*mechanikus.*" The meeting also chose six alternate committee members: Vilém Šťastný, master bookbinder; Antonín Macourek, merchant; Emanuel Pštross, trader in hides; Josef Vyličil, upholsterer; Václav Řivnáč, furrier; and Petr Vnouček, resident burgher and brewmaster. Hugo Kašpar, resident burgher and medical doctor, was elected treasurer, and František August Brauner, doctor of laws, was chosen as the society's convenor. These are gentlemen of a class that had not been conspicuous for its part in the *obrození* hitherto.

The Beseda ceremonially inaugurated its activities with a banquet on 31 January of the following year, at which 103 members were present. The guests of honor were the city *hejtman* (captain) Count Maurice z Deymů, Mayor of Prague Knight Josef z Müllerů, and Josef Jungmann, Pavel Josef Šafařík, František Palacký, and Jan Svatopluk Presl. The young journalist Karel Havlíček Borovský (1821–56) reported on the event in *Pražské noviny* the next day, describing the speeches, toasts, and singing of Czech songs in approving detail. "Our most serene king and lord the most gracious Ferdinand V, under whose fatherly governance the sciences, arts, and industry are flowering and prospering" of course had his health drunk first, and after him the governor of Bohemia, the city *hejtman*, and the mayor. Confident that he would be understood, the mayor delivered his own toast to the success of Měšťanská beseda in German. Then "our Palacký spoke many serious words about our history," and "after him our Šafařík raised his glass to the toleration of all nations and languages in the Austrian monarchy." These events, Havlíček thinks, require no commentary. They "sufficiently speak for themselves. It is enough to say that the Prague burghers have for the first time stood up in greater glory in a completely Czech spirit, taking a firm step toward the unceasing profession of their nationality before the world."[2] It was, as Havlíček recognized, a crucial symbolic moment. From an esoteric concern of "modest enough numbers" of priests and intellectuals, a Czech identity was finally being publicly embraced by "the heart and core of the nation," as the Czech-speaking middle classes were redefining themselves to be. The lexicographers and historians were sharing the stage with millers, manufacturers, brewers, and builders, and the burghers recognized the scholars' arcane preoccupations as having some relevance to themselves.

In that marriage of convenience much of the story of Czech nationalism—

and of Czech nationality—in the later nineteenth century is prefigured. It was modernization that gave the ideas of the *buditelé* a new pertinence and purchase, and it was the Czech middle classes who were to become their most enthusiastic advocates. It is perhaps not hard to see why. The social landscape of the Czech lands was utterly transformed between 1850 and 1914. A modern and prosperous civil society was built. For the ever-increasing numbers of officials and clerks (of whom the imperial bureaucracy required legions), school and university teachers, publishers and journalists, doctors and lawyers, entertainers and actors, manufacturers, bankers, merchants, and shopkeepers whose livelihoods depended on purveying goods and services to the Czech-speaking masses, language, in particular, became an urgently practical question. Which tongue, Czech or German, was to be employed in classrooms and offices, councils and courts, stores and banks, newspapers and magazines, was an issue of opportunities gained or denied—on both sides. Modernization also changed the terms of the national game in two other critical respects. It generated a population capable of being newly nationalized, a population that increasingly lived in towns and cities or had easy access to their products, could read and write, and had money in its pocket. And it developed the many material instruments—schools, cheap newsprint and technologies of book illustration, a postal service, railroads, banks, insurance companies, art galleries, exhibitions, theaters, political parties, public buildings and public parks, and much else—through which the project of nationalization could be practically accomplished.

By 1913 the Czech lands (including the rump of Silesia) had a combined population of 10.3 million people, around a fifth of that of Austria-Hungary as a whole and 36 percent of that of the Austrian half of the empire. They also contained over half the latter's industrial plants and employed fully 57 percent of its industrial labor force.[3] Agriculture, forestry, and fishing occupied 51 percent of Bohemia's workforce in 1869. By 1910 only 34 percent still worked the land, and industry, trade, and transportation between them accounted for half of all employment.[4] Agriculture nonetheless prospered, not least because of the abolition of the *robota* in 1848; between 1870 and 1913 yields per hectare doubled, and Czech peasant farmers thrived.[5] This *sedlák* class was to be a key fixture of the political landscape until after 1945. Major industries—whose owners were often, though by no means always, German or Jewish—included coal mining, iron and steel, light and heavy engineering, chemicals, textiles, paper, brewing, and food processing. Along with industrialization went massive movements of population. Between 1869 and 1900 Plzeň (with its suburbs) grew from 26,000 to 83,000 people, Brno from 95,000 to 164,000. Moravská Ostrava, a coal and steel town in northern Moravia on the Silesian border, exploded from 23,000 to 115,000 over the same thirty years (and to 150,000 by 1910).[6] Rates of urban growth were well above those for the population as a whole; Czechs were moving out of the countryside and into the towns. As late as 1843 only two cities in the Czech lands, Prague and Brno, had more than 20,000 inhabitants, and almost five-sixths (83.5 percent) of the Bohemian population still lived in settlements of less than 2,000 people.[7] By the end of the century this latter figure had fallen to 57 percent.[8] This mass inmigration from the Czech-speaking countryside (rural emigrants from German regions went more often to Munich or Vienna) altered more than just the social structure of the towns and cities of Bohemia and Moravia. Decisively for Czech nationalism, it equally dramatically reshaped their linguistic—or, as it increasingly becomes appropriate to call it as the century wears on, their ethnic—composition.

This was not a process that was uniform in its effects. Rather, it exacerbated and exaggerated differences, mapping linguistic boundaries onto the new urban spaces and creating a polarized ethnic geography. Most of the cities of the *pohraničí* remained predominantly German. Liberec [Reichenberg], for example, had 28,263 German-speaking inhabitants and only 1,613 Czechs (and one Pole) in 1890. It also shrunk in relative importance. In 1840 it had been the second city in Bohemia, with 16,000 inhabitants. Fifty years later it had fallen to sixth place, behind Prague, Plzeň, and the mushrooming Prague suburbs of Žižkov, Vinohrady, and Smíchov, which were counted as independent cities until 1922. There were also "islands" of German preponderance in the interior of the Czech lands. In Moravia, the capital city of Brno (48,591 Germans, 32,142 Czechs in 1880), the bishop's seat of Olomouc (6,194 Czechs out of a total population of 19,761 in 1900, a proportion that had actually fallen since 1870), and the royal city of Jihlava (4,117 Czechs, 19,325 Germans in 1890) continued to show a face that was more German than Czech. The Moravian industrial town of Přerov, on the other hand, which by 1900 had two sugar refineries, two breweries, and more than thirty factories supplying agricultural machinery and other goods to the region, counted not a single German among its 17,005 inhabitants. Plzeň city had a population of 57,806 Czechs as against 8,008 Germans in the same year; if its suburbs were included in the figure, the disparity would be still more marked. In Bohemia as in Moravia, outside the borderlands and established German "islands" [*ostrovy*]—an interesting term, because it implies a surrounding sea[9]—the rapidly growing smaller towns were overwhelmingly Czech. In 1900 there were only 89 Germans living among Příbram's 13,475 Czechs, 216 Germans in Pardubice, a town of 17,031 inhabitants, and just 13 Germans in the 5,519-strong little town of Poděbrady, the birthplace, nearly five centuries earlier, of the Hussite king Jiří z Poděbrad.[10]

Nowhere was this Czechization more striking than in the Bohemian capital. In 1851, Prague was a walled city of around 150,000 people of whom (maybe) 41 percent were German-speakers, with an insignificant suburban hinterland.[11] By 1900 the walls had long since come down, and the conurba-

6. The Palacký Bridge, with Josef Myslbek's statues of legendary Czech heroes on the nearer pylons, photographed from Podskalí around 1884. On the opposite bank, under Petřín Hill, lies industrial Smíchov.

tion boasted over half a million inhabitants, 93 percent of whom identified their language of everyday intercourse as Czech.[12] Here, Czech encirclement of Bohemia's "Germans" was literal. Those who claimed German as their everyday language had their principal location[13] in the five central boroughs that until 1883 made up the city of Prague in official fiction if not in demographic fact. This presence was amplified out of all proportion to mere numbers by the continuing and visible German dominance of key institutions of Prague's commercial and cultural life,[14] and, more mundanely but no less significantly, by how the city presented itself to the eye in such details as the names on its shop-fronts.[15] Emperor Franz Josef, visiting in 1868, complacently remarked that "Prague has a thoroughly German appearance." It was an observation that did not please Czechs, but was not so wide of the mark considering the date and the parts of town where he spent his time.[16] As late as 1880, "Germans" still formed 22 percent of the population of Staré město (the Old Town), 16 percent in Nové město (the New Town), 20 percent in Malá strana (the Little Quarter), 9 percent in Hradčany, and 39 percent in the former Jewish ghetto of Josefov.[17] The burgeoning suburbs, whose combined population exceeded that of Prague proper by 1890, were by contrast crushingly Czech. Working-class Žižkov had a population of 824 Germans amid 58,112 Czechs at the turn of the century. Holešovice-Bubny, which was officially incorporated into the city in 1884, had an entirely Czech-speaking population of 15,352 in 1890. Libeň, added in 1901, counted only 159 Germans among its 12,536 people (1890). Nusle, the village setting for Tyl's and Škroup's *Fidlovačka* in the 1830s, had grown to a sizable town of over 20,000 by 1900 and was separated from Prague by administrative imagination rather than green fields. Only 307 of these people identified themselves as German-speakers.[18]

There is a luminous passage in Franz Kafka's diaries for 1911 in which he registers this estrangement at the city's heart. As is usual with Kafka, he could be talking about anywhere in the modern world. A precise eye for detail goes along with a total disembodiment from any particular time and place, making his vision universal. But he happens to be writing explicitly for once about his hometown, a place where at that date a ride on a streetcar was also a journey through uneasily intersecting zones of class, language, ethnicity, and (since Kafka was Jewish, and in the language of the day) "race":

> Yesterday in the factory. Rode back on the trolley, sat in a corner with legs stretched out, saw people outside, lights in stores, walls of viaducts through which we passed, backs and faces over and over again, a highway leading from the business street of the suburb with nothing human on it save people going home, the glaring electric lights of the railway station burned into the darkness, the low, tapering chimneys of a gasworks, a poster announcing the guest appearance of a singer, de Treville, that gropes its way along the walls as far as an alley near the cemeteries, from where it then returned with me out of the cold of the fields into the livable warmth of the city. We accept foreign cities as a fact, the inhabitants live there without penetrating our way of life, just as we cannot penetrate theirs. . . . The suburbs of our native city, however, are also foreign to us, but in this case comparisons have value, a half-hour's walk can prove it to us over and over again, here live people partly within our city, partly on the miserable, dark edge of the city that is furrowed like a great ditch, although they all have an area of interest in common with us that is greater than any other group of people outside the city. For this reason I always enter and leave the suburb with a weak mixed feeling of anxiety, of abandonment, of sympathy, of curiosity, of conceit, of joy in traveling, of fortitude, and return with pleasure, seriousness, and calm, especially from Žižkov.[19]

When Kafka returned from that trip, it was to his parents' apartment at 36 Mikulášská (from 1926 Pařížská) třída, or as his mother would have called it Niklasstrasse, the most elegant boulevard in all Prague, which runs from the Old Town Square, Staroměstské náměstí, to the recently opened art nouveau Svatopluk Čech Bridge (1908). The street was pan-Slavically named thus after the Russian czar Nicholas [Mikuláš] II.[20] Mikulášská had been punched through the centuries-old Jewish ghetto at the beginning of the century, as the showpiece of one of the most extensive slum-clearance schemes on the Continent.

The next year the family was to move to the Oppelt House on the corner of Staroměstské náměstí itself, where Kafka's father Herman had a notions shop on the ground floor of the baroque palace of the Kinskýs. Kafka's mother Julie had herself grown up on Staroměstské náměstí, in the house where, some years earlier, the young Bedřich Smetana had once had a music school. Franz himself spent part of his early childhood in the Dům U Minuty (House at the Minute) beside the Old Town Hall, which separates Staroměstské náměstí from Malé náměstí (the Small Square). Among the Renaissance sgraffiti uncovered beneath layers of plaster on its facade in 1919, alongside Adam and Eve in the garden of Eden, a bacchanalian procession, the noble Roman Gaius Mucius Scaevola extending his hand into the flames burning on the sacrificial altar of Lars Porsena, and a gallery of fifteen French kings, is a Talmudic legend in which the youngest of three sons, by refusing to join his brothers in an archery competition in which his father's exhumed corpse is the target, gains the inheritance.[21] This is a historical and semiotic landscape of enormous complexities. But they were even then being ironed out by its reclamation for Czechness; and as with any palimpsest, new texts were inscribed at the cost of erasures of the old.

The Affordable National Library

The events of the "stormy year" [bouřlivý rok] of 1848 have often been mythologized in subsequent recollection, especially by Czech communists. One example is the inscription "1848—1948" high up on the facade of the erstwhile Hotel International, today a Holiday Inn, Prague's finest example of Stalinist architectural pomposity; a legend that links, one could well say, two equally ersatz revolutions. That of 1848 proved to be something of a damp squib in the Czech lands. If it showed anything, it was the political ineptitude of nationalist intellectuals and the shallowness of their popular support. Such disorders as there were in Prague were put down with the aid of a little shelling of Staré město from Hradčany by General Windischgrätz, and the few concessions to Czech national aspirations wrung from the monarchy in 1848–49 mostly disappeared for the duration of the centralizing and authoritarian regime of Emperor Franz Josef's tough interior minister Alexander Bach. Even Bach's fall in 1859 and the revival of constitutionalism with the October Diploma of 1860 and the February Patent of 1861 were not taken much political advantage of by Czech nationalists. The Old Czech party, which was led by Palacký's son-in-law František Ladislav Rieger (1818–1903), high-mindedly and ineffectually boycotted the Imperial Reichstag from 1863 to 1879. As in the pre-March days, the favored terrain of nationalist endeavor for long remained culture rather than politics.

The difference now was that a wide range of civil institutions, both public and private, was developed through which the idea of nationality was pervasively stitched into the fabric of everyday life. Despite occasional moments of Austrian heavy-handedness (and vigorous Bohemian-German resistance), this cultural Czechization of the social landscape was never seriously disrupted after 1860. It was becoming too deeply ingrained, in and as subjectivities. Entailed in this colonization of the quotidian was a subtle but far-reaching transformation. Taken-for-granted features of the life-world (language, customs, nursery rhymes, dress) acquired a novel significance. They were subsumed under organizing master narratives of nationality, of whose truth they now came to furnish the daily existential confirmation. From incidental aspects of personal existence they were reconfigured as essential elements of a social identity. And with this, they came increasingly to mark lines of demarcation between Bohemia's ever-more nationalized populations, making them into self-evident and mutually exclusive "communities." The demographic movements just discussed undoubtedly provided the basis for this nationalization, but they do not in or of themselves wholly explain it. Bohemia also experienced a profound *cultural* revolution in the later nineteenth century, in which Czech-speakers were welded into a Czech nation and German speakers were in the same process themselves ethnicized, to become a bounded "national minority." The instruments of this revolution were mundane, material, and quintessentially modern.

When Maria Theresa had first introduced her elementary and secondary schools in the mid-1770s, and modern "defenses of the Czech language" were already beginning to appear, perhaps four-fifths of Bohemia's servile population could not read or write in any language.[22] A century later, we are dealing with an almost wholly literate public; according to the 1890 census, only 4.6 percent of males (over the age of six) and 6.9 percent of females could neither read nor write.[23] But as significant was the language in which they read. Only in 1848 did the Ministry of Education finally decree that the language of instruction in elementary schools would henceforth be the mother tongue. Two years earlier, Karel Havlíček Borovský could still ask the question: "How many hundreds (they certainly cannot be reckoned in the thousands) of Czechs yet know how to write correctly in their own language? Not to be able to write German correctly is regarded here as a great shame for anybody who wants to be considered educated. And Czech?—"[24] By 1890, a total of 576,963 elementary school pupils were being educated (in all subjects) in Czech, as against 332,041 in German.[25] There is, perhaps, no more powerful means of nationalizing a population, in the double sense of homogenizing them internally and differentiating them externally, than compulsory schooling through the medium of a "national language." Nor, indeed, is there any more authoritative and effective way of "reviving" that language itself.

The difficulty earlier on, about which we have seen Jungmann (and before him Dobrovský) complaining, was that there had been no way a Czech child could progress beyond the elementary grades in the education system without first having mastered German; and often that meant additional years of schooling, of which the results were frequently less than perfect.[26] Havlíček repeats the same complaint here. Before 1848 there was not a single high school teaching in Czech in Bohemia. The first to do so was Prague's Academic Gymnasium during 1850–53, but it again reverted to German until 1861. The cause was as much a shortage of textbooks and teachers as it was "Bach's absolutism." As late as 1841 there were still no textbooks in Czech suitable for gymnasium use, and the first entirely Czech teachers' training college did not open in Prague until 1849. But in the 1860s twelve gymnasia switched to Czech as their language of instruction, and a further two taught in a mixture of Czech and German. Laws of 1866 and 1868 segregated high schools, requiring them henceforth to use one language or the other. By 1890 there were forty-nine Czech gymnasia and technical high schools in Bohemia with 13,390 students—more than their German language equivalents.[27] The first girls' gymnasium in the Austro-Hungarian Empire, called Minerva after the ancient Roman goddess of wisdom, opened its doors in Prague that same year. Started by the author, feminist, and fierce patriot Eliška Krásnohorská (1847–1926), who among other things wrote several of the libretti for Smetana's operas, it too taught in Czech.

Minerva's object was to prepare girls for entry to university. Addressing the first graduating class in 1895, Krásnohorská concluded with an exhortation that is typical of her in its mix of feminist and patriotic ardor: "Dear girls, Czech girls, future workers for light and good, leaders of our female patriots on the future road to knowledge! Turn your sight and heart toward the Goddess of Wisdom and bow down before her: beneath her shield you will find the keys to true greatness. Success to you! Blessings be with you on your life pilgrimage!"[28] The first Czech female to gain a Ph.D at Prague university was Marie Baborová in 1901; the first Czech female medical doctor was Anna Honzáková a year later. By the winter semester of 1904–5 there were fifteen girls studying in the Medical Faculty and 149 in the Philosophy Faculty (but none before 1921–22 in the Faculty of Science).[29] The university itself offered only 22 out of its 187 lecture courses in Czech in 1861.[30] It split into separate Czech and German institutions in 1882. The ancient Karolinum and Klementinum were internally sundered with dividing walls, and when it was necessary for Czechs and Germans to use the same facilities, as at convocations, they did so at different times. By 1891 the Czech university had 142 faculty, only 10 fewer than the German university, and 2,308 students.[31] The first lectures in Czech at Prague's Polytechnic Institute, the school set up by the Estates in 1806, were given in 1861–62, and it too formally divided in 1869–70. By 1904 the Czech university had 209 faculty and 3,184 students, the German university 202 faculty and 1,283 students; the Czech polytechnic had 93 faculty and 1,420 students, the German polytechnic 67 faculty and 571 students.[32]

Earlier we saw the parlous state of the Czech-language press in the pre-March period. There was an explosion of Czech journalism in 1848–49. At the beginning of "the stormy year" there were still only two Czech political newspapers, *Pražské noviny* and *Slovanské noviny* (*Slav News*). A year later there were thirty. The most influential was Karel Havlíček Borovský's *Národní noviny* (*National News*), which he defiantly continued to publish until January 1850.[33] With the reimposition of absolutist rule they were all suppressed, and Havlíček himself was exiled, without trial, to the small town of Brixen in the Austrian Tyrol in December of 1851. He was finally permitted to return to Bohemia in 1855 only to face bitter disappointment. His wife Julie died in Prague a few days before his arrival, and many erstwhile patriots, in the general climate of fear induced by Bach's police, avoided his company. Palacký and the novelist Božena Němcová (1820–62) were honorable exceptions. Havlíček died of tuberculosis (brought on, many believed, by his exile) the following year, aged only thirty-five. His funeral was the first of many that were to remind Czechs who they were over the next century and a half: Němcová, Palacký, Rieger, Jirásek, Masaryk, Čapek, Mácha, Opletal, Beneš, Palach, Patočka, Seifert. As on many of these occasions, the mourners assumed the secret police of the day to be present.

"So yesterday, at six o'clock in the evening," wrote Božena Němcová to a friend, "we laid to rest our Havlíček. . . . I had a beautiful crown made for the coffin lid from pin cherry leaves and a demi-wreath for his head from laurel, also I had passionflower blossom ordered for Friday. I managed to get it, two blooms just out, and immediately I went down and laid it in Havlíček's hands. He was a lover of flowers, and this one was particularly suited to him." It was so well suited, perhaps, because in Czech as in English the passionflower is so named [*mučenka*] because its parts are supposed to recall the instruments of Christ's Passion. In Karel Havlíček the Czech national cause had its first modern martyr. She continues,

> From Friday morning people walked up as if in procession, where he lay in his coffin already—I tell you, the sight was upsetting to tears. It was not idle curiosity these people coming, what sort of coffin, what clothes, to look the place over—the old, the young, men, women, *clergy*, *soldiers*, simple tradesmen and laborers, each came quietly, with extraordinary respect, and the tears that flowed by his coffin were not faked. . . . But on Friday he was already very blue, especially around the forehead and his ears were cornflower blue—and from his mouth blood was oozing, the odor was becoming very strong.—They had to

carry him down to the entrance passageway [*průjezd*] and asperged him with holy water there because upstairs there was no room for all the folk. . . . There was an enormous number of people, it was hardly possible to get through; as far as the eye could reckon, over five thousand, and all classes and estates were represented, even those you would not expect. No policemen or gendarmes in sight, but no doubt there were plenty of them among the folk, in plain clothes. If they heard what I did—and it resounded from all sides fearlessly, they had sufficient to report:—"Since Hus there has not been a man like this born, who would dare tell them the truth like this!" . . . "He has done much for us, it was only him, who opened our eyes, previously we did not even know what we are and who we belong to!"—"That one knew how to tell the truth, that's why they poisoned him!"—"Nay, this is our martyred saint, well he has a martyr's crown on his coffin!" "No, that's not a martyr's crown, it means that he was a writer, a poet as well!" . . . Such voices echoed among the general folk, we ourselves were quiet as mice and just looked around almost timorously, hoping the sad procession would not be interrupted in any way. God knows where any disruption would lead, there were people in the procession itching to settle scores. They carried him down Poříč, around Saint Joseph's and Prašná brána to Hybernácká ulice, then through Senovážní Square to the New Gate. The ramparts were swarming with spectators—When the coffin was about to be placed in the hearse, the cry went up: "Not in the carriage, we will carry him ourselves as far as the cemetery!"—It was the people of Podskalí.[34]

Němcová's husband Josef got eight days in jail for his participation in the funeral.[35]

It was a considerable loss. Havlíček was brave, intelligent, and very much more levelheaded than most Czech nationalists of the time. A spell in czarist Moscow in the 1840s had cured him of the romantic and uncritical pan-Slavism that afflicted so many of his contemporaries. "Russian frosts and other Russian things extinguished in me the last spark of pan-Slav love. . . . I returned to Prague a *Czech*, a mere inflexible Czech," he wrote in 1846.[36] This essay, which is entitled "A Slav and a Czech" [*Slovan a Čech*], could have been read with profit by starry-eyed Slavophiles in the Czech lands on many occasions since, not least after World War II. Havlíček had first made himself notorious a year earlier with a savage review of Tyl's vacuously patriotic *Poslední Čech.*[37] One of his epigrams, entitled "To Very Many Czech Poets," reads:

> Eternal your song: "What bliss
> It is to love the Czech homeland!"—
> But if she is to profit from your love,
> Don't send your songs to the press.[38]

Not a single nongovernmental Czech newspaper appeared in Bohemia throughout the 1850s.[39] As with high schools, a regular Czech-language press also emerged only after 1860 with the newspapers *Čas* (*Time*) and *Národní listy* (the *National Paper*), whose first issue came out on 1 January 1861. *Národní listy* was edited by Julius Grégr (1831–96), who was later to become a leading figure in the Young Czech party, and was backed by among others Palacký, Purkyně, Rieger, and Palacký's pupil the historian Václav Vladivoj Tomek. It went on to become the leading Czech-language daily, with a circulation of over ten thousand.[40] Other new Czech papers included *Hlas* (the *Voice*), founded in 1862, which merged with *Národní listy* three years later, and Palacký and Rieger's own *Národ* (the *Nation*, 1863–66), which was succeeded by *Pokrok* (*Progress*), a daily published from 1867 until it changed its name to *Hlas národa* (*Voice of the Nation*) in 1886. From 1866 there was also a government daily, *Pražský denník* (the *Prague Daily*). In Moravia the daily *Moravská orlice* (the *Moravian Eagle*) and the thrice-weekly *Olomoucké noviny* (*Olomouc News*, after 1869 *Našinec*, the *Compatriot*) started up in 1863 and 1865 respectively. By the end of the decade a socialist press was also making its appearance (*Dělník*, the *Worker*, 1867; *Oul*, the *Beehive*, 1868–69; *Český dělník*, the *Czech Worker*, 1869). *Dělnické listy* (the *Workers' Paper*) was published from 1872 as the official organ of the Czech Social Democrats.

Not every such venture, of course, survived. Nevertheless by 1890 there were seventeen dailies, one four-times-weekly, two thrice-weekly, thirty twice-weekly, and seventy-five weekly papers coming out in the Czech language.[41] By 1904 Prague alone was served by twelve daily papers.[42] In 1875 there were 195 periodicals and magazines being published in Bohemia, 99 of them in Czech; by 1890 there were 418, of which 253 were in Czech as against 157 in German. Quite as important as the number of these publications is the range of interests to which they catered. It is one indication of the variety of walks of life in which it was becoming possible routinely to function in civil society in Czech and as a Czech. Apart from politics, which was the largest single category, there were magazines devoted to national economy, trade and business, pedagogy and youth, literature and entertainment, diocesan affairs, music and theater, geography and statistics, law and administration, military matters, medicine and science, stenography, advertising, and local news. By this date there was even one Czech magazine specifically "for women," *Ženské listy* (the *Women's Paper*).[43] It had been edited since 1875 by Eliška Krásnohorská, the founder of the girls' gymnasium Minerva.

Periodicals like *Zlatá Praha* (*Golden Prague*), which appeared weekly from 1884 and expired finally in 1929, gave to the rapidly broadening educated Czech public the opportunity to participate in literate culture in its own tongue, in a way that would have been impossible a few decades before. They also quietly defined that culture, doing much to create what they purported merely to represent, in and through the very act of its representation. *Zlatá Praha* was seldom aggressively political or vociferously nationalistic, but it was all the more effective for that. It published poetry and fiction in Czech (Alois Jirásek, Jaroslav Vrchlický, Eliška Krásnohorská, and many others) and reproduced the work of Czech painters, among them Alfons Mucha.[44] It subtly reoriented political and cultural geographies away from Austria-Hungary through its regular column "The Slav World" [*Slovanský svět*] and its frequent special features on Bulgaria, Russia, and other Slav lands; photography now allowed "*Slovanstvo*" (Slavdom) to step off the poetic page and assume visual concreteness and immediacy. It transcended the Habsburg administrative division of the Kingdom of Bohemia and the Margravate of Moravia—since Maria Theresa these had been separate provinces, governed independently of one another from Vienna—by treating both as parts of a single national space, unified by its shared Czechness. It reviewed Czech books, concerts, plays, exhibitions and operas, manifesting the vitality of a Czech culture week in, week out. It gave face and body to the nation in its lengthy obituaries and special birthday tributes to prominent Czechs.[45] It covered newsworthy events in Prague and the Czech provinces, and in so doing redefined what was newsworthy by its place in a national frame of reference: the opening of a new Czech school, for example, was something that always merited attention.

Just as important, for the most part it pointedly ignored German Prague and all its works. As much by omission as commission, it represented Golden Prague as precisely what Mayor Tomáš Černý (1840–1910) notoriously said it was in his inaugural speech of 8 October 1882, a speech that provoked the resignations of the last remaining German members from the city council: "Our historic city, our hundred-towered, our ancient, our beloved, *golden Slavonic Prague*."[46] In 1885, the year after its launch, *Zlatá Praha* already had a circulation of 8,500. Celebrating its one thousandth issue in January 1903, the magazine gave a detailed statistical breakdown of its contents to date. It noted with satisfaction that it had so far carried 2,171 original Czech poems (527 of which were by Jaroslav Vrchlický) and 395 domestic prose works, including five full-length novels by Alois Jirásek. Of its 9,205 illustrations over the same period "there were no less than 3,819 pictures by domestic artists reproduced in *Zlatá Praha*! . . . From these numbers it is evident that *Zlatá Praha* always placed the chief weight on indigenous work. It was always above all original, Czech."[47] These figures eloquently testify to the flowering of Czech literature and art in the later nineteenth century, as they are intended to. But the very act of compiling them speaks equally expressively to what was involved in materializing the idea of the Czech nation.

Zlatá Praha was part of the stable of the indefatigable Jan Otto (1841–1916), whose career ably illustrates the growth and nature of Czech publishing during these years.[48] Having inherited a press from his father-in-law Jaroslav Pospíšil (son of Jan Hostivít Pospíšil, the Hradec Králové publisher

ROČNÍK XVII.   ČÍSLO 8

ZLATA PRAHA

7. Viktor Oliva's turn-of-the-century masthead for the magazine *Zlatá Praha.*

whom we met earlier) in 1871, Otto built it into the biggest Czech publishing house before World War I. He popularized authors like Jirásek, Adolf Heyduk, Vrchlický, and Karolina Světlá in cheap editions with such titles as Enlightenment of the People [*Osvěta lidu*] and The Affordable National Library [*Laciná knihovna národní*]. He introduced translations from other literatures into Czech in his Collection of World Poetry, World Library, Russian Library, and other series, still a critical matter if Czech were to rival German as a "language of the educated." Apart from *Zlatá Praha*, Otto also published several other influential magazines, including at one time or another the literary review *Lumír* and the current affairs *Světozor* (*Worldwatch*). From the 1880s the firm began to put out richly illustrated luxury works, mostly on patriotic themes. Prominent among these were Vrchlický's *The Legend of Saint Prokop*, another Czech patron saint, and the multivolume *Čechy* (*Bohemia*), a lavish description of the land and people of Bohemia billed as "a cooperative venture of Czech artists and writers," whose first editor was the novelist Alois Jirásek. Equally noteworthy were two mementos of great national occasions, František Adolf Šubert's *Národní divadlo*, a celebration by its first director of the opening of the National Theater in 1881, and the official souvenir volume of the Czechoslavic (*sic*, not "Czechoslovak") Ethnographic Exhibition [*Národopisná výstava českoslovanská*] of 1895.[49] Both of these are beautifully produced books. The heavy paper, the color plates protected by tissue, the richly tooled gold leaf on the binding, their weight, their amplitude—all underline the substantiality of that which they are documenting. Otto himself was one of the moving spirits behind the Czechoslavic Ethnographic Exhibition, as he was for the great Jubilee Exhibition of 1891, staged on the centennial of the industrial exhibition of 1791. Ostensibly a festival of one hundred years of Czech industry, this was in reality a jamboree of Czech nationalism, on which grounds most German businesses in Bohemia boycotted it. The Jubilee Exhibition had 2,432,356 visitors, over 80,000 of them on one Sunday, July 26.[50]

The undoubted jewel in Otto's crown was the monumental encyclopedia *Ottův slovník naučný*, whose twenty-eight majestic volumes were published from 1888 to 1909. Alfons Mucha had a well-thumbed set of them in the living room of his opulent house on Hradčanské náměstí.[51] Long before the project was launched, Otto had dreamed of such a work as "the culmination of my publishing activity."[52] František Palacký had been advocating a large Czech encyclopedia on explicitly nationalist grounds since 1829,[53] as had Josef Jungmann; this was one of the original aims of Matice česká. The idea was first realized in the shape of the ten-volume *Riegrův slovník naučný* (*Rieger's Encyclopedia*) which came out from 1860 under the (largely nominal) editorship of František Ladislav Rieger, who had himself been one of Jungmann's pupils at the Old Town Gymnasium.[54] But it is *Ottův slovník naučný* that remains the greatest of Czech works of reference, unsurpassed by anything published since. In its time it was one of the largest encyclopedias in the world, second in the number of its entries and illustrations perhaps only to the *Encyclopaedia Britannica*.[55] The brainchild of future Czechoslovak president Tomáš Masaryk, who was then a young philosophy professor, it is a work of considerable scholarship. For so manifestly patriotic an endeavor Otto was able to draw on the expertise of virtually the entire faculty of the newly autonomous Czech University of Prague, as well as authors from the Czech Polytechnic, Czech gymnasia, and other specialized schools. Among the more notable contributors were Josef Pekař (1870–1937) and František Xaver Šalda (1867–1937), by common consent the greatest historian and the greatest cultural critic of their day. *Ottův slovník naučný* aimed to compare with the best of foreign encyclopedias in its comprehensiveness and scientific authority, and it probably did. It tells us all about Julius Caesar, Victor Hugo (a six-page entry), and Thomas Alva Edison; it even has a substantial entry headed "Women's Emancipation." However, "it was not a copy of a foreign work adapted to our conditions. It was a work through and through Czech, original, written from our national and Slavonic standpoint."[56]

The Czech and Slavonic nation that provides this vantage point is itself compendiously delineated in Otto's many thousands of pages. Josef Pekař's entry on František Palacký, "awakener, Czech historian and politician, Father of the Nation," is thirty-two pages long, a substantial critical minibiography in itself. Every community of any size in the Czech lands merits an individual statistical and historical description, providing, at the least, the latest census figures on the "language of everyday intercourse" of its inhabitants, and usually very much more. The entry "Bohemia" [Čechy] runs to 570 double-columned, closely typed pages, complete with fourteen fold-out colored maps and illustrations. The land and its people are exhaustively detailed, from its flora and fauna to its customs and cooking.[57] There are geological, political, and demographic maps, maps of churches, maps of schools—broken down, of course, by nationality—maps of industry, maps of the Czech kingdom in 1175, 1400, and 1751. There are also color plates of the Czech crown jewels (the frontispiece to the volume) and Czech "national" costumes [národní kroje], a topic that alone gets a seven-page article. Interestingly, after 108 pages describing the land (its mountains, rivers, geology, mineralogy, botany, zoology) and 99 pages that provide a richly informative survey of the life and institutions of contemporary Bohemia, over half the entry is devoted to history of one sort or another: political history, cultural history, legal history. It is as a subdivision of the latter, under the heading "constitutional history," that current institutions of governance are dealt with, rather than—as we might expect—in the earlier contemporary description. This encyclopedic representation is one that has, above all, historical depth, and it is accordingly tendentious. It is the continuity of the nation in its link with the homeland across the centuries that unifies this account and in the process intimates the ephemerality, the contingency, and by implication the incongruity of present political arrangements.

The entry on Moravia occupies another 113 pages, that on the city of Prague 134 pages. In the case of Prague the state-of-the-art scientific visual aids include what can only, in view of the accompanying commentary, be called triumphant pie charts showing the decline of German and ascendancy of Czech in each of the city's boroughs between 1880 and 1900 ("Prague is today a Czech city, so Czech, that it was perhaps more Czech only during the Hussite times and the times which immediately followed," it begins).[58] A two-volume popular abridgement from the larger work, Malý Ottův slovník naučný (Otto's Shorter Encyclopedia), followed in 1905. So did a pocket edition (Kapesní Ottův slovník naučný); it required capacious pockets. Otto was not the only large Prague publisher producing patriotic works of reference, or (re)defining the patria in national terms thereby. Josef Vilímek issued a Who's Who—of great Czechs rather than of notable inhabitants of the Kingdom of Bohemia—in 1900 under the title Národní album (National Album). It has more than fourteen hundred entries, which range from leading figures of the obrození like Dobrovský and Palacký (whose portrait opens the volume) to engineers, actresses, schoolteachers, and other foot soldiers of the national movement. A curious, but as we shall see perhaps not an inexplicable omission from this gallery is future "president-liberator" Tomáš Masaryk. There are 280 pages of photographs, framed by decorations very much in le style Mucha. On the pretty art nouveau cover is a dark-haired, bare-shouldered young woman with an open book on her knee, who is holding up a mirror to two small children.[59] The pedagogic symbolism is obvious: this is an exercise in moral education, a nationalist *Life of the Saints*.

Little Golden Chapel on the Vltava

Back in 1833, Josef Linhart Knoll, professor of Austrian history at the university of Prague, had written to Czech Supreme Chancellor Antonín Bedřich Count Mitrovský warning of the threat to imperial unity posed by the cultural activities of František Palacký and his associates. He was a man who clearly appreciated the dangers of his own discipline:

> Four times already frightful, destructive Czechism has risen up against Germany and Austria: during the Hussite Wars, under Jiří z Poděbrad, against Ferdinand I during the Schmalkaldic War, and under Rudolf II, Matyáš, and Ferdinand II. . . . History hides a fresh, quickening source with which to arouse and enthuse the nation for the old independence and freedom, for the former grandeur and fame; the national language then points the right road through which this could be accomplished. Czechs will always consider as the golden age of their national glory the times when the Czech language expelled Germans from the Karolinum, when King Jiří spoke Czech with the Utraquist lords, and finally when the Czech Estates defiantly demanded the right to make treaties with neighbors despite the right of their monarchs, [and] to hire and raise armies.[60]

Knoll objected as strongly to nationalist inroads into the Bohemian Royal Society. Among the developments that alarmed him were the election as fellows of Josef Jungmann, the Presl brothers, and the first librarian of the National Museum Václav Hanka (1791–1861). He also protested against Palacký's publication of the Society's *Annals* [*Letopisy*] in Czech from 1829, and the revision of its statutes five years later to give Czech equal rights with German, Latin, and French in its lectures and publications. The Royal Society, he wrote, "is now merely an outpost, a colony of the committee of the Czech National Museum, which has for its aim the propagation of Slav books and the re-Czechization of the land."[61]

More measured criticism of the new directions taken by the museum came a decade later from Rudolf Glaser, the editor of the magazine *Ost und West* (*East and West*). Though he welcomed its support for Czech language and literature, Glaser bitterly complained that "the *Patriotic* [*Vlastenecké*] Museum in Bohemia continuously focuses its activity solely on the Slav element, completely ignoring the German element in the homeland," likening it to "a body, one of whose legs has been prematurely amputated." In particular he lamented the demise of the German-language museum journal in 1831, a publication, he says, that "was originally devoted to awakening sympathy for the museum among the German population of Bohemia."[62] The German magazine in fact went under as much because of the attentions of the censor as of any animus on Palacký's part, but Knoll and Glaser were quite right about which way the wind was blowing.[63] Palacký was chosen executive director of the museum in May 1841, and in the words of František Kop "from an originally aristocratic institution arose a national and popularly Czech institution."[64] The museum's mission, as articulated by Palacký the next year, became "to collect and exhibit in a scientific arrangement all that characteristically distinguishes the Czech land [českou zemi] in regard to its natural character and conditions and the spiritual activities of its inhabitants in the past and present." "The museum," he said, "must grow into a scientific portrait of our homeland."[65] His son-in-law František Ladislav Rieger was more explicit as to the national rather than territorial reference of the adjective "Czech" in "Czech land" in 1873: "The task of the museum of the Czech Kingdom is to collect, safeguard, and bring to the knowledge of the nation and the educated world everything that facilitates a thorough knowledge of our nation in the past and our homeland in the present. . . . It should be a sacred reliquary of the mementos and remains from our forebears. . . . Whoever then feels himself to be a Czech, whoever feels for the honor of the Czech name, for the uplifting of his homeland, for the elevation of the Czech nation, every such person is called upon and obligated to support the institution."[66]

Reliquary is the appropriate word. By the end of the century the project of displaying the nation had become monumentalized, and employed media that extended well beyond the sciences. The museum moved in 1890 into new premises closing off the upper end of Wenceslas Square, where, previously, one of the old city gates had been. The centerpiece of Josef Schulz's imposing neo-Renaissance building (so imposing that Soviet troops shelled it in 1968, assuming it to be the headquarters of Czechoslovak Radio) is the domed Pantheon. Beneath four lunettes depicting glorious moments of Czech legend and history by František Ženíšek ("The Calling of Přemysl the Plowman to Government" and "Saint Methodius Completes His Translation of the Bible into the Slavonic Language Before Dying in Rome in 885") and Václav Brožík ("Charles IV Founds Prague University in 1348" and "Jan Amos Komenský Submits His Didactic Works to Amsterdam Town Council in 1657"), are statues and busts of the great men and women—to be precise, two women, Božena Němcová and Eliška Krásnohorská—of the Czech nation.[67] It was here that Karel Hynek Mácha's remains lay in state in 1939 in what was by then a long-established funeral ritual for eminent Czechs. It was this hall, too, that the museum said it lacked the coal to heat for Karel Čapek in the miserable Christmas of 1938. The cemetery at Vyšehrad, where Mácha was taken from the Pantheon and Čapek made his way despite it, was equally a medium through which the idea of a Czech national community was realized and its tradition made manifest in the later nineteenth century. (Some) Czech monarchs had indeed been buried there centuries before, but as we have seen it was a location whose memory as a royal seat was already so distant as to need recovery at the coronation of Charles IV in 1347. The Hussites had had no compunction about sacking the fortress in 1420. Vyšehrad's consecration as a *national* shrine dates, like so much else, from the 1860s. The Slavín vault in which Alfons Mucha is buried was commissioned two decades later by Petr Fischer, mayor of Smíchov, as "a burial place for the most notable men, those excelling above others in their efforts for the Czech nation, those who by their brilliant writings or artistic endeavors, important inventions or uncommon sacrifices, arduous battles or beneficial successes helped to spread the glory and honor of the Czech nation even beyond the borders of this our motherland."[68] The sacredness of Vyšehrad has nothing to do with Christianity.

Until 1848 Václavské náměstí, where the National Museum stands, had been simply the Horse Market [*Koňský trh*], the name it had borne since Charles IV laid it out as part of the New Town in the mid–fourteenth century. The square was renamed after Bohemia's patron Saint Václav at the suggestion of Karel Havlíček Borovský in that revolutionary year. Completing its refurbishing as a landscape of national memory was Josef Myslbek's equestrian statue of Saint Václav attended by four other Czech patrons: Saint Vojtěch, Václav's grandmother Saint Ludmila, Saint Prokop, and the Blessed Anežka.[69] Significantly absent from this company is the baroque Saint Jan Nepomucký. Whatever Nepomucký's image may or may not have done for the preservation of Czech language and Czech identities during the dark years of the eighteenth century, by the end of the nineteenth he had become an unwelcome interloper, at least in nationalist eyes. The Saint Václav statue, which Myslbek (1843–1922) had worked on since 1887, was placed at the top of the square in front of the museum in 1913. Inscribed on its pedestal are the words Balbín adapted from the Saint Václav chorale, "Do not let us or our descendants perish!" It was beneath this statue five years later, on 28 October 1918, that the Czechs were to celebrate their independence from Vienna. It is a sight familiar to Western television viewers from the events of August 1968 and November 1989 when, draped in banners, flags, and hand-lettered posters, Saint Václav once again became a national rallying point. Myslbek's statue was but one of many such patriotic monuments which by 1918 abounded in Czech towns large and small. Among the more important in Prague are the Jungmann (1877), Palacký (1912), Mácha (1912), and Hus (1915) memorials.

Street names, too, began methodically to embody Czechness, recalling the heroes of the national present and past. Prague's Staré město renamed a street after Jan Hus in 1870, and in 1895 streets were renamed in honor of Palacký, Havlíček, and the writers Karolina Světlá and Jan Neruda. In the newer sub-

8. Václavské náměstí (Wenceslas Square), formerly the Horse Market, in the 1890s. The new National Museum building closes off the head of the square.

urbs there was much more scope for such commemoration. Žižkov's streets systematically recalled the battles and personalities of the Hussite Wars.[70] In neighboring Vinohrady one of the largest squares, built in 1896, honors the Hussite king Jiří z Poděbrad. By 1914 the conurbation contained eleven Havlíček streets, nine Palacký streets, and nine Hus streets. The city's most famous landmark, Charles Bridge, was renamed thus (previously it had been known simply as Prague Bridge or the Stone Bridge) only in 1870, more than half a millennium after the Father of the Homeland had ordered it to be built. The language of Prague's street signs changed in these years too. Joseph II had first required street names to be displayed in 1787. Czech names had appeared then on signs beneath German, but this order was reversed in 1861, the same year as Czech became an official language of all city offices and Prague elected František Václav Pštross (1823–63) its first Czech mayor of modern times. After 1893—and a bitter court challenge from Prague Germans—the city's street signs were in Czech only, and the black-on-yellow lettering of the empire was replaced by the Czech national colors of red and white.[71]

Banking and insurance, both fields in which Czech capital was strong (the

earliest Czech savings bank, the Česká spořitelna, was founded in 1824),
appealed to consumers on an ethnic basis, and their buildings also often bore
patriotic motifs. The Zemská banka (Land Bank) building on Na příkopě, for
example, which was erected in 1895, has a mural by the young Max
Švabinský in the vestibule that depicts Saint Václav, and mosaics laden with
Czechness on the facade by Mikoláš Aleš. His subjects include "Prague and
the Vltava" and "Love for the Homeland."[72] There was an obvious challenge
in this. Na příkopě, known to German Praguers as Am Graben, was the
German Corso, and next door to the Zemská banka stood the Deutsches
Kasino, founded in 1862, the hub of German society in Prague with its
restaurants, reading room, and assembly halls.[73] Antonín Wiehl and Osvald
Polívka's Městská spořitelna (City Savings Bank) building of 1891–94—later
to become the home of the Klement Gottwald Museum—is likewise richly
decorated with pastoral scenes by Aleš, together with sculptures by Myslbek
and murals by Ženíšek and other leading Czech artists of the day. All of this
amounted to a very tangible nationalization of the routine settings of everyday urban life.

Czech cultural institutions blossomed in the later nineteenth century. The
National Theater [Národní divadlo] opened in 1881, although a Provisional
Theater had existed since 1862, since which time the Stavovské divadlo had
been a purely German-language venue.[74] This was a supreme moment of
national identification: the Národní divadlo was funded entirely by public
donations, and its completion was the culmination of a campaign begun in
1845. Money was given by rich and poor from the largest to the smallest and
most remote settlements across Bohemia and Moravia, a point of national
pride (and a powerful means of welding these places *into* a self-conscious
nation). Mikoláš Aleš provided a sweetly sentimental drawing of country
people contributing to the collection for Šubert's souvenir volume *Národní
divadlo*.[75] That the theater burned down after only twelve productions and
was rebuilt, again from voluntary subscriptions, to reopen in 1883, only
added to its status as the "little golden chapel on the Vltava" [zlatá kaplička
nad Vltavou] of Czech nationhood, the "cathedral of Czech art" [chrám českého umění]—as the novelist Alois Jirásek described it in a speech of 16 May
1918, in the Pantheon of the National Museum, at a ceremony commemorating the laying of the foundation stones for the theater fifty years earlier.[76] The
Academy of Fine Arts, originally founded by the Society of Patriotic Friends
of Art in 1799, was transformed into a center for national art from the re-
arrangement of the school in 1887, after which Mařák, Brožík, Myslbek, and
Hynais, patriotic artists of the "Generation of the National Theater"—as it
became known—joined the staff.[77] The Academy was formally nationalized
by the Land government in 1896. The Czech Academy of Arts and Sciences
was founded in 1891,[78] the Czech Philharmonic in 1894. By the time the
Modern Gallery [Moderní galerie] opened in Prague in 1902, it was quite

natural that it should be administered and exhibit contemporary art in separate Czech and German divisions.[79]

Czech artists had long organized themselves into private associations separate from (and often hostile to) the Academy of Fine Arts. Josef Mánes (1820–71), who is described in a recent Czech biographical dictionary as "one of the greatest European painters of his time, for us in addition a painter national in his very being [malíř bytostně národní],"[80] was a leading light of Umělecká beseda (the Artistic Society), founded in 1863. This society was devoted to the cause of national music and literature as well as the visual arts. It counted the writers Jan Neruda and Jaroslav Vrchlický among its luminaries, and Karel Jaromír Erben served with Bedřich Smetana and Josef Mánes on its first committee. Umělecká beseda had 359 members contributing a total of 1,017 crowns in its first year, and 3,236 members contributing 97,564 crowns by 1912.[81] It organized lectures, discussions, and readings; staged concerts, recitals, and art exhibitions; published books, magazines, and graphic albums; and sponsored memorials and commemorative plaques. Among those plaques it erected in Prague—apart from, inevitably, one commemorating Jan Hus (1869)—were memorials to Kramérius (1868), Mácha (1868), Havlíček (1870), Čelakovský (1872), Jungmann (1873), Mánes (1874), Erben (1875), Šafařík (1875), and Palacký (1885). The buditelé were now themselves being pantheonized, a national canon was in the making. The first art exhibition arranged by Umělecká beseda was of Lessing's picture "Hus Before the Border" in 1863, the second was of three portraits of a Montenegrin princely family by Jaroslav Čermák in 1865; its first graphic album was a folder of illustrated folk songs [Illustrované písně národní] in 1865; its first concert, which took place on 21 March 1886 at Prague's Rudolfinum concert hall, began with the Overture to Smetana's Libuše. It should not surprise us to find that the "Statistical Survey of the Activities of Umělecká beseda," appended to the society's fiftieth anniversary history of 1913, lists its lectures on literature (of which there had been several hundred through the years) under the headings "Czech," "Russian and Little Russian," "Polish," "South Slav," "Slavonic," and "Foreign."[82]

Another mainstay of Czech cultural life, the Spolek výtvarných umělců Mánes (the Mánes Fine Artists' Society), was set up in 1887 by a group of students at the Academy of Fine Arts who were dissatisfied with what they saw as the stagnation of Umělecká beseda. Their magazine Volné směry (Free Directions), published from 1896, was the first regular Czech art periodical.[83] Though by it was no means insensitive to international or modernistic artistic currents, SVU Mánes was no less patriotic in inclination than Umělecká beseda had originally been. Mikoláš Aleš (1852–1913) was chosen as its first president; he is conventionally considered to be "the founder of the national tradition in painting, our most Czech [nejčeštější] artist."[84] In 1912 Aleš was the subject of a biography in the Zlatoroh (Golden Horn) series published by

SVU Mánes under the general editorship of Max Švabinský; the earlier volumes had been devoted to Mánes, Neruda, Smetana, Havlíček, Němcová, Jungmann, Palacký, and the painter Hanuš Schwaiger. Commenting on the "consistency and constancy" of Aleš's art, Karel B. Mádl situates his subject in a timeless landscape of Czechness:

> Aleš comes from the people, that is from the countryside, from the region which we call South Bohemian not merely in the geographical but in the ethnic and ethical sense. The country is here as it were an opposite pole to the big city, whose cultural plenitude is nourished almost entirely by the healthy blood of the choice influx from the countryside. . . . Aleš's birthplace Mirotice is a town, but one of those in which the farmer has not yet been transformed into a burgher, where work is often half crafts and half in the fields, where the waves of the peasant countryside lap the town square. Mirotice is also a South Bohemian small town in that it is entirely Czech in its surroundings, undisturbed by any foreign elements. Sixty and fifty years ago, Mirotice was an old-world little town where life went on evenly and quietly, if not always contentedly, from century to century. Everything disquieting and dangerous, which was usually short-lived, arrived from outside and abroad; and here also everything foreign became something out of the ordinary, disturbing and conspicuous, be it a squadron of cuirassiers or a gypsy caravan.[85]

Appropriately, it is one of Aleš's drawings of Saint Václav that forms the frontispiece to Jan Otto's patriotic album *Čechy*.

In this highly musical land choral societies like Prague's Hlahol (1860) and the Moravian Teachers' Choir (1903) were also extremely popular, and Smetana, Janáček, and many others whose names are less well known wrote suitably patriotic compositions for them. Karel Bendl (1838–97), Hlahol's onetime choirmaster, offered "*Svoji k svému*" (Each for His Own), a title that was also to be the slogan of an anti-Semitic boycott in the 1890s; Arnošt Bohaboj Tovačovský (1825–74) shifted his creative focus from settings of German lyrics to such Czech texts as "*Vlasti*" (To the Homeland) after the revolution of 1848; Arnošt Praus (1873–1907), a pupil of Antonín Dvořák's, was rewarded with three years compulsory military service in Krakow for his "Chorale of the Czechs" [*Chorál Čechů*] of 1894.[86] A Union of Czechoslavic [*Českoslovanských*] Choral Societies was formed in Prague in 1868. The word "*hlahol*" means a joyful musical outpouring, like a peal of bells, but it also conjures up older and specifically Slavic associations. *Hlaholice* was the oldest Slavonic script, which Saints Cyril and Methodius had brought with them to Great Moravia. The motto on Hlahol's Secession building on Masaryk Embankment in Prague reads "Let the song reach the heart—Let the heart reach the homeland."[87] By 1888 Bohemia boasted 655 male, female, and mixed-voice choral societies, and Hlahol alone had 609 members. That year there were in all 10,547 registered private clubs and societies of one kind or an-

9. Viktor Oliva's poster advertising tours to the 1900 World Exhibition in Paris.

other in Bohemia. Cultural societies were not the only crucibles of a national consciousness. The most popular clubs were volunteer firefighters' societies, of which there were 2,187. It is quite characteristic of the period that three years later their association too split along national lines, with Germans and Czechs going their separate ways.[88]

Probably the most influential, and certainly the most celebrated of popular Czech patriotic organizations was the gymnastic society, Sokol—"*sokol*" is Czech for falcon—which was founded by Miroslav Tyrš (1832–84) and Jind-řich Fügner (1822–64) in 1862. Sokol had its own uniform, a romantic elaboration of Czech peasant attire originally designed by Josef Mánes; Tyrš himself was an art historian by trade. The organization sought to embody the national ideal in a very literal sense, as photographs of its muscular male gymnasts graphically show; its aim was "the physical and in part also the moral education and improvement of all the nation, its nurturing for the enhancement of its strength, bravery, refinement, and defense."[89] From 1882 Sokol staged mass jamborees every few years in Prague, whose centerpiece was huge collective gymnastic displays. At the time of the second jamboree in 1891 there were 24,268 Sokols in Bohemia, of whom 7,926 were active gymnasts; 11,095 Sokols in costume and 6,705 gymnasts took part in the fourth jamboree ten years later.[90] By 1914 Sokol claimed 194,321 men, women, and schoolchildren as members in the Czech lands and had branches among Czech émigrés in Austria, North America, and elsewhere.[91] Tomáš Černý, the nationalist mayor of Prague mentioned earlier, was a Sokol founder-member and one of "Our Three Stars" profiled alongside Tyrš and Fügner in the society's twentieth anniversary celebratory volume in 1883.[92] One sign of how deeply Sokol penetrated Czech life is the way its ritualized salutation "*Na zdar!*" (To success!) has passed into the Czech language in the shape of the common greeting "*nazdar!*" The origin of the phrase lies in the campaign slogan "*Na zdar Národního divadla!*" (To the success of the National Theater!).

Looking back in 1888, the "old patriot" (as he was by then styling himself) František Ladislav Rieger measured how far the national revival had progressed since the midcentury. A Czech ball was first organized by Rieger himself, Tyl, and others in 1840 and thereafter became an annual Prague event. Rieger explains to a younger generation, who could by now take their Czech nationality for granted, the significance of something seemingly so trivial:

> So it is, of course, if we look at it only from the standpoint of entertainment or financial profits; however the *národní beseda* also always worked beneficially for the revival of national consciousness. For at that time the very occurrence and appearance of this first large public ball—at which, against a public opinion which considered the German language exclusively to be the speech and badge of the cultivated, Czech alone was spoken—was a great event. It was a serious and significant, even so to speak a revolutionary moment in the story of our national awakening. It was an act, with which a long enchanted gate was broken open, so that Czech nationality could come out into the free air of the public realm. With this event the slur of vulgarity and aspersion of ignorance was removed from the patriotic Czech, and the Czech language, once the language of famous monarchs, powerful magnates, and great thinkers, went again from the workers' workshops and the servants' quarters to the salons of the educated.[93]

By the end of the nineteenth century, Czech nationality had done very much more than come out into the public realm. It had become the principle on which—for Czechs—much of that public realm was ordered. It was the space in which they moved, the air they breathed. This newly nationalized social space was, of course, a set of cultural representations institutionally imposed upon a demographic reality which was still, as a matter of fact, "multiethnic." But such terms themselves need qualification: ethnicity is not a given. The Czech "revival" was at the same time a process in which Bohemia's Germans and Jews were increasingly forced to define *their* identities in ethnic terms too as they were progressively extruded from the nation thus constructed.[94]

A Cathedral and a Fortress

What, then, was the content of this Czechness? *How* was the Czech national community imagined in the later nineteenth century?

Central to the *obrození* was the "revival" of the Czech language itself, high points of which were were the grammars and dictionaries of Dobrovský and Jungmann. It was its language that above all else came to delineate the renascent community of the Czech nation, becoming, in Pavel Eisner's apt phrase, its "cathedral as well as its fortress."[95] The nation's tongue became its totem, and the resurrection of Czech as a written language took on all the qualities of a modern foundational myth. Recall here the poet Josef Hora's words at Karel Čapek's funeral. "The native language," he said, "is a sacred instrument hallowed by tradition and leading us to a new life." Classical Arabic and Church Latin are or were sacred instruments for Islam and medieval Christendom in the clear sense that they were set apart from the profane world.[96] That a vernacular language should be imbued with the same qualities of sanctity is a more difficult notion to grasp, and it is particularly so, perhaps, for native speakers of English. We may revere Shakespeare, but we do not normally sanctify the very language in which he wrote. His immortality is seen as lying in the genius with which he used English rather than in English itself.

Karel Čapek was an undoubted master of written Czech, but it was as a servant of his language that Hora eulogized him. English is not spoken solely by the English and cannot therefore become a symbol of their national uniqueness. Only Czechs speak Czech as their mother tongue, and there have never been that many of them. It is their property alone, and it is in consequence a property that sets them apart from others and defines them. English has also never been in danger of extinction. The Czech language plumbed such depths in the seventeenth and eighteenth centuries that its rebirth seemed little short of miraculous.[97] It is scarcely surprising that for Czech patriots of the nineteenth century (and since), the fortunes of their language became a barometer of the fate of their nation. Even the tireless

Jungmann at times despaired of the prospects of reviving Czech as a cultured language and a language of the cultured. Nowhere is the magnitude of that task more poignantly illustrated than in the lives of many of the leading *buditelé* themselves. Few of them born before 1850 were altogether at home in the language they wished to reclaim as their own.

Karel Hynek Mácha wrote to his girlfriend Lori and the young Bedřich Smetana (1824–84) kept his diaries not in Czech but in German. As late as the 1860s Smetana gives pencil drawings in his sketchbook titles in German ("*Nussle bei Prag*," portraying Nusle, the setting of Tyl and Škroup's operetta *Fidlovačka*, is one).[98] Karel Havlíček Borovský, who is fairly considered to be the founder of modern Czech journalism, and whose own complaints about educated Czechs' inability to write their own language we encountered earlier, wrote to a friend in 1839 that he earnestly desired "to be a Czech both in speech and actions. To this end I take the magazine *Květy* and read only Czech books, although as you will see from my spelling mistakes, I have had scant success in this."[99] Havlíček was seventeen at the time. Four years later, during which time he had lived in Prague and continuously moved in patriotic circles, he confessed that he was still "as yet unaccustomed" to expressing himself on paper in what he had described in that letter of 1839 as his "sacred sonorous mother tongue."[100] Havlíček acquired his facility in the language as a foreigner might, by copying down lists of words from Jungmann's dictionary and learning them by heart.[101] Here "to be a Czech" is a project, something one might aspire to, not something one simply and unproblematically is. To the end of his life Havlíček wrote to his parents in German. Josef Mánes, that painter "national in his very being," patriotically illustrated Czech folk songs; but their texts are riddled with elementary linguistic errors.[102] The art historian Antonín Matějček explains that "the struggle with the Czech language was Mánes's chief difficulty in the realization of his artistic plan. In the fifties he mastered Czech only in ordinary conversation, in the following decade he considerably extended his vocabulary, but he never learned to write well to his death, he lacked a knowledge of the language grounded in cultural literacy."[103] Of Mánes's published letters, a volume of 254 pages, only 4 were originally written in Czech, and that Czech is truly appalling.[104]

That "Father of the Nation" František Palacký should have published the early volumes of his *History of the Czech Nation* in German (1836) before he did in Czech (1848) is comprehensible enough in the circumstances of the time. But he only began to write the book in Czech after 1848; and he spoke German at home with his wife and children.[105] Neither of the founders of Sokol were born into Czech-speaking households. Miroslav Tyrš was baptized Friedrich Emanuel Tirsch and came from a family in Děčín in the *pohraničí* that had spoken German for generations; in 1860, two years before Sokol was established, he was still signing his name in its Germanic form.[106]

When Jindřich, née Heinrich Fügner was asked by his incredulous six-year-old daughter Renata whether he "had been a German" when younger, he replied: "No, little one, I wasn't a German, I was a Praguer, a German-speaking Praguer."[107] Tyrš and Fügner spoke together mostly in German because Fügner's "kitchen Czech" (as he himself described it) was not up to the elevated subjects of their discussions.[108] Within the conceptions of national identity that Sokol itself did so much to help crystallize, these two born-again Czechs might both have been classified as ethnic Germans had they come into the world two or three decades later. Jaroslav Vrchlický (1853–1912), probably the most important Czech poet of the later nineteenth century, entered life as Emil Frida, and there has been persistent speculation over the years as to whether he was not Jewish.[109] Even the future founder of independent Czechoslovakia, Tomáš Masaryk, did not grow up in a Czech-speaking family; with his Slovak father he spoke Slovak, with his Moravian-German mother he spoke German.[110] Born in Hodonín on the Moravia-Slovakia border, he got his high school education at the German gymnasium in Brno and in Vienna, in which city he went on to university. The languages of Masaryk's own household were for a time English and German; he married an American, Charlotte Garrigue, in New York in 1878, and they lived for the next five years in the Austrian capital. It was from Charlotte that he took his very un-Czech middle name. To complicate things still further, Masaryk's son Jan later said that the family always thought of themselves as Slovaks![111] The reconstructions of identity, linguistic and otherwise, entailed in the Czech national rebirth began first of all with its authors' own subjectivities.

The Czech language was likewise as much reconstructed as it was rediscovered by the *buditelé*. Much more was entailed in the revival of Czech as a written instrument than a merely passive transcription of preexisting oral realities. Josef Jungmann's celebrated translation of Milton's *Paradise Lost*, a task to which he devoted a full four years, is one of the glories of revivalist Czech literature and a cornerstone of the modern written language. To produce it, Jungmann worked not just from the humble spoken Czech of the time but vastly extended its vocabulary by drawing from medieval Czech literature, borrowing from other Slavonic languages, and coining an abundance of neologisms of his own. All these in their turn found their way into his *Dictionary*. Jungmann came under fire for this from various contemporaries, among them Antonín Puchmajer, who wrote him in 1816: "You import virtually the whole of Linde, Heym, and other foreign-Slav [*cizoslovanské*] dictionaries, something of which I can in no way approve. This will no longer be a Czech dictionary but a general Slavonic dictionary."[112] Dobrovský was similarly disapproving of Jungmann's and Presl's terminological innovations in *Krok*. As with Erben's efforts in the legal field later, there were clear practical justifications for these. If Czech were indeed to become "a language of the educated," words would have to be made up for things that existed neither in the pages of the *Bible kralická* nor in the everyday speech of unlettered Czech peasants. But Jungmann's linguistic program was as much ideological as it was pragmatic. He was inspired by pan-Slavist sentiment in all he translated, anthologized, and lexicographed, as he makes clear in his preface to *Paradise Lost*: "But, do I hear somebody say, why so many unknown words?—Unknown? He who diligently occupies himself with reading good books, especially the Holy Scriptures, will find little here that is unknown. 'But there are also words from other Slavonic languages here!' One or two; all of them in the end explained. . . . Dear patriot, do not let a sublime poem be sullied by everyday language; rather, being yourself a Slav, get better acquainted with the Slav language, and demand, along with others who know, that we Czechs too might slowly embrace a *universal Slavonic literary language*."[113] That grandiose chimera was never to be realized, but it overshadowed how the Czech language was rewritten in the early nineteenth century and what, in the course of time, it actually became.

Jungmann's great *Dictionary* was not a record of the Czech spoken at the time, nor was all the Czech spoken at the time recorded in its pages. Much as he wished to survey all the main Czech dialects, he simply did not have the resources to do so. It is better regarded as a blueprint for an edifice that did not yet exist. Spoken and written Czech differ considerably to this day in both grammatical forms and vocabulary, and there are multiple dialects of the spoken language. Jungmann's borrowings and innovations are merely a particularly graphic illustration of the fact that any act of standardizing a written language is as much an act of creation as it is of simple transcription. *The Oxford English Dictionary* is no more a description of what any real human collectivity has ever actually spoken. Dictionaries and grammars map, define, and bound these various speakers into a single abstract linguistic community, superimposing fixity on fluidity, clamping uniformity upon multiple shades of difference. In the written language they create an instrument of power that enables those who have mastery of the word to speak to and for all the others whom they have subsumed under its mantle, and they confer authority on their utterances; to elevate one mode of expression as the standard is at the same time to vernacularize others as "dialect," "slang," or simply manifestations of illiterate ignorance.

Linguistic standardization establishes frontiers between the imagined communities thus delineated, where formerly there had been less determinate horizons. In time those frontiers come to seem natural; they appear as boundaries that simply reflect preexisting linguistic differences, rather than lines drawn by men on maps through the very process of differentiating languages itself. Obviously such differentiation cannot be wholly arbitrary. Languages are not just the artifacts of linguists. But it is not by any means as straightforward a matter as, say, the family tree of Indo-European languages at the back of *Webster's New World Dictionary of the American Language* represents it to be.[114] Nor, as a rule, is it an issue simply of linguistics. In the case of Czech in the early nineteenth century, the borders of the linguistic community represented in the dictionaries and grammar books were both uncertain and contested. Jungmann sought to push its frontiers outward, to the boundaries of Slavdom [*Slovanstvo*]. If the artifice of this seems—in retrospect—to be plain, we should remember that Dobrovský too, who was certainly no pan-Slavist romantic, classified what would nowadays be seen as distinct Slavonic languages as mere dialects of a single language. When Havlíček famously argued in 1846 that Poles, Russians, Czechs, and Illyrians no more constitute a single "Slav nation" by virtue of the affinities of their languages than Germans, Danes, Swedes, Norwegians, Dutch, and English make up a single "Germanic nation" or Spaniards, French, Portuguese, and Romanians form a single "Romance nation," he was challenging what was, at the time, a conventional wisdom among Czech patriots. Havlíček himself wished to draw the borders of the nation very much more narrowly, to encompass only those whom he called "Czechoslavs" [*Českoslované*], the Slavic inhabitants of Bohemia, Moravia, Silesia, and Slovakia. "All," he wrote, "are Czechs, Czechs in the kingdom [Bohemia], Czechs in Moravia, Czechs in Slovakia. Don't the inhabitants of Provence, the Vendée, and Burgundy want to be called French, and don't the Saxons and the Prussians call themselves Germans?"[115] Havlíček's own conceptions of this Czech linguistic community, it should be said, were no more innocent of politics than Jungmann's. He had a profound suspicion of Russian expansionist ambitions, of which he saw pan-Slavism as an unwitting tool.

But this apparently commonsensical mapping of languages and the nations that spoke them was even then being challenged from within. It was self-evident to Havlíček that Czech and Slovak are simply dialects of one language in a way that, say, Czech and Russian are not. Then as now, Czech and Slovak were for the most part mutually intelligible, their differences being not much greater than those between some Czech dialects themselves. The poet Jan Kollár had used written Czech for *Slávy dcera*, although he was by modern criteria a Slovak. Two decades later Ľudovít Štúr (1815–56) formalized a separate written Slovak, a development Kollár, Šafařík, and Havlíček himself strenuously resisted. A century and a half after that, during the brief life of the Czechoslovak Federal Republic set up in the wake of the 1989 Velvet Revolution, the Czech words on the presidential standard which had flown above Prague Castle since 1920, "*Pravda vítězí*" (Truth will prevail; popularly held to be Jan Hus's last words at the stake), had to be replaced by the Latin motto "*Veritas vincit*" in deference to Slovak national sentiment.[116] Much may hang on a difference of one vowel: in Slovak, the motto would read "*Pravda víťazí*." Thus may linguistic codifications of imagined communities in the course of time become instruments in their realization as political subjects. Today, if we speak of the Czechs in Slovakia we are speaking— equally self-evidently—of resident aliens.

The "Slovak question" was to complicate Czech identity for long years, and we shall return to it. Nevertheless it was above all as a linguistic community that the Czech nation was imagined in the earlier nineteenth century, and the linguistically divided schools, press, theaters, art galleries, firefighters' societies, and gymnastic associations of the second half of the century were the practical instruments with which that blueprint was eventually translated into an experiential reality. Implicit in this identification of the nation through its language was a pregnant conceptual relocation of the Czech lands. Pan-Slavism as political ideology, especially in its overtly Russophile forms, by no means commanded universal support among nineteenth-century Czech nationalists. *Slovanstvo* (Slavdom) as a matrix of identity was another matter. Palacký, for example, warned in April 1848: "Imagine the Austrian Empire fragmented into a multitude of greater and lesser republics—what a nice basis for universal Russian monarchy."[117] He nevertheless chaired the Slavonic Congress in Prague two months later, the event that provoked riots in the streets and Windischgrätz's shelling of Staré město, and was one of those (Rieger was another) who in 1867 made an ostentatious "pilgrimage" to Moscow on the occasion of a large pan-Slavic ethnographic exhibition.

Havlíček notwithstanding, being a Slav became an essential part of being a Czech, in a way it had not noticeably been previously. As a matter of simple fact, the history of Bohemia and Moravia had been that of the lands of the Holy Roman Empire since the tenth century. Since the time of Cyril and Methodius, Czechs had been variously Catholic and Protestant, but never Orthodox; their language had been written in Roman and Gothic scripts, but never in Cyrillic. Regrounding Czech identity in language established a new set of affinities, which were then claimed to be primeval and therewith more essential to identity than the mere contingencies of a thousand years of history. The Czech lands were disentangled from their "Germanic" integument and relocated as the most westerly outlier of an imagined "Slavic" civilization. Borders to the west hardened as frontiers to the east expanded. Linguistic kinship supplanted historical experience, or rather provided an instrument for its reconfiguration. The construct of *Slovanstvo* furnished an altered vantage point from which that experience could be reappropriated and its significances reordered. It is in this context that Šafařík's *Slovanské starožitnosti*, which excavates and re-presents a common Slavic prehistory, was such a significant book.

The centrality of the Czech language to Czech self-awareness was equally consequential internally. It laid the ground for the ethnicization of the German-speakers in the Czech lands—who in 1890 still constituted 37 percent of Bohemia's population[118]—and their definitive extrusion from this emergent community of the nation. The frontiers between Czech and Slovak, or Czech and "the Slavonic language," may have long remained uncertain, blurred, and disputed. The line between Czech and German, on the other hand, was crystal clear to all. With the reconstitution of Czech as a written language, a new parity was established with German. Formerly Bohemia's social divisions had been articulated as a contrast between a world language of culture, civility, and state, and a multiplicity of ignorant local vernaculars. The consolidation of written Czech transformed that axis of social difference into a dividing line between two national communities, each now identified and solidified by its own language. Count Nostic, as we saw, could without contradiction put the motto "*Patriae et musis*" on his mostly German-speaking Gräfliches Nationaltheater in 1783. By the later nineteenth century, such a conjunction of Bohemian patriotism and the German language had become offensively oxymoronic. On 17 November 1920, two years after Czechoslovak independence, the same theater was occupied by a Czech mob and its German players forcibly evicted under the slogan "The Stavovské to the nation!" That nation now plainly meant, as it had for Jungmann, a nation of Czech-speakers only, and the theater duly became the second stage of the Národní divadlo.[119]

An unsavory, but telling, aspect of the same phenomenon (if scarcely one confined to the Czech lands) was the respectability afforded to anti-Semitism by Czech writers of the stature of Jan Neruda (1834–91) and Petr Bezruč (1867–1958). We do not need to go to the hook-nosed, money-grabbing stereotype of Jews in what is usually seen as a jewel of Czech literature, *Tales from the Malá strana* [*Povídky malostranské*, 1878], to indict Neruda. His 1869 article "'The Jewish Fear'" ["'*Pro strach židovský*'"] is unashamedly anti-Semitic, calling for "emancipation from the Jews" and repeatedly drumming home the message that Jews are foreigners. Neruda's Czech patriotism does not prevent him, on this occasion, from invoking the authority of "the great composer and still greater German and liberal Richard Wagner" in support of his views.[120] Havlíček had similarly stressed Bohemian Jews' foreignness twenty-five years previously when rejecting Seigfried Kapper's appeal for common cause between Czechs and Jews against the oppressions of Vienna. In his own words: "We must regard [Jews] as a separate, Semitic nation which lives only incidentally in our midst and sometimes understands or knows our language . . . and this bond which ties them together is stronger than the bond to the land in which they live. . . . He who wants to be a Czech must cease to be a Jew."[121] Kapper (1821–79) had been the first to translate Mácha's *Máj* into German, hailing its merits at a time when the poet's literary compatriots were dismissing it as "un-Czech."

Mikoláš Aleš's *Špalíček* (two volumes, 1907, 1912), a charmingly illustrated collection of "national songs and rhymes" that is to a Czech childhood

10. A page from Mikoláš Aleš's *Špalíček*, the Czech *Mother Goose*.

what *Mother Goose* is to a North American, has as offensive a physical caricature portraying "Our Jew Liebermann" as one can find in anybody's literature.[122] Bezruč's *Silesian Songs* [*Slezské písně*, 1899–1900] is a seminal work of
modern Czech poetry. Here is how it maps out the Moravian landscape:

> On their farms dwell the peaceful peasants.
> The good emperor lives somewhere in Vienna,
> Germans under the mountains, in the towns the Jews.[123]

Franz Kafka (1883–1924), who was born and spent most of his life within a stone's throw of Staroměstské náměstí, gives an alternative perspective on the Prague riots of November 1920. The Stavovské divadlo was not the only target of Czechs' patriotic wrath. Many Jewish properties were attacked, and the medieval Jewish Town Hall in the former ghetto of Josefov was put under the protection of the United States embassy. "I have been spending every afternoon outside on the streets, bathing in anti-Semitic hate. . . . Isn't it natural to leave a place where one is so hated?" wrote Kafka to his Czech translator and lover Milena Jesenská.[124]

These letters—and this relationship—speak sadly to the brutalities (and absurdities) involved in making polyglot Prague into a world of imagined monolithic solitudes, a place inhabited by people who were indelibly either Czechs or Germans and could be unambiguously differentiated as such by the language they spoke. Milena Jesenská (1896–1944) was a true daughter of the Czech revival, and it bored her unutterably. Her father Jan Jesenský (1870–1947) was a zealous, not to say bigoted, Czech nationalist professor of dentistry at the Czech university of Prague, who according to (unsubstantiated) family legend was a descendant of the university rector of the same name so theatrically executed on Staroměstské náměstí in 1621. Her aunt was the novelist, playwright, and poet Růžena Jesenská (1863–1940), of whom Kafka's friend and biographer Max Brod later wrote "Because of her chauvinistic Czech attitudes and philistine outlook she was held in distaste in our circles." Růžena Jesenská's plays were staged at the National Theater, and she was a frequent contributor to Zlatá Praha. She was also one of the very few women ever to be elected to the Czech Academy of Sciences and Arts, a select company indeed.[125] Milena herself was one of the "Dear girls, Czech girls" who graduated from Eliška Krásnohorská's Minerva. Her family did not much approve of her consorting with Prague's German-Jewish literati.

They would probably have chuckled at the cartoon "New-Age Tourney in Our Old Prague" in the satirical magazine Šípy (Arrows) in 1893, depicting two jousting knights under the banners "Na příkopě" and "Graben." In this war of the street names, the top-hatted and business-suited German champion was drawn with stereotypically Jewish features, and lest the significance of his hook nose by chance be missed, he sported a Star of David on his saddlecloth.[126] In Czech eyes during this period Germans and Jews were routinely assimilated, as they were in the disturbances of November 1920, and as they had been in the earlier riots of November 1897, when Czech mobs evenhandedly smashed every window in both the Neues Deutsches Theater and the synagogues in Smíchov and Žižkov. The Prague poet Oskar Baum was blinded as a child by being hit over the head by a pencil box in one of the many fights that took place between Czech and "German" schoolboys. Gustav Janouch's apocryphal Conversations with Kafka may be a dubious source (though Max Brod found it completely believable), but the words

Janouch puts in Kafka's mouth are accurate enough, whether or not Kafka actually uttered them: "The Jew Oskar Baum lost his sight as a German. As something which in fact he never was, and which he was never accepted as being."[127]

This German-Jewish hyphenation was not entirely groundless. Outside of the *pohraničí* and other German "islands," a substantial proportion of the (self-declared) urban German-speaking population was made up of Jews— close to half in Prague itself in 1900.[128] *Ottův slovník naučný*, gloating in 1903 over the "second Czechization of Prague," comments sourly that things would be still rosier if "Prague Jewry, who were mostly born in Czech regions, would at long last stop seeing material advantage in declaring their language of everyday intercourse to be German upon moving to Prague."[129] Bohemian Jews' gravitation to German is historically comprehensible. It goes back to the double-edged terms on which Joseph II, in the interests of building a loyal Austrian citizenry, had "emancipated" them a century earlier. Czech anti-Semitism in the latter half of the nineteenth century, whether in the shape of riots or in its more "moderate" manifestations, like the boycott of Jewish businesses organized in 1892 under the slogan—which had originally come from Palacký—"*Svůj k svému!*" (Each for his own!), did little to persuade most Jews that their interests would be better served by abandoning the imperial cosmopolitanism which speaking German had previously represented and opting instead for a Czech national affiliation. Their tragedy, however, was that by this date the German language too was being ethnicized and transformed into the badge of a "national" community of which Jews were no more allowed to be a part than were Czechs. The empire's Germans were in general no more favorably disposed toward Jews than were its Slavs; witness the election of the rabidly anti-Semitic Karl Lueger (whose appointment had four times previously been vetoed by Emperor Franz Josef) as mayor of Vienna in 1897. The Jews were the most palpable victims of the radically altered significance of language in relation to identity in later nineteenth-century Bohemia. One response to the impasse in which they found themselves was the emergence of Zionism.[130]

Early in his acquaintance with Milena, who was living at the time with her (Jewish) first husband Ernst Pollak in Vienna, Kafka writes: "Of course I understand Czech. I've meant to ask you several times already why you never write in Czech. . . . I wanted to read you in Czech because, after all, you do belong to that language, because only there can Milena be found in her entirety . . . whereas here there is only the Milena from Vienna. . . . So Czech, please."[131] He continues in the same vein the following month: "I have never lived among Germans. German is my mother tongue and as such more natural to me, but I consider Czech much more affectionate, which is why your letter removes several uncertainties; I see you more clearly, the movements of your body, your hands, so quick, so resolute, it's almost like a

11. Turn-of-the-century postcard, showing the demolition of the former
Jewish ghetto of Josefov during the slum clearance. The legend reads:
"Greetings from Prague!"

meeting."[132] Kafka's reference here to German as his "mother tongue" is quite
literal. His mother Julie, née Löwy, who came from a prosperous bourgeois
family in Poděbrady, preferred to speak German. He himself, however, never
felt wholly at home in that mother tongue of which he is one of this century's
greatest prose writers. In his diary of 1911 we read:

> Yesterday it occurred to me that I did not always love my mother as she deserved
> and as I could, only because the German language prevented it. The Jewish
> mother is no "Mutter," to call her "Mutter" makes her a little comic (not to
> herself, because we are in Germany), we give a Jewish woman the name of a
> German mother, but forget the contradiction that sinks into the emotions so
> much the more heavily. "Mutter" is peculiarly German for the Jew, it uncon-
> sciously contains together with the Christian splendor Christian coldness also,
> the Jewish woman who is called "Mutter" therefore becomes not only comic but
> strange.[133]

Kafka's father Herman, on the other hand, was happier in Czech. He was the
son of a kosher butcher in the entirely Czech-speaking little village of Osek
in southern Bohemia.[134] Franz's own Czech seems to have been fluent.[135] The
family member to whom he was closest, his youngest sister Ottla, married a
Czech Catholic—and Sokol activist—Josef David, against her parents' oppo-

sition and with her brother's wholehearted support. His sister Valli was involved in founding the first Jewish public elementary school in Prague in 1920, whose language of instruction was Czech.

Was Kafka then a Czech or a German? Or both? Or neither? To what language did he belong, where could he be found in his entirety? Assuredly he was Jewish, but what that meant in relation to nationality was no clearer at the time. When in the first Czechoslovak state census of 1921 people were for the first time allowed to declare "Jewish" as their nationality, barely a fifth (5,900) of those in Prague who listed their religious faith as Judaism chose to do so. A quarter (7,426) described their nationality as "German," more than half as "Czechoslovak" (16,342).[136] Twenty years later, all three of Kafka's sisters were to perish in the Holocaust at the hands of occupying Germans for whom it was quite clear that Jewish and German were mutually exclusive identities. Before she was transported to Terezín (which is better known by its German name of Theresienstadt), and thence to Auschwitz, Ottla Davidová had to divorce her husband Josef in order to protect their daughters Věra and Helena. Mercifully perhaps, Franz himself did not live to see his family massacred on the altar of "racial purity." He died of tuberculosis in 1924 and is buried in Prague's New Jewish Cemetery. He was not reclaimed for the national memory after 1945. For much of the latter part of this century his name was obliterated and his books banned in the "national state of Czechs and Slovaks" that rose from the ashes of World War II. When he was recalled at all—occasional moments of "thaw" aside—it was briefly and dismissively as "a Prague Jewish author writing in German"[137]—a double exclusion. As for Milena Jesenská, we shall meet her again. She had a life, and a death, of her own, beyond being "mistress to Kafka."[138]

A Procession of Servant Girls

Definition of the Czech national community in terms of its language also gave a distinctly plebeian cast to rhetorics of Czechness—something which is also very evident in Petr Bezruč's poetry—welding together *národ* (nation) and *lid* (people). If Czech is a "sacred instrument," so the argument runs, Karel Čapek and others were able to write in it only because the people, above all the country people, had kept the flame alive while the towns and the upper classes were being "Germanized" through the long centuries after Bílá hora. There is more than a hint here of society's upper echelons being bought off, of their having sold the mother tongue that was their birthright for the mess of pottage represented by imperial favor and favors. Rudolf Medek drew upon this conventional wisdom in his speech at Karel Hynek Mácha's funeral. He hails Mácha as having been the first in modern times to transform the roughness of spoken Czech into verse, giving it "real poetic

melody." But he is also clear that "in the simple people was the living sparkling faith in the future."[139] Here "the people" becomes the repository of
identity and seat of patriotism, and what is *lidové* is by that very fact also
intrinsically *národní*.

Folk songs are interchangeably referred to both as *lidové písně* and as
národní písně in the titles of nineteenth-century Czech collections. The ornate
costumes of Bohemian and Moravian villagers, too, are at once *lidové* and
národní kroje, even though their most striking feature is their minute regional
and local variety. This says much for what the idea of the *český národ* came
eventually to convey. It took on class as well as ethnic connotations, and its
favored imagery was sturdily rural. The aristocracy, in particular, was readily
portrayable as an alien element imposed upon the nation after Bílá hora, and
German or at least unhealthily cosmopolitan in affiliation, notwithstanding
its considerable earlier contributions to the *obrození*. František Ladislav
Rieger, interviewed in 1902, recalled how at the opening of the National
Theater he had sat beside "Countess Kaunic, née Countess Thun, wife of
Albert Kaunic, oldest brother of Count Dr. Václav Kaunic. The enthusiasm
was stupendous. It was really a majestic and sublime moment. Countess
Kaunic turned to me and said: 'Believe me, doctor, I am ashamed. Here
something so beautiful is coming into being, and we [that is, the Czech
aristocracy] contributed nothing to it.'" The countess spoke, of course, in
German. The parenthesis was added to the Czech translation of her words
either by Rieger, or by his interviewer, or by later editors, it is not clear from
context which; but nor does it really matter.[140] Similar rhetorics were to be
used later about the Czech bourgeoisie, a class whom the communists tarred
with national betrayal after Munich and wartime collaboration. In both cases
social distance from *lid* easily translated into foreignness from *národ*.

Malost (littleness) became an essential component of *národnost* (nationality): this was a nationalism centered on the little Czech [*malý český člověk*]
from a small nation [*malý národ*], sometimes humorously and self-depre-
catingly so. The phrase "*malé, ale naše*" (little, but ours) is one Czechs often
use when poking fun at themselves. The lookout tower on Petřín Hill in
Prague is a structure inspired by the Eiffel Tower in Paris but very much
smaller (it is sixty meters high). It was erected to coincide with the Jubilee
Exhibition of 1891. The tower is pictured in a hundredth anniversary book
on the exhibition with the caption "*Česká Eiffelovka—malá, ale naše.*"[141]
Marxists have often somewhat mechanically attached the epithet "petit bourgeois" to nationalism, but in much of its imagery Czech nationalism was
precisely and rather proudly that. The poet, feuilletonist, and sometime editor of *Světozor*, *Lumír*, and the belles lettres monthly *Květy*[142] Svatopluk Čech
(1846–1908), whose hugely popular *Songs of a Slave* [*Písně otroka*, 1894]
went through a record twenty-four editions in one year,[143] mercilessly lam-
pooned the *malý český člověk* of his day by uncomfortably dumping his fic-

tional Prague landlord Mr. Brouček first on the moon, then back in the
Hussite fifteenth century of which he was so inordinately proud. Mr. Brouček
was small and round, and his name is a diminutive—it means "little beetle";
"*brouček*" is what Czech mothers call their babies. On a more vulgar note, the
satirist Jiří Suchý, whom the film director Miloš Forman exaggeratedly once
claimed was the only Czech dramatist apart from Václav Havel not to have
been honored by the communist state in the post-1968 years of normalization,[144] published a little book in Prague in the early 1990s entitled *For Gentlemen Only* [*Jen pro pány*]. Dedicated to celebration of the female derriere, it
would doubtless be judged supremely tasteless in today's North America. But
it has some harmless and affectionate fun with imageries of Czech identity,
and in so doing, of course, reinforces them. Accompanying a drawing of one
plump behind, described as "*česká lidová*" (Czech popular), is the legend:
"Typical in a healthy Czech girl, but not exclusively so—this is panslavism
materialized. The ideal Mařenka from *The Bartered Bride* is guaranteed not to
have sat on anything else. It will engage us at first sight by its roundness and
fullness. It is excellently suited to national costume, if less so to the miniskirt." This is followed by a still more ample exemplar of what is described
as "*česká velmi lidová*" (Czech very popular). Among the forms Suchý goes on
to depict are the "baroque," the "merry peasant," and—how could he resist?—"*malá, ale naše*."[145]

This *český lid* was nonetheless in large part a construction of the urban
intelligentsia—as, perhaps, "the people" as a collectivity are always and everywhere. Cultivation of matters *lidové* was a very general facet of nineteenth-
century Czech nationalism. We have already encountered the collection of
folktales and folksongs by Karel Jaromír Erben and others, the same sort of
songs as Čelakovský's poetry claimed to echo. Josef Mánes may not have
been able to speak much Czech, but he painstakingly portrayed Bohemian
and Moravian villagers wearing embroidered and bobbin-lace local costumes,[146] and brought their presence into the very center of "Germanized"
Prague. His ornamental calendar disk for the centuries-old astronomical
clock on the Old Town Hall, painted in 1866, sentimentally portrays the
agricultural year.[147] Just around the corner in Malé náměstí, bucolic scenes of
reapers and blacksmiths by Mikoláš Aleš adorn the Rott House, then a hardware store.[148] They were painted in 1896–97. Renata Tyršová (1854–1937),
daughter of one founder of Sokol (Fügner) and wife of the other (Tyrš),
became a noted collector and propagandist of folk art [*lidové umění*], and an
expert on folk costumes. Her Czech was a good deal better than her father's.
It was she who designed the popular Czech homestead [*česká chalupa*] exhibit for the Jubilee Exhibition of 1891, at which 110 of Josef Mánes's pictures were also on display.

Božena Němcová published folktales and ethnographic travelogues, as well
as writing the most beloved of all nineteenth-century Czech novels, *Babička*,

12. Veruna Čudová, drawn by Josef Mánes in 1854 in "national costume."

whose heroine is a country grandmother. Set in Ratibořice in northeastern
Bohemia in the 1820s, *Babička* is subtitled "Pictures from Country Life." One
measure of its resonance in Czech culture (and continuing centrality to the
imagery of Czech identity) is the fact that when Sixty-Eight Publishers, Josef
Škvorecký's and Zdena Salivarová's Toronto-based publishing house that did
so much to keep contemporary Czech literature alive after the Soviet invasion of 1968, brought out its hundredth book, it was Němcová's *Babička*.[149]
Božena Němcová herself was by the standards of her time an extraordinarily
emancipated woman, a kind of George Eliot figure.[150] She was illegitimate,

unhappily married to a husband many years her senior, beautiful, and she had a string of lovers; it was the unconventionalities of her personality and lifestyle, as much as her nationalism, that raised the hackles of her contemporaries, even in Czech patriotic circles. Her biography is as apt a metaphor as any for this overlay of sentimental rural representations on increasingly modern and urban realities. She certainly did not live like the simple rural folk she so fondly depicted, even if her own childhood experience provided her—at a very nostalgic distance—with the settings and characters for *Babička*.

Smetana, Dvořák, and Janáček all employed real and invented elements of folk song and dance in their music. Dvořák's *Slavonic Dances* are well known. Bedřich Smetana's opera *The Bartered Bride* [*Prodaná nevěsta*, 1866] invokes a timeless rural Bohemia, offering a cast of canny farmers, pretty country maidens, traveling circuses, and a stuttering simpleton. One of its liveliest choruses extols the virtues of good Czech beer. It is somewhat pathetic that this should be familiar to opera audiences the world over as a tale of Hans and Marie rather than of Jeník and Mařenka, for *Prodaná nevěsta* is *the* Czech national opera; even if the author of the libretto, Karel Sabina (1813–77), a friend and early champion of Karel Hynek Mácha's and a regular lecturer for Umělecká beseda, was subsequently exposed as an Austrian police informer.[151] It chalked up its hundredth performance in 1882, and between 1883 and 1983 had no less than 2,881 more[152]—an average of 29 per year—in the National Theater alone. Emil Pollert (1877–1935), the most famous of all Czech basses, who incidentally was Jewish, sang the buffo role of the marriage broker Kecal there 449 times.[153] It was *Prodaná nevěsta* that was staged at the Stavovské divadlo on the night it was occupied in 1920, a message obvious to all.[154]

Leoš Janáček (1854–1928), who is nowadays hailed by some Western critics as the greatest of all modern opera composers,[155] also collected folk songs, and endeavored to create an operatic language out of the everyday rhythms of northern-Moravian dialect. His most famous opera *Jenůfa* (1904; known as *Její pastorkyňa*, Her Stepdaughter, to Czechs) is also set in a (Moravian) village, though one portrayed in much darker hues than Smetana's. It tells the story of the pregnancy of the unwed Jenůfa and the murder of her baby by her stepmother, the village sextoness. Responding to a questionnaire in 1899 from *Moravská revue* (*Moravian Review*) on the foundation of a National Theater in Moravia, Janáček makes the link between language, *lid*, and identity truly elemental:

> We need to plunge to the depths to find the truth: even the tone of our actors' language, in fact the speech melodies of actors' language, have to be *genuinely Czech, genuinely Moravian*.
> The melody of the Czech language, that which rings out from its speech,

which pleases, or touches, which roars with thunder and whispers with tenderness, this florid attire of thought, and its embodiment, this melody, however, is debased through our contact with the Germans and, alas, also through all our schooling, from the very beginning to the end.

What is often spoken on our stage is not the soft Czech language, gentle in all its delicate turns. It is simply not genuine Czech.

The actors need to go back to that rare and inexhaustible school, the life of the people, to regenerate and purify themselves.[156]

Two decades later, writing in *Lidové noviny*, Janáček measures Czechness in microseconds, with the aid of a device known as Hipp's chronoscope, in the difference between the Czech [*Moravany*] and German [*Morawaan*] names for a railroad station in Pardubice, as he heard them shouted by a guard on 18 August 1917. "How the different 'spirit' of both languages shone through here. Our version is ranged in the notes of a warm triad D flat—F—A flat. The German version cut harshly and roughly in the same triad, with a dissonance of a seventh; it has crushed the third syllable and torn off the last one; it has ground into grumbling the sweetness of the first two." "Speech melody," he continues, "calls for a Czech in the bosom of his land; it calls for his life, rolling through the centuries with equal sorrow and harshness. It is not inherited song-like boasting, a boasting of the green baize. It is the vigor of broad fields and the worthlessness of the dust, dark ages and the spark of a thousandth fraction of a single second!"[157]

The opening scene of Antonín Dvořák's opera *The Jacobin* [*Jakobín*, 1889] is set in the arcaded market square of a small country town, with a church in the background, a pub to the left, and a view of the château in the distance. The sound of singing comes from the church. Bohuš, long-absent son of the owner of the lordship, enters with his wife Julie and (according to Dvořák's stage directions) "they look around them with emotion." "Hark, Czech song!" sings Bohuš. "Oh, ring out to me, ring out! Your welcoming voice sounds so sweet to me! The greeting of the homeland embraces us!" Throughout the opera, Czech song comes to stand in for the Czech land. In the most famous number in the score, "*My cizinou jsme bloudili*," Bohuš and Julie relate how:

> We wandered lost through alien lands,
> Ah, for long years, long years,
> Tears of homesickness dimmed our sight
> And longing welled up in our hearts.
> Who counted our sighs,
> Who will console the exiles?
> From the depths of our soul
> We sung to ourselves a Czech song
> And the gloom disappeared from the soul,
> The distress fled from the heart. . . .

> In song alone, in song alone,
> We found sweet relief.[158]

Like many Czech cultural artifacts, *Jakobín* has had a checkered fate during this century. It was banned under the Nazi occupation, it seems because the villain of the plot is named Adolf. An offer to alter the name to Rudolf did not placate the authorities. Communist critics, on the other hand, disapproved of both the opera's counterrevolutionary sentiments and what they saw as the offensive portrayal of the village schoolteacher and choirmaster Benda.[159] Benda is a good-hearted and simpleminded rustic, a stock figure who is both comic and lovable, but far too subservient to feudal authority to serve as an appropriate role model in a progressive state governed by the working people. He is pivotal to the fond nostalgia that Dvořák (who among other things sought through this opera to recapture the landscape of his own childhood) was conjuring up. The choirmaster embodies the survival of the nation in and through its ordinary country folk, and his simplicity and his humility are integral to that representation. The librettist for *Jakobín* was Marie Červinková-Riegrová (1854–95), daughter of F. L. Rieger and granddaughter of František Palacký. When Dvořák reworked parts of the opera in 1897, Rieger made a contribution of his own, writing Terinka's song "In fall among the hazel groves love no longer gives any joy." Terinka is objecting to Benda's plans to marry her off to the old burgrave Filip. In the end she of course gets her way and her young Jiří, who, she says, warms her like the rays of the springtime sun.

A high point of this representation of Czechness in terms of the popular was the Czechoslavic Ethnographic Exhibition [*Národopisná výstava českoslovanská*] of 1895.[160] The roots of the adjective "*národopisný*," which is normally rendered in English as "ethnographic," lie in the noun "nation" [*národ*] and the verb "to write" [*psát*]. Transcribing custom into texts of nationality is exactly what the exhibition was about. The same year as Alfons Mucha's poster for *Gismonda* mesmerized Paris, this "Czechoslavic" spectacle drew two million visitors to Stromovka park on the outskirts of Prague. On view were meticulous reconstructions of Czech farmsteads and cottages, village magistrates' houses, mills and churches; a multitude of Bohemian, Moravian, Silesian, and Slovak peasant costumes, all carefully classified as to their regions of origin; ceramics and glass, furniture, leather work, textiles and lace, religious artifacts, popular song, music and dance, hand-painted Easter eggs, and very much more. Sections were devoted to Czech literature, theater, music, clubs, schools, and "the Czech woman." Czechs abroad were not forgotten (there was a model of the first Czech church in St Louis), and neither was "modern industry." The main emphasis, however, was domestic, rural, and inward-looking. Displays illustrated "age-old customs and habits" like marriage rituals and the Christmas, New Year, Shrovetide, and Easter

13. The "village square" at the Czechoslavic Ethnographic Exhibition of 1895.

festivities which "despite all the influences of Western culture . . . the Czech people have preserved almost to the present day." One of the most famous of these was the colorful Whitsuntide Ride of the Kings [*Jízda králů*], which at that point survived only in a few areas of Moravia. The study of such customs, the catalogue tells us, is "a very important tool for getting to know the spiritual life of the nation."[161]

The brief of the exhibition was to "depict in a wide variety of appropriate ways, strictly in accordance with reality and truth, the life and state of the Czech nation at the close of the nineteenth century, as well as its historical development."[162] Whether this representation at all accorded with "reality and truth" of either present or past is questionable. It offered an idealized portrait of a rural mode of life that many of its visitors had irrevocably left behind them, and it essentialized a particular conception of Czechness on that basis. While the individual elements out of which the exhibition was composed were doubtless for the most part "authentic" enough, the totality constructed out of their combination was another matter.[163] The boy who played the part of the king in the *jízda králů* was dressed in women's clothing and carried a rose between his teeth, as tradition demanded.[164] What this ride had originally signified is lost in the mists of time; most probably the flight of the Hungarian king Mathyas Corvinus after his defeat by Jiří z Poděbrad in 1468. What it *now* signified was a function of its juxtaposition alongside

14. The Ride of the Kings display at the Czechoslavic Ethnographic
Exhibition of 1895.

rooms devoted to Čelakovský, Jungmann, Havlíček, Palacký, Kollár, Neruda,
and Purkyně, the "Old Prague" exhibit which comprised a full-scale reconstruction of Malé náměstí as it was thought to have looked at the end of the
sixteenth century, and displays of Hussite military hardware. Like them, the
jízda králů had become but a sign of the common Czechness all of these
diverse particulars were held to possess, a mirror of identity and a means of
identification. The Czechoslavic Ethnographic Exhibition was all the same a
splendid show that evidently more than satisfied its mainly urban consumers. Encouraged by its success, a permanent Ethnographic Museum was
founded in Prague the following year in the gardens of the Kinský family
under Petřín Hill.[165]

The handsome souvenir volume of the exhibition published by Jan Otto, a
copiously illustrated work of over six hundred pages, has a section analyzing
the political significance of the event. "The Exhibition," it says, was "*a manifestation of the cooperative participation and well-organized work of the whole
nation*, without distinction of opinions or parties." It is in support rather than

in contradiction of this claim that it goes on to stress that "the government could not but see that the exhibition brought us an invigoration and enlargement of *the idea of nationality* in that the work accomplished here was exclusively Czech. At the exhibition too the Czech language alone officially held sway. For the first time at a large enterprise, which could not fail to attract the attention of the wider world, our usual bilingualism was dispensed with." Equally important was the fact that "it was brought about *without any participation of the aristocracy. . . . The exhibition had a completely democratic character.*" This latter was quantifiable:

> The great discrepancy in numbers of visitors between working days and on Sundays, thus between visits of well-heeled bourgeois and working people, was striking. Out of 162 days when the exhibition was open twenty-nine fell on holidays and Sundays, during which there were 1,143,000 visits, over 55 percent of the total (2,065,000). . . . Most visitors came on the days when something really popular [*něco hodně lidového*] was on show. Thus the procession of servant girls enticed to the exhibition over 70,000 visitors, the exhibition's festival modeled on the Nusle *fidlovačka* over 57,000, and so on. . . . From all this it is evident which social layers make up our life, which are for us the most significant. . . . It is our duty to ensure a proper education for our least privileged people. In it is for us the heart, in it lies our future, and that future will be the more secure, the better this people is educated.[166]

We are a long way from aristocratic land patriotism, and rather firmly in the modern world.

Palacký's Looking-Glass

Another and equally consequential strand in the skein of Czech identity being woven in the nineteenth century was historiographic. The central figure here was František Palacký (1798–1876), who was appointed official Land historian by the Bohemian Estates in 1831 and went on to become, with Josef Jungmann, one of the first members of Vienna's Academy of Sciences in 1847. Palacký was much more than just a historian; he towers over mid-nineteenth-century Czech cultural and political life. He was instrumental in the founding of the journal of the National Museum, which he edited, in 1827, and of Matice česká in 1831, as well as being involved in launching the newspapers *Národní listy*, *Národ*, and *Pokrok* in the 1860s. He chaired the committee set up to raise funds for the building of the National Theater in 1850. Such endeavors, like his longtime advocacy of a Czech encyclopedia, are at least as significant contributions to the development of a Czech national awareness as his role in the revolution of 1848, when he presided over the first pan-Slav Congress in Prague and led the Czech delegations to the

Vienna and Kroměříž constitutional assemblies, or his political activities in the Old Czech party after 1860. His principled refusal to participate in the Frankfurt parliament of the German Empire in 1848, on the other hand ("I am not a German, at least I don't feel like one. . . . I am a Czech of Slavonic stock"),[167] supplied a proud image of national self-assertion that was to be much milked later. His point in that same *Open Letter* that "if the state of Austria had not already long existed, in the interests of Europe, indeed of humanity, we would have to immediately exert ourselves to bring it into existence"[168] was more easily forgotten. But it was through his historical writings that František Palacký had his deepest and most enduring impact on modern Czech self-perceptions.

In 1836, the same year as Karel Hynek Mácha's *Máj* appeared, Palacký published the first part of his monumental *History of the Czech Nation in Bohemia and Moravia* [*Dějiny národu českého v Čechách a v Moravě*].[169] It took him another thirty years to complete his great work. By 1848 he had taken the story of the Czechs to 1419; by 1860 he had reached 1471 and the death of Jiří z Poděbrad. The fifth and last volume, dealing with the Jagellon kings, came out in 1867. The *History* is based upon an awesome mastery of primary sources. Palacký worked in over seventy European archives and copied some four hundred documents in the Vatican library alone; besides Greek and Latin, he read German, French, English, Russian, Hungarian, Italian, Spanish, and Portuguese. His book was massively authoritative, a Czech counterpart to Guizot or Macaulay. He spelled out the point of this enormous labor in his preface to the 1848 Czech edition. It was certainly not scholarship for its own sake. "From my early youth I had no higher wish for my earthly life than to serve my beloved nation by giving a faithful account of its past, in which it would recognize itself as in a mirror and regain consciousness [*vzpamatovat se*] of what it needs."[170] In this, as the founder of Czech positivist historiography Jaroslav Goll (1846–1929) later remarked, the *History* was as much a mirror of its author and its own time as of the Czech past. Conceived above all as a pedagogical instrument, "It was composed in the service of the nation; it was meant to be a means of its awakening and education, it was written for its instruction."[171]

Palacký's great achievement—in a time in which except as one of the nominal crowns and lordships by which the Habsburgs defined their dominions, the Kingdom of Bohemia had been wiped from the maps and the consciousness of Europe for over two hundred years—is to have reconstituted the Czech nation as a historical subject, a national community possessed of a past and destined to have a future. This was no small feat. Friedrich Engels, for one, was contemptuously dismissing the Czechs as late as 1849 as a "historically absolutely nonexistent 'nation'" who "have never had a history of their own,"[172] a view that was to embarrass Czech communists a century later.[173] Palacký's overall message is summed up in one of his most frequently quoted axioms: "We were here before Austria, and we will also be here after it!"[174] Implicit in this deceptively simple statement is a profound dislocation of nineteenth-century temporal geographies. It refocuses Czech history on Prague instead of Vienna, and it marginalizes the previous three centuries as an anomalous disruption of a much longer continuity. It also implicitly undermines Palacký's own preferred "Austroslav" federalist politics insofar as it provides a historical grounding for eventual claims to national sovereignty, pitting the essence of identity against the ephemera of Realpolitik. Not for nothing is Palacký known to Czechs as "the Father of the Nation." He did much to (re)invent it. We might, however, register a pregnant difference between this sobriquet of *Otec národa*, granted to Palacký in the nineteenth century, and that of *Otec vlasti*, "Father of the Homeland," which was bestowed on Charles IV at his funeral five hundred years earlier. As Petr Pithart acidly puts it, "The *vlast* [homeland] also included the Germans in Bohemia, whereas the *národ* [nation] comprised only 'Czech speakers.'"[175] Palacký's choice of title for his magnum opus is equally instructive. His is a history of the Czech nation in Bohemia and Moravia, not a history of the Kingdom of Bohemia and its inhabitants.

Enthused by Palacký's example, other historians followed in his footsteps like Václav Vladivoj Tomek (1818–1905), a onetime private tutor in the Palacký household, whose twelve-volume history of Prague remains unmatched to this day in the wealth of its empirical detail.[176] Among his other works are a monograph on Jan Žižka.[177] Tomek became a member of the Bohemian parliament from 1861 to 1870 and was chosen first rector of Prague's Czech university after the split of 1882. An academically less distinguished writer, but one who was no less important if we are considering the media through which history was inscribed in the nineteenth-century present, was Karel Vladislav Zap (1812–71). Zap was another Czech patriot whose first language was not Czech, but he more than amply overcame that handicap later. His activities were many-sided. In 1835, at the age of twenty-three, he wrote the first guidebook to Prague to be published in Czech.[178] During the next eight years he lived in Galicia, where he put Slav reciprocity into practice. He translated Gogol's *Taras Bulba* into Czech, sent ethnographic reports on the region's Polish and Russian inhabitants to *Květy*, the *Časopis Českého musea*, and other magazines, put together an annotated collection of Russian and Polish stories which he called *A Mirror of Life in Eastern Europe* [*Zrcadlo života ve východní Evropě*, 1843–44], and found himself a Polish wife. Returning to Prague in 1845, he updated his *Guide* and supplied the Czech nomenclature for Bedřich Krečmar's maps of the sixteen Czech districts. During the 1850s he chiefly devoted himself to writing geography textbooks and atlases that would meet the needs of Czech schools. From 1854 to 1867 he also edited the National Museum's archaeological magazine, where he published numerous articles of his own on buildings in Prague, Hradec Králové,

Tábor, and other historic places in the Czech lands. He was a founder-member of the Jednota Svatovítská, a society whose objective was to "complete" the building of Charles IV's Saint Vitus's Cathedral, which had been "interrupted" by the Hussite Wars four and a half centuries previously.

Zap's largest work is the *Czech-Moravian Chronicle* [*Česko-Moravská kronika*], whose first edition came out in 1862. Tomek was an early supporter of the project, a debt Zap acknowledges in his preface. This grandiloquently begins: "Noble is the mission of a national chronicle, something which should stand immediately after the Bible in the family chest in every home, which should be the domestic treasure-vault, from which every son and daughter of the nation could draw knowledge of the fate of the homeland, of the deeds of their ancestors, of their character, thinking, and conditions of life. A national chronicle should consequently be a source of love for the homeland and for the family, it should fan the spark of the sacred ardor, which we call patriotism, which binds an individual to the land of his fathers and to his brothers." The nation here is at once sacralized—its history belongs beside the Holy Scriptures—and thought of in familial terms, and just as in Karel Čapek's *The Mother* that family includes the dead. Zap goes so far as to define his task as "bringing to life and explaining the past, in which the whole of our national being consists." We have traveled a long way from Bolzano! Zap made no pretense at original research and fully acknowledged his reliance on Pelcl, Tomek, and above all "the immortal work of our patriarch [*starosta*] among Czech historians," Palacký's *History*. He dismisses older chronicles as inadequate for the needs of the modern reader, because they lack narrative coherence. "A chronicle that merely related events without attending to their inner connections . . . would certainly not satisfy our times or the needs of the people,—a chronicle has today to be a real *history*, but of course popular [*prostonárodní*]. . . . The main need is that a chronicle should be written in a simple style, so that the things related in it would be sufficiently comprehensible and therefore clear to every reader."[179] He need not have worried. The *Chronicle* proved to be enormously popular. Sections of it were republished as independent books, and the whole was enlarged by others and reissued in 1880.

By the later years of the century Palacký's rendition of Czech history had penetrated popular culture in the shape of the historical fictions of Alois Jirásek (1851–1930) and others, where it was even more ideologized and simplified. The intellectual shortcomings in Palacký's own work criticized later by Goll and Pekař from the point of view of a more "scientific" historiography—anachronism, essentialism, teleology, romanticism—were precisely what became magnified in Jirásek's powerful popularizations. The critic F. X. Šalda, writing in 1930, the year of the novelist's death, pinpoints the significance of what Jirásek accomplished through his translations of history into fictional realism. Simultaneously the past becomes a living presence and contemporary agendas gain enormous, even if largely spurious, historical depth:

> Much, much more than Palacký, Jirásek gave Czech history a liberationist meaning according to the then politically free-thinking liberal outlook; to him Czech history is above all a struggle against all types of tyranny, against the tyranny of the Church as well as against feudal oppression; a struggle for freedom of conscience, as well as for a higher standard of material life; Jirásek's later novels are to a certain extent and in some sense novels of the social, because the people [lid] are their protagonist; by this understand the little folk without historic titles and functions in their everyday struggle with the soil, in their everyday struggle for the crust of bread.[180]

Jirásek's many novels and plays relate the epic story of the Czech nation in these terms over a millennium, from its mythical beginnings in the arrival of the "Old Slavs" in central Europe (*Staré pověsti české*, *Old Czech Legends*, 1894) to the revolution of 1848 (*Filosofská historie*, *A Philosophical History*, 1878). His favored periods, as we might expect, are the Hussite era and the *obrození*, both of which he portrays on a scale worthy of Tolstoy. He wrote two *obrození* chronicles: the five-volume *F. L. Věk* (1890–1907) brings to life the world of Kramérius and the Thám brothers, the four-volume *U nás* (*Here*, 1897–1904) recreates the rural environs of Jirásek's own birthplace Hronov, and has as its leading character a *buditel*-priest. Jirásek devoted three trilogies of novels[181] as well as a trilogy of plays—*Jan Hus* (1911), *Jan Žižka* (1903), and *Jan Roháč* [z Dubé] (1913–14)—to the Hussites, and was at work on the second volume of *The Hussite King*, whose hero is Jiří z Poděbrad, at his death [*Husitský král*, 1920, 1932]. It is perhaps not without significance that one famous period of Czech history to which Jirásek does not pay comparable attention is the "golden age" of Charles IV, though he paints an unflattering picture under that ironic title of Rudolf II's Prague [*Ze zlatého věku*, 1882].

The Dogheads [*Psohlavci*, 1883–84], which, like *A Philosophical History*, Jirásek wrote as a young gymnasium teacher in Litomyšl, relates the story of the peasant rebellion in Domažlice in 1692–93. An episode already addressed by both Božena Němcová and Karel Jaromír Erben in their collections of folktales, this conflict between the Czech *sedlák* (yeoman) Jan Sladký Kozina and the German landlord Lamminger is redolent with symbolism. Domažlice was then the only place in the *pohraničí* where the Czech element in the population reached as far as the border,[182] and (as Jirásek tells the story)[183] the Chodové, as the people there are known, were a clan of free peasants who had guarded the frontier with Bavaria for centuries. They took the name "Dogheads" from the device on their standards. They helped Břetislav I repel Emperor Henry III in 1040, and "It is certain that they were not idle in the rest of the struggles, in particular the Hussite times of glorious memory." For these services the Chodové received special rights and privileges, which were confirmed by successive Czech kings. They owed no labor services to any lord, they could hunt in the forests they guarded, they were permitted to bear arms, and no aristocrats were allowed to purchase or settle on their lands. "Then came the battle of Bílá hora . . ." The following year, dominion over the Chodové was handed over to Wolf Wilhelm Lamminger, "who was one of the imperial commissioners and directors of the horrible tragedy of 21 June 1621," when the twenty-seven Czech lords were publicly executed on Staroměstské náměstí. Nine years later, "the Chodové were sold to the same Lamminger for 56,000 gulden in full hereditary ownership. The new lord of course did not want to recognize and did not recognize their rights and privileges, and treated them as if they were serfs."[184]

The rising of 1692–93 was thus no ordinary local revolt but an event of national significance. It was a struggle to restore ancient Czech freedoms, violently usurped by foreign—and specifically, German—overlords. Jan Sladký Kozina is in the end executed; but on the scaffold he prophesies that Lamminger will also stand before God's judgment throne in a year and a day, an event that duly comes to pass. *The Dogheads* is transparently an allegory of the contemporary situation of the Czech nation. Characteristically, Jirásek (in his own words) "regularly and systematically" explored the Domažlice region before he wrote about it, painstakingly researching its customs, costumes, and dialect in order to render them with greater realism and fidelity.[185] He dedicated the book "to the memory of Božena Němcová," and only contractual problems with publishers prevented Mikoláš Aleš's illustrations for it from appearing sooner than they did (1900). With its author's approval, *The Dogheads* went on to form the basis of an opera of the same title by Karel Kovařovic (1862–1920), which won a National Theater competition for new works (against Fibich's *Šárka* and Foerster's *Eva*, operas whose musical value has proven to be very much more lasting), and was premiered in 1898. A no less telling illustration of the power of Jirásek's fictions to reinscribe the past in the living present is the fact that a monument to Jan Sladký Kozina was unveiled in 1895 on the hill above his home village. It testifies to anything but the unbroken continuity of "popular memory." Fifty years earlier, when she was collecting her "folktales," Božena Němcová had described a very different Domažlice in a letter to her friend Antonia Bohuslava Čelakovská, wife of the poet František Ladislav Čelakovský:

> Although I am in Bohemia, not far from our little mother [*matička*] Prague, I am yet low in spirits; here the folk are still so backward, it horrifies one. *They speak Czech, because they do not know how to speak German*; but of any higher level of literacy, of national consciousness, they don't know the slightest. And what am I to say about the peasant folk! In one village there teaches a bricklayer, here again a cabinet-maker, elsewhere somebody who cannot even read properly and who

has to have a sample written out for him when he requires the children to write. You can surmise for yourself where this leads. One could cry bloody tears over these folk. How many talents, how many a quick mind will perish without reaching the right consciousness? They do feel it, they would be willing to learn, but what can they do when no one sends them a Messiah? Few know anything about history or would have ever read a book in their lives; but now they come from the villages where I am known, unbidden, to ask for books, and they read them in flax-spinning bees on winter nights. . . . What the real devastation is in several villages here is the damned-to-hell Jesuitism. Near here there are two Jesuits, from the so-called brotherhood, the fools! But you have no notion how they have bamboozled the poor folk, led them into impoverishment, so that now they walk around like stray sheep.[186]

Jirásek's works were staged at the National Theater and serialized in *Květy*, *Světozor*, *Lumír*, and—most frequently—*Zlatá Praha*. He was a prolific writer, and his books were extraordinarily popular. By 1921 *The Dogheads* was in its twentieth edition, and his *Collected Works*, published by Jan Otto from 1890, had reached their forty-third volume.[187] Jirásek is known, not unjustly, as "the Czech Walter Scott." He was chosen as one of the first cohort of members of the Czech Academy of Arts and Sciences in 1890, elected to the Royal Society of Bohemia in 1901, named an honorary citizen of Hronov, Litomyšl, and in 1918 Prague, and awarded a doctorate *honoris causa* by Charles University in 1919. It was not only through the word, however, that the national history was brought to life in the later nineteenth century. Historical painting, too, was much in vogue. A famous example is Václav Brožík's "national monumental work"[188] "The Sentencing of Master Jan Hus" (1883), which hangs opposite his "The Election of King Jiří z Poděbrad" (1898) in the council chamber of Prague's Old Town Hall. In the latter picture Brožík (1851–1901) paints what are recognizably nineteenth-century Czech patriots, among them Šafařík, Rieger, Tomek, Tyrš, and Fügner, in the guise of fifteenth-century electors.[189] We could ask for no more perfect a metaphor for this historicization of the present and contemporization of the past. It goes without saying that Alfons Mucha was later to use Palacký's *History* as a principal source for his *Slovanská epopej*.

Palacký also left his mark on the landscape of everyday life. Žižkov, then a new district on the outskirts of Prague, had a population of 4,336 and 202 buildings in 1869. By 1880 there were 21,212 people living there; by 1900 there were 59,326, most of them workers. Žižkov became administratively separate from neighboring Vinohrady only in 1875 and received its present name in 1877. In 1881 it was granted the status of an independent city. By 1907, when it had a population of over 72,000, most of whom lived in its 16,000 or so tenement apartments, Žižkov was in its own right the third-largest city in Bohemia.[190] It took its name from Jan Žižka z Trocnova, the one-eyed Hussite commander who is portrayed on the coat of arms granted it in 1898. Within its boundaries lies Vítkov, the hill where Žižka defeated Emperor Zikmund's crusading army on 14 July 1420. Thoroughfares within Žižkov were given names that recalled the Hussite struggles, and many of the area's tenements sport Hussite decorative motifs.[191] This graphically exemplifies the way in which by the later nineteenth century history had become mobilized as a storehouse of symbols of contemporary identity, and the imagined community of the nation back-projected a thousand years. This thoroughly proletarian, entirely modern, and almost entirely Czech quarter of Prague was where the past was most insistently and systematically recalled. Without Palacký it is doubtful whether such a thing could have happened. These names that now formed a quotidian part of the city's geography—Hus, Jeroným Pražský, Žižka, Prokop Holý, Tábor, Lipany, and Domažlice all lend their names to Žižkov's grimy streets—would hardly have signified much at all to most Czechs, least of all a national identity in which they themselves partook, half a century earlier.

The Hussite movement, which Palacký interpreted both as a struggle for religious freedom and as an assertion of Czech nationality in the "age-old" conflict of Slavs and Germans, lies at the heart of his narrative. In both respects he saw it as a harbinger of the national struggle of his own time. He sought to identify the common features of Hussitism and the *obrození* (as he saw them) with what he claimed to be original "Slavic" virtues that had necessarily been modified by contact with the "Germanic" world, but threaded their way through Czech history nevertheless. Foremost among these were a love of freedom, democracy, egalitarianism, and pacifism. To detect a nationalist element in Hussitism is not in itself by any means anachronistic, as we saw earlier. A more pertinent question (as Josef Pekař later argued against Tomáš Masaryk)[192] is whether the content of fifteenth- and nineteenth-century Czech nationalisms was in any meaningful sense the same. The Hussites were medieval soldiers of God, not modern democrats; if they were nationalistic, it was as a latter-day chosen people, God's elect nation. Freethinkers they decidedly were not. But what matters here is less the propriety of treating the past as a mirror for the present than its consequences.

Palacký successfully grounded modern Czechness in the recovered memory of an independent medieval state whose governance had extended at various points almost to Trieste and beyond Berlin, a kingdom ruled for four hundred years by the Czech Přemyslids. Prague was celebrated as Charles IV's imperial capital rather than the provincial backwater it became after 1620. Jan Hus was reappropriated less as a religious dissident than as a national hero, the Hussite Wars represented as a moment when, a century before Luther, *Czechs* stood up "against all" (*Proti všem*, the title of one of Alois Jirásek's Hussite trilogies. Alfons Mucha read this during his 1905 voyage to America and immediately determined to put something similar on canvas.)[193] Through this identification of present and past *národ* and *lid* were indissolubly wedded to *vlast*, the homeland whose gentle landscape was abundantly sentimentalized in poetry, painting, and song in these years, and that Bohemian and Moravian *země* (land, earth, soil) became eternally and exclusively Czech, no matter how long others had lived there too. The land was nationalized and title reclaimed in retrospective perpetuity. This conception was not without its long-term political consequences. It was the basis for the assertion of "historic state right" that was to justify the incorporation of majority German-speaking areas into the Czechoslovak Republic in 1918, whatever the wishes of their inhabitants; a plebiscite was refused and Czech troops drafted in. Therein lay the seeds of Munich.

Though Palacký's *History* covers only the medieval Czech kingdom, the structure of his narrative offered a framework within which later events could also in turn be reconceptualized in terms of violations of this millennial identity. The revolt of the Czech Estates of 1618–20 became simplified as a national insurgency rather than a combination of a Protestant/Catholic conflict (whose dynamics were not a simple replay of the earlier Hussite struggles) and a defense of Czech aristocratic and burgher privileges against a monarchical centralization that had gone on since the Bohemian crown passed to the Habsburgs in 1526. Unlike its Hussite predecessors, the "Czech" army that lost at Bílá hora consisted largely of foreign and mercenary troops, and its command was entirely German. The post–Bílá hora period was similarly represented in terms of straightforwardly national persecution by a Germanic power rather than as an era conditioned as much by the impulses of continent-wide religious struggles and modern state formation as by any specifically ethnic factors. A good half of the burgher families who fled Prague in 1624–27 for religious reasons, including the richest ones, were in fact German, not Czech.[194] But once again the issue is not the accuracy of nationalist historiography so much as its effects. The twenty-seven Czech lords so bloodily executed on Staroměstské náměstí in 1621, and the émigrés like Jan Amos Komenský who left their beloved Bohemia and wandered homeless through the labyrinth of the world rather than renounce their Protestant faith, were retrospectively conscripted as timeless and contextless *Czech* patriots pure and simple. It was an emotive martyrology.

Consider this passage, from what is probably Alois Jirásek's most widely read work, *Staré pověsti české*. It comes from a section of the book entitled "Sad Places," and deals with the executions of 1621. On Staroměstské náměstí, Jirásek relates,

> There were once sixteen great stones arranged in a square. The old Czechs, when they passed through these places, never trod on these stones, nor even laid a foot on them. They always avoided them or went around them, out of consideration

15. Staroměstské náměstí, photographed around 1870. The Old Town Hall is to the left, the Mary Column in the right foreground. The Kinský Palace can just be seen on the extreme right. The spires in the background are those of Saint Nicholas's Church. All of the buildings on the north side of the square were to be demolished during the slum clearance.

for the sad place and the spilled blood of the Czech lords. In these places, it is said, these executed noblemen and burghers appear, once a year that is, on the night before the day on which they met their end at this place of execution. They all assemble, in the lead the eldest among them, the nearly ninety-year-old Lord Kaplíř of Sulevice. . . . They assemble at the place of execution and then quietly, without a sound, cross the square to the Týn Cathedral. There they kneel before the altar and reverently accept the body of the Lord in both kinds. And then they disappear.[195]

It is a masterly piece of mythmaking, sinewing together images of the fifteenth and seventeenth centuries in a single figure of eternal return, and reclaiming the heart of Prague for Czechness. As they crossed the square, after 1897, the Czech lords would have been overseen by the protective gaze of Saint Václav, painted on the front of Štorch's bookstore to Mikoláš Aleš's design.[196] Franz Kafka, too, must have witnessed this ghostly procession. His boyhood bedroom in Celetná ulice looked directly into the nave of the Týn Cathedral.

A symptomatic feature of Palacký's and Tomek's books is the time span they cover. Tomek ends in 1608 and Palacký in 1526, the year the Habsburgs acceded to the throne of Bohemia.[197] So does Zap. The claim for essential continuity between the medieval Czech state and the *obrození* is much strengthened by overlooking what came in between. It becomes simply "Darkness" (*Temno*, the title of another of Alois Jirásek's novels), an interruption, during which the nation like some Sleeping Beauty awaited its awakening, not having aged a day in the meantime. "*Buditel*," the term that Czechs use to describe their revivalists, comes from the verb *budit*, to wake up. To shine a critical historical light on the intervening darkness (as Josef Pekař was to do later) would raise the awkward question of whether the Habsburgs and Jesuits had not succeeded in reshaping this supposedly hibernating Czech essence beyond all recognition, as they had the external landscape. Like towns up and down Bohemia and Moravia, "old" Prague is visually predominantly a baroque city, and its fabled beauties are largely a legacy of the Counter-Reformation. Even the famous Hradčany skyline that Alfons Mucha was to use on the first independent Czechoslovakian postage stamp as a symbol of national sovereignty (on his second he drew a Hussite priest with a chalice) was a legacy of Maria Theresa's remodeling of the ancient and frequently reconstructed castle.[198]

An architectural equivalent of the historiographic erasure of the period of "Darkness" is the Gothicization of many Prague buildings in the late nineteenth century, extending at times to makeovers of surviving genuinely Gothic structures like the Powder Gate [*Prašná brána*] at the end of Celetná ulice. One casualty was the Church of Saint Peter and Saint Paul at Vyšehrad, where the funeral services for Mucha and Mácha took place. The baroque building dating from the later seventeenth and early eighteenth centuries was almost entirely destroyed between 1885 and 1903 to make way for a purist neo-Gothic edifice more in keeping with the reconstituted Czechness of the "most sacred place."[199] It is a very baroque Gothic; every inch of the walls is decorated, and the sinuous female figures above the arches in the nave, whose golden halos gleam dully in the half-light, could have been painted by Alfons Mucha. This rebuilding occurred during a period of massive demolition of historic Prague, including every structure except for the Town Hall and a handful of synagogues in the former Jewish ghetto of Josefov in the name of slum clearance [*asanace*].[200] Symbols of a constructed past were multiplying exactly as the evidence of the real past was everywhere being destroyed. Similar incongruities are almost comically evident in Mikoláš Aleš's plans for his uncompleted cycle "Three Ages of the Czech Land." He described them to the art critic Emanuel Svoboda in 1912:

> The main pictures and among them insertions. (And at this he sketched with his finger on the table how he imagined it all.) *Vyšehrad* in glory and opposite *Petřín* with the [Old Slav] god Perun. *The Přemyslids*—in the center Otakar with his standard—the homeland bows down at the sarcophagi in Saint Vitus's Cathe-

dral—that is what I was thinking of then—perhaps more than necessary—*The Hussites*—highest in the heavens Christ, at his sides Hus and Jeroným [Pražský]. In the clouds Žižka and commanders—and down below the armed Hussite people—*The Thirty Years' War*—a motto of three executed young men, who had opposed the clerics, then the execution of the lords. Valdštýn [Albrecht z Valdštejna] riding a horse points in the distance to a shining star—all around, skulls. I wanted to depict in more depth the *resurrection and awakening*. Oh, my boy, it is vain to talk of these plans. And from all this came only one sheet—the fragment "*A ta naše lípa*" (And That Lime-tree of Ours, 1891).[201]

Try to imagine, for a moment, any *Protestant* artist painting Christ in his heaven with Martin Luther at his right hand and John Calvin at his left. The grammar of the picture is eternally, indeed almost blasphemously, at odds with its purported message. Aleš's sensibility remains irrepressibly baroque.

Certainly there were few Protestants in the Czech lands by the time Palacký was writing, unlike in 1620. The Jesuits who flooded into Bohemia after Bílá hora to purge the kingdom of heresy had done their work thoroughly. Palacký himself, the son of a Lutheran pastor, was an exception, as was Tomáš Masaryk (and even Palacký permitted his children to be raised as Catholics, while Masaryk converted to Protestantism only after his marriage to Charlotte Garrigue). Such technicalities in no way dampened the growing cult of Jan Hus. His significance had long since ceased to have very much to do with religion. To the surprise of that city's inhabitants, there was a "national pilgrimage" to Konstanz in 1868 of four hundred Czechs, among whom were Bedřich Smetana and Karel Sabina, with representation from Umělecká beseda, Sokol, Hlahol, and several other patriotic societies. The next year was celebrated as the five hundredth anniversary of Hus's birth. There was a ten-thousand-strong commemoration in Prague on 5 July, the eve of the date of Hus's immolation. That evening an unauthorized crowd of "workers, women, children, and servants" assembled in Betlémské náměstí on the site of the Bethlehem Chapel in which Hus had preached, and the gathering was broken up by the police when it burst into patriotic song.[202] Tomáš Masaryk reclaimed Hus as a precursor for his own projects of moral reclamation,[203] Brožík and others painted the stations of his cross on enormous canvases, and Ladislav Šaloun (1870–1946) sculpted his expressionist memorial in the middle of Staroměstské náměstí. Hus is presented here as the pivot around which Czech history revolves. To one side of him, the Týn Cathedral side, proudly stand the soldiers of God at the highest point of the circle; to the other, at its lowest, cower post–Bílá hora Czech emigrants, who face toward the execution place of 1621; completing the circle, ascending again toward the peaks of Hussite glory, a mother quietly nursing her babies represents the *obrození*. Šaloun himself wrote of his memorial: "Hus signifies for the Czech nation a vehement, irreconcilable struggle or at least unceasing

16. Šaloun's Jan Hus Memorial and the Kinský Palace on Staroměstské náměstí,
1915. Herman Kafka's store is in the right-hand corner of the palace.

strife with the world around and in our own core, the ultimate endeavor as
well as a near-fatal plunge."[204]

The foundation stone for the Hus monument was laid on 5 July 1903.
Jirásek's play *Jan Žižka* was premiered the night before at the National Theater in honor of the occasion. Josef Pekař contributed a subtle and moving "In
Memoriam" to the book that commemorated the event. He concluded with a
reminder of the multiple associations of time with place:

> [The Hus monument] will stand on Staroměstské náměstí which will thus be
> enriched by a great reminder of the painful contrasts of our history. . . . It will
> stand not far from the place at which a victorious king bloodily punished a revolt
> of our nation [i.e., the Rising of 1618–20] for which the first foundations were
> laid by Hus's activities. . . . It will stand not far from the place where the statue
> of the Virgin Mary Victorious, a monument celebrating this victory of legitimacy
> and Catholicism over a heretic kingdom, was erected. . . . It is the self-same
> statue of Virgin Mary Victorious, only slightly changed and enlarged, which
> stands in the main square of gay and lively Munich, whose inscription directly
> thanks the mother of God for the triumph at Bílá hora; "*Rex, regnum, regimen,
> regio, religio—restaurata sunt sub tuo presidio*". . . . This, too, the fact that the

Virgin Mary is celebrated as a victor over Hus's nation, is a bitter historical mis-
conception. Jan Hus was a devotee of the Virgin Mary, the cult of the Virgin Mary
is an expression of moralist reformatory efforts of the fourteenth and fifteenth
centuries, and it was with the Song of Mary on his lips that Master Jeroným
[Pražský] went to the pyre.

Let both monuments stand here beside each other, as witnesses to our greatness and our defeat, testaments to the tragic contrasts of our history. The edge of
that tragic contrast has been blunted by centuries but the shadow of its grief still
reaches into our hearts.[205]

Pekař's plea for Czech history to be remembered in all its tragic complexity
fell on deaf ears. Šaloun's completed monument was eventually unveiled on
6 July 1915, the quincentennial of the burning of Hus at Konstanz.[206] This
was in the depths of World War I; worried enough about Czech loyalties
already, the Austrian government forbade any ceremonies or speeches, and
press coverage of the event was heavily censored. For three short years the
reformer and the Virgin Mary gazed at each other across the square. She had
stood there, on a tall column, since 1650, in thanks for the delivery of the
city from besieging Swedes two years before. But on 3 November 1918, less
than a week after independence, demonstrators returning from a meeting on
the site of the battle of Bílá hora tore her down as a symbol of Habsburg
oppression.[207] Had they not been prevented by the city authorities, they also
would have toppled Saint Jan Nepomucký from Charles Bridge into the
Vltava for a second time. The statistical likelihood is that most of them were
(at least nominally) Roman Catholics,[208] even if the mob was led by a drinking companion of the anarchistic and utterly profane Jaroslav Hašek, creator
of the good soldier Švejk.[209]

The national Hussite Church [Československá církev], set up two years later
with the blessing of the new Czechoslovak state, succeeded in wooing only
half a million souls from Rome.[210] There are multiple ironies here. The main
Prague site of this "Czechoslovak" Church is not, as we might expect, the
soaring gothic Týn Cathedral where Konrad Waldhauser preached in the time
of Charles IV, where the heads of the executed Czech lords were buried in
1631, and where until Jesuit students destroyed them in 1623 a stone chalice
and a statue of Jiří z Poděbrad had decorated its western face. It is Saint
Nicholas's Church on the opposite corner of Staroměstské náměstí, an ex-
travagant confection built to the design of the architectural prince of the
Prague baroque, Kilián Ignác Dienzenhofer, in 1732–35. Disused after 1787,
Saint Nicholas's became a warehouse (and for a time a military concert hall),
and was later leased out for Russian Orthodox services, earning it the
nickname of "the Russian Church." Modern Czech reference books seldom
neglect to mention that Dienzenhofer (1689–1751), as his name suggests,
was of German origin.

17. The destruction of the Mary Column in Staroměstské náměstí, 3 November 1918. Note the new buildings on the north side of the square.

A Discovery in Dvůr Králové

As history was transformed into nationalist myth, so ancient and not so ancient myth fused seamlessly, in popular and public representations at any rate, with nationalist history. Libuše, the Czech princess invoked by Max Švabinský at Mucha's funeral and by Rudolf Medek at Mácha's, reigned, according to legend, sometime before the first documented Prince of Bohemia Bořivoj, who died in (perhaps) 894. From her seat at Vyšehrad she is said to have one day gazed across the Vltava to the wooded heights of Petřín Hill and prophesied the future glory and sufferings of the city of Prague. "I see a great city, whose glory will reach the stars" are the words attributed to her by Alois Jirásek in *Staré pověsti české* and known ever after to every Czech schoolchild.[211] Libuše took for her husband the plowman Přemysl, thereby founding the Přemyslid dynasty as well as the mother of cities. According to Jirásek, at least, Přemysl was appropriately *lidový*: he brought his bast shoes with him to Vyšehrad so that his princely descendants should not forget their beginnings, "since we are all equal."[212] In the later nineteenth century Libuše was celebrated in sculpture, painting, poetry, and music. Perhaps the most famous portrait of her is Karel Vítězslav Mašek's symbolist masterpiece of 1893, which today hangs in the Louvre in Paris.[213] Alfons Mucha painted her in 1917. It was Bedřich Smetana's opera *Libuše* that won the competition to inaugurate the National Theater in 1881, and was played again for the reopening after the fire in 1883. Smetana had composed it in 1870–72—to a libretto first written in German—"not to be included among repertory operas, but kept as a festive work for special commemorative days."[214] This day was special enough to justify the work being performed for the first time, a full decade after it was written.

In golden letters above the proscenium arch of the National Theater is the motto "*Národ sobě*" (The nation to itself). The building's splendid decorations, by the mostly young artists known thereafter as the Generation of the National Theater, represent the nation to itself largely through its myths. Mikoláš Aleš and František Ženíšek (1849–1916) paint Czech legends and Julius Mařák (1832–99) Bohemia's "sacred places," including Vyšehrad, Blaník (whose sleeping knights led by Saint Václav will save the nation in its hour of greatest need), and Říp, the mountain from which the mythical forefather of the nation, *Praotec* Čech, having led his people from the east, looked out and decided the *vlast* had at last been reached. It was to this site that Prague Sokol had its first outing on 27 April 1862; the seventy-three participants, then "only partly in uniform," included Miroslav Tyrš, Jindřich Fügner, and future mayor of Prague Tomáš Černý.[215] The "foundation stone proper" of the National Theater, laid with much pomp and circumstance by Palacký on 16 May 1868, a month before his seventieth birthday, was quarried at Říp and brought to Prague in ceremonial procession.[216] Other foundation stones laid that day come from Blaník and other Czech "sacred places," including Prácheň and Trocnov, locations linked respectively with the memory of Jan Hus and Jan Žižka, and Vítkov in Prague, the scene of Žižka's famous victory over Emperor Zikmund in 1420. The legend on the stone donated by Czechs in Chicago the next year reads sadly in the light of the experiences of later generations of Czech émigrés: "What blood unites, the sea will not sunder!" [*Co krev pojí, moře nerozdvojí*].[217] Also embedded in the theater's foundation is a small casket said to contain stones taken from the jail in which Jan Hus was imprisoned in Konstanz.[218]

Smetana's great symphonic poem *Má vlast* (My Homeland) also starts in Vyšehrad and ends with Blaník.[219] In between the composer weaves some more authentic history. The most dramatic movement, "Tábor," named after the southern Bohemian city founded by the radical wing of the Hussite movement, employs the melody of the Hussite hymn "Ye who are the soldiers of God." So does the finale of *Libuše*. Here the princess prophesies with remarkable accuracy among others Charles IV, Jan Žižka, and Jiří z Poděbrad. Few people at Alfons Mucha's funeral will have missed the echo when Max

18. Mikoláš Aleš, sketch for mural in the vestibule of the Old Town Hall, 1904. Libuše is looking out from Vyšehrad. The silhouette she sees of Saint Vitus's Cathedral is that of its "completion" as envisaged by the architect Josef Mocker, not that which existed in her time, Mikoláš Aleš's time, or any other time.

Švabinský spoke of the Czech meadows and woods [*luhy a háje*] flowering again; it is of another movement of "*Má vlast*," the sweetly lyrical "From Bohemia's Meadows and Woods" [*Z českých luhů a hájů*]. Smetana's composition is completed by two other movements. "Šárka" recalls a heroine of the Girls' War [*Dívčí válka*] that supposedly followed Libuše's death. Led by Libuše's handmaid Vlasta the Czech girls rebelled against male governance and were duly defeated, since which time, according to the medieval chronicler Kosmas, "our women have been under the power of men."[220] "Vltava," well known in the West as a popular concert piece called "The Moldau," pictures Prague's river. Its main theme is based on the tune of a Czech nursery rhyme, "*Kočka leze dírou*" (The cat is crawling through the hole). All in all it is an interesting bundle of associations, and a powerful answer to the question "*Kde domov můj?*"

The earliest written mention of Princess Libuše is in Kosmas's chronicle, which dates from the early twelfth century.[221] Other Czech legends go back no further than the second decade of the nineteenth century, and a curious episode that in its way says much about the whole *obrození*. In 1816 the future editor of *Zvěstovatel* and *Pražské noviny*, the then twenty-seven-year old Josef Linda (1789–1834), "discovered" the manuscript of a purportedly medieval Czech poem, "Song Beneath Vyšehrad" [*Píseň pod Vyšehradem*], in the binding of a large book he used as a footstool. A year later his friend and fellow lodger Václav (or Váceslav) Hanka, who was then twenty-five, had an even more spectacular "find." According to his own account, on 16 September 1817, while examining a bundle of arrows said to have come from Jan Žižka in a vault under a church tower in the town of Dvůr Králové, he stumbled across a bundle of parchment, which subsequently became famous as the *Rukopis královédvorský* (Dvůr Králové manuscript).[222] The following year yet another manuscript, the *Rukopis zelenohorský* (so called because it hailed from the town of Zelená hora), was sent anonymously to the mayor of Prague. These purported to contain Czech poetry dating respectively from the thirteenth and tenth centuries, some of it about Libuše and Vyšehrad. The manuscripts appeared physically to authenticate the antiquity of Czech history and Slav culture, putting both on a par with their German equivalents. Their publication caused tremendous excitement. In his introduction to the thirteen-language edition of the *Rukopis královédvorský*, which he published in Prague under the title *Polyglotta* in 1852, Hanka's estimate of their importance knew no bounds. Like Homer and Aeschylus, he wrote, "Our Lumírs and Zábojs sung the glorious deeds of ancient heroes," which, he is convinced, "are founded in historical events."[223]

Further manuscripts turned up over the next three decades, among them "Libuše's Prophecy" [*Libušino proroctví*], which Hanka made public in 1849. Josef Dobrovský included the *Rukopis královédvorský* in the updated editions of his *History of Czech Language and Literature*, but he considered the *Rukopis zelenohorský* to be a forgery from the start, and said so in print. It was not his skepticism that prevailed. Indeed, because of this indiscretion his reputation suffered in patriotic circles long thereafter. Václav Hanka was showered with honors at home and abroad, most notably from Russia, whose Academy awarded him a silver medal weighing a pound. The manuscripts were translated into many languages, among them English. The first Czech encyclopedia *Riegrův slovník naučný* begins its entry on Hanka with the words: "Hanka Václav (Váceslav), a man with every right counted among the most respected and most beloved of the Czech-Moravian nation, whose name is forever linked with the Královédvorský manuscript."[224] Indeed. Doubts on the manuscripts' authenticity were again publicly cast in the 1850s, and Šafařík and Palacký stoutly stepped forward in their defense. In 1858 Hanka was openly accused of forgery in one of Prague's two leading German newspapers, the *Tagesbote aus Böhmen*, leading him (successfully) to sue for libel David Kuh, its Jewish editor. The case contributed to anti-Jewish rioting in Prague in 1861. The *Tagesbote*, incidentally, had been one of the very few Prague newspapers to give Karel Havlíček Borovský a decent obituary two years earlier; the Czech press, such as it was, was too cowed by Bach's police.[225]

Only in the 1880s was the manuscripts' fraudulence finally put beyond all reasonable doubt, and Linda and Hanka established as their most probable authors, in a series of articles in Tomáš Masaryk's review *Atheneum* by Masaryk himself and the philologist Jan Gebauer (1838–1907). The manuscripts had become so totemic by then that as a result of the controversy Masaryk had little choice but to resign his job as editor-designate of *Ottův slovník naučný* and was pilloried in the more nationalistic press as a traitor to the Czech nation.[226] The battle lines here were by no means simple. Eliška Krásnohorská, the founder of Minerva, was an unfailing progressive on matters of gender, but she came out strongly in defense of the manuscripts' authenticity in *Ženské listy*.[227] Masaryk himself went on the offensive less out of a desire to repudiate Czech nationalism than from a wish to moralize and modernize it, to set it on new foundations.[228] The "main elements" of a contemporary Czech national program, he wrote in *The Czech Question* [*Česká otázka*, 1894], should be "humanism, nationality, constitutionality, social reform, education of the people."[229] He intensely disliked "Old Slav" mythologizing, instead seeking "the meaning of Czech history"—a no less mythical construct, as Josef Pekař pointed out[230]—in the specifically Czech and Protestant heritage of Hus, Komenský, and the Union of Brethren. Unsurprisingly, the figure among his immediate predecessors for whom Masaryk had most time was Karel Havlíček Borovský, who had also derided his contemporaries' search for the essence of Czech identity in the pages of Šafařík's *Slovanské starožitnosti* (and explicitly taken issue with the ubiquitous "mirror" metaphor).[231]

Masaryk was to find himself in similar trouble with superpatriots again some years later, when in 1899 he championed the cause of a Jewish vagrant, Leopold Hilsner, who was convicted of what was alleged to be the "ritual murder" of a nineteen-year-old Czech girl, Anežka Hrůzová, in a wood outside Polná in southeastern Bohemia.[232] In large part because of Masaryk's intervention, Hilsner's death sentence was commuted to life imprisonment. Hilsner was almost certainly an innocent victim of Czech anti-Semitism. It is possibly this cause célèbre that accounts for the future president's otherwise puzzling omission from Vilímek's *Národní album* the next year. But here, too, Masaryk's stance was more complex that it might at first sight appear. His relation to "the Jewish question" was not simply founded in his humanism. His support for Zionism was in part a consequence of his endorsement of Havlíček's position that Jews were *not* Czechs but a separate nationality.[233] He intervened in the "*Hilsneriáda*," as it became known, not only to defend Hilsner but also to defend the reputation of the Czech nation against the slur of backward superstition. In his old age, recalling the anti-Semitic milieu in which he was raised as a boy, he confessed to Karel Čapek: "When did I overcome in myself this popular anti-Semitism? Sir, in feeling perhaps never, only intellectually."[234]

Forged medieval manuscripts were not uncommon in early nineteenth-century Europe. Seldom, however, can they have had so deep or lasting an impact on the imagination of a nation as in the Czech case. The Dvůr Králové and Zelená hora manuscripts inspired generations of Czech artists. Josef Mánes and Mikoláš Aleš both reverently illustrated them, Aleš's illustrations appearing in 1886, the same year as *Atheneum* exposed Hanka.[235] Josef Myslbek's statues of Záboj and Slavoj, two wholly fabricated heroes of the *Královédvorský rukopis*, stand in Vyšehrad beside Libuše and Přemysl; they were originally sculpted in 1881–92 for the Palacký Bridge in Prague, where they stood until they were damaged by bombing during World War II. Emanuel Chvála's opera *Záboj* was premiéred at the National Theater in 1918; its libretto comes from a poem of the same title by Jaroslav Vrchlický. According to Hanka, Václav Tomek assigned Záboj and Slavoj to the first half of the eighth century, most probably between 728 and 748.[236] There is not a shred of evidence for their existence other than that furnished by the manuscripts themselves. Palacký used the manuscripts as a historical source in his *History of the Czech Nation*, as did Šafařík in his *Slav Antiquities*. It comes as no surprise that parts of the libretto for Smetana's *Libuše* are based on the *Zelenohorský rukopis*, nor that in the National Theater are a sculpture of Záboj and a painting of Dvůr Králové, the latter in Aleš and Ženíšek's cycle *Vlast* in the grand foyer.

Among the theater's foundation stones laid in 1868 is one from Hostýn in Moravia, "famous for the wondrous victory over Kublai Khan"[237] in 1241. Whether such a battle ever took place is more than doubtful, but the sole authority for believing it did is the ballad "Jaroslav" in the *Královédvorský rukopis*. Palacký quotes the last stanzas of this poem in his account of the Tartars in Moravia in his *History*, as the testimony of a "near contemporary poet."[238] Karel Hynek Mácha, too, was deeply influenced poetically by the manuscripts (as he was also by the Scottish forgery "Ossian"), while Jindřich Fügner's reading of the *Rukopis královédvorský*—in German translation—was, in his own words, "a huge experience" that "helped me to discover the road to the Czechs."[239] The consensus in much later Czech commentary is that irrespective of their dubious origins, the manuscripts contain poems of high literary merit that made a positive contribution to the development of the Czech national culture. Positive or not, the contribution is indisputable. So is the trauma caused by their unmasking as forgeries. However overwhelming the evidence against Hanka, the controversy has never died. Along with criticisms of Hitler's Nazis as way too socialist and Mussolini's fascists as insufficiently anti-Semitic, the Czech 1930s fascist organization Vlajka (The Flag) included defense of the manuscripts in its political platform.

The first burial of modern times in Vyšehrad Cemetery, and the one that marks the beginning of its transmutation into the "most sacred place," was that of Václav Hanka. He died in 1861, reportedly with Russian words on his lips, and was given a fine funeral, at which the choral society Hlahol performed for the first time in public. The following year subscriptions raised enough for the erection of a pillar over his grave inscribed with the legend "Nations will not perish, so long as the language lives." Hanka was a key figure of his time, and thoroughly representative of the *obrození* in the range of his interests. A man of modest habits, he lived quietly with his wife, mother, and sister in Prague, and devoted his life to the national cause. He was a pupil of Dobrovský's, whose dictionary he helped finish, and a friend of Jungmann's. He wrote lyrical poems, whose popularity was such that they became virtual folk songs (*znárodnit* is the Czech term), as well as translating popular poetry from Serbian, Russian, and Polish. A fervent pan-Slav and Russophile, he took to styling himself in the Russian fashion Váceslav Váce-slavič; there is no such use of patronymics in Czech. He translated Rühs' *Short History of the Slav Nations* (1818), kept up a voluminous pan-Slavic correspondence, participated in the Slavonic Congress in Prague in 1848, and wrote textbooks of Polish (1839) and Russian (1850). He compiled and published a six-volume collection of Czech medieval texts, many of them from Dobrovský's own archive [*Starobylá skládanie*, 1817–24]. He successfully modernized Czech spelling [*Pravopis český*, 1817] and unsuccessfully pioneered a pan-Slavic alphabet that mixed Roman and Cyrillic characters. In 1848 he was chosen as the first president of the patriotic society Slovan-ská lípa (The Slav Linden; the lime tree is another national symbol) and was a delegate to both the Land and imperial parliaments. Above all, he was the first librarian and custodian of manuscripts—which he had an unfortunate habit of "improving"[240]—at the National Museum, a post he held for four decades, from 1819 to his death.

Václav Hanka was in all probability a forger; but he was also an undoubted *buditel*. As must be obvious by now, in the Czech nineteenth century the line between the two was not always entirely clear.

Memories of Ivančice

Alfons Mucha's sensibilities were molded by all this. The son of a court usher, he was born in 1860 in the small town of Ivančice in southern Moravia, whose main claim to fame was that the *Bible kralická* was printed there in 1578. As a boy Mucha imbibed the nationalistic gospel from those stock characters of the *obrození*, a patriot-schoolteacher named Novotný and a *buditel*-priest, Beneš Metoděj Kulda, who was later to become a canon at Vyšehrad. He got his education as a choral scholar, drinking in the baroque splendor of Saint Peter's Cathedral in Brno, and was a fellow pupil of Leoš Janáček's at the Brno gymnasium. Rejection by Prague's Academy of Fine Arts rather than wanderlust took him first to Vienna, where he painted theatrical scenery, and later as a student to Munich (1885–86) and then (1887) to Paris. In Munich he chaired the Slavonic painters' club Škréta, named for a Czech artist whose family was forced to flee Bohemia after Bílá hora (though Karel Škréta himself was eventually to return). On its behalf he sent a congratulatory diploma to Mikoláš Aleš, who was then under attack from "progressive" quarters in Prague for his illustrations for Hanka's manuscripts; Julius Grégr, proprietor of the Young Czech daily *Národní listy*, wrote that "work so shallow, superficial, and ugly is not worth either the paper it's printed on or the expense."[241] Mucha hastened to reassure Aleš "We always understood you and shall always understand you, just as everyone certainly will in our Czech nation who is not a reactionary and retains a last ounce of sense."[242]

One of Mucha's earliest commissions, while he was still a student in Munich, was a painting of Saints Cyril and Methodius for the Church of Saint John of Nepomuk [Jan Nepomucký] in the little Czech settlement of Pisek, North Dakota. Throughout his long sojourn abroad—in Germany, in France, and in the United States—he eagerly threw himself into Czech and Slavonic society and societies. He was a founder-member of the American Slav Society. In Paris his circle of friends included Vojtěch Hynais (1854–1925), who created the curtain for the National Theater and the first Czech poster for the 1891 Jubilee Exhibition; Václav Brožík, for whom Mucha had boundless admiration; and the young Czech painters Luděk Marold (1865–98) and Jan Dědina (1870–1955). Among Luděk Marold's most famous paintings is the gigantic panorama *The Battle of Lipany*—it measured eleven by ninety-five meters—which he and several assistants executed in a specially constructed circular pavilion thirty meters in diameter for the third of the great Prague public exhibitions of the decade, the Exhibition of Architecture and Engineering of 1898.[243] In the late 1880s and early 1890s Mucha regularly contributed to Czech magazines[244] and illustrated Svatopluk Čech's *Adamité* (a poem about the Adamites, the dissident Hussite sect purged from Tábor by Jan Žižka) for the Prague publisher Šimáček.[245]

After his rise to international fame with his poster for *Gismonda*, Mucha continued to work on Czech subjects whenever he could. He designed a new masthead for the literary magazine *Lumír* in 1898, which also evoked the world of "old" Slavonic myth.[246] In 1902 he and Jan Dědina illustrated Poggio-Bracciolini's *Jan Hus Before the Council of Konstanz*, which they published in Prague with Jan Otto but at their own expense.[247] Among Mucha's most

19. Alfons Mucha's 1911 poster for the Moravian Teachers' Choir.

charming posters are two for agricultural-industrial exhibitions at Vyškov in Moravia (1902) and Hořice in northeastern Bohemia (1903). Both feature pretty peasant girls wearing "national" costume, and the trademark Mucha halo plays in the first case on the Moravian eagle and in the second on the Bohemian lion, which are old heraldic symbols of the Czech lands. His 1911 poster for the Moravian Teachers' Choir, an organization with which Leoš Janáček had a long and fruitful involvement, is similar in style. Another

Czech commission, Mucha's 1907 poster for the Slavia insurance company, is famous;[248] the same design was later used on the hundred-crown bill of 1920. Mucha intended to employ it again as the centerpiece of his stained-glass window for Saint Vitus's Cathedral, which relates the story of Cyril and Methodius, but persuaded that so pagan a figure as Slavia was out of place in a house of God, he finally substituted Saints Ludmila and Václav. Slavia is a symbol of the Slav peoples; the ring she holds may symbolize Slavonic unity.[249] This poster was executed during Mucha's time in the United States. So was the melancholic "Memory of Ivančice" (1909), with its motif of departing swallows.

Arguably there is also a deeper Czechness in Mucha's art that lies less in its subjects than in its very style. His bold use of line strikingly recalls Mikoláš Aleš, and his decorative forms have clear affinities with some of the work of Josef Mánes (for instance, the latter's 1862 banner for Prague Sokol).[250] A good part of the charm of Mucha's women lies in their candor of face and solidity of body. These are neither pale Pre-Raphaelite lovelies nor the remote society beauties of Gustav Klimt, but "an unnerving amalgam of Slavic peasant girl and the Queen of Heaven," as one commentator puts it.[251] One is tempted to say they are more *lidové*. Alfons's son Jiří Mucha (1915–91) finds in the panel "Summer" from the 1896 quartet *The Seasons* more than a hint of *vlast*: "Needless to say, the scene . . . was no Queen of the Summer sleeping in her great solitude, but rather a realistic evocation of a Moravian summer afternoon, with a girl sitting in a typical manner, her head garlanded with wild poppies, her feet dangling in the pool, half dreaming, half thinking with voluptuous languor of the lads who are coming down to water their horses. Few of Mucha's *panneaux* are so truly southern Moravian, so close to the slow love songs of those parts sung by the village girls in peculiar harmonic intervals, exploited with such success by Janáček."[252] Perhaps father and son are equally romanticizing here, but if so, the romanticization is of a piece with that of the Czechoslavic Ethnographic Exhibition of the year before. No less a connoisseur of all things *lidové* than Renata Tyršová appreciated Mucha's work for the echoes of Moravian folklore she discovered in it.[253]

After his return to Bohemia in 1910, Mucha could give his patriotism free rein. His ceiling for the Mayoral Hall in Obecní dům, entitled *Slavonic Concord*, is an allegory of pan-Slav unity, and his designs for other murals there bear the captions "Accept love and enthusiasm from your son, mother of the holy nation!" and "Though humiliated and tortured, you will live again, my country!" These were made into postcards to commemorate the building's opening. In the same chamber are two exquisite murals entitled "Prague in Chains" and "Dreaming of Freedom."[254] Mucha's banknotes are a real feast of Czechness. In the words of one recent Czech commentator, "In contrast to the 'Germanic' types of girls and women on Austro-Hungarian banknotes he prefers a more substantial female physiognomy, bordering on the corpulent, with broad cheekbones, whose simultaneous Slavness [*slovanskost*] and 'folk-ishness' [*lidovost*] is also signified by floral garlands on their heads and flowers in their hair, 'folk' costumes ['*lidové*' *kroje*] or more accurately his creations on this theme, and the frequent appearance of lime leaves or sprigs."[255] Mucha also employs the two-tailed Bohemian lion, the falcon (Sokol's emblem), the legionnaire's head (commemorating the Czechoslovak Legions that fought on the Allied side in World War I), and the dove of peace, then held by pan-Slavists to be a peculiarly Slavic virtue. His five-hundred-crown bill of 1919 depicts an "ancient Slav" family reminiscent of Mánes's and Aleš's illustrations for Hanka's manuscripts. Behind it stands the silhouette of modern Hradčany, suggesting age-old continuity. As a curiosity, we might note that among the symbols of *lidovost* that Mucha weaves into his fifty-crown bill of 1929 are a hammer and a sickle. Though it is highly unlikely that the artist had any communist associations in mind, this did not escape the notice of Czech fascists, who in May 1939 called for the bank-note's withdrawal and legal action against its author. Mucha's later Czech posters employ similar elements; "national" costumes, heraldic devices repre-senting Bohemia, Czechoslovakia, and the city of Prague, lime leaves, the Czech national colors, Slavia.

We have encountered Mucha's postage stamps already. Other miniatures of his art in the service of the nation include the decorations he drew for the honorary doctorates awarded to Presidents Poincaré and Wilson by Prague university in 1919, and his "Reconciliation of the Czechs and Slovaks," which was painted for a calendar celebrating the tenth anniversary of the Czechoslovak Republic in 1928 (and subsequently made into a postcard).[256] But the apotheosis of Mucha's patriotism in art is undoubtedly the majestic cycle which he returned to Bohemia in 1910 to paint, the *Slovanská epopej*.[257] For this he mined Palacký's *History*, consulted with the renowned historian of Bohemia and Czechophile Ernest Denis in Paris, and journeyed through Russia and the Balkans meticulously researching the background to his pic-tures. Simply to call these "historical" paintings, however, is wrong; it under-states their power and originality. Their style is not that of Brožík, Čermák, or other nineteenth-century Czech historical painters. Mucha transposes his historical subject matter into another dimension, a timeless realm of essential truths that stands above the ephemera of mere events. He distances himself from simple historical illustration by his palette, which is as striking as it is in "Gismonda," and by his use of symbolism. Colors are not used realistically, but to convey mood and meaning. Spirits float in the air above his mortal men and women, lime leaves recur like Wagnerian leitmotifs, lacing episodes separated by centuries (and modern national boundaries) into a unified mythic whole.

The *Epopej* has twenty paintings, ten on Czech subjects, ten on broader Slavic themes. The first depicts "The Slavs in Their Original Homeland [*pra-

20. Alfons Mucha, "Dreaming of Freedom." Mural in Obecní dům, 1911.

vlast]" and carries the subtitle "Between the Knout of the Turks and the Sword of the Goths." The last is "The Apotheosis of the History of the Slavs." In between this somber beginning and transluscent ending, Mucha paints an odyssey that runs from paganism through "The Introduction of the Slavonic Liturgy (Praise God in Thy Native Tongue)"—a portrayal of Saints Cyril and Methodius—to "The Abolition of Serfdom in Russia, 1861 (Liberated Labor, the Foundation of the State)." He depicts the Bulgarian czar Simeon (888–927), the coronation of the Serbian czar Stephen Dushan (1346), and the defense of Sziget against the Turks by the Croatian hero Nicholas Zrinský (1566). But it is his choice of Czech subjects which is most interesting. Six of the canvases are on broadly Hussite themes ("Jan Milíč of Kroměříž 1372," "Master Jan Hus Preaching in the Bethlehem Chapel 1412," "The Meeting at Křížky 1419," "After the Battle of Vítkov 1420," "Petr Chelčický at Vodňany 1433," and "The Hussite King Jiří z Poděbrad 1462"). Two more ("The Printing of the Kralická Bible at Ivančice 1578" and "Jan Amos Komenský—Last Days in Naarden 1670") invoke the legacy of the Union of Brethren and the tragedy of Czech Protestant exiles after Bílá hora. Přemysl Otakar II, perhaps the most famous of the Přemyslid kings, is also included for "Unity of the Slav Dynasties 1261."

The whole cycle is animated by a powerful Christian and pacific vision, whose embodiment is the Slavic peoples. At the top of "The Apotheosis," behind men waving lime sprigs and women in peasant costume, is a haloed Christlike figure. The picture bears the subtitle "Slavdom for Humaneness!" [or humanity; *Slovanstvo pro lidskost*], and the universal resonance of the Slav experience is pointed up by the inclusion of (among other symbols) an American flag. This latter juxtaposition is not so singular as it might at first sight appear. A fascinating *National Songbook* [*Národní zpěvník*] published in Prague soon after 1918, for instance, contains "a selection of the most popular patriotic Sokol, social, love and national Czech songs," operatic arias both Czech and foreign, and "hymns of free nations," including "The Marseillaise" and "The Star-Spangled Banner."[258] The overall effect of the *Slovanská epopej* is to (re)locate Czech history squarely in a pan-Slav context, while placing the Hussite drama at the heart of both. That Mucha freely mingles pagan, Orthodox, Catholic, and Protestant references in a paean to Slavism is interesting. On one level his indiscriminate plundering testifies to just how secularized religion had by then become. But it equally witnesses the ascension of the national and the ethnic into the realm of the sacred.

Mucha's *Slovanská epopej* can serve as a metaphor for much more. He wrenches historical events out of their diverse contexts and reinscribes them in a new space, which is that of the epic of his title. This space has its own parameters and coherence, which is not that of the times and the places in which these events actually occurred. The paintings are *tableaux vivants*, referring intertextually to one another rather than to the worlds from which they were abstracted. They are not historical illustrations but the exact opposite: history serves in them as itself the illustration of the national and Slavonic Idea that animates them. But Mucha paints with such power and beauty that this space, and the Idea which structures it, becomes real; very much more real, in its immediate and imposing presence, than the distant history it reorders (and disorders). The same is true, mutatis mutandis, of Jungmann's writing of the Czech language, of Palacký's grand narrative of the Czech national odyssey, of Erben's and others' compilations of Czech folktales, songs, or costumes, or of the representation of Czech identity at the Czechoslavic Ethnographic Exhibition. In each case an ideal coherence is hypostasized out of fragmented, fluid, and localized particulars, then variously reified and compellingly re-presented. Henceforth, it is only *within* the semantic space thus reconstructed that these particulars—a girl's dress, a nursery rhyme, a legend, a date, a manner of speaking—come to signify at all.

FIVE

MODERNISMS AND MODERNITIES

Futurist Manifestos

THE CZECHNESS of Alfons Mucha's work—as defined by the legacy of the *obrození*—is undeniable. But by the end of the nineteenth century by no means all Czech artists and intellectuals, not to speak of the populace, were content to let their identities be thus defined, least of all by a man who had spent a quarter century living abroad. In October 1895, while Mucha was reaping plaudits for "Gismonda" in Paris, F. X. Šalda, F. V. Krejčí, J. S. Machar (1864–1932), Otakar Březina (1868–1929), and other literary Young Turks published a "Manifesto of Czech Modernism" [*Manifest české moderny*] in Prague. One of the targets of this patricidal proclamation was Jaroslav Vrchlický, who had first coined the term "*česká moderna*" as an abusive epithet, and whose 527 poems published in the first thousand issues of *Zlatá Praha* were to be proudly instanced a few years later as testimony to that magazine's indelible Czechness. Not unlike Bedřich Smetana in music, Vrchlický had sought to provide Czech literature with native exemplars of all poetic forms from the sonnet to the epic (which, paradoxically, made him extremely sensitive to the latest literary trends abroad).

Šalda and company roundly denounced "old directions" in art and politics alike, demanding universal suffrage, workers' rights, and "entry into cultural and social life for women." In art the manifesto stood for "individualism." Mocking "imitation national songs, versified folkloristic baubles," "Hey Slaving," and "Where is my home-ing,"[1] it took a decidedly heretical position on the national question:

> In no way do we accentuate Czechness [*českost*]: be yourself and you will be Czech. . . . We have no fear for our tongue. We are nationally so far advanced, that no power in the world can tear it away from us. Its preservation is not for us an aim, but a means to higher ends. That is why we condemn the brutality perpetrated by the German side under the slogan of nationality exactly as we would were it to be perpetrated by us. . . . We will seek mutual understanding with our German countrymen. . . . Do we count the workers as part of the nation? Even when they proclaim that they are internationalist? Yes. Nationality is not a patent of the Young Czechs or the Old Czechs.[2]

Before long events bore out the currency of the social issues the manifesto had so rudely laid on the table. On 28 November 1905 a general strike in support of universal suffrage culminated in a demonstration of over two hundred thousand people on Staroměstské náměstí.

A more sustained attempt to modernize the national discourse, published a year before the *Manifest české moderny*, was Tomáš Masaryk's much-debated *The Czech Question*. Masaryk rejected "historicism" in favor of what he called "realism." He did not deny the importance of history to modern Czech self-awareness, describing Palacký's *History* as "a national act" that "made us aware of the meaning of our history in its full extent—he presented the endeavors of our Czech Brethren to us as our ideal, he showed us Kollár's philosophical and Slavonic idea as a Czech idea, as our true national program."[3] But Masaryk also wished to move beyond this grounding of modern Czech identity in a recaptured past. "History is really the teacher of life and must be so for us more than for others. And so it was—but the main teacher of life is the present, life itself. And it cannot be denied that thus far we have been more diverted from the present toward the past than is good for us, and this one-sidedness hides a serious danger for the national cause. Šafařík and Kollár one-sidedly turn our minds to the Slavonic past; Palacký only in part rectifies this one-sidedness, in that he shows us a Czech past. But above all we need comprehension of the present."[4]

Masaryk is quite candid about the nature of his own historical excursions. "I occupied myself with history and relics from past times," he says, "always only as backing and proof for my sociological observations."[5] Dismissive of the "empiricism" of historians, he favors what he calls an "organic" appropriation of history from the standpoint of the needs of the here and now. He sees the significance of Hus, the Brethren, and Komenský as lying chiefly in their opposition to clerical obscurantism and their anticipations of modern humanism; he marginalizes aristocratic land patriotism because of its lack of any specifically Czech content; he prefers Dobrovský to Jungmann for his more scientific temperament. He contrasts Havlíček and Palacký in terms of their "progressiveness":

Havlíček was more democratic and as a matter of fact more populist [*lidovější*] than Palacký. Palacký tried not only in theory . . . but also in practice to come to an agreement with the Czech nobility, the bearers of political power; he was socially more conservative, as is most clearly witnessed by his rejection of universal suffrage. Against this Havlíček, although he adhered to older national-economic views, was in favor of universal suffrage. Havlíček is more progressive, Palacký more conservative. This connects . . . with the fact that Palacký inclined to historicism, Havlíček to realism. Palacký makes an attempt to reconcile historical right with natural right, Havlíček did not have to undertake this attempt. Palacký in practice and in theory made concessions to the nobility and sometimes even to their clerical conservatism and reaction, concessions which on the basis of his philosophical views he ought not to have made. Havlíček was more nationalist, Palacký was more for state right, which was political in its essentials. That is why Havlíček wrote only in Czech, Palacký wrote in German as well, and spoke both German and Czech in parliament.[6]

This is a relentlessly present-centered and future-oriented appropriation of the past.

This was not the only respect in which *The Czech Question* foreshadows positions that Czech communists were later to take to their logical conclusions. Masaryk's own reconstruction of Czech nationalism focused on the people, understood through modern socioeconomic categories. He was no Marxist—his book *The Social Question* [*Otázka sociální*, 1898] is among the classic critiques of historical materialism—but he held that in "the social question" is "the kernel and the only resolution of the Czech question."[7] Discussing nineteenth-century Czech literature, he praises Němcová, Světlá, Neruda, and others for the "social direction" of their work. "Especially Neruda," he says, "renders several types of Czech individual in a masterly fashion and is a hitherto unsurpassed Czech and Slavonic poet, Slavonic because he is Czech, and Czech because he is popular and directly social." "In place of pre-Kollárian and Kollárian patriotism and Slavism, younger writers and poets . . . are seeking a more concrete Czech human being, and they are naturally discovering him in the Czech countryside and in those classes of the people who were least touched by cultural development. It is a healthy direction, a more popular direction, nationality is perceived as the popular. In the popular [*lidovost*], Czechness [*českost*] and Slavness [*slovanskost*] are definite, concrete, living."[8] He adds that "on the artistic side *lidovost* manifests itself as realism," a view that would not have been at all out of place in the Stalinist 1950s.[9] Masaryk is much less enamored of Czech progress in the visual arts, noting that many Czech artists are trained abroad and sponsored by foreigners. He tartly observes that "a historical and patriotic picture is not always Czech and really national. . . . The historical subject, even if it is patriotic, of course does not in any way guarantee a real national character."[10]

A year later, in *Our Current Crisis* [*Naše nynější krize*], Masaryk summarized his overall conception of the modern evolution of Czech nationality thus:

> I showed in *The Czech Question* how among us *the idea of nationality* gradually through the development of the revival *altered*, in such a way that the nation always more and more came democratically and more certainly to understand itself as *the people* [*lid*], that it comprehended itself in popular terms; I showed that this is not merely a change of terminology. From these reasons and causes the concept of *the state* has similarly altered, so that today among us, as elsewhere, we comprehend the state too *not only democratically* [*demokraticky*] *but popularly* [*lidově*]. Against the older constitutional liberalism we today formulate

our more correct modern viewpoint in the statement: we must *socialize* politics and the state. With this we are consciously resisting two tenets of liberalism: on the one hand the omnipotence of the state, which was adopted by liberalism from absolutism and reaction, and on the other we understand socialization not only as *the broadening of political rights to the widest layers* (which is already happening), but principally that the state and political work has to have regard for *the needs of all classes* and of course those of the biggest class of *the people*.[11]

Masaryk's successor as president and fellow sociologist Edvard Beneš was later to use the same contrast of *"demokracie"* and *"lidovláda"* (people's government) in his justification of the 1945 Košice Program, which laid the groundwork for the 1948 communist coup.[12] One issue, however, on which Masaryk did sharply disagree with socialists of his day was whether Czech workers were, in fact, "internationalist." "I am convinced," he wrote, "that our bourgeois society is not any more national than the working class, if indeed it is not less national."[13] His remained emphatically a national program.

One of the issues underlying the many splits between traditionalists and modernists in Czech artists' societies in the early years of this century was artistic cosmopolitanism versus cultural nationalism.[14] The Osma (the Eight), who first exhibited together in Prague in 1907, included both Czech and German-Jewish artists. Their most favorable review came not from Czech circles but from the Prague Jewish writer Max Brod (1884–1968), who was later responsible for bringing international attention not only to Franz Kafka but also to Leoš Janáček. He hailed "a spring in Prague" and expressed the hope that "some Berlin gallery, like Cassirer, might open its space to this rich new art."[15] More typical of Czech establishment reaction was that of Arnošt Procházka, who greeted the group's second exhibition the next year in *Moderní revue* (*Modern Review*) with the comment "these pictures do not belong to creative art."[16] The Osma and its successor the Skupina výtvarných umělců (the Group of Fine Artists), who seceded from SVU Mánes in 1911, marked the eruption of the modern international currents of fauvism, expressionism, and cubism into Czech cultural life. Many great names of twentieth-century Czech art got their start here. The painters Bohumil Kubišta, Emil Filla, and Vincenc Beneš were members of the Osma, the sculptor Oto Gutfreund, the painters Josef Čapek and Václav Špála, and the architects Josef Chochol, Pavel Janák, and Josef Gočár leading figures in the Skupina.

A series of major art exhibitions in Prague brought contemporary westerly influences home. The Rodin exhibition of 1902 and the Munch exhibition of 1905, both of which were organized by SVU Mánes, had a huge impact on younger Czech artists.[17] The society also showed "French Impressionists" (including Cézanne, Gauguin, and Van Gogh, with a catalogue introduced by F. X. Šalda) in 1907, and "*Les Indépendants*" (among them Bonnard, Braque,

Maillol, Matisse, Vlaminck, Redon, and most controversially Derain, whose "Bathers" caused the biggest storm) in 1910.[18] "Then I took the notion," recalled Emil Filla later, "that Derain's picture—it cost 800 crowns—should be kept for Prague. So we went around the cafés with a subscription form and collected five-to-ten crowns, until we had gotten together the 800 crowns."[19] The Skupina's third exhibition, in April 1913, took place in Munich; its fourth, in Prague the following month, included five Derains, eleven Braques, nine Picassos, and two canvases by Juan Gris. One of the city's last prewar exhibitions, the "Survey of Modern Art" staged by SVU Mánes in 1914, introduced to the Czech public, among other artists, Robert Delaunay, Archipenko, Piet Mondrian, and Constantin Brancusi.[20]

A Czech "futurist" manifesto entitled "Opened Windows," signed by the poet Stanislav Kostka Neumann (1875–1947) and published in August 1913 as a feuilleton in the newspaper *Lidové noviny*, captures something of the irreverent modernism of the younger generation:

> Long live:
> the liberated word, the new word, fauvism, expressionism, cubism, pathetism, dramatism, orphism, paroxysm, dynamism, plastic art, onomatopoeism, the poetry of noise, the civilization of inventions and of journeys of discovery!
> Long live:
> machinism, sports fields, Frištenský, the Českomoravská Machine-Tools Works, the Central Slaughterhouse, Laurin and Klement, the crematorium, the future cinema, the Circus Henry, the military concert on Střelecký Island and in Stromovka Park, the World Exhibition, railroad stations, artistic advertisements, steel and concrete!

Among the even longer list of things Neumann prescribes "Death To!" are "folklore, Moravian-Slovak embroidery, Alfons Mucha [and] old Prague sentimentality."[21] Frištenský was a renowned Czech boxer, Laurin and Klement the earliest Czech automobile manufacturer; their cars and motorcycles were displayed prominently at the first Prague international automobile exhibition held on Žofín Island in 1904. The first Czech football club, AC Královské Vinohrady, later AC Sparta Praha, dated from 1893; a tennis club had been founded a year earlier; the city had ten ice hockey clubs by 1908.[22] The Central Slaughterhouse was built in Holešovice in 1895. This "futurist" manifesto, of course, is not entirely serious. It departs from the values and demeanor of the Generation of the National Theater as much in that fact as it does in its celebration of these everyday ephemera of modernity.

By the time Czechoslovakia became independent in 1918 Jaroslav Hašek (1883–1923), whose genius Brod was also among the few to recognize, was speaking with a very different voice in his *Good Soldier Švejk* from that sentimentally ascribed to the *český lid* in the previous century. Hašek was doing the exact opposite of what Medek claimed for Mácha, or Rieger for the Czech

21. Josef Čapek's linocut "Children Under a Lamp," 1919.

balls. Scurrilous, vulgar, profane, he took the Czech language back from the "salons of the educated," which he detested, to the barracks, the brothels, and the bars.[23] In the two upcoming volumes of *Švejk*, he promised readers in the pugnacious epilogue to the first volume, "The soldiers and civilian population will go on talking and acting as they do in real life. . . . this novel is neither a handbook of drawing-room refinement nor a teaching manual of expressions to be used in polite society. It is a historical picture of a certain period of time." He continues: "We cannot expect the inn-keeper Palivec to speak with the same refinement as Mrs Laudová, Doctor Guth, Mrs Olga Fastrová and a whole series of others who would like to turn the whole Czechoslovak Republic into a big salon with parquet flooring, where people go about in tail-coats, white ties and gloves, speak in choice phrases and cultivate the refined behavior of the drawing-room. But beneath this camouflage these drawing-room lions indulge in the worst vices and excesses."[24]

Palivec is arrested at the beginning of the novel for referring in the hearing of a secret policeman to the circumstance of flies shitting on the portrait of Emperor Franz Josef that used to hang in his bar. The name of Palivec's pub, "The Chalice" [*U kalicha*], should also perhaps give us pause for thought.

There is nothing remotely heroic about Švejk; he accommodates, he lacks principles, and mostly he triumphs by feigning stupidity. Then as later, Hašek's portrayals of Czech character were not always appreciated among the "cultivated." Such tensions continued into the first republic. Karel Čapek writes respectfully enough about Josef Mánes in 1920, but he cannot resist pointing out that in the same year as Mánes was painting his folksy calendar disk for the astronomical clock in Prague, Manet was scandalizing Paris with his "Olympia."[25] Ferdinand Peroutka's *What We Are Like* [*Jací jsme*, 1923], which he calls "polemics against some popular ideas about the Czech national character," dissects and dismisses just about every nineteenth-century shibboleth of Czech identity. He concludes that "humanity" [or humaneness; *humanita*] cannot be a specifically Slavic virtue because "it is a thing as civil and international as the telegraph and telephone."[26] This is a perfect foil to the subtitle of the last picture of Alfons Mucha's *Slovanská epopej*.

Small wonder that Mucha's young wife Maruška (Marie) Chytilová, a Czech art student twenty years his junior whom he married in 1906, sought to temper his distant patriotic enthusiasm with the observation "You write about 'the people' [*lid*]. Darling, 'the people' is either too broad or too narrow a conception."[27] In December 1909 she warned him, "You haven't lived in Bohemia so long, you don't know how things have changed."[28] During his twenty-five years away, Mucha's patriotism never wavered. But this patriotism became petrified by exile, increasingly identified with static symbols of Czech nationality while ever more cut off from the realities of the rapidly changing Czech lands. Mucha was in fact utterly removed from Czech art in Bohemia, and could comprehend its contemporary development only in terms of national betrayal. "In twenty years of service to the foreign master and foreign models," he wrote later, "the old, original tradition and the ancient, unadulterated, exquisite forms were almost forgotten. . . . since 1900 the Czech nation has had no art of its own."[29] Such sentiments were scarcely calculated to endear Mucha to an avant-garde who saw what he viewed as the "organic evolution" of the "national tradition" as merely the empty recycling of outmoded kitsch. It might indeed be argued that a truly distinctive Czech modern art first emerged with the Osma exhibition in 1907. That same year, in as telling an illustration of changing times, the nationalist Young Czech party, which had dominated official Czech political life for three decades, went down to humiliating defeat in the first Bohemian elections fought on universal manhood suffrage by opponents who appealed to the interests of class rather than nation. The Social Democrats took 39.8

percent of Czech votes, the Agrarians 22 percent, the Young Czechs only 11.3 percent. Results were similar in the last prewar elections of 1911.[30]

What made things worse for Alfons Mucha was his very fame. He was not just (from the point of view of those who saw themselves as "progressive") a living anachronism. His stature was such that he was still in a position to insinuate his own conceptions of Czechness into the fabric of everyday life: in his banknotes, his postage stamps—of which the far from radical magazine *Umění* (*Art*) wrote in 1919 that they pleased nobody[31]—and his decorations for public buildings, for example. His patriotic idealism was interpreted as arrogance. When he was offered the contract to decorate Obecní dům in 1909, Mucha himself saw this as an opportunity to "serve his nation" and demanded that the fee be calculated in such a way that he make no personal gain from the venture ("The very thought of deriving profit from the sacred cause was always abhorrent to me"). He also saw the commission as a chance to fight against what he persisted in viewing as "the Germanization of Prague through the Secession."[32] But all hell broke loose in Prague itself, where more bread-and-butter concerns were at stake. SVU Mánes and Jednota umělců výtvarných (the Union of Fine Artists)[33] unleashed a vicious campaign, supported almost unanimously in the Czech press, in which Mucha was accused of using his international renown to prevent local talent from reaping its just rewards.

In the end a compromise was patched up. Mucha got to decorate the Lord Mayor's Hall, and the rest of the building was entrusted to prominent domestic artists. Among them were Aleš, Švabinský, and Ženíšek, by now scarcely avant-garde painters. Švabinský's two lunettes, bearing the title "Czech Spring" [*České jaro*], portray cultural giants of the nineteenth-century Czech renaissance: Myslbek, Aleš, Mánes, Smetana, and Dvořák; Svatopluk Čech, the novelist and poet Julius Zeyer, Vrchlický, Neruda, and (looking improbably demure beneath her parasol) Božena Němcová.[34] But such iconographies were already rapidly becoming passé. Obecní dům was the last major Secession building to go up in Prague; younger architects and artists were moving toward a different kind of spring, and one that was not very evidently or self-consciously Czech. Prime examples of the new modernist sensibility are Josef Gočár's department store "At the Black Mother of God" (1911–12) on the corner of Ovocný trh and the mainly baroque Celetná ulice, Josef Chochol's celebrated apartment block on Neklanova ulice beneath Vyšehrad (1913), and Pavel Janák's gracefully undulating Hlávka Bridge (1909–11), whose pillars are adorned with Oto Gutfeund's reliefs. All are cubist in inspiration and were, in their time, internationally pioneering in design. Cubism was to leave as deep an imprint on Prague's architecture as on that of any city in the world.[35]

The Obecní dům episode is symptomatic of the difficulties of Mucha's

22. Josef Chochol's cubist apartment block on Neklanova ulice, Vyšehrad, 1913.

position—and his patriotism. In 1916 František Ženíšek died, leaving vacant a professorship at the Academy of Fine Arts. Mucha was turned down by the Viennese authorities because "it would be like naming Kramář for it."[36] Karel Kramář (1860–1937) was a Young Czech leader (and earlier a cofounder with Tomáš Masaryk of the Realist party) who preached a modernized pan-Slavism [novoslovanství] and in that spirit had convened a Slavonic Congress in Prague in 1908. An organizer of the domestic resistance against Vienna during World War I, he was then under sentence of death for treason. Amnestied the next year, he went on to lead the National Committee that proclaimed Czech independence on 28 October 1918, and was chosen as Czechoslovakia's first prime minister. He did not last long in the job, losing out to a red-green coalition of Social Democrats and Agrarians the following July. But Mucha was not to be given a chair at the Academy under the Czechoslovak Republic either. Like Kramář, who never again sat in government, he seemed out of place among the new realities of national independence, a throwback to a time whose mantras had lost their meaning.

When the first eleven pictures of the *Slovanská epopej* were shown at the Brooklyn Museum in New York in 1921, there were over six hundred thousand visitors and critical reaction was almost universally ecstatic. In Prague two years previously the critical reception had been lukewarm, and downright hostile from the modernists. The same thing happened when the completed cycle was ceremonially exhibited at Veletržní palác in 1928.[37] Though gifted by Mucha to Prague, the *Slovanská epopej* never found a permanent exhibition site in his lifetime (nor, in Prague, since). The fact is that whatever may have been his own "feeling, conviction, and patriotism," the Alfons Mucha who returned to Bohemia in 1910 in many ways *was* Czech only by birth and origin—less because he had changed while wandering lost through alien lands than because he had not. His compatriots—or, at least, the modernists among them—no longer recognized themselves in his "work for the nation." It was an image, an identification, out of kilter.

Guten Tag und auf Wiedersehen

The social and economic profile of the Czechoslovak Republic that arose from the ashes of World War I did not remotely correspond to the portrait that had been painted, even then inaccurately, at the Czechoslavic Ethnographic Exhibition a quarter century before. Czechoslovakia was by now home to some three-fifths of the industrial capacity of the former Austrian Empire, and the bulk of these mines and factories were situated in the Czech lands. In 1921 industry employed 50.7 percent of the workforce in Czech Silesia, 41 percent in Bohemia, and 35 percent in Moravia.[38] The workers referred to in the Manifesto of Česká moderna were not just a figment of "progressive" intellectuals' imagination. For much of the interwar period they had real enough grievances, and these soon found political expression. The years immediately following World War I were economically extremely grim. A letter of 19 March 1920 from U.S. President Herbert Hoover thanks Adolf Kašpar (1877–1934), a much-loved illustrator of Božena Němcová's *Babička* and several of Alois Jirásek's novels, for a watercolor entitled "We Gratefully

iii Czechoslovakia between the world wars, 1918–38 borders

Remember Mr. Hoover over the Ocean." The picture is bucolic in its imagery. But the gratitude was for gifts of food and clothing to the value of over six million dollars from the American Relief Administration to the charity Czechoslovak Child Relief [*Československá péče o dítě*] chaired by Tomáš Masaryk's daughter Alice, which went largely to alleviate urban misery.

Czechoslovak Child Relief maintained 2,613 soup kitchens in the Czechoslovak Republic during 1919–20 and fed 500,000 children daily on its rations of milk, rice, fat, and flour.[39] Finance Minister Alois Rašín's savagely deflationary policies stabilized the crown, but at considerable cost to ordinary people. Like Karel Kramář, Rašín (1867–1923) had been condemned to death for treason in 1916, and was one of the "Men of 28 October" who fashioned Czechoslovak independence two years later. He was nevertheless to die at the hands of a Czech anarchist assassin in Prague in 1923. It took until 1925 to recover prewar levels of manufacturing output. Rapid growth in living standards thereafter was halted by the onset of the Great Depres-

sion. Unemployment was below 50,000 in 1929; by March of 1933, over 978,000 people were officially registered as jobless. The count remained above half a million until 1937.[40] It is not surprising that through these two decades many Czechs supported parties that regarded national independence less as an end in itself than as the starting point for another kind of social reconstruction. Dissatisfaction with a merely nationalist agenda had already been voiced before the war in electoral support for the Social Democrats, and that war, as elsewhere in Europe, rewrote the script of left politics. The echo now being heard from Russia was not that of Čelakovský's lidové písně but Lenin's lidová revoluce.

Tomáš Masaryk's Czechoslovakia was launched on a promise not just of national independence but also of social justice. A number of radical social reforms were pushed through parliament in the foundational years of the Czechoslovak state. Not only was the Habsburg succession repudiated, so was the ancient Bohemian monarchy itself. The reborn national state would be a modern democratic republic. German and Austrian monopolies were nationalized, the working day limited to eight hours, and state unemployment benefits established. Aristocratic titles were abolished. Landed estates were broken up (the limit on ownership was 150 hectares of agricultural land and 250 hectares of land of any kind) and redistributed among smallholders; the Czech nobility were amply repaid for their perceived lack of patriotism in the past. The Czech Social Democrats won the 1920 national elections with 25.7 percent of the vote, almost twice as much as their nearest rivals the Agrarians, who polled 13.6 percent; third were the German Social Democrats with 11.1 percent.[41] Altogether left parties took 47.5 percent of the votes cast. Soon afterward the Czech Social Democrats split. The year ended with a general strike led by the Marxist wing of the party that some hoped to turn into a social revolution on the Bolshevik model. Red guards occupied factories, railroad stations, and other buildings, and martial law was proclaimed in Moravia. The strike was put down only at the cost of several lives in Prague, the northern Bohemian town of Most (where nine people were killed), and elsewhere.

In 1921 the Marxist faction of the Social Democrats officially reconstituted themselves as the Communist party of Czechoslovakia [*Komunistická strana Československa*, hereafter KSČ]. The KSČ gained 13.2 percent of the vote and 41 seats in the 1925 national election, making it the second largest party behind the Agrarians, who took 13.7 percent of the vote and got 46 seats. In the Prague local elections in 1923 the KSČ received 70,202 votes (19.17 percent of the total cast) and took 73 out of 318 seats on the city's borough councils.[42] Many of these representatives were, indeed, sons and daughters of the working class. In Prague VIII (Libeň, Bohnice, Kobylisy, Střížkov, Troja-Podhoří), for example, nine out of twenty-four council members were communists. The first deputy mayor, Antonín Trousel, was a typographer. Josef Červenka and Čeněk Hruška describe themselves simply as "workers" [*dělníci*], the one woman elected, Františka Štěpánková, gives no occupation. Josef Hejna was a locksmith, Jan Kocourek an instrument maker, Rudolf Luskacz a factory clerk, František Mach a lathe operator, Antonín Pech a leather dyer.[43]

Although the KSČ never took part in any of the coalitions that governed interwar Czechoslovakia, it remained one of the strongest political parties throughout the first republic. In the 1925 election it received 933,000 votes, in 1929, 753,000, and in 1935, 849,000. The communists' claim that they, and the working classes for whom they spoke, were nonetheless systematically excluded from the political nation during these years was not implausible. The weakness of all the parties individually—none took more than 15.2 percent of the vote in the 1925, 1929, or 1935 national elections, and that percentage was gained by Konrad Henlein's separatist Sudeten German party in 1935[44]—dictated coalition as the normal form of government. The effect was to leave that government in the hands of a remarkably stable oligarchy of party leaders. Edvard Beneš (1884–1948), a National Socialist, remained foreign minister from 1918 until he succeeded Tomáš Masaryk as president in December 1935, despite fourteen changes of administration. The so-called Pětka (the Five), an informal grouping of the leaders of five major parties intended to manage relations between them and hammer out a common agenda for government, was one instrument through which this stability was maintained. Set up in 1920, its original members were Antonín Švehla for the Agrarians, Alois Rašín for the National Democrats, Jan Šrámek for the People's party, Rudolf Bechyně for the Social Democrats, and Jiří Stříbrný for the National Socialists. It was not difficult for the communists to portray Czechoslovakian parliamentary democracy as an exclusive bourgeois dance, whose invisible conductor was the Živnostenská Bank.

Communism was not simply some alien ideology imported into Czechoslovakia after World War II on the heels of the Red Army, whatever was agreed at Yalta regarding spheres of influence (and whatever may have been the case elsewhere in central and eastern Europe). It had strong indigenous roots in the (real) *český lid*, and it especially thrived among organized manual workers. In the working-class districts of Prague VIII (Libeň), IX (Vysočany), and XI (Žižkov), the KSČ gained less than 20 percent of the vote only once during interwar elections (14.09 percent in Žižkov in 1931). More often its totals were closer to 30 percent. In 1923 the KSČ polled over 36 percent in Prague VIII and IX. In the last prewar borough elections in May and June of 1938, it took 18.42 percent of all Prague votes and won 69 out of 366 seats; in no Prague district did it receive less than 10 percent of the ballot.[45] People had no reason to be deluded as to what they were supporting when they voted communist. At its founding congress in 1921 the KSČ accepted the twenty-one conditions for entry into the Communist International, and a thoroughgoing "Bolshevization" of the party was carried through under its leader Klement Gottwald (1896–1953) in 1929.

Gottwald made KSČ objectives, and loyalties, abundantly clear in his maiden speech to the Czechoslovak parliament on 21 December that year. They were not conspicuously patriotic. The party held other social solidarities to be more binding than nationality:

> You say finally, that we are under the command of Moscow and that we go there to get our savvy. Well! It's like this: you are under the command of the Živnobanka [the Živnostenská Bank]. . . . And we, we are the party of the Czechoslovak proletariat and our highest revolutionary headquarters really is Moscow. And we go to Moscow to learn, you know what? We go to Moscow to learn from the Russian Bolsheviks how to wring your necks. (Shouts) And you know the Russian Bolsheviks are masters in that. (Noise, shouts). . . . The working people will recognize that it is necessary and possible to completely settle accounts with

your regime: by armed uprising, social revolution, dictatorship of the proletariat. . . . We will pursue this struggle regardless of sacrifice, doggedly, single-
mindedly, until your lordship is swept away.[46]

Side by side with tensions of class, interwar Czechoslovakia was riven by
fault lines of ethnicity. The Czechoslovak state set up in 1918 contained
6,800,000 Czechs, 3,124,000 Germans, 1,967,000 Slovaks, 745,000 Hungarians, 462,000 Ruthenes, Ukrainians, and Russians, 181,000 Jews (345,000
if reckoned by religion rather than declarations of Jewish as a nationality),
76,000 Poles, and a smaller number of Rumanians, "gypsies," and others.[47]
Czechs themselves formed a bare majority (51 percent) of the population,
while people of "Czechoslovak" nationality (that is, Czechs and Slovaks put
together) made up only two-thirds of the republic's inhabitants. This mélange
is described by one Western historian of Czechoslovakia as "a curious creation, similar in composition to the defunct Habsburg Monarchy, only on a
microscopic scale. . . . from the beginning in 1918, it was obvious that minority problems and conflicts would be inherited from the Monarchy."[48] But
this misses an important point. For Austria-Hungary was not a nation-state,
but a dynastic ᵉmpire. First, within it no single ethnic group constituted a
demographic majority. Second (and crucially), the monarchy's legitimacy as a
polity was never predicated upon a claim to be the state of any single nation;
Emperor Franz Josef used to begin his addresses "To my nations . . . "
Czechoslovakia was completely different. Although its creation was in part
an artifact of Allied diplomacy, its animating ideas and its entire legitimacy
derived from precisely such a claim.[49] The difficulty was that the nation in
question was—in practice—the *Czech* nation, and the cultural boundaries of
this imagined community had come to be rather sharply drawn over the
preceding century to exclude, in varying degrees, 49 percent of the population now governed from Prague. They became "minorities" not because of
their numbers alone, but because nationality and statehood had become intertwined in a new way. Consider, for instance, so mundane a moment of
state as Alfons Mucha's postage stamps. For whom, exactly, were Hradčany
and the Hussites' chalice meaningful symbols of identity?

Certainly not the 23.3 percent of Czechoslovakia's population who in the
1921 census asserted their nationality to be German. In Bohemia the proportion of self-described Germans was still higher, at 32.6 percent, or one in
every three people.[50] Their incorporation into the new state had been reluctant. The day after Czechoslovak independence was declared in 1918, the
Bohemian-German representatives at the imperial parliament in Vienna invoked the same right to national self-determination as had been pleaded by
the Czechs and Slovaks, and proclaimed the establishment of the independent province of Deutschböhmen in the German-majority regions of northern Bohemia. An independent Sudetenland in northern Moravia, Deutsch-

südmähren in southern Moravia, and Böhmerwaldgau in southern Bohemia followed within days. Vienna recognized these as part of Austria, claiming also the German "islands" around Brno, Olomouc, and Jihlava. After negotiations broke down, taking its stand on "historic state right" the Czech government decided to occupy the *pohraničí* by force. Most was retaken on 29 November, Liberec on 14 December, Znojmo on 16 December, and Opava on 18 December. By the end of 1918, the whole of the "historic Czech lands" were once again in Czech hands, but bitterness persisted. Czech troops broke up a demonstration in Most on 4 March 1919, killing forty Germans.

Richard Weiner, Paris correspondent of the Brno newspaper *Lidové noviny*, relates a chance encounter in what was soon to be renamed the Square of the Republic [*náměstí Republiky*] but was then still Franz Josef Square, which says much about the atmosphere in Prague at the time:

> Monday, 28 October [1918], evening.
>
> In front of Obecní dům, now the seat of the National and Military Committee [i.e., the domestic interim government], I meet a German acquaintance. It is drizzling and he muffles himself up in his overcoat.
>
> "How are you? What do you say to all this?"
>
> "My sister cried bitterly when she heard that Austria has collapsed."
>
> On this day not a word of German was to be heard. Not until Wednesday did the Germans take their mother tongue into the streets again. We too spoke with Germans that we knew in Czech.
>
> Motorized units, scouts, Sokols sped in front of Obecní dům, soldiers crossed and passed. An elegant limousine drew up, two generals got out and took themselves off to the National Committee.
>
> How did the German take this? It looked as if he felt foreign, and a sort of hostage. I took a notion to relieve his feeling of loneliness. When we parted, I said to him: "*Guten Tag und auf Wiedersehen.*"
>
> "Thank you," he replied in Czech, and his eyes said that he was thanking me for more than just the greeting.[51]

Richard Weiner (1884–1937) himself is a thoroughly, sadly Bohemian figure. A poet, though one who received little honor in his own land, he moved to Paris in 1912, where (the war years apart) he remained until 1936. It was he who first brought together the young French painters who then called themselves Les Simplistes and the Czech artist Josef Šíma to form the group Le Grand Jeu in 1927. Returning to Prague, gravely ill, in 1936, he died an anonymous death the following year. "Neither a Jew, nor a Czech, nor a German, nor a Frenchman," he once wrote of himself.[52]

In fact the Czechoslovak Republic, unlike many other states in the region, went to some lengths to guarantee minority rights. The language law of 1920—which was counted as part of the constitution—allowed national minorities to use their own tongue in dealings with officialdom in all the administrative districts where they made up 20 percent of the population. Germans had their own schools, universities, press, theaters, and other institutions, and German political parties had ministers in most interwar cabinets. Tomáš Masaryk refused ever again to set foot in the Stavovské divadlo after its occupation in 1920. But none of this overcame the basic alienation inherent in the very conception of a state that was Czechoslovak in name and for the most part Czech in substance. The more heavily industrialized German north suffered disproportionately during the Great Depression, and popular anger was mostly vented in the shape of ethnic politics, especially after the Nazi triumph in Germany in 1933. Konrad Henlein's Sudeten German party, which sought unification of the *pohraničí* with the Third Reich, received 67.4 percent of all German votes in the national election of 1935.[53]

Nationality problems were not confined to the German minority. Although centered on the historic lands of Bohemia, Moravia, and what was left of Czech Silesia, the Czechoslovak Republic also embraced two large regions that had never been part of the domains of the medieval Czech crown, Slovakia and Podkarpatská Rus. Its borders extended almost a thousand kilometers east of Prague to the Ukraine. The populations of these newly acquired territories presented different problems than did Czechoslovakia's Germans, but problems that were to prove no less intractable for the putative nation-state. During the nineteenth and early twentieth centuries Slovaks had frequently been incorporated within the discourse of Czech nationalism. A nice example is the magazine *Naše Slovensko* (*Our Slovakia*), published in Prague from 1907 and written for the most part in Czech. We have seen Havlíček's earlier characterization of Slovaks as "Czechs in Slovakia." Mikoláš Aleš and Josef Mánes both traveled through Slovakia in search of the popular; Mánes's "Slovak Family" is one of his most celebrated pictures.[54] Božena Němcová's ethnographic travelogues encompass Slovakia as well as Bohemia and Moravia; the Czechoslavic Ethnographic Exhibition displayed Slovak "national costumes" beside their Bohemian and Moravian counterparts.[55] The historical connections between Slovakia and the Czech lands were nonetheless far more tenuous than was generally much acknowledged at the time on either side. This mattered because historical reminiscence had become a defining ingredient in Czech national self-imagery. Czechs might conceive the establishment of the Czechoslovak Republic as renewal of statehood. Slovakia, however, had been an integral part of the Kingdom of Hungary for a millennium. The sovereignty being renewed was not a Slovak sovereignty, and its historical symbols did not speak to Slovak experience. Jan Hus was not a Slovak hero nor Bílá hora a Slovak tragedy; Saint Stephen meant more to most Slovaks than Saint Václav. Such commonalities as there were between Czechs and Slovaks rested on the flimsy foundations of linguistic kinship and pan-Slavist sentiment, and like pan-Slavist ideology itself were mostly of comparatively recent historical origin.

The gap was bridged, when it was bridged at all, mainly in the biographies of prominent—and untypical—individuals. Jan Kollár, the Slovak author of *Slávy dcera* who wrote in Czech, is one whom we have met already; Pavel Josef Šafařík, the author of *Slovanské starožitnosti*, is another. Šafařík was born in Slovakia in 1795 and moved to Prague only in 1833. This did not stop *Ottův slovník naučný* from describing him in 1906 as "one of the most remarkable *Czech* men and writers,"[56] a detail that says a lot about the relations between these nations at the time. But to claim Šafařík simply as a Slovak, as communist books of reference do, is just as problematic. For one thing, his books too were written in Czech (or German), for another, what it meant to be Slovak in the mid–nineteenth century is even less clear than what it meant then to be Czech. Palacký spent his youth in Slovakia, though he said of himself that "being Moravian by birth I am Czech by nationality."[57] Masaryk's father was a Slovak, but Tomáš himself was born and raised in Moravia, his mother's country. The Slovak astronomer Milan Rastislav Štefánik (1880–1919) was with Masaryk and Beneš one of the troika who organized the Czechoslovak foreign resistance during World War I. His connection with Slovakia was already by then pretty attenuated: he was educated at Prague's Czech Polytechnic and University from the age of nineteen, emigrated to France in 1904, and became a French citizen in 1912. He was awarded the Legion of Honor and rose in World War I to the rank of a general in the French army. Štefánik became Czechoslovakia's first minister of defense. His death in an air crash in 1919 robbed Slovakia of its most powerful voice in Prague, but just how Slovak that voice would actually have been is open to question.

Czechs and Slovaks indeed had come together in the Czechoslovak Legions, recruited from prisoners, deserters, and émigrés, which by the end of World War I had eighty-five thousand men under arms fighting on the side of the Allies. But the statement in the so-called Washington Declaration of 18 October 1918 that "we demand for Czechs the right to be linked with their Slovak brothers in Slovakia, which once was part of our national state [and] was later torn off from the body of our nation and fifty years ago annexed to the Hungarian state of the Magyars" is historical nonsense, as its signatories Masaryk, Beneš, and Štefánik must have known very well.[58] The last (and only) time Czechs and Slovaks had been part of a common "national" state was during the brief heyday of the Great Moravian Empire during the ninth century, a full thousand years earlier. Josef Pekař acknowledged this in the textbook *Czechoslovak History* [*Dějiny československé*, 1921], which he patriotically wrote for use in first-republic high schools. He tries hard to cover events in Slovakia throughout the book, making it something more than a purely Czech history, but his task is complicated by the fact that after 906, in his own words, "Slovakia was lost to national unity for more than ten centuries."[59] In the case of Podkarpatská Rus, still farther to the east, there were no historical ties to Prague whatsoever. Out of its total population of 606,568 in 1921, there were only 19,737 Czechs and Slovaks, most of whom can safely be assumed to have moved there after 1918.[60] The region was to be unceremoniously annexed by the Soviet Union after World War II, with the unanimous agreement of the Czechoslovak parliament.

As important as the differences in historical experience of Slovakia and the "historic lands" of the Bohemian crown was the enormous gulf between them at independence as kinds of societies. They were two worlds. The Czech lands had all the accoutrements of a modern civil society: large cities and abundant middling-size towns, a literate public, established political parties, trade unions and chambers of commerce, a multitude of voluntary clubs and societies, a vigorous press, universities, high schools, theaters, art galleries, and so on. Poor and rural Slovakia for the most part did not; in particular, it lacked an indigenous educated elite. The same was still more true of Podkarpatská Rus. In 1921 only 14.9 percent of the employed population in Slovakia and 10.5 percent in Podkarpatská Rus worked in industry,[61] as against 60.6 and 66 percent respectively in agriculture and forestry. Figures for agricultural employment in the Czech lands in the same year were 38.6 percent in Moravia, 29.6 percent in Bohemia, and 21.8 percent in Silesia.[62] Twice as many Czechs (45.7 percent) as Slovaks (23.9 percent) then lived in agglomerations of 2,000 inhabitants or more.[63] A decade later, in 1930, of the thirty-eight conurbations of 20,000 or more people in the republic, only six were in Slovakia and two in Podkarpatská Rus. Just two Slovak cities, Bratislava with 142,516 people and Košice with 70,232, and one Ruthenian town, Užhorod with 33,124, contained over 30,000 inhabitants. In the Czech lands at the same date there were twenty such settlements, and Prague had 848,081 people, Brno 263,646, Ostrava 175,056, and Plzeň 121,344.[64] Even these figures do not fully bring out the contrast in modes of life between Czechs and Slovaks, for within Bratislava itself Slovaks were very far from a majority of the population at the time it became the Slovak capital (and acquired its present name). The 1921 census details its ethnic makeup as being 39.75 percent "Czechoslovak," 27.72 percent German, 22.24 percent Hungarian, and 10.29 percent other.[65] Thirty years earlier (when greater Prague's population was already 397,268)[66] there were 52,411 people living in Pressburg, as Bratislava was then called. Only 8,707 of them were Slovaks, a majority of whom would have been in menial occupations.[67] In 1900 the proportion of Slovaks had actually fallen to 14.6 percent.[68]

The Washington Declaration was, however, correct in one particular. It is not just socioeconomic "backwardness" that is indexed here but systematic political repression. From 1867 (when Austria-Hungary officially became a "dual monarchy," leaving Slovakia to be administered entirely from Budapest), the development of any Slovak national consciousness had been actively stunted by deliberate Magyarization. The 1868 Hungarian nationality law defined Hungary as a "single Magyar political nation," rendering the political expression of minority nationality claims potential treason. In 1876 the Slovak patriotic society Matica slovenská (founded in 1862 with similar objectives to its Czech counterpart Matice česká) was abolished and its assets, which according to its articles should have gone to "the Slovak nation" in the event of the association ceasing to function, were turned over to a Magyar patriotic society on the grounds that "the Slovak nation does not exist."[69] The official justification for the Matica's suppression was that "this society from its inception did nothing but endeavor to serve the political movement known throughout the world as pan-Slavism."[70] There were trials of Slovak activists for separatist agitation in 1894, 1899–1900, and 1906. But where Magyarization was most sustained and most devastating in its impact—and where the contrast with Czech experience during the same period is sharpest—was in education.

Of thirty-nine high schools in Slovakia in 1909, not one was teaching in Slovak. Students stood to be expelled from school for "pan-Slavism" if books in Slovak were found in their bags. In 1874–75 the Hungarian government had closed the only three Slovak gymnasia because of their "unpatriotic spirit," and no more Slovak high schools were to be opened until after 1918. At the turn of the century there were all told 4,134 elementary schools in Slovakia; of these, 519 taught in Slovak and another 1,189 taught in a mixture of Slovak and Hungarian. The population at the time was around 55 percent Slovak.[71] In 1902 a new government decree required that a minimum of eighteen hours weekly (that is, between two-thirds and three-quarters of the school week at the time) must be taught in Hungarian in all schools. This was stiffened by a school law of 1904, which allowed for disciplining of teachers who could not prove their competence in Hungarian. After further legislation in 1907 only 344 Slovak elementary schools survived in Slovakia as compared with 3,242 Hungarian,[72] and they were bound by the eighteen-hour rule. Of the six thousand schoolteachers working in Slovakia in 1919 only one-tenth even spoke Slovak; Minister for Slovak Affairs Vavro Šrobár told the Czechoslovak parliament that on independence "we found there perhaps three hundred Slovak elementary school teachers and perhaps twenty Slovak high school teachers who were faithful to their origin."[73] A Hungarian university was established in Pressburg in 1912. It officially became a Slovak institution (with the name Komenský University) in 1919–21, but it is plain that at that date it lacked any infrastructure within the Slovak elementary and secondary school system.

Prague sent in 1,650 Czech schoolteachers in 1919–21, who (so it was officially claimed) were soon teaching fluently in Slovak.[74] Within a few years such efforts were paying off. By 1929 there were 2,830 Slovak elementary [l'udové] schools[75] and 52 Slovak high schools,[76] 4 of them teaching a total of 1,579 pupils in Bratislava alone.[77] But inherent in these achievements was a new source of grievance. Where gymnasium pupils in the Czech lands were required merely to have "acquaintance [*seznámení*] with the major dialects of the Czech [sic] language, especially with literary Slovak," pupils in Slovak high schools were expected to have "knowledge [*znalost*] of literary Czech" in addition to the same acquaintance with the dialects of what is in this case described as "the Czechoslovak language."[78] Like their Czech peers, thirteen-year-old Slovak children had to read Němcová's *Babička*, Svatopluk Čech's *In the Shadow of the Lime Tree* [*Ve stínu lípy*], and Jirásek's *The Dogheads*. Czech boys and girls, however, were not obliged also to read Hviezdoslav and other Slovak writers, as were their Slovak counterparts (who had five hours of language per week to the Czechs' three). Older Czech students read Shakespeare, Mickiewicz, Gogol, and Turgenev, but despite a general instruction that "in all classes appropriate attention should be devoted to Slovak," not a single work in Slovak appears in the list of set books to be read in school or under supervision at home for Czech gymnasia (of 1922) for any grade.[79] In the comparable list for Slovak schools we find, among others, Mácha, Vrchlický, Rais, Světlá, Neruda, Winter, Čelakovský, Machar, Dyk—in short "the whole company of our great minds." Though the lists are not exhaustive, and Czech students would encounter writing in Slovak in their readers, the imbalance is palpable. These syllabi speak to much more.

Inevitably, given the character of Slovak society in 1918, the relationship between the Czech lands and Slovakia was in many respects bound to be effectively a colonial one. In education, as in most other walks of life, Czechs provided the resources and set the agendas for "modernizing" (or, as many of them undoubtedly saw it, "civilizing") Slovakia. Even the Slovak National Theater in Bratislava was founded by a Czech company from Pardubice and long played in Czech for a lack of Slovak actors. A national consciousness itself was something the Czechs felt they had to import into their newly acquired eastern lands. At the end of 1919 the government carried out a census in Slovakia to try to ascertain how many new Slovak schools would be needed. In one enumerator's recollections we catch a distant echo of the Prague census of 1851:

> With the greatest eagerness we anticipated the response to the nationality question. "Are you Slovak?" A blank stare. Excepting one village the answer everywhere was: "I speak both Slovak and Hungarian." "I did not ask which language you speak, but whether you are a Hungarian or a Slovak." Here, as a rule, there ensued a prolonged negotiation. The person had a Slovak name, the children would speak Slovak, the face would be Slovak, and he did not know whether he was a Slovak or a Hungarian.
>
> We devised various criteria: what language they pray in with the children, what language they use at home, what prayer books they use (if literate), and so on, and on this basis we ourselves had to ascribe [literally, write: *napsat*] him a

nationality. Often a horrifying answer would sound: "It's the same difference! If the bread is buttered on the Hungarian side, I am Magyar, if it is buttered on the Czech side, I am Slovak."

We heard this "It's the same difference" [*A to šicko jedno*] so often and in all the villages that it became to us an almost all-embracing characteristic of eastern Slovakia. If you go to one village, then a second and a third, and everywhere you hear that "it is all the same," the horror you experience on behalf of these people will be greater than that you would feel on behalf of those condemned to death.[80]

This says as much about *Czech* understandings of the importance of nationality as a ground of identity by 1919 as it does about the Slovaks; death row is a strong simile. We have come a long way from 1851. The irony, of course, is that the awareness of national identity that Czech paternalism eventually did call forth among Slovaks was not of the sort they had bargained for. It was to be shaped in large part by specifically anti-Czech resentment.

The ubiquitous fiction of a "Czechoslovak" nationality (that is, an ethnic identity of Czechoslovak, as distinct from Czechoslovak state citizenship, which the country's Germans, Hungarians, and so on equally enjoyed) was a fundamental legal category of the first republic. It was sewn, improbably, into the language law, which made "the Czechoslovak language"—an entity whose existence, since Štúr, Czechs and Slovaks are apt equally hotly to deny—into the sole official language of the republic.[81] Official statistics likewise for many purposes simply homogenized Czechs and Slovaks. Part of the rationale behind this unitary category was to represent the state as more coherently national than it in fact was, in order to underline the minority status of the Germans as a Teutonic island within a Slavonic sea. But not only did this hybrid nationality efface Slovak specificities. The very success of nineteenth-century Czech nationalism in reconstituting the subjectivity of the Czech nation meant that the only position available for a "brother Slovak" within this discourse was that of a little brother [*bratříček*]. Czechoslovakia was no tabula rasa. Slovaks were for the most part assimilated into an already existing and institutionally entrenched Czechness, which provided the new state with much of its governing imagery. The heritage in which the Slovaks were expected to feel national pride was essentially Czech. Interwar Czechoslovakia's centralized administrative structures routinized this relationship. Only Podkarpatská Rus had a measure of autonomy, despite guarantees given to the Slovaks in the Pittsburgh Agreement of 30 May 1918 that Slovakia would be given its own administration, parliament, and courts.[82] The justification for reneging on this promise—a not entirely unreasonable one in the circumstances—was that in the absence of an indigenous educated Slovak class, to devolve power to Bratislava would in practice mean to return it to Hungarians or Magyarized Slovaks.[83] Major decisions affecting Slovakia were thus made from Prague, a city whose Slovak population was minuscule; in the entire Czech lands Slovaks made up 0.2 percent of the population in 1921 and 0.4 percent in 1930.[84] There is no need here to trace the long story of twentieth-century Slovak nationalism, whether between the wars or after. Suffice it to record that Andrej Hlinka's separatist Slovak People's party took 28.5 percent of Slovak votes in 1929 and an even higher proportion in 1935.[85]

As for Podkarpatská Rus, a communist deputy complained in parliament on 13 September 1928, a month before the tenth anniversary of Czechoslovak independence was to be lavishly celebrated in Prague, of unprovoked police brutality against Ukrainian workers and peasants in Hust-Boroňava. The cause of this, he said, was "the colonial system, which could not be darker in Africa, and which with its bloodthirsty and sadistic details worthily ranks with the vilest cases of Bulgarian, Rumanian, and Hungarian white terror." His speech was quoted—with a reminder to the censor that such quotations carried parliamentary immunity—in *ReD*, the "Illustrated Monthly for Modern Culture" of the Devětsil group of Prague avant-garde artists and writers. Accompanying it was a photograph of six men, baring their apparently soundly caned buttocks to the camera. Dr. Gáti's speech concluded: "Do then the people of Podkarpatská Rus have reason to celebrate the tenth anniversary of the lordship of the bourgeoisie? Have this people, whose rights of sovereignty were taken away, rights contained in the [Versailles] Peace Treaty and the constitution, whose forests and land the Czech Agrarian party hands over to its vote catchers, whose state citizenship was cast into doubt, whose schools were Czechized, who constantly go hungry, and whose majority is persecuted for its political convictions, do these people have a reason to celebrate?"[86] The cane marks on the photograph look suspiciously painted. Still, the KSČ took 15.2 percent of the vote in Podkarpatská Rus in the national election the following year, its highest total in any of the twenty-two electoral regions of the republic except for Louny in northwestern Bohemia (15.9 percent), and Nové Zámky (16.8 percent) and Košice (15.7 percent) in Slovakia.[87]

The Completion of Saint Vitus's

Such tensions of class and ethnicity did little to inhibit the sewing of a very self-conscious Czechness into the public life of the Czechoslovak Republic, particularly in its earlier years. Popular illustrated magazines like *Český svět* (*The Czech World*) seldom lost an opportunity to cloak that world in a folkloristic garb, and President Masaryk could reliably expect to be greeted by maidens in peasant costume wherever he officially went.[88] The date of the martyrdom of Jan Hus, 6 July, was made a state holiday, and Catholic religious instructors in schools were quietly banned from teaching medieval history.[89] State involvement in the Hus celebrations made papal nuncio Marmaggi quit Prague in protest in 1925, and relations with the Vatican were very sour for two years after. A Universita Karlova was born again in Prague—after 267 years—in February 1920, when the Czech university established in 1882 was declared by the new state to be the sole legitimate successor to Charles IV's medieval foundation and invested with its buildings, archives, registry, "ancient insignia, seals, books, pictures, and other objects of historical note which belonged to Prague university . . . before 1882."[90] This act of legislative fiat masked a turbulent history of anything but institutional continuity; if anything it was the Czech university that was the newcomer. The German university was not allowed to keep the name Karl-Ferdinand University; it was too reminiscent of a more immediate past in need of forgetting.

Sokol's membership exploded from 194,321 on the eve of World War I to 559,026 two years after independence, and 818,642 the year before Munich.[91] So emblematic had the gymnastic society become of the nation that there were proposals to rename the currency the *sokol*, and eminent artists designed coins accordingly.[92] Sokol staged festivals in Prague in 1920—funded by a gift of 2,500,000 crowns and a matching loan from its American branches—and in 1926, 1932, and 1938. These were splendidly national and ostentatiously Slavic occasions. No less than 143,177 gymnasts, including representatives from other Slav countries and soldiers from the armies of the Little Entente,[93] participated in the ninth Sokol jamboree in 1932, which also commemorated the centennial of founder Miroslav Tyrš's birth.[94] For the eighth jamboree six years earlier, Brother Alfons Mucha, as he described himself on the poster he designed for the occasion,[95] was entrusted with organizing a spectacular historical pageant on the Vltava. "The pan-Slavic concept will be there with six of my pictures from the *Epic*. . . . There will be sixty boats which will transport the various scenes, to the accompaniment of music and all kinds of lighting, one by one, down the river to the stage itself, located on Střelecký Island. . . . I only hope it doesn't rain!" It did, and the ensuing chaos was such that the Prague police forbade any such entertainments on the Vltava thereafter.[96]

Prague itself was duly transformed into a national capital after 1918. A law of 6 February 1920, which came into effect on 1 January 1922, linked thirty-eight neighboring communities, among them the hitherto independent cities of Karlín, Smíchov, Žižkov, and Vinohrady, to the existing districts of Prague I to VIII to form Hlavní město Praha, Capital City Prague. The city's official population count therewith expanded from 223,700 (on the 1910 census) to 676,700 (on the 1921 census).[97] Much more was involved here than a mere administrative reorganization, overdue as that might have been. Integration of the Prague conurbation had been a bone of political contention throughout the previous sixty years, in part because of its implications for the bal-

23. Alfons Mucha's design for a thousand-crown bill, 1919.

ance of power between Czechs and Germans, who as we saw earlier were mainly concentrated in the historic parts of the city. The city council's official *Almanac* for 1922, the first to be published since 1914, begins with a preface entitled "Prague the Great" [*Veliká Praha*]. It portrays the previous few decades as a history of unending conflict between "those who had Prague's welfare in mind [and] strove for her to join with neighboring settlements . . . to lay new foundations for the well-being and good fortune of the whole nation" and "the animosity of Vienna and the state, as well as the Germans [who] created obstacles and sought to break the natural development." The capital was unified, it argues, in "repeated hard battles with the wrath of enemies," and through its integration the city could now finally aspire to become "ideally Czech, faithfully republican and really democratic."[98] This overlooks a long history of equally hard battles with Czech suburban administrations, who were loath to surrender their municipal autonomy. Karel Baxa (1863–1938) was the new capital's first lord mayor. He had played a less than savory role in the "ritual murder" trial of Leopold Hilsner in 1899, acting free of charge as a prosecuting lawyer on behalf of the murdered girl's mother.[99] States need capital cities; but this "mighty body, having roots in the people, founded in the spirit of the republican constitution on democratic bases and laws as the powerful capital of the Czechoslovak state, as its expression and support,"[100] was demographically remarkably unrepresentative of those whom it now aspired to represent symbolically. It remained emphatically a Czech capital.

The year 1929 was (perhaps) the thousandth anniversary of the murder of the Czech patron Saint Václav by his brother Boleslav, and in any event provided an excuse to celebrate what the guide to the commemorative exhibition held in the Vladislav Hall of Prague Castle called "our thousand-year culture."[101] Sufficient paraphernalia documenting the Wenceslas cult through the ages—altarpieces, statues, breviaries, coins, medals, and much else—was assembled to fill 104 display cases. Exhibits ranged from eleventh-century illuminated manuscripts to such foreign curiosities as "A Bibliophilic 1927 Christmas Gift of the Artist George F. Trenholm in Boston with the Song 'Good King Wenceslas' and the Etching 'Saint Wenceslas Collects Wood for the Poor.'"[102] Portrayals of the saint from the nineteenth century were plentiful, with Mikoláš Aleš's work much in evidence. So were images of Saint Václav on wood, glass, and other media of *lidové umění*, which "will please our eyes with the charming naïveté with which our people represented to themselves their beloved patron."[103] "Through the image of Saint Václav," according to a long article in *Umění* published for the jubilee, "the Czech nation lived spiritually, and that is why the unique image that it forms is not only a memorial to Saint Václav but also the history and memorial of the nation."[104] Czechoslovak Post issued special stamps with reproductions of paintings of the saintly monarch by Josef Mánes and Mikoláš Aleš to mark the anniversary,[105] and Charles IV's Saint Václav crown, together with the rest of the Bohemian crown jewels, were put on public display in Saint Vitus's Cathedral in Hradčany.

Ordinarily these jewels were kept in a chamber in the cathedral above Saint Václav's Chapel, in a cabinet secured by seven locks whose keys were dispersed among separate guardians. This is a fine example of retouched tradition. The chamber had indeed originally been built in 1380 by the Gothic architect Petr Parléř for the crown jewels, but the jewels themselves had spent little time there since. During the Hussite Wars King Zikmund took them with him to Hungary, from 1436 to 1618 they were kept in Karlštejn Castle, the Thirty Years' War saw them secreted in various hiding places in Prague, and from 1646 to 1791 they languished in the imperial treasury in Vienna. The chamber above Saint Václav's Chapel was reconstructed in 1867–68 after the jewels' ceremonial return from another sojourn in Vienna, this time in retreat from the invading Prussian army, and the mystique of the seven locks dates only from then.[106] The jewels have been publicly exhibited just eight times in this century, most recently in February 1993.[107] This was in conjunction with Václav Havel's inauguration as first president of the Czech Republic that came into existence on 1 January of that year following the breakup of Czechoslovakia. Exactly the same phrase was being used then to describe Czechoslovakia's dissolution as had been applied to describe its birth seventy-five years previously—*obnovení českého*

státu, the renewal of the Czech state. It begs some questions. The leaflet accompanying the 1993 exhibition (which many thousands of Praguers queued
long hours in bitter weather to visit)[108] glosses over this and many earlier such
upheavals. The crown jewels, it asserts, are "a national cultural memorial sym-
bolizing the centuries-old tradition of the Czech state."[109] In 1929 visitors were
also told that the jewels, exhibited "in the place where the remains of Saint
Vojtěch have rested through the ages," "belong to the most precious historical
and artistic artifacts of our nation."[110] Which state, and whose nation? The
boundaries of both changed several times over in the decades that separated
these exhibitions, let alone the preceding "ages." But it is exactly this contingency of identity that all such rituals forcefully deny. Like Alfons Mucha's *Slovanská epopej*, they create a time and a space all of their own.

Saint Vitus's Cathedral itself, begun (in its present form) in the time of
Charles IV, was "finished" and ceremonially reconsecrated in that same symbolic jubilee year, 1929. This building, the largest church in Prague, is as
much a national as a religious monument. It is a strange marriage of old and
new. The choir, the body of the bell tower, and the surrounding chapels are
the work of the Gothic masters Matyáš of Arras and Petr Parléř during the
fourteenth and fifteenth centuries, but building was stopped because of the
Hussite Wars. Petr Parléř, incidentally, is how the architect's name is normally
spelled in the Czech literature, but he was in fact called Peter Parler and was
a German, born in Cologne. A provisional wall erected to enclose the finished parts of the medieval edifice was to last, in the event, until 1924. A
Society for Completing Saint Vitus's Cathedral [*Jednota pro dostavění chrámu
sv. Víta*] was set up in 1859,[111] and the foundation stone for the proposed
additions laid in 1873. Around half the cathedral (the entire western portion,
including the nave and the western facade with its twin towers) was built
between then and 1929. Decorations went on into the 1930s. Alfons Mucha's
window was one of a number designed by prominent contemporary Czech
artists—none of them evident modernists—among them Max Švabinský, Cyril Bouda, and Karel Svolinský.

From an aesthetic—or a conservationist—point of view this "completion"
might well raise eyebrows. Certainly several structures that would undoubtedly be classed today as historical monuments were demolished to make way
for it, including an eleventh-century chapel of Saint Maurice and a sixteenth-
century chapel of Saint Vojtěch.[112] Architect Josef Mocker's original plans included re-gothicizing of the great bell tower, whose present gallery and spire
date from 1560–62 (restored 1770)—a quite breathtaking piece of cultural
hubris.[113] In the event the reconstruction did not go that far. But the *obrození*
version of Czech history was duly etched into the Prague skyline. What
testimony to the continuity of Czech identity could be more compelling than
this realization of Charles IV's project after a five-hundred-year hiatus? It
triumphantly confirmed, in a language all could read, that "We were here
before Austria, and look, here we are after it!" Mikoláš Aleš's mural "Libuše

24. Saint Vitus's Cathedral in the mid–nineteenth century.

Prophesies the Glory of Prague,"[114] executed for the foyer of the Old Town
Hall in 1904–6, duly closes the representational circle. It is the silhouette of
Hradčany with the new twin-towered west end of the cathedral and unrealized Gothic spire that furnishes the backdrop to the princess's prophecy,
not the truncated building with the oddly divorced bell tower that had over-

25. The "completion" of Saint Vitus's Cathedral as envisaged in 1884 by
Josef Mocker.

looked the Vltava for centuries. Alfons Mucha used the same visual conceit
in his murals for Obecní dům. The old cathedral stands in the background to
"Prague in Chains," but it is Mocker's neo-Gothic fantasy that graces "Dreaming of Freedom."

Completion of Saint Vitus's was part of a wider transformation of Hradčany into an eminently representational space after 1918. Throughout the nineteenth century both the castle of Hradčany and the quarter of the city to which it gave its name were somewhat ambivalent locations. If historically Czech, they were nonetheless the highly visible citadel of Habsburg authority. Increasingly depopulated while the rest of the city mushroomed, Hradčany was an enclave of barracks and bureaucracy. Some of this ambivalence comes out in Jan Neruda's *Tales of the Malá strana*, the "Little Quarter" of Prague over which Hradčany looms. The situation of the castle, which according to *The Guinness Book of Records* is the largest in the world, may also have inspired Franz Kafka's famous novel. But when the first Czech head of state moved in since the last of the Přemyslids over six hundred years before—Jiří z Poděbrad apart—Hradčany, just like the jewels of the repudiated monarchy, became a symbol of this reconstructed Czech(oslovak) sovereignty. The presidential standard, which bore the heraldic devices of Silesia, Moravia, Slovakia, and Podkarpatská Rus,[115] with the Bohemian lion in the center, flew over its ramparts emblazoned with the Hussite motto "*Pravda vítězí.*" Much of the castle complex, including its gardens and the former royal palace, was renovated and opened to the public for the first time during the 1920s, claiming and proclaiming a renewed identity between state and subjects.[116] The same thing has happened since 1993, with the emphasis this time being put on democratic openness and governmental visibility after four decades of communist oppression. Prominent in the current plans for restoration and exhibition are Tomáš Masaryk's presidential apartments.[117]

Inculcation of that identity between state and subjects was also, predictably, a major concern of the nicely named Ministry of Education and National Enlightenment [*Ministerstvo školství a národní osvěty*]. The victory of truth, though, was not the most obvious priority of the extensive reforms of school curricula that took place between 1919 and 1921. In the best imperial tradition the resulting syllabi were extraordinarily detailed, specifying the number of hours each week to be spent on every subject, the material to be covered, even the precise exercises to be done by pupils in the obligatory weekly two hours of physical education. All textbooks—including unchanged reprints—had to be approved by the ministry, as did wall maps and pictures and atlases, before they could be used in schools. Textbooks published abroad were inadmissible.[118] Textbooks [*učebnice*] in this context mean books pupils were required to read. Other books could be employed in the classroom without such approval as ancillary reading [*pomocné knihy*], but pupils could not be compelled to study them. Nor was it deemed necessary to vet the "texts of Roman and Greek classics, so long as they are complete (with the exception of Ovid, who is always subject to approval)."[119] Of course. We catch a rare glimpse here of a continuity that is more substantial and less visible than the sort broadcast in the grand public symbols and rituals of state. Boundaries, populations, regimes, and ideologies of the polities of which Prague has been the capital city have changed repeatedly over the past two centuries. But governmental licensing of school textbooks—and thus of the content of compulsory education—has an unbroken history stretching from Maria Theresa to Gustáv Husák.

Občanská nauka, which roughly translates as "civic education," was not a separate subject in first-republic schools, but the term comes up again and again in instructions for how history and geography are to be taught. The objectives of the history syllabus for secondary schools were set out in 1921 as follows: "*Aim*: particular emphasis is to be laid on those historical personalities and events which have importance for the Czechoslovak state. In all classes—especially of course in the higher grades—the objective is that social and political problems should be elaborated in relation to civic upbringing [*výchova*]; thus, commensurate with the pupils' capacities, moments of state formation [*momenty státotvorné*] should be stressed, and the development of constitutions should also be noted."[120] In Grade 1 of the gymnasium, ten- and eleven-year-olds would gain a first acquaintance with the past by way of "the most significant and most beautiful legends" and "rounded pictures" of people and events, above all those "that have importance for [the Czechoslovak state]." All the words here other than those in square brackets were inherited from the former Austrian syllabi. It is not the state-serving function of historical education that is new, only its particular content. In Grade 3, where medieval and modern history were to be taught up to the Peace of Westphalia, room for "special emphasis on Czech and Slav history" is made by reducing the time spent on "migration of nations, German dynastic history, and the history of discoveries. In Czech history proper care should be devoted to the history of the Hussite period and the history of the Reformation. The post–Bílá hora era should be dealt with in detail and especially its spirit brought out." In Grade 4, where the story was brought up to the present, the emphasis is again put on Czech history, and "presentation of Habsburg lordship should be correspondingly abbreviated and filled with a wholly Czech spirit." In Grade 6, "apart from Czech history the history of other Slavs should also be emphasized, to which end German and Austrian history should be limited." In Grade 8, "the history of the Austrian lordship should be dealt with from the standpoint of liberated Bohemia" (*sic*: not Czechoslovakia, nor even the Czech lands).[121] This is history as a mirror of identity, as Palacký would have wished, with a vengeance. Only now, the mirror is that of the new national state, in which its subjects are, shall we say, energetically encouraged to see themselves reflected.

New Hussite Armies

Alongside such nationalizations of the past, the *buditelé* who during the preceding century had done so much to give that past a contemporary significance themselves became icons of modern nationhood. The square in front of Prague's Rudolfinum, originally a complex of concert halls and exhibition rooms on the right bank of the Vltava that served (to the chagrin of some artists) as the parliament building during the first republic, was renamed for Bedřich Smetana and the embankment behind it after Mikoláš Aleš. Josef Mánes and (after his death) Alois Jirásek added their names to the city's bridges. New monuments went up to Svatopluk Čech (by Jan Štursa, 1923), Miroslav Tyrš (1926), Josef Mánes (1930), Eliška Krásnohorská (1931), and Jaroslav Vrchlický (1936). Tyrš, Fügner, Smetana, Dvořák, and Mácha all appeared on Czechoslovak postage stamps. Tomáš Masaryk, who was styled "president-liberator" [*President-osvoboditel*] and "Little Father" [*Tatíček*], was the object of a widespread, if benign, personality cult. A Masaryk Embankment appeared in Prague as a result of a decision of the city council on 12 February 1919, the same day Aleš and Smetana were similarly honored. This tribute to Masaryk was unusual in that Prague streets were rarely named after living people in the first republic, unlike later. What became Masarykovo nábřeží was Prague's oldest embankment, built in 1841–49 and named after Austrian emperor Francis I in 1894, which runs from the National Theater to Charles Bridge and commands the familiar picture-postcard view of Hradčany and the Malá strana. Francis's statue was quietly removed to the lapidarium of the National Museum in 1918. So was that of a once-famous Czech who had distinguished himself by what was now deemed unpatriotic service to the empire, Marshal Václav Radecký (1766–1858), the hero of the Austrian victories in Italy in 1848–49. Radecký's memorial had stood in Malostranské náměstí for sixty years.

More modern figures than Saint Václav were also the subjects of jubilee commemorations, often under state patronage. In 1920 SVU Mánes, the Museum of Arts and Crafts [*Uměleckoprůmyslové muzeum*], the Society of Patriotic Friends of Art, and other bodies held a large exhibition (610 works in all) at Obecní dům and two other Prague venues to mark the centennial of the birth of Josef Mánes. Max Švabinský did the poster for the event. The aged Josef Myslbek was the honorary president of the organizing committee, and Tomáš Masaryk himself participated in the opening ceremonies, solemnly wreathing Mánes's bust in the Pantheon.[122] Mikoláš Aleš's biographer Karel B. Mádl and Max Švabinský gave speeches; Masaryk made his entrance and exit to the strains of a fanfare specially composed for the occasion by Josef Bohuslav Foerster.[123] Myslbek, who died in 1922, was himself given a comparable retrospective at Veletržní palác in 1929 as part of the Saint Václav celebrations, which was organized by Umělecká beseda. Over two hundred of his sculptures and reliefs were displayed; the earliest, dating from 1867, bore the title "Apotheosis of the Královédvorský Manuscript."[124]

Bedřich Smetana had his jubilee duly celebrated in 1924, all nine of his operas[125] being staged that season at the National Theater, six of them in new

26. The Radecký monument in Malostranské náměstí, covered up prior to its removal in November 1918.

productions. *Libuše* was performed on 12 May, the anniversary of his death. The previous day there had been a memorial celebration at his grave at Vyšehrad at which the main speaker was Zdeněk Nejedlý (1878–1962), whose contorted attempts to turn Josef Dobrovský into a latter-day Czech patriot we encountered earlier. We will meet Nejedlý again in a later incarnation as a communist cultural gauleiter. He was best known then as a critic and musicologist; he first gained fame for his magisterial *History of Hussite*

Song (1904–13). He went on to write a multivolume biography of Smetana and two out of six volumes of the handsome *History of the National Theater*,[126] published for its fiftieth anniversary in 1933, another jubilee that was lavishly commemorated during these years.[127] He also penned a long (uncompleted) biography of Tomáš Masaryk. Needless to say, *Má vlast* was performed in 1924 at a gala concert with the president of the republic in attendance. Even the Neues Deutsches Theater broke with custom to stage Smetana's opera *Hubička* (*The Kiss*), following this up the next year with *Prodaná nevěsta* and in 1926 with Janáček's *Jenůfa*.[128] Smetana's artistically undistinguished amateur drawings were reverently exhibited at Umělecká beseda; Zdeněk Nejedlý wrote the hagiographic preface for the exhibition catalogue.[129]

A competition was held in 1926 for designs for a Smetana memorial on Masarykovo nábřeží. Had it been built, it would have replaced the missing statue of Francis I, whose pedestal remains there, empty, to this day. One of three proposals to which the jury awarded prizes was by the architect Pavel Janák, the painter František Kysela, and the sculptor Oto Gutfreund. The model was unconventional, comprising ten freestanding sculptural groups. In the center Smetana rises up above a composition entitled "The Genius of Music Revives the Nation." Fanning out to either side are allegories of Dance, Victory, Song, the Czech Countryside, the Past, Love, Struggle, Nature—"the voices of the land, to which Smetana hearkened," according to Oto Gutfreund's submission to the jury.[130] The memorial was to be enclosed on three sides by a "monumental wall" with mosaics of Smetana's life and work, whose central portion would visually echo the sequence of subjects in *Má vlast*. The statue of the composer stands between "The Czech Countryside" and "The Past." According to a 1962 monograph on Gutfreund, these two are "conceptually linked: the deepest history of the national past is bound up with the work of country people."[131] Even if the communist gloss here is transparent, this is a link we have come across before.

Gutfreund died in a drowning accident the next year at the age of thirty-seven, and the project remained unrealized. The episode shows that patriotism and artistic modernism were not always at odds, for Gutfreund was among the most original and inventive Czech sculptors of this century. A member of the Skupina výtvarných umělců, he was among the earliest practitioners of cubist sculpture anywhere in the world ("Anxiety," 1911–12; "Viki," 1912–13). After the war, he made a sharp turn to civic realism, working mostly in colored plaster and baked clay and often taking his themes from industrial and commercial life. He did leave behind him some patriotic monuments, notably the frieze "Return of the Legions" on the facade of the Legiobanka on Na poříčí in Prague (1923) and the memorial to Božena Němcová's *Babička* in Ratibořice above Česká Skalice in northeastern Bohemia (1922), which affectionately, if unconventionally, portrays the old lady and her grandchildren. The latter did not meet with universal approval. The

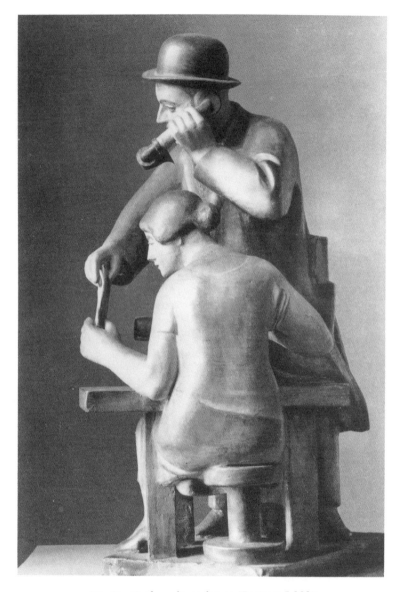

27. Oto Gutfreund's sculpture "Business," 1923.

poet Otakar Březina, for one, fumed: "Gutfreund's *Babička* in this valley in Česká Skalice is something so vulgar, ugly, foreign, un-Czech, un-Slav, and you see, the times are such that this sculptor is accepted among us."[132] Whether there is an implied reference to Gutfreund's Jewishness here is open to debate, but it would not be altogether surprising.

The eightieth anniversary of Mikoláš Aleš's birth provided the occasion for another jubilee exhibition, under the patronage of the Government of Czechoslovakia and Prague City Council, which ran from October 1932 to February 1933 in the art society SVU Myslbek's pavilion on Na příkopě. This was one of the largest exhibitions mounted in interwar Prague; 497 works were shown. The members of the honorary committee included Mayor Karel Baxa, director of the Modern Gallery (and former prime minister) Karel Kramář, the rectors of the Academy of Fine Arts and Charles University, the president of the Czech Academy of Sciences and Arts, the venerable Renata Tyršová, and Aleš's widow Marie Alšová. This is an unusually fulsome roster of the great and the good, which underlines Aleš's status by this time as an official emblem of Czech identity. Tomáš Masaryk was among those who lent works from their collections, among them Aleš's 1891 cycle "The Life of the Old Slavs." The two-volume catalogue gives detailed information on every picture and has seventy-two reproductions; it is an impressive souvenir by the standards of the time.[133] One drawing reproduced here that is especially poignant, in the light of subsequent Czech history, is entitled "The Fate of Talent in Bohemia." It depicts a departing young man on horseback, taking leave of his distraught sweetheart.

V. V. Štech's preface acknowledges that as an artist Aleš was judged to be "behind the times, even reactionary" by many of his contemporaries even in the 1880s, and later was thought of as "above all a patriotic painter . . . unconnected with the development of contemporary art. He became a patriarch outside time, a representative of times which are irrevocably gone." Štech makes a case for there being an innate artistic strength in Aleš's work, of course, but locates this less in its form, about which he is faintly apologetic, than in its content and motivation. Aleš's enduring value, he says, lies in his provision of a link with "the past, continuity, tradition." "We no longer feel the backwardness in Aleš's form, which mattered earlier, because we understand that the peculiar freshness of this painter is the result of pure sincerity, the fruit of an intensively lived youth, of his experience, of his ideals, to which he adhered even if they were romantic and uncontemporary."[134] That these are not the sort of terms in which we would expect to see a Manet or a Picasso critically appraised at a major retrospective is one more indication that we are dealing here with something more than just an art exhibition.

Karel Čapek, as so often, went to the heart of the matter in a short article in *Lidové noviny*, entitled "Old Master," whose publication coincided with the jubilee show. It calls for quotation at length:

> Yes, it is a national idyll: children, the people [*lid*], song, countryside. And right beside the Hussite captain [*hejtman*] on his South Bohemian horse, Saint Václav, the Turkish wars, strong Bivoj, Jiří z Poděbrad, sabers, coats of arms, pagan prehistory and standards flying in the wind. Next to monumental frescoes little

pictures for a children's reader; alongside almanacs, heroic myths. Father Aleš has everything all together in one bundle: national idyll and national epic, the beetle in the grass and the knights in combat, nature and history, children and the king, animals and elements, present and prehistory; for all this echoes together when we say and feel the word home. This is the second great simultaneity that speaks to us out of Aleš's work: the presence of everything that home means to us; home is the world of our childhood, nature, the people and the critters in the fields, a girl's song and a grandmother's wisdom, men's work and grandfathers' learning, the native region, myths, legends and history, people and kings, the blessings of peace and the clash of weapons. Mikoláš Aleš had to draw it all, for he wanted to portray home as a whole, overlooking nothing. To him the Hussite *hejtman* was as much a piece of home as the boy whittling a pennywhistle, as a butterfly, as the seasons of the year, as the rippling of a field. It is this fullness and wholeness that makes Aleš classical. . . . There is and can be no national art without such wholeness, which brings together heaven and earth, nature and myth, the ages and the seconds, the greatest things and the smallest things in one single reality which is presented to be seen and loved. This is what both Aleš and Smetana are to us.[135]

There is not one urban or contemporary referent in this litany of "everything that home means to us"; which is not to disagree with a word Čapek says. We might, however, register his persistent equation of countryside and childhood. Home, here, is very much a landscape of nostalgic remembrance.

Sadly, Mikoláš Aleš did not live to see Czech independence. He died in 1913. His old friend Alois Jirásek not only witnessed the momentous events of 1918, but was himself a notable participant in them. Jirásek's name was prominent on the list of signatories on the "Manifesto of Czech Writers" protesting against Vienna's suppression of Czech public life in May 1917.[136] It was Jirásek who, after the singing of the Hussite hymn "Ye who are the soldiers of God," rose in the Smetana Hall of Obecní dům on Saturday 13 April 1918, "like a living incarnation of an old *hejtman* of the immortal Hussite revolution,"[137] to pronounce the "National Oath of the Representatives of Czech Cultural and Political Life." This condemned the war "which we did not want and for which we are not responsible" and promised "for today and for the entire future: we shall remain, where we stand! Faithful in work, faithful in struggle, faithful in suffering, faithful to the grave! [*Zůstaneme, kde jsme stanuli! Věrni . . .*] We shall endure, until we win! We shall endure, until we greet the independence of our nation!"[138] It was Jirásek, too, who was chosen to welcome home Tomáš Masaryk on behalf of the nation at Prague's Woodrow Wilson Station—formerly Emperor Franz Josef Station—when on 21 December 1918 the exile returned in triumph as the first president of independent Czechoslovakia. By then Masaryk was sixty-eight, Jirásek sixty-seven. The aging novelist became a member of the National Assembly and headed the National Democrats' slate of candidates for the senate.

All of this was recalled in the many speeches at his funeral in March 1930. It was said then that "there is not a schoolchild in our nation who does not know the name of Alois Jirásek. . . . His historical novel became the new Bible of the nation."[139] This may have had much to do with the packaging of excerpts from Jirásek's works in textbooks and readers,[140] and was not entirely voluntary; pupils were required to read many of his books in full, beginning with *Staré pověsti české.*[141] But in any event, this parting of the Czech nation with one of its latter-day patriarchs offers as sharp a picture of the official self-imagery of the Czechoslovak Republic as we could possibly ask for.[142] Notably, the Church played no part in the ceremonies; as *Lidové noviny* explained to its readers, "Alois Jirásek, bard of the chalice and evoker of the strangling darkness, was without confession. He left the Church in order to gain the right to his conception of Czech history."[143] Just about everyone else in Czech public life was there. Jirásek's lying-in-state in the Pantheon, darkened by black draperies, attracted fifty thousand mourners on the afternoon of 14 March alone. Beneath Myslbek's statue of Saint Václav a huge cenotaph was erected, on which rested a "symbolic coffin" wrapped in the Czechoslovak flag and surrounded by vessels of "Greek fire." Here, on the evening of Saturday 15 March, chairman of the senate Dr. Soukup and former Prime Minister Karel Kramář remembered Jirásek. The ceremony began with "Ye who are the soldiers of God," played by a military band, and ended with "*Kde domov můj?*" and the Slovak anthem "*Nad Tatrou sa blýska.*" The neon signs of Václavské náměstí were obscured by black banners, the National Museum illuminated, the whole upper half of the square densely packed with throngs of people.

The funeral took place the next day. It began, as had by then become traditional, with a ceremonial parting in the Pantheon:

> Not long ago we saw shuffling on his walk a small, suffering old man, with a fur cap on his head and an unkempt beard; there was nothing to him, and he took up hardly any space with his old man's walk. Under the vault of the Pantheon he is now surrounded by everything which represents nation and state: president of the republic, government, houses of parliament, highest state officials, representatives of the army, rectors and deans of the universities, writers, artists . . . the whole nation, which comes to bow its head before that black coffin. The whole nation: which is to say, the whole state too.[144]

President Masaryk arrived at ten o'clock sharp, top hat in hand. "He stands before the catafalque and with a deep bow of the head bids farewell to the man who twelve years before greeted him on behalf of the whole nation not far from this place. He gazes intently at the black coffin, as if remembering."[145] The minister of education spoke (in Slovak) for the government, the poet

28. Gutfreund's memorial to Božena Němcová's *Babička* in Ratibořice, 1922.

29. Alois Jirásek's funeral, Václavské náměstí, March 1930. In the foreground is the cenotaph, guarded by uniformed Sokols; behind it Josef Myslbek's statue of Saint Václav; in the background the National Museum.

Jaroslav Kvapil—himself a veteran of "the glorious time of the National Oath and Manifesto"[146] and a onetime editor of Zlatá Praha—for Czech writers, Rudolf Medek for the army. Kvapil (1868–1950) urged Czechs not to mourn Jirásek overmuch, for "to bow before his coffin came the liberator of the homeland, the successor, chosen by the nation, to our Hussite king, and over this coffin fly the victorious banners of the new Hussite armies. Lipany is redressed, Bílá hora redressed."[147]

Beneath the ramp of the National Museum, three hundred soldiers from the Jirásek Regiment were drawn up. From Fochova třída came the sound of marching. Led by two mounted officers, sixteen-strong rows of police, the first row on black stallions, entered Václavské náměstí. Behind them marched Czechoslovak legionnaires from the French, Italian, and Russian fronts; Sokols, preceded by thirty-six huge standards, each draped in black; volunteer firemen, rescue, and riflemen's associations; members of guilds in historic costumes, the Vltava rivermen [Vltavané] in blue with top hats, the green-jacketed malt makers, the black chimney sweeps with white scarves and silver shovels slung over their shoulders; workers' gymnastic associations; scouts, and "girls, tiny and big." From Mezibranská ulice entered another procession headed by the banners of political parties: the National Socialists, National Democrats, Agrarians, National Fascist Community, and "the radical parties." Behind them came theatrical and other societies; fifty standards, carried by the seventh and eighth graders of Prague's Jirásek gymnasium, each bearing the title of one of his works; Jirásek's own pupils; and delegations from Litomyšl and other places associated with his writing, among them the Dogheads of Domažlice, bearing their symbolic axes. Wreaths were laid, beginning with one from the president of the republic. It took 350 men to carry all the bouquets. Borne by four Sokols, Masaryk's wreath was a circle of laurel decorated with a floral bouquet, beneath which was a book fashioned out of leaves. Wildflowers spelled out the words "U nás." Not only is this the title of one of Jirásek's obrození chronicles. "U nás" is a phrase full of homely potency: it can mean "at our home," "in our country," "among us," or simply "here." "U nás se to nedělá," which might be said to a child who persists in talking with her mouth full, means "We don't do that here." Not all languages provide so economical a means of expressing the identities whose assertion is so fundamental to modern national statehood.

The coffin, resting on the shoulders of Sokols, emerged from the museum. Troops presented arms as it was carried to the cortege. Jirásek's last journey through Prague was led by twelve noncommissioned officers with dipped weapons, under the command of a captain, and twelve Sokols with drawn rapiers. Beside the cortege, pulled by six black horses, walked twelve Czech writers; behind it a staff officer carried Jirásek's Revolutionary Medal. Then came his family, followed by the entire government—the prime minister, the chairmen of both houses of parliament, ministers—the leaders of Czech political parties, representatives of Czechoslovak universities in full academic regalia, Czechoslovak writers and poets, a deputation of the Thirtieth Infantry Regiment (which bore Jirásek's name), and others. A full-scale military procession followed. The cortege made its way through Prague, stopping at the National Theater, Jirásek's own house on Rieger Square, Otto's publishing house, and the Vinohrady Theater before arriving at Olšany Cemetery, the burial place of Tyrš, Fügner, and Havlíček. At each of these sites there was further ceremony. At Olšany, Jirásek was cremated to the strains of "Ye who are the soldiers of God" and, finally and fittingly, "*Kde domov můj?*" His ashes were then reverently transported (and by no means by the most direct route) through more than a score of Czech towns, at each of which there were more crowds, more ceremony, until at last he was laid to rest in the earth of his native Hronov in the far northeastern corner of Bohemia.

"Jirásek's Country," as this region had by then been baptized, provided Karel Čapek with the title for the brief tribute he wrote for *Lidové noviny* on 14 March 1930. It is a masterly exercise in a geography that is at once historical and emotional. "That corner of the foothills between the Úpa and the Metuje," he begins, "was the world of our own childhood; one of our grandfathers had a smallholding above Babička's valley and used to know the mad Viktorka herself." The *babička* in question is Božena Němcová's heroine, Viktorka a character in her novel, the valley the place where Gutfreund's memorial had stood since 1922. These personages and places are presented matter-of-factly, as every bit as real as the "red sandstone hills [which] rise gently, speckled with silvery birch and dark spruce and pine . . . where still in our childhood . . . hand looms were clattering from morning to night." Hard by "runs the meandering line of the linguistic border, which beyond Náchod breaks into Prussia. . . . That linguistic border was like the end of the world, beyond which there is nothing. The very near border of the empire was also the gate through which the religious emigration came and went." The land falls toward the "military and Theresian towns" of Hradec Králové and Josefov; "few of our places have so much war in their past as this gentle country; Jirásek's historicism is directly the local tradition." Čapek recalls his other grandfather, who owned the Hronov mill, and who used to ferry small loaves of bread and small sums of money from the bakers Jirásek to the young Alois when he was a student in Hradec; scribes, spiritualists, and sectarians; ducal houses, insubordinate mayors, and enlightened parish priests; Jesuits and *buditelé*; a teacher in Hradec who spent a whole year instructing twelfth graders, Čapek's own father among them, on the French Revolution instead of Austrian history. In just four, beautifully written paragraphs, he sinews together "the greatest things and the smallest things in one single reality," unerringly tapping the keys of identity: history, literature, land, language, *lid*.

The name of Alois Jirásek conjures up all this; it has become nearly synonymous with the very landscape itself:

> If the country around Hronov is known as Jirásek's, it is done so rightfully; this honorary possessive is worthy of both Jirásek and his country. Even though Jirásek belongs to all the nation and is loved by it, he captured in all his work that almost natural beauty and intimacy of his country between Brendy and Hejšovina: a country without grandiosity, naively open and mild, modest and delicate; a country that historically suffered in its people more than it led, but which silently and steadfastly held onto its typical Czechness at the very border of our national region. From the coffin of our most essentially national writer must not be absent a posy of saxifrages and buttercups from the damp meadows above Hronov.[148]

The International Style

The power of such occasions and images is palpable. But it was never either total or unchallenged. The critic F. X. Šalda, for one, interjected a sharply dissonant note into this official national rhapsody, just as he had a few months previously with regard to the Saint Václav jubilee. On that occasion he had written, "This was not a national celebration, as was for instance the laying of the foundation stone for the National Theater, it was a celebration of just one single national class, the most conservative and the wealthiest class."[149] He was no less scathing about the pomp and circumstance surrounding Jirásek's funeral, mocking those literary critics who "before Jirásek's coffin gave up their analytic function, threw away their scalpel and other professional tools, and capitulated under the pressure of this collective imperative" to make of the man a myth.[150] He coolly—but not ungenerously—goes on to dissect Jirásek's writing. He gives the novelist his due for his "good, quiet, sober art, which promises no more than it can deliver." But he places Jirásek in his time and place, that of "an already completely closed chapter in literary history."[151] Jirásek's work, he says, is good popularization rather than great art, and will not stand the test of time. "Soon it will be, I am afraid, a historical document. It will be in a museum case and above it will be written: The official literary style of the first decade of the republic."[152]

Šalda reserved his greatest scorn not for Jirásek but for the "official republican world" that canonized him:

> Here is a young state and for its building this state has a huge need of legend and myth. . . . It is no longer a question here of a man who wrote such and such books of such and such value, it is a question of a social symbol. . . . A state needs in its foundations an array of such figures, just as not so long ago great monumental buildings needed an array of sculptures on the facade, which were

everything but faithful likenesses of definite concrete persons; well then, this mystique of state usage dictates its own requirements, and reality is recomposed, the finished poetic composition tailored to prescribed dimensions and profiles.[153]

"The Czech nation," Šalda went on, "is really saturated with historicism; and historicism can very easily become its danger today, just as yesterday it was its goad and spur."[154]

Šalda's distaste for official Czechness in general and its historicizing predilections in particular was shared by a good many Czech intellectuals between the wars. If anything, the dominant note of the urban cultural life of the period was cosmopolitan modernism, though there also were plentiful exceptions to this generalization. The war, national independence, and—for some—the Bolshevik revolution seemed to have changed the world so utterly that a figure like Jirásek came to belong to a past as distant as that about which he wrote. Introducing an English edition of *Staré pověsti české* in 1931, Karel Čapek affectionately relates how he used to read it, as a boy of eight or nine, perched up in an oak tree with a wooden sword hanging from his belt, "the best way to read heroic legends of your land."[155] Čapek's own patriotism is unimpeachable. Nonetheless here, as in his tribute to Mikoláš Aleš quoted earlier, he places "*starý pan Jirásek*," old Mr. Jirásek, in the irretrievable world of childhood—a fitting object for fond remembrance, but not a figure with anything much to say to the present. Others, like Ferdinand Peroutka in *What We Are Like*, used the imagery of age less charitably to suggest that the nationalist culture of the later nineteenth century belonged to a societal adolescence that sorely needed to be outgrown.[156]

One way to get a sense of this shift in sensibility is to thumb through Josef Kroutvor's excellent history of the Czech poster.[157] With Josef Čapek's "Radicals Read *Červen*" of 1918 we feel ourselves quite suddenly in a new world. The poster uses only two colors, black and red, the design is sharp and angular, the technique (linocut) is direct, and the subject—a figure framed by urban high-rises—is urgently contemporary. All of the decorativeness and mysticism of the Secession has vanished. Not only Alfons Mucha's "Princess Hyacinth" of 1911, but Oldřich Koníček's poster for the SVU Mánes members' exhibition of 1914, with its artfully twining lime branches, seem an epoch away. In subsequent pages we come across Zdeněk Rykr's advertisements for the Kolín Oil Refinery (1920), whose cars, trains, and planes come at you head-on; Václav Špála's poster for an "Exhibition of World Fashion" at the Museum of Arts and Crafts in 1921, a modish young lady in a short summer dress captured in a few swift lines of black on beige; an abundance of images that suggest the excitement and pace of modern times—radio, film, travel, fashion, jazz. As the 1920s move on photographs are montaged into posters and words become an integral element of visual design. The boundary between art and advertising, culture and commerce blurs. In its

30. Josef Čapek's poster "Radicals, Read *Červen*," 1918–19.

intention, at least, this is a public, democratic, mass art, and above all it is a self-consciously modern art. It speaks of, for, and to a society light-years away from that portrayed at the Czechoslavic Ethnographic Exhibition twenty-five years previously; even if it remains in some ways a society just as imagined. For we should not forget that outside of this modernist palisade there still existed the Czech countryside, not to mention backwoods Slovakia and faraway Podkarpatská Rus.

This is also an art that repeatedly refers in text and image to a world beyond Czechoslovakia's borders, a world to which, it is implied, modern Czechs rightfully belong. Posters advertise "The Dandy" men's outfitters, "Macháček's American Dancing Hall" (offering "*thé dansant*" and "*souper dansant*"), the "Grand French Restaurant," and an assortment of nightclubs and cabarets with names like Montmartre, Pigall's, Sport Bar, and Bar Chat-noir. František Zelenka's 1930 placard for "*Jazzové revue*" at Jiří Voskovec and Jan Werich's Liberated Theater [*Osvobozené divadlo*] centers the word "girls"—in English. Viktor Oliva's celebrated poster for the 1900 Paris World Exhibition had portrayed an elegant Parisienne holding out a leather-gloved hand to a Czech ingenue in village costume. In Alexej Hrstka's 1930 poster for the new Barrandov Terraces overlooking the Vltava just south of Prague, the elegantly gloved lady sipping a cocktail under a sunshade is (presumably) herself a Czech, and the text is multilingual: "*Terasy Barrandov. Za Prahou a přece v Praze* [outside Prague and yet in Prague]. *Visit Barrandov. Visitez Barrandov. Besuchet Barrandov.*" The Barrandov Terraces were a fashionable haunt which could be pleasantly reached by a short steamboat ride up the river. Designed by Max Urban, a founder of the Skupina výtvarných umělců, they were built by future Czech president Václav Havel's father, an engineer and real estate developer, also named Václav, in 1929.[158] The Havels were then one of Prague's most prominent and richest families. The president's Uncle Miloš is known as the father of Czech film, an industry that was centered on the Barrandov film studios. His paternal grandfather, another Václav, built the Lucerna complex on Václavské náměstí, containing a huge concert and assembly hall, arcades, restaurants and bars, and one of Prague's first cinemas, in 1911. Lucerna was the first building in Prague to make use of the state-of-the-art technology of reinforced concrete in its construction. The president's maternal grandfather Hugo Vavrečka (1880–1952) was at one time or another an editor of *Lidové noviny*, Czechoslovakia's ambassador to Hungary and Vienna, and business director for the Baťa footware empire.

The "garden city" around Barrandov was one of many so-called villa quarters that sprung up on the perimeter of Prague between the wars. The most famous of these is Baba, above Dejvice in the city's northwest, which was built between 1928 and 1933. It affords a stunning view of the Prague basin. Baba was a planned development by Svaz československého díla (the Union of Czechoslovak Workmanship), a "center for quality manufacture" estab-

31. Alexej Hrstka's poster advertising the Barrandov Terraces, 1929.

lished in 1920 with the aim of improving design quality in all areas of every-day living. The plan, by Pavel Janák, called for thirty-three two- and three-story villas, constructed from reinforced concrete and other modern building materials, on three parallel streets one above the other on the hillside. In terms of its price Baba was an eminently bourgeois location, but there is nothing stuffy or conventional about these houses. They are bold, refreshing, and unashamedly modern, their geometric exteriors and rational interiors proclaiming the "international style" of functionalism.[159] Prague boasts many such monuments to architectural modernism. So does the Moravian capital of Brno. Among the more celebrated Prague constructions are the Müller Villa designed by Adolf Loos in Střešovice (Loos himself was born in Brno and took Czechoslovak citizenship in 1930), the huge factory-like Veletržní (Trade Fair) Palace in Holešovice for whose ceremonial opening Alfons Mucha's completed *Slovanská epopej* was—somewhat incongruously—exhibited in 1928, the glass-fronted "Universal Department Store" Bílá labuť (the White Swan) on Na Poříčí, and Tomáš Baťa's nine-story shoe emporium on Václavské náměstí.

This latter temple of consumerism provided while-you-wait shoe repair in the basement and offered pedicures and a buffet on the top floor. On its facade was the slogan "Our Customer—Our Master" [*Náš zákazník—Náš pán*]. Baťa's production for the masses made it the biggest shoe manufacturer in the world; by the end of the 1930s the company was turning out two hundred thousand pairs daily. Zlín in Moravia, Tomáš Baťa's company town, is a showpiece of designed modern living. Its administrative building, a seventeen-story skyscraper built in 1937–38, may well have been the tallest building in Europe at the time. Still more distinctive was Baťa's provision of standardized family houses and apartments for his workers and a range of social amenities from "Masaryk Schools" to hospitals to community centers. Rents for Baťa apartments in the late 1920s were a nominal one crown per week—cheap, but a tie that very effectively binds. "*Baťovci*" candidates took seventeen out of thirty seats on Zlín City Council in the elections of 1923 and twenty-five out of thirty in 1927, a fact Tomáš Baťa does not neglect to mention in his *Thoughts and Speeches* [*Úvahy a projevy*] published in Zlín in 1932. With headings like "Organizer," "Economist," "Educator," "Citizen," "Statesman," "Co-Worker," and "Human Being," this collection is not entirely unreminiscent of Mao Zedong's famous little red book: homespun snippets of practical morality from a great helmsman, in this case a captain of modern industry and therewith an indisputable champion of progress.[160]

Renamed Gottwaldov—after KSČ leader Klement Gottwald—in 1948, Baťa's purpose-built town is, in its way, as much an experiment in totality as the national one Gottwald's communists were to attempt later. The town architect František L. Gahura summed up the Baťa architectural philosophy in 1933:

> From the beginning of its construction we have endeavored to have the town grow stylistically in an organic way out of industrial architecture, the latter being a new form for the architect to express his conceptions of the life and work of an industrial city. Zlín's appearance is influenced by the industrial object, that is to say, the factory building. It is the main motif of Zlín's architecture. This motif is repeated in different variations in other buildings serving public purposes; in schools, residential training schools, the Community House, the Welfare and Health Institute, and others. The architect's creativity had always to resolve the problem of adapting the disposition of a building meant for public use to the factory construction standard. This standard is the module (element) of Zlín's architecture. It is a construction plane, the dimensions of which are 6.15×6.15 meters. From this unit ground plans of all the buildings are formed. The exterior appearance of Zlín's architecture is accordingly distinguished by a stylistic unity, with many variations.[161]

It is an eminently modernist vision, which the visiting Le Corbusier, for one, much appreciated.

SVU Mánes moved in 1930 to a new functionalist building on Slovanský ostrov in the Vltava, just south of the National Theater. Slovanský ostrov means Slav Island; formerly called Žofín Island, after Emperor Franz Josef's

32–34. The Baťa store on Václavské náměstí, 1928–30 (top left); Baťa advertisement, 1923 (top right); Baťa workers' housing in Zlín, around 1936 (bottom).

mother Archduchess Sophia, it was renamed thus in 1925 in honor of the Slavonic Congress held there in 1848. A striking feature of the gallery and restaurant designed by Otakar Novotný is the way the uncompromisingly modern lines of the white concrete building incorporate the tower and onion dome of a water mill built in 1489. The building is in its way symbolic of what the society became between the wars. The 1920 Josef Mánes jubilee discussed earlier was not representative of its work. SVU Mánes did stage occasional retrospectives of nineteenth-century Czech artists, but not many.[162] The biggest was the exhibition "One Hundred Years of Czech Art 1830–1930," with which it celebrated its move to Slovanský ostrov. It marked its fiftieth birthday in 1937 not with genuflections to nineteenth-century Czech classics but with three large exhibitions called "French Painting from Manet to Today," "Fifty Years of Mánes," and "Mánes Today." The great majority of Mánes's 189 exhibitions between the foundation of the republic and the German invasion of 1939 were devoted to contemporary art, both Czech and foreign.

Munch and Picasso were shown in 1922, Juan Gris in 1924, Chagall, Kokoschka, and other representatives of "Contemporary German Art" the same year, "Modern Austrian Art," including Klimt and Schiele, in 1928. The guests featured at the society's hundredth exhibition in 1926 at Obecní dům included Braque, Bonnard, and Derain. Two notable Mánes exhibitions were those of "Contemporary French Art" in 1931 (Léger, Matisse, Maillol, and Modigliani, among many others) and "Poesie 1932," the first international surrealist exhibition in Prague (and one of the earliest surrealist exhibitions anywhere in the world outside France). Here 155 works were exhibited. Side by side with Arp, Dalí, Giacometti, Ernst, Klee, De Chirico, Miró, and Tanguy were the Czech artists Muzika, Štyrský, Toyen, Wachsmann, Šíma, Makovský, and others.[163] When this show finished, SVU Mánes followed it up with an exhibition of contemporary architecture in the USSR. The story was not too different at Umělecká beseda. Even if its repertoire was more limited, more domestic, and generally rather more conservative than that of SVU Mánes, still the old patriotic society exhibited Dufy and De Chirico, Štyrský, Toyen, and Šíma.[164] Josef Čapek was instrumental in mounting the Umělecká beseda exhibition "*L'école de Paris*" at Obecní dům in 1931, at which 525 works were shown. It was a display of the best and most contemporary in Parisian modern art: the exhibitors included Bonnard, Braque, Derain, Dufy, Ernst, Chagall, De Chirico, Léger, Maillol, Matisse, Miró, Picasso, Rouault, Tanguy, Vuillard, and Suzanne Valadon.[165]

Earlier, we examined the nationalistic publishing activities of Jan Otto in the later years of the nineteenth century. An equally vigorous, but quite differently oriented entrepreneur of the 1920s was Otakar Štorch-Marien (1897–1974). Aventinum, the firm he founded in Prague in 1919, became a leading outlet for contemporary Czech and foreign literature. By the mid-

1920s Aventinum was bringing out sixty titles a year, by the end of the decade ninety. A mainstay of the firm's list, and a major reason for its success, were the brothers Čapek. Karel's plays *R. U. R.* (*Rossum's Universal Robots*, 1920) and *The Makropulos Case* [*Věc Makropulos*, 1922]—the source of Leoš Janáček's opera of the same name—were notable Aventinum books. So was Josef's *The Most Modest Art* [*Nejskromnější umění*, 1920]. *R. U. R.* gave the word "robot" (from the Czech *robota*, originally meaning servile labor) to the English language. Like much of its author's work it belongs to the same genre as Aldous Huxley's *Brave New World*, interrogating the moral dilemmas of an unstoppable modernity empowered and endangered by triumphant scientific rationalities.[166] There is a wonderful caricature of Karel Čapek by "Dr. Desiderius" (Hugo Boettinger): with his hair slicked down, a cigarette holder in his mouth, and a phonograph record in his hands, Čapek is the very epitome of a thoroughly modern man.[167]

The Most Modest Art is devoted to a much broader and more urban and contemporary *lidové umění*—a term that should be translated, here, as popular art rather than folk art—than that which was normally recognized as such at the time. Among the vulgar art forms in which Josef Čapek seeks inspiration are posters, billboards, film, and the documentary (as distinct from contrivedly "artistic") photographs in the new popular magazines like *Weekly Variety* [*Pestrý týden*]. His later book *The Art of Natural Nations* [*Umění přírodních národů*] celebrates the art and artifacts of African, Native American, Australasian, and other non-European peoples. Like his brother Karel, Josef Čapek too was not above writing for children. His much-loved *Stories About Doggie and Pussycat As They Keep House Together and About All Sorts of Other Things As Well* was another Aventinum first and has since become a Czech children's classic. Čapek dedicated it to his daughter Alenka (Alena) and all children. Here is what the dog and the cat baked into their birthday cake:

> flour, egg, milk, sugar, salt, butter, *tvarůžky* [a very pungent cheese from Olomouc], a few strips of smoked pork skin, nuts, a pickle, lots of bones, four mice, several peppery sausages, a pot of whipped cream, an onion, chocolate, gravy.
>
> Also included: garlic and pepper, lard and candies, pork scratchings and cinnamon, semolina and quark, gingerbread and vinegar, cocoa and cabbage, one goose head and sultanas.
>
> No bread—doggies and pussycats don't like that too much.[168]

Fortunately for them, another dog—a bad dog—stole their cake and ate it. Needless to say, it was not a confection that agreed with his stomach.

The Čapeks were not the only reason for Aventinum's success. The firm had a broad list, ranging from "progressive" older Czech writers like F. X. Šalda, J. S. Machar, Antonín Sova, and S. K. Neumann to leading figures of the younger Czech avant-garde, born around 1900, like Adolf Hoffmeister, Karel Teige, Vladislav Vančura, and Vítězslav Nezval. Where Jan Otto's labors had centered on a national encyclopedia and the patriotic album *Čechy*, the flagships of the Aventinum reference library were external in reference and often in origin. H. G. Wells's *History of the World*—which became the company's biggest commercial success—Elie Fauré's *History of Art*, and an (uncompleted) fifteen-volume series The Geography of the World were among them. Štorch-Marien echoed Otto's edition titles, but little else, with his "*Lidová knihovna Aventina*" (Aventinum Popular Library) of 1924. This series offered contemporary novels, both Czech and foreign, with boldly constructivist cover designs. Aventinum's translation program was geared more to modern literature than to classics, though it published the entire works of Flaubert in a single day in 1931, a decision that contributed to the financial crash of the firm not long afterward. Yeats, Galsworthy, Gide, Valéry, Apollinaire, Ehrenburg, Cocteau, and Yesenin all appeared on Štorch-Marien's list. The company also produced an edition of contemporary Czech novels in French translation through the Paris firm Bernard Grasset called "*La collection Tchéque.*"

When Aventinum published Czech classics it contemporized them with modern artwork. Jan Zrzavý (1890–1977) illustrated Mácha's *Máj* in his highly individual magic realist style. But with Václav Špála's sparse linocut illustrations for Božena Němcová's *Babička*, which were commissioned by Štorch-Marien in 1923, we enter the realm of blasphemy. Of the 664 exemplars of the book, 440 were returned by irate booksellers within two weeks. "You have raped our most beautiful literary work and should be banned from publishing books," wrote one. In a small bookstore in southern Bohemia, Štorch-Marien was greeted with the words "It's you, who published that frightful *Babička*? And you have the nerve to show your face here? Get out of here, Sir, get out, or I won't be responsible for my actions."[169] Along with Josef Čapek, Jan Zrzavý, Rudolf Kremlička, and Vlastislav Hofman, Václav Špála (1885–1946) was a member of the Tvrdošíjní (the Obstinates), who in April 1918 reasserted the values of prewar artistic modernism with a Prague exhibition called "And Yet . . . [*A přece!*]."[170] Some of this work was aggressively social in its content: recurrent motifs in Josef Čapek's art in this period are sailors, prostitutes, and beggars of both sexes. The Tvrdošíjní pioneered a stylistic synthesis of cubist and expressionist influences that is—in retrospect—peculiarly Czech. Václav Špála, in particular, is the most lyrical of painters, and both he and Josef Čapek were in time to return to the national mainstream with rural subjects, albeit in a modernist idiom. But that was not how matters were widely seen in 1923, at least where "our book of books"[171] was concerned. The irony is that the "classic" illustrations of *Babička* which Špála polluted, those of Adolf Kašpar, date only from the fiftieth anniversary edition of 1903.[172] Tradition may be timeless, but it is not necessarily old.

35. Václav Špála's linocut "Autumn," around 1920.

High-quality artistic layout, from covers to illustrations to typographics, was a hallmark of Aventinum books, even if they were mostly affordable paperbacks. Apart from members of the Tvrdošíjní, Štorch-Marien drew upon an array of talents from both the prewar (Kobliha, Bílek) and postwar Czech avant-gardes. The latter included František Muzika, Otakar Mrkvička, Karel Teige, Josef Šíma, and Toyen (Marie Čermínová). These names might be much better known in "the West"—as many of them were in their time, when Paris and Prague were a good deal closer to one another than they are today—had it not been for the postwar political events that redrew Europe's maps. They span a range of artistic standpoints running from constructivism to surrealism, and Aventinum's jackets and illustrations were just as varied. Josef Čapek, who had a share in the visual design of more than two hundred Aventinum titles,[173] usually employed linocut techniques and geometric or primitivist motifs. Teige, Mrkvička, Hoffmeister, and Muzika favored photomontage, or a clear, direct constructivist style where the impact comes mainly, and sometimes entirely, from the typography itself.[174] Šíma's and Toyen's illustrations move us closer to the dreamlike, inner visions of surrealism.

Štorch-Marien's involvement with the visual arts was not confined just to "the beautiful book." Aventinum published an influential art magazine, *Musaion,* whose first editor was Karel Čapek, and in November 1927 Štorch-Marien established his own art gallery, the Aventinská mansarda (Aventinum Loft) in the baroque Zedwitzovský dům. Entry to the opening was by invitation only; the tickets were printed in both Czech and French. This venture shook the complacency of SVU Mánes, by now the official bastion of Czech art: Štorch-Marien became the exclusive agent for the works of Josef Čapek, Špála, Filla, Zrzavý, Kremlička, Šíma, Muzika, and Hoffmeister. The Aventinum Loft offered a reading room with new books and the biggest selection of magazines in Prague, and it was the venue for concerts, literary evenings, and lectures, as well as art exhibitions. These latter were without exception contemporary. Toyen (1902–80) and Jindřich Štyrský (1899–1942), the founders of Czech surrealism, had their first Prague exhibition at Aventinská mansarda in 1928. Josef Šíma (1891–1971), another expatriate and a founder-member of the Paris group Le Grand Jeu, showed his work there in the same year. Štorch-Marien also mounted exhibitions of modern photography and launched the first Czech film review, *Studio,* as well as publishing an entertainment magazine with the English title *Gentleman.* He edited the *Rozpravy Aventina (Aventinum Discussions),* "A Monthly for Culture, Art, Criticism and Particularly Literature," himself. It first appeared in 1926, went fortnightly a year later, and became a weekly fixture of the city's literary and artistic scene from 1929 to 1933.

Aventinum was the most successful of the quality publishing houses that sought in the 1920s to bridge the gap between the established, and now for the most part very staid, "official publishers"—firms like Otto, Šimáček, Topič, and Vilímek who had enjoyed state-licensed franchises under the empire—and the smaller "private publishers" whose limited bibliophilic editions had been the main outlet for contemporary literature during the first two decades of the century. But it was far from the only one. Twenty-three such firms banded together in 1926 to form "Kmen," the Club of Modern Publishers.[175] Štorch-Marien wrote Kmen's first public proclamation. Distinguishing themselves from both "the official traditional firms which lack any relation to the artistic present and offer their readers the works of older authors" and "the publishers of worthless or even bad books, which we want to thoroughly suppress with our activities," Kmen stood for "the *beautiful book*." It also looked outward. "We are national [*národní*], but we want to be cosmopolitan [*světový*] in the best sense of the word. We want to be a bridge between domestic and foreign culture and with the beautiful book on our escutcheon make our mark wherever there is genuine culture."[176] They made good on this promise. Between 1 January 1928 and 15 September 1930 alone, Kmen affiliates between them published 225 foreign authors in Czech translation,[177] who included Babel, Baudelaire, Bulgakov, Jarry, O. Henry, Pirandello, Rimbaud, Upton Sinclair, Maurois, George Bernard Shaw, and Virginia Woolf. Odeon, the avant-garde publishing house set up by Jan Fromek and Zdenka Fromková in 1925, had a foreign list that included Marcel Proust's *À la recherche du temps perdu* and D. H. Lawrence's *Lady Chatterley's Lover*. Václav Petr offered James Joyce's *Ulysses* and Vladimir Mayakovsky's *150,000,000*, for which Václav Mašek supplied stark linocuts of the modern metropolis and its restlessly mobile masses. Melantrich brought out Maxim Gorky and Thomas Mann. André Breton, Colette, Alberto Moravia, E. M. Forster, Aldous Huxley, Sinclair Lewis, Boris Pasternak, and John Dos Passos were among other modern authors translated into Czech by Kmen publishers between the wars. The club produced an annual *Almanac* [*Almanach Kmene*] from 1930 whose successive editors included F. X. Šalda, Karel Teige, Josef Čapek, and Jaroslav Seifert. It provided an excellent sampling of the best in contemporary Czech and world literature.

It is noteworthy, too, that Bohemian-German writers were not absent from Kmen's lists. Franz Werfel and Franz Kafka both appeared in Czech, Kafka's *The Castle* coming out as an SVU Mánes book in 1936. Kafka had first been translated into Czech by Milena Jesenská in 1920 for a magazine that coincidentally was also entitled *Kmen*, whose editor was the poet Stanislav Kostka Neumann. Neumann concurrently edited *Červen* (*June*), the magazine for which Josef Čapek did the poster discussed earlier. *Červen* was a major vehicle for Tvrdošíjní graphics; it appeared from 1918 to 1921 with mottos like "Proletkult—Communism—Literature—New Art"[178] on its masthead. Neumann himself was a perpetual enfant terrible of Czech letters. We read his not entirely serious salute to the poetry of noise and the Central Slaughterhouse in Holešovice earlier. He was also behind two key modernist manifestos, both influential in their day, the *Almanac of the Secession* (1896) and the *Almanac for the Year 1914*, to which the Čapek brothers had also contributed. His intellectual odyssey led him by way of decadence, symbolism, and Satanism in the 1890s through anarchism and eventually to communism. He was a founding member of the KSČ in 1921. The one thing Neumann could be relied upon to be was unfailingly progressive. The translator of *The Castle*, Pavel Eisner (1889–1958), is an interesting figure for rather different reasons. He recalls a Prague that has vanished almost beyond imagining, a Prague whose voices were not heard at such gatherings of "the whole nation; which is to say, the whole state too" as Alois Jirásek's funeral. Eisner was a German Jew who translated freely from Czech to German and vice versa; his writings include a study of Czech women (beginning with Princess Libuše) as celebrated in German poetry, and a long, learned, and loving paean to the Czech language, *Chrám i tvrz* (*A Cathedral as Well as a Fortress*).[179] This Prague was destroyed in World War II and its aftermath. The Germans murdered the Jews, the Czechs expelled the Germans, and the communists did their utmost to obliterate the very memory of both. *Chrám i tvrz* did not appear in Czech bookstores again until 1992, and Eisner's work joined the long list of books that were removed from Czech libraries, among which were the anguished imaginings of Franz Kafka.[180]

But things were once otherwise, and not only on the cultural fringes. The updated *Ottův slovník naučný nové doby* (*Otto's Contemporary Encyclopedia*) published in the 1930s includes Franz Kafka in its discussion of literature in the Czechoslovak Republic. He is hailed (along with Rainer Maria Rilke, another German Praguer) as a writer "who already belongs to world literature" but proudly claimed for his native city. His novels and stories are said to portray "a typically Prague fate."[181] Eisner, meanwhile, wrote the lengthy chapter on German literature since 1848 in the territories of the Czechoslovak Republic for another major encyclopedia of the time, *Československá vlastivěda*, a title that literally means "Czechoslovak Homeland-Science." The same volume has substantial entries on literature on the soil of the *vlast* in Hungarian, Slovak, Polish, and Ruthenian.[182] Bernard Bolzano would surely have approved. This was not an intellectual culture that was conspicuously inward- or backward-looking; and we have yet to speak of its youngest and most avowedly revolutionary cohorts.

Emily Comes in a Dream

It was on a boat trip up the Vltava in the summer of 1926—not to Barrandov, that had not yet been built, but to the village of Zbraslav—in the company of Karel Teige, Adolf Hoffmeister, and other young artistic radicals of the Devětsil group, that Milena Jesenská met the architect Jaromír Krejcar and seduced him away from her friend Jarmila Fastrová, who never forgave her.[183] They got married the following year, with Karel Teige officiating as Milena's witness at the wedding, and moved into a two-room apartment above Jaromír's mother's little confectioner's shop on Spálená ulice. Here, on Saturdays, "bought-in sausages were warmed up, white coffee brewed, rolls devoured, and the gramophone played," and Milena hosted the cream of the Prague avant-garde.[184] Once they were honored by a visit from F. X. Šalda himself, now sixty. Milena's friend Jaroslava Vondráčková describes this meeting of the young radicals ("The age has divided in two. Behind us remains the old time, which is condemned to molder in libraries, and in front of us sparkles a new day," began Devětsil's first public proclamation)[185] and the old veteran of Česká moderna. "Spálená 33! . . . Teige and Fučík pulled Šalda up the winding narrow stairs of the old house. They supported, almost carried him. The rest of us stood as a guard of honor at the top and bottom of the stairs lighting the scene with flashlights. We loved Šalda, and Spálená 33 was proud that it drew him there."[186]

Karel Teige (1900–1951) was the dean of the Prague avant-garde; a founder of Devětsil and its leading theoretician, he penned its major manifestos[187] and edited its journal *ReD* [*Revue Devětsilu*, 1927–31]. His copious writings on all areas of the arts, from film to architecture, from poetry to typography, are a barometer of Czech avant-garde life and preoccupations over three decades. Their central concern with art in the machine age anticipates the problematic of better-known (because Western) cultural critics like Walter Benjamin. Teige was also a highly original artist in his own right, experimenting in various media from his own specialty of typography to surrealist collage.[188] Julius Fučík (1903–43) was a bright young star of communist journalism. From 1929 to 1938 he co-edited the KSČ daily *Rudé právo* (*Red Right*), as well as the cultural magazine *Tvorba* (*Creativity*). *Tvorba* had been started in 1925 by Šalda, who turned it over to the KSČ in 1928 as a protest against censorship of the communist press. Devětsil (the word is the name of a flower but also puns on the Czech for "nine forces," possibly a reference to the nine muses of antiquity) became one of the longest-lived of Europe's interwar avant-gardes. Founded in Prague's Café Union on 5 October 1920, it survived splits, defections, and polemics to last until 1931. It dominated Prague avant-garde cultural life in the twenties, and provided its 1930s successors, like the Czechoslovak Surrealist Group and the Left Front [*Levá fronta*], of which Karel Teige was the first president, with their founding members. It was closely, if at times uneasily, linked with the KSČ. One of the events that led to the group's eventual disintegration was the expulsion of seven prominent Czech writers, Vladislav Vančura, Ivan Olbracht, Marie Majerová, Helena Malířová, Josef Hora, S. K. Neumann (who soon returned), and Jaroslav Seifert (who did not), from the party in 1929 for their "radically petit bourgeois views." Teige and Fučík were among those who at the time publicly denounced their former comrades' "grave error," in their own words, "not in order that we may correct their mistake—but to emphasize that here our ways part."[189]

Devětsil's membership[190] included some (if not most) of the foremost creative artists of their generation. The poets Jiří Wolker, Jaroslav Seifert, František Halas, Konstantin Biebl, and Vítězslav Nezval were all at one time or another participants; so were the prose writers Vladislav Vančura, Jiří Weil, and Karel Schulz, and the painters František Muzika, Alois Wachsmann, Jindřich Štyrský, Toyen, Adolf Hoffmeister, Otakar Mrkvička, and Josef Šíma. Devětsil's architectural section (ARDEV) was particularly strong. Seven Devětsil architects participated in the Bauhaus Exhibition in Weimar in 1923, and Karel Teige taught at Hannes Meyer's personal invitation at the Bauhaus on typography, advertising, and the sociology of architecture in 1930. Josef Chochol (1880–1956), the pioneer of Czech cubist design, was also counted as an honorary Devětsil member. Whether they knew it or not, so were Charlie Chaplin, Douglas Fairbanks, and Harold Lloyd, a detail that tells us a lot about Devětsil's orientation. In their early statements they repeatedly single out film as the epitome of an art for the modern world. The group contained several journalists, one of them the "furious reporter" Egon Erwin Kisch (1885–1948), another representative of German-Jewish Prague; Roman Jakobson (1896–1982), founder of the Prague Linguistic Circle and intellectual precursor of structuralism; photographers and composers, theater directors and actors, and even one dancer, Mira Holzbachová. The Liberated Theater of Jiří Voskovec and Jan Werich ("V + W"), which became a hugely popular vehicle for social and political satire in the 1930s, first gained fame under the direction of Jindřich Honzl as Devětsil's theatrical section in 1925.[191] Among its early productions—apart from premieres of avant-garde Czech plays—were Apollinaire's *Les Mamelles de Tiresias* in a translation by Jaroslav Seifert (1926), Alfred Jarry's *Ubu roi* (1928), and works by Cocteau, Breton and Soupault, and Marinetti. Many of these works had their first foreign stagings anywhere in the world in Prague.

Milena Jesenská herself epitomized rebellious *jeunesse dorée*. After graduating from Minerva she dropped out of medical school and music conservatory, experimented with drugs filched from her father's practice, and generally scandalized her elders. She mixed with the German-Jewish literary set around Franz Werfel, Willy Haas, and Max Brod, who frequented the Café Arco on Hybernská ulice. Her liaison with one such "Arconaut," Ernst Pollak, led her father, who was vehemently anti-Semitic, to have her committed to a sanitarium for several months. That, at any rate, is how Max Brod tells the story; Jaroslava Vondráčková says there were equally compelling reasons for hospitalizing her in order to avoid the embarrassment of prosecution, since she was singularly free with the property of others.[192] As soon as she got free

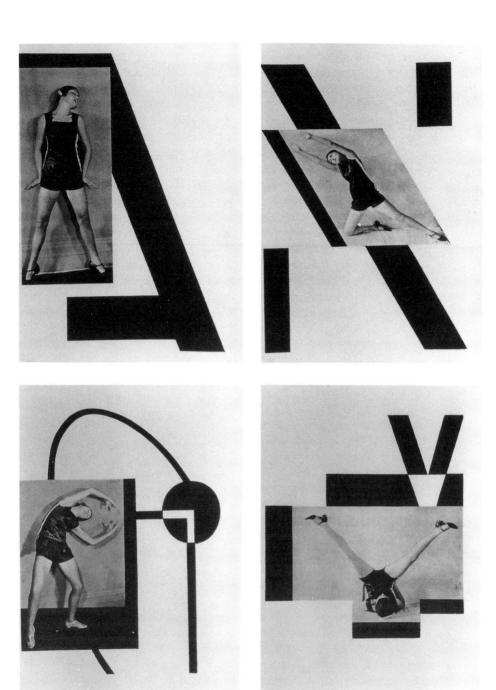

36. Milča Majerová dancing the letters A, N, O, and V for Vítězslav Nezval's poem *Abeceda* (Alphabet), typography and photomontage by Karel Teige, 1926. This multimedia composition was performed at the Osvobozené divadlo before being turned into a book.

of the asylum, Milena married Pollak with her father's reluctant acquiescence and moved to Vienna. She was unfulfilled there, not least because Pollak was more comfortable practicing fashionable doctrines of free love than she.[193] She was not drawn home by national independence. It was during her time in Vienna that Milena had her famous affair (which apart from two brief trysts was carried on entirely through the mail) with Franz Kafka. Divorced, she returned to Bohemia in 1925, chafed at what she saw as Prague's "provincialism," danced the night away in jazz clubs, and supported herself as a journalist. She wrote for *Lidové noviny, Národní listy, Tribuna, Pestrý týden*, the communist illustrated weekly *Svět práce* (*The World of Labor*), and eventually Ferdinand Peroutka's *Přítomnost* (*The Present*). In the early 1930s she became an active member of the KSČ. Reportedly Klement Gottwald himself, whom on one occasion Milena obligingly hid in her Prague apartment from the police, sponsored her party application. The gulf between Milena's world and that of her staunchly nationalist father and Aunt Růžena was—obviously—vast. By all accounts, including Kafka's, Milena was a remarkable individual: determined, clever, courageous, emancipated. But she was also not altogether untypical of her class, her generation, and her time.

Jaromír Krejcar (1895–1949), Milena's second husband, was a leading light of modernist Czech architecture. A pupil of the pioneering Czech modernist architect Jan Kotěra, he moved through purism and constructivism to functionalism. With Karel Teige he edited the 1922 miscellany of Czech modernism *Život II* (*Life II*: subtitled "A Collection of New Beauty"), and with Teige and Jaroslav Seifert he edited *Disk*, a Devětsil magazine that appeared the following year. He was the accredited Czechoslovak representative of the Bauhaus and a founder of the Club for New Prague [*Klub za novou Prahu*], whose name satirizes that of the influential Club for Old Prague [*Klub za starou Prahu*], set up in 1900 to oppose what its members saw as reckless modernization of the city. Like many of his contemporaries, Krejcar was smitten by the Leninist romance of Soviets plus electrification. He had a keen interest in Soviet architecture and participated in the international architecture exhibition in Moscow in 1927. He worked in the USSR from 1934 to 1935. In Moscow he lived in the run-down Hotel Lux on Gorky Avenue where foreign sympathizers were quartered. Many disappeared by night into the *gulag* or to execution.[194] Krejcar's project—a workers' spa—fell foul of Soviet bureaucracy, but he did find himself a new wife, and Milena found herself divorced for a second time. Lucky to get back home in the circumstances at all, and thoroughly disillusioned by his Soviet experience, Krejcar designed the critically acclaimed Czechoslovak pavilion for the 1937 World Exhibition in Paris, for which he was awarded two grand prizes and a gold medal. He fled Czechoslovakia after the communist coup in 1948 and taught at the Architectural Association School in London. He died there the following year.

One of Krejcar's best-known (though never realized) designs, originally intended for Žižkov, appeared in *Revoluční sborník Devětsil* (*Revolutionary Miscellany Devětsil*) in 1922. The *sborník* was Devětsil's first major group publication and had the character of a manifesto; it contained Teige's "New Proletarian Art," Honzl's "On Proletarian Theater," Černík's "Russian Creative Art," poetry by Jiří Wolker, Jaroslav Seifert, and Vítězslav Nezval ("The Wonderful Magician," one of his most famous poems), and prose by Vladislav Vančura and Karel Schulz. It begins with a ringing declaration:

> The great French Revolution announced the dawning of the epoch, at whose grave we stand today. The World War was a cruel, depressing agony of this epoch. On the threshold of the new epoch is the Russian Revolution, which out of the great eastern empire created the homeland [*vlast*] of the proletariat and the cradle of the new world. . . . The Russian Revolution and today's revolutionary ferment in all parts of the world announce the beginning of the great and glorious future. They open the way to a clear goal: for a socialist society, and when this goal is attained there will arise *a new style, a style of all liberated humanity* [*lidstvo*], *an international style*, which will liquidate provincial national culture and art.[195]

It was not, however, from Soviet Russia that Krejcar's design drew its inspiration. A proposal for a large market hall between twin skyscrapers, it bore the title "Made in America."[196] Krejcar's Olympic Department Store on Spálená ulice (1925–28) also evokes transatlantic images. The facade of the building, which is largely made out of plate glass, is crowned by three receding terraces with steel railings. They recall the decks of the ocean liner, that perfect symbol of form following function, as well as of open horizons and the New World. It was considered an appropriately progressive place to take the Soviet poet Vladimir Mayakovsky when he visited Prague in 1927, as Vondráčková relates: "Mayakovsky arrives and goes with us to the Národní Café. Then we photograph him on the roof of Krejcar's Olympic. God, that Mayakovsky, what a hunk of a guy! Then he was at Mařka Majerová's [Marie Majerová, a communist writer, 1882–1967], she roasted him a goose. Soon after that came the news of his suicide. We are horrified, uncomprehending. Why, we asked, only why? Nobody explained it to us."[197]

The ocean liner was a common motif in Czech avant-garde art in the 1920s, as were other symbols of travel and tourism. It figures in Karel Teige's 1923 collage "*Odjezd na Kytheru*" (Departure to Kythera), a "pictorial poem" whose text reads "*Au revoir!*" "*Bon vent*," and "American Line."[198] There is also a liner (together with an airplane) at the top of Otakar Mrkvička's 1923 photomontage cover for Jaroslav Seifert's *Samá láska* (*Only Love*).[199] The latter is a brilliant conceit; it superimposes an American skyscraper on a photograph of Václavské náměstí and sits a five-pointed red star atop the skyscraper. Seifert's book was a classic of Czech *proletkult*. This montaging of

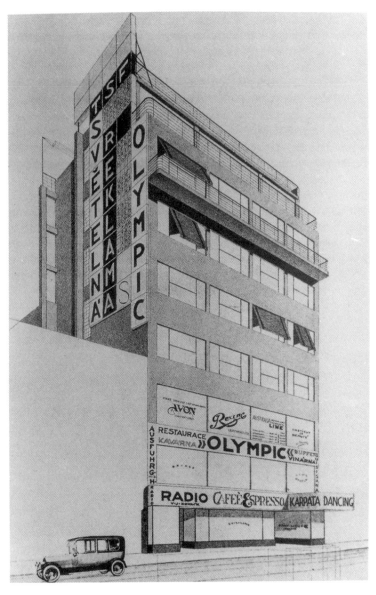

37. Jaromír Krejcar's design for the Olympic Department Store on Spálená ulice, 1925–26.

capitalist America and revolutionary Russia beneath Myslbek's Saint Václav statue says much about the avant-garde sensibility of the time. It is an exuberant, not to say indiscriminate affirmation of the modern, the radical, the new. It is also a powerful counterpoint to the messages sent out from that same location at Jirásek's funeral, when the neon signs of Václavské náměstí were blacked out by the resurrected shades of the nationalist past. For the Prague avant-garde the world existed to be changed, and that past was precisely history. Their orientation was to "the great and glorious future." Their *vlast* was the new international homeland they were imagining into being, a paradise without borders, and they spoke of *lidstvo* (humanity) rather than of the *český lid*. *ReD* carried on its masthead Vladislav Vančura's motto—proclaimed in his preface to Seifert's first volume of poetry, *City in Tears*, in 1920—"New, new is the star of communism, and outside it there is no modernity!"[200]

When the Czechoslovak Surrealist Group had its first exhibition in January 1935 at the SVU Mánes gallery on Slovanský ostrov, it was Karel Teige who wrote the preface to the catalogue. It is typical of him. One of the few constants in his artistic and political pilgrimage through primitivism, poetism, the "end of art," constructivism, and surrealism was the impulse to break down all barriers between art and life, and reconstruct both from scratch. "In front of the doors of the first exhibition of the group of Czechoslovak surrealists, above the entrance to the exhibition hall in which the paintings, sculptures, photographs, and montages of Toyen, Jindřich Štyrský, and Vincenc Makovský are installed," he begins,

> there should be placed a sign reminding us that:
> SURREALISM IS NOT AN ARTISTIC SCHOOL.
> To surrealists, [he goes on to explain,] art, painting, poetry, and theatrical creation and performance are not the aim, but a tool and a means, one of the ways which can lead to liberation of the human spirit and human life itself, on condition that it identifies itself with the direction of the revolutionary movement of history. . . . The philosophy and worldview of surrealism are dialectical materialism. . . . And if surrealists pronounce the word REVOLUTION, they understand by it exactly the same thing as the followers of that social movement which is founded upon the dialectical materialist worldview.[201]

The Surrealist Group's manifesto had been accompanied by two letters. One was from Vítězslav Nezval (1900–1958), perhaps the most inventive Czech poet of his generation, to the father of surrealism, André Breton. The other was to the Agitprop Section of the KSČ.

Štyrský and Toyen are presented here as part of "the revolutionary movement of history." A few years before they were thus elevated they had written a tourist guide to Paris, (where they spent the years 1925–28), which was published by Odeon, Devětsil's house firm, in 1927. Eight hundred pages

38. Karel Teige, untitled collage, 1938. The background to Teige's composition is the National Theater in Prague.

long, it may be one of the best guides to that city ever written. Apart from the standard fare (visas, hotels, restaurants, sights, transportation) it contains detailed sections on "Czech Paris" (the Czech community in France then numbered over eighty thousand), "Musical Paris," "Fashionable Paris," "Literary Paris," and—of course—"Artistic Paris." Štyrský and Toyen tell us the museums are not especially good, but they give very detailed guidance to private galleries and collections, even listing the addresses of artists' ateliers. They also enlighten us, in passing, as to what *thé dansant* is: "The hour of tea with dance begins at four and ends at seven. *Thé dansant* is a place of select society, a rendevous of all elegant Parisian and foreign ladies, a salon, where the latest novelties of Paris fashion are surveyed."[202] The book is a practical guide, and Odeon clearly expected it to find a market; the company advertised it in *ReD* with the blurb "Paris, center of science and art, focus of contemporary culture, cradle of modern architecture."[203] It is the coincidences of Mayakovsky on the Olympic roof, the red star of communism and the American skyscraper on Václavské náměstí, dialectical materialism and *thé dansant* that need to be taken in. They speak of forgotten horizons, of a Prague that had not yet been enclosed in "Eastern Europe," a world that had not yet become Manichaean, a country whose borders, physical and conceptual, were open. These cultural coordinates—Paris, Moscow, an America everybody fantasized but nobody had ever seen—by which the Prague avant-garde defined its position and identity were decidedly not those of official Czechness. Nor were they to survive the next war. The darkness was already falling, and not only in neighboring Nazi Germany.

In January 1936, a year after the first Czechoslovak Surrealist Group exhibition in Prague, an anonymous article appeared in the Soviet daily *Pravda* under the title "Chaos Instead of Music" attacking Dmitry Shostakovich's opera *Lady Macbeth of Mtsensk*. It proved to be the start of a sustained campaign against so-called artist formalism, whose casualties included Eisenstein, Pasternak, Babel, Mandelshtam, and the theater director Vsevolod Meyerhold, with whom the Devětsil directors Emil Burian and Jindřich Honzl had enjoyed close relations. Constructivist architecture was also singled out for vitriolic attack. In October 1937, Soviet censors gutted an official representative exhibition of Czechoslovak art in Moscow. All of Max Švabinský's pictures were removed on grounds of their "immorality" (Švabinský had a taste for the lush female nude), along with paintings and sculptures by Špála, Filla, Zrzavý, Makovský, and others. Also excised from the show were every single exhibit of Štyrský and Toyen. This campaign coincided with the first of the three great Moscow trials of the 1930s; Zinoviev, Kamenev, and fourteen others were executed in August 1936. That same year André Gide's *Return from the Soviet Union* consternated the European left with its frank portrayal of contemporary Russian realities. Milena Jesenská, who quit the KSČ in protest against the Moscow trials that September, later recalled the pressures under which Czech socialist intellectuals were put: "In the interest of the people the KSČ insisted that all its members begin to think about things otherwise than they had up till then. People found themselves in serious conflict with their conscience and character—and it was just this conflict that the KSČ called treachery, 'Trotskyism,' villainy, mendacity."[204]

Some found it easy enough to shed their previous skins. The poet S. K. Neumann, who was by this time in his sixties, manfully took up the cause of "a positive, clear, healthy, truthful, clean and indomitable relation to objective reality."[205] His *Anti-Gide, or, Optimism Without Myths or Illusions* is by any standards a scurrilous piece of writing. He applauds the Moscow trials, in which, he says, far from Stalin ridding himself of his opponents, "*the Soviet proletariat rid itself of saboteurs.*"[206] He defends recent Soviet laws against abortion and homosexuality, the former on the grounds that "the Soviet proletariat has an interest in the growth of its socialist strengths as well as of its proletarian army," the latter by way of an innovative distinction between "natural homosexuality" and "learned homosexuality."[207] But his choicest invective is reserved for "petit bourgeois 'intellectuals'" and the Prague avant-garde in particular. He derides "bourgeois 'isms,'" "modernist little games," "decadent saints," and "the noisy Teigeism [halasná Teigovština] that for several years worked its conjuring tricks among us with Marxist quotations."[208] "The socialist revolution," he assures his readers, "has nothing in common with today's aesthetic 'revolutions' in the intellectuals' teacup, which is merely a big-city, coffeehouse, tepid, badly filtered, every which way sweetened, perfumed, and colored beverage for the upset stomach of an isolated caste."[209] This demagoguery was echoed by Fučík and Nezval (whose creations during this period included an "Ode to Stalin") among others.

The following year Neumann took on the visual arts, accusing Emil Filla of "cruel deformation of the human body amid technical refinement," mocking Špála's and Muzika's "postimpressionist artistic wandering," and condemning Štyrský and Toyen's depraved use of "sexually pathological literature and erotic photography" in terms that would warm the heart of the most respectable petit bourgeois. He likely had in mind the in-your-face eroticism of Štyrský's collage-series Emily Comes to Me in a Dream [Emilie přichází ke mně ve snu], published in Prague in 1933 in a private edition of sixty-nine exemplars since otherwise it would undoubtedly have engaged the attentions of the censor; or maybe it was Toyen's unladylike drawings of penises that so disturbed him.[210] "Snobismus" became one of the commonest terms in the vocabulary of artistic, literary, and theatrical criticism in the pages of Tvorba and Lidová kultura (Popular Culture). This was an anti-intellectualism, as some of Neumann's critics pointed out at the time, which represented that most pliant of intellectuals' grand abstractions "the people" as congenitally incapable of appreciating anything other than the most anodyne artistic pablum. The Devětsil theater director Emil Burian ridiculed the "popular artist" [lidový umělec] as conceived by Neumann as "a kitsch-maker, a wage slave, who reproduces, repaints, and restages only that which is already commonplace. . . . lidovost in art is a counterfeit concept of the cognoscenti of kitsch and a mockery of the taste of today's individual, at best it is pulp. . . . 'People's artists' forget that the foundations of popular culture lie somewhere other than in a popular taste dictated from above and injected by education. . . . This people's artist serves capital, even if he fights against it, by the forgery of popular culture through symbols from outside the popular."[211]

Burian was not alone in being unwilling to dance to Moscow's drum. Roman Jakobson, Vladislav Vančura, Jindřich Štyrský, Jaromír Krejcar, František Halas, and Emil Filla were among others on the left who disavowed the KSČ's new cultural policy. But it was Karel Teige who pushed his critique the furthest. In September 1936 he publicly, if still somewhat cautiously, questioned the verdicts in the first Moscow trial, repeatedly using the word "tragedy."[212] The following January, refusing to be blackmailed by the charge that

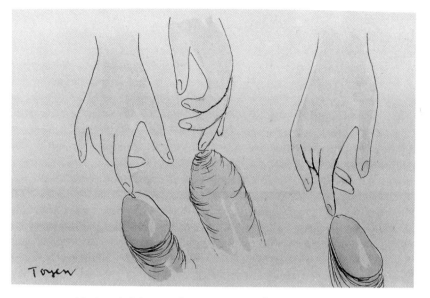

39. Untitled drawing by Toyen (Marie Čermínová), 1937.

any criticism of the Soviet Union succored the forces of fascism, he defended André Gide's *Return from the Soviet Union* at a public debate organized in Prague by *Přítomnost*.[213] When in January 1938 he introduced another exhibition of Štyrský and Toyen at Topič's Salon, he pointed out, against Neumann, that there may be more to "objective reality" than immediately meets the eye, and more to art than mere mechanical depiction. But as significant is his characterization of the political setting in which these aesthetic disputes were occurring: the moment of, in his own words, "the crusade, announced against independent art and the international avant-garde simultaneously in Berlin and Moscow . . . the wave of terror, aimed at that creativity which in Germany is called 'depraved art' and in the Soviet Union 'monstrous formalism.'"[214] Whatever their private doubts about Soviet developments, for many on the Czech left this was an unthinkable equation of totalitarianisms. Teige was deranging a moral and political cosmology that had located them for twenty years, scandalously tarring the sanctum of progress with the same brush as the citadel of reaction. It was too much for Vítězslav Nezval, who spluttered "If Karel Teige was able . . . to toss Berlin and Moscow into one basket, this testifies not only to a moral, but also—and above all—to an intellectual mistake."[215] Two months later Nezval unilaterally dissolved the Czechoslovak Surrealist Group (which promptly reconstituted itself without him). Teige responded with his *Surrealism Against the Current* [*Surrealismus proti proudu*], published in May 1938, which goes well beyond a mere defense of avant-garde artistic freedom. It is a full-fledged critique of Stalinist socialism, whose analysis foreshadows such postwar works as Arthur Koestler's *Darkness at Noon*.

Jaroslav Seifert, who had never mended his fences with the KSČ after his breach in 1929, was another who did not mince his words. In January 1937 he published a short poem entitled "The Moscow Trial" in the newspaper *Právo lidu* [*People's Right*]:

> What you can read in the newspapers
> Is a play, not to be believed
> And the scenes, from which come horror, fear
> Are whispered from the prompter's box.
>
> What you can read in the newspapers
> Is a play, let the world amuse itself.
> Only the end—the smell of human blood
> Is unfortunately, however, genuine.[216]

The last word—a valediction on an era of bright modernist hopes that had metamorphosed into something altogether dreadful—should perhaps be given to F. X. Šalda, whose visit had aroused so much excitement among the eager young radicals of Spálená 33 not so very long before. His article "The Age of Iron and Fire," published in his own magazine *Šaldův zápisník* (*Šalda's Notebook*) in October 1936, six months before his death, begins with General Franco in Spanish Morocco and moves on, quite smoothly and naturally it seems, to the gallows of Moscow. Šalda is as lucid, and as acerbic, as ever; the years have not dimmed his caustic intellect. But beneath what he has to say, as he compares his own time to that of the religious intolerances of the fifteenth and sixteenth centuries, lies a profound sadness. The prose drips with contempt:

> The point here is that in this trial was demonstrated a fundamental disrespect and disdain for the human spirit and the human conscience, and above all these the crude, brutal reality of power and violence towered to the skies. The idealistic (albeit completely mistaken) revolutionary direction was definitively kissed good-bye, having first been contemptuously trampled upon by the heavy hobnailed boots of the "realists," whose realism consists—in a loaded gun. It is this that now joins Stalin with the rest of the "positive" West European reactionaries, be they German, be they Italian, who respond to arguments with a bullet from a Browning or the hempen rope of the scaffold. Such, then, is the time in which we live: a time of iron and fire, or perhaps not even that; a time of a secret poison, which is surreptitiously poured into the drink of the condemned, so that it could strip them of their selves even before their execution and send them out, transformed into liars and cripples, to the ridicule and mockery of all.[217]

SIX

ETERNAL RETURNS

The Art of Remaining Standing

IT WAS NOT self-evidently ridiculous for Jan Baťa, stepbrother and successor to the shoe magnate Tomáš Baťa, to publish a book as late as 1937 entitled *Let Us Build a State for 40,000,000 People!*, which he thought could be "culturally and economically the healthiest, strongest, and richest state in Europe."[1] Central to his vision of the future was a superhighway running the entire length of the country from west to east and passing, of course, through the Baťa company utopia of Zlín. But his prognosis was perhaps a trifle optimistic. What might have happened had Czechoslovakia's internal conflicts not become intermeshed with international geopolitics is anybody's guess, but this faraway country has the misfortune to be located in the heart of Europe. That same year the venerable Tomáš Garrigue Masaryk, who had resigned the presidency on health grounds two years previously, died at the age of eighty-seven. In his speech over Masaryk's coffin, President Beneš struck a far more somber note. He appealed to the varied centrifugal forces which, as he saw it, were threatening to tear Masaryk's creation apart:

> I call you all without exception, from the left to the right, from the most remote hamlet to this capital city, from Aš [in the west] to Jasiňa [in the east], all of you, who think mostly about the social problems of this state, and you, who dedicate yourselves mostly to nationality problems—I call all of you without difference, in the spirit and memory of our first president, to the fulfillment of his bequest and the completion of his work—to the building of our just, staunch, unconquered, developing humanitarian democracy. . . . President-liberator, to the bequest which you placed in our hands, we will remain faithful! [*věrni zůstaneme*].[2]

It was not to be. Konrad Henlein's Sudeten German party took no less than 86 percent of the German vote in the local elections of 1938,[3] and Adolf Hitler made what he assured the world was his last territorial demand in Europe. Beneš mobilized but did not fight, despite considerable popular will to do so; a quarter of a million people demonstrated in Prague and were addressed in front of the Rudolfinum by Klement Gottwald (the Molotov-Ribbentrop pact had not yet been signed). Within a week of the government's reluctant acceptance of the Munich ultimatum, Slovakia became an autonomous republic within a now federated Czechoslovakia. Its secession six months later under German tutelage was the signal for Nazi occupation of what remained of the Czech lands. Twenty-four hours after Father Josef Tiso's declaration of Slovak independence on 14 March 1939, the Wehrmacht entered Hradčany. By then Czech democracy was largely dead anyway. Beneš had abdicated on 5 October 1938 and fled to England, and in the ensuing weeks the KSČ was banned and its property seized, its members ejected from parliament (and the Prague City Council), Voskovec and Werich's Liberated Theater closed down, and the new government headed by army general Jan Syrový empowered to rule by decree. The National Theater's refusal to fly a black flag in Karel Čapek's memory was eloquent testimony to the more general climate of fear and demoralization.

And so we return to where we began: the sad time of the burials in Vyšehrad Cemetery of a poet who had died a century earlier and a painter who, as far as Czech modernists were concerned, might just as well have done. Mácha and Mucha were nonetheless resurrected as symbols around which to coalesce, instruments for affirming the continuity of Czech identity in the face of the practical extinction of Czechoslovak sovereignty. Three years earlier Czech surrealists had claimed "the great revolutionary romantic" Mácha for their own, angrily protesting what they saw as the hypocrisy of official commemorations of the hundredth anniversary of his death with their collection *Neither the Swan Nor the Moon* [*Ani labuť, ani Lůna*], whose title is taken from one of Mácha's variations on "national songs."[4] But the moment for such fractiousness had passed. Like the legendary knights of Blaník, the shades of the past rode to the rescue of the present. This phenomenon was more general. One example was the large art exhibition that opened at five sites in Prague, including Obecní dům, on 12 November 1939. "The Nation to Its Creative Artists,"[5] as the event was called, was jointly organized by most of the leading Czech art societies in conjunction with the cultural council of the Národní souručenství (National Partnership), the only political organization permitted to exist under the Protectorate. Similar shows were simultaneously staged throughout the Czech lands.[6] Bitter arguments that had long divided generations and political adversaries were declared suspended in the interest of displaying a common national front.

The exhibition catalogue proclaims that "the most enduring manifestation of national being is the national culture"[7]—a national culture whose very existence, in the face of the class divisions of the first republic, F. X. Šalda had not long before publicly questioned in his 1936 "Meditation for the 28th of October."[8] Like Tomáš Masaryk, Šalda died in 1937; his passing, as much as Masaryk's own, could be seen as marking the end of an era. This catalogue makes it seem as if he had never lived. It recalls those "names most beloved of the Czech people," Josef Mánes, Josef Myslbek, and Mikoláš Aleš, who are taken as "classic representatives" of "what creative art meant in our national development." The artists represented in the exhibition, it goes on, "make up a united whole, nothing more and nothing less than purely Czech artists.

There is no barrier between them of artistic directions or ideological view-points, such as divided them in the past, they have transcended these will-ingly and joyfully in order to manifest before the whole public their united will to serve the nation and its culture. . . . All are imbued with the con-sciousness that they belong together and go by different paths to a single end, which also illuminated Mánes and Smetana and Neruda and which is forever embodied in the name of Smetana's apotheosis *Má vlast.*"[9] Max Švabinský—by then long a byword for artistic conservatism—was one of nine members of the honorary committee, together with the rectors of Charles University, the Czech polytechnic, and the Academy of Fine Arts, the president of the Czech Academy, mayor of Prague Dr. Otakar Klapka, and other notables. The official poster for the show, designed by František Muzika, employed Švabinský's woodcut of Saint John the Baptist [*Sv. Jan Křtitel,* 1930].[10]

Two things might be observed about the flurry of patriotic symbolization in this and other events of the time.[11] Neither is particularly surprising, but both were to be consequential. First, the modernist sensibility that had dom-inated interwar Czech artistic and cultural life went out the window. The "national tradition" was resurrected in its most self-consciously nationalist and historicist forms. For the most part this meant a leap back to the nine-teenth century. The names that came once again to stand for the nation—consider Švabinský's roll call over Mucha's grave: Smetana, Dvořák, Vrch-lický, Myslbek, and "the great Mikoláš Aleš"—were those whom progressives of various stripes had been consigning to the reliquary (or, as Karel Čapek did with Jirásek and Aleš, to the national nursery) for fifty years. Second, although it was the multiethnic, cosmopolitan state of Czechoslovakia that had perished, it was Czechness as a national identity that was being affirmed through this ritual recalling of the "whole company of our great minds." Despite (or because of) the German assault on Czech sovereignty and cul-ture, symbols of a Czechness with which Alfons Mucha would have felt thoroughly at home enjoyed a much less disputed presence in Czech public life in 1940 than they had for most of the preceding two decades of Czechoslovak independence. It is one of the more tragic ironies of modern Czech history that because events of 1938–45 so brutally confirmed the old stereotypes of the *obrození*—Germans as the oppressors, the Czechs as an exposed Slav peninsula jutting into the indifferent seas of Western Europe, Russians as liberators—this nineteenth-century discourse could be revived and mobilized as a central component of postwar reconstruction and eventu-ally used to legitimate a revolution whose methods and objectives would have horrified most *buditelé* themselves.

The war provided fresh images of national oppression to set beside Bílá hora and the martyrdom of Jan Hus, which testified to the eternal purchase of the earlier nationalist discourse while inflecting it in harsher and more radical directions. Czechoslovakia did not suffer as much as many other European countries during World War II, if we measure suffering by deaths or material destruction alone. Prague and other Czech cities were relatively unscathed by bombing. Some 360,000 Czech and Slovak nationals perished in the war. Of these—it is immediately necessary to add, since communist sources mostly do not—perhaps 260,000 were men, women, and children killed for no other reason than that they were Jewish.[12] The single largest slaughter of Czech citizens in modern history took place far from Bohemia on 8 March 1944, when 3,792 inmates of the "family camp" at Auschwitz-Birkenau, almost all of them Czech Jews, were gassed in a single night.[13] Reportedly they went to their deaths singing "*Kde domov můj?*"[14] But there was brutality and humiliation enough in the Czech lands to sear new names and dates into collective memory, and these were carefully, if selectively, cultivated by the KSČ after the war ended. One such name is Jan Opletal, one such date 17 November 1939, known ever after as "the day of the students."[15] Opletal, a medical student, was shot and seriously injured when the police broke up a demonstration in Prague on 28 October 1939, the anniversary of the founding of the Czechoslovak Republic twenty-one years earlier. He died on 11 November and was buried on 15 November, three days after the opening of "The Nation to Its Creative Artists." After Opletal's funeral, students roamed through Prague skirmishing with baton-wielding police and chanting anti-German slogans. They sang patriotic songs, including those nineteenth-century anthems out of whose titles Česká moderna had concocted mocking neologisms back in 1895, "*Hej Slované!*" (*Hey, Slavs!*) and "*Kde domov můj?*" On Masaryk Embankment the students ripped German-Czech bilingual route maps from the sides of trams and threw them into the Vltava.[16]

Two days later, Protector Konstantin von Neurath issued a proclamation in German and Czech that made the price of such patriotism clear. It announced that "Czech institutions of higher education have been closed for a period of three years, nine perpetrators have been shot, and a larger number of participants put in confinement."[17] In the small hours of 17 November, student dormitories in Prague, Brno, and Příbram were stormed and 1,200 students randomly arrested. Subsequently they were deported to German concentration camps. One of them, who was then a twenty-five-year-old graduate student of civil engineering in Brno, was my wife's father, Ladislav Borůvka. The ten Czech institutions that were closed included Charles University and the Academy of Fine Arts. Altogether 1,223 staff and 17,556 students (12,248 of them in Prague) were affected. The buildings were taken over by SS and German army units, and library collections were dispersed or destroyed.[18] An incomplete list compiled in September 1945 names forty-nine Czech students who died in or as a result of their time spent in German camps, a further three who survived the camps but died on the Prague barricades in May 1945, and seventy faculty who died in the camps or were shot.[19] The ban on Czech higher education was tightly enforced. Among the twenty-two executed men and five women listed in State Secretary Karl Hermann Frank's daily report to Berlin of 1 June 1942, for example, is "one professor for continuing higher educational instruction after the closure of Czech institutions of higher education."[20] Czech universities and colleges were not to reopen their doors until after the war.

Mayor Otakar Klapka (1891–1941) was not on the committee for the sequel to "The Nation to Its Creative Artists" mounted under the same title in 1940,[21] with Max Švabinský this time as one of two honorary presidents. By then he had been arrested by the Gestapo for resistance activities. Klapka was shot in October 1941, shortly after the arrival in Prague of von Neurath's replacement as Protector Reinhard Heydrich, head of the SS and architect of the "final solution." But even the unified representation of Czech art in the first show was already compromised by events. Conspicuously missing from the 662 exhibits was the work of Josef Čapek, for one. He had been arrested on 1 September 1939, the day that Germany invaded Poland and World War II officially began for the rest of the world. By the time the nation was celebrating its creative artists in Obecní dům, Čapek was in Buchenwald. Later he was moved to Sachsenhausen, where most of the Czech students seized on 17 November 1939 were interned, and thence in 1945 to Bergen-Belsen. In the 1930s, like his brother Karel, Josef had been an active antifascist. Among his creations most likely to have incensed the Nazis were three biting cycles of satirical drawings, many originally published in *Lidové noviny*, called "Modern Times," "Dictators' Boots," and "In the Shadow of Fascism."[22] Emil Filla (1882–1953), whom we earlier encountered scouring Prague's coffeehouses in 1910 for subscribers to buy Derain's "Bathers," was arrested on the same day as Čapek and also spent the war in the camps. Though two of Filla's pictures were on show in 1939 at Obecní dům, the records would not show it; his name was expunged from the list of exhibitors published in the official commemorative catalogue issued the following year.[23]

The artist Vojtěch Preissig (1873–1944), who had worked with Alfons Mucha in Paris at the turn of the century, died in Dachau. From 1910 to 1930 he had lived and taught in the United States; he put his talents at the service of the national resistance during both world wars, making posters for the Czechoslovak Legions in World War I and graphic designs for the illegal magazine *V boj!* (*To Arms!*) during World War II, for which he was arrested in 1940. His daughter, too, was arrested along with other members of the family and executed in Berlin in 1942. Max Švabinský was later criticized by some for accepting the so-called Saint Václav Prize for services to art from the occupation authorities, awarded to him in 1939 for his massive stained-glass window "The Last Judgment" in Saint Vitus's Cathedral.[24] Possibly he wanted to avoid the fate of his ex-wife Ela, who was the subject of many of his best-known early paintings, including the hauntingly beautiful "*Chudý kraj*" (Poor Countryside, 1899). She spent the war in Ravensbrück.[25] Milena Jesenská, who was also involved with *V boj!*, was arrested in November 1939 and died in the same camp in 1944. Whether or not she was a descendant of the Jan Jesenský executed so theatrically on Staroměstské náměstí in 1621, it was her father's nationalist xenophobia rather than her own cosmopolitanism that seemed vindicated by this modern replay of ancient oppressions.

Milena wrote some extraordinarily moving articles for Ferdinand Peroutka's *Přítomnost* during the dark summer of 1938 and in the early months of the occupation. She became the magazine's de facto editor after Peroutka's arrest in March 1939. It says a lot for her consistency of moral perspective—and for the variety of ways in which it is possible to be a patriot—that when complimented by a man "with whom just a year ago I would certainly have greatly differed in worldviews" with the words "Let your opinions be what they may, I see that above all, you are a Czech," Milena replied: "I am *self-evidently* a Czech, but I try *above all* to be a decent human being."[26] But Czech she was. In "The Czech Mom" [*Česká maminka*] she locates national identity in the little things of life, and roots the nation's continuity in the female line. This article is remarkable among other things for its proud assertion of the value and power of the traditionally feminine in human existence, though for that reason it would probably not pass muster in some North American feminist circles today. "Trifles," Milena writes, "become big symbols. And since it is woman, who wields in her hand the trifles, she reigns also over the big symbols. Czech song and the Czech book. Czech hospitality. The Czech language and old Czech customs. Czech Easter eggs, little Czech gardens and clumps of Czech roses." She fondly recalls her grandmother, who "looked like Božena Němcová's *Babička*, just as did all your grandmothers"—of course—and who during World War I obstinately kept her household clocks an hour behind the official imperial summer time, which she held to be an "Austrian invention."[27]

Milena's relations with her father had been checkered, to say the least—though she did dedicate her first book, published in 1926, to "Dear Dad." But we glimpse another side of both of them in "On the Art of Remaining Standing." Milena relates how, as a little girl, she and her mother, who was gripping her hand "more tightly than was necessary," watched from the window of their apartment on the corner of Václavské náměstí and Na příkopě as what had been a ritualized Sunday morning confrontation between Czech and German promenaders turned nasty. The police intervened, shots were fired, the marchers fled. At the end of it, beside a fallen Czech demonstrator, "there remained standing before the guns one man—my Dad. I remember clearly, absolutely clearly, how he stood. Calmly, with his hands by his side." She continues:

I witnessed something similar once again later. It was, of course, under completely different circumstances. It was in the war and in the theater. At that time, Czechs did not yet have their own sovereignty in mind and no such things were happening. Only their Czechness was wedged in their hearts like the thorn of a mallow from a Czech garden. Tyl's *Fidlovačka* was on the stage—on the whole a naive, out-of-date, and unentertaining work. But then suddenly they started to sing "*Kde domov můj?*" You know, not a state anthem, not at all, but a national, Czech tune it was back then. But suddenly somebody stood up in front of me. Some gentleman, without a sound and calmly, with his hands by his side. I don't know what he wanted to express, but the act was as if to honor the Czech song. In a while another stood up. Then several more. And then all of us were standing. Then we were singing. That song was played several times over then, and it was played in such a sincere and heartfelt way, like a prayer. "*Kde domov můj*" was not a song against anyone, but for something. It did not wish for anybody's destruction, but for our continued existence. It is not a warrior song, but a song of our Czech home, that land without anything grandiose about its countryside, a land of hills and hillocks, fields and leas, silver birches, weeping willows and broad-crowned lime-trees, a land of fragrant boundaries between fields and tranquil little streams. The land where we are at home. It was beautiful to stand by her, because it is always beautiful to love one's home.[28]

Franz Kafka was right. Whatever her many dissatisfactions, in the end Milena did belong to her own language, and could not be found in her entirety anywhere else.

Grave Far Away

Of 118,310 people in the Protectorate of Bohemia and Moravia deemed to be "of Jewish race" (as defined by the Nuremberg Laws) on 15 March 1939, 26,111 managed to emigrate, 14,045 survived the war, and 78,154 perished at German hands.[29] The great majority of Czech and Moravian Jews were interned first in Terezín, an old Bohemian fortress town sixty kilometers north of Prague built by Joseph II and named for his mother, Maria Theresa. Reinhard Heydrich expelled the Czech population in November 1941 and turned the town into a camp for Jews from the Protectorate, as well as for prominent Jews from elsewhere in occupied Europe and from Germany itself. Among the latter were Rabbi Leo Baeck. Terezín was unique among Nazi concentration camps, at once an efficient cog in the machinery of genocide and a surreal theater of its public denial. The International Red Cross was invited to inspect this "model ghetto" in July 1944; it was also the setting for a propaganda film entitled *Theresienstadt: A Documentary on the Jewish Settlement District* [*Siedlungsgebiet*]. But for the Jews themselves, Terezín was merely a way station on the long journey to the ramp at Auschwitz. Of

139,517 inhabitants of the camp between 24 November 1941 and 20 April 1945, 87,063 were sooner or later transported to the East. Not that the model ghetto (whose prewar Czech population had never exceeded 7,000) did not have an impressive death rate of its own: 33,521 people lost their lives there over the same period.[30]

Among the many artists who died in Terezín or in the gas chambers to which it led were Emil Fritta (1907–44), whose drawings of life in the camp were exhibited by SVU Mánes after the war ended, and František Zelenka. Zelenka (1904–43) is best known for his stage sets and advertisements for Voskovec and Werich's Liberated Theater. It was he who did the "*Jazzové revue*" poster discussed earlier. Zelenka prepared sets and costumes for twenty-five theatrical productions in Terezín, not all of which were allowed to be staged. One was of Smetana's *Prodaná nevěsta*, whose camp premiere took place in 1943.[31] Cultural life flourished behind the fortress walls so long as there was any life left to live at all. Half-starved women compiled recipe books from their memories of normality, oftentimes forgetting ingredients.[32] Their children, whom the adults made every effort to provide with schooling despite everything, were encouraged to draw pictures. The novelist Jiří Weil (1900–1959) describes the things they saw and drew, the food lines, the SS men strutting the sidewalks, the coffins on carts, and the rest of Terezín's routines. He goes on:

> But they also saw that which the adults did not want to see—the beauty beyond the gates of the citadel, green meadows and bluish hills, the road, unwinding into the distance with the imagined sign "Praha" [Prague], animals, birds, butterflies—all that was beyond the gates and not in town, they could look at everything only from a distance, from the barrack windows and the fortress ramparts, where they were sometimes let to go. And they saw different things too, things that the grown-ups were not even able to see—princesses with tiaras on their foreheads, wicked witches and sorcerers, jesters and little bugs with human faces, a land of plenty, where for the entrance fee of one crown it was possible to get everything—cakes, sweetmeats, suckling pig with a fork stuck in it, where streams of pop and milk flowed. They also saw their former rooms complete with little curtains and the cat by its saucer of milk, they transported them to Terezín, there had to be stoves though and lots of pots, because in those pots should be food. All this they drew and painted and lots more besides; they liked to paint and draw, maybe from morning to night.[33]

Of those fifteen thousand Jewish children, perhaps as many as one hundred returned home. Arnošt Lustig (b. 1926), who passed his own adolescence in Terezín, Buchenwald, and Auschwitz, paints an unforgettable portrait of one such survivor in his novel *Dita Saxová*.[34] Eighteen years old when the book begins in 1947, tall and blonde, with lovely blue eyes, Dita smiles a bright public smile. Her motto is "Life is not what we want but what we have."

Jiří Weil's own life cannot be seen as typical of anything—it was too extraordinary for that—but it was, in its way, emblematic of his times. The son of a maker of frames for pictures and mirrors, Weil entered Charles University in 1919 as a student of Slavonic philology and comparative literature. He was one of F. X. Šalda's favorite pupils. He joined the youth wing of the KSČ in 1921 and made his first pilgrimage to the Soviet Union, aged twenty-two, the following year. Through the 1920s he worked as a translator in the press section of the Soviet mission in Prague. His *Russian Revolutionary Literature* of 1924 was one of the first books to introduce the Soviet avant-garde in Europe. He followed this up with the anthology *Sborník sovětské revoluční poesie* (1932). Vítězslav Nezval recalls that Weil was "the only one of us who knew Russian and the first to translate for us Mayakovsky's verse. He showed us various Soviet avant-garde reviews, which later, when Teige got hold of them, had a great influence on the typographic layout of our avant-garde magazines."[35] Weil was a member of Devětsil and one of those who theatrically parted company with the seven writers expelled from the KSČ in 1929. It was he, too, who initiated the meeting between Julius Fučík, Josef Hora, and F. X. Šalda at which Šalda agreed to put *Tvorba* at the disposal of the party. Weil coedited *Tvorba* alongside Fučík until 1933.

That year he went again to the Soviet Union, where he worked first in Moscow translating Lenin into Czech. In circumstances that are still not clear, he joined and was subsequently expelled from the Bolshevik party and later the KSČ itself; his letters home, complaining among other things about shortages of coffee in the people's paradise, may have had something to do with it.[36] Narrowly escaping the noose after Kirov's assassination, he was exiled to Alma-Ata. Later he spent six months serving as a reporter "attached" to a labor camp in Soviet Central Asia. He was permitted to return to Czechoslovakia in 1935. In 1937, at Fučík's suggestion, he published a memoir of his Soviet experiences under the title *Czechs Are Building in the Land of the Five-Year Plan*. His novel *Moskva—hranice* (*Moscow—The Border*), which came out in Prague that same year, was altogether less conventional. It is the first work of European fiction to bring to life the Moscow of Stalin's show trials. It proved as unpalatable to the communist left as André Gide's *Return from the Soviet Union*, and Fučík duly savaged it in *Tvorba*. *Moskva—hranice* is an experimental work, written in a deliberately "Sovietized," staccato prose style. It is also a roman à clef. One of its central characters, Ri, is modeled on the daughter of a Prostějov factory owner (and first love of the poet Jiří Wolker) Hella Galasová, who married an engineer in Moscow. The couple got caught up in the machinery of the trials, and (as Petr Nový puts it) "the publication of *Moskva—hranice* only confirmed their fate: the producers of the play very quickly realized who Weil was writing about. Both were executed."[37] Weil did not even attempt to publish his sequel to *Moskva—hranice*, *The Wooden Spoon* [*Dřevěná lžíce*, 1938], in which he scored yet another first, in this case the first novel to be set in the gulag. *Dřevěná lžíce* was first published in Italian translation in 1970, and then in *samizdat* in 1977. The first legal domestic publication was in 1992.[38]

Although, Nový continues, Jiří Weil grew up in an Orthodox Jewish household, the children "'weren't into that any more.' The arrival of the Germans thus meant for him a thorough shock: he is suddenly and publicly designated as a Jew and he cannot comprehend why he is somebody other than he was before."[39] To stave off the inevitable, he married his longtime and properly Aryan lover Olga on 19 March 1942. It was the last "mixed marriage" permitted in the Protectorate. In the evenings Weil wrote and wrote, in the daytime he was forced into Jewishness whether he liked it or not, cataloguing the stolen artifacts arriving daily at the Jewish Museum. The summons finally arrived for him to present himself at Veletržní palac for his transport to Terezín. With the help of Olga and her coworkers he faked suicide from Hlávka Bridge, and the authorities recorded him as dead. He survived the rest of the war in hiding, weighing just forty-four kilograms at its end. During these years he wrote a historical novel set in the eighth century whose theme is the false prophet *Makanna: Father of Wonders*, which was published, with a foreword by Pavel Eisner, in 1946. After the war he became editor of the celebrated publishing house ELK (European Literary Club), until it was nationalized in 1949. His novel *Life with a Star* [*Život s hvězdou*], set in occupied Prague and published that same year, proved to be no more to the taste of the KSČ than *Moskva—hranice* had been. It was considered too "subjectivist" and insufficiently heroic. Banned from publishing, Weil once again found himself a reluctant employee of what had in the meantime become the State Jewish Museum. His *Elegy for 77,297 Victims* came out in a miserly edition of seven hundred copies in 1958.[40]

Jiří Weil's last work, *Mendelssohn Is on the Roof*, was published posthumously in 1960. Also set in wartime Prague, its final text is a mutilated patchwork; already seriously ill, Weil was told the book would not see the light of day at all unless it was modified to emphasize the communist resistance and the heroic Red Army. He hurriedly excised many passages, including one whole chapter, and inserted others written to order.[41] The book begins with a fine piece of Prague grotesque on the Rudolfinum roof where they are searching among the statues of composers for the Jew Mendelssohn. Unfortunately, the statues are not labeled. "How are we to recognize this Mendelssohn?" asks the despairing Bečvář. Protector Heydrich is a cultivated man who knows his classical heritage, and a mistake could mean the eastern front. Schlesinger finally hits on an idea. "Go round the statues one more time and look carefully at their noses. The one that has the biggest nose, that'll be the Jew." Schlesinger had learned this from slides he had been shown in lectures at a course he took on "racial science." They inspect the statues once again. "Over there," shouts Bečvář, "that one with the beret, no other statue has a nose like that!" They begin to haul down Richard Wagner.[42]

The worst repression of the war, as far as non-Jewish Czechs were concerned, followed the assassination in Prague of Reichsprotektor Reinhard Heydrich on 27 May 1942 by Czech parachutists based in Britain. Between 28 May and 4 July the press published daily lists of people who had been condemned to death by Prague and Brno courts and executed—in all, 1,381 Czech men and women.[43] One prominent victim was Vladislav Vančura (1891–1942). The first president of Devětsil, and one of the seven writers condemned by Jiří Weil and Karel Teige in 1929 for his petit bourgeois heresies, Vančura had turned his talents from avant-garde fictions to writing a patriotic epic, Pictures from the History of the Czech Nation [Obrazy z dějin národa českého, 1939–40], following the occupation. He was also active in the resistance. This tally for executions does not include those slaughtered in one of the most infamous of all Nazi reprisals during World War II, which took place on 10 June 1942 at the village of Lidice twenty kilometers from Prague. Let the German communiqué speak for itself:

> During the search for the murderers of Obergruppenführer Heydrich it was conclusively proven that the inhabitants of the community of Lidice by Kladno provided support and help to a network who are likely to have perpetrated this crime. The relevant evidence was obtained without the help of the local population. The attitude toward the assassination shown by this is underlined by further actions hostile to the Reich, such as the discoveries of antistate printed matter, stores of arms and ammunition, illegal transmitters and an extraordinarily large quantity of rationed goods, and the circumstance that citizens of this settlement are in active enemy service abroad. Because the citizens of this community by their actions and support of the murderers of the SS Obergruppenführer Heydrich broke proclaimed laws in the grossest manner, the grown men were put to death by shooting, the women were transported into concentration camps, and the children were taken to be appropriately raised. The buildings in the village were razed to the ground and the name of the village was erased.[44]

Lidice had 167 families, 503 inhabitants, 106 houses, a baroque church dating from 1729–32.[45] One hundred ninety-two men and seven women—relatives of those "in enemy service abroad"—were shot, and 205 women shipped to Ravensbrück and other camps, from which 60 of them never returned. Of Lidice's ninety-six children, eighty-one died in the gas chambers. A detachment of Jewish prisoners was drafted in from Terezín to bury those who had been summarily executed; detailed lists were drawn up of all property seized ("a so far unascertained quantity of chickens and rabbits," reads one item);[46] according to the relevant report to Prague, "perhaps 20,000 man-hours" were put in by around one hundred workers between 11 June and 3 July to obliterate all traces of the settlement.[47] The people of Lidice almost certainly had no involvement whatsoever in Heydrich's assassination. The same fate befell the smaller village of Ležáky (32 killed, 11 transported) two weeks later. Though such massacres were not repeated thereafter, terror became normalized. The guillotine installed in Prague's Pankrác prison in the spring of 1943 claimed 1,075 lives before the war ended.[48]

The destruction of Lidice provoked immediate international outcry. It also touched the hearts of two prominent Czechs then in exile. One was "the most beautiful and charming Metropolitan Opera star," as her American posters billed her, Jarmila Novotná. Novotná (1907–94) was the best known of Czech sopranos between the wars. She made her debut at the National Theater as Mařenka in Smetana's *Prodaná nevěsta* at the age of seventeen in June 1925.[49] From 1929 to 1933 she sang in the Staatstheater in Berlin, from 1933 to 1938 at the Staatsoper in Vienna, from 1940 to 1956 at the Met in New York. The dates are significant: it was the onward tramp of totalitarian boots, not the search for stardom, that explains Miss Novotná's itinerary. The other refugee was Jan Masaryk (1886–1948), son of Tomáš Masaryk, ambassador to Britain from 1925 to 1938 and minister of foreign affairs in the Czechoslovak government-in-exile in London from 1940. His words introduced the record album he and Novotná made together in May and June of 1942, which was issued in the United States that summer under the title "Songs of Lidice":

> This is a selection of a very few, simple, but to my mind, lovely folk songs of my nativeland. Jarmila Novotná used to sing these songs to my father, and if I happened to be in Prague, I accompanied her. Today, both Jarmila and I are refugees from Hitler's vulgar terribleness and we did these songs once more for ourselves. Some kind friend suggested that they should be recorded, and with great trepidation I agreed to do my part. Our recording coincided with Heydrich's arrival in Prague, with his thousand-times deserved death, and with the unbelievable horror of Lidice. The simple, immortal folk of that unhappy village sang all these songs, and it is in their memory that Jarmila Novotná is offering them to the American public. . . . And when we rebuild Lidice, these songs will come back through pure Czech and Slovak air, cleansed once and for all from the destroyers of music.[50]

Would he were right. Despite the KSČ's own cult of *lidovost* and cynical use of the Lidice massacre as propaganda for many years after,[51] Jarmila Novotná's "Songs of Lidice" were not heard in Czechoslovakia until Supraphon issued them on a compact disk in 1992, exactly fifty years after they were recorded at 78 rpm. The sleeve notes explained that plans for their domestic release had been blocked on two previous occasions—in 1948, following the communist coup, and in 1968, following the Soviet invasion.[52] Novotná herself lived long enough to visit Prague for the 1992 launch, discovering a city in which few people remembered her. She had been in exile, for a second time, since 1948.

Beside the executions and transportations we must also put sustained cultural warfare, the deliberate destruction of Czech symbols of identity. A quarter of the books (150,000 out of a collection of 600,000) were removed from Prague City Library.[53] The National Museum was pointedly renamed the Land Museum [*Zemské muzeum*], its halls used for Nazi propaganda exhibitions, and the statues of Hus and Masaryk confiscated from the Pantheon.[54] Among the memorials that disappeared from Prague streets were those to Havlíček, Rieger, Svatopluk Čech, and the French historian of Bohemia Ernest Denis, as well as Stanislav Sucharda's majestic—if somewhat overblown—Palacký monument, which had been erected on the banks of the Vltava in 1912.[55] The Jan Hus monument in Staroměstské náměstí was left to stand but was obliterated by flags with swastikas.[56] A gigantic "V" for victory (*Viktoria* in German, *vítězství* in Czech), trumpeting German successes on the eastern front, was inlaid in the cobblestones of the ancient square in the summer of 1941.[57] One October night that same year, SS men removed the remains of the Unknown Czechoslovak Soldier that had been installed in the chapel of the Old Town Hall in 1922 and threw them into the Vltava downstream of the city at Troja.[58] Street names were purged wholesale. Národní třída (National Avenue), in the latter part of the nineteenth century Ferdinandova třída, the Czech Corso, where the National Theater sits, became třída Viktoria (Victory Avenue). Paris [*Pařížská*] Avenue—which until 1926 had been Mikulášská třída, where Franz Kafka's family lived—became Nürnberg Avenue. Revolution Avenue became Berlin Avenue, Masaryk Embankment became Vltava Embankment and then Heydrich Embankment, the Jirásek Bridge became the Dienzenhofer Bridge, the Bridge of the Legions became Smetana Bridge.[59]

Smetana's music was less repressed during the occupation than later sources often imply. The Nazis tried where possible to appropriate Czech figures, from Saint Václav to Josef Pekař, for their own ends, and censored selectively rather than wholesale. If, as a post-1989 *History of the Lands of the Czech Crown* states,[60] the "Tábor" and "Blaník" movements of *Má vlast* were ultimately banned, this must have occurred very late in the war indeed. The entire symphonic cycle was performed in what was still the Smetana Hall of Obecní dům under the baton of Václav Talich on 12 May 1944, and the program notes for the concert are overtly patriotic. They begin: "Along with the opera *Libuše*, with which it makes up a single conceptual whole, *Má vlast* is Smetana's greatest work, dedictated to the celebration of the creator's homeland." The commentary on "Blaník" also strikes an unexpected note. In place of "Saint Václav's army," which Jirásek had sleeping under the hill in *Staré pověsti české*, it has *Hussite* warriors waiting "in deep sleep for the moment, when they have to come to the aid of the *vlast*."[61] This concert, one of a cycle of seven, was part of a "Smetana Year," the 120th jubilee of his birth and the sixtieth of his death, which also saw special performances in the

40. Jarmila Novotná personifying the Czechoslovak Republic, with phrygian cap intact, on Max Švabinský's hundred-crown banknote, 1931.

National Theater of six of his operas (though conspicuously not of *The Brandenburgers in Bohemia* or *Libuše*). Smetana, it seems, is a man for all seasons: when in 1952 the KSČ, too, decided to rename Masaryk Embankment, it became Smetanovo nábřeží. What Czech could possibly object to honoring Bedřich Smetana? But events like the Smetana Year were at best a thin veneer on a national humiliation that was deliberate, insistent, and ubiquitous. The Germans imposed themselves on signs, route maps, official documents, and commercial letterheads, which had to be bilingual with the German text put first. Given the protracted language wars of the nineteenth century, this was an especially unpleasant pill for Czechs to swallow. Emblems of Czech sovereignty were struck from insignia, stamps, and banknotes. Jarmila Novotná had sat for Max Švabinský as the model for the female figure of the Republic on the hundred-crown bill issued in 1931.[62] When the same design was used on the fifty-crown Protectorate bill of 1941, the Phrygian cap of liberty had been removed from her head on the orders of the German overlords of the national bank.[63] A small detail, no doubt, in a sea of death, but the kind of everyday reminder that could not be escaped.

When spring finally did come again to the meadows and woods of the Czech land, it was a spring edged with bitterness. Prague was liberated by the Soviet army on 9 May 1945, a day after the official German surrender in Berlin. It was the last significant fighting of World War II in Europe. Four days later Smetana's *Prodaná nevěsta* was sung at the National Theater in a performance dedicated to the memory of the fallen.[64] The official reopening of the theater came on 27 May, when *Libuše* was ceremonially staged in the presence of President Edvard Beneš, newly returned from six years in (his second) exile.[65] *The Brandenburgers in Bohemia* followed soon afterward; its contemporary resonance was clear enough.[66] On 17 June the Stavovské divadlo reopened with Alois Jirásek's *Lucerna*.[67] There was symbolism in this, and an echo of a much older battle. *Lucerna* (*The Lantern*) had been the last play to be performed in Czech at the Stavovské on 1 July 1939 before, for the duration of the war, it once again became a purely German theater. But these affirmations of a restored national freedom did not herald a simple restoration of the prewar status quo ante. There had been too many losses and too many betrayals for that, starting with Munich.

Some came in the very last week of the war. The Prague uprising of 5–8 May 1945 took 1,691 Czech lives, and 436 Soviet soldiers also perished in the battle for the city. Many of the city's architectural and cultural monuments, especially in and around Staroměstské náměstí, were badly damaged in the fighting. Among them were the ancient astronomical clock on the Old Town Hall for which Josef Mánes had painted the calendar disk, Mikoláš Aleš's fresco of Saint Václav on the Štorch bookstore, and Charles IV's Emmaus Abbey. The city archives in the Old Town Hall were destroyed along with its neo-Gothic wing. "Very valuable indeed," had read a prewar guidebook, "are the collection of city charters from the year 1316 and the great collection of city books from 1310 to 1850, for in these is a picture of all the city's law and all the legal life of the city, complicated and many-sided."[68] Some of the dead Russians were buried in the square in front of what had been from 1941 the headquarters of the German administration, the Rudolfinum, from whose roof Mendelssohn had had to be removed. Formerly Smetana Square, this bore the German name Mozartplatz (*alone*, without Czech translation) during the occupation. It was renamed the Square of the Red Army Soldiers [*náměstí Krasnoarmějců*] in 1952. It is now náměstí Jana Palacha, honoring the young student Jan Palach who burned himself to death in January 1969 beneath Myslbek's statue of Saint Václav in protest against yet another invasion of his country; and the Soviet soldiers' graves are unmarked. But long before that, in 1945, before Palach was born, the street leading from this square to the Svatopluk Čech Bridge had been renamed 17 November Street in memory of what the Nazis did to an earlier generation of Czech students.

Prague's first three postwar art exhibitions opened on 20 July 1945. The graphic art society SČUG Hollar organized a posthumous retrospective of Vojtěch Preissig, while SVU Mánes displayed previously unexhibited paint-

41. Staroměstské náměstí, May 1945.

ings and drawings of 1938–39 by Emil Filla, who survived his six years in the camps. Josef Čapek did not. The exhibition "Josef Čapek *in Memoriam*" in the Aleš Hall of Umělecká beseda showed Čapek's last paintings, two cycles from 1938–39 entitled *Oheň* (Fire) and *Touha* (Longing). They are among the most powerful works in modern Czech art, in spirit, if not in their style, which is pure Josef Čapek, a Czech *Guernica*. *Oheň* portrays "a threatening, bellicose woman," against a background in most of the pictures of burning or broken buildings and fleeing human figures. *Touha* depicts "a woman, who, he [Josef Čapek] said, is looking with longing on the severed countryside of the *pohraničí*." These descriptions are those of Čapek's wife, Jarmila.[69] A larger Čapek retrospective was mounted by Umělecká beseda in September and October of the next year.[70]

A casual glance through the list of graves in the official guidebook to Vyšehrad Cemetery would lead us to believe that like his brother Karel, Josef Čapek too is buried in "the most sacred place" amid "the whole company of our great minds."[71] But the headstone tells us otherwise:[72]

Here would have been buried Josef Čapek, painter and poet
Grave far away
18 23/3 87 19 -/4 45

Josef died in Bergen-Belsen, probably of typhus, probably in mid-April 1945. Nobody knows exactly. His body was never found, so there is no grave. Emil Filla contributed his memoirs of his own time in the camps to the catalogue for "Josef Čapek *in Memoriam*." He ends: "We came back and spoke of good fortune—but we never saw Josef Čapek again——Shamefully they stole from us so many works, which he would have created for us, they stole from us a poet, a great human being, a patriot, whom today we need so much."[73]

Bílá hora Redressed—Again

The tone of postwar Czechoslovak politics was set by the Košice Governing Program, which was adopted by the provisional National Front government on 5 April 1945. Elaborating on the program that same day in newly liberated Košice in eastern Slovakia, President Beneš promised a radically different social order. "We are all fully aware," he said, "that the renewed republic should not be a simple return to what existed before Munich." He concluded his speech, all the same, with a poignant reminiscence of the past: "It has been said in recent speeches that our new democracy [*demokracie*] will really rest only on the people, that it should be a new real *people's government* [*lidovláda*]. This is my decided wish too. I believe that after this war we will have all the conditions to bring about this new people's government. It is up to you alone—all of you. To this program—as I already promised in Prague Castle on the day of Masaryk's funeral—I myself remained faithful under all circumstances, and faithful I shall remain [*věren zůstanu*]."[74]

Beneš's association of the radicalism of the Košice Program with the memory of Tomáš Masaryk is typical of the political imagery of the fateful period in Czech history between liberation and the KSČ coup of "Victorious February" [*Vítězný únor*] 1948. These years abound with what seem, in retrospect, improbable conjunctions. In 1947, for example, Czechoslovak Post issued stamps that commemorated the tenth anniversary of Masaryk's death (and the 950th of Saint Vojtěch's) side by side with the Two-Year Plan, the First World Festival of Democratic Youth in Prague, and the thirtieth anniversary of the "Great October Socialist Revolution." In 1948 it marked the fifty-second birthday of by then "first workers' president" Klement Gottwald with a special first day cover that exhorted Czechs to "be still more unanimous, united, and resolute, and your will, the will of the people, will be the law in this land."[75] The same year two issues of stamps, both designed by Max Švabinský, celebrated the eleventh Sokol jamboree in Prague. One bore "a symbolic drawing of the republic, Sokols and Hradčany," the other carried portraits of two revered Sokol leaders of the past, Jindra Vaníček and Josef Scheiner.[76] Writing in the first issue of the government magazine *Československo* (*Czechoslovakia*; edited by Marie Majerová) in 1945 Zdeněk Nejedlý, who was now minister of education and national enlightenment, emphasized the "deeply popular" character of the "national culture" which "from the Hussite era to modern times always served the people and never the aristocracy, whether of birth or intellect." As leading exemplars of this dedication to the people he lists "Komenský, Kollár, Palacký, Smetana, Němcová, Mánes, Jirásek, Aleš, Masaryk."[77] The same issue has two photographs of the 1938 Sokol jamboree with the caption "an uplifting and binding memory of the Sokol festival, the last before the German invasion."[78] Binding that memory was not to be; the eleventh Sokol jamboree of 1948 was to be the last until 1994. Sokol was unceremoniously dissolved by the communist government soon afterward, for the third time; it had been banned by Austria in World War I and the Nazis in World War II. Every attempt would be made over the next few years to erase all traces of Tomáš Masaryk from the public mind. But Czechs were not to know this at the time. These couplings of the old and the new did not jar; it is only in hindsight that they seem unthinkable. At the time, socialism paraded itself in impeccably national costume.

In fact, neither the new "people's government" agreed upon by the two centers of wartime foreign resistance, London and Moscow, nor its policies bore much resemblance to the Masarykian legacy to which Beneš had sworn eternal fidelity back in 1937. Eight out of twenty-five government members, among them two deputy prime ministers and the ministers of the interior, agriculture, labor, education, and information, were communists. The ministry of information under the former journalist Václav Kopecký (1897–1961) was a particular plum; it gave the KSČ control over Czechoslovak Radio and such propaganda media as Československo. The party also wielded strong influence at defense, where the minister, army general Ludvík Svoboda (1895–1979), was a communist sympathizer, and at Jan Masaryk's foreign ministry through the KSS (Communist party of Slovakia) Secretary of State Vladimír (Vlado) Clementis (1902–52). No other party held more than four positions in the government, and the norm was three. Prime Minister Zdeněk Fierlinger and the ministers of industry and food were Social Democrats, who worked closely with the KSČ in these years. Consistently with this leftward turn in the government's composition, the Košice Program also announced a major (and, it envisaged, a permanent) shift in international orientation: "The Czechoslovak-Soviet treaty of 12 December 1943 . . . will determine for the whole future the foreign policy position of our state."[79] Memories of Western betrayal at Munich were still fresh and raw.

Mindful of prewar tensions between Czechs and Slovaks, the Košice Program broke with the unitary "Czechoslovakism" of the first republic, recognizing the Slovaks as a "sovereign nation." It offered them a National Council that would be not just symbolic but a genuine "bearer of state power in Slovak territory"; a promise, in the event, that was honored more in form than substance, just as similar undertakings had been after 1918. The KSČ kept a very tight rein on Slovakia in the 1950s, ruthlessly suppressing what it called "bourgeois Slovak nationalism." One casualty was future president Gustáv Husák (1913–91), who spent the entire decade in prison (and according to legend swore to get even with "those Czech bastards"). Another was Vlado Clementis, who was to dangle at the end of a hangman's rope in December 1952, one of only three non-Jewish victims of the gaudy show trial of former KSČ General Secretary Rudolf Slánský. Clementis was permitted to write a farewell letter to his wife Lída on the morning of his execution: "I am smoking a last pipe and I am listening. I hear you clearly singing the songs of Smetana and Dvořák."[80] At the local level, the Košice Program promised replacement of the "former bureaucratic administrative apparatus [which was] distant from the people" by "national committees elected by the people." Dominated for the most part by communists, these ad hoc committees were extremely powerful in the disordered conditions following liberation. Another new organ of "popular power" mooted in the program (and legally established by a presidential decree of 19 May 1945) was "extraordinary people's courts," operating "in conjunction with national committees" to deal with "traitors, collaborators, and fascist elements from the ranks of the Czech and Slovak nation." By May 1947 these courts had handed out 713 death sentences and 20,629 terms of imprisonment, 741 of them for life.[81]

"Universal, secret, and direct elections" to a new constituent assembly were promised as quickly as practicable. The voting age was lowered to eighteen, and the franchise extended to members of the armed forces. This did not mean that prewar parliamentary life would resume as before, however. Only those parties represented in the National Front government, that is, the KSČ, National Socialists, Social Democrats, and People's party in the Czech lands, and the KSS and the Democratic party in Slovakia, were allowed to resume their activities after the war. The Agrarians and other prewar "right-wing" parties were banned on grounds of their alleged betrayal of the interests of the republic before and after Munich. This was far more than a simple matter of outlawing a fascist fringe. The Agrarians had topped the polls among Czechoslovak voters in every national election since 1925,[82] and parties made illegal after the war had between them received over half the votes in the last prewar national election of 1935.[83] The elections to the constituent assembly were scheduled for May 1946. Meantime, a provisional assembly nominated by legal parties and "mass organizations" like the KSČ-dominated labor union congress ÚRO [Ústřední rada odborů] convened in Prague in October of 1945. Up until then, the National Front governed by presidential decree. These decrees[84]—whose validity the provisional assembly immediately ratified—swiftly and dramatically altered prewar Czechoslovakia's ethnic composition and class structures. Their first target, not altogether surprisingly, was the country's German minority.

In June 1945 Monsignor Bohumil Stašek, the canon of Vyšehrad who had delivered the sermon at Karel Hynek Mácha's reburial six years before, declared that "once in a thousand years the time has come for settling accounts with the Germans, who are evil and to whom the commandment to love thy neighbor therefore does not apply."[85] This peculiar revision of Christian doctrine may owe something to the fact that Stašek himself spent the war in Dachau, where he was sent after preaching an anti-Nazi sermon at a "national pilgrimage" to the shrine of Saint Lawrence [sv. Vavřinec] in Domažlice in August 1939, and where he lost an eye. The canon rejoiced in "the coming of the most glorious Slav epoch under the leadership of Russia" when "Kollár's idea of the triumphant *Slávy dcera* will be fulfilled, an invincible Slavonic camp brought into being. The Czechoslovak and Soviet anthems together with the Saint Václav chorale ring out with the promise that Catholic folk will work for the truth, honesty, and justice of Czechoslovakia."[86] Prokop Drtina, a leader of the National Socialist party who was familiar to Czechs from his wartime broadcasts from London as "Pavel Svatý" (Paul Saint), struck similar notes at that party's congress held on 17 May 1945 in the Lucerna palace on Václavské náměstí; a property that was not to belong to the Havel family for very much longer. His speech was interrupted by loud applause after almost every sentence:

> The bestiality and vandalism which the Germans committed at the last moment in Prague . . . these customary atrocities of the nation of *Kulturträger* [bearers of culture] themselves show us what is and must be the first task in laying down the basis for a new life: to clean out the republic as a whole and completely of Germans. This is the order of the moment for every one of us, it is the historical task of our generation. . . . Our new republic cannot be built as anything other than a purely national state, a state of only Czechs and Slovaks and of nobody other than Czechs and Slovaks! . . . Although our land is beautiful, fecund, rich, it is small and there is no room in it for anybody other than us. The Germans are foreigners in it, carpetbaggers [*přivandrovalci*] and colonists. . . . The Germans were always a foreign ulcer in our body. . . . In our new republic no more than these three little German words should be permitted: *Heim ins Reich!*[87] To achieve this end we must begin to expel the Germans from our lands at once, immediately, by all methods, nothing must be allowed to make us falter or hesitate. . . . Every one of us must help in the cleansing of the homeland [*čistění vlasti*].[88]

Prime Minister Zdeněk Fierlinger called for the "cleansing" [*očista*] of the land from Germans on 14 May, adding that "the united will of all the people will resolve once and forever this problem that has burdened us for a whole millennium." Zdeněk Nejedlý proclaimed that "we do not have progressive Germans and we do not know them." Similar sentiments were expressed by Deputy Prime Minister Josef David, Minister of Food Václav Majer, Minister of Justice Jaroslav Stránský, and many others.[89] Klement Gottwald, now also a deputy prime minister, spoke in Brno on 23 June on the need push back "once and for ever beyond the borders of our land . . . an element hostile to us," and called for Czech resettlement of the *pohraničí*, describing this as "redressing Bílá hora" and correcting "the mistakes of our Czech kings, the Přemyslids, who invited the German colonists here for us."[90] President Beneš sent out the same message in Staroměstské náměstí on 16 May: "It will be necessary . . . to liquidate out [*vylikvidovat*] especially uncompromisingly the Germans in the Czech lands and the Hungarians in Slovakia, in whatever way this liquidation can further the interest of a united state of Czechs and Slovaks. Let our motto be: to definitively de-Germanize [*odgermanizovat*] our homeland, culturally, economically, politically."[91] At Lidice three weeks later, on the anniversary of the massacre, he justified this by a clear principle of collective guilt: "I know that there were individual Germans who were aware of these horrors. But it is a question of the direct guilt of the overwhelming majority of Germans, and that is why the Germans as a whole are responsible."[92]

Modern Czech history is rich in ironies; not the least of them is this consensus, in the spring and summer of 1945, between the KSČ and so many of its imminent victims on "the order of the moment." Canon Bohumil Stašek (1886–1948) was no apolitical priest. He was a prewar leader of the People's party, editor of its newspaper *Lidové listy* (*The People's Paper*), and a member of parliament from 1925 to 1939. By the time he died in August 1948, communist persecution of the Catholic Church was well under way.[93] Its properties were sequestered, monks and nuns forcibly driven from monasteries and convents and interned in "concentration cloisters," members of the hierarchy confined and in some instances put on trial. In one notorious case (which forms the centerpiece of Josef Škvorecký's novel *The Miracle Game*) the secret police rigged a "miracle" during a mass in a small country church, then tortured to death the unfortunate incumbent, Father Josef Toufar, attempting to extract his confession to the fraud.[94] Prokop Drtina (1900–1980) survived longer, to his cost. A longtime member of the National Socialist party that won the biggest single share of Prague votes in the last prewar city council elections (26.17 percent in May 1938; the KSČ came in second with 16.62 percent),[95] Drtina was Edvard Beneš's private secretary from 1936 to 1938 and one of his closest associates during his London exile. He became minister of justice in the National Front government from November 1945 and was one of the so-called bourgeois ministers whose collective resignation in 1948 provided the excuse for Victorious February. He attempted suicide a few days later, was taken to Bulovka hospital in Prague, and detained on remand until 1953 when he was sentenced to fifteen years in prison. Amnestied in 1960, he was "fully rehabilitated" in 1969; a rehabilitation only to be revoked two years later as the "normalization" imposed after the Soviet invasion tightened its grip. Drtina ended his life as a supporter of the 1977 "dissident" manifesto *Charta 77* (*Charter 77*), which called upon the Czecho-slovak government to implement the Helsinki accords—to which it was a signatory—on human rights.[96] His angry autobiography is aptly titled *Czechoslovakia My Fate.*[97]

Josef David (1884–1968) and Jaroslav Stránský (1884–1973) were also National Socialists. David quit politics altogether after Victorious February. Stránský, between the wars owner of the Borový publishing house and publisher of the newspaper *Lidové noviny*, with which both Čapek brothers had a long and close association, was another "bourgeois minister" of 1948. He emigrated after the coup. So did Václav Majer, the only Social Democrat to support his "bourgeois" colleagues in the 1948 crisis. His leader, Zdeněk Fierlinger (1891–1976), a former ambassador to both Washington and Moscow, went over to the KSČ and was richly rewarded for his services by a seat in its presidium and a string of high state offices. But in 1945 such conflicts lay still in the future. With an eye to the upcoming elections, the National Front parties outbid one another in vengeful Czech patriotism. Their support for a permanent solution to "the German problem" was loud and unanimous, and public voices of opposition few and far between. Some individuals did have the moral courage to stand up and say that perhaps collective vengeance was not the national legacy of Komenský and Masaryk, but they were in a decided minority, and not to be found within the National Front.

Beneš's decrees put the property of "Germans, Hungarians, traitors, and collaborators" under state control (19 May 1945), expropriated their lands (21 June 1945) and later their movables (25 October 1945), authorized resettlement of Czechs and Slovaks in the *pohraničí* (20 July 1945), deprived Germans and Hungarians of Czechoslovak citizenship (3 August 1945), and dissolved all German institutions of higher education, among them the German university of Prague (18 October 1945). The decree of 3 August 1945 formed the legal basis for the *odsun*, the forcible deportation of Czechoslovakia's German minority to occupied Germany and Austria. By that time perhaps 600,000 Germans had already been driven out of the country in the wild *odsun* [*divoký odsun*] that followed liberation, when Czechs followed Prokop Drtina's advice and took ethnic cleansing into their own hands. The policy of wholesale expulsion was endorsed by the Allies—reluctantly by the United States and Britain, adamantly by the USSR, whose strategic aims it suited—at the Potsdam Conference of July 1945, though it went far beyond anything agreed during the war (or even proposed in the Košice Program). Thereafter the "transfer" proceeded in a more orderly fashion. On 24 October of the following year Minister of the Interior Václav Nosek informed parliament that the exodus was basically over, a further 2,165,135 Germans having been deported in the meantime. Those left were either proven antifascists or essential workers in industry or mining. By December 1946, Foreign Minister Jan Masaryk, Miss Novotná's pianist on "Songs of Lidice," reported that

2,256,000 Germans had been removed since August 1945.[98] By the time of the 1950 census, people declaring their national identity as German made up a mere 1.8 percent of the population of the Czech lands. In the last prewar decennial census of 1930 the comparable figure had been 29.5 percent. The Hungarian population of Slovakia (where, in the event, the policy was less stringently applied) fell from 17.6 to 10.3 percent over the same period.[99]

Just how many Czechoslovak Germans were deported or perished during the *odsun* remains a matter of controversy to this day. Three million is a fair estimate of the total population loss—in the Czech lands, between a quarter and a third of the inhabitants. There was abundant brutality, especially during the wild *odsun*. One of the worst incidents occurred in the town of Ústí nad Labem in northern Bohemia in July 1945. An explosion and fire in a munitions warehouse that killed twenty-eight people (among whom were both Czechs and Germans) was blamed on German saboteurs. One deportee, the German Social Democrat and undoubted antifascist Alois Ullman, recounts what followed:

> When work finished at 3 P.M. and the workers, mainly from the firm Schicht, had to go home across the Elbe bridges, the wildest mobs were rampaging in the vicinity of the market square. They tossed women with baby carriages into the Elbe, and these became targets for soldiers, who fired on the women until they no longer came to the surface. They also threw Germans into the water reservoir at the market square and pressed them under with poles whenever they came up. Only around 5 P.M. did some Russian officers show up, who attempted to clear the streets. . . . On the evening of 31 July the dead were collected in three places and taken away on trucks. In these three places there were around four hundred dead.[100]

German sources name 18,889 people who died in the *odsun*, 5,596 of them violently. Unnamed casualties would raise the real count to perhaps 50,000, while the final total of those who "died prematurely as a consequence of the *odsun*" may be as high as a quarter of a million; but all figures, in this matter, are uncertain and contested.[101]

Contemporary with the *odsun*, and in part made possible by it, was a parallel assault on Czechoslovakia's prewar propertied classes. What to do with the confiscated lands of "Germans, Hungarians, traitors, and collaborators" became a matter of political dispute within the National Front. The KSČ organized demonstrations in favor of wide redistribution to smallholders and agricultural laborers under the slogan "We will redress Bílá hora." The same slogan had been used in the earlier agrarian reform of 1919–20;[102] we might also remember Jaroslav Kvapil's use of the phrase in his speech at Alois Jirásek's funeral. Though the center parties in the coalition warned (rightly, as it turned out) that the economic consequences of such a redistribution would prove catastrophic, the communists' demagoguery proved irresistible. Around 28 percent of the agricultural land in Bohemia and Moravia changed hands: 2,946,395 hectares (of which 1,295,379 hectares was forest land) was confiscated in all, the bulk of it (around 2,400,000 hectares) lying in the Czech lands.[103] The phrase *"po Němcích"* (after the Germans, as in *po babičce*, after Granny) entered the language as a description of a mode of acquiring property. By way of comparison, some 1,800,000 hectares had been redistributed or sold, very much more gradually, as a result of the 1919–20 land reform, which took almost ten years to implement.[104] Equally damaging to the power of the prewar propertied classes was a presidential decree of 24 October 1945 that was ceremonially proclaimed from the ramp of the National Museum. One of Beneš's last legislative acts before the convening of the provisional national assembly, this nationalized all banks, mines, insurance companies, and major utilities, key industries like ironworks, chemicals and food processing, and most larger enterprises of any kind, down to "the manufacture of gramophone records." Altogether 2,119 firms were affected, which between them accounted for 75 percent of all manufacturing output and employed 62 percent of industrial workers.[105]

These expropriations were both justified by a rhetoric that seamlessly sewed together the patriotic and the "progressive," just like the postage stamps discussed earlier. Karel Kaplan, who is certainly no fellow traveler, recounts how the nationalization decree "was celebrated as an event of historic significance, which put the republic in the vanguard of progressive Europe, an event of a Czechoslovak character, which answered to the national tradition, experience, and needs, which came into being without any copying of foreign models."[106] The language here is peculiarly reminiscent of that in which, half a century earlier, *Zlatá Praha* and *Ottův slovník naučný* had patted themselves on the back for their unsullied Czechness. Beneš's decree was greeted by mass demonstrations of support in over two hundred Czechoslovak towns and cities. The 1946 New Year's editorial in *Tvorba*, once F. X. Šalda's journal, now the KSČ's "Weekly for Culture and Politics," looked back on "the first year of peace and freedom" with considerable satisfaction:

> Only for enemies of the nation can the historic measures of the National Front government mean nothing—these measures which broke the economic power of occupants and traitors by confiscation and national control [of their property], which divided their land among small agricultural workers, which punish crimes against the national honor, which with the establishment of national committees gave the power of the old bureaucratic apparatus into the hands of the people, and with the nationalization of the commanding heights of the economy guaranteed the people that the whole nation will reap the benefits of their work, all the working people.
>
> Why *above all* did the government, with the enthusiastic agreement of the

people, go for these measures? So that Munich will never be repeated, once and for ever to neutralize all traitorous elements, who aided it, who prepared it in cooperation with foreign fascism and who so shamefully served the Nazi invaders; so that we would never again live through the terrible years of oppression and humiliation.[107]

Tvorba's new editor was the ever-progressive S. K. Neumann.

Munich had by now become a capacious signifier. Glossed over here is the fact that nationalization affected *all* firms in certain sectors or of a certain size, irrespective of whether their individual owners had been patriots or collaborators. As in the case of the Germans, guilt is attributed collectively. A simple equation is drawn between social class and national treachery; the bourgeoisie was, so to speak, "Germanized" as a class. Populism had never been far from the surface of Czech nationalism, as we have oftentimes seen. The treatment of Czech aristocrats after World War I, though less brutal, in many ways parallels what happened on a much broader scale after World War II. The difference was that after 1945 identification of *národ* with *lid*, in the restrictive sense of the "popular classes," became the common currency of the only permitted politics. In the cabinet vote on the nationalization decree there was only one abstention, from Mgr. Jan Šrámek of the People's party, and nobody voted against. Those who might have done so had already been excluded from the political nation. Šrámek (1870–1956) paid dearly for his indiscretion. He was arrested trying to flee the country three years later and was interned until his death in 1956. He had been a member of the National Committee that declared Czech independence in 1918, was one of the original members of the Pětka, served as a minister in every Czechoslovak government from 1921 to 1938, vigorously opposed the Munich agreement, and headed the Czechoslovak government-in-exile in London from 1940 to 1945. Of such stuff are traitors made. But we should perhaps remember the fate of Marshal Radecký's statue in Malostranské náměstí.

These revolutionary measures were undeniably popular, and the KSČ, which had most consistently championed them, reaped the benefits. The communists won the May 1946 national elections—which were "free and fair," if we disregard the banning of the "right-wing" parties—convincingly, easily becoming the largest party, and capturing 38.12 percent of the vote nationally and 40.17 percent in the Czech lands. They emerged as the strongest party in the villages, and of the 43 (out of 156) electoral districts in which they took over 50 percent of the vote, the majority lay in the resettled *pohraničí*.[108] Their advocacy of land reform had clearly delivered them a significant proportion of the prewar Agrarian party vote. The Social Democrats took a further 12.1 percent (15.58 percent in Bohemia and Moravia), giving the left an absolute majority in the constituent assembly. The National Socialists came in a distant second with 18.37 percent of the vote (23.66 percent

42. Victorious February on Staroměstské náměstí, 1948.

in the Czech lands). The only fly in the communist ointment was Slovakia, where the Democrats won a resounding 62 percent (as against 30.37 percent for the KSS).[109] Although the next government remained a National Front coalition, it was now headed by Klement Gottwald. With this popular mandate the road to Victorious February was open. We need not go into the details of the 1948 putsch here. Suffice it to say that it was publicly justified by the same notions of "*lidovláda*" as the other parties in the National Front, not to mention Edvard Beneš, had so eagerly embraced three years earlier themselves. Their collusion in the "national revolution" lost them the social (and moral) basis from which this final ascent of "the people" to state power might—perhaps—have been prevented. Summoned by the KSČ, the nation converged on Myslbek's statue on Václavské náměstí, in the shape of column upon column of armed workers from Prague's factories. Who could now resist their claims, or deny their legitimacy?

Three weeks after the KSČ coup, in the early hours of the morning of 10 March 1948, there occurred a third defenestration of Prague. Jan Masaryk committed suicide by jumping from a bathroom window high up in the foreign ministry building, the Černín Palace. He was momentarily unhinged, it was officially suggested, by Western charges of treachery at his acquiescence in Victorious February. Or maybe—though it seems less likely—he was pushed. In any event, he was given a properly solemn state funeral, just like his father. The ceremonies began, inevitably, in the Pantheon of the National Museum. Klement Gottwald parted with the last bourgeois minister in his government in the name of the Czechoslovak people. *The World in Pictures* [*Svět v obrazech*] put out a special souvenir entitled "Jan Masaryk as We Knew Him," reassuring its readers that "to his legacy we shall remain faithful" [*zůstaneme věrni*]. On the back cover, beneath Jan Masaryk's smiling portrait, his public reaction to Victorious February is prominently quoted: "Czechoslovakia always got by and is getting by today. The people of Czechoslovakia have spoken. I always went with the people and will go with them today too."[110] But (assuming he was not murdered) the fact is that he chose not to go any further with them on this occasion. It was an ignoble end, and an inauspicious beginning.

These tumultuous years left a profound legacy for the imagining of the Czech nation. Henceforth, it was as if Germans had never been anything but outsiders in the Czech lands. As a result of the *odsun*, and of the destruction of Czechoslovakia's thousand-year-old Jewish community during the war and by postwar emigration of Holocaust survivors,[111] it would be a very different population that images of the nation sought to capture from now on. Having always been exclusive of "foreign elements," the rhetorics of Czechness could finally become *inclusive* of all inhabitants of the Czech lands as well. With the forcible removal of the "alien" ethnicities whose presence had for centuries complicated questions of the identity of the land and its populace, the tropes of Czech nationalism acquired a self-evidence of empirical purchase, an obviousness of reference, an immediacy of relevance that had been impossible during the first republic. Other postwar measures similarly homogenized the country's social structures. Before the war, class and nation could be construed as alternative loyalties, and official Czechness represented as a tool of capitalist domination, as it had been by Šalda and many others on the political left. No longer. For the first time in modern Czech history *národ*, *vlast*, and *lid* were made to coincide experientially, rather than merely rhetorically, and to coincide moreover with the boundaries of the political state (though there remained the minor problem of the Slovaks). That coincidence was to change the terms of Czech political life. It was the foundation upon which the communists built that singular edifice Czechs call *totalita*, totality—a system whose very essence is the erasure of all boundaries between the personal and the political, society and state.

Reminders that things had ever been otherwise disappeared in short order. The record of the Germans' centuries-long presence in Bohemia and Moravia was erased from Czech maps. The town of Německý Brod, which now became Havlíčkův Brod after its most famous son Karel Havlíček Borovský, was but one of sixty-four settlements to lose the prefix "*německý*," which means

"German." A directory of communities that were renamed (or incorporated into other jurisdictions) between 1945 and 1964 runs to 102 pages; the biggest single category of changes were those eliminating names with German connotations.[112] No longer would Prague have a Neues Deutsches Theater; this neo-Renaissance jewel, built by the city's German community in 1886–87, was nationalized and eventually renamed the Smetana Theater. What else? The much fought-over Stavovské divadlo lost both its German and its aristocratic associations, becoming the Tylovo divadlo (J. K. Tyl Theater) after the author of "*Kde domov můj?*" The Deutsches Kasino building on Na příkopě, for over seventy years the social hub of German Prague, was pointedly, if somewhat preposterously, reborn as Slovanský dům (the Slavonic House). Familiar Czech landmarks disappeared at the same time: Baťa's shoe shops, the Česká spořitelna, the Grand Hotel Šroubek on Václavské náměstí, the Živnostenská bank, and many other everyday reminders of prewar bourgeois society went the way of the German university and the *Prager Presse*. What was left was a denuded landscape, shorn of its ethnic and social complexities and ripe for the imposition of a unitary national script.

SEVEN

FUTURE PERFECT

Neither the Swan nor the Moon

AND WHAT OF THAT "great artist and great Czech" Alfons Mucha, to whom Max Švabinský, in the name of "Prague and the Czech nation," had promised eternal remembrance at Vyšehrad Cemetery a few short years before? Between 1945 and 1990 there were 740 art exhibitions in Prague organized by the National Gallery, an institution formed by the amalgamation and nationalization of the Collection of Old Masters, the Modern Gallery, and the graphic collection of the Hollareum (founded in 1863) after the war.[1] Works by Alfons Mucha appeared in just ten of them. During the same period Josef Mánes featured in 32 exhibitions, Aleš in twenty-nine, Švabinský in twenty-eight, Brožík in twenty-two, and Mařák in twenty. The bulk of these artists' appearances were during the 1950s and early 1960s, when Mucha might as well never have existed. After an exhibition of works in the ownership of the city of Prague in 1947, at what was then still a private artists' society SVU Purkyně, not a single Mucha was shown by the National Gallery in Prague until 1963, when he emerged at the Museum of Arts and Crafts. The occasion was an exhibition of *French* drawings of the nineteenth and twentieth centuries. Of Mucha's other eight appearances, many were as a minor player within some other framework: art and postage stamps (1978), theater in Czech modern art (1983–84), an exhibition of a private collection gifted to the National Gallery (1989).

Mucha figures in none of the many exhibitions over this period devoted to what were represented as nineteenth- or twentieth-century Czech classics. The centennial of his birth was not commemorated in 1960, unlike anniversaries of Aleš (1952), Mánes (1971), Mařák (1949, 1972), Švabinský (1953, 1973), and others. Between the end of the war and the fall of communism in November 1989 Prague saw just *one* National Gallery exhibition devoted entirely to Mucha's work, the retrospective at the Riding School at Hradčany in 1980, and this was organized jointly with the Musée d'Orsay and shown first in Paris and Darmstadt. Over the same period the National Gallery mounted seven exhibitions in Prague of Josef Mánes and Max Švabinský, six of the Czech impressionist painter Antonín Slavíček (1870–1910), and five of Mikoláš Aleš.[2] In considering these figures, we should take into account the fact that between 1960 and 1980 works by Mucha were included in thirteen exhibitions in Paris, six in London, six in Germany, and five in the

United States, and he had solo exhibitions in London (three times), Paris (twice), Zurich (twice), Brussels, Vienna, Milan, New York, Baltimore, Tokyo, and elsewhere.[3] Alfons Mucha is without a doubt the best known of all Czech painters outside his homeland; even if he is rarely known, as he would undoubtedly have wanted to be, as a *Czech* painter.

There is an interesting discrepancy between the policies of the National Gallery toward exhibiting Mucha at home and abroad. Until 1968 the pattern of neglect is identical. Not a single work by Mucha was included in any of the seventy-two foreign exhibitions organized by the National Gallery between 1946 and 1967. But between 1968 and 1989, Mucha featured in thirty-two such exhibitions that were shown altogether in seventy-one locations. Only a handful of other Czech painters, all apart from Švabinský modernists (among them Emil Filla, Josef Čapek, Václav Špála, Josef Šíma, Bohumil Kubišta, and Jan Zrzavý) rack up similar figures. No less than thirteen of these exhibitions, including a retrospective for the fiftieth anniversary of Mucha's death that toured ten Japanese cities in 1989, were devoted wholly or very largely to Mucha. Equally significantly, for external purposes the National Gallery *was* happy to include Mucha within the Czech national canon. Among the foreign exhibitions in which his works appeared were "Traditions of Modern Art of Czechoslovakia," "Three Hundred Years of Painting in Prague," "Czech Art of the Twentieth Century," "The Czech Avant-Garde 1900–1939," and "Ten Centuries of Czech and Slovak Art." The author of many of the catalogues for these foreign exhibitions, Jiří Kotalík, was not only the director of the National Gallery from 1967 to 1990 but also a connoisseur of Czech art nouveau. It was Kotalík (1920–96) who was among the first to revive domestic interest in the latter with the exhibition "The Czech Secession (Art 1900)" at the Aleš South-Bohemian Gallery in 1966. He lacked knowledge (and appreciation) neither of Mucha's work nor of the international revival of his reputation from the 1960s, and it likely was his influence that was responsible for Mucha's prominence in the National Gallery's foreign exhibits after 1968. All of this throws Mucha's domestic neglect into even sharper relief. So does the fact that the one large exhibition Mucha did have in Prague during these years, that of 1980, was possibly the most popular show ever staged by the National Gallery, attracting 214,480 visitors in the two months it ran.[4] Whatever the reasons may have been for Mucha's official neglect, they certainly did not include lack of interest on the part of the Czech public.

Apart from Jiří Mucha's writings on his father, which were not published until the late 1960s, discussions of Mucha in Czech during the communist period are scarce.[5] The Odeon series of critical studies on individual painters "*Malá galerie*" (Little Gallery) reached number forty-three in 1990 with Vojtěch Hynais. Mucha was not among the subjects of the previous forty-two volumes. He lacked even the minor recognition of a memorial plaque on any building in Prague, a city that abounds in them, although the street named after him in 1947 in Dejvice was permitted to remain Muchova ulice. Most tellingly of all perhaps, the *Slovanská epopej*, which despite modernist coolness had been more or less continuously exhibited in Prague and Brno between 1928 and the outbreak of war, remained rolled up in storage (where it was put to protect it from the Germans) for over a quarter of a century. Even then, it was not exhibited to the people of Prague for whom Mucha had painted it but instead was housed in a château in the small town of Moravský Krumlov in his native region of southern Moravia. Only three out of the twenty canvases from the *Epopej* were included, along with some smaller studies for the series, mostly from the personal collection of Jiří Mucha, in the 1980 retrospective.

An article by Jana Brabcová in the catalogue for the latter dismisses the whole enormous cycle as an "artistic mistake." Mucha's "personal tragedy," she explains,

> was that he did not understand his talent and forsook the expression most personal to him in the interest of illustration of an idea. For Alfons Mucha was above all a great decorative talent. His major contribution remains confined to the short period of his Paris activity, and the core of Mucha's production lies in the realm of the poster and decorative work. Here on the boundary of genius and banality he contrives to create truly consequential and contemporary works. On the other hand in the areas where he thought to address the time in which he lived and future generations he lost his way in ideals coming from the preceding century and his outdated message found no spectators and listeners. It would be a disservice to Mucha's talent if we were to disguise this fact, which cannot in any way lessen his significance for the face of Paris around the year 1900.[6]

What is dismissed here is precisely that art in which Mucha presumed to Czechness; in an ironic mirroring of his standard location in Western commentary, he is firmly positioned in the fin de siècle Paris on which he himself turned his back in order to better "serve his nation." The *Slovanská epopej* undoubtedly is an artistically contentious work. Brabcová ignores the six hundred thousand spectators at the Brooklyn Museum in 1921, however, and the New York critics who compared Mucha then to Tiepolo. The authors of the catalogue for the 1980 exhibition (who include Jiří Kotalík) were taken to task over this by at least one French critic: "This single canvas from the Slav Epic [The Slavs in their Original Homeland] happens to be a masterpiece" wrote Pierre Mazars in *Le Figaro*, concluding "This is Mucha whom we would like to get to know better."[7]

Brabcová is, in any case, being somewhat disingenuous when she chides Mucha for his "outdated message." The period in which Mucha was most comprehensively "forgotten," from 1948 to the early 1960s, was a time in which the "national art" of the nineteenth century was being massively revived and artistic modernism as thoroughly reviled on all sides. Josef Mánes, Mikoláš Aleš, and the nineteenth-century Czech classics were thrust down Czech throats ad nauseam. Monumentalism was all the rage. This had been presaged well before Victorious February. The catalogue to an exhibition staged by SVU Mánes in the summer of 1947 under the nicely punning title "The Monumental Task of Contemporary Graphic and Plastic Art" [*Monumentální úkol současného výtvarnictví*] conceptualized the requirements of the time thus: "The exhibition . . . arises from a simple cause. Its object is to present to the public the given artistic task on a scale, in a situation, and in a conceptual direction that is expressly nonintimate, nonprivate, from the viewpoint of both the spectator and the artist himself. It is a task that is assuredly greater, as well as more responsible, as compared with (it could be said) normal artistic activity. It is also a more topical task. It is the problem of contemporary art.[8] The exhibits were appropriate to the theme: Břetislav Benda's bronze "Victory (for the City of Stalingrad)," Karel Dvořák's sculpture "Revolution," Karel Pokorný's "Memorial for 9 May," Miloš Malina's fresco "The Harvest," with its massive female bodies and its mighty sheafs of wheat.

The aged Max Švabinský, whose rather different but no less monumental rendition of a harvest ["Žně," 1927][9] had attracted exactly the same charges of anachronism, academicism, and so on from prewar modernist critics as Mucha's *Slovanská epopej*, was now the most revered of living artists. He was entrusted with official portraiture, design of postage stamps, and the poster for the huge and bombastic 1955–56 exhibition "Ten Years of the Czechoslovak Popular Democratic Republic in Creative Art."[10] His 1950 portrait of Julius Fučík is famous. The communist journalist was executed by the Gestapo in 1943 and later canonized by the KSČ as a model of socialist patriotism with the aid of his prison writings, which were carefully doctored before their publication under the title *Report from the Gallows* [*Reportáž psaná na oprátce*]. Milan Kundera (b. 1929) describes the portrait in his novel *The Joke* [*Žert*, 1967]:

> The drawing of Fučík on the wall was the work of Max Švabinský, the wonderful old virtuoso art nouveau painter of allegories, plump women, butterflies, and everything delightful; after the war, so the story goes, Švabinský had a visit from the Comrades, who asked him to do a portrait of Fučík from a photograph, and Švabinský had drawn him (in profile) with infinite grace of line and inimitable taste in such a way as to make him seem almost virginal—fervent, yet pure— and so striking that people who had known him personally preferred Švabinský's noble drawing to their memories of the living face. . . . Fučík's face hung on the wall as it hung in a thousand other public places in our country, and its expression was so striking, the radiant expression of a young girl in love, that it made me feel inferior for my appearance as well as my crime.[11]

This is embodiment of the idea, with a vengeance. Ferdinand Peroutka suggests that Fučík (who in fact talked to the Gestapo, as passages censored out of *Report from the Gallows* make clear) was chosen over the executed writer Vladislav Vančura to play this martyr role in part because of his romantic good looks; Vančura was "unpleasantly bald.[12] The crime to which Kundera's hero refers, incidentally, was writing a postcard to his rather earnest girlfriend saying "Optimism is the opium of the people! A healthy atmosphere stinks of stupidity! Long live Trotsky!"—the "joke" of the novel's title.

Not that Kundera himself did not contribute to the Fučík cult. Among his literary creations from the 1950s is an epic poem entitled "The Last May" [*Poslední máj*, 1955]. It dramatizes the episode in *Report from the Gallows*, a kind of *malé, ale naše* variant of Christ's temptation on the mountain, in which the Gestapo chief Böhm takes Fučík from Pankrác prison through the streets of Prague and up Petřín Hill, where he wines him and dines him and tells him how all this beauty can be his if he only will cooperate. Fučík is deaf to all such blandishments:

> He heard only the Vltava play on its weir's dulcimer
> And it seems to him, that he is walking in a vast comradely crowd,
> And it seems to him, that they are spreading far across the land,
> Where from the partisans' mountains the rebels are singing!
>
> He was still turning after them with a smiling glance—
> When behind him shut the gates of Pankrác.[13]

As for Švabinský's drawing, a slightly different (and quite possibly apocryphal) version of the same story also made the rounds in Prague; that the old master talked of being commissioned to portray "some Fouček," of whom he had clearly never heard, and was rewarded by a van-load of French burgundy, a commodity in scarce supply in Czechoslovakia at the time. Despite his wartime indiscretion over the Saint Václav Prize (and in a time in which people were fingered for collaboration for very much less), Švabinský was one of the first recipients of the newly created title National Artist [*Národní umělec*] in 1945 and was honored by President Antonín Novotný (1904–75) with the Order of the Republic in 1958. The "wonderful old virtuoso"—as he indeed was—died at the ripe old age of eighty-nine in 1962. Throughout his long life he had stayed faithful to an artistic vision forged in the symbolist 1890s, depicting satyrs and nymphs frolicking in primeval forests, the birth of a Venus altogether more mobile and mischievous than Botticelli's, and noons over the treetops as skies spilling over with sweet naked women. Švabinský's biography is one reminder that human life spans seldom neatly coincide with political periodizations of national histories, and of the moral dilemmas for individuals that discrepancy can set up. Fučík was by no

43. Noon above the treetops as seen by Max Švabinský, 1936.

means his first official commission; he had been drawing portraits of prominent Czechs since the 1890s. The first stamp he designed, back in 1920,
bore the president-liberator's head. In 1933 the magazine *Umění* had approvingly dissected the artistic means Švabinský employed on his hundred-crown
bill—the same bill Jarmila Novotná graced and the Nazis censored—to represent Masaryk as "teacher, liberator, and leader of the nation," noting how
the two children bracing his portrait are "symbols of the future of the nation
raised by the president-teacher, an allegory of love for the father and the

head of state."[14] But states can be fickle things. A commemorative volume entitled *Švabinský's Czech Pantheon* was issued in 1985. Absent from this gallery of one hundred portraits of great Czechs from Hus to Fučík were many leading cultural and political personalities of the first republic drawn by Švabinský, among them, needless to say, Tomáš Garrigue Masaryk.[15]

In stark contrast to this revival of the "national tradition," until the late 1950s the tradition of Czech modernism was officially tabooed. The approved artistic watchwords of the time were "realism" and "comprehensibility."[16] The first exhibition after 1945 of the early twentieth-century avantgarde by the National Gallery, "Founders of Modern Czech Art," staged in Brno in 1957 and in Prague a year later, met with near-hysterical condemnation in some quarters of the press.[17] A follow-up on the Czech interwar avant-garde organized in Brno by the same curators, Miroslav Lamač and Jiří Padrta, the following year never made it to Prague, and books by Lamač and Padrta on the Osma and the Skupina výtvarných umělců written during the short-lived cultural thaw of the mid-1960s were withheld from publication for many long years after the 1968 Soviet invasion.[18] Devětsil had to wait until 1986 for any Prague collective retrospective exhibition, by which time many of their works had been lost.[19] Prewar left critics of KSČ cultural policy, as we might expect, got particularly short shrift from the party after 1948. Seifert and Teige were the targets of bitter hate campaigns.[20] By the time František Halas died at the age of forty-eight in 1949, he too was an object of official odium; his poem "*Staré ženy*" (Old Women), with its merciless images of the ravages of age, was particularly repugnant to the compulsory optimism of the day and its facile cult of youth.[21] Halas's father had inscribed on his prematurely dead son's gravestone the epitaph: "Here he sleeps, fortunate in his death. . . . He lived in a time, when others were dead while living."[22] It was not permitted to remain there for long.

Others who were less prominent suffered worse fates. Záviš Kalandra (1902–50) had joined the KSČ in 1923, at the age of twenty-one. With Julius Fučík and future Minister of Information Václav Kopecký he went on to become one of the renowned group of young communist journalists known as the "Karlín boys" [*Karlínští kluci*], after the location of the KSČ Central Committee building in Prague. He was a sometime editor of both *Rudé právo* and *Tvorba*. Kalandra's interest in reconciling Marx and Freud brought him into close association with the Czechoslovak Surrealist Group; he contributed an article on Mácha and Palacký to their 1936 Festschrift for Karel Hynek Mácha, *Ani labuť, ani Lůna*, alongside Vítězslav Nezval and Karel Teige. That same year he broke with the party over the Moscow trials and went on to edit a left opposition journal *Proletář* (the *Proletarian*). He is also said to have drafted a famous anti-Stalinist manifesto of the period, entitled "We Protest!" [*Protestujeme!*], whose signatories included Halas, Seifert, Teige, and the distinguished critic Václav Černý.[23] Having spent the entire war in

44. Tatíček Masaryk on Max Švabinský's one-hundred-crown bill, 1931.

German concentration camps and survived, Kalandra was arrested for "Trot-skyism" in 1949. Incongruously, given his pure Bolshevik politics, he found himself indicted as one of the defendants in the notorious show trial of the National Socialist deputy Milada Horáková, as a co-conspirator with people he had never even met. André Breton called publicly upon the French com-munist (and onetime surrealist) poet Paul Éluard to protest, and Éluard equally publicly refused. Breton's "Open Letter" begins by reminding Éluard that "It is fifteen years since we, you and I, went to Prague at the invitation of our Czech surrealist friends." A photograph, shot in Karlovy Vary in 1935, recalls that visit. They are all posing together, Toyen, the young Czech psy-choanalytic theorist Bohuslav Brouk (1912–78), Jacqueline and André Bre-ton, Vítězslav Nezval, Vincenc Makovský, Jindřich Štyrský seated in front of the group, and on the right of the picture Paul Éluard with his arm around Karel Teige's shoulder. Breton ends: "How can you in your soul bear such a degradation of a human being in the person of he who was your friend?"[24] Kalandra was hanged in June 1950 in Pankrác prison for treason and espio-nage.

The reasons why Alfons Mucha was all but obliterated from official na-tional memory after 1948, in short, cannot have been those for which his work was criticized earlier by his more modernistic Czech contemporaries. Antimodernism and a conception of art as the "illustration of an idea" were the reigning orthodoxies of postwar cultural policy. After the war, and partic-ularly after Victorious February, we are in a different ballpark. The media through which art was made public were controlled by the state, that is to say the Communist party of Czechoslovakia. The art galleries were nationalized. Among the 220,000 to 250,000 posts whose appointees had now to be ratified by the Central Committee of the KSČ were the rectors and all the professors of the Academy of Fine Arts and the Museum of Arts and Crafts, the director of the Institute for Theory and History of Art of the Czechoslovak Academy of Sciences, the president and secretary of the Union of Czechoslovak Creative Artists (into which, after 1948, formerly independent artists' societies like SVU Mánes were unceremoniously absorbed), and the director of the National Gallery. Editorial boards of artistic publishing houses and magazines were (like all others) controlled by the same *nomenklatura* system. The Central Committee also exercised a veto over bestowal of the title National Artist, a postwar creation which itself says much about altered expectations of the place of the artist in society.[25] If an artist of Mucha's stature was "forgotten" it was not by accident. Nor will it have had overly much to do with questions of aesthetics. Alfons Mucha was an incidental casualty of a much wider war for the soul of the nation.

Prayer for Marta

State-sponsored amnesia has a long history in the Czech lands. A name well known to Czech patriots of the nineteenth century was that of Antonín Koniáš, the Jesuit writer and leader of the literary Counter-Reformation in Bohemia whose enthusiastic book burning we encountered earlier. Koniáš published his *Key for Recognizing Heretical Errors* in Hradec Králové in 1729. This contained a two-hundred-page-long alphabetically arranged "Index of Prohibited or Dangerous and Suspicious Books." The former were to be destroyed, the latter expurgated and/or "improved." The basis of Koniáš's list was the Vatican Index, whose principles he applied to local Bohemian circumstances. An anathema was proclaimed every Maundy Thursday "against whomsoever has a heretical book, written or printed, is harboring it, even unread, hides it in somebody else's dwelling, prints it or helps with publishing or printing it, copies it, distributes it, lends it, sells it, obstructs its incineration, in any way whatsoever approves of its contents, suggests it does not deserve burning, and against anybody who reads any page of it, either deliberately or from mere curiosity."[26] A second edition of the *Key*, with its Index now enlarged to 420 pages, followed in 1749, and a third, under the official imprint of the archbishop of Prague, in 1770.[27]

When in 1917 Czech representatives at the imperial parliament in Vienna compiled a list of over two hundred Czech books censored, confiscated, or banned by the Habsburg authorities during World War I, it was the name of Koniáš they recalled. The tendency of the new censorship, they said, "was and is the same. To wipe out the memory of the illustrious Czech past, of Jan Hus and the Hussite period, of the sufferings of the Czech nation in the time of Bílá hora, to curtail the upsurge of freethinking and progressive movements, to extinguish the Sokol idea and Czech awareness of belonging to the Slav people, to root out the conception of a united nationality of Czechs and Slovaks, and to proclaim as traitors the bearers of these opinions."[28] Contemporary subversives like future Prime Minister Karel Kramář and the journalist and poet Josef Svatopluk Machar (one of whose articles had led to the formation of Česká moderna) were obvious targets. Imprisoned during the war, Machar went on to become a high Czechoslovak military functionary after independence. Other books banned included works on the Hussites, Havlíček's writings, and Ernest Denis's *Bohemia After Bílá hora* (1902). The serialization of Alois Jirásek's novel *The Hussite King* in *Národní politika* was stopped on police orders in 1916.[29] Though written by a Frenchman, *Bohemia After Bílá hora* was the true spiritual successor to Palacký's *History of the Czech Nation*; it was with a passage from Denis emblazoned on its front cover that *Zlatá Praha* hailed independence in 1918,[30] and one of the first acts of the new Czechoslovak parliament was to send a flowery address of thanks to this "incomparable historian, friend, and teacher of the Czechoslovak nation."[31] Denis was to fare less well under the communists. His statue was not one of those restored to Prague's streets after the German occupation; remembrance of French connections was no more to the taste of the KSČ than it had been to the Nazis.

Censorship did not by any means cease with Czechoslovak independence, though it was less extensive—or centralized—during the first republic than at most times before or since. Its object was not the ghosts of the past so much as present threats to bourgeois property and Catholic propriety. The courts' ban on the Czech edition of Isidore Ducasse, Comte de Lautréamont's *Chants de Maldoror*, which was published by Odeon in 1929, as "a danger to public morality," became an international cause célèbre.[32] The surrealists claimed the symbolist poet Lautréamont as their direct precursor: it was he who coined the famous simile "He was as handsome as . . . the fortuitous encounter on a dissecting table of a sewing machine and an umbrella."[33] Jindřich Štyrský was the book's illustrator, Karel Teige its translator. The KSČ daily paper *Rudé právo*, founded in 1920, celebrated its thousandth censor's "confiscation" of copy on 6 May 1928.[34] Among those who between 1918 and 1928 had texts proscribed by one Czechoslovak court or another on grounds of obscenity or offense to religion were Hus, Komenský, Havlíček, Vrchlický, Machar, and even President Masaryk himself.[35] But in no case were the writings of any one individual extirpated in their entirety, with the intention of wiping their very memory from public consciousness. The communist press was undoubtedly often harassed, but it was never banned outright (until after Munich and the end of the first republic). For a parallel in scale or systematicity with Koniáš's depredations we have to look to another period of totalizing reformation of the world and its inhabitants.

A set of "Instructions for Screening of Book Collections in Libraries of All Kinds" was issued to Czech and Slovak libraries in 1953. These instructions, which were marked "Confidential!," begin with a brief word of explanation:

> For the building of socialism in our country and in the struggle to maintain world peace libraries are an ever-more important tool for making new socialist human beings. To fulfill this task and diligently extend and consolidate the scientific worldview, progressive science and art, libraries may not from now on freely lend books and articles which by their content retard or impair our journey to socialism.[36]

Committees were to be formed for all libraries, comprising the head librarian and KSČ and local government representatives. The librarian would be held personally answerable for carrying out of the "Instructions" before 25 September 1953. Along with the "Instructions" came two separate lists of "objectionable" [*závadná*, also translatable as "defective" or "faulty"] literature. Works on the first list were to be dispatched "by registered mail and directly only to the Institute of the History of the KSČ in Prague." Works on the second list were to go to a range of university, institute, and large public libraries, where they were to be securely kept, separate from the main collection, pending orders from relevant ministries on their "classification, division, and circulation." Signed reports on the screening had to be submitted, and the two lists of prohibited works returned at the end of the process. Unlike Koniáš's *Key*, the KSČ Index was not published. There were no bonfires of books in the streets, empty white spaces in the newspapers, or highly publicized court cases to advertise the ubiquitous presence of authority.

Works removed from (or never permitted to enter) Czech public libraries during the communist period are listed in the "Catalogue of Formerly Prohibited Literature" kept in the National Library in Prague.[37] A fitting location, perhaps; the National Library is housed in the Klementinum, the Jesuit College that took over the library of the university in 1622, two years after Bílá hora. In 1992, when it was still described as "provisional"—documenting the KSČ's ravages took time—this catalogue occupied seventeen drawers of standard-sized index cards. The cards were in turn compiled from large handwritten notebooks, divided alphabetically and filled in as material was proscribed. There are two main series of these notebooks, for literature in Czech and for works in other languages, just as in Koniáš's *Key*. Separate volumes cover "Legionnaires" (works on the Czechoslovak Legions of World War I), "Freemasons," "Fascists," "Occult Literature," and "Erotica"—an intriguing bestiary. Within the main Czech alphabetical series the Masaryk family (Tomáš's wife Charlotte, son Jan, and daughter Alice, as well as Tomáš himself) and Edvard Beneš each warrants an individual notebook to themselves. The list of proscribed works by or about the Masaryks fills thirty-

45. First page of questionnaire from Ladislav Borůvka's *Kádrový spis* (Cadre File), 1950. Question 23 inquires into time spent abroad, wanting to know where, when, and for what purpose. Engineer Borůvka's answers read: "Germany—Oranienburg"; "17.11.1939–20.xii.1940"; "in a concentration camp."

seven pages. One of them is the (unfinished) multivolume biography of Tomáš Masaryk by Minister of Education Zdeněk Nejedlý.

Much of what is listed in this latter-day *Index Bohemicorum librorum prohibitorum* is exactly what we might expect: Pope John Paul II's encyclicals; Winston Churchill's history of World War II; *The World Christian Encyclope-*

dia, The International Who's Who, and *Books in Print*; a bevy of "Western Marxists" from Gramsci to Marcuse;[38] *The Fontana Dictionary of Modern Thought,* and virtually anything else foreign with the word "modern" in the title. We have met Jiří Mucha previously as the biographer of his father. He appears here as the author of *Cold Sun* [*Studené slunce*, 1968], a novel set in the uranium mines of Jáchymov which the communists employed as a forced labor camp. Mucha wrote from experience: he passed through Jáchymov during his own 1951–55 imprisonment. Koniáš had proscribed all books by "arch-heretics," whatever they were about, and all books by "heretics" dealing with religion, whether or not they actually contained any theological errors.[39] The KSČ applied these same principles to émigré and "dissident" authors. On this basis works at one time published quite legally in socialist Czechoslovakia were retrospectively pulled from library shelves. Karel Čapek's *War with the Newts* [*Válka s mloky*, 1936] and a German edition of *Macbeth* were both removed because they had prefaces written by onetime director of Czechoslovak Television (1955–57) and later prominent dissident Pavel Kohout (b. 1928), who himself amasses over eighty separate entries in the catalogue. Keeping company with him are Milan Kundera, Josef Škvorecký, Ludvík Vaculík, Arnošt Lustig, Lenka Procházková, Eva Kantůrková, and many of the other leading names of postwar Czech literature. Some other entries are perhaps more surprising. Tacitus's *Germania*, Sappho, and Catullus rub shoulders with *The Guinness Book of Records*, Kant's *Prolegomena to Any Future Metaphysic*, and *Lee Wade's Korean Cookbook*. Storehouse of the Czech language as it may have been, the *Bible kralická* proved no more sacrosanct than *The New English Bible*. We would doubtless expect to encounter Samuelson's *Economics*, but possibly not Friedrich Engels's *On Religion*, nor volumes 1, 22, 27, 37, 38, and 39 of the (Czech) *Collected Works of Marx and Engels*.

The "Catalogue of Formerly Prohibited Literature" reveals much about KSČ attempts to massage the national memory. This was an ongoing, authentically Orwellian process; the past was routinely updated. Among works absented from library shelves were the published proceedings of dozens of city, district, and regional conferences of the KSČ of various dates, plus many other reports by party or state organs; *Contributions to the History of the KSČ* for 1957, 1959, 1960, 1964, and 1965 put out by the State Publishing House for Political Literature; a history of the KSČ published in 1961 in an enormous edition of 150,400; prewar KSČ documents; and successive editions of once ministry-approved school textbooks of Czech history from the 1950s and 1960s. Transcripts of the trials of Milada Horáková (1901–50), a National Socialist parliamentary deputy and the first woman to be executed this century (the victims of the Nazi occupation apart) in Czechoslovakia, former KSČ General Secretary Rudolf Slánský (1901–52) and other defendants in the 1950s show trials were distributed at the time in massive numbers. Later they too were proscribed, along with four speeches of Zdeněk

Nejedlý's for Czechoslovak Radio on the "antistate conspiratorial center" that Slánský was accused of heading. Milada Horáková's trial was one of the most shameful episodes in the tawdry postwar history of Czech communism, which provoked worldwide protests and appeals for clemency from Albert Einstein among others.[40] Like many other KSČ victims, Horáková had been active in the wartime resistance, and spent 1940–45 in German camps and prisons. After the war she became president of the Council of Czechoslovak Women, and vice president of the Union of Liberated Political Prisoners. Rudolf Slánský, who met his end two years later, was one of those who did most to establish the KSČ machinery of state terror that devoured her. Since 1991, Milada Horáková has had a commemorative gravestone in Vyšehrad Cemetery.

It goes without saying that writings from the 1968 Prague Spring and everything that led up to it (like the proceedings of the 1963 Liblice Conference on Franz Kafka and the 1967 Fourth Congress of the Union of Czechoslovak Writers)[41] were in due course also banned. But as critical to the laundering of memory, apparently, was the removal of material by Klement Gottwald (his articles and speeches of 1949–50, and his *On Our Resistance* with Viliam Široký)[42] and even by the "president of forgetting" Gustáv Husák himself (*Speeches and Articles*). Husák's predecessor as Czechoslovak president, army general Ludvík Svoboda, was prevented from publishing the second volume of his war memoirs while still in office in Hradčany. Husák, then KSČ general secretary, wrote to him personally on 5 April 1972, explaining that in view of Svoboda's position in the party and the state it was necessary "to proceed very cautiously and delicately, so as not to create confusion in the explanation of our past among members of our party and our population at home or open up the possibility of the misuse of your person by foreign propaganda."[43] Not only was the second volume of Svoboda's *Through Life's Journeys* not published until twenty years later, the second edition of the first volume, then in press, was pulped. What adds particular piquancy to this is the fact that in 1965 Svoboda was awarded the coveted title Hero of the Soviet Union for his military record during World War II.

Propaganda works intended to frame popular memory crop up often in this index. Among them are books about World War II and the German occupation, the Prague uprising of 1945, and the liberation of Czechoslovakia by the Red Army.[44] The ritual recalling of Czechoslovak wartime sufferings, resistance, and liberation was integral to the structure of communist legitimation, but that recall was highly selective and repeatedly reviewed. That works on Lidice produced at the time by Czechs in Western exile or by foreign sympathizers abroad should later have been deemed "offensive" is predictable, even if (in view of the KSČ's own propagandistic use of the massacre) obscene. The irony in the disappearance of *Unforgettable Spring:*

Memoirs of Soviet Soldiers in the Liberation of Czechoslovakia must be uninten-tional. Works of reference—which of course construct the past too—also had short half-lives. Vítězslav Macháček's *Fifty Czech Authors of the Last Fifty Years* proved as transitory as Rudolf Havel and Jiří Opelík's 1964 *Dictionary of Czech Writers*: both were in due course banned. Their successor, the "dictio-nary handbook" *Czech Writers of the Twentieth Century*, which went into its third edition in 1985, is 830 pages long and covers 279 authors. Conspic-uous by their absence are Václav Havel, Ludvík Vaculík, Ivan Klíma, Pavel Kohout, Arnošt Lustig, Milan Kundera, and Josef Škvorecký, to take but a few names known from translations into English.[45] This is as if a dictionary of modern American writers were to omit the names of Baldwin, Morrison, Mailer, Kerouac, Salinger, Updike, and Welty. Jiří Mucha is likewise "over-looked." Caught between the conflicting imperatives of the totalization of politics (the personal and just about everything else was political) and the evanescence of the politically correct, it is no surprise that the Encyclopedia Institute of the Czechoslovak Academy of Sciences never succeeded in pro-ducing a socialist successor to *Ottův slovník naučný*. The best it could manage was the six-volume *Malá československá encyklopedie* (*Small Czechoslovak En-cyclopedia*) of 1984–87, which is as scanty as it is tendentious.[46]

Apart from regularly spring-cleaning their own past, the communists equally determinedly purged the record of what preceded them, especially the history of the first (or as it was now invariably known, the "bourgeois") republic of 1918–38. Alongside transcripts of the trials of Horáková and Slánský, they removed from libraries material on the trials of Karel Kramář and other Czechs sentenced to death for treason by the Habsburg authorities in 1916. The 1920 Czechoslovak constitution was off limits, as were celebra-tory publications for the tenth anniversary of independence like the richly informative three-volume set *Ten Years of the Czechoslovak Republic*.[47] Also forbidden were the prewar programs of other political parties, writings of and about major political figures of the period like Alois Rašín and Milan Rastislav Štefánik, and the quarterly journal *Naše revoluce* (*Our Revolution*), a magazine devoted to the history of the Czech liberation struggle against Vienna, which was founded in 1923. Materials on the "first resistance" (i.e., that during World War I) and in particular on the Czechoslovak Legions abroad—which as we have already seen were classified with fascists and pornographers—were an object of particular scrutiny. Among objectionable works was the catalogue of the exhibition "Our Resistance," commemorating the first anniversary of Czechoslovak independence, which had opened on 28 October 1919 at Obecní dům, where a year previously the National Com-mittee had proclaimed Czech sovereignty. The fine anthology *Naše umění v odboji* (*Our Art in the Resistance*), published by the European Literary Club[48] on 15 August 1938, an act of some courage and patriotism considering the date, was also thought unfit reading for later generations. It is no surprise to find that the index proscribes an abundance of works touching on the history of Bohemian Germans and their postwar expulsion.

The more distant past was comprehensively "screened" too. The historian Josef Pekař, whom we might remember reflecting sadly on the monuments in Staroměstské náměstí in 1903, gets one of the longest entries in the catalogue. Pekař was from 1918 chief editor of the leading Czech historical journal *Český časopis historický*, rector of Charles University in 1931–32, and a prospective candidate to succeed Tomáš Masaryk as Czechoslovak president in 1935 (he declined to run). His many writings cover the complete span of Czech history from its early legends through the Hussite Wars, Bílá hora, and the subsequent period of "Darkness" (upon which he did much to shed light). He also wrote the standard gymnasium textbook of Czechoslovak history used in the first republic. He insisted that the Hussite storms were a *medieval, religious* struggle, and denied any relation between Hussitism and modern Czech national and social movements. Tomáš Masaryk's attempt to anchor his own nationalism in an alleged Hussite and Protestant legacy was Pekař's prime target here. Though he saw Bílá hora as a national tragedy, Pekař had a more positive view of baroque culture and specifically of the Catholic contribution to modern Czech identity (recall here Beneš Metoděj Kulda's influence on the young Alfons Mucha). An advocate of historic state right and an opponent of pan-Germanism before World War I, during the first republic Pekař argued for rapprochement between Czechs and the German minority on the basis of land patriotism. These positions were quite compatible, and equally unacceptable to those who sought to ground nationality in ethnicity. Just as consistently, given his revisionist analysis of the "Darkness," Pekař opposed the confiscations of aristocratic estates that in 1919 began the long history of twentieth-century expropriations in Czechoslovakia in the name of *národ* and *lid*.[49] Notoriously, he had refused to sign the May 1917 Manifesto of Czech Writers. An arch-heretic indeed. Regrettably, these were also views that the Nazis were able to twist to their own ends during the occupation, and this allowed the KSČ to construct Pekař, who died in 1937, as a posthumous collaborator.

Purging libraries was not the only means of control of the written word, nor was control of the written word the only instrument for state manipulation of memory. Thanks to the fact that the KSČ Index has been made public since 1989, it is merely among the easier to document. Printing presses, newspapers, magazines, and publishing houses were "publicly" owned, and their editorial boards were disciplined through the *nomenklatura* system of politically vetoed appointments before any formal censorship came into play.[50] "Objectionable" literature for the most part simply did not get published at all, unless in *samizdat* form. Just as important, this state of affairs led to a

widespread and corrosive self-censorship, even on the part of non-establish-
ment writers like Bohumil Hrabal, who is perhaps best known in the West
for his screenplay for Jiří Menzel's 1967 Oscar-winning film *Closely Observed
Trains* [*Ostře sledované vlaky*]. Hrabal (1914–97) is widely acknowledged to
be the most original Czech writer since the war. Renowned for holding court
in his last years in his favorite Prague hostelry, "The Golden Tiger" [*U zlatého
tygra*], he died falling from a fifth-floor window in Bulovka Hospital in 1997
while trying to feed the birds. Several of his books have now been translated
into English. The novella *Too Loud a Solitude* makes surreal poetry out of the
story of Haňťa, whose job is the pulping of books. "For thirty-five years
now," Haňťa introduces himself, "I've been compacting old papers and
books, living as I do in a land that has known how to read and write for
fifteen generations; living in a onetime kingdom where it was and still is a
custom, an obsession, to compact thoughts and images patiently in the heads
of the population, thereby bringing them ineffable joy and even greater woe;
living among people who will lay down their lives for a bale of compacted
thoughts."[51]

Works that were published had frequently been through a Koniáš-style
process of "cleansing" [*očistit*] and "improvement" [*polepšit*] before they finally saw the light of day. A ninth-grade modern history textbook approved
by the Ministry of Education in 1970, for instance, informs Czech teenagers
that "the poets Jaroslav Seifert, S. K. Neumann, Josef Hora, Fráňa Šrámek,
František Halas, Vladimír Holan, and others wrote their poetry against the
occupation [of 1939–45]." The second, "reworked" edition of the same
book, approved (as a "provisional teaching text"!) in 1972, contains the identical sentence, but with Seifert's name left out.[52] The reason for the change
had nothing to do with Seifert's resistance to the Germans and everything to
do with his resistance to the Soviet occupation of 1968. Seifert's "Eight Days"
[*Osm dní*], a cycle of poems written as a requiem for Tomáš Masaryk in 1937,
had been provocatively reissued a month after the invasion, with the date
"September 1968" prominent on the title page.[53] The work is as famous for
its illustrations as its text; their author was Josef Čapek. Seifert was elected
president of the Union of Czechoslovak Writers in 1969, but that organization was soon dissolved (later it was reconstituted after being purged). Unable to publish any new poetry legally throughout the 1970s, he became a
signatory of the first proclamation of Charta 77. When, in 1982, his memoirs
All the Beauties of the World were finally permitted to appear in Prague, many
passages had been stripped from the edition published by Zdena Salivarová
and Josef Škvorecký in Toronto the year before.[54] Seifert's title, *Všecky krásy
světa*, is taken from the marriage broker Kecal's aria in act 2 of Smetana's
Prodaná nevěsta. He had first used this title sixty years earlier, for the final
poem in *Samá láska*. It was a favorite Devětsil motto during the 1920s, af-

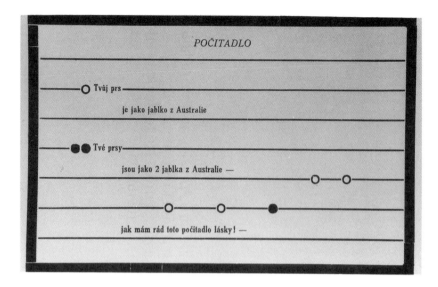

POČITADLO

O Tvůj prs

je jako jablko z Australie

Tvé prsy

jsou jako 2 jablka z Australie —

jak mám rád toto počítadlo lásky! —

46. Jaroslav Seifert's poem "Abacus," from his 1925 book *On Radio Waves*, typography by Karel Teige. The poem translates: "Your breast / Is like an apple from Australia / Your breasts / Are like two apples from Australia— / How I like this abacus of love!—"

firming a modernity that then seemed pregnant with promise; a promise Seifert, the working-class boy from Žižkov, had then identified with the "*vlast* of the proletariat." Back in 1926, at the age of twenty-five, he had affirmed his muse thus: "I believe that there is no modernity outside communism. When I was in Moscow, on the day of the anniversary of the revolution, I found myself caught up in the current of the enthusiastic crowd, which was rolling toward Red Square. In that moment I was dying with longing to become the poet of this people."[55]

Because Seifert indeed was in the forefront of cultural resistance to the Nazi occupation, and a hugely popular poet of his own people, he could not be so easily erased after Victorious February as, say, the unfortunate Záviš Kalandra. This did not stop Ivan Skála, editor of *Rudé právo*, from denouncing him in *Tvorba* in 1950 in an article entitled—significantly—"A Foreign Voice." The occasion was the publication of Seifert's *Song About Viktorka* [*Píseň o Viktorce*]. The Viktorka in question was the deranged girl, abandoned by her faithless lover, who met a tragic end in Božena Němcová's *Babička*, and who was allegedly personally known to Karel Čapek's grandfather. Skála finds a new use for her:

Seifert appeals often in his verses to Jan Neruda and Božena Němcová. These were great artists, who never deserted their people, who did not betray their interests. All our preeminent artists took this road.

Seifert, who in the present time, when the people are victoriously realizing their revolutionary ideals, does not see these stupendous changes, but sees only the crazy Viktorka, does not have the right to abuse the names of Němcová and Neruda and does not have the right to abuse the honorable title of poet, he does not have the right to abuse poetry against the people, to deride everything that is great and dear to our working people.[56]

Skála (b. 1922) went on to become a stalwart of post-1968 "normalization," heading the flagship literary publishing house Československý spisovatel (the Czechoslovak Writer) from 1970 to 1982. One of his first actions there was to tear up the signed contract for Ludvík Vaculík's novel *The Guinea Pigs* [*Morčata*], on the grounds that it no longer corresponded to "the newly-established tasks of the publishing house." Vaculík was the author of the famous 1968 manifesto "Two Thousand Words." Československý spisovatel was belatedly to publish *Morčata* two decades later, after the fall of communism. It is prefaced by a letter from the publishing house to its readers thanking Vaculík, who, it says, "for long years in Edice Petlice"—a *samizdat* press—"maintained the continuity of Czech literature in place of us."[57] Founded in 1972, Edice Petlice had published around four hundred original titles by 1989.[58] The word *petlice*, by the way, means a latch fastening a door or a gate.

Among the passages excised from the first domestic edition of *Všecky krásy světa* were parts of Seifert's account of Karel Teige's death of a heart attack in Prague on 1 October 1951. Seifert calls the chapter *"Danse Macabre* in Smíchov"; Teige was followed to the grave by his common-law wife, Jožka Nevařilová, on 2 October and his mistress, Eva Ebertová, the illegitimate daughter of J. S. Machar, on 12 October. Both of them committed suicide. Prudery rather than politics seems to have dictated this cut, since Karel Teige's name is not excised from the book altogether. A few days after their deaths, both Teige's and Ebertová's apartments were ransacked by the state security police, who carted away some seven hundred books and five hundred packages of manuscripts and press cuttings.[59] In lieu of an obituary *Tvorba* published a three-part denunciation entitled "Teigeism [*Teigovština*]— a Trotskyist Agency in Our Culture."[60] Teige was cautiously rehabilitated in the mid-1960s, only to fall foul of normalization after the 1968 invasion. There were small exhibitions of his art in Prague in 1966 and Brno in 1967. A first volume of his writings from the 1920s came out in 1966 under the title "The World of Building and Poetry"; most copies of the second volume, entitled "Struggles over the Meaning of Modern Creativity" and containing

47. Karel Teige's cover for *The Smallest Apartment*, 1931. Teige's book was a paean to a thoroughly socialized lifestyle, in which superfluous personal living spaces would be minimized.

among other 1930s writings *Surrealism Against the Current* and "The Moscow Trial," were pulped before they reached the bookstores in 1969; though ready for the press that same year, a proposed third volume never appeared (until 1994).[61] The first comprehensive retrospective exhibition devoted to this towering figure in interwar Czech cultural life (not to mention in interwar left politics) did not take place until 1994 at the Gallery of the City of Prague.[62]

As on previous occasions in Czech history, these battles were waged not only on the terrain of "high culture" but also in the prosaic landscapes of everyday life. Among the many names expunged from the bridges, embankments, and squares of Prague between 1947 and 1952 were those of Masaryk, Beneš, Rašín, Kramář, Štefánik, and Švehla, all of them founders of Czechoslovakian statehood. Beneš Square became the Square of the October Revolution, Rieger Embankment became Gottwald Embankment, Štefánik Square became the Square of the Soviet Tank-Crews. In 1951 the statues and busts of Tomáš Masaryk (for the second time in a decade), Edvard Beneš, and František Ladislav Rieger were removed from the Pantheon of the National Museum. So were those of Count Kašpar Šternberk (whose idea the museum had been in the first place), Petr Parléř and Kilián Ignác Dienzenhofer (those two German architects who left so enduring a mark on Prague), and Josef Pekař.[63] Czechoslovak Post specialized in appealing stamps of high artistic quality, issuing many more special sets than had been customary before the war and employing leading artists in their design and execution. Many commemorated—and thus conferred significance and order upon—people and events of the past. The anniversary of Czechoslovak independence in 1918 was celebrated in 1948, 1968, and 1978 by stamps utterly innocent of all reference to those whose achievement it was. In 1958 it was not marked at all. In 1950, postage stamps commemorated the 130th anniversary of Božena Němcová's birth, the seventy-fifth anniversary of S. K. Neumann's, the hundredth anniversary of composer Zdeněk Fibich's, and the twentieth anniversary of the death of Soviet poet Vladimir Mayakovsky. The centenary of Tomáš Masaryk's birth in 1850 was not recalled. The president-liberator did not appear on a single stamp throughout the entire communist period, not even during 1968–69, when M. R. Štefánik, Franz Kafka, Alfons Mucha, and others briefly emerged from their habitual obscurity. Analysis of coins, banknotes, or commemorative medallions would tell much the same story.[64]

One final example of enforced forgetting can speak for all. Marta Kubišová (b. 1942) was one of the most popular young Czech singers of the later 1960s. She looked just like her Western counterparts in those days, long hair, mascara, miniskirt, and bare feet. One of her biggest hits was a Czech cover version of the Beatles' "Hey Jude"; it can be heard (together with much Janáček) on the sound track to Philip Kaufman's film of Milan Kundera's *The*

Unbearable Lightness of Being. Kubišová has a glorious voice, a rich contralto of operatic proportions. The KSČ silenced it in 1970 for twenty years. Banned from radio and TV, the recording studio, and public appearances, and heavily persecuted in the private life that was left to her, Marta Kubišová, too, eventually became a spokesperson for Charta 77. What had occasioned her official obliteration were the lyrics of a song she recorded in November 1968, called "Prayer for Marta":

> Let peace remain long with this land,
> Malice, envy, hatred, fear, and discord,
> Let them pass,
> Let them pass already,
> Now, that the lost government of your affairs
> Returns to you, people,
> Returns to you.
> The cloud slowly passes away from the sky,
> And each one reaps what he sowed.
> Let this prayer of mine, let it speak to hearts
> Which have not been burnt,
> Like blossoms by frost,
> By the time of malice.[65]

The relevance of "Prayer for Marta" to the events of 1968 is perhaps obvious enough. But there is more to the song (and to what makes it so "objectionable") than first meets the eye. The words "the government of your affairs returns to you, people" were those with which Tomáš Masaryk began his first speech as president to the Czechoslovak National Assembly on 22 December 1918, and Václav Havel in turn was to end his first speech as president seventy-two years later on 1 January 1990. But the words are neither Masaryk's nor Havel's. Earlier, they were inscribed on the pedestal of Ladislav Šaloun's Jan Hus memorial in Staroměstské náměstí. They come from a prayer by the last bishop of the Jednota bratrská Jan Amos Komenský, whose lonely death in Naarden in 1670 Alfons Mucha painted in the *Slovanská epopej*, and whom Antonín Koniáš had done his utmost to extirpate from Czech memories, forever, through his *Key for Recognizing Heretical Errors.*[66]

The Lineup for Meat

Mention was made earlier of a grand exhibition of historical documents—over seventeen hundred of them, from the Prague Fragment of the Gospel of Saint Mark with which Josef Dobrovský first made his name, to the text of the Warsaw Pact—which was staged at Hradčany in 1958 under the title "From the Heroic Past Toward the Victory of Socialism." Introducing the exhibition catalogue, Zdeněk Nejedlý summarized his view of history and its uses thus: "To us, history is not the dead past, indeed it is not the past at all, it is an ever-living part of the present too."[67] In view of the foregoing, we might be tempted to say: evidently.

But it would be wrong to think that the KSČ's relation to history was limited only to excising those bits of it that were "objectionable." Side by side with censorship of the past went vigorous cultivation of a preferred version of it, and while the censorship was invisible the cultivation was highly public. Historicism was at least as pronounced a facet of public discourse under the communists as it had been, to the chagrin of Šalda and other modernists, in the first republic; it is one of the most visible (and important) features of the period. Forgetting was less an end in itself than a tool in the fabrication of *memory*; a cultural counterpart of the *odsun*, it cleared the landscape of obstacles that might give the lie to its approved representations. The past was purged not (simply) to rid the record of alternative political visions but in order to make possible, and render plausible, a positive reconstruction of Czech history. This ambitious archival exhibition is one small example. According to its catalogue, the exhibition "shows the *continuity* of the past and the efforts of the Czechoslovak people today to complete the building of socialism, in which they are realizing the desires and dreams of past generations."[68] History is rewritten in such a way that the communists can represent themselves as (in the title of another, famous article of the omnipresent Zdeněk Nejedlý's) "The Heirs of the Great Traditions of the Czech Nation."[69] Three very public sites in Prague illustrate, in different ways, how (and at what cost) this was accomplished.

The Czech capital once boasted one of the largest memorials to Josef Stalin in the world, on Letná Plain overlooking the historic city center across the Vltava. A competition for designs, for which there were ninety-five entries, was held in 1949. The architects Jiří Štursa and Vlasta Štursová and the sculptor Otakar Švec (1892–1955) triumphed with their idea for a gigantic collective statue. There is a distinguished lineage here. Jiří Štursa (b. 1910) is the nephew of perhaps the greatest Czech sculptor of this century, "the young Jan Štursa" (1880–1925) buried at Vyšehrad, to whom Max Švabinský referred in his speech at Mucha's funeral. Jan Štursa was Josef Myslbek's assistant and successor at the Academy of Fine Arts. His work can be seen on the pylons of Prague's Hlávka Bridge, in the shape of two vigorous and powerful groups "Humanity" and "Work," or on the facade of the Bank of the Legions on Na poříčí, on which he cooperated with Oto Gutfreund. He died by his own hand in 1925. Švec, who was also a pupil of Myslbek's, had in turn been Jan Štursa's assistant. His "Sunbeam Motorcyclist" of 1924 is a classic of Czech civic realism. He too committed suicide, in 1955, causing considerable embarrassment when in consequence he failed to show up for the ceremonial unveiling of his colossal homage to the generalissimo. The

48. "With the Soviet Union for all eternity!" or, "It must go quickly, there mustn't be much of a bang, and it must be seen by as few people as possible"—the Stalin Memorial on Letná Plain.

official commemorative brochure describes the monument thus: "In the forefront [is] the figure of J. V. Stalin, behind him marching on one side representatives of the Soviet people and on the other side representatives of the Czechoslovak people. By this means the unity of Stalin's person with the people and the eternal brotherhood of the Czechoslovak people with the Soviet people in the struggle for the realization of the great ideas of peace and socialism are expressively conveyed."[70] Praguers interpreted the symbolism more vulgarly, dubbing the monstrosity the "lineup for meat" [fronta na maso].

The intention, however, was to locate Stalin very squarely within the emotional landscape of Czech history. The foundation stone was laid on the Soviet leader's seventieth birthday on 21 December 1949. Prime Minister (from 1953 President) Antonín Zápotocký (1884–1957) reminded Czechs that "this friendship proved itself, proved itself always just in the worst times and in the moments of gravest danger. This friendship did not let us perish [*Toto přátelství nedalo zahynouti nám*]. That is why we will make this friendship with the Soviet Union and its great leader generalissimo Stalin ever stronger, since this friendship is to us a firm guarantee that it will not let our descendants perish either [*že nedá zahynouti ani budoucím*]." He is playing, of course, on the words Bohuslav Balbín had taken from the Saint Václav chorale in his despairing prayer of 1673. Zápotocký ended his speech with the words "to Stalin, the Soviet Union and socialism, we will remain faithful"— *věrni zůstaneme*, those same words that Bohumil Stašek had uttered over Mácha's coffin in 1939, and Edvard Beneš over the body of Tomáš Garrigue Masaryk two years before that, and which had more recently graced the banners of Czechoslovak battalions on both eastern and western fronts in World War II.[71] These were not the only such echoes of the past used rhetorically to insert Stalin into the national epic. Embedded in the monument's foundation, in a supreme piece of kitsch that deliberately recalls the foundations of the National Theater, were engraved stones from all Czech administrative districts [*okresy*].

Work on the colossus began in 1952. Its construction consumed fourteen thousand tons of granite, 495 days, six hundred workers, and twenty-three stonemasons. It stood a full thirty meters high, and the block from which Stalin's head was carved alone weighed fifty-two metric tons.[72] The memorial was built with maximum panopticalism in mind. As Vlasta Štursová explained,

> The political significance that the government of the Czechoslovak Republic attributed to the Stalin Memorial was already expressed by the chosen site on the edge of Letná Plain, on the axis of the Svatopluk Čech Bridge. The chosen site commands all the most significant views from the Prague basin, upstream on the Vltava from beyond the National Theater, as well as from the Smetana and Old Town Squares, and downstream from the embankment as far as Libeň. The monument is a pronounced architectural dominant, which marks out Letná from both close and distant vantage points (from Vítkov, from Vinohrady), and is a sovereign element in panoramic pictures of the city. At the same time the monument commands the space of Letná Plain from the south and will thus become a significant component in its future architectural development.[73]

Standing in Staroměstské náměstí on the spot where on 21 June 1621 twenty-seven Czech aristocrats and burghers were executed—crosses in the pavement mark the place—in front of the missing neo-Gothic wing of the Old Town Hall burned down by the Germans in May 1945, one could gaze directly down Pařížská třída to this monument "to its liberator from the Czechoslovak people"; and one might remember the remark of Mikoláš Aleš, often enough quoted in these years, that "with us it will be well, when the cossacks are in the Old Town Square."[74] The intention to utilize Prague's topography to reorder the significances of its history was made quite explicit. Stalin was to be "a new landmark, linking with places that hitherto dominated the Prague basin and which are most deeply inscribed in the history of the city and the nation—with Žižka's Mountain at Vítkov, ancient Vyšehrad, and Hradčany."[75] Pictures of the monument, which was unceremoniously blown up in 1962,[76] later became hard to come by. One surviving record is Cyril Bouda's tapestry "Praga regina musicae," which hangs in the lobby bar of the former Hotel International (1952–56) in Dejvice, itself a landmark of Stalinist architecture, all gilt, marble, and heavy draperies. Bouda sharply exaggerates the vertical perspective to achieve just this linking effect. Today, Jiří Štursa's steps sweep purposefully up the steep slope to Letná from the Svatopluk Čech Bridge to an incongruously empty but still monumental plinth. Lest it too disappear from historical memory, it should be recorded that in 1996 the plinth was briefly occupied by a ten-meter-tall inflatable water-filled replica of Michael Jackson, an American singer inordinately popular in his time. It was advertising the Prague gig on his new world tour, a tour that was called, appropriately enough, "History."

The fate of the National Memorial on Žižka's Mountain across the Vltava from Letná, which Stalin's monumental presence was once intended to counterpoint, is equally instructive. The memorial is closely bound up with the life of Rudolf Medek (1890–1940), the army general who spoke at both Mácha's and Jirásek's funerals. The son of a private entrepreneur, Medek was until 1914 a teacher in Hradec Králové. Joining the colors at the beginning of the war, he went over to the Russians as an Austrian officer in 1915. The following year he entered the Czech Legion in Russia as a simple volunteer but was promoted that September to lieutenant. He saw action in Galicia and the Carpathians and was twice decorated in 1917 by the Russian provisional government. In 1919 he was made head of military administration of the Czech Legions in Russia by the new Czechoslovak state and sat on a special three-man committee for military affairs that effectively created the Czechoslovak national army. In June 1920 he was appointed director of the Památník odboje (Memorial of the Resistance), the proposed museum and archive of the Czechoslovak Legions. This organization, which was Medek's own creation, was renamed Památník osvobození (Memorial of the Liberation) in 1929. Medek remained its director throughout the interwar years, winning promotion to colonel in 1923 and to general in 1931.

Rudolf Medek was not just a military man. The son-in-law of the impressionist painter Antonín Slavíček, he built a fine collection of modern Czech art, including (apart from Slavíčeks) paintings by Vincenc Beneš and Rudolf

Kremlička, graphic sheets, and bibliophilia. He was an honorary member of the Czech Academy, a member of Umělecká beseda and the Czech Pen Club, and president of the Circle of Czech Writers. He was also a prolific poet, novelist, and playwright. Three of his plays were staged at the National Theater in the 1920s and 1930s. In Kiev and Siberia between 1917 and 1920 Medek founded and edited the magazine *The Czechoslovak Soldier* [*Československý voják*]. His drama *Colonel Švec* (which played at the National Theater 110 times between 1928 and 1934)[77] and his cycle of novels *The Epic of the Legions* [*Legionářská epopej*] draw on his own experience in Russia. The latter went through no less than ten editions in the 1920s.[78] Needless to say, *The Epic of the Legions* features in the "Catalogue of Formerly Prohibited Literature," along with everything else Medek wrote. He does not merit an entry in *Czech Writers of the Twentieth Century*. As a brief entry in the *Malá československá encyklopedie* explains, his writings created "a nationalistic and anti-Soviet focused apotheosis of the struggle of the Czechoslovak Legions in Russia."[79]

Medek was vice president of the Committee for Building a Memorial of National Liberation and a Monument to Jan Žižka of Trocnov on Žižka's Mountain in Prague. Žižka's Mountain, also known as Vítkov, was the site of the celebrated Hussite victory over Emperor Zikmund's invaders in July 1420. It offers a panoramic view of the city, and the edifice built here between 1927 and 1932 can be seen for miles around. Seeking to render in stone the founding struggles of modern Czech statehood and identify them with the glories of the national past, the original memorial complex was made up of "Žižka's monument with a mausoleum and the museum of 'Památník osvobození,' a museum of the Legions, the military museum of the Czechoslovak Republic, the military archive of the Czechoslovak Republic, the archive of the Legions, [and] the archive of the national liberation." This is how the memorial is described in a Czech tourist guide of 1930.[80] That guide's successor, published in March 1950, retains some fidelity to the original intent of the liberation memorial in its description of what was then still known as the Památník osvobození. "The monumental granite building of the Pantheon is intended as the resting place for the remains of the most notable representatives and heroes of both resistances [i.e., World War I and II]."[81] But by 1955, virtually all of the threads tying what had now been renamed the Národní památník (National Memorial) to the world of Rudolf Medek and the Legions had been snapped. Václav Hlavsa's *Prague: A Guide to the City* devotes three pages to Vítkov without once mentioning the Czechoslovak Legions by name. (Some time after, Prague's Bridge of the Legions was also to be renamed Bridge of the First of May.) Moving smartly from Jan Žižka's victory over "the crusading forces, which the united reaction of the entire then existing world stood up against the Czechs"—a sentence quite beautiful in its brutal simplicity—through the barest details of the original

49. The National Memorial at Vítkov, with Bohumil Kafka's statue of Jan Žižka.

construction of the monument, Hlavsa informs us that "after the occupation the Národní památník received a new calling. In 1949 the remains of the Unknown Czechoslovak Soldier, exhumed from the battlefield at Dukla Pass, were placed there, and from 1951 the greatest sons of our working class, who dedicated their whole lives to the struggle for the victory of the working people, find their last resting place here."[82]

The KSČ cannibalized the Památník osvobození for its own. In faithful imitation of all things Soviet, Klement Gottwald's embalmed body was displayed in its mausoleum from June 1954; Gottwald died a few days after Stalin himself, attending his mentor's funeral in Moscow. Reportedly Jan Zázvorka, the architect of the original building, was forced by the StB [*Státní bezpečnost*, the secret police] in the days after Gottwald's death to design a "hospital" underground where, every night, a seventy-member team of specialists worked to make his mummy endure.[83] Their efforts were unsuccessful. Gottwald's decaying corpse had to be cremated in 1962, and his ashes were deposited in a red marble sarcophagus in the central hall of the mausoleum. Presidents Zápotocký and Svoboda were also in due course laid to rest here (Zápotocký's successor, Antonín Novotný, did not make it). The Columbarium, originally built for Czech legionnaires, became a "red Slavín." Its urns bore the ashes of the writers Marie Majerová, Ivan Olbracht, and S. K. Neumann, and other communist luminaries. A Hall of the Soviet Army, with remains of an Unknown Soviet Soldier and soil taken from the battlefield at Stalingrad, was added to the building and opened on the tenth anniversary of the liberation of Czechoslovakia in 1955; a solemn materialization of the ubiquitous slogan of the time "With the Soviet Union for all eternity!" [*Se Sovětským svazem na věčné časy!*].

Josef Malejovský sculpted reliefs for the doors of the monument, in best socialist realist style, with "subjects from the history of the revolutionary struggles of the Czechoslovak people" from the Hussites onward. Malejovský (b. 1914) is also the author of the exquisitely lyrical "Spring" [*Jaro*, 1983] in the courtyard of the National Theater; not all artists who loyally served the KSČ, as did Malejovský, who held a string of high positions in Czech art organizations under the post-1968 regime of "normalization," were devoid of talent.[84] Inside the mausoleum, almost inevitably it seems, there is a hauntingly beautiful mosaic by Max Švabinský, completed in 1939. It adorns the walls of the Chapel of the Executed Legionnaires. Beneath each of its panels is a legend by Rudolf Medek. The last text reads: "Once again, homeland, you govern yourself freely. Do not weep for us! We live on."[85] Guarding this desecration is the largest equestrian statue in the world. Erected in 1950, the year the KSČ hanged Milada Horáková, Bohumil Kafka's bronze sculpture (which was commissioned under the first republic and erected posthumously) stands 18.6 meters tall and weighs 16.5 metric tons. Seated on the horse is Jan Žižka z Trocnova.

But perhaps the most surreal communist reappropriation of the national past is a literal reconstruction. Among the memorials to Czech communism in its Stalinist heyday, pride of place must surely be given to the Bethlehem Chapel in Prague, where Jan Hus preached from 1402 to 1412. The Betlémská kaple was originally built in 1391. According to folklore, funds for such a chapel, where the gospel would be delivered in Czech, were first donated by Prague prostitutes moved by the appeals of the Moravian reformer Jan Milíč z Kroměříže. The chapel went through mixed fortunes after Hus's death; communist accounts rarely neglect to mention that Thomas Müntzer preached there in 1521, perhaps because (in the guise of a class warrior) Müntzer is the hero of Friedrich Engels's book *The Peasant War in*

Germany. Bethlehem was bought by the Jesuits in 1661 and used thereafter for Catholic services. Following the dissolution of the Jesuit order, the chapel was finally demolished in 1786. Another house was later built on its site. In 1919–20 it was discovered that three of the original exterior walls had been utilized in neighboring buildings in ways that preserved the outlines of the medieval windows and entrances. Other traces of the old building, including a well, the base of a pillar, and some fragments of biblical texts which Hus had had inscribed on its walls, also survived. Not long after, plans of the chapel dating from 1661 and 1783 were found. There were suggestions at the time, among them from the cultural committee of the Czechoslovak parliament, to rebuild Bethlehem, but they remained unrealized until after the war.

At Zdeněk Nejedlý's urging the communist government committed itself on 30 July 1948 to full restoration. While every effort was made to ensure the historical accuracy of the reconstruction with the aid of old descriptions, plans, and pictures, inevitably much was pure guesswork: little is known, for instance, of which texts actually adorned the interior. But the true betrayal of authenticity is not of an architectural kind. The chapel was finished in 1954 and "handed over to the Czech people" on 5 July of that year, the day before the state holiday marking Hus's death.[86] Bethlehem then joined Hradčany, Vyšehrad, the National Theater, and other such "sacred places"—among them the Národní památník on Vítkov—as an officially designated "national cultural memorial." On a pillar inside the chapel is a prominent plaque bearing this inscription:

> Master Jan Hus
> waiting in prison for death
> laid down this charge on the 10th of June 1415
> to all faithful Czechs:
> Be kind to the Bethlehem Chapel.
> In fulfillment of this bequest,
> we restored this cradle
> of the Czech people's movement
> under the government of the people
> and by its will
> in the years 1948–1954.[87]

Another plaque thanks Zdeněk Nejedlý for his part in the project of "the renewal of Bethlehem."[88]

What is surreal in this is not the simple fact of the restoration, nor even the elevation of a latter-day replica to the ranks of the monumentally national. It is that Hus's "charge" should be so painstakingly honored by a murderously atheist government, which at the time was busy killing, imprisoning, and torturing priests on a grand scale, and which cheerfully al-

50. Saint Michael's Church, Prague, photographed in May 1990.

lowed many of the country's ancient churches—genuine historic monuments, which is to say, monuments of a genuine rather than a refurbished
history—to fall into utter ruin. One sad exemplar stood not fifty yards from
the lovingly antiqued facades of Staroměstské náměstí, the baroque Church
of Saint Michael. It is apt, then, to recall what Jan Hus actually did beseech

in that letter of 10 June 1415, written in the night of the Monday before the feast of Saint Vitus, addressed "To all faithful Czechs, *who love and will love the Lord God*": "I beg you especially, Praguers, to love Bethlehem, so long as the Lord God permits that the word of God be preached in it. For the Devil was angry with this place and has inflamed priests and canons against it, for he saw that in this place his kingdom was crumbling. I believe the Lord God will preserve this place according to his will and in it will bring about greater successes through others than he has done through my weak self."[89] God's word was not to be preached again in the "restored" Bethlehem Chapel until after the Velvet Revolution of 1989. It is, however, an undeniably beautiful building, of a pure, stark simplicity, which gives every appearance of piety toward the national past.

The KSČ certainly endeavored to reinvent tradition and imagine the Czech nation anew. But no more than their nineteenth-century predecessors did the communists paint on a blank canvas. They refashioned *existing* narratives, motifs, and symbols of identity, suffusing them with a socialist content. The two-tailed Czech lion remained at the center of the state insignia, but in 1960, when the country was given a new constitution and officially renamed the Czechoslovak Socialist Republic, his golden crown was replaced by a five-pointed red star; on coins and military badges he was often framed by what was said to be a "Hussite shield."[90] The ubiquitous marriage of wheat fields and smokestacks on coins, banknotes, and elsewhere came to symbol-ize the class alliance of urban and rural "working people," but such iconogra-phy was not in itself novel; Oto Gutfreund had long ago depicted factory chimneys behind five ears of wheat, without any connotations of class strug-gle, on his 1925 design for a five-crown piece.[91] A set of eight postage stamps issued in 1950 in celebration of "the fifth anniversary of the Czechoslovak popular democratic republic" located new-age socialist heroes in timeless scenarios of Czechness. One portrayed "a Soviet tank driver and Hradčany," another "the central Bohemian countryside with Říp mountain, tractors, and an agricultural worker"—Říp, from whose summit *Praotec* Čech had looked out and told his people, in the words of Jirásek's *Staré pověsti české*, "We have found the land, where we will remain and establish our dwellings. Behold, this is that land, which you have sought. . . . This is that promised land, full of animals and birds, abounding in honey."[92]

October 28 remained a public holiday, but it was now listed in calendars as "the Day of Nationalization" [*Den znárodnění*]. In this guise it commemo-rated Edvard Beneš's 1945 nationalization decree as much as Czechoslovak independence in 1918, sinewing the two together as successive milestones on a single journey of national self-realization.[93] Sokol may have been dis-solved, but mass gymnastic festivals still took place from 1955 in Prague under the name of Spartakiáda (after Spartacus), and the spirit of Miroslav Tyrš continued to preside over them as before.[94] In this guise the five-yearly jamborees became living embodiments of socialist values; the form is after all tailor-made for the glorification of collectivism. *The New Guide to Czecho-slovakia* published in March 1950 reassured its readers that "the tradition of the former student festival '*Majáles*' continues in the 'Joyous Days of Youth' of the Czechoslovak Union of Youth . . . with a rich cultural and physical education program in the socialist spirit."[95] This guidebook itself, an official publication written "with the cooperation of the ministry of information" and local officialdom, employs exactly the same cover design as the prewar guides of the (private) Club of Czechoslovak Tourists. Familiar names of once-private publishing houses like Melantrich and Odeon were similarly purloined. Earlier we encountered a *National Songbook* published soon after 1918. *The Czech Revolutionary Songbook* of 1953, which contains "revolution-ary, folk, workers', and socialist-construction [*budovatelské*] songs from the oldest times to the present day," mimics such compilations.[96] But alongside "Ye who are the soldiers of God" and "*Hej, Slované!*" we now find "The song of the agricultural brigade," "A song to Stalin," and—with uplifting lyrics by the young Pavel Kohout—"A song to Julius Fučík." The scouting movement, which had been very popular in Czechoslovakia between the wars, was dis-solved after Victorious February and replaced in 1949 by the Pioneers, a branch of the KSČ youth wing the ČSM (*Československý svaz mládeže*, the Czechoslovak Union of Youth). The new organization's "fundamental fea-tures" were said to be "its mass character [*masovost*], unity, and voluntari-ness"; this last should be taken with an enormous pinch of salt. The Pioneers aimed to "bring up children for creative work, for the formation of noble personal qualities and for socialist patriotism and proletarian international-ism."[97] But their uniforms, activities, and rituals (Leader: "Be prepared!" Pi-oneers: "Always prepared!") bore an uncanny resemblance to those of their imperialist counterparts, even if the boys' and girls' scarves had now turned "the color of spilled proletarian blood."[98]

The retail furnishing chain Krásná jizba (the Beautiful Room) had been founded in 1927 under the auspices of the publisher Družstevní práce (Co-operative Work) as a showcase for modern interior design. Its original aim, like that of Pavel Janák's Svaz československého díla, was to elevate the qual-ity of mass-produced goods for everyday living, and its aesthetic ethos was uncompromisingly functionalist.[99] Krásná jizba's shops in Prague, Bratislava, Brno, and elsewhere sold furniture, glass, porcelain, and textiles from leading Czech and foreign companies, among them goods made in Czechoslovakia under license from the Bauhaus. They also carried modern graphic art and posters. After 1948 a Krásná jizba was still to be found on Prague's Národní třída, occupying the premises that had borne that name since 1936, and in city centers up and down the country. But it now purveyed a very different kind of beauty. This erstwhile center of international modernist design had metamorphosed into an outlet mainly for domestic "folk"-inspired art and crafts. Marcel Breuer's tubular steel furniture, Adolf Loos's glass tableware, and Antonín Kybal's bold geometric carpets in primary colors were supplanted by hand-woven and hand-dyed draperies, fabrics, and clothes whose designs had their source in "traditional" local patterns, hand-stitched and hand-embroidered tablecloths and doilies, hand-painted majolica plates and bowls, handmade wooden toys and hand-colored Easter eggs. With its emphasis on fine craftsmanship and use of natural raw materials (wood, cotton, linen, hemp) the new Krásná jizba remained a bastion of good taste, and its prices were by no means low. But good taste had now been redefined in terms that were closer to the ideological heart of the communist regime. These were *Czech* products, rooted in timeless forms, living proof of *popular* creativity [*lidová tvořivost*]. What was now being elevated was not an international modernist aesthetic of machine production but "*zlaté české ručičky*," golden Czech hands. With each item sold came a card naming both the designer and the individual craftsman or craftswoman who made it. Alfons Mucha would no doubt have approved; recall his lament for "the old, original tradition and the ancient, unadulterated, exquisite forms."

It might be said that these are trivia, the small change of social life. But that is exactly why they matter. Historic sites and public monuments, popular festivals and national holidays, coins, postage stamps, the designs of book covers and the names of their publishers, the shops on the street, the rituals and uniforms of the organizations that take children on summer camp—these are everyday media that routinely bound social identity. They give shape and meaning to the surrounds, delineating the spatial and temporal parameters of the community within which individuals live their lives and in terms of which they locate themselves. They unobtrusively yet authoritatively map out boundaries of belonging, etching their shape and weight into the contours of the quotidian. These little mutations in the landscape of the everyday bear eloquent witness to what Czechs call the *totalitní* character of the KSČ's revolution, its determined penetration into every nook and cranny of human existence. They also testify to something else. Even while it was turning the world upside down, that revolution assiduously draped itself in the reassurances of time-honored language and borrowed costumes";[100] and as it did so, it comprehensively reshaped the legacy of the past. Tradition was reordered. Its elements were comfortingly familiar, but they were newly related to one another to form a totality that was barely recognizable. The community of the nation was reimagined as a caricature of its former self, and the instruments of that makeover were above all its own traditions and history.

In the Land Where Tomorrow Already Means Yesterday

One vantage point on this pastiche of earlier imageries of Czech identity is afforded by the Klement Gottwald Museum, which opened with much fanfare in Prague on 23 November 1954. The museum was situated in the former headquarters of the Prague City Savings Bank [*Pražská městská spoři-telna*] on the corner of Rytířská ulice and Na Můstku, which lies on the ancient route from Václavské náměstí to Staroměstské náměstí. It was a pointed choice of location. The Dům spořitelny had been a palace of commercial pride, proclaiming the solidity of a venerable Czech financial institution founded in 1825. Buried in the foundations was a pot containing two hundred gold coins. Embellished with the artistry of Myslbek, Ženíšek, Sucharda, and Aleš, Wiehl and Polívka's stately neo-Renaissance building had stood there since 1894. This "first great political museum," according to its guidebook, "documents the historical process and development of our society by modern exhibition methods, with the help of original documents, models, maps, and graphs. By its arrangement and individual exhibits the museum leads the visitor on the trail of the glorious revolutionary traditions of our nations from the Hussite times up to the history of our glorious Communist Party. Thus the museum links together two basic mottoes of the cultural revolution. The visitor educated by traditions, will more easily and fully comprehend today."[101] The Gottwald Museum no longer exists, though Wiehl and Polívka's structure still stands; it now houses another bank, the Česká spořitelna, whose glossy brochures on the building's history tactfully omit any reference to its postwar fate.[102] In a way it is a pity; left just as it was, with its confident mastery of past, present, and future preserved for posterity like a fly in amber, this would have made a wonderful monument to totality.

On the main floor, the visitor entered a hall devoted to "The Hussite Revolutionary Movement," which, the guidebook tells us, was "one of the greatest antifeudal uprisings in the Middle Ages. The rural and urban poor here for the first time tried to realize their ideas of a classless society. The Hussites, however, did not struggle only for the realization of a socially just order, but strove to safeguard the happy development of our homeland." Hall II was devoted to peasant uprisings, demonstrating that "the class struggle between exploiters and exploited formed the chief feature of the entire feudal order." Hall III depicted "The Revolutionary Year 1848," Hall IV "The Beginnings of the Workers' Movement in our Lands" from 1848 to 1917. Thus primed, spectators were led through the landmarks of twentieth-century Czechoslovak history. On the second floor, the story of the first republic was told in successive rooms with exhibits entitled "The Echo of the Great October Socialist Revolution," "The Founding of the KSČ," "Bolshevization," and "Crisis and the Struggle Against Fascism." This was followed by "The National Liberation Struggle [of World War II]." The third floor guided visitors through the present and onward into the future; the tour concluded with a display entitled "The Victory of Socialism in Czechoslovakia and Perspectives on Building a Developed Socialist Society," which it brought to life through documents showing "the recent past, the present, and"—really—"the future too." Side by side with scale models of Czech-made cars and trucks and a copy of the 1960 constitution of the Czechoslovak Socialist Republic were incontrovertible knowledges of an equally up-to-date variety. Where once we might have had a natural cabinet divided according to species and genera, or, rather later, an ethnographic map, now we find a statistical table depicting "The Class Composition of the Population of the ČSR." This conclusively demonstrated that by comparison with 1930, workers had by 1958 risen from 61.4 percent of the population to 89.5 percent, while "capitalists (*kulaks*, entrepreneurs, rentiers)" had declined from 9.2 percent to 0.3 percent. Thus "the exploitation of man by man," against which Czechs had been heroically struggling from the Hussites onward, "was practically eliminated."

It is superfluous to comment upon what is "left out" of Czech history as represented here. As interesting as the content of this standing exhibit is its form. History is presented as a stage upon which an Idea inexorably unfolds, an Idea that was present from its very beginning. This is a flat, planar space, with no differentiation of past and present beyond that furnished by mere chronology. There is endless progress, but in their essentials the dramatis personae never change. The guidebook gets to the heart of the matter when it approvingly quotes an (alleged) entry in the visitors' book: "This isn't a museum—it's a school, a university of the history of our nation—the history of the construction of socialism here."[103] The history of the nation is the history of the construction of socialism, and by the same token the history of the construction of socialism is the history of the nation. Identity is established by analogy and extended across the centuries, enfolding past, present, and future in a single seamless narrative. Communists *are* latter-day Hussites, and the Hussites were communists *avant le mot*. In this fairy tale of the eternal return of the ever-same, the past becomes a merely figurative space, to be plundered for metaphoric equivalences. The one thing it emphatically is not is a foreign country, where they do things differently,[104] a territory that demands to be explored and understood in its own specificity and difference. We have encountered this narrative structure before, of course. It was that of Palacký's mirror. Only in this case, the mirror is tilted a little to the left. The consequence in both cases is the same. Contemporary agendas acquire an ancient pedigree, and ancient heroes and villains rise again to play new roles in contemporary dramas.

It is from this point of view that we must understand an otherwise puzzling set of commemorative postage stamps, the first of many such issues over the years, which appeared in 1949 under the title "Cultural and Political Personalities."[105] The stamps show the nineteenth-century Slovak writer Pavol Országh Hviezdoslav (1849–1921) and five Czechs. Four of the latter are communists or fellow-travelers. Julius Fučík (in Max Švabinský's portrait) and Vladislav Vančura we know; Jiří Wolker (1900–1924) was a *proletkult* poet and early Devětsil member who had the inestimable advantage, as far as subsequent uses of his name for political ends was concerned, of dying romantically young; Jan Šverma (1901–44), who like Fučík was a communist journalist, froze to death during the Slovak National Rising of 1944–45. It is the last "cultural and political personality" that is so discordant. It is none other than—old Mr. Jirásek. What jars here is the association of Alois Jirásek with radical writers of that 1920s generation whose unflattering opinion of his work was so devastatingly expressed by F. X. Šalda on the occasion of his death in 1930. Viewed as purely literary figures, Jirásek and Vančura are polar antitheses. As political personalities these are equally strange bedfellows; Jirásek, after all, had been a parliamentary deputy for the National Democrats, one of the many "right-wing" parties banned in 1945, and was a colleague of Monsignor Jan Šrámek's on the National Committee of 1918, the same Jan Šrámek who had been indefinitely interned as a traitor to the Czech nation the year before these stamps were issued. The condition of this coupling is a violent abstraction from these men's lives, times, and beliefs. But the ground on which they are brought together here is not that of literary history, or indeed of any history whatsoever. The unifying principle of this discordant menagerie is that all these writers were retrospectively deemed, in the jargon of the age, "progressive" [pokrokoví].

Through a variety of media, from stamps to street names, theatrical productions to school textbooks, such discords were harmonized, until the old-new canon of the "progressive" was habituated as the very heart of the national heritage. Alois Jirásek was not the only nineteenth-century patriot to find his way onto socialist Czechoslovakia's postage stamps. Into the future, side by side with Lenin and Stalin, miners and construction workers, S. K. Neumann and student girls bearing doves of peace, strode a long procession of buditelé. Havlíček appeared in 1946, Palacký and Rieger in 1948, Smetana in 1949, Němcová in 1950, Dvořák and Jirásek (again) in 1951, Kollár, Myslbek, Čelakovský, and Aleš in 1952, Erben, Kramérius, Dobrovský, and Josef Mánes in 1953, Neruda in 1954, Šafařík in 1955. This is by no means a complete list, but even so it far outstrips the philatelic homages of the first republic, when we might have expected such nationalist pantheonization to be in full flood. The Jirásek centennial set of 1951 resuscitated images of a still more distant Czech past, seen through the eyes of the later nineteenth century. One stamp portrayed the novelist himself, the others "Legends and Fates" and "Tábor"—Old Slavs and Hussites as sketched by Mikoláš Aleš for his cycle Vlast in the National Theater. Saint Vojtěch, Charles IV establishing the university of Prague in 1348, Hus, and Komenský were duly commemorated in these years too. The thirtieth anniversary of the founding of the KSČ was celebrated in 1951 with a stamp collaging together those comrades-in-arms across the centuries, "a worker-militiaman and a Hussite warrior." It is a strange turn of events. The young radicals of Devětsil had condemned "the old time" to molder in libraries in 1920; visiting the Soviet Union for the first time in 1930, Julius Fučík had sung its praises as "the land where tomorrow already means yesterday."[106] Twenty years later, that slogan could be read ironically; yesterday and tomorrow had now become one, and it was the nationalist icons of the past that lit up the road to the glorious communist future.

In the 1950s the State Publishing House for Belles-Lettres, Music and Art [SNKLHU, formerly Orbis][107] put out a 32-volume edition of Jirásek, a 20-volume edition of Tyl, a 15-volume edition of Němcová, a 38-volume edition of Neruda, and substantial collections of Karolina Světlá, Jaroslav Vrchlický, Karel V. Rais, and other nineteenth-century writers. SNKLHU's largest series was the National Library [*Národní knihovna*], which kicked off in 1948 with František Ladislav Čelakovský's *An Echo of Russian Songs* and *An Echo of Czech Songs*. This was immediately followed by Němcová's *Babička*, Erben's *Kytice*, and Jan Neruda's *Tales from the Malá strana*. The mandate of this series, which was planned to reach 150 volumes, was to provide "cheap and reliable" texts of Czech classics in order that "every Czech will be able gradually to build up a library, in which may be found the most fundamental works of our literary culture."[108] It is a publishing program that is disconcertingly reminiscent of Jan Otto's nationalist endeavors of the 1880s and 1890s in both its titles and its aspirations, and a million miles from Otakar Štorch-Marien's Aventinum. Only now, the stimulus for the series came from the publications division of Václav Kopecký's Ministry of Information and Enlightenment, and the publishing house—if we may still use the term to describe what was effectively a branch of government—boasted that its series "will certainly not be the smallest contribution to the fulfilment of the cultural five-year plan." We may be forgiven for wondering whether the selection of Čelakovský's two collections of poems (rather than, say, Mácha's *Máj* or the most obvious choice, Němcová's *Babička*) to launch the series was not a diplomatic as much as a literary decision; but it serves to remind us, as it doubtless reminded Czechs, that there was an authentically Czech legacy of pan-Slavist Russophilia to be drawn upon in cementing new alliances. The single largest number of translations from any foreign literature in SNKLHU's lists, 242 books over the ten years 1953–62, came from the Russian.[109]

There is an elegiac passage in Milan Kundera's *The Book of Laughter and Forgetting* in which he reflects on the transience of Prague's street names and the ephemerality of the city's memorials, a theme that has understandably preoccupied many Czech writers of his generation:

> The street Tamina was born on was called Schwerin. That was during the war, and Prague was occupied by the Germans. Her father was born on Černokostelecká Avenue—the Avenue of the Black Church. That was during the Austro-Hungarian Monarchy. When her mother married her father and moved there, it

51–53. Three designs for communist-period banknotes, respectively portraying Jan Žižka (top), a young worker and Říp Mountain (middle), and Hussites with their distinctive weaponry (bottom).

bore the name of Marshal Foch. That was after World War I. Tamina spent her childhood on Stalin Avenue, and when her husband came to take her away, he went to Vinohrady—that is, Vineyards—Avenue. And all the time it was the same street; they just kept changing its name, trying to lobotomize it.

There are all kinds of ghosts prowling these confused streets. They are the ghosts of monuments demolished—demolished by the Czech Reformation, demolished by the Austrian Counterreformation, demolished by the Czechoslovak Republic, demolished by the Communists. Even statues of Stalin have been torn down. All over the country, wherever statues were thus destroyed, Lenin statues have sprouted up by the thousands. They grow like weeds on the ruins, like melancholy flowers of forgetting.[110]

Praguers eventually took to mockingly calling what is now officially Vinohradská třída the Avenue of the Marshals. Yet even blandly naming the street after the district through which it passes did not entirely escape the long reach of old struggles for power; as Franz Kafka once remarked of Prague, "This little mother has claws."[111] Before 1948, Vinohrady had been known as Královské Vinohrady, the *Royal* Vineyards. Its main square was also symbolically democratized after Victorious February. What had from 1896 to 1948 been known as náměstí krále Jiřího (King Jiří's Square) was rechristened náměstí Jiřího z Poděbrad (the Square of Jiří of Poděbrady). No detail, it seems, was too trivial to be worthy of political scrutiny and correction.

But the process of refurbishing the symbolic streetscape of Czech towns and villages after 1948 was also somewhat more complicated than Milan Kundera suggests. It was far from being just a matter of demolitions and erasures. The flowers of forgetting were as often as not unimpeachably Czech. Certain figures and periods in Czech history—those retrospectively deemed "progressive"—were very insistently recalled. New statues sprang up in Prague not only of Lenin, Gottwald, Zápotocký, and Šverma (after whom the Štefánik Bridge, which had begun life in 1868 as the Franz Josef Bridge, was renamed in 1951), of Fučík, Bezruč, Vančura, and Wolker, but also of Němcová (1955), Jirásek (1960), Vrchlický (1960), Jan Evangelista Purkyně (1961), Neruda (1970), Aleš (1985), and Smetana (1984). The Smetana statue, which overlooks the Vltava at the Staré město side of Charles Bridge from Smetanovo nábřeží, is another creation of Josef Malejovský's. The Hussites, in particular, were pervasively materialized in these years in bronze and stone. In 1960 a statue of the firebrand preacher Jan Želivský was installed outside the Town Hall of the New Town, whence he had incited the defenestration of 1419. Another bust of Želivský, also dating from 1960, graces the wall of the Old Town Hall in Staroměstské náměstí, the scene of his execution at Utraquist hands in 1422. It is strategically placed near the 1911 plaque remembering the Czech lords executed by Ferdinand II in 1621, injecting progressiveness into the heart of this old landscape of martyrdom.

Želivský fell, the inscription tells us, "because he stood in the road of the bourgeois [*městácká*] reaction." A statue of Jan Roháč, executed leader of the last die-hard resistance to Zikmund's return as Czech king, was unveiled in front of the Old Town Hall the same year.[112] Nine years later, the courtyard of the Jirásek Museum in Hvězda Castle—a location to which we will return—was furnished with a statue of "A Hussite Woman." Generic rather than specific in its celebration of the progressiveness of the past, this commemorates (as Milan Krejčí's 1979 guide to *Prague Sculptures and Monuments* puts it) "the heroic part of women in the Hussite struggle."[113]

The KSČ was more than content to retain Žižkov's Hussite street names, and it perpetuated the prewar custom of naming streets in Braník after the titles and characters of Alois Jirásek's plays and novels. But even here it engaged in some discrete retrospective purging. Mladoňovicova ulice in Žižkov, which had originally been named after Hus's companion on the journey to Konstanz Petr Mladenovic (or Mladoňovic), was renamed in honor of the more acceptably radical Jan Želivský in 1951. Jakoubkova ulice, which since 1875 had commemorated Jakoubek ze Stříbra, was rechristened after Karel Sabina, Bedřich Smetana's librettist for *Prodaná nevěsta*, in 1952. Evidently it was preferable to remember a nineteenth-century radical democrat and patriot, even one who subsequently turned Austrian police informer, rather than an Utraquist critic of Tábor, notwithstanding the fact that Jakoubek had preached communion in both kinds in the Bethlehem Chapel before Hus. To continue to display the name of the commander of the victorious Utraquist forces at the battle of Lipany on socialist Prague's street signs was unthinkable: Nusle's Bořkova ulice, which was originally named after Diviš Bořek z Miletínka (who had led the then-unified Hussites to victory over Zikmund's forces at nearby Pankrác in November 1420) was renamed for Václav Runczík, "a progressive teacher and illegal worker of the KSČ" who was executed in Mauthausen in 1942.[114] Josef Myslbek proved an ideal replacement for the aristocratic champion of historic state right Jindřich Jaromír Count Clam-Martinic (1826–87) on the street signs of Střešovice, while Josef Šafář z Postřižína, an executed leader of the peasant uprising of 1775, was a convenient historical icon with which to displace the more recent and threatening memory of "the ideological originator of the program of the Agrarian party"[115] Alfons Ferdinand Šťastný (1831–1913), who had lent his name to a street in Hostivař from 1947 to 1952.

The first postwar director of the National Theater was Václav Vydra, the actor who read from *Máj* at Karel Hynek Mácha's funeral. After his replacement in 1949, there was a striking nationalization and historicization of the theater's repertoire.[116] Thirteen new operatic productions were offered in the 1949–50 season, all but five of which were by nineteenth-century Czech composers. Škroup's *Dráteník* (*The Tinker*, 1826) was followed by Dvořák's *Šelma sedlák* (*The Cunning Peasant*, 1882), Fibich's *Blaník* (1881) and *Šárka*

(1897), Foerster's *Eva* (1899), Kovařovic's *Na starém bělidle* (1901), and Leoš Janáček's most accessible and least modernistic opera, *Její pastorkyňa* (*Jenůfa*). Premiered at the Stavovské divadlo on 2 February 1826, *Dráteník* is generally reckoned the first original Czech opera; it is appropriately folkish in its locations and melodies. Škroup also composed operas on the legendary themes of *Oldřich and Božena* and *Libuše's Wedding*, as well as cooperating with Josef Kajetán Tyl on *Fidlovačka*. Less often remembered is the fact that—not uncharacteristically of his time and place—the author of the music for "*Kde domov můj?*," who was Kapelmeister at the Stavovské divadlo from 1837 to 1857, had gone on to write several operas to German libretti, as well as providing liturgical music to Hebrew texts for the Prague Jewish community. One of his German operas, whose subject is Christopher Columbus [*Kolumbus*], was premiered at the National Theater in 1942, nearly a century after it was written; communists were not the only ones with an interest in recycling the Bohemian past. Needless to say, *Kolumbus* has never played in the Národní divadlo since.

Dvořák's *Šelma sedlák*, Foerster's *Eva*, and Janáček's *Její pastorkyňa* are also set in the Czech or Moravian countryside. Kovařovic's *Na starém bělidle* (*The Old Bleaching-Ground*) conjures up the most archetypally Czech of all sentimental landscapes. It is a not entirely successful musical adaptation of Němcová's *Babička*, which takes its title from the name of the house in the valley in Ratibořice in which the action of the novel takes place. Fibich's two operas pluck other strings in the nineteenth-century weave of Czech identity, bringing to the stage the same mythical locations and characters as Smetana's *Má vlast*. *Blaník*, whose librettist was Eliška Krásnohorská, gives the old legend of the knights sleeping under the hill a Hussite twist; the opera begins in Staroměstské náměstí in 1623, with the chalice being stripped by Jesuits from the facade of the Týn Cathedral. In 1880 *Blaník* had won second prize behind Smetana's *Libuše* in the competition for a work suitable to inaugurate the Národní divadlo. With his later *Šárka*, which was inspired by Vrchlický's long poem on the same legendary subject, Fibich (1850–1900) set out to write "a true national opera, which will consolidate my place as a Czech composer."[117] *Šárka* was a heroine of the Girls' War who used her beauty to entrap the warrior Ctirad to his death. Myslbek's sculpture of the two of them stands in Vyšehrad, and Jirásek tells their tale in *Staré pověsti české*. Leoš Janáček's first operatic composition (to a text inspired in this case by Julius Zeyer), also entitled *Šárka*, dramatized the same story.

Of the foreign works produced that season, two were by Mozart, the other three by Glinka, Rimsky-Korsakov, and Tchaikovsky. This pattern was to continue. Between 1950 and 1955 the operatic literature of nineteenth-century Czech revivalism dominated the theater's stage, while foreign operas, with the conspicuous exception of those by Slavic and in particular Russian composers, were well-nigh absent from the repertoire. There were no "Western" works at all among the new productions of 1950–51. Instead, Czechs were offered Dvořák's *Rusalka* (1901) and *Dimitrij* (1882), Smetana's *Hubička* (*The Kiss*, 1876), and Kovařovic's *The Dogheads*, leavened with Tchaikovsky and Mussorgsky. *Rusalka* is a Czech variant of Hans Christian Andersen's tale of the little mermaid, set in Bohemia's woods and fields rather than on the Scandinavian seashore. Its libretto was written by the then thirty-two-year-old Jaroslav Kvapil, who had already made a name as editor of *Národní listy* and *Světozor*. The opera opens with a trio of sylvan maidens singing in the moonlight and teasing a *vodník* or *hastrman*, a well-known inhabitant of Czech lakes, ponds, and streams who drowns unwary trespassers in his watery domain and keeps their souls under mugs in his underwater cupboard. When a *vodník* takes on human form, you can always tell him by the drips of water falling from the left-hand corner of his frock coat. There is an obvious echo here of the opening scene between the Rheinmaidens and Alberich in Wagner's *Das Rheingold*, which begins his Ring cycle. But the musical mood is utterly different. *Rusalka* is pastoral, light, a little sad, indelibly Czech. It is no portentous saga of gods and heroes, warring over the fate of the world, but a modest tale of that unpretentious countryside we saw Milena Jesenská and Karel Čapek so emotively describing earlier. The scale is domestic, not epic. Smetana's *Hubička*, like his *Bartered Bride*, is another peasant romance. *The Dogheads* was discussed earlier; this story of Jan Sladký Kozina and Count Lamminger, told by Němcová and Erben and retold by Jirásek, went through no less than four new productions between 1945 and 1962.

The same biases were if anything even more evident in the National Theater's selection of plays. Though Shakespeare and Molière remained staples, it was overwhelmingly Russian classics that dominated the foreign repertoire after 1948, such as it was. In many seasons between the wars foreign plays had outnumbered Czech, and their authors ranged from Ibsen and Strindberg to Cocteau and Pirandello. Works by the Čapek brothers were among the earliest to be put on by the Národní divadlo immediately after liberation—unsurprisingly, in view not only of their authors' fates but also of their enormous popularity with audiences before the war.[118] *The Mother* was produced in October 1945, a run discontinued in July 1948. *The Insect Play* [*Ze života hmyzu*] followed in 1946, ending its run after eighty-eight performances in April 1949. Thereafter no Čapek work was to be performed at the National Theater, let alone made the object of a new production, until 1954. Nor was much other Czech prewar drama in evidence. Instead, along with Alois Jirásek, Josef Kajetán Tyl's *The Kutná Hora Miners* [*Kutnohorští havíři*, 1848], *Jan Hus* (1848), and *The Obstinate Woman* [*Tvrdohlavá žena*, 1849] were clearly considered healthier fare for the emancipated masses. *The Kutná Hora Miners* strikes notes that had once again become thoroughly contemporary; it was described in *Ottův slovník naučný* in 1906 as "our first social drama, in which the workers' question, with all its horrific images, violence, a strike, bloodshed, were very effectively brought to the stage."[119] Tyl's play also provided the basis for one of only two new Czech operas premiered at the Národní divadlo during these years, Zbyněk Vostřák's *Králův mincmistr* (*The Royal Mint-Master*), which ran for eleven performances in 1955 and thereafter slipped into oblivion. *The Obstinate Woman* belongs to a Czech theatrical genre best translated as dramatized folktales [*pohádkové hry*]. The only occasions on which it had previously been performed at the National Theater were in 1903, when it ran for ten performances, and in 1922–23, when it managed twenty. It played 205 times between 1952 and 1960.

The story was similar at the National Gallery. Twentieth-century Czech painters were for the most part absent from the gallery's exhibitions during the decade after 1948. The occasional exceptions served only to confirm the antimodernist rule. Max Švabinský had solo exhibitions in 1948, 1951, twice in 1953, and 1954. Josef Lada (1887–1957), who is known in the West for his humorous illustrations for Jaroslav Hašek's *The Good Soldier Švejk*, had a show of gouaches and watercolors at Prague City Library in 1953; but Lada's art is full of self-conscious *lidovost*. The 1975 *Encyclopedia of Czech Art* describes his style as a fusing of "contemporary planar drawing with the popular experience of the baroque, folk primitivism, and the Czech Mánes-Aleš tradition of draftsmanship."[120] Many Czech children's picture of a *vodník* will be Josef Lada's; he drew a *hastrman* sitting gloomily by the waterside, smoking a pipe, many times. Lada paints the Czech countryside and its inhabitants in a contrived simplicity, and the same stock motifs recur in picture after picture:[121] children, animals, grandmothers, the village square, the church on the hill, the pub, the village band, Czech Christmases with their vats of live carp and their nativities, Czech Easters with their gaily colored eggs, *koláče* (little cakes), and beribboned *pomlázky*. A *pomlázka* is a rod made out of plaited twigs with which, traditionally, Czech lads visiting house to house on Easter Monday whack Czech girls across their behinds, in the interests, it is said, of stimulating fertility. The girls then give the boys eggs. Božena Němcová affectionately describes this "bad day for the female sex" in *Babička*.[122] The book's most famous illustrator Adolf Kašpar, whose work also embellished Jirásek's *Filosofská historie*, was another "popular" artist (in both senses of the word) who was exhibited by the National Gallery at the Kinský palace on Staroměstské náměstí in 1953.

Little was shown in these years of Western, especially modern Western painting, but there were several fraternal exhibitions of Russian and Chinese art. Apart from propagandistic shows of contemporary socialist realism, it was once again the legacy of the Czech nineteenth century that was most prominently on display. Individual exhibitions were devoted to Josef Mánes (1948, 1950, 1951), Karel Purkyně (1949), Julius Mařák (1949), Václav Brožík (1951), Antonín Slavíček (1951), and other nineteenth-century painters. There were also repeated collective retrospectives, which authori-

54. Josef Lada's "December," from a calendar of the Czech year, 1941.

tatively ordered tradition in the way that all such groupings do. "Czech Classics of the Nineteenth Century" ran at the Mánes building on Slovanský ostrov from June to October 1948. "Czech Art of the Nineteenth Century from the Collections of the National Gallery and Prague Castle" was open from March 1950 to February 1951 at the Riding School of Prague Castle (and was reprised in 1954). "Czech Landscapes of the Nineteenth Century" was offered in 1951, another show on the same theme in 1953. "Czech Masters of the Nineteenth Century (New Acquisitions)" ran from November 1950 to December 1951 at the Šternberk palace. Many of these "new acquisitions" are likely to have been confiscations. The National Gallery substantially boosted its collections by this means after Victorious February, picking up among other treasures Josef Mánes's "Josefina," one of his most celebrated paintings. It used to belong to the now-exiled soprano Jarmila Novotná, once the most famous Mařenka of her generation.[123]

Here, the process of displacing the artifacts of a national culture and reinserting them into a different field of significances is by no means a matter merely of discourse. Collections were physically dispersed, and with this the individual stories each might have told in its integrity and by its particularity were fractured, to be overwritten by a legend of a generic cultural heritage watched over by a beneficent national state.[124] These dismembered stories were, of course, primarily those of the Church and the aristocracy, stretching back over a thousand years of a history from which both were now being retrospectively written out. State libraries acquired 1,227,970 books and the National Gallery received 624 paintings and 249 sculptures from the suppression of Czech monasteries and convents in 1950. There were more recent casualties, too; the state expropriated the buildings and collections of Sokol in 1952, while many of the exhibits of Czech majolica in Trojský zámek, a baroque château in the Prague suburbs belonging to the Šternberk clan that is now part of the Gallery of the City of Prague, turn out originally to hail from the collections of the Havel family.[125] The National Gallery's outstanding collection of Braques and Picassos was "donated" by the pioneering collector of modern art and early patron of Czech cubism Vincenc Kramář (1877–1960); voluntarily, says the gallery, under threat of imprisonment and expropriation, say his descendants.[126] Abstracted from their original contexts, stolen properties were recombined in the great galleries of state to provide a mirror in which the nation could, yet again, re-cognize itself anew.

Father Aleš and Old Mr. Jirásek

By far the most ambitious artistic spectacle of this period—indeed, it may well be the largest artistic exhibition ever staged in Prague—was the Mikoláš Aleš centennial celebration of 1952, which was officially declared "Aleš Year" [Alšův rok]. The exhibition lasted for six months and occupied four separate venues. Four hundred seventy-five of Aleš's paintings, drawings, cartoons, and preliminary studies were displayed at the Riding School of Prague Castle, along with photographs, letters, and other memorabilia. Sketches and studies were exhibited at Slovanský ostrov for Aleš's frescoes and sgraffiti adorning, among many other Czech buildings, the Štorch and Rott houses, Obecní dům and the Old Town Hall in Prague, and the town halls of Plzeň and Náchod (148 exhibits). Five hundred three of Aleš's drawings were shown at the Kinský palace on Staroměstské náměstí, while the National Museum mounted a 767-item exhibition documenting the artist's "Life and Work for the Czech Book and Theater." The Aleš Year was also celebrated with exhibitions in Brno, Kolín, Olomouc, Hradec Králové, Náchod, Písek, Liberec, and Plzeň, and the Ministry of Information helped stage shows of reproductions of Aleš's work in over a dozen other Czech towns. The president of the honorary committee for the Prague exhibitions was Zdeněk Nejedlý, its honorary patron Klement Gottwald himself. Nejedlý was by this date president of the (reorganized) Czechoslovak Academy of Sciences, a post he kept until his death in 1962, as well as minister of education, science, and arts, as his portfolio had been renamed. A quotation from Klement Gottwald provides the frontispiece to the exhibition catalogue: "In order to elevate our individual spiritually and morally, we want to make accessible to him all the great cultural treasures of the past and throw wide open to him the gates of knowledge and beauty."[127]

In view of the communist state's predatory behavior toward "the national cultural heritage," it is not altogether surprising that the organizing committee had considerable difficulty in persuading private owners to part with their possessions for the exhibition. In a meeting of 10 January 1952, just four months before the show opened, V. V. Štech stated that "nobody will respond to the letter requesting them to lend works; we will need a string of personal measures, visits, interventions." Evidently they were successful. He was equally worried about whether it would be possible to prepare an adequate catalogue in the short time available, warning that "a bad catalogue, unprepared, hastily done, is of no value."[128] It was Štech (1885–1974) who wrote the introduction to the catalogue for the Aleš eightieth jubilee exhibition at SVU Myslbek in 1932. One of the century's leading Czech art historians, he was also a stalwart of the conservationist Klub za starou Prahu. A catalogue did eventually get written in time for the 1952 show, to which Štech again contributed; whether it is of any value, other than as a symptomatic document of its times, is debatable. But certainly it is of interest to the cultural historian.

František Nečásek frames Aleš very differently in his introduction than Štech had done twenty years earlier. While praising the eternal freshness of Aleš's art, Štech had placed him firmly in the past, "a patriarch outside time, a representative of times which are irrevocably gone."[129] Nečásek relentlessly contemporizes Aleš as a living embodiment of the český lid, an artist who has only now, after Victorious February, come into his own along with them. He takes us on a metaphoric pilgrimage from darkness to light:

> The hundredth anniversary of Mikoláš Aleš's birth is an auspicious and glorious year for his work. It is as if the mists had dispersed, the dark clouds been torn asunder, and the sun of Aleš's genius risen up high over its homeland, illuminating it all.
> And hard, nay cruel, was the fate of Aleš himself and his work in the past. They drove him out of the National Theater, they drove him out of the exhibi-

tions, they would not allow him to decorate the National Museum, they insulted him, they killed him off. And then still worse—official recognition and in reality cold indifference. To be sure, not from the people; no, Aleš knew the love of simple people during his lifetime, and the succeeding generations likewise loved the creator of enchanting little pictures in primers and readers, in Jirásek's and Rais's writings. It was the Czech parvenu masters, their sons and grandsons, who drove Aleš back to the cottage whence he came, and who did not wish to admit him into the "holy of holies" [svatyně] of the nation.[130]

In fact, the list of owners of Aleš's works lent—rather more willingly, one presumes—for the 1932 jubilee exhibition reads like a Who's Who of inter-war Czech high society. It includes President Masaryk and former Prime Minister Antonín Švehla; Cyril Bartoň-Dobenín, Josef Sochor, and several other factory owners, managers, and "large industrialists"; Jan Otto and František Topič, publishers; the writer Jaroslav Kvapil and the graphic artist T. F. Šimon, professor at the Academy of Fine Arts; Antonín Tille, deputy director of the Živnostenská Bank, which back in 1929 Klement Gottwald had accused of pulling the strings of Czech government; the "large landowner" (as he is described in the acknowledgments) K. Schablin; and an assortment of senators, professors, lawyers, doctors, architects, engineers, and "ladies."[131] These are just the sort of people whom we might expect to hang the unde-manding and sentimental art of Mikoláš Aleš rather than, say, Toyen or Štyr-ský on their walls. Among the institutional donors of works were the Slavia Bank and Rudolf Medek's Památník osvobození, both in their different ways pillars of bourgeois Czechoslovakia, and the government of the day had offi-cially sponsored this exhibition too. But what of it?

> Yes, that is how it was. And today we are opening the exhibition of Aleš's work in the place most dear and sacred to the nation, in Prague Castle. Aleš is our first artist whose life-work has been exhibited in Prague Castle. . . . The government of the republic itself is watching over Aleš's jubilee year.
>
> And what is the cause of this turnaround, what storm has dispelled the fogs and torn apart the dark clouds? Self-evidently the cause of the new, high regard for Aleš's work is not just the incident of the jubilee. There were enough of these even earlier. It really is a question here of a storm, which swept out the former masters, the enemies of our people and of Aleš's talent. This is why the arrival of Aleš to Prague Castle is directly symbolic: he could come there only when our working people came there and seized the reins of government. Aleš could come from the cottage to Prague Castle only when another son of the cottage came there too, the faithful son and leader of our people—Klement Gottwald. . . .
>
> Today, his art rings out to us in new tones than before, in the capitalist past. Aleš's "Sirotek" [The Orphan] or "Za chlebem" [In Search of Bread], these really are already narrations of a past, which will not return; his cossacks with the Soviet star on their caps indeed did come to Staroměstské náměstí and have

brought us freedom; his Hussites really have come back to life today in our people, in our mighty struggle for peace and the building of socialism; and happily, as never before, the joyful shrieks of Aleš's children and the songs of his skylarks ring out over the freshly green hereditary field of our nation.

That is why our people will experience festive, beautiful moments among Aleš's works. And today surely is also finally beautiful for Aleš himself in the homeland he loved and celebrated so much. Today it truly is his homeland, because it is the homeland of the people.[132]

This scarcely requires commentary. We might, however, pause to recall the terms in which Karel Mádl rhapsodized in his 1912 biography about the thatched cottage in which Aleš was born, locating the artist's hometown of Mirotice in a countryside ethnically and ethically Czech. Nečásek's assertion that for Aleš "the national cause was always the cause of the simple people"[133] might also bring to mind Tomáš Masaryk's characterization in *The Czech Question* of the source of Jan Neruda's greatness; a writer "Slavonic because he is Czech, and Czech because he is popular and directly social." This catalogue was ploughing a well-manured furrow.

As for that other son of the cottage, with whom Aleš is here inextricably semantically intertwined, *Czech for Grade Three*, a language arts textbook approved by the Ministry of Education for use in elementary schools in 1977, contained a comprehension exercise entitled "The Birthplace of Klement Gottwald." Its author was the selfsame František Nečásek. Under a sweet watercolor of a typically Czech *chalupa* surrounded by trees, exactly the kind of *česká chalupa* Renata Tyršová had been in charge of reconstructing for the 1891 Jubilee Exhibition, the exercise read:

> On 23 November 1896 president Klement Gottwald was born in just such a quite ordinary little house. When he was twelve his poor mother had him apprenticed as a cabinetmaker. The boy liked the trade. He worked gladly. He was still a child, but he had to work until long into the evening. On Thursdays and Fridays he even worked until two and three in the morning.
>
> Our first workers' president knew the hard youth of poor children on his own skin. That is why later he struggled so bravely to make their life better.

Pupils were instructed:

1. *Read the article.*
2. *Look at the picture and describe it.*
3. *Describe the picture again according to the instructions given; you may use the following expressions:* we stopped, our attention was caught, it stands along, we enter through the doorway, on the main wall we count, the roof of the house is made from, above the roofs are, the cottage is connected to, in the orchard are green . . .

4. *Complete these sentences:*

> The birthplace of Klement Gottwald is . . .
> He knew on his own skin, that . . .
> He knew on his own skin, how . . .[134]

Earlier in the year, Czech eight-year-olds learning their grammar and spelling from the same book would have been applying themselves with equal diligence to an old *vodník*'s reminiscences of the time when "the whole of Bohemia was underwater and you could go nicely under the water say from Brno to Prague without ever getting your feet dry. Folks, those were the days!"[135] This passage was taken from a story by Karel Čapek, who by this date was persona grata again, though neither his *Conversations with T. G. Masaryk* nor—equally to the point—his translations of modern French poetry were scheduled for inclusion in his *Collected Works*, published by Československý spisovatel.[136] It is Čapek's observations on Mikoláš Aleš, written on the occasion of the eightieth anniversary exhibition in 1932, that come to mind here. This children's reader, too, puts "everything all together in one bundle . . . the greatest things and the smallest things in one single reality which is presented to be seen and loved."

From Father Aleš it seems natural, if not positively obligatory, to pass on to old Mr. Jirásek. F. X. Šalda could not have been more wrong when in 1930 he predicted that the historical novelist's works would soon be in a museum case as exemplars of the official literary style of the first decade of the first republic. Even more than Aleš, it was Alois Jirásek whose schoolmasterly visage decorated the facades of post-1948 communism. But Šalda's explanation of Jirásek's official popularity between the wars—when he counted Jirásek, along with K. V. Rais, as an author typically read by "the conservative bourgeois"[137]—applies equally well to the first decade of communist Czechoslovakia: "Here is a young state and for its building this state has a huge need of legend and myth." On 10 November 1948, in the presence of Zdeněk Nejedlý, Minister of Information Václav Kopecký, and president of the Alois Jirásek Society Albert Pražák, Klement Gottwald ceremonially launched what was called the "Jirásek Action" [*Jiráskova akce*]. His speech—which was issued as a pamphlet with illustrations by, of course, Mikoláš Aleš—stressed the "very contemporary" nature of the "cultural task" of "emphasiz[ing] the significance of the works of our great national, popular writer for today's times, and giv[ing] them into the hands of our people."[138] Publishers, theaters, and filmmakers obediently complied.

The first work in SNKLU's thirty-two-volume Jirásek's Legacy to the Nation, edited by Zdeněk Nejedlý, appeared in May 1949. The series was said to give "a continuous chronological picture of the Czech past from mythological times, from old Czech legends up to work from the author's own times.";[139] Its first volume was *Staré pověsti české*. Every cover carried an illustration by Mikoláš Aleš. The standard print run in this library was a claimed fifty-five thousand copies, and many volumes went through more than one printing. Between 1953 and 1962 SNKLU alone additionally published eighteen individual books by Jirásek outside the Legacy series.[140] Jirásek's presence in the socialist landscape was not confined to the printed page. His play *M. D. Rettigová* was produced at the National Theater in the 1947–48 season (84 performances between 1947 and 1952), *Lucerna* in 1948–49 (42 performances between 1949 and 1950), *Jan Žižka* in 1949–50 (88 performances between 1950 and 1953), *Vojnarka* in 1950–51 (156 performances between 1950 and 1956), *Lucerna* again in 1951–52 (199 performances between 1952 and 1957), *Samota* (*Solitude*) in 1952–53 (63 performances between 1953 and 1955), and *Otec* (*The Father*) in 1955–56 (43 performances between 1956 and 1957).[141] The Theater of the Czechoslovak Army staged the Hussite trilogy *Jan Hus*, *Jan Žižka*, and *Jan Roháč* in 1951–52. The army also provided many of the extras in the numerous films of Jirásek's works made in people's democratic Czechoslovakia: among them were *Jan Roháč* (1947), *Temno* (1950), *Staré pověsti české* (1953), *Jan Hus* (1955), *Jan Žižka* (1956), and *Proti všem* (1957). *F. L. Věk*'s panorama of *obrození* Prague hit Czech TV screens in the early 1970s.

These are, of course, measures of the importance the communist state attached to Jirásek, rather than, in any straightforward sense, indexes of his popularity. This was not a free market. Actors may well have been playing to empty houses (or bused-in audiences of schoolchildren and collective farm workers). To have a set of "Jirásek's Legacy to the Nation" on the bookshelf was politically de rigueur, especially for KSČ members, but that does not mean that the books were read—outside the schools, at least. The 1952 Aleš centennial exhibition provides convincing testimony that much of this revivalist activity aroused no great enthusiasm among the *český lid* whom it was intended to inspire. A paltry 13,233 visitors turned out for the main Aleš show at Prague Castle, an average of just 71 people a day.[142] This compares with 161,071 for another Josef Mánes retrospective in 1971, 101,608 for "Baroque Art in Bohemia" in 1982, and 98,517 for the 1990 exhibition "Czech Art 1908–1968," a first postcommunist attempt to set the record straight on twentieth-century Czech art. By 1979, Aleš mustered 132,486.[143] Alfons Mucha, as we saw, attracted over 200,000 visitors in 1980. When and where they could, large numbers of people evidently voted with their feet. This does *not* mean, however, that we can dismiss such activities as merely ritualistic and therefore inconsequential. Not all power rests upon the consent of the governed. In this case (as, perhaps, in most others), a hegemony is established less through inculcating a conformity of belief than by controlling the media through which the bounds of identity can be publicly articulated, and that control was close to absolute. This representation of the national culture may have been in many ways a Potemkin's village, but the fake facades effectively blocked the view of anything that might lie beyond. With the passage of time they became the only reality most Czechs knew, especially if they were born after, say, 1939.

Vladimír Borský's rendition of Jirásek's *Jan Roháč* was the first full-length Czech feature film to be made in color. Jiří Trnka's marionette film of *Staré pověsti české* is deservedly famous for different reasons. Trnka (1912–69) is one of the most original Czech artists to have emerged since the war, and he has taken the old (and thoroughly *lidové*) Czech art of puppet theater into quite new artistic dimensions. His films have won gold medals at both the Cannes and Venice film festivals, and his paintings, prints, puppets, and sculptures have been exhibited in London, Paris, Munich, Amsterdam, Montreal, and other Western centers. Among his puppet films are Hans Christian Andersen's story of *The Emperor's Nightingale* (1948), a ballet of Shakespeare's *A Midsummer Night's Dream* (1957), and Jaroslav Hašek's *Švejk* (1954). Trnka has also illustrated around a hundred books, many of them for children, including the tales of Andersen,[144] the brothers Grimm, and Karel Jaromír Erben. One Czech critic, Jan Poš, describes the "difficulty" and the charm of Jiří Trnka's art thus: "Because of the broadness of his interests and the richness of his talents, he also became the scourge of all manufacturers of definitions, who could fit him into their schemas only with difficulty. He was no less of a headache to those who were accustomed to divide art into traditional = representational and modern = abstract. And they could not at all get their heads around the fusion of poetic, folk, and traditional elements in Trnka's art with its expression in modern cinematic language. But audiences the world over accepted him completely spontaneously. Children and poets above all."[145] Jiří Trnka was not representative of those who sought to transform Jirásek into a contemporary figure (though, perhaps, he succeeded better than most). Modernity has harsher languages than that of children's cinema.

The dust-jacket blurb to Jirásek's novella *On the Island* [*Na ostrově*, 1888], which was reissued in the People's Library [*Lidová knihovna*] in 1948, begins with a sharp reminder of both the recent and the more distant past. "In the time when we have forever finished with the German question in the border regions of our land," it baldly starts, "it is well to recall the history of the penetration and strengthening of the German element in our country. Jirásek as the eternal conscience of the nation dedicated all his work to the rousing of the national consciousness, and consecrated to it this slim volume from the Czech *pohraničí* in the second half of the last century." *Na ostrově* is unusual among Jirásek's writings in being set in his own time. It is presented here as an eternal parable about class as much as nationality, or, more precisely, confirmation of the timeless indissolubility of the two:

[Jirásek] reminds us here how national indifference or, conversely, national consciousness always went hand in hand with the economic standing of the individual in society. Czech capital is almost nonexistent, capital in the hands of albeit Czech-speaking but nationally indifferent people puts up German factories, and the Germanized factory owner puts the talented boys of his Czech foremen through German schools with the clear intention of suppressing even in the womb everything healthy in the Czech element, which threatens by its talent to build a future dam against German expansion; the wife of a Czech landowner forces her daughter to marry an owner of German factories, who calculates that with his wife's dowry he can acquire Czech land as well, which he will use to expand his German factories and thus by economic pressure support the Germanization of the region.

The blurb goes on to remind readers "how slowly the national idea penetrated to the strata of the 'better sort,' who gladly aped German society in both language and fashion."[146]

Zdeněk Nejedlý supplied an afterword, as he was later to do for many of the volumes in Jirásek's *Legacy to the Nation*, in which he amply embroiders on this theme. He also takes the opportunity to settle some old scores with Czech modernists. The context in which Jirásek turned his pen from the past to the contemporary borderlands, Nejedlý tells us, was "a time of great political and national stagnation," when "the inner life of the nation was transformed into empty patriotizing, hollow phrases, talk and rhetoric, and a no less sterile proliferation of clubs, which were capable only of wasting time, money, and energy in witless celebrations and entertainments." *Na ostrově* was written on the eve of the nationalist nineties, five years after the triumphant reopening of the Národní divadlo and three years before the great Jubilee Exhibition; it hails from the same year as František Ladislav Rieger's well-satisfied remarks on the progress of the Czech language quoted earlier. But no matter. "The culmination of all this," Nejedlý continues,

was that in the boom period the newly rich Czech bourgeoisie felt they had achieved their goal, and fearing the new power of the people, began to propagate the fable that the security of the nation was assured, and that it was possible to turn to other, more pleasant things. This bourgeoisie gave birth to a cultural generation which even gave programmatic expression to this in the notorious Manifesto of Czech Modernism of 1894, in which it was expressly proclaimed that the time of national struggles, the time of rebirth, is over, the existence of the nation guaranteed, and the gates are thrown wide open to the decadence of Western bourgeois culture.[147]

Klement Gottwald was still cruder in his contemporary application of Jirásek's oeuvre in the greeting he sent to those assembled in the National

Theater on 22 August 1951 to celebrate the hundredth anniversary of the novelist's birth.[148] Once again, as at his funeral in 1930, when Tomáš Masaryk came to bid his last farewell, Jirásek was surrounded by "everything which represents nation and state." On the stage, behind tubs of flowers, was a dais on which sat two rows of dignitaries; framing them, to the left, six enormous Czech flags; to the right, six Soviet flags. In the center, in front of the dais, a drapery with a hammer and sickle; behind it, a gigantic fatherly portrait of Jirásek, wreathed by intertwined lime leaves, bearing the legend "100." Gottwald played leadenly on the titles of Jirásek's works:

> Accept my greetings on this evening of celebration in honor of the hundredth anniversary of the birth of Alois Jirásek, with which I join the salutations to this our great artist. Jirásek's work rings out today with a powerful voice for freedom and the independence of our land, for the building of a better life for our people, for world peace and the brotherly coexistence of nations, and it rings out no less powerfully against all [proti všem] enemies of our homeland and of our peaceful construction, against the instigators of new crusading wars as well as against homegrown ruling-class traitors, who would in foreign service [v cizích službách] like once again to flood our land with blood and enthrone in her the government of a new darkness [temno]. Let us therefore continually ensure that our people draw strength, courage, and fighting spirit from the great and beautiful work of Jirásek in their labors for the construction of socialism in our homeland, as well as in the global struggle for the maintenance of peace, in which our Hussite land is engaged side by side with all the progressive forces of the world and under the leadership of the great Soviet Union![149]

We are a long way from the funeral ceremonies of 1930, yet not altogether in another world. Then, too, there was much talk of "new Hussite armies."

The pinnacle of the "Jirásek Action" was the opening of the Alois Jirásek Museum in Letohrádek Hvězda (Star Castle) on the western outskirts of Prague on 2 September 1951. The architect for the renovations to the Renaissance hunting lodge, a building that dates from 1555–56, was Pavel Janák, cofounder of the Skupina výtvarných umělců and creator of the functionalist villa colony at Baba. Mikoláš Aleš joined his old friend in the museum in 1964. It is an appropriate enough venue for them both, and was not selected arbitrarily. Hvězda stands on the site of the battle of Bílá hora. By now it will not be unexpected that at the museum's dedication ceremonies on 12 March 1951, Jirásek's portrait above the entrance was flanked by those of Gottwald and Stalin. The inscription on the marble plate greeting visitors in the entrance hall, once again by Klement Gottwald, should also hold no surprises. It begins: "We claim Jirásek, and he is close to us—closer than to the old capitalist society."[150] We might, though, wish to reflect upon how this homage to old Mr. Jirásek is ordered. Though the museum is ostensibly a monu-

55. The opening of the Alois Jirásek Museum at Hvězda Castle, 1951.

ment to an individual, it is not arranged biographically, as the real-life story of "a man who wrote such and such books of such and such value." Once again the mystique of state usage dictated its own requirements, once again reality was recomposed and poetically tailored to prescribed dimensions and profiles. The exhibition took the visitor on an excursion through Czech history as presented in Jirásek's books, beginning in the mists of Old Slav legend, then progressing (as Ctibor Rybár's *What's What in Prague* puts it) "from Hussitism, through the time of Darkness, up to the *národní obrození*."[151] What better preparation could any Czech have for a tour through the Klement Gottwald Museum on the other side of town?

Children's Eyes and Fiery Tongues

The long life of Max Švabinský, a life obstinately devoted to the artistic values he formed in the 1890s and seemingly indifferent to the vicissitudes of Czech politics, was instanced earlier as a warning against taking historians' divisions between "periods" too literally. Švabinský died on 10 February 1962, which coincidentally was Zdeněk Nejedlý's eighty-fourth birthday. Nejedlý himself departed this earth a month later. His biography, too, is testimony to the fact that the iron curtain that after 1948 cut off Czechoslovakia from Western Europe by no means so neatly severed the country's present from its past. In the 1950s derisive jokes used to circulate in Prague about how on sunny days Professor Nejedlý could be seen walking along the banks of the Vltava with an opened umbrella—the explanation being that it was raining in Moscow. But the future minister of education had not always been viewed by his compatriots in such disrespectful terms. He celebrated his seventieth birthday in Victorious February, and had already turned forty before the Czechoslovak Republic achieved its independence. Before the war, and indeed before the war before that, he had been one of his country's most eminent scholars. He was also a staunch Czech patriot, of a decidedly nineteenth-century vintage.

The son of a schoolmaster and amateur composer, Nejedlý was born in Litomyšl in 1878. Litomyšl lies in the extreme east of Bohemia, close to the Moravian border. It is a little town steeped in Czechness; it was the birthplace of Bedřich Smetana and the place where, as a young gymnasium teacher, Alois Jirásek wrote his *Filosofská historie* and *Psohlavci*. Both Magdaléna Rettigová and Božena Němcová spent time there. Nejedlý himself was later twice to write its history (1901, 1903), as well as devoting his talents to extensive studies of its two favorite sons. He describes the town with obvious affection in his entry on it for *Ottův slovník naučný*, published in 1900. Litomyšl is mentioned, he says, in Kosmas's chronicle, as a settlement dating from 983; Diviš Bořek z Miletínka, the future victor at Lipany, was made its *hejtman* by Jan Žižka in 1421; in the later fifteenth century it became one of the chief strongholds of the Jednota bratrská and was the seat of their bishop Jan Augusta. It was here, in the great fire of 1546, that the Brethren lost their first archive. The town boasts one of the finest Renaissance châteaus in the Czech lands, built by Vratislav z Pernštejna in 1568–73, as well as one of the oldest gymnasia, founded in 1640, where Alois Jirásek was later to teach. "There is a rich enough literature on the history of Litomyšl," Nejedlý concludes, "but the most popular historian of Litomyšl is Jirásek with his *Small Town Histories*, especially the *Philosophical History*."[152] At the time Nejedlý was writing this, Litomyšl remained as Czech as ever; of its 8,066 inhabitants, only 50 counted themselves as German.

Nejedlý left his hometown to study in the Philosophical Faculty of the Czech university of Prague in 1896. It is one measure of his precocity that he should have been entrusted with this contribution to the great national encyclopedia at so tender an age. He became a pupil of the renowned positivist historian Jaroslav Goll and was an early contributor, alongside Josef Pekař and others, to the *Český časopis historický*. He simultaneously studied music, privately, with the composer Zdeněk Fibich. In 1905, at the age of twenty-seven, he was made a reader [*docent*] in musicology at the university. Two years earlier he had been elected a fellow of the Bohemian Royal Society, one of the youngest people ever to receive that honor. This was followed in 1907 by election to the Czech Academy of Sciences and Arts. He was promoted to full professor at the university in 1909. Nejedlý was a prolific writer. His *History of Hussite Song*, biography of Smetana, contributions to the *History of the National Theater*, and biography of Tomáš Masaryk have been mentioned already. These were but the tip of an enormous iceberg. There was an unfinished *General History of Music* (1916–30), a history of Czech music (1903), and monographs or long articles on Wagner (1916), Mahler (1913), Richard Strauss (1911, 1913), Fibich (1901), Foerster (1910), and Vítězslav Novák (1921). A fair summary of Nejedlý's views on Czech composers would be to say that he worshiped Smetana, adored the neoromantics Fibich and Foerster, disliked Dvořák, and loathed the modernistic Janáček. It says much about the man and his mission that amid these more weighty projects he found the time to write the history of the Prague choral society Hlahol (1911).

Beside his musicological works, Nejedlý was the author of monographs on Alois Jirásek (1911, 1921) and Božena Němcová (1922), whom he reverently situates in their respective environs of Litomyšl and Ratibořice. He intervened in the famous historiographic polemic between Masaryk and Pekař with his *Argument over the Meaning of Czech History* (1914). His interest in the Hussites extended well beyond their song: among his early publications were an article on the youth of the Utraquist archbishop Jan Rokycana in the *Časopis Českého musea* in 1899, and an edition of Táborite letters, speeches, and tracts in 1900. To all this we must add his copious journalism and reviews. Characteristically, Nejedlý founded and edited both the musical magazines *Smetana* (1911) and *Hudební sborník* (*Musical Miscellany*, 1913) and the radical populist newspaper *Var* (*Foment*, 1922), half of whose contents, according to F. X. Šalda, he wrote himself.[153] He was the founder and first president of the Society for Cultural and Economic Rapprochement with the New Russia [*Společnost pro kulturní a hospodářské sblížení s novým Ruskem*], set up in 1924. But it was also Nejedlý who, five years later, established Prague's Bedřich Smetana Museum.

Šalda was one of a distinguished group of contributors to a Festschrift published in honor of Nejedlý's fiftieth birthday in 1928; others included the aged Jaroslav Goll, J. B. Foerster, and Zdeněk Fibich's son Richard. Alois Jirásek apologetically declined to participate on grounds of ill health. J. S. Machar extricated himself more humorously, expressing a horror of "all questionnaires, jubilee publications, celebratory numbers, etc.," and adding that "otherwise it wouldn't hurt me in the least bit not to write about Nejedlý."[154] Aside from personal reminiscences, much of the volume, as we might expect, is given over to discussions of Nejedlý's wide-ranging scholarship. Less typical of the contents of academic Festschriften, but no less appropriate where Zdeněk Nejedlý is concerned, was this short greeting from the writer Helena Malířová (1877–1940), herself an active feminist and socialist and one of the seven writers expelled from the KSČ in 1929:

HONOR TO LABOR! [PRÁCI ČEST!]

I received a letter from a working-class woman B. M. from Německý Brod. She relates her wretched childhood and her great, vain longing for education. She was at a lecture of Professor Nejedlý's on the USSR. She got to know that there in Russia, everybody learns, the old, the young. She got to know something else as well. She listened with her whole soul and then she said to herself: "Such a lecture here—this is also a small piece of a workers' university." I send my friend Zdeněk Nejedlý this statement of a poor woman with sincere greetings for his fiftieth.[155]

Šalda, too, paints a portrait of a man who "is not only a university teacher, but an apostolic popular lecturer as well, who spends the majority of his Sundays and holidays in the country in the reeking saloons of taverns and pubs, filled with noise and tobacco smoke."[156]

Šalda's essay is perhaps the most penetrating in the book. He is not unappreciative of the merits of Nejedlý's work, but he is by no means uncritical either. He begins by paying tribute to "its enormous extent and uncommon, rich variety" of subject matter, style, and genre, and to Nejedlý's inexhaustible energy and faith in both his own capacities and the importance of the project in which he is engaged. He cites Nejedlý's own avowal (in the foreword to the second volume of the Smetana biography) that his is "a lifework, in the same sense as Jungmann's *Dictionary*, Šafařík's *Slav Antiquities*, Palacký's *History of the Czech Nation*, or Gebauer's *Historical Grammar* and *Dictionary of Old Czech* are life-works." The comparisons are apt: there is something very nineteenth-century about the proportions of so heroic an enterprise, as Nejedlý himself was very well aware. He is disdainfully out of tune with the nervous temper of his times, times in which, he thinks, there is a lack of "the courage to create a plan for a whole lifetime's work" or "even confidence in the possibility of such a long labor," times when scholarship occupies itself with ephemera "calculated for the immediate present." And yet, as Šalda goes on, "against this proud vital élan, against this quasi religion of enthusiasm for work, there stands, unfortunately, a simple gray fact . . . the sober reality that the great majority of Zdeněk Nejedlý's works, and precisely the works which aspire toward monumentality and grand synthesis, have remained and likely will remain only a torso." The obverse of Nejedlý's "steadfast industry and diligent conscientiousness" is an "*impatient haste*" and "*predilection for change and alternation.*"

Šalda next turns to the more difficult question of the "intensity" of Nejedlý's work, its historiographic standpoint and method. "One thing, I think, is characteristic of Nejedlý. . . . From the beginning he is *interested in the people*, he has the warmest *empathy* toward them; he regards the people as the constitutive element of history; as the bearer of its peculiar creative life, which if it erupts and thrusts its way to the surface, will endow the entire flow of events, the entire epoch, with its particular significance and mean-ing." He notes that recognition of this "collective agent" as the subject of history is a modern phenomenon, and in particular the creation of romanti-cism. Nejedlý's true spiritual precursor is Jules Michelet, who—not coinci-dentally, he thinks—was the greatest literary stylist among nineteenth-cen-tury French historians. The condition of romantic historiography, Šalda continues, is the ability of the historian to empathize emotionally with "the people," to feel himself into their place, "the capacity to live and feel a life that is petty, ordinary, humble, oppressed, but of course a life that is also full of bustle and variety." For this the historian must have "a *new* historical imagination." Much more than a mere dry chronicler of events, he becomes a "*new, young* artist or poet." This may seem an odd characterization of the pedantic Zdeněk Nejedlý; but contrary to the appearances of his "stilted and gray prose," "the roots of the collectivistic conception in Nejedlý's histo-riography are to be sought in his artistic feeling." This feeling is most trans-parent in his musical writings, where it is precisely to the great romantics, both domestic (Smetana, Fibich, Novák, Foerster) and foreign (Beethoven, Wagner, Berlioz), that Nejedlý is drawn.

"Well then," Šalda concludes, "to the romantic, emotion always was and will be closer than the will and the will closer than the intellect, woman closer than man, the subconsciousness and half-consciousness of the mass closer than the leader's focused consciousness and purposeful farsighted-ness." There is, indeed, a unity to Nejedlý's multifaceted endeavors, a single impulse that threads its way equally through his diverse literary enterprises and his revolutionary politics: "Both sides of this activity, seemingly hetero-geneous, are brought together in the higher union of the romantic core of his personality." The foundation and object of Nejedlý's intellectual and political project is a poetic fiction of the *český lid*.

In another of the more substantial contributions in the book, entitled "Zdeněk Nejedlý: Historian," Václav Novotný (1869–1932), professor of his-tory at Prague university since 1908 and like Nejedlý a pupil of Jaroslav Goll, arrives at a very similar conclusion, though with a slightly different twist. It is Nejedlý's Czechness he chooses to emphasize. He gives notice at the start that he does not intend to discuss Nejedlý's politics, for which he has little time. Novotný himself was a longtime adherent of Tomáš Masaryk's Realist party. Nonetheless he ends his essay—which is, in the main, extremely com-plimentary—with these, somewhat rueful, words: "*Nejedlý's book on Smetana must be read. . . . it is a book that is truly Czech, Czech in a way that few books in our literature are. And is there not also to be found in this aspect of it the key to understanding Nejedlý's political activity, to which I deliberately do not want to refer here?*"[157]

It is to Nejedlý's positivist method, which is superficially at odds with any such romanticism, that Šalda finally turns. He begins by observing that "perhaps in no other of our historians, not even in V. V. Tomek, will you find such a host of facts, smaller facts and still smaller facts [*faktů, faktíků i faktíčků*] as in the books of Zdeněk Nejedlý, especially in his great monograph on Smetana." The use of the diminutive here is a shade derisory, and Šalda's discussion continues in the same vein. He concurs with Nejedlý that all historians must seek objectivity, but he makes the obvious point that the same facts may support varied interpretations: "The *punctum litis* is that positivism, with its cult of '*petits faits,*' in no way *guarantees* objectivism, nor even, in particular, delivers it." Not only is a positivist method quite compatible with a romantic inspiration, it may very effectively mask it. He then poses a provocative question:

> Whether I have to know the Smetana family back to the sixteenth century, as Nejedlý with indefatigable diligence traces and in almost eighty pages of his monograph relates it, whether I have to know *down to the smallest detail* the life stories of his parents and siblings, whether the historian has to describe for me over 115 quarto pages down to the smallest components and elements the economic, moral, social, educational, national and ecclesiastical life of contemporary Litomyšl, over almost 100 pages the same life of Jindřichův Hradec, and later of Německý Brod, Plzeň, Prague, Göteborg, in order to comprehend—Smetana's *creative* genius?

Šalda's answer is emphatically negative.

> *Every* artist takes "the facts" for his work from "reality," since they simply do not exist anywhere else . . . but the only thing that matters here is what he *creates* out of these facts. . . . For the poet phenomenal reality is nothing more than the storehouse of words, the vocabulary of his mother tongue, his dictionary; it is the common property of all poets of a given land and time. But how far it is from a dictionary to *poetry!* If I want to comprehend a poem of Březina's or Wolker's, surely I do not begin with a description of all the words which the poet could have heard in his little hometown?

To reduce an artist to his milieu, in short, is to overlook exactly that which makes art what it is. Nejedlý's romanticism and positivism perfectly complement one another. The particularities of individual agency are lost, displaced onto an abstract collective subject, which exists nowhere but in the artist-historian's romantic imagination. Positivism then cloaks this imagined subjectivity with all the empirical appurtenances of being, speciously concretizing it through the encyclopedic recitation of endless "facts"—a project that can, of its very nature, never be concluded.

It was a long and cluttered past that Zdeněk Nejedlý brought with him to the Ministry of Education and National Enlightenment, and we ignore that past to our detriment. Nejedlý's activities in government were, quite palpably, a *continuation* of the "life-work" that Šalda describes. All that had changed was the opportunity to translate intellectual aspiration into social policy. For Nejedlý, *Var* and *Hudební sborník*, the Czech-Soviet friendship society and the Smetana Museum, evening lectures for workers and the *History of the National Theater* had always been two sides of the same coin. So, after the war, were the restoration of the Bethlehem Chapel and the *odsun*, the Jirásek Museum and Victorious February, SNKLHU's National Library and the hanging of Milada Horáková, the All-State Exhibition of Archival Documents and the confidential instructions to libraries on the making of new socialist human beings. If we ask from what conceivable standpoint these discordancies can be reconciled—from what standpoint, in other words, "nationalist" and "communist" perspectives cease to appear as self-contained, mutually exclusive, and conveniently divided, for purposes of historiographic orderliness, by the coup of 1948—the answer is that furnished twenty years earlier by F. X. Šalda and Václav Novotný in this innocent Festschrift for a manifestly talented if somewhat quixotic musicologist. The standpoint is that of the *český lid*, as that imagined community had been variously corporealized over the previous two centuries, in poetry and in prose, on canvas and on the stage, as the subject of historians' narratives and the object of grand exhibitions, on the facades of stately banks and the frescoes of humble tenements.

An interesting counterpoint to Zdeněk Nejedlý—but one who, if we leave aside Nejedlý's "gray prose" and focus instead on what Šalda sees as his romantic soul, might well be regarded as his alter ego—is the poet Jiří Wolker. Wolker was a good Catholic boy, as well as a communist and apostle of *proletkult*. He saw no contradiction in this; and perhaps there was none. One of his greatest poems, "Svatý Kopeček," invokes "great Russia and the brave Lenin" in the same breath as the Blessed Virgin. Svatý Kopeček lies a few miles outside Olomouc in Moravia; the name means "the holy little hill." Or it did, until in 1950 it was changed to Kopeček u Olomouce (the Little Hill by Olomouc). It was—is—a picturesque place of steep streets and red-tiled roofs tumbling down the hillside, high above the fertile farmland of the Haná plain. In the year of Wolker's birth it had 105 houses and 815 inhabitants, all of them Czechs.[158] Crowning the hill is a fine baroque church of the Virgin Mary, built in 1669–79. For centuries it was a site of pilgrimages and miracles. Wolker, who used to spend all his holidays there as a boy, returns from afar. He would have traveled the last seven kilometers from Olomouc down a majestic avenue of ancient chestnut trees, planted long ago in the days of Empress Maria Theresa;

> And I am a procession eager for the word of God,
> I come from faraway Prague and my home Prostějov
> A grown-up young man, a student and a socialist
> Believing in myself, in steel inventions, and in the good Jesus Christ.

At the end of the poem he asks the church on the hill to watch over the future as it has the past:

> Svatý Kopeček, church billowing on the green mountain,
> Standard of this tranquil and blessed land,
> Just strength, children's eyes, and fiery tongues give us this day,
> So that what we believe in today we carry out tomorrow.[159]

Everything is all together here, once more, in one bundle: Jesus and Lenin, class struggle and lyrical poetry. And although Jiří Wolker was a good Catholic boy, the Hussites were bundled somewhere in there too, just as they had been for Mikoláš Aleš. "Communism," his editor explains, "was only a necessary step further down the road which our Reformation marked out for us, which our best people proclaimed. Utopian Christianity metamorphosed into practical life, the afterlife, superterrestrial, unreal kingdom of God—brought down to earth and made human. The heritage of the fifteenth century interpreted in the language of today. That is communism."[160] No, this is not a gloss from the 1950s. It comes from the introduction to a slim volume of Wolker's poetry and essays published in 1925, a year after he died, in the words of the epitaph he wrote for his own gravestone, "twenty-four years young."[161]

None of this is to say that communism was *the* natural, necessary, or inevitable terminus of nineteenth-century romantic nationalist projects. That would be absurd. There are few (if any) inevitabilities in human history, and there have been many twentieth-century ways of being Czech. But it *is* to insist that there is no cultural canyon dividing prewar and postwar Czech history. Nejedlý was scarcely revolutionary in collectivizing (or nationalizing) historical agency. Take, for instance, the figures and events with which we began, at Vyšehrad Cemetery in 1938–39. Alfons Mucha had agonized over his own worldly successes in exile because he saw himself as "sinfully misappropriating what belonged to my people." Josef Hora remembered Karel Čapek, first and foremost, for the enduring "Czechness" of his art, a Czechness that lay not only "in the language, which he used with respect," but also—to quote a portion of Hora's speech not given earlier, but relevant here—"in his democratic feeling and social awareness [*sociálnost*], in his eulogy to working people."[162] Rudolf Medek rooted Karel Hynek Mácha's genius ultimately in "the simple people," the ordinary Czech-speaking country folk, like Dvořák's schoolmaster Benda, who had obdurately kept Czech language and identity alive with their "living sparkling faith in the future." Politically speaking, Mucha, Medek, and Hora, not to mention Karel Čapek and Zdeněk Nejedlý, were poles apart. But the left and right of politics is not what is at issue here. These individuals inhabit a shared discursive territory, a common sociality marked out by Čelakovský's *Echoes* and Tyl's *Fidlovačka*, Aleš's cottage and Babička's valley in Ratibořice, Mánes's agricultural calendar and Rieger's conversation with Countess Kaunic, Masaryk's *Česká otázka* and the parade of servant girls at the Czechoslavic Ethnographic Exhibition. The KSČ was able to identify the progress of the class struggle with the fortunes of the nation only because of the extent to which the *český lid* had already been constructed out of such imageries of the popular.

Hus, Žižka, and the Táborites could be recycled as class warriors because, for a century and more, they had been thoroughly contemporized and secularized as heroes of this "popular" nation. When the Central Committee of the KSČ addressed its announcement of Klement Gottwald's death to "the Hussite and Gottwaldite, strong and brave *československý lid*,"[163] it was doing nothing new. The nineteenth-century heritage of Czech pan-Slavism, with its conceits of *holubičí národy* (dovelike nations), could likewise be mobilized anew after 1948 to give emotional substance to the notion of the "peace-loving socialist camp." It was, after all, the Roman Catholic canon Bohumil Stašek, not Gottwald or Nejedlý, who in June 1945 had coupled together "*Kde domov můj?*" and the Soviet anthem in a latter-day apotheosis of Kollár's *Slávy dcera*. When Chopin, Tolstoy, and Pushkin appeared on Czechoslovak postage stamps, or Lvov, Minsk, and other Soviet cities lent their names to Prague's postwar streets, this could plausibly be represented as a realization of long-held and long-frustrated national affinities, because, in many ways, that was exactly what it was. There is a splendid mosaic in what is today Anděl, but was not so long ago Moskevská (Moscow) subway station in Smíchov, which melts together the Prague and Moscow skylines.[164] It is movingly employed in Jan Svěrák's Oscar-winning 1996 film *Kolja*. The station was opened in November 1985, in touching tandem with a new Prague station on the Moscow metro. Obviously it was a monument to fraternal normalization, but its symbolism was not without abundant historical precedent; in Jungmann's grandiloquent plans for a "universal Slavonic literary language," for example, or in Václav Hanka's failed pan-Slavic alphabet, in *Zlatá Praha*'s weekly column "The Slav World," in Mikoláš Aleš's cossacks in Staroměstské náměstí. Not to mention in Alfons Mucha's *Slovanská epopej*. In its *lidovost*, its pan-Slavism, its historicism—to come back to Šalda, in its comprehensive romanticism—Czech communism in the 1950s looks time and again like a misbegotten child of the *obrození*; an ill-favored child perhaps, lacking its parent's refinement and civility, but bearing an unmistakable family resemblance. Zdeněk Nejedlý's boast that the communists were "the heirs to the great traditions of the Czech nation" had more than a touch of truth in it. Certainly Nejedlý himself was.

But the importance of Šalda's critique of Nejedlý goes beyond this. It is not just specifics of imagery or ideology that unite nineteenth-century nationalist and (postwar) Czech communist projects, but a more fundamental commonality of structure. The structure is that we encountered in Alfons Mucha's *Slovanská epopej*, whereby a collective subject is concocted out of a multiplicity of related and unrelated particulars, and these particulars are then replayed as manifestations of that collective agency. In the hands of an Alfons Mucha, this furnished a recipe for a series of masterly paintings that transport the commonplaces of pan-Slavist romanticism into an altogether more transcendent realm; although, even so, critics like Jana Brabcová have ultimately found the cycle unsatisfying because Mucha subordinated his art to "the expression of an idea." In the hands of a Jungmann, or a Palacký, or an Erben, it provided a mold for equally inspiring works of the human imagination, works that gave real substance to that collectivity they were depicting into existence. Jiří Wolker fashioned out of it sublime lyrical poetry, even if he was too young to know much about anything at all. He remains one of the best-loved poets in the language. In the more workaday hands of Zdeněk Nejedlý, what resulted was something very much more prosaic. He describes a landscape apparently teeming with colorful diversity, alive with *fakty, faktíky,* and *faktíčky,* which in the end turns out to be a gray terrain of relentless monotony. Whatever his ostensible subject, whether it be Hussite song, or Němcová, or Jirásek, or Smetana, it is the same story that Nejedlý tells over and over again; albeit he tells it with sincere feeling and heartfelt empathy.

But such banality plays supremely well in the corridors of power—at least as power is organized in modern states, where rule is configured in terms of representation of the imagined community of the governed. For what is created in this confluence of the generic and the particular is, precisely, a presumption of *identity:* the immediate identity of an artist and his milieu, of a poem and the "natural tongue" in which it is written; the identity of the times and spaces of individuals' biographies and nations' histories; the identity of a national community and all those—artists, poets, politicians—who are now claimed to be speaking in its name. A closed circle comes to enfold self and society, endlessly mirroring the one to the other. Such simplifications are integral to the very possibility of modern politics. It is this presumption of identity that constitutes the ubiquitous collective subjects of modernity— "the Nation," "Society," "the Working Class," "Women," choose your poison—whose spectral presence (they are invariably spoken of and for) authorizes the exercise of power. The more total the social transformation envisaged, the simpler and more encompassing these representations of identity have to be. The corollary, of course, is ever-sharper demarcations between Us and Them; horizons become frontiers, frontiers become borders, borders require guards. If we want to know why the discourse of the *obrození* was so conducive to the KSČ after 1945, where it notably had not been between the wars, the likely answer lies here.

Revolution requires a more substantial footing than the futuristic fantasies of the modernist intellectuals who, in Czechoslovakia as elsewhere, provided communism with its progressive veneer between the wars. Rule of whatever sort can only be exercised over definite places and peoples, states and subjects, not over some amorphous republic of the mind. Like the Hussites before them, the nineteenth-century *buditelé* had provided a ready-made template for a community homogenized in culture and belief, uncomplicated by the inconsistent liberalism, uneasy acknowledgment of ethnic and social differences, and cosmopolitan ambivalences of location of the first republic. In KSČ hands, this romantic nationalist legacy was refashioned into a script of totalizing power, a screenplay for a world in which there were no spaces left for ambiguity, for heterogeneity, and least of all for multiple or divided loyalties; a world in which the boundaries of identity were prescribed and policed *down to the smallest detail*, so that, for example, Jaroslav Seifert's "objectionable" use of *Babička*'s mad Viktorka could make of him "a foreign voice." There was no man better prepared by temperament and training to direct such a production than the energetic, confident, dedicated, meticulous, encyclopedically knowledgeable, incurably impatient, and in the end rather simpleminded Professor Nejedlý, stalwart champion of the *český lid* for half a century and more.

Love Is at Work It Is Tireless

In *The Book of Laughter and Forgetting*, Milan Kundera describes a dance inside this fairy ring. "It was June 1950, the day after Milada Horáková had been hanged," and "one or another of those anniversaries of God knows what." So "the streets of Prague were once again crowded with young people dancing in rings. . . . And knowing full well that the day before in their fair city one woman and one surrealist"—Záviš Kalandra—"had been hanged by the neck, the young Czechs went on dancing and dancing, and they danced all the more frantically because their dance was the manifestation of their innocence, the purity that shone forth so brilliantly against the black villainy of the two public enemies who had betrayed the people and its hopes." Kundera knew by then, he says, that he "belonged to Kalandra, not to them . . . but even though I did not belong to them, I could not help looking on with envy and nostalgia."[165]

Kundera writes luminously and honestly about nostalgia, which is a recurrent theme in his work. At the beginning of *The Unbearable Lightness of Being* he catches himself out feeling warm and cozy when looking at faded photographs of Adolf Hitler, for no other reason than that they bring back his Brno childhood.[166] It is an outrageous juxtaposition—and one that immediately rings true. It is this keen sense for paradox and irony that goes a long way toward making Kundera so fine a writer. He refuses the norms of kitsch, which would sanitize away all such improper couplings. By kitsch he means something more than just a mawkish work of art. Kitsch is an *attitude*, which he characterizes as "the need to gaze into the mirror of the beautifying lie and to be moved to tears of gratification at one's own reflection." (Think of Disney's *Pocahontas* or the opening ceremonies of the Olympic games.) The locus classicus of kitsch, he says, is the terrain in which the word first emerged, Germany and central Europe in the nineteenth century, with its great flowering of "sentimental romanticism."[167] Kundera's portrayals of the early years of Czech communism are so disturbing not because he unsparingly catalogues their litany of horrors—plenty of others have done that equally capably—but because he unsparingly captures their romance.

"What actually remains of that distant time?" he asks in *Life Is Elsewhere*:

> Today, people regard those days as an era of political trials, persecutions, forbidden books, and legalized murder. But we who remember must bear witness: it was not only an epoch of terror, but also an epoch of lyricism, ruled hand in hand by the hangman and the poet.
>
> The wall behind which people were imprisoned was made of verse. There was dancing in front of it. No, not a danse macabre! A dance of innocence. Innocence with a bloody smile.
>
> You say it was a period of shabby lyricism? Not quite! The novelist, who wrote about this period with the blind eyes of a conformist, produced mendacious, stillborn works. But the poet, who merged with his epoch just as blindly, often left behind beautiful verse. As we mentioned earlier, through the magic of poetry all statements become the truth, provided they are backed by the power of emotion. And the poets certainly felt so deeply that their emotions smoldered and blazed. The smoke of their fiery feelings spread like a rainbow over the sky, a beautiful rainbow spanning prison walls . . .[168]

The book's original title, which Kundera has several times expressed regret at abandoning at the urging of his Paris publishers who found it too abstruse, was to have been *The Lyric Age*. The lyric age, he explains, is youth, understood not as a time of life but as "a *value* that transcend[s] any concrete age." That person is young "who marches in step with the youth of the world," "who is walking with the future, and who refuses to look back."[169]

Finished in Bohemia in 1969 and first published in France in 1973, *Life Is Elsewhere* may be Kundera's bitterest book. Certainly it is among his funniest. Its hero, Jaromil (the name means "lover of spring"), is a nineteen-year-old poet—by no means a bad poet, Kundera hastens to assure us, not at all, "Jaromil is a talented poet, with great imagination and feeling. And he is a sensitive young man. Of course, he is also a monster."[170] The crux of the action is Jaromil's betrayal to the secret police of his girlfriend's brother, who plans illegally to flee the country. Kundera savors the scene. As Jaromil leaves police headquarters the winter sun was shining and "an unwritten poem was . . . soaring over the rooftops."[171] The redheaded girl is duly arrested. Walking out of the police building again the next day into another "sunny, frosty morning," Jaromil once again "sucked in the icy air and felt big and filled with destiny." Only now, "it occurred to him that through his decisive act he had *entered the realm of tragedy*." He realizes his girl will be interrogated, maybe tortured. "All these ideas and images filled him with a kind of sweet, fragrant and majestic substance, so that he felt himself growing bigger and striding through the streets like an animated monument of grief."[172] Jaromil is a cruel fiction; but he is also[173] Rimbaud, Shelley, Lermontov, Mayakovsky, František Halas, and, of course, Jiří Wolker, all of whom make cameo appearances in *Life Is Elsewhere*. Kundera's dry comment on Halas's lines:

> A fugitive from the realm of dreams
> I'll find my peace in crowds
> And to curses change my songs

is: "And it is not at all true that he was an exile from the realm of dreams. On the contrary, the crowds he was writing about were the realm of his dreams."[174] Remember the twenty-five-year-old Jaroslav Seifert, sinking himself in the throngs in Red Square in Moscow in 1926?

More particularly, Jaromil is the great French poet—as Kundera insists he was—Paul Éluard, who publicly renounced his old surrealist friend Záviš Kalandra after Kalandra had been sentenced to death. It was in that giddy dance in the streets of Prague the day after the KSČ hanged Kalandra and Horáková that *Life Is Elsewhere* had its genesis.[175] To return to *The Book of Laughter and Forgetting*. "And that is when I saw him," Kundera continues, "right in front of me! He had his arms around their shoulders and was singing those two or three simple notes and lifting first one leg, and then the other. Yes, there was no doubt about it. The toast of Prague. Paul Éluard!"

> And suddenly the people he was dancing with stopped singing and went on with their movements in absolute silence while he intoned one of his poems to the rhythm of their feet:
>
> > We shall flee rest, we shall flee sleep,
> > We shall outstrip dawn and spring
> > And we shall fashion days and seasons
> > To the measure of our dreams.

And then suddenly they were all singing the three or four simple notes again, speeding up the steps of their dance . . . and before long not one of them was touching the ground, they were taking two steps in place and one step forward without touching the ground, yes, they were rising up over Wenceslas Square, their ring the very image of a giant wreath taking flight . . . and down below—Prague with its cafés full of poets and its jails full of traitors, and in the crematorium they were just finishing off one Socialist representative and one surrealist, and the smoke climbed to the heavens like a good omen, and I heard Éluard's metallic voice intoning,

> *Love is at work it is tireless.*

As for Kundera himself, "I ran after that voice through the streets in the hope of keeping up with that wonderful wreath of bodies rising above the city, and I realized with anguish in my heart that they were flying like birds and I was falling like a stone, that they had wings and I would never have any."[176] The circle, he says, is a magical figure; "once a circle closes, there is no return." He himself has "been falling ever since. Some people remain in the circle until they die, others smash to pieces at the end of a long fall. The latter (my group) always retain a muted nostalgia for the circle dance."[177]

It is an unforgettable portrait of an era—an era of innocent certainties and beautiful simplicities, presided over by a writer of historical fictions and a painter of enchanting little illustrations in children's readers whom a previous generation of modernist intellectuals had relegated to the nurseries and the elementary schools. But at least as interesting as Kundera's description of the delirium of the dance itself, with its recurrent metaphors of taking wing into the heavens, is his repeated use of this biblical figure of the Fall. He is too literary a man not to be aware of the echoes of Milton's *Paradise Lost*; the more so when, in the hands of Josef Jungmann, that marvelous poem was transmuted into a cornerstone of the Czech *obrození* as *Ztracený ráj*. But it is another poem, closer to home, that these pages might more readily bring to mind for the Czech reader: one of the most famous poems in the Czech language, Viktor Dyk's fiercely, not to say savagely patriotic "The Land Speaks" [*Země mluví*]. Dyk (1877–1931) was a fervent Czech nationalist. Before World War I he had been editor of the review *Independence* [*Samostatnost*, 1910–14], whose title is self-explanatory. He wrote "*Země mluví*" in a Viennese jail in 1917, awaiting his trial for treason (in the event he was amnestied and released). This is the final stanza of the poem. It culminates in a celebrated couplet:

> Heed words of warning:
> Do not sell your birthright for a mess of pottage.
> Maybe you will leave me,
> I shall not perish.
> But do you know,
> How many shadows will come here?
> How many times your descendant will clench his fist
> And how many times your son will curse you?
> I shall not perish, eternal am I,
> But I shall live with painful astonishment:
> How have you forgotten your hereditary part?
> How could you hesitate? And how could you betray?
> How is it possible to do an accursed deed knowingly?
> You could betray yourself; but your descendants?
> As long as you could breathe, why did you surrender?

What were you afraid of?
What is death?
Death means to come to me.
Your mother the land
Opens her arms; is it possible, that you could spurn her?
Come, you will learn how soft is this embrace
For he who fulfills what she expects.
I, your mother, beg you; for yourself, defend me, son.
Go, maybe it is difficult for you to die.
If you leave me, I shall not perish,
If you leave me, you will perish.
[*Opustíš-li mne, nezahynu,*
opustíš-li mne, zahyneš.][178]

Now consider another poem, a communist variant on the same theme. There are other echoes here, too, apart from Dyk: a timeless little town in southern Bohemia, where the waves of the peasant countryside lap the town square, and everything disquieting and dangerous arrives from outside and abroad; Bohuš and Julie, wandering hand in hand like two lost children, one imagines, through alien lands; if we listen attentively enough, we might even catch the distant murmurings of a gathering of defenders of God's truth and the Czech language, some three thousand in number, in the Year of Our Lord 1469. The poem appeared in 1953 in a volume published by Československý spisovatel bearing the title *Man the Expansive Garden* [*Člověk zahrada širá*]. It is called "Christmas" [*Vánoce*], which is a festival we should undoubtedly visualize here as painted by Josef Lada in all its pristine Czechness, a time of carp swimming in the bathtub, midnight masses in onion-domed little village churches, Baby Jesus [Ježíšek] bringing Czech children their presents, and the bustle of Czech mothers busily baking a dozen different kinds of fragrant Christmas cookies:

> The star of Bethlehem came to rest
> Above the tops of the white trees.
> Mommy, all roads today
> Lead home to you.
>
> The blowing snow will sweep away from our brow
> Everything erroneous, everything foreign.
> From those, who betrayed,
> Let even the dogs turn away.
>
> The star of Bethlehem came to rest
> Above the tops of the white trees.
> Today all roads, all of them today,
> Ah, they all lead home.

The heads of the traitors out there, abroad,
Weigh heavy and fall.
Today their solitude
Becomes a coffin.[179]

The author? A young poet by the name of Milan Kundera.

Kundera was a reluctant émigré who did not abandon ship for seven years after the invasion of 1968 because, as he told Ian McEwan in 1984, "I thought that a writer couldn't live anywhere else except in his homeland."[180] The fall he describes in *The Book of Laughter and Forgetting* was temporarily arrested; kicked out of the party in 1950, he was reinstated in 1956. He had three collections of verse published domestically between 1953 and 1957, as well as the short story collection *Laughable Loves* (1963) and his first novel *The Joke* (1967), which was made into a film the following year. Stripped of employment and banned from publishing in the 1970s, he finished *The Book of Laughter and Forgetting* in exile in 1978, three years after he accepted a position as visiting professor at the University of Rennes, and one year before he was officially stripped of Czechoslovak citizenship. Kundera has always insisted that his books are not "about" Bohemia—the name he uses, interestingly, in preference to Czechoslovakia, which in his words is "too young (born in 1918), with no roots in time, no beauty."[181] They are, he is adamant, *novels*. That is to say, they are investigations of "existential situations," not analyses of particular times or places. Still less are they political tracts: "The novelist is neither historian nor prophet: he is an explorer of existence."[182] Maybe. Nevertheless it is striking that up until *Immortality*, which was published in 1990, Kundera's books continued to be set in the homeland he had forsaken.

Kundera's "*Vánoce*" was not the only literary work of the 1950s to recall Dyk's "*Země mluví*." Much better known, at any rate to Czechs, is Zdeněk Pluhař's novel *Opustíš-li mne* (*If You Leave Me*), which takes its title directly from Dyk's final, brutal couplet. *Opustíš-li mne* won Pluhař the Klement Gottwald State Prize in 1957 and was into its seventh edition (with an imprint of twenty-three thousand copies) by 1985. The plot is a simple one, as befits such black-and-white times. Pluhař tells the story of three young men, Václav, Jarda, and Honzík, who illegally flee the homeland in September 1948. Václav, a medical student expelled from his faculty and sent to work in a factory on account of his class origin, wishes to continue his studies. Jarda, whom Victorious February deprived of his small auto-repair shop, dreams of becoming an entrepreneur; his flight also frees him both from his fiancée and from the likelihood of going to prison for theft from the state enterprise in which he now works. The typographer Honzík, the youngest and most sympathetic member of the trio, simply seeks adventure.

What instead awaits them in the West is internment, interrogations, a squalid refugee camp in the outskirts of Nuremberg, penury, and inexorable moral degeneration. Václav eventually commits suicide. Jarda gets in trouble with the police and is given the choice of imprisonment or becoming a spy for the West. He perishes in a botched espionage expedition into Czechoslovakia, shot by a fellow refugee, Pepek. Other characters in the novel fare no better. The onetime university professor Markus ends up working as a domestic tutor. Katka, who left her country in search of her husband, becomes a prostitute. Honzík winds up in the French Foreign Legion. This is how the sorry saga ends:

"Halt, verfluchte!"

The white border stone shines on the ridge, all good powers of the world, stand by us, don't let us fall thirty steps from the homeland, twenty, ten. . . .

Ratatatatat!

A white splinter of wood broke off from a tree trunk on their right, that terrible whistle of steel death deafened them, torn-off needles of swivelling branches plummeted down to the ground.

Ratatatatat!

She sank, as if mowed down, in wild terror he took her in his arms, tripped, his knee hurting piercingly, he rose again, the white stone flashing past him.

"Halt, halt!"

Honzík races on down the hill, blinded by stinging sweat, his shirt clinging to his chest and in his throat a corrosive gagging, he is choking and he cannot hear, pain and sorrow tear at his insides and in place of lungs he has a fiery pouch which just burns, burns till he can hardly endure it.

Ratata-tata-tat!

He collapsed with exhaustion, for God's sake, they are shooting over to our side—no, Honzík cannot run any more, if those two dare to come here, they will finish them off like poachers do wounded game in the bush.

"Katka!"

Blood is gushing from a slash on her cheek, some twig that was, no, this is not death, not these few crimson drops.

"Katka, what's up?"

He strokes the smooth purple cheek, crazily kisses the salty dampness of tears and sweat in the eyes, cold forehead covered in droplets, throat, bosom, mouth.

"N-no, nothing . . . is the matter . . . at least I don't think . . ."

He picked her up again, runs heavily down through the woods, squeezing her in his arms, in his knee pain stabbing sharply, Honzík limps more and more, he laid Katka down on the ground, rolled over with his face in the moss, his hands pressing on his groin, doubling up with the pain.

"What . . . happened, where are we, Honzík?"

He lost sense of time, the breath wheezes through his burning throat, at last he gathered enough strength to lift his head, he saw her uncomprehending, exhausted face.

"We are—home, Katka."

Something welled up in him sharply, a stream of tears burst out of him, his chin shook comically, his mouth twisted in an uncontrollable grimace of wild, crazy happiness without limits, he sank his sobbing face into the soft moss as a child would into a mother's lap—in clenched fingers he felt the Czech land.

From below, from a clearing in the woods, came the sound of quick-running feet, Czech voices, and the eager bark of a dog.[183]

"Kde domov můj?" asked Josef Kajetán Tyl in 1834. Honzík and Katka know. So does Milan Kundera, whether in *"Vánoce"* or *The Book of Laughter and Forgetting*. Home is a place difficult to leave and still more difficult to return to, a protective family circle, outside which there is eternal fall and no redemption; a take-it-or-leave-it, all-or-nothing kind of a place. It is no longer Karel Čapek's "crossroad of Europe," an uncertain and shifting location, open to all comers, defined only by being betwixt and between. William Shakespeare located Bohemia as "a desert country near the sea" in order to situate it clearly in the realms of pastoral fantasy. It took the KSČ finally to give that imagined Arcadia a coastline. It was guarded by minefields, barbed-wire fences, and tall watchtowers with machine guns. It was guarded by unobtainable exit visas and a nonconvertible currency. It was guarded by the so-called *Kádrový spis* (Cadre File), an annual report that required employees to detail, along with their name, date of birth, marital status, nationality, education, employment, and class origin, the names and particulars of relatives abroad, all other contacts abroad, and any visits abroad.[184] It was guarded by a battery of censors working tirelessly to keep out everything alien and undesirable. It was guarded by the indictments in the Slánský trial, which were careful to document the fact that the former general secretary himself and ten of the other thirteen accused were "of Jewish origin."[185] It was guarded by ancient memories of foreign oppressions and fresh experiences of foreign occupation, by monuments to newly martyred heroes and museums on the sites of old battles. It was guarded by the Hussites of Tábor and the Dogheads of Domažlice, the knights of Blaník and the cossacks in Staroměstské náměstí with the Soviet stars on their caps. It was jealously watched over by the whole company of our great minds, arbiters of all that was ethnically and ethically Czech. And it was fortified by Kundera's wall of beautiful, *new, young* verse, joyfully celebrating the recovered identity, after all these centuries, of *národ, lid,* and *vlast,* the closing of the circle of the dead, the living, and the still to be born.

Behind these formidable defenses, the happy shrieks of Aleš's children rang out over the freshly green hereditary field of the Czech nation. To the east, the mighty bulwark of *Slovanstvo*, disappearing into the endless vastness of the Russian steppe. And Alfons Mucha? What of him! A bourgeois cosmo-politan. A Frenchman. Let him stay out there, in the West, with all the rest of you who ran away. *Opustíš-li mne, zahyneš.*

56. Untitled collage by Karel Teige, 1948 (road sign for Prague).

NOTES

BEARINGS

1. William Shakespeare, *The Complete Works*, ed. Stanley Wells and Gary Taylor (Oxford: Clarendon, 1986), 1256.

2. BBC radio broadcast of 27 September 1938, reported in the *Times* (London), 28 September 1938.

3. Shakespeare, *Complete Works*, 1241.

4. *The Compact Edition of the Oxford English Dictionary: Complete Text Reproduced Micrographically*, vol. 1 (London: Book Club Associates/Oxford: Oxford University Press, 1979), 242, entries "Bohemia" and "Bohemian." The information on Puccini's *La Bohème* is taken from the Earl of Harewood, ed., *Kobbé's Complete Opera Book* (London: Putnam, 1979), 1157–58; on *"böhmische Dörfer"* from *Langenscheidt's Concise German Dictionary* (London: Hodder and Stroughton, 1973), 115. A literal translation of the German would be "It's all Bohemian villages to me." On the origins of the word "Bohemia" see below, p. 29.

5. This is reproduced in *Český kubismus 1909–1925: malířství, sochařství, umělecké řemeslo, architektura*, exhibition catalogue, ed. Jiří Švestka and Tomáš Vlček (Prague: Národní galerie/Stuttgart: Gerd Hatje, 1991), 87.

6. See below, p. 161.

7. Guillaume Apollinaire, *Alcools: Poems by Guillaume Apollinaire*, trans. Donald Revell (Hanover, N.H., and London: Wesleyan University Press, 1995), 8. I have retranslated this line.

8. John Foxe, *Foxe's Book of Martyrs* (Springdale, PA: Whitaker House, 1981).

9. "Bohemia Newly described by John Speed. Anno Dom: 1626. Are to be sold in popshead Alley by G. Humble." Consulted in William C. Wonders Map Collection, University of Alberta.

10. This is rich, considering the book's subtitle. Frederick Karl, *Franz Kafka: Representative Man. Prague, Germans, Jews, and the Crisis of Modernism* (New York: Ticknor and Fields, 1991).

11. William S. Rubin, *Dada, Surrealism and Their Heritage* (New York: Museum of Modern Art, 1968).

12. *Výstava Poesie 1932*, exhibition catalogue, introduction by Kamil Novotný (Prague: SVU Mánes, 1932). The exhibition took place at the Mánes building on Slovanský ostrov from 27 October to 27 November 1932. The only mention in *Dada, Surrealism and Their Heritage* of any significant collective surrealist exhibition outside France before this date in is the exhibition at the Wadsworth Atheneum in Hartford, Connecticut, in November 1931, which was reprised at the Julien Levy Gallery in New York in January 1932. This was one-third the size of the Prague show, with a total of fifty exhibits.

13. Stephen Bann, ed., *The Tradition of Constructivism* (New York: Viking Press, 1974, reprinted as a Da Capo paperback, 1990), 97–102. The first page of the Czech text is (fortunately) reproduced as a plate. The full Czech text is given in Štěpán Vlašín et al., (eds), *Avantgarda známá a neznámá*, vol. 1, *Od proletářského umění k*

poetismu 1919–1924 (Prague: Svoboda, 1971), 483–87, and in Jindřich Štyrský, *Každý z nás stopuje svoji ropuchu* (Prague: Thyrsus, 1996), 9–10. The latter, a photoreprint, preserved Štyrský's original layout and typographics. The original publication was in *Disk*, 1, December 1923, and not, as Bann asserts, May 1923.

14. *Štyrský, Toyen, artificialismus: 1926–1931*, exhibition catalogue, text by Lenka Bydžovská and Karel Srp (Prague: Středočeská galerie, 1992), 44–45. For further literature on Štyrský and Toyen in the broader context of Czech surrealism see ch. 5, note 201.

15. On this seminal surrealist exhibition see Bruce Altshuler, *The Avant-Garde in Exhibition: New Art in the Twentieth Century* (New York: Abrams, 1994), 116–35. The most famous exhibit was probably Salvador Dalí's "Rainy Taxi."

16. It is perhaps relevant to record here that Sigmund Freud was born and spent his early years in Příbor in Moravia; Adolf Loos was born in the Moravian capital, Brno, and later became a Czechoslovak citizen; Gustav Mahler was born in Kaliště u Humpolce, in Bohemia; Egon Schiele's mother was a Bohemian, and his paintings of Český Krumlov, her hometown, are famous.

17. Whatever its inaccuracies, an exception in this regard is Hilary A. James and Jiří P. Musil, *Prague, My Love: An Unusual Guide Book to the Hidden Corners of Prague* (Prague: Crossroads of Prague, 1992). The *domeček* is discussed in detail in the articles published in the Czech press in the Prague Spring of 1968 and reproduced in Antonín Kratochvil, ed., *Žaluji*, vol. 1, *Stalinská justice v Československu* (Prague: Česká expedice/Dolmen, 1990), 73–84. "Tomato puree" [*rajský protlak*] is not my term but the torturers'; an alternative name for the procedure was "calf's bleating" [*telecí bečení*]. It is one of the list of tortures given by Filip Jánský in his article "Obavy" (Fears), first published in *Literární listy*, 5, 28 March 1968, reprinted in this same volume, p. 210.

18. Arnošt Lustig, "Clock Like a Windmill," trans. Josef Lustig, in Arnošt Lustig, *Street of Lost Brothers* (Evanston, Ill.: Northwestern University Press, 1990), 167.

19. See Václav Havel, *Open Letters: Selected Writings 1965–1990* (New York: Knopf, 1991), passim, especially the long essay "The Power of the Powerless"; I have counterposed Havel to Gramsci elsewhere in my paper "Everyday Forms of State Formation: Dissident Remarks on 'Hegemony,'" in G. Joseph and D. Nugent, eds., *Everyday Forms of State Formation: Revolution and the Negotiation of Rule in Modern Mexico* (Durham, N.C.: Duke University Press, 1994), 367–77.

20. See below, p. 128.

21. Percy Bysshe Shelley, "Ozymandias," in Denys Kilham Roberts, ed., *The Centuries' Poetry*, vol. 3, *Pope to Keats* (London: Penguin, 1950), 200.

CHAPTER 1

1. This is how "Gismonda" is described in Jack Rennert and Alain Weill, *Alphonse Mucha: The Complete Posters and Panels* (Boston: G. K. Hall, 1984), 48.

2. See Jiří Mucha, *Alfons Mucha* (Prague: Mladá fronta, 1994), 141.

3. Quoted in Michel Laclotte et al., *Alfons Mucha 1860–1939*, exhibition catalogue (Prague: Národní galerie, 1980), 102–3.

4. See Jiří Mucha, *Alphonse Maria Mucha: His Life and Art* (New York: Rizzoli, 1989), 181–83.

5. Between 1892 and 1897 Mucha had illustrated Charles Seignebos's *Scénes et episodes de l'histoire de l'Allemagne*.

6. Quoted in Jiří Mucha, *Alphonse Maria Mucha*, p. 145. The Czech text is given in Jiří Mucha, *Kankán se svatozáří: život a dílo Alfonse Muchy* (Prague: Obelisk, 1969), 194–95. The addressee is not identified nor the date given.

7. Jiří Mucha, *Alfons Mucha*, 343–44.

8. Mucha had only two major foreign exhibitions during his lifetime thereafter: of the *Slovanská epopej* in Chicago and New York in 1921, and a large retrospective with František Kupka at the Jeu de Paume in Paris in 1936. Along with Mucha, Kupka (1871–1957) is perhaps the best known of Czech modern artists outside his homeland. Having made his home in Paris from 1895, he is little discussed here. He is an interesting counterpoint to Mucha in his relations to things Czech. Though an anti-militarist, he served the Czech resistance in France during World War I, first as a volunteer at the front—he fought in the battle of the Somme—and later as organizer of the Czechoslovak Legions and president of the French Czechoslovak colony. He rose to the rank of captain in the Czechoslovak army. In recognition of these services he was made a professor at the Prague Academy of Fine Arts in 1922, but he never settled back in Bohemia. Kupka was one of the founders of twentieth-century abstract art; his first nonfigurative works date from as early as 1910. Ludmila Vachtová, *František Kupka* (Prague: Odeon, 1968), is a comprehensive study of his life and work; see also Miroslav Lamač, *František Kupka* (Prague: Odeon, 1984). Kupka's early viciously satirical paintings and drawings on social and political themes (their targets include "Money" and "Religion") are also of interest: see *Album Františka Kupky*, ed. Karl Eugen Schmidt (Prague: B. Kočí, n.d. [1905?]).

9. Letter from William Goodyear, quoted in Jiří Mucha, *Alfons Mucha*, 413.

10. I quote from Max Švabinský's graveside speech, which is given in full in Ludvík Páleníček, *Max Švabinský: život a dílo na přelomu epoch* (Prague: Melantrich, 1984), 164–66.

11. For a history of the Vyšehrad Cemetery and Slavín see Bořivoj Nechvátal, *Vyšehradský hřbitov* (Prague: Národní kulturní památka Vyšehrad, 1991). This provides a complete list of graves.

12. From Páleníček, *Max Švabinský*, 166. Páleníček wrongly dates Mucha's funeral as April 1939: see *Československo biografie* (Prague: Státní tiskárna, serie 21, doplněk, 22 August 1939); Jiří Mucha, *Kankán*, 321.

13. BBC radio broadcast of 27 September 1938. The text was published the next day in the *Times*.

14. "My good friends, this is the second time in our history that there has come back from Germany to Downing Street peace with honour. I believe it [the Munich Agreement] is peace for our time. . . . And now I recommend you to go home and sleep quietly in your beds." Neville Chamberlain's words again, speech from window of 10 Downing Street, 30 September 1938, reported in the *Times*, 1 October 1938.

15. Jiří Mucha, *Alphonse Maria Mucha*, 293.

16. Among notable public funerals over this period were those of the journalist Karel Havlíček Borovský (1856), the novelist Božena Němcová (1862), the historian and "Father of the Nation" František Palacký (1876), his son-in-law the politician František Ladislav Rieger (1903), the novelist Alois Jirásek (1930), and President Tomáš Masaryk (1937). Several of these are discussed in detail below. On the signifi-

cance of such occasions in modern Czech history, see Jindřich Pokorný, "'Zemřel, ale žije v nás,'" in *Revolver Review*, 26, 1994, 294–302.

17. Karel Čapek, "Národní světoobčan," *Lidové noviny*, 8 July 1934, reprinted in his *Spisy*, vol. 19, *O umění a kultuře III* (Prague: Československý spisovatel, 1986), 582–83.

18. Karel Čapek, preface to *At the Crossroads of Europe*, written for the 1938 Pen-club Congress in Prague. Reprinted in Eva Wolfová et al., *Na křižovatce Evropy: Karel Čapek a Penklub*, exhibition catalogue (Prague: Památník Národního písemnictví, 1994), 22–27.

19. Karel Čapek, "Poznámka překladatele," in "Francouzská poezie," *Spisy*, vol. 24, *Básnické počátky—překlady* (Prague: Český spisovatel, 1993). Like Čapek's *Conversations with T. G. Masaryk*, correspondence, and some other writings, this material was not planned to be issued in his *Collected Works* before the revolution of 1989. On the enormous influence of these translations on the development of modern Czech poetry, see Alfred French, *The Poets of Prague: Czech Poetry Between the Wars* (Oxford: Oxford University Press, 1969), ch. 1. The source of the quote from Milena Jesenská is her obituary article "Poslední dny Karla Čapka," published in *Přítomnost*, 11 January 1939, as reprinted in Milena Jesenská, *Zvenčí a zevnitř* (Prague: Nakladatelství Franze Kafky, 1996), 28.

20. Ferdinand Peroutka, "Osud Karla Čapka," in his *Budeme pokračovat* (Toronto: Sixty-Eight Publishers, 1984), 39–40.

21. Ferdinand Peroutka, *Jací jsme/Demokratický manifest* (Prague: Středočeské nakladatelství, 1991).

22. Ferdinand Peroutka, *Budování státu*, 4 vols. (Prague: Lidové noviny, 1991).

23. Peroutka, "Osud Karla Čapka," 40. *R.U.R.* premiered at the Národní divadlo in 1921, playing 63 times, and was revived in 1939, playing 25 times, the last on 4 April, shortly after the German invasion; *Ze života hmyzu* (*The Insect Play*) premiered in 1922 (93×) and was revived in 1925 (36×) and 1932 (13×); *Loupežník* (*The Robber*) premiered in 1925 (13×) and was revived in 1938 (13×); *Adam Stvořitel* (*Adam the Creator*) premiered in 1927 (31×); *Lásky hra osudná* (*A Fateful Game of Love*) premiered in 1930 (6×); *Bílá nemoc* (*The White Disease*) premiered in 1937 (83×); *Matka* (*The Mother*) premiered in 1938 (32×). Hana Konečná, ed., *Soupis repertoáru Národního divadla v Praze 1881–1983*, 3 vols. (Prague: Národní divadlo, 1983).

24. Quoted in Jiří Opelík, *Karel Čapek ve fotografii* (Prague: Středočeské nakladatelství, 1991), 170.

25. Contemporary (unnamed) journalist's account, quoted in Jindřich Pokorný, "'Zemřel, ale žije v nás,'" 298.

26. This is available in English as Karel Čapek, *Dashenka, or, The Life of a Puppy* (London: Allen and Unwin, 1933).

27. Most of Karel Čapek's novels and plays have been translated into English, among them the dystopias *Krakatit*, trans. Lawrence Hyde (New York: Macmillan, 1925), and *War with the Newts*, trans. Ewald Osers (London: Unwin, 1985). The latter relates an extremely funny conversation between a giant salamander and a Czech writer on the Galápagos Islands on the subject of Czech history. The mutated reptile had learned his history from a book entitled *Czech for Newts*, which chance had brought his way. It goes, in part: "'So you are fascinated also by our history?' . . .

'Certainly, sir,' the Newt replied. 'Especially by the disaster of the White Mountain and the three hundred years of servitude. . . . No doubt you are very proud of your three hundred years of servitude. That was a great period, sir!'" They part like this:

"And what message, Mr . . . Mr . . ." I said, not knowing our friend's name.

"My name is Boleslav Jablonský [a patriotic nineteenth-century Czech poet, discussed below, pp. 51–52]," the Newt shyly informed us. "In my opinion it is a beautiful name, sir. I chose it from my book."

"And what message, Mr. Jablonský, would you like to send to our nation?"

The Newt thought for a while. "Tell your fellow countrymen," he finally said with deep emotion, "tell them . . . not to fall back into the age-old Slav discord . . . but to keep the battle of Lipany and especially the White Mountain in grateful memory . . ." (151–52).

28. Milan Kundera, *Testaments Betrayed* (New York: HarperCollins, 1995), p. 193.

29. Mácha was described thus in the report in the popular illustrated weekly *Pestrý týden*, vol. 14, no. 19, 13 May 1939, which also contains numerous photographs of his funeral.

30. Emil Hácha (1872–1945) was a lawyer who rose to become president of the Supreme Court in Prague from 1925 to 1938. On 30 November 1938 he was chosen president of the post-Munich republic as an independent, nonpolitical candidate; on 16 March 1939 he became "state president" of the Protectorate of Bohemia and Moravia. Following liberation in May 1945, he was arrested at the presidential country seat of Lány and imprisoned in Pankrác prison in Prague, where he died less than three weeks later. He was reviled under the communists as a traitor and collaborator. Post-1989 revisionism is more inclined to stress his endeavors in the early years of the Nazi occupation to salvage what he could of Czech sovereignty and protect Czech lives. After the arrest of General Alois Eliáš (1890–1942), head of the Protectorate government from April 1939, in September 1941 for cooperation with the Czech resistance, Hácha was effectively sidelined, and health problems completely incapacitated him from 1943. Eliáš himself was executed in June 1942. Hácha wrote poetry and translated from English Jerome K. Jerome's *Three Men on the Bummel* (which has an amusing chapter on Prague), among other works. Four of his poems, from a private (and anonymously authored) bibliophilic edition of fifty numbered copies published in Prague in 1939 under the title *Mistakes and Delusions* [*Omyly a přeludy*], are reprinted in Pavel Kosatík, *Osm žen z hradu* (Prague: Mladá fronta, 1993), 146–47. For a recent assessment of Hácha's wartime role, see Dušan Tomášek and Robert Kvaček, *Causa Emil Hácha* (Prague: Themis, 1995).

31. I quote here and draw throughout this section from coverage in *Lidové noviny*, 7 and 8 May 1939. Some later secondary accounts, for example, Zdeněk Míka et al., *Dějiny Prahy v datech* (Prague: Panorama, 1988), 282, or Ivan Borkovský et al., *Dějiny Prahy* (Prague: Nakladatelství politické literatury, 1964), 614, wrongly date Mácha's burial in Vyšehrad as having taken place on 9 May.

32. Beneš's speech is given in full in Jasoň Boháč, ed., *Odkaz T. G. Masaryka* (Prague: Práce, 1990), 101–5. See also Karel Hájek, *Poslední cesta TGM* (Prague: Orbis, 1947); an interesting collection of photographs of Masaryk's funeral, with commemorative poems by among others Jaroslav Seifert, Josef Hora, Fráňa Šrámek, and—opening the book—Vítězslav Nezval.

33. "Kde domov můj?" remains the national anthem of the Czech Republic established on 1 January 1993. Bedřich Smetana said of it: "That song which the people itself elevated as its hymn, will also remain its hymn. Up till now the song 'Kde domov můj' is the hymn of the Czech people—let it be sung so long as our people has not taken another to its heart." Quoted in Ljuba Horáková, ed., *České korunovační klenoty: pamětní vydání ke vzniku České republiky MCMXCIII* (Prague: Kancelář presidenta České republiky, 1993), vi.

34. "Byl pozdní večer—první máj—večerní máj—byl lásky čas." Karel Hynek Mácha, *Dílo*, vol. 1 (Prague: Československý spisovatel, 1986), 15. *Máj* has been translated into English: see William E. Harkins, "Karel Hynek Mácha's *May*," *Cross Currents*, vol. 6, 1987.

35. Mácha, *Dílo*, vol. 1, 37. The alliteration to which I refer is on the dipthong "ou."

36. See Ivan Březina, "Causa Karel Hynek Mácha," *Reflex*, no. 9, 1993, 65.

37. Karel Čapek, *The Mother*, trans. Paul Selver (London: Allen and Unwin, 1939), 9.

CHAPTER 2

1. Josef Erben, ed., *Statistika královského hlavního města Prahy*, vol. 1 (Prague: Obecní statistická kommisse královského hlavního města Prahy, 1871), 122.

2. See Benedict Anderson, *Imagined Communities: Reflections on the Origin and Spread of Nationalism*, rev. ed., (New York: Verso, 1991), 9–22. I do not intend to slight Anderson's book, which I consider a major contribution to the literature on nationalism; but the tacit assumption that nations are imaginable as communities only under conditions of modernity, which Anderson shares with many others, needs in my view to be seriously rethought.

3. For a sharp critique of this conventional rhetorical device of historians see Michael Taussig, "Violence and Resistance in the Americas: the Legacy of Conquest," *Journal of Historical Sociology*, vol. 3, no. 3, 1990, 216–19; more generally Ana Maria Alonso, "The Effects of Truth: Re-presentations of the Past and the Imagining of Community," *Journal of Historical Sociology*, vol. 1, no. 1 (1988), 35–57.

4. Anderson, *Imagined Communities*; Eric Hobsbawm and Terence Ranger, eds., *The Invention of Tradition* (Cambridge: Cambridge University Press, 1983).

5. See Pope John VIII's Bull to the Moravian prince Svatopluk of 880, in Zdeněk Veselý, ed., *Dějiny českého státu v dokumentech* (Prague: Victoria Publishing, 1994), 21–22.

6. Ibrahim, syn Jaquba, "Zpráva o městě zvaném Fraga," A.D. 965, in V. Schwarz, ed., *Město vidím veliké . . . Cizinci o Praze* (Prague: Borový, 1940).

7. I have argued the case regarding England elsewhere; see Philip Corrigan and Derek Sayer, *The Great Arch: English State Formation as Cultural Revolution* (Oxford and New York: Blackwell, 1985); Derek Sayer, "A Notable Administration: English State Formation and the Rise of Capitalism," *American Journal of Sociology*, vol. 97, no. 5 (1992), 1382–419. See also, from an enormous literature, Patrick Wormald, "Engla Lond: The Making of an Allegiance,", *Journal of Historical Sociology*, vol. 7, no. 1, (1994), 1–24; James Campbell, "Stubbs and the English State," University of Reading, Stenton Lecture, 1989; G. E. Aylmer, "The Peculiarities of the English State," *Journal of*

Historical Sociology, vol. 3, no. 2 (1990), 91–108; and the recurrent discussion of medieval England's differences with continental Europe in Marc Bloch, *Feudal Society* (London: Routledge, 1967).

8. "František Pražský: *Kronika*," in Marie Bláhová, ed., *Kroniky doby Karla IV.* (Prague: Svoboda, 1987), 84.

9. Karel IV., "Vlastní životopis," in Bláhová, *Kroniky doby Karla IV.*, 27.

10. Ibid.

11. "Téhož roku [1358] pan císař, maje zvláštní úctu k svatému Václavovi, svému hlavnímu ochránci a pomocníku, obložil hlavu tohoto světce ryzím zlatem, zhotovil mu náhrobek z ryzího zlata, vyzdobil ho nejdražšími drahokamy a vybranými kameny a tak ho okrášlil, že se takový náhrobek nenajde na celém světě." Beneš Krabice z Weitmile, "Kronika pražského kostela," in Bláhová, *Kroniky doby Karla IV.*, 232.

12. Ibid.

13. "Obřady korunovační, jak je stanovil Karel IV.," in Horáková, *České korunovační klenoty*, 40.

14. Kosmas has subsequently been interpreted as referring to this song in his description of Dětmar's enthronement; see, for example, *Ottův slovník naučný*, vol. 6 (Prague: Otto, 1893), 362, which is categorical. All Kosmas actually says is that "the simpler people, unversed in song, called out 'Kyrie'" [prostější pak a zpěvu neznalý lid volal "Krlešu"]; *Kosmova kronika česká* (Prague: Svoboda, 1972), 45. Josef Dobrovský identified this with the song "Hospodine pomiluj ny" in his *Dějiny české řeči a literatury* (Prague: Československý spisovatel, 1951, 36–37; translation of first edition, in German, of 1792). For fuller discussion see Zdeněk Nejedlý, *Dějiny husitského zpěvu*, vol. 1, *Zpěv předhusitský* (Prague: Československá akademie věd, 1954), 315–27. Nejedlý dates the song from the twelfth century. It was first explicitly mentioned by name in 1249, and first written down only in a ms. of 1397 (Nejedlý, 324).

15. "Kronika pražského kostela," 224.

16. "Listina Karlova," 7 April 1348, in František Kop, *Založení University Karlovy v Praze* (Prague: Atlas, 1945), 12–15.

17. Quoted in Pavel Augusta et al., *Kdo byl kdo v našich dějinách do roku 1918* (Prachatice: Rovina, 1992), 209.

18. The so-called *Bible drážďanská* or *leskovecká*. From the fifteenth century, twenty-four whole Czech Bibles and approaching one hundred parts of the Bible and fragments have survived. See Mirjam Bohatcová et al., *Česká kniha v proměnách staletí* (Prague: Panorama, 1990), 98.

19. "Stížný list českých a moravských pánů do Kostnice," in Amadeo Molnár, ed., *Husitské manifesty* (Prague: Odeon, 1986), 48–52.

20. "Osvědčení Pražské univerzity o Husovi a Jeronýmovi," in Molnár, *Husitské manifesty*, 53–56.

21. "Univerzitní deklarace schvalující kalich," in Molnár, *Husitské manifesty*, 57–60.

22. "Páni a Pražané všem Čechům," in Molnár, *Husitské manifesty*, 67–70.

23. "Čtyři artikuly pražské," 3 July 1420, in Veselý, *Dějiny českého státu v dokumentech*, 83–85.

24. This is the title of a famous novel on the Hussites by Alois Jirásek. I discuss Jirásek more fully in chapter 4.

25. Josef Pekař, *Dějiny československé* (Prague: Akropolis, 1991), 65–66. This is a

textbook, approved by the Ministry of Education of the first Czechoslovak Republic; a class analysis of Hussitism is not a communist gloss but the conventional wisdom. For a Western example compare J. F. N. Bradley, *Czechoslovakia: A Short History* (Edinburgh: Edinburgh University Press, 1971), 49–50. Pekař, however, never reduced the Hussite storms to a socioeconomic (or national) "basis," insisting that they remained *religious* struggles that could be understood only in their medieval context. Fuller assessments of the Hussite period can be found in many other of Pekař's writings, notably his long monograph *Žižka a jeho doba* (Prague: Odeon, 1992). See also the essays "K boji o Husa" and "O Husovi a husitství" in his *O smyslu českých dějin* (Prague: Rozmluvy, 1990), and the lecture "O době husitské" in his *Postavy a problémy českých dějin* (Prague: Vyšehrad, 1990).

26. "Provolání k boji na obranu pravdy," in Molnár, *Husitské manifesty*, 229–40. Nowadays *pravda* means truth; then it also had connotations of justice or right.

27. Bohatcová, *Česká kniha*, 121–23, 154–57, 216.

28. Quoted in Pekař, *Žižka a jeho doba*, book 1, 265.

29. Josef Pekař estimates that by the second half of the sixteenth century, perhaps two-thirds of Bohemia's inhabitants (Germans included) were New Utraquists or Lutherans, and a further 5 to 10 percent were adherents of Jednota bratrská, discussed below. Old Utraquist strength was negligible; among the aristocracy, he thinks, only 3 percent (though higher in Prague). Pekař, *Dějiny československé*, 91.

30. Quoted in *Ottův slovník naučný*, vol. 13 (1898), 165.

31. Quoted in Petr Čornej et al., *Dějiny zemí koruny české*, vol. 1 (Prague: Paseka, 1992), 241.

32. *Ottův slovník naučný*, vol. 13 (1898), 169.

33. On these executions see Josef Petráň, *Staroměstská exekuce* (Prague: Mladá fronta, 1971).

34. Pekař, *Dějiny československé*, 110.

35. "Rekatolizační patent Ferdinanda II.," in Veselý, *Dějiny českého státu v dokumentech*, 193–94.

36. See Veselý, *Dějiny českého státu v dokumentech*, 193; Pekař, *Dějiny československé*, 111; Zdeněk Míka et al., *Dějiny Prahy v datech* (Prague: Panorama, 1988), 124.

37. Pekař, *Dějiny československé*, 123.

38. Ibid., 112.

39. Jan Amos Komenský, *The Labyrinth of the World and the Paradise of the Heart*, trans. Count Lützow (New York: Dutton, 1901; reprinted New York: Arno Press, 1971), 53. This is quoted from Komenský's opening dedication to Karel ze Žerotína, *zemský hejtman* of Moravia from 1608 to 1615, who had sheltered Komenský during the writing of the book on his estate at Brandýs. Unlike the rest of the book, the dedication was written in Latin.

40. Ibid., *Labyrinth*, 53–54.

41. Quoted in Bohatcová, *Česká kniha*, 283.

42. *Ottův slovník naučný*, vol. 24 (1906), 196.

43. I take this phrase from Josef Škvorecký, "Bohemia of the Soul," *Daedalus*, vol. 119, no. 1, 1990, where he reflects on the theme of emigration in Czech history.

44. See Bohatcová, *Česká kniha*, 273–77.

45. *Ottův slovník naučný*, vol. 14 (1899), 700.

46. Dobrovský, *Dějiny české řeči a literatury*, 125.

47. Quoted in Bohatcová, *Česká kniha*, 279.

48. The original song as recorded by Beneš Krabice z Weitmile in his "Kronika pražského kostela" had three verses (240). The Litoměřický graduál of 1473, a collection of Hussite songs, adds six more verses, one of which includes the words taken up by Balbín. The song itself may be as old as the twelfth century. See Pavla Obrazová and Jan Vlk, *Maior gloria: svatý kníže Václav* (Prague: Paseka, 1994), 152–53, 167–72; Balbín's prayer is also given here (191). Josef Pekař comments very perceptively on the song, its history, and its national significance in his essay "Svatý Václav," in his *O smyslu českých dějin* (Prague: Rozmluvy, 1990), 58–62.

49. Dobrovský, *Dějiny české řeči a literatury*, 127.

50. This is inferred from surnames as declared in an imperfect census. Eduard Šebesta and Adolf L. Krejčík, eds., *Popis obyvatelstva hlavního města Prahy z roku 1770* (Prague: Rodopisná společnost československá, 1933), xix.

51. Quoted in František Ruth, *Kronika královské Prahy a obcí sousedních*, vol. 1 (Prague: Körber, 1903), 506.

CHAPTER 3

1. "Provolání k založení Národního muzea," in Jan Novotný, ed., *Obrození národa: svědectví a dokumenty* (Prague: Melantrich, 1979), 190–94.

2. See *Ottův slovník naučný*, vol. 1 (1888), 573. Josef Haubelt, in what is in general an extremely scholarly study, maintains that there is not a single contemporary source that confirms this. Josef Haubelt, *České osvícenství* (Prague: Svoboda, 1986), 307. But Nostic certainly patronized the researches of František Martin Pelcl and Josef Dobrovský, both of whom he employed as tutors of his four sons.

3. The root of the word is the verb *rodit*, "to give birth." To me the translation "revival," though etymologically perfectly acceptable, has religious associations in English that are absent from the Czech.

4. Josef Hanuš, *Národní museum a naše obrození* (Prague: Národní museum, 1921), book 2, 37.

5. The adjective *vlastenský* has fallen out of modern Czech usage; it is omitted from smaller dictionaries and is marked "archaic" in larger ones. These give its primary meaning as "pertaining to the homeland," and a secondary meaning as "patriotic" (= *vlastenecký*). The adjective *vlastenecký* straightforwardly means patriotic, and always did. In the early nineteenth century both words were current in the language (see the titles of the Societies mentioned in this section for uses of *vlastenecký*); therefore, presumably choice of one or the other was not arbitrary. In the Czech of the day *Vlastenské museum* would have been a direct equivalent of the German *vaterländisches Museum*. Significantly, perhaps, the only use of *vlastenský* as synonymous with *vlastenecký* at this period that is recorded in the eight-volume *Slovník spisovného jazyka českého* is by Jungmann himself. Of course, in neither meaning would *vlastenský* pertain to *národ* as distinct from *vlast*, though in due course in the Czech lands as elsewhere patriotism came to imply nationalism.

6. "Základy pro společnost vlastenského muzeum [sic: not muzea] v Čechách," reproduced (in modernized Czech transcription) in František Kop, *Národní museum: památník našeho kulturního obrození* (Prague: Družstvo Vlast, 1941), 177–79.

7. "An die vaterländischen Freunde der Wissenschaften," dated "Prag am 15. April

1818," signed Franz Graf von Kolowrat, Oberstburggraf. I have to thank paní Věra Beňová for sending me a photocopy of this text from the archives of the Národní muzeum.

8. Kolovrat, "Provolání k založení Národního muzea," in Novotný, *Obrození národa*, 194.

9. Jiří Hilmera, *Stavovské národu!* (Prague: Stavovské divadlo), 13. The first production at the Stavovské divadlo in Czech, a translation of a German play, took place in January 1785, the first original Czech production in January 1786; see Míka, *Dějiny Prahy v datech*, 153. See also Vladimír Procházka, ed., *Dějiny českého divadla*, vol. 2 (Prague: Academia, 1969), 11–26.

10. "Základy pro společnost," in Kop, *Národní museum*, 178, Article 13.

11. Dobrovský's speech—including material not delivered before Leopold but printed in the press at the time—is reprinted in Novotný, *Obrození národa*. The relevant sections are on pp. 76–78.

12. František Josef Kinský, *Erinnerung über einen wichtigen Gegenstand von einen Böhmen* (Prague, 1773), quoted in *Ottův slovník naučný*, vol. 14 (1899), 243. Though remembered later primarily as a "defense of Czech," this book was in fact a wider reflection on the making of man. Language is considered within the field of a general educational theory that stresses the importance of experience in the formation of character. Kinský sees the mother tongue, whatever it may be, as a far more effective medium of instruction than a second language. For the same pedagogic, rather than patriotic, reasons he believes the homeland should be the starting point for the study of both history and geography. See Haubelt, *České osvícenství*, 313–17.

13. Hanuš, *Národní museum*, book 2, 36–37.

14. Ibid., 37. He suggests the example of the Moravia-Silesia Museum, founded in 1816, and the influence of Dobrovský as reasons for the shift of emphasis.

15. Procházka, *Dějiny českého divadla*, vol. 2, 18.

16. Novotný, *Obrození národa*, 163.

17. Quoted in Arnošt [Ernest] Denis, *Čechy po Bílé hoře*, vol. 2 (Prague: Bursík a Kohout, 1905), 104.

18. Bernard Bolzano, "O lásce k vlasti," in Novotný, *Obrození národa*, 128–29.

19. Bernard Bolzano, "O poměru obou národností v Čechách," in Novotný, *Obrození národa*, 174–75.

20. Ibid., 165–66.

21. Ibid., 167–68.

22. Ibid., 174.

23. On these disputes see Haubelt, *České osvícenství*, 333–51.

24. See Andrew Lass, "Presencing, Historicity and the Shifting Voice of Written Relics in Eighteenth-Century Bohemia," *Bohemica*, vol. 28, no. 1 (1987), 92–107. See also his "Romantic Documents and Political Monuments: The Meaning-Fulfillment of History in 19th-Century Czech Nationalism," *American Ethnologist*, vol. 15, no. 3 (1988), 456–71.

25. See Frederick G. Heymann, "The Hussite Movement in the Historiography of the Czech Awakening," in Peter Brock and H. Gordon Skilling, eds., *The Czech Renascence of the Nineteenth Century* (Toronto: University of Toronto Press, 1970). Palacký's comment is from his "Ocenění starých českých dějin," in his *Dílo Františka Palackého* (Prague: Mazáč, 1941), 74. He discusses Hájek, and Dobner's critique, in detail later in the book, pp. 294–308.

26. This claim—which I see no particular reason to dispute—is made in the entry on Hájek in Augusta, *Kdo byl kdo v našich dějinách*, 91.

27. Palacký, "Ocenění," 76.

28. "Dedukce o právní nepřetržitosti ústavních práv a svobod českých stavů," in Veselý, *Dějiny českého státu v dokumentech*, 220.

29. Zdeněk Šamberger et al., *Celostátní výstava archivních dokumentů: od hrdinné minulosti k vítězství socialismu*, exhibition catalogue (Prague: Ministerstvo vnitra, 1958), 15. I discuss this exhibition below, pp. 270–71.

30. *Ottův slovník naučný*, vol. 7 (1893), 707.

31. Quoted in Robert Auty, "Changing Views on the Role of Dobrovský in the Czech National Revival," in Brock and Skilling, *Czech Renascence*, 17. Dobrovský made himself similarly unpopular by his skepticism over the notorious *RKZ* forgeries; see below, pp. 144–47.

32. František Palacký, "Josefa Dobrovského život a působení vědecké," in his *Dílo Františka Palackého*, vol. 3, 266n, 252–53.

33. Dobrovský, *Dějiny české řeči a literatury*, 138–39. I quote the first edition of 1792; the relevant passage is omitted from the third edition of 1818. Whether Dobrovský had become more optimistic in the interim I do not know, but Palacký's testimony speaks against it.

34. Zdeněk Nejedlý, *Dějiny národa českého*, 1949, quoted in the introduction to Dobrovský, *Dějiny české řeči a literatury*, xxxii, n1.

35. "Toleranční patent Josefa II.," in Veselý, *Dějiny českého státu v dokumentech*, 205–06.

36. "Patent Josefa II. o zrušení nevolnictví," in Veselý, *Dějiny českého státu v dokumentech*, 209–10.

37. Dobrovský, *Dějiny české řeči a literatury*, 138–39.

38. See Hillel J. Kieval, *The Making of Czech Jewry: National Conflict and Jewish Society in Bohemia 1870–1918* (New York: Oxford University Press, 1988), 4–6.

39. "Dezideria českých stavů," in Veselý, *Dějiny českého státu v dokumentech*, 211–12.

40. Dobrovský, *Dějiny české řeči a literatury*, 135.

41. See Haubelt, *České osvícenství*, 413–14. The generally very detailed, if thoroughly communist, chronology in Míka et al., *Dějiny Prahy v datech*, for example, makes no mention of this chair, though it does of Pelcl's.

42. Preface to *Básně v řeči vázané*, quoted in *Ottův slovník naučný*, vol. 25 (1906), 321.

43. See Haubelt, *České osvícenství*, 412–13.

44. *Ottův slovník naučný*, vol. 13 (1898), 674–75.

45. Josef Jungmann, "Z předmluvy k česko-německému slovníku," in Novotný, *Obrození národa*, 290–91.

46. These may be found in Karel Hynek Mácha, *Dílo*, vol. 1, 212–60. One of them, "Ani labuť ani Lůna," was to be taken up a century later by Czech surrealists as the title of a famous collection; see below, pp. 222 and 225.

47. Karel Jaromír Erben, *Prostonárodní české písně a říkadla* (Prague: Evropský literární klub, 1937).

48. Dobrovský, *Dějiny české řeči a literatury*, 134, 14.

49. See Tomáš G. Masaryk, *Česká otázka* (Prague: Svoboda, 1990), ch. 2.

50. "Dalimil": the author is in fact unknown. Václav Hájek z Libočan wrongly assigned authorship to Dalimil Mezeřycký, a canon in Stará Boleslav, hence the traditional designation. See Dobrovský, *Dějiny české řeči a literatury*, 62.

51. Quoted in Haubelt, *České osvícenství*, 435.

52. Dobrovský, *Dějiny české řeči a literatury*, 85–86. Contrary to many subsequent (especially communist) accounts, Dobrovský did not rate the Hussite period as the "golden age" of Czech; that epithet he explicitly reserved (109) for the period 1520–1620.

53. Ibid., 85. Dobrovský is specifically discussing the hymn "Ye who are the soldiers of God."

54. Quoted in Haubelt, *České osvícenství*, 436. See also Heymann, "The Hussite Movement in the Historiography of the Czech Awakening," 228–29.

55. See Haubelt, *České osvícenství*, 420.

56. Josef Volf, "Dějiny novin a časopisů do roku 1848," in *Československá vlastivěda*, vol. 7 (Prague: Sfinx, 1933), 415. He gives a figure of 900 subscribers for 1788, based on a letter from Pelcl to Dobrovský.

57. Pavel Bělina et al., *Dějiny zemí koruny české*, vol. 2 (Prague: Paseka, 1992), 45.

58. *Ottův slovník naučný*, vol. 15 (1900), 63.

59. Bohatcová, *Česká kniha*, 355.

60. This is the feminine form of the noun *buditel*, "awakener." Rettigová is one of the subjects of Wilma A. Iggers, *Women of Prague: Ethnic Diversity and Social Change from the Eighteenth Century to the Present* (Providence, R.I., and Oxford: Berghahn Books, 1995), which gives extracts from her memoirs and correspondence. Rettigová's *Home Cookery* was reprinted, complete with successive patriotic prefaces, as Magdaléna Dobromila Rettigová, *Domácí kuchařka* (Prague: Odeon, 1986).

61. Arne Novák, *Literatura česká 19. století*, vol. 3 (Prague: 1905), 205, as translated in Iggers, *Women of Prague*, 45. Novák (1880–1939) was the leading Czech literary historian of his age: he was literary editor for *Ottův slovník naučný nové doby* and author of the book-length entry on Czech literature in *Československá vlastivěda*, two major reference works of the 1930s, and a literary reviewer for the newspaper *Lidové noviny* from 1921 to 1939. The entry in *Československá vlastivěda* (as updated by Antonín Grund in 1946) has been translated into English: Arne Novák, *Czech Literature*, trans. Peter Kussi, ed. and with supplement by William E. Harkins (Ann Arbor: Michigan Slavic Publications, 1976). Novák is more charitable about Rettigová's character in his monumental (1,800-page) and since unsurpassed *Historical Survey of Czech Literature*, describing her as a "refined practical homemaker" and "an ardent *buditelka*," but he still has little time for her literary efforts, which he dismisses as "shallow little verses" and "honeyed and moral tales." Jan Novák and Arne Novák, *Přehledné dějiny literatury české od nejstarších dob až po naše dny*, 4th ed. (Olomouc: R. Promberger, 1936–39), 393.

62. *Ottův slovník naučný*, vol. 21 (1904), 609.

63. Bohatcová, *Česká kniha*, 357.

64. Stanley B. Kimball, "The Matice česká, 1831–1861: The First Thirty Years of a Literary Foundation," in Brock and Skilling, *Czech Renascence*, 61, 57.

65. For a detailed analysis of the social makeup of the Czech national movement before 1848, see Miroslav Hroch, "The Social Composition of the Czech Patriots in Bohemia, 1827–1848," in Brock and Skilling, *Czech Renascence*, 33–52.

CHAPTER 4

1. František V. Schwartz, ed., *Památník Besedy měšťanské v Praze na oslavu pade-sátileté činnosti spolku 1845–6—1895–6 (Prague: Měšťanská beseda, 1896), 1.*

2. Ibid., 3–9.

3. Karel Půlpán, *Nástin českých a československých hospodářských dějin do roku 1990*, 2 vols. (Prague: Univerzita Karlova, 1993), 118.

4. Miroslav Buchvaldek et al., *Dějiny Československa v datech* (Prague: Svoboda, 1968), 482.

5. Bradley, *Czechoslovakia*, 131.

6. *Československá vlastivěda*, Řada II, *Národopis* (Prague: Sfinx, 1936), 37. The source is census figures; the totals for Plzeň and Moravská Ostrava here include suburbs.

7. Ibid., 20.

8. Ibid., 29–30.

9. This sea and its islands were carefully charted from the later nineteenth century onward. For example, the entry on Bohemia in *Ottův slovník naučný* (vol. 6, 1893) has an extremely detailed description of German *ostrovy* (pp. 122–25) as well as a chart (110–11) breaking down each *okres* (district) by area, population density, sex, and nationality (under the headings Czech, German, Other). The *Atlas Republiky československé* (Prague: Česká akademie věd a umění, 1935), 16–17, likewise has very precise prettily colored ethnographic maps.

10. All population figures given in this paragraph are from censuses, based on declarations of language of everyday intercourse. The source is *Ottův slovník naučný*, various volumes, entries under name of town or city.

11. I say maybe, because of the problems with the relevant census. As well as uncertainties among respondents about what nationality meant, they included alleged underreporting of Czech tenants by German landlords. This figure includes German-speaking Jews. See Erben, *Statistika královského hlavního města Prahy*, vol. 1 (1871), 122–23, and discussion above, p. 29. I have elaborated on the qualitative quagmire underlying quantitative data on nationality in late nineteenth- and early twentieth-century Bohemia in more detail elsewhere; see Derek Sayer, "The Language of Nationality and the Nationality of Language: Prague 1780–1920," *Past and Present*, no. 153 (1996), 164–210.

12. Greater Prague, as calculated on the boundaries established in 1922, had 514,345 inhabitants in 1900. See Václav Vacek, "Praha—na hlavní evropské křižovatce," *Československo*, vol. 1, no. 3, 1946, 33.

13. Even here they tended to live within enclaves, like in the lower New Town. There were also significant German pockets in the *předměstí* of Karlín (the oldest suburb), Smíchov, and the generally upscale Vinohrady. Karlín had 16,260 Czechs and 2,911 Germans in 1890; Vinohrady 47,056 Czechs and 4,769 Germans in 1900; Smíchov 49,376 Czechs and 3,463 Germans in 1904. These are census figures, based on declarations of language of everyday intercourse. Many of these German-speakers (and a smaller number of Czech-speakers) would have been Jewish. According to declarations of religion, there were 1,241 Jews in Karlín, 3,450 in Vinohrady, and 1,165 in Smíchov in these same years. My source for all these figures is relevant volumes of *Ottův slovník naučný*.

14. See on this visibility the famous reminiscence by the "furious reporter," as he was known, Egon Erwin Kisch. He writes: "Who did not have a title or was not wealthy did not belong to her. German Prague! It was almost only great burghers, owners of brown coal mines, managing directors of mining enterprises and Škoda [engineering] establishments, hop-growers who used to go to and fro between Žatec and America, sugar refiners, textile barons and owners of paper mills, directors of banks, and in their society used to move professors, higher military officers, and state officials. A German proletariat did not exist. Twenty-five thousand Germans, that is only 5 percent of the total Prague population, had two excellent theaters, a huge concert hall, two institutions of higher education, five gymnasia and four technical high schools, two daily newspapers which came out in the morning and evening, large social buildings, and a very active social life." "Češi a Němci," in *Vždycky na levém křídle* (Prague: Naše vojsko, 1953), 20. We are speaking here, however, emphatically of *perceptions*. Gary Cohen's excellent study of Prague German society in the later nineteenth century, *The Politics of Ethnic Survival* (Princeton, N.J.: Princeton University Press, 1981), concludes from census data for 1910 that one-third of Prague's German-speakers then in fact "fell into the laboring or lowest middle-class strata" (122). It was exactly they, however, who were most likely to assimilate to the Czech majority, as victims of German self-definitions as a cultural elite. Their invisibility again demonstrates the constructedness of Prague ethnicities in this period.

15. The classic published sources on the visual appearance of Prague in the later nineteenth century are the six-volume *Zmizelá Praha*, compiled by V. V. Štech, Zdeněk Wirth, and others (Prague: Václav Poláček, 1945–48), and Wirth's *Stará Praha: obraz města a jeho veřejného života v 2. polovici XIX. století podle původních fotografií* (Prague: Otto, 1942). More recent works include Pavel Scheufler, *Praha 1848–1914: čtení nad dobovými fotografiemi* (Prague: Panorama, 1984), and *Fotografické album Čech 1830–1914* (Prague: Odeon, 1989). For photographs of the large area in Staré město and Josefov (the erstwhile Jewish ghetto) destroyed in the slum clearance that began in the 1890s, see *Zmizelá Praha*, 3, 1947 (ed. Hana Volavková) and more recently *Acta Musei Pragensis*, 93, *Pražská asanace* (Prague: Muzeum hlavního města Prahy, 1993).

16. Quoted in A. J. P. Taylor, *The Habsburg Monarchy, 1809–1918* (London: Penguin, 1990), 181.

17. Census figures. My source here is Cohen, *The Politics of Ethnic Survival*, 92–93, which tabulates census data on "Germans" for Prague and its suburbs for 1869, 1880, 1890, 1900, and 1910.

18. Census figures. My source is relevant volumes of *Ottův slovník naučný*.

19. *The Diaries of Franz Kafka*, ed. Max Brod (London, Penguin, 1964), 119.

20. And not, as we might otherwise assume, after the Saint Nicholas Church on the corner where the street meets Staroměstské náměstí, which I discuss below, p. 140. A Saint Nicholas Church had stood on this site since perhaps the thirteenth century. See Jiří Čarek et al., *Ulicemi města Prahy od 14. století do dneška* (Prague: Orbis, 1958), 289.

21. Michal Tryml, *Staroměstské náměstí* (Prague: Oswald, 1991), 17. For a contemporary description of the uncovering of the sgraffiti, see K. Guth, "Sgrafita na domě 'U minuty' v Praze," *Umění*, vol. 1 (1918–21), 446–49, and the photograph on p. 451.

22. Haubelt, *České osvícenství*, 411. He estimates that in 1770 perhaps a quarter of children of school age were actually attending elementary schools.

23. *Ottův slovník naučný*, vol. 6 (1893), 114.

24. Karel Havlíček Borovský, "Slovan a Čech," in Novotný, *Obrození národa*, 341.

25. Jan Šafránek, "Školství obecné a měšťanské," in J. Kafka et al., eds., *Sto let práce: zpráva o všeobecné zemské výstavě v Praze 1891*, exhibition catalogue, 3 vols. (Prague, 1892–95), vol. 3, 519. These figures are for public elementary [*obecné*] schools only. Broken down by nationality of pupils, there were 590,590 Czechs and 318,414 Germans, which means that 13,627 Czech children were still being educated in German.

26. See, for example, Václav Vladivoj Tomek's 1848 article "Jak může uvedena být stejnost práva české i německé národnosti ve školách?" in Novotný, *Obrození národa*, 386–91.

27. Data from Kafka, *Sto let práce*, vol. 3, 513–46, and *Ottův slovník naučný*, vol. 6 (1893), 196–97.

28. Eliška Krásnohorská, "Slovo k prvním abiturientkám našim," in Albina Honzáková, ed., *Československé studentky let 1890–1930* (Prague: Ženská národní rada a Spolek Minerva, 1930), 16.

29. Honzáková, *Československé studentky*, 59, and unpaginated statistical supplement. By 1927–28 there were 2,870 girls studying in Czechoslovak universities: *Ročenka Československé republiky*, vol. 9 (1930), 70.

30. *Ottův slovník naučný*, vol. 6 (1893), 360.

31. Ibid., 198–99. The latter figure is for the second semester of the academic year 1890–91.

32. *Almanach královského hlavního města Prahy*, vol. 9 (Prague: Archiv královského hlavního města Prahy, 1906), statistical supplement, 36.

33. Kafka, *Sto let práce*, vol. 3, 575–76.

34. Božena Němcová, letter to Dušan Lambl, 2 August 1856, in Karel Havlíček Borovský, *Stokrát plivni do moře* (Prague: Československý spisovatel, 1990), 303–4. and (more fully) in Božena Němcová, *Z dopisů Boženy Němcové*, ed. Jana Štefánková (Prague: Státní nakladatelství dětské knihy, 1962), 141–45. Podskalí was a poor district of Prague, at the south end of the New Town on the right bank of the Vltava. The gates and ramparts were those of the city walls, then still standing. Havlíček was buried in Olšany Cemetery.

35. See letter from Božena Němcová to her son Karel, 28 August 1856, in Němcová, *Z dopisů Boženy Němcové*, 147–50, also partially translated in Iggers, *Women of Prague*, 72–73.

36. Karel Havlíček Borovský, "Slovan a Čech," 333.

37. The whole furor is described, and Havlíček's review extensively quoted, in Slavomír Ravik, *K. H. Borovský (portrét bojovníka)* (Prague: Pražská imaginace, 1991), 29–34.

38. "Velmi mnohým českým básníkům," in his *Stokrát plivni do moře*, 42.

39. Kafka, *Sto let práce*, vol. 3, 575–76.

40. Augusta, *Kdo byl kdo v našich dějinách*, 87.

41. Kafka, *Sto let práce*, vol. 3, 577.

42. *Almanach královského hlavního města Prahy*, vol. 9 (1906), 38. This figure includes both Czech and German papers.

43. *Ottův slovník naučný*, vol. 6 (1893), 358. The categories are theirs.

44. According to the bibliography of Mucha's illustrative work in the catalogue of

the Prague 1980 retrospective exhibition, his work was featured in *Zlatá Praha* in 1889, 1893, 1894, 1898–1901, 1903, 1907, and 1910–18 (Laclotte, *Alfons Mucha 1860–1939*, 122).

45. A good example is the fiftieth birthday tribute to Alois Jirásek in 1901, a double issue bearing his photograph on the cover. It begins with a poem to him by Vrchlický, a long biographical piece "To Alois Jirásek and About Him," by Zikmund Winter, and a poem "You Are to the People Soothsayer, Leader, Teacher," by Adolf Heyduk; it continues with reminiscences by Josef Sládek, Karel V. Rais, Viktor Dyk (beginning "I am Jirásek's pupil"), and others; it carries a multitude of greetings, many of them in verse, from, among others, Eliška Krásnohorská and Růžena Jesenská; and it has articles about Jirásek and Litomyšl, where the novelist taught at the gymnasium from 1874 to 1888, by the young Zdeněk Nejedlý, and Jirásek and Hronov, his home-town. Complementing these, besides family photographs, are reproductions of illus-trations from Jirásek's books by Mikoláš Aleš and others, and photographs of charac-ters in his plays, whose interpreters include the celebrated actress Hana Kvapilová. *Zlatá Praha*, vol. 18 (1901), no. 42–43.

46. Quoted in the obituary by Jindřich Šolc, "Tomáš Černý," *Almanach královského hlavního města Prahy*, vol. 13 (1910), 269; emphasis in original.

47. *Zlatá Praha*, vol. 20 (1903), no. 12, 143–44. This special issue gives a richly detailed history of the magazine.

48. Information on Otto is drawn from Bohatcová, *Česká kniha*, 386–87, and Otto publications as cited below.

49. František Adolf Šubert, *Národní divadlo v Praze: Dějiny jeho i stavba dokončená* (Prague: Otto, 1881–83); K. Klusáček et al., eds., *Národopisná výstava českoslovanská v Praze 1895*, exhibition catalogue, Výkonný výbor národopisné výstavy českoslovanské a Národopisná společnost českoslovanská (Prague: Otto, 1895).

50. Kafka, *Sto let práce*, vol. 2, 284, and graph between pp. 288 and 289. On this exhibition see also the official catalogue, *Všeobecná zemská výstava 1891 v Praze . . . Hlavní katalog*, ed. Josef Fořt (Prague, 1891), and the memorial volume *Jubilejní výstava zemská království českého v Praze 1891* (Prague: Šimáček, 1894). Relevant sec-ondary literature includes Milan Hlavačka, *Jubilejní výstava 1891* (Prague: Techkom, 1991); Pavel Augusta and František Honzák, *Sto let jubilejní* (Prague: Státní na-kladatelství technické literatury, 1991).

51. The interior of the house, which is today much as it was when Mucha lived there, is generously photographed in Suzanne Slesin, Stafford Cliff, and Daniel Rozensztroch, *Mittel Europa: Rediscovering the Style and Design of Central Europe* (New York: Clarkson Potter, 1994), 180–86. Beside the bookcase is the harmonium that used to stand in Mucha's Paris studio, at which Mucha once famously photographed Paul Gauguin sitting.

52. *Ottův slovník naučný*, vol. 27 (1908), unpaginated afterword by Jan Otto enti-tled "Některé poznámky o vzniku 'Ottova Slovníku Naučného.'"

53. F. Palacký, "První návrh o slovníku naučném" (1829), in his *Úvahy a projevy* (Prague: Melantrich, 1977), 233–39. See also his "O českém slovníku naučném" (1850), idem, 240–55, or in his *Dílo Františka Palackého*, vol. 4, 75–89; and Vladimír Smetana, "František Palacký: průkopník českého naučného slovníku," *Malá řada En-cyklopedického Institutu ČSAV* (Prague, 1969).

54. [Riegrův] *Slovník naučný*, 10 vols. (Prague: Kober, 1860–72).

55. Such, at any rate, is the claim of Bohumil Němec, the chief editor of the additional volumes published through the 1930s. *Ottův slovník naučný nové doby*, vol. I/1 (Prague: Otto, 1930), unpaginated preface.

56. Ibid.

57. *Ottův slovník naučný*, vol. 6 (1893), 3–572.

58. *Ottův slovník naučný*, vol. 20 (1903), 488. The graphs face p. 489.

59. J. J. Benešovský-Veselý et al., *Národní album: sbírka podobizen a životopisů českých lidí prací a snahami vynikajících i zasloužilých* (Prague: Vilímek, n.d. [but marked "Completed 6 December 1899"]).

60. Quoted in Hanuš, *Národní museum*, Book 2, 468–69.

61. Quoted in ibid., 471.

62. Quoted in ibid., 473.

63. See Joseph F. Zacek, "Metternich's Censors: The Case of Palacký," in Brock and Skilling, *Czech Renascence*, 95–112.

64. Kop, *Národní museum*, 27.

65. František Palacký, "Verhandlungen des vaterländischen Museums," in *Das vaterländische Museum in Böhmen im Jahre 1842* (Prague: 1842). Quoted (in Czech translation) in Kop, *Národní museum*, 27–28.

66. F. L. Rieger, "Museum království českého," reproduced in Kop, *Národní museum*, 39–40.

67. These are listed (together with their dates of entry and, in some cases, exit) in full in Lubomír Sršeň, *Budova Národního muzea v Praze 1891–1991: architektura, umělecká výzdoba a původní uměleckořemeslné vybavení* (Prague: Národní muzeum, 1991), 102–6.

68. Quoted in Ruth, *Kronika královské Prahy*, vol. 3 (1904), 1147.

69. Saint Anežka (Agnes of Bohemia, ?1211–1282), youngest daughter of King Přemysl Otakar I, was the founder and abbess of Prague's Anežský klášter, which now houses the National Gallery's collection of nineteenth-century Czech painting. She was pronounced "Blessed" by the Church in 1870 and canonized as a saint by Pope John Paul II on 14 November 1989. See Bohumil Svoboda, ed., *Blahoslavená Anežka česká: sborník k svatořečení* (Prague: Česká katolická Charita, 1989). This event occurred three days before the outbreak of the Velvet Revolution. The novelist Jaroslav Putík wrote in his diary: "Near and far church bells are ringing, the last time I heard them like that was sometime in Easter of 1946. What is going on, what has happened so exceptional that the whole land is ringing out? Has the government fallen or Husák resigned? But then I remembered that on this day the Pope is canonizing Anežka česká and the Czech land is celebrating her with the voices of bells. Although I am a nonbeliever, sacred feelings take hold of me. And admiration for the foresight of the Church, that it chose just this day. If freedom soon returns to us, it will be henceforward linked with Anežka česká." Jaroslav Putík, *Odysea po česku* (Prague: Prostor, 1992), 291.

70. The history of Žižkov's street names is discussed more fully below, pp. 133–34 and 289. Unless otherwise stated, information on street names in this book is taken from Ruth, *Kronika královské Prahy*, and Čarek, *Ulicemi města Prahy*. The introduction to the latter traces the history, and explains the principles, of naming of streets in different districts of Prague up to 1958. There has of course been a major purge since the Velvet Revolution of 1989. See *Co je nového v Praze: nové názvy ulic, náměstí,*

nábřeží, sadů, mostů a stanic metra (Prague: Gabriel, 1991) for an annotated list of postcommunist name changes up to that date.

71. Red and white were the Czech national colors and those on the first postindependence flag in 1918. Blue was added to represent Slovakia in 1920. For detailed discussion of the extended arguments over the symbolism of the flag and other state insignia in 1918–20, see Zbyšek Svoboda, *Československá státní a vojenská symbolika* (Prague: Federální ministerstvo obrany, 1991).

72. Most of these are reproduced in Mikoláš Aleš, *Nástěnné malby* (*Dílo Mikoláše Alše*, vol. 3) (Prague: Státní nakladatelství krásné literatury, hudby a umění, 1955), and discussed on pp. 104–6. The text comments: "Aleš took for the theme of his lunettes . . . economic life. But it would not have been Aleš, if within the economic scenes he did not place allegory with a national content" (104).

73. On the founding of the Deutsches Kasino see Cohen, *Politics of Ethnic Survival*, 66–70.

74. Šubert's *Národní divadlo* is an excellent history that also gives relevant documents and the financial accounts of the fund-raising collection. See also the first two volumes of the six-volume fiftieth anniversary celebratory history *Dějiny Národního divadla* (Prague: Sbor pro zřízení druhého Národního divadla v Praze, 1933–35), by Jan Bartoš and Antonín Matějček, respectively. A thick—if highly tendentious—general history of Czech theater is the four-volume *Dějiny českého divadla* published by the Czechoslovak Academy of Sciences from 1969 to 1983.

75. See Šubert, *Národní divadlo*, 40.

76. "Řeč Al. Jiráska," in *Za právo a stát: sborník dokladů o československé společné vůli k svobodě 1848–1918* (Prague: Státní nakladatelství, 1928), 298–300. Published for the tenth anniversary of independence by the State Publishing House, this thick (580-page) collection begins with the legend: "Since gratitude passes more quickly than time, let this book at the same time be a reminder that memories of the merits of the foreign and domestic [resistance] workers are a source for the deeds of their successors. It would be a misfortune for the Czechoslovak nation if for insufficiency of memories and gratitude new deeds were unable to blossom from it." This is followed by two pages of quotations from "Hospodine, pomiluj ny," Dalimil, "Píseň svatováclavská," Hus, "Ktož sú boží bojovníci," Žižka, Komenský, Balbín, Dobrovský, Kollár, and Šafařík.

77. See Jiří Kotalík et al., eds., *Almanach Akademie výtvarných umění v Praze k 180. výročí založení (1799–1979)* (Prague: Akademie výtvarných umění/Národní galerie, 1979).

78. See Otto Wichterle et al., *Sto let České akademie věd a umění* (Prague: Československá akademie věd, 1991).

79. On the history of the Modern Gallery see *Moderní galerie království českého v Praze* (Prague: Unie, 1907), which was the first catalogue of the gallery; R. Musil et al., *Moderní galerie tenkrát 1902–1942*, exhibition catalogue (Prague: Národní galerie, 1992); Lenka Zapletalová, ed., *Czech Modern Art 1900–1960* (Prague: Národní galerie, 1995), the catalogue of the standing exhibition in the recently reopened Veletržní palác; and Anna Janištinová, "Praha a Čechy," in Hana Rousová, ed., *Mezery v historii 1890–1938: polemický duch Střední Evropy—Němci, Židé, Češi*, exhibition catalogue (Prague: Galerie hlavního města Prahy, 1994), 44–49.

80. Augusta, *Kdo byl kdo v našich dějinách*, 193.

81. These figures are for living members only in the relevant years, and cover all categories of membership, including honorary, corresponding, and country.

82. H. Jelínek, ed., *Padesát let Umělecké besedy* (Prague: Umělecká beseda, 1913), Statistické přehledy. See also F. Skácelík, ed., *Sedmdesát let Umělecké besedy 1863–1933* (Prague: Umělecká beseda, 1933); and Jiří Kotalík, *Umělecká beseda: k 125. výročí založení*, exhibition catalogue (Prague: Národní galerie, 1988).

83. On the history of this magazine see the beautifully illustrated book by Roman Prahl and Lenka Bydžovská, *Volné směry: časopis secese a moderny* (Prague: Torst, 1993).

84. Aleš is described thus in Prokop Toman, *Nový slovník československých výtvarných umělců*, unchanged reprint of third edition of 1947–50 (Ostrava: Chagall, 1993), 10. The fullest dictionary of Czech artists ever produced, this book first came out in 1927.

85. Karel B. Mádl, *Mikoláš Aleš* (Prague: SVU Mánes, 1912), 13–15.

86. All of these choruses can be heard on the Supraphon record album 1112 4095 G (1987), *Kytice písní společenských/Czech Revival Male Choruses.*

87. *Zpěvem k srdci—srdcem k vlasti.* Personal observation.

88. These figures are all from *Ottův slovník naučný*, vol. 6 (1893), 207.

89. Josef Scheiner, ed., *Pátý slet všesokolský pořádaný v Praze . . . 1907* (Prague: Česká obec sokolská, 1907), 6.

90. Ibid., 12.

91. *Ottův slovník naučný nové doby*, vol. VI/1 (1940), 98. By 1920 this figure had risen to 559,026, by 1937, to 818,642.

92. Josef Müller and Ferdinand Tallowitz, eds., *Památník vydaný na oslavu dvacetiletého trvání tělocvičné jednoty Sokola Pražského* (Prague: Sokol, 1883).

93. F. L. Rieger, "První národní bál. Ze vzpomínek starého vlastence," in *Almanach Národní Besedy* (Prague: Národní Beseda, 1908), 11. Rieger's article is reprinted "in place of a preface."

94. On this see Cohen, *The Politics of Ethnic Survival*, and Kieval, *The Making of Czech Jewry.*

95. Pavel Eisner, *Chrám i tvrz: kniha o češtině* (Prague: Lidové noviny, 1992; photo-reprint of edition of 1946). Eisner is discussed below, p. 208.

96. See Anderson, *Imagined Communities*, 12–19.

97. See here Jungmann's two famous dialogues on the state of the Czech language, first published in the magazine *Hlasatel* in 1806, reprinted in *Josefa Jungmanna vybrané spisy* (Prague: Vojtěch Hrách/Jan Otto, 1918), 41–68, under the title "O jazyku českém." The first of these is an imaginary conversation between the sixteenth-century Czech scholar Daniel Adam z Veleslavína, a contemporary Czech, and a German. The Czech's abilities in his own language are caricatured viciously, for example: "Na, na, pan! ja Šech je, a v Šechy narotil" (No, no, Sir! I am a Czech, and was born in Bohemia.) Apart from spelling mistakes in nearly every word, this hilariously mixes up grammatical cases and persons. It should read "Ne, ne, pane! Já jsem Čech, a narodil jsem se v Čechách."

98. These drawings are reproduced in *Kresby Bedřicha Smetany* (Prague: Umělecká beseda, 1925). Exhibition catalogue, with an introduction by Zdeněk Nejedlý.

99. Letter to a friend, quoted in Tomáš Feřtek, "Causa K. H. Borovský," *Reflex*, no. 41, 1993, 50. The same letter is quoted in unmodernized Czech, and the addressee

identified as Mořic Příborský, in Jiří Morava, *C. k. disident Karel Havlíček* (Prague: Panorama, 1991), 19.

100. Letter to František Jirgl, 1842, quoted in Ravik, *K. H. Borovský*, 13.

101. Ravik, *K. H. Borovský*, 13; Morava, *C. k. disident Karel Havlíček*, 19. Ravik claims Havlíček copied out the entire (4,500-page) dictionary.

102. See Antonín Matějček, *Dílo Josefa Mánesa*, vol. 1, *Národní písně*, 2d enlarged edition (Prague: Jan Štenc, 1928), where these are copiously reproduced.

103. Ibid., vol. 1, 42.

104. Jan Kühndel, ed., *Dopisy Josefa Mánesa* (Prague: Odeon, 1968).

105. Podiven [pseudonym for Petr Pithart, Petr Příhoda, and Milan Otáhal], *Češi v dějinách nové doby (pokus o zrcadlo)* (Prague: Rozmluvy, 1991), 71.

106. Zora Dvořáková, *Miroslav Tyrš: prohry a vítězství* (Prague: Olympia, 1989), 7, 23. On Tyrš's own struggles with Czech, see the reminiscences of his wife, Renata Tyršová, *Miroslav Tyrš: jeho osobnost a dílo* (Prague: Český čtenář, 1932–34), 34–35.

107. Quoted in Dvořáková, *Tyrš*, 29.

108. Dvořáková, *Tyrš*, 24–25.

109. See the discussion in Natalia Bergerová, ed., *Na křižovatce kultur: historie československých Židů* (Prague: Mladá fronta, 1992), 120.

110. F. V. Krejčí, "Život a činnost T. G. Masaryka," originally published in a series of articles on Masaryk in *Právo lidu*, 14–22 December 1937, reprinted in Boháč, *Odkaz T. G. Masaryka*, 12.

111. According to the reminiscences of Masaryk's daughter Alice, Czech became the language of the household only after Tomáš and Charlotte moved back to Prague from Vienna in 1882, but Charlotte learned Czech rapidly and well. Alice's own first languages were German and English, both of which she later forgot. Alice Masaryková, *Dětství a mládí* (Prague: Ústav T. G. Masaryka, 1994), 15. Jan Masaryk said "We, the Masaryks, are Slovaks and Slovakia was my greatest love" in a speech broadcast in the United States on 17 March 1939, quoted in Vladimír Vaněk, *Jan Masaryk* (Prague: Torst, 1994), 110. There was some justification in this. Though originally of Czech origin, several generations of the Masaryk family had lived in Slovakia before Tomáš's father moved to Moravia.

112. Puchmajer to Jungmann, letter of 1816, quoted in *Ottův slovník naučný*, vol. 13 (1898), 671.

113. "Předmluva" to first edition of Jungmann's translation of *Paradise Lost*, in *Josefa Jungmanna vybrané spisy*, 155; emphasis in original.

114. *Webster's New World Dictionary of the American Language*, 2d college edition (New York: Prentice Hall, 1986), endpapers.

115. Karel Havlíček Borovský, "Slovan a Čech," 342.

116. See Svoboda, *Československá státní a vojenská symbolika*, 55.

117. Palacký, "Psaní do Frankfurtu (O poměru Čech i Rakouska k říši Německé)," in his *Úvahy a projevy*, 163.

118. Figure from 1890 census, in *Ottův slovník naučný*, vol. 6 (1893), 122. In the Czechoslovak Republic established in 1918 (according to the 1921 census), the German population of Bohemia was 2,173,000, the Czech 4,382,800. In the republic as a whole—excluding Podkarpatská Rus, ceded to the Soviet Union after World War II—Czechs formed slightly more than half of the whole population (6,800,000 out of 13,007,000); Germans (3,124,000) easily outnumbered Slovaks (1,967,000). Figures

from *Ottův slovník naučný nové doby*, vol. I/2 (1931), 1082–83. See further below, p. 168.

119. See Hilmera, *Stavovské národu!* for a detailed account of these events.

120. "'Pro strach židovský,'" in Jan Neruda, *Studie krátké a kratší* (Prague: L. Mazač, 1928), 248. Substantial extracts from this are translated in Wilma Abeles Iggers, ed., *The Jews of Bohemia and Moravia: A Historical Reader* (Detroit: Wayne State University Press, 1992), 183–90. A recent English translation of Neruda's *Povídky malostranské* is Jan Neruda, *Prague Tales*, trans. Michael Henry Heim, intro. by Ivan Klíma (London: Chatto and Windus, 1993).

121. Quoted in T. G. Masaryk, *Karel Havlíček*, 3d ed. (Prague: Jan Laichter, 1920), 446–47. Part of Havlíček's review of Kapper's *České listy*, in which this passage appears, originally published in *Česká včela*, November 1946, is translated in Iggers, *Jews of Bohemia and Moravia*, 134–35.

122. Mikoláš Aleš, *Špalíček národních písní a říkadel* (Prague: Orbis, 1950), 93.

123. Petr Bezruč, "Hanácká ves," in *Slezské písně* (Brno: Nový lid, 1928), 10.

124. Franz Kafka, *Letters to Milena*, ed. and trans. Philip Boehm (New York: Schocken, 1990), 212–13. At the suggestion of my wife, Alena, I have altered the translation here; "wallowing in anti-Semitic hate" seems an unnecessarily embellished rendition of Kafka's straightforward "Die ganzen Nachmittage bin ich jetzt auf den Gassen und bade im Judenhass." The original German may be found in Franz Kafka, *Briefe an Milena* (Frankfurt: Fischer Verlag, 1986), 288.

125. Brod is quoted from his *Franz Kafka: A Biography* (New York: Schocken, 1963), 222. Between its foundation in 1890 and 1948 there were 648 domestic members (ordinary, extraordinary, and corresponding) elected to the Czech Academy. Of these, just 10 were women. Eight were writers (Božena Benešová, Růžena Jesenská, Eliška Krásnohorská, Marie Majerová, Gabriela Preissová—who wrote the libretto for Janáček's opera *Jenůfa*—Marie Pujmanová, Anna Maria Tilschová, and Božena Viková-Kunětická), one a historian at Prague university (Milada Paulová), and one a composer and conductor (Vítězslava Kaprálová). Jiří Mucha, Alfons Mucha's son, writes about Kaprálová (1915–40) and her circle, which included the composer Bohuslav Martinů, in Paris before the outbreak of World War II in his memoir *Podivné lásky* (Prague: Mladá fronta, 1988). Milena's father, Jan Jesenský, was also a member of the Academy. For a biographical listing of the latter see Alena Šlechtová and Josef Levora, *Členové České akademie věd a umění 1890–1952, Práce z dějin Československé akademie věd*, vol. 3, series B, (Prague: Ústřední archiv ČSAV, 1989).

126. *Šípy*, 12 May 1894. This is reproduced on the front cover of *Res Musei pragensis*, vol. 4, no. 2, 1994.

127. Gustav Janouch, *Conversations with Kafka: Notes and Reminiscences* (London: Derek Verschoyle, 1953), 67. On Janouch himself see Josef Škvorecký, "Franz Kafka, Jazz, and the Anti-Semitic Reader," in his *Talkin' Moscow Blues* (Toronto: Lester and Orpen Dennys, 1988), 157–62.

128. The Austro-Hungarian censuses (from 1880) did not directly ask about nationality but "language of everyday intercourse." Yiddish was for these purposes counted as a dialect of German. In 1890, 73.8 percent of Prague's Jews (as identified by declarations of religion) gave their "language of everyday intercourse" as German; in 1900, this figure had fallen to 45.3 percent. In both censuses Jews made up 46 percent of all declared German-speakers, which means, among other things, that a

similar proportion of *non*-Jews had switched linguistic allegiance over the decade. It is difficult to think of a better example of the shifting sands beneath the apparent solidities of ethnolinguistic identity than the virtual realities constructed by these statistics. These census data are tabulated in Cohen, *The Politics of Ethnic Survival*, 102, table 3/3. See, further, my "Language of Nationality."

129. *Ottův slovník naučný*, vol. 20 (1903), 488.

130. Kieval's *The Making of Czech Jewry* is a superb account of these dilemmas, packed with detail. See more generally Tomáš Pěkný, *Historie Židů v Čechách a na Moravě* (Prague: Sefer, 1993); Bergerová, *Na křižovatce kultur*; Ctibor Rybár et al., *Židovská Praha* (Prague: Akropolis, 1991); Altshuler, *The Precious Legacy*, especially the chapter by Hillel Kieval; and Society for the History of Jews from Czechoslovakia, *The Jews of Czechoslovakia*, 3 vols. (Philadelphia: 1967, 1971, 1984).

131. Kafka, *Letters to Milena*, 8.

132. Ibid., 14.

133. *The Diaries of Franz Kafka*, 88.

134. The 1890 census listed 381 inhabitants, all Czech. *Ottův slovník naučný*, vol. 18 (1902), 906.

135. See, for example, the facsimile of his letter to Josef David of 22 or 23 August 1901, in his *Letters to Ottla and the Family*, ed. N. N. Glatzer, trans. Richard and Clara Winston (New York: Schocken, 1982), 78. For fuller discussion see my "Language of Nationality."

136. Figures given in Josef Šiška, "Populační a bytové poměry," in Václav Vojtíšek, ed., *Praha v obnoveném státě československém* (Prague: Rada hlavního města Prahy, 1936). This was a thick official volume commemorating Prague's achievements as capital of independent Czechoslovakia since 1918. Šiška's own distaste for Jews is undisguised. He comments: "Although living compactly, with a high economic, social, and to some extent cultural level, the Prague Jewish minority has only a small fraction within it that possesses any crystallized national awareness," and sees Jewish desertion of German schools for Czech after 1918—a course of action Czech nationalists had been urging Jews for decades—as merely "a contribution to the study of [Jews'] national character" (74). I believe this is what is called a double bind: Šiška himself (rightly) sees Prague Jews' actions as "an accurate barometer of powerful political conditions."

137. I quote from the communist *Malá československá encyklopedie*, vol. 3 (Prague: Academia, 1986), 256.

138. This is the title of the biography of Jesenská by her fellow inmate in Ravensbrück, the German writer Margarete Buber-Neumann. Margarete Buber-Neumann, *Mistress to Kafka: The Life and Death of Milena*, introduction by Arthur Koestler (London: Secker and Warburg, 1966). The German title is *Kafkas Freundin Milena*. Buber-Neumann knew no Czech and had never visited Prague at the time she wrote the book, which is littered with errors. Her own biography, however, is as illuminating of its times as Milena's own. It includes stints in both Soviet and Nazi camps; see Koestler's introduction.

139. *Lidové noviny*, 8 May 1939, 2.

140. Interview with R. J. Kronbauer, in *Národní divadlo*, vol. 29, no. 3 (1953–54), 18. What is significant, given the date of this reprint, is that it was these words that were chosen for quotation in the context of a seventieth anniversary commemoration

of the theater's reopening. The communists' postwar recycling of the tropes of nine-teenth-century nationalist discourse is discussed at length in Chapter 7.

141. Augusta and Honzák, *Sto let jubilejní*, 47.

142. Not the same magazine as the *Květy české* discussed previously, this was foun-ded by Čech himself in 1879.

143. Josef Galík et al., *Panorama české literatury* (Olomouc: Rubico, 1994), 138.

144. In the 1991 film documentary *Why Havel?*, shown on CBC TV in Canada.

145. Jiří Suchý, *Jen pro pány: pojednání o zadních partiích žen, slečen, dívek a holek* (Prague: Klokočí, 1994), 11–12.

146. These are fulsomely reproduced and discussed in František Žákavec, *Dílo Jo-sefa Mánesa*, vol. 2, *Lid československý* (Prague: Jan Štenc, 1923). See also Jaromír Pečírka's handsome volume *Josef Mánes: živý pramen národní tradice* (Prague: SVU Mánes/Melantrich, 1939).

147. See Jan Loriš, *Mánesův orloj* (Prague: Orbis, 1952); and on the broader history of the clock, Zdeněk Horský, *Pražský orloj* (Prague: Panorama, 1988). Compare the much-romanticized account, which places such nineteenth-century additions to the *orloj* as the crowing cock back in the Middle Ages, in Alois Jirásek's *Staré pověsti české* (Prague: Papyrus, 1992), 162–67.

148. See Aleš, *Nástěnné malby*, 116–119, and plates 320–41.

149. *Katalog Sixty-Eight Publishers* (Prague: Společnost Josefa Škvoreckého, 1991), 28.

150. Some of Němcová's correspondence, along with contemporaries' reactions to her multiple unconventionalities, is translated into English in Iggers, *Women of Prague*, 49–89.

151. See Slavomír Ravik, *Karel Sabina (portrét konfidenta)* (Prague: Pražská imag-inace, 1992).

152. Calculated from Konečná, *Soupis repertoáru Národního divadla v Praze*.

153. Alexandr Buchner, *Opera v Praze* (Prague: Panton, 1985), 148.

154. For a detailed account of the event see Hilmera, *Stavovské národu!*, 32–38.

155. See, for example, Michael Kennedy, "The Operas of Janáček," in Alan Blyth, ed., *Opera on Record*, vol. 2 (London: Hutchinson, 1983), 326–44.

156. "The Language of Our Actors and the Stage," in Mirka Zemanová, ed. and trans., *Janáček's Uncollected Essays on Music* (New York: Marion Boyars, 1989), 37.

157. "Moravany! Morawaan!" in Zemanová, *Janáček's Uncollected Essays on Music*, 40, 42.

158. Marie Červinková-Riegrová, libretto to Antonín Dvořák's *Jakobín*, with record album set Supraphon 1112 2481/3 (1980), 15, 35.

159. Jaromír Paclt, "Jedna perla za druhou," in Jan Dehner, ed., *Antonín Dvořák: Jakobín* (Prague: Národní divadlo, 1993), 39 (theater program).

160. Information on this exhibition is mainly drawn from two sources: Klusáček, *Národopisná výstava českoslovanská*; and Josef Kafka, ed., *Národopisná výstava čes-koslovanská v Praze 1895: hlavní katalog a průvodce* (Prague, 1895).

161. Kafka, *Národopisná výstava českoslovanská . . . hlavní katalog*, 137.

162. Klusáček, *Národopisná výstava českoslovanská*, Doklady a poznámky, VI.

163. See here the sharp analysis of the preparations for the exhibition and the negotiations over what counted as ethnographic realities that they entailed in Andrew Lass, "What Keeps the Czech Folk 'Alive'?" *Dialectical Anthropology*, vol. 14, no. 1 (1989), 13–16.

164. The *jízda králů* is a key motif in Milan Kundera's novel *The Joke* (London: Penguin, 1984); and he provides a detailed account of its symbolism in Part 7 of the book.

165. Its catalogue is extraordinarily informative. Starting with a thumbnail sketch of the "Czechoslovak nation" (an interesting construct given the date, 1910), it goes on to provide a detailed history and bibliography of ethnographic studies in the Czech lands, broken down according to the various divisions of the museum. August Žalud, ed., *Národopisné museum v Praze: průvodce sbírkami*, 3d ed. (Prague: Společnost Národopisného musea českoslovanského, 1913). See also the German version: *Čechoslavisches ethnographisches Museum in Prag: Führer durch die Sammlungen* (Prague: Verlag der Gesellschaft des Čechoslavischen ethnographischen Museums in Prag, 1915).

166. Klusáček, *Národopisná výstava českoslovanská*, 540–43.

167. F. Palacký, "Psaní do Frankfurtu," in his *Úvahy a projevy*, 158–59.

168. Ibid., 161.

169. *Sic*. Today this would be written *Dějiny národa českého v Čechách a na Moravě*, underlining what was said earlier about the fluidity of Czech in the earlier nineteenth century and the effects of standardizing written languages.

170. F. Palacký, *Dějiny národu českého v Čechách a v Moravě*, 6 vols. (Prague: Kvasnička a Hampl, 1939), vol. 1, vii.

171. Jaroslav Goll, "František Palacký" (1898), in his *Vybrané spisy drobné*, vol. 1 (Prague: Historický Klub, 1928), 104.

172. Friedrich Engels, "Democratic Pan-Slavism," in K. Marx and F. Engels, *Collected Works*, vol. 8 (New York: International Publishers, 1977), 362–78.

173. See Vladimír Macura, *Šťastný věk: symboly, emblémy a mýty 1948–1989* (Prague: Pražská imaginace, 1992), 58–63, on these contortions.

174. Palacký, "Idea státu rakouského" (1865), in his *Úvahy a projevy*, 387. The context of this remark is a defense of the idea of a federative, rather than a centralized or dualistic, Austrian state, and a warning of the disintegrative consequences of the monarchy's ignoring of Slav national aspirations.

175. Petr Pithart, "Neklidný život pražských pomníků a soch," in his *Dějiny a politika: eseje a úvahy z let 1977–1989* (Prague: Prostor, 1990), 261. Pithart was a prominent dissident who became prime minister of the Czech Republic (within the then Czechoslovak federation) after 1989; he is also a refreshingly revisionist historian. Currently (1997) he is speaker of the Czech senate.

176. Wácslaw Wladiwoj Tomek, *Dějepis města Prahy*, 12 vols. (Prague: Řivnáč, 1879–1905).

177. Václav Vladivoj Tomek, *Jan Žižka*, photoreprint of Otto edition of 1879 (Prague: V ráji, 1993).

178. Revised and enlarged as *Popsání hlavního města království českého* (Prague: I. L. Kober, 1868).

179. Karel Vladislav Zap, "Předslovo" to *Česko-Moravská kronika* (Prague: I. L. Kober, 1862).

180. F. X. Šalda, "Alois Jirásek: čili mythus a skutečnost," in *Šaldův zápisník*, vol. 2 (1929–1930), 248.

181. These were *Mezi proudy* (*Between the Currents*), consisting of *Dvojí dvůr, Syn*

ohnivcův, and *Do tří hlasů* (1891); *Proti všem* (*Against All*), consisting of *Skonání věků*, *Kruciata*, and *Boží zástup* (1894); and *Bratrstvo* (*Brotherhood*), consisting of *Bitva u Lučence* (1900), *Mária* (1905), and *Žebráci* (1909).

182. Eduard Maur, *Kozina a Lomikar*, Slovo k historii 20 (Prague: Melantrich, 1989), 35. Domažlice had symbolic significance for nationalists not only as the site of the historically attested battles of 1040 and 1431 but also as the legendary location of Sámo's seat Vogastisburk and the utterly mythical Záboj's victory too. On Záboj and the *RKZ* manuscript forgeries, see below, pp. 143–47.

183. Jirásek exaggerates the degree of freedom of the Chodové by the time of Bílá hora, and thus the extent to which "Germans" were responsible for the degradation of their condition. See Maur, *Kozina a Lomikar*, 1–8.

184. Alois Jirásek, *Psohlavci* (Prague: Československý spisovatel, 1980), 18–20.

185. Alois Jirásek, *Z mých pamětí* (Prague: Mladá fronta, 1980), 380–81.

186. Letter to Antonia Bohuslava Čelakovská, 14 February 1846, in Němcová, *Z dopisů Boženy Němcové*, 26–28. This is also partially (and differently) translated in Iggers, *Women of Prague*, 53–54.

187. This information is taken from František Páta, "Bibliografie Jiráskova díla," in Miloslav Hýsek and Karel B. Mádl, eds., *Alois Jirásek: sborník studií a vzpomínek na počest jeho sedmdesátých narozenin* (Prague: Otto, 1921), 477–505.

188. The painting is described thus in Prokop Toman, *Nový slovník československých výtvarných umělců*, 104.

189. Václav Vojtíšek, *The Old Town Hall of Prague* (Prague: Corporation of Prague, 1936), 23.

190. These figures from *Ottův slovník naučný*, vol. 27 (1908), 877–84.

191. For Žižkov street names see Čarek, *Ulicemi města Prahy*. For discussion and illustrations of decorations on Žižkov buildings see Jiří Všetečka and Petr Klučina, *Praha husitská* (Prague: Naše vojsko, 1986).

192. See the essays "O Husovi a husitství," "Jan Žižka z Kalicha," and "Smysl českých dějin," in his *O smyslu českých dějin* (Prague: Rozmluvy, 1990).

193. Laclotte, *Alfons Mucha 1860–1939*, 105.

194. Josef Pekař, "Bílá hora," in his *O smyslu českých dějin*, 206.

195. Jirásek, *Staré pověsti české*, 186–87. A recent English translation of this book is Alois Jirásek, *Old Czech Legends*, trans. Marie K. Holeček (London and Boston: UNESCO/Forest Books, 1992).

196. This is reproduced in Aleš, *Nástěnné malby*, plates 367–71.

197. Palacký at first intended to cover the whole of Czech history and later hoped to go as far as Bílá hora (1620). See Jaroslav Goll, "Palacký," 95.

198. Mucha's stamps are reproduced in Alois Dušek et al., *Příručka pro sběratele československých známek a celin* (Prague: Svaz československých filatelistů, 1988), 27, 62. Unless otherwise stated, all information on Czech postage stamps in this book is taken from this source, which details all Czechoslovak postage stamps from 1918 to 1985, the wartime period of German occupation excepted.

199. See Emanuel Poche and Zdeněk Wirth, *Zmizelá Praha*, vol. 4 (Prague: Poláček, 1947), 22–23, and photographs 6–8.

200. See Hana Volavková, *Zmizelá Praha*, vol. 3 (Prague: Poláček, 1947), and Jiří Hrůza et al., *Pražská asanace*.

201. Quoted in Emanuel Svoboda, "Doslov o historii cyklů," in Jaromír Neumann, *Mikoláš Aleš: cykly* (Prague: Státní nakladatelství krásné literatury, hudby a umění, 1957), 360.

202. Alois Kubišek, *Betlémská kaple* (Prague: Státní nakladatelství krásné literatury, hudby a umění, 1960), 8; his source is the police report in the Ministry of the Interior archive.

203. Masaryk, *Česká otázka*, especially ch. 5; *Jan Hus: naše obrození a naše reformace* (Prague: JK, 1990).

204. Quoted in Emanuel Poche et al., *Praha našeho věku* (Prague: Panorama, 1978), 191.

205. Josef Pekař, "In memoriam," in *Pamětní list . . . k slavnosti položení základního kamene k Husovu pomníku* (Prague: Spolek pro zbudování "Husova pomníku," 1903), 7. This brochure begins with a poem to Hus by Svatopluk Čech.

206. See the account and photographs in *Zlatá Praha*, vol. 32, no. 40 (1915). It has been heavily censored (476–77, for instance, are entirely blank). The previous issue of the magazine was also given over almost entirely to coverage of the Hus quincentennial.

207. For their own justifications of this action, see Josef Žemla's pamphlet *Historie sloupu Mariánského na Staroměstském náměstí*, Knihovna 28. října, no. 3 (Prague: V. Rytíř, dated "16. dne republiky [12. listopadu 1918].")

208. The 1921 Czechoslovak census gives 10,384,833 Roman Catholics (76.2 percent) and 535,450 Greek-Catholic, as against 990,300 for all evangelical denominations combined (7.2 percent). Almost half the latter were in Slovakia. In the historic Czech lands only 3.7 percent of the population belonged to evangelical confessions. *Ottův slovník naučný nové doby*, vol. I/2 (1930), 1083.

209. Petr Pithart, "Neklidný život pražských pomníků a soch," 263.

210. The 1921 census gives 525,333 members of the Czechoslovak Church (10 percent of the Czech population in Bohemia, 3.5 percent in Moravia and Silesia) as against 10,384,833 Roman Catholics. *Ottův slovník naučný nové doby*, vol. I/2 (1930), 1083.

211. Jirásek, *Staré pověsti české*, 41. Compare the prophecies as rendered by the medieval chroniclers Kosmas (*Kosmova kronika česká*, 23–24) and "Dalimil" in *Kronika tak řečeného Dalimila* (Prague: Svoboda, 1977), 26.

212. Jirásek, *Staré pověsti české*, 39. Cf. Kosmas, *Kosmova kronika česká*, 20–21.

213. This is reproduced in Tomáš Vlček, *Praha 1900: studie k dějinám kultury a umění Prahy v letech 1890–1914* (Prague: Panorama, 1986), p. 39.

214. Bedřich Smetana, quoted in Ladislav Šíp, *Česká opera a její tvůrci* (Prague: Supraphon, 1983), 40.

215. Müller and Tallowitz, *Památník vydaný na oslavu dvacetiletého trvání tělocvičné jednoty Sokola pražského*, 201.

216. For a detailed contemporary account of these ceremonies, see "Slavnostní položení základního kamene k budově Národního divadla," in Servác Heller, *Jubileum velké doby: obraz našeho národního rozmachu před padesáti lety* (Prague: Pražská akciová tiskárna, 1918), 7–67. Heller draws here mainly on his own earlier description of events, which was first published in 1868.

217. Personal observation.

218. See Alois Jirásek, speech of 16 May 1918, in *Za právo a stát*, 298–300.

219. On this work see Mirko Očadlík, *Smetanova Má vlast* (Prague: Orbis, 1953).

220. Kosmas, *Kosmova kronika česká*, 25.

221. Ibid., pp. 14 onward.

222. Váceslav Hanka, *Polyglotta kralodvorského rukopisu* (Prague: F. Řivnáč, 1876), v–x; see also J. Karlík and V. Seykora, eds., *Rukopis královédvorský a Rukopis zeleno-horský* (Prague: Rukopisný fond vědecký, 1936), 22–28. For a more recent assessment of the *RKZ* controversies, together with facsimiles of the mss. and a copious bibliography, see Mojmír Otruba, ed., *Rukopisy Královédvorský a Zelenohorský: dnešní stav poznání* (Prague: Národní muzeum/Academia, 1969) (*Sborník Národního muzea*, Řada C, vol. 13, nos. 1–5). Andrew Lass perceptively relates the whole *RKZ* episode to the preceding eighteenth-century Enlightenment context, with its stress on scientific objectivity and physical evidence, in his "Presencing, Historicity and the Shifting Voice of Written Relics in Eighteenth-Century Bohemia."

223. Hanka, *Polyglotta kralodvorského rukopisu*, v, ix.

224. [Riegrův] *Slovník naučný*, vol. 3 (Prague: I. L. Kober, 1863), 630.

225. See Ravik, *Karel Havlíček Borovský*, 149–50.

226. See Jan Otto, "Některé poznámky o vzniku 'Ottova slovníku naučného,'" unpaginated afterword in *Ottův slovník naučný*, vol. 27 (1908), and Masaryk's own testimony in Karel Čapek, *Hovory s T. G. Masarykem* (*Spisy*, vol. 20), (Prague: Československý spisovatel, 1990), 106.

227. Eliška Krásnohorská, "Slovo našim čtenářkám o Rukopisech královédvorském a zelenohorském," *Ženské listy* (1886), 94–96, reprinted in Drahomíra Vlašínová, *Eliška Krásnohorská* (Prague: Melantrich, 1987), 187–89.

228. See Karel Čapek, *Hovory s T. G. Masarykem*, 107–8, 143–44. Masaryk links together his various struggles: "When the manuscript wars broke out, it was the Catholic daily *The Czech* that came out most sharply against me; and during the Hilsner affair it was again the clerical press that played the lead role. Sure, they could not forgive me because I take up the Czech Reformation and in place of falsified old Slav culture stressed the domestic Czech culture. I take up our Reformation, which was above all a moral and religious movement, not a theological one. Hus, and before him Štítný, stood for a reform of morals" (143–44).

229. Masaryk, *Česká otázka*, 186.

230. See note 192.

231. Karel Havlíček Borovský, "Slovan a Čech," 337–38.

232. On the "Hilsneriáda," as it became known, see Jiří Kovtun, *Tajuplná vražda: případ Leopolda Hilsnera* (Prague: Sefer, 1994).

233. See T. G. Masaryk, *Karel Havlíček*, 3d ed. (Prague: Jan Laichter, 1920), 445–51.

234. Čapek, *Hovory s T. G. Masarykem*, 22. For fuller discussion see Michael A. Riff, "The Ambiguity of Masaryk's Attitudes on the 'Jewish Question,'" and Steven Buller, "The Hilsner Affair: Nationalism, Anti-Semitism and the Individual in the Habsburg Monarchy at the Turn of the Century," both in Robert B. Pynsent, ed., *T. G. Masaryk (1850–1937)*, vol. 2 (London: Macmillan, 1989).

235. Josef Mánes's illustrations can be found in Karlík and Seykora, *Rukopis královédvorský a zelenohorský*, or Antonín Matějček, *Dílo Josefa Mánesa*, vol. 3, *Rukopis královédvorský* (Prague: Jan Štenc, 1927); Aleš's in his *Ilustrace české poezie a prózy* (*Dílo*, vol. 11), ed. Hana Volavková (Prague: Státní nakladatelství krásné literatury a

umění, 1964). For other examples of the impact of the *rukopisy* on the Czech artistic landscape, see Miroslav Míčko, *Výtvarné dědictví rukopisů* (Prague: Vyšehrad, 1940).

236. See Hanka, *Polyglotta*, ix.

237. Heller, *Jubileum velké doby*, 45.

238. Palacký, *Dějiny národu českého*, vol. 1, 448–51.

239. Quoted in Dvořáková, *Miroslav Tyrš*, 29.

240. *Ottův slovník naučný*, vol. 10 (1896), 847.

241. Quoted in Volavková, *Mikoláš Aleš: ilustrace české poezie a prózy*, 224.

242. Quoted in ibid., 224.

243. See Jana Brabcová, *Luděk Marold* (Prague: Odeon, 1988), 66–74.

244. Among them were *Zlatá Praha, Světozor, Dvacátý věk, Máj*, and *Věstník zahraniční domoviny*.

245. Svatopluk Čech, *Adamité* (Prague: Šimáček, 1897).

246. See Laclotte, *Alfons Mucha 1860–1939*, 27–28, and plate.

247. Poggio-Bracciolini, *Mistr Jan Hus na Koncilu kostnickém, Jeho výslech, odsouzení a upálení dne 6. července 1415* (Prague: Otto, 1902).

248. All of these are reproduced in Rennert and Weill, *Alphonse Mucha: The Complete Posters and Panels*.

249. This is asserted in ibid., 322. The ring may also be a Masonic symbol, as Bohumil Nuska suggests in "K symbolice na platidlech: Slované, zednáři a Mucha," *Umění a řemesla*, 4 (1992); the two are not of course exclusive. The Saint Vitus's Cathedral window is photographed in Marie Kostílková, *Katedrála Sv. Víta*, vol. 2 (Prague: Správa Pražského hradu, 1994), 61.

250. Reproduced in Hana Volavková, *Josef Mánes: malíř vzorků a ornamentu* (Prague: Odeon, 1981), 153. Volavková, like other Czech critics, accuses the famous Belgian Secession architect and artist Victor Horta of plagiarizing Josef Mánes's design.

251. *Drawings of Mucha* (New York: Dover Publications, 1978), v (Publisher's Note; no author is credited).

252. Jiří Mucha, *Alphonse Maria Mucha*, 103.

253. See Laclotte, *Alfons Mucha 1860–1939*.

254. Mucha's work for Obecní dům is amply illustrated in Sarah Mucha, ed., *Alphonse Mucha: Pastels, Posters, Drawings and Photographs. An Exhibition at the Imperial Stables, Prague Castle*, exhibition catalogue (London: Mucha Foundation, 1994); Arthur Ellridge, *Mucha: The Triumph of Art Nouveau* (Paris: Terrail, 1992); and Dalibor Kusák and Marta Kadlečíková, *Mucha* (Prague: BB/Art, 1992). See also the photographs in Slesin, *Mittel Europa*, 212–15.

255. Bohumil Nuska, "K symbolice na platidlech," 22.

256. The designs for the honorary degree certificates were published in *Zlatá Praha*, vol. 36, no. 37–38 (1919), 292–93; I have not seen them reproduced elsewhere. The 1928 postcard is reproduced in Ellridge, *Mucha*, 217.

257. The entire cycle is reproduced in both Kusák and Kadlečíková, *Mucha*, and Jiří Mucha, *Alphonse Maria Mucha*. For further information on the background to the individual pictures of the *Epopej*, see the guidebook to the standing exhibition of the paintings in the château in Moravský Krumlov: *Slovanská epopej—historie Slovanstva v obrazech—Alfons Mucha*, no author credited (Moravský Krumlov: Městské středisko v Moravském Krumlově, n.d.). This contains Alfons Mucha's own comments on the finished cycle in Prague in 1928. He says, among other things, that "I am convinced

that the development of every nation may proceed with success only if it grows organically and continuously from the nation's own roots and that for the preservation of this continuity knowledge of its historical past is indispensable. . . . This work, now completed, I considered as my duty." (2).

258. František J. Peřin, ed., *Národní zpěvník* (Prague: B. Stýblo, n.d.).

CHAPTER 5

1. The Czech is: "zhnuseni hejslovanstvím a kdedomováním procitli jsme." F. V. Krejčí et al., *Česká moderna*, in F. X. Šalda, *Kritické projevy—2, 1894–1895*, Soubor díla F. X. Šaldy 11 (Praha, Melantrich, 1950), 361–63.

2. Ibid.

3. Tomáš Masaryk, *Česká otázka*, 80.

4. Ibid., 124.

5. Ibid., 125.

6. Ibid., 96.

7. Ibid., 184, 180.

8. Ibid., 112–16.

9. Ibid., 115.

10. Ibid., 116.

11. Tomáš Masaryk, "Naše nynější krise," with *Česká otázka*, 217.

12. See below, p. 237.

13. Tomáš Masaryk, *Česká otázka*, 182.

14. For general surveys of this period in Czech artistic life see Petr Wittlich, *Umění a život—doba secese* (Prague: Artia, 1987); Petr Wittlich, *Česká secese* (Prague: Odeon, 1985); Petr Wittlich, *Prague: Fin de Siècle* (Paris: Flammarion, 1992); Bohumír Mráz and Marcela Mrázová, *Secese* (Prague: Obelisk, 1971); Tomáš Vlček, *Praha 1900: studie k dějinám kultury a umění Prahy v letech 1890–1914* (Prague: Panorama, 1986); Miroslav Lamač, *Osma a Skupina výtvarných umělců 1907–1917* (Prague: Odeon, 1988); Jiří Padrta, ed., *Osma a Skupina výtvarných umělců 1910–1917: teorie, kritika, polemika* (Prague: Odeon, 1992), which contains texts by the artists, and Lamač's essay on book and poster illustration in the period. Equally valuable are exhibition catalogues, notably: *Zakladatelé moderního českého umění*, text by Miroslav Lamač, Jiří Padrta, and Jan Tomeš (Brno: Dům umění, 1957); *Czech Modernism 1900–1945*, texts by Jaroslav Anděl and others (Houston: Museum of Fine Arts/Bullfinch Press, 1989); Švestka and Vlček, *Český kubismus*; *Český kubismus: architektura a design 1910–1925*, texts by Lamarová, Wittlich, Kroutvor, and others (Weil am Rhein: Vitra Design Museum, 1991); *Le Cubisme à Prague*, text by Claude Pétry and others (Paris: Jacques London, 1991); *Grafika české avantgardy 1907–1918*, text by Jana Wittlichová (Prague: Národní galerie, 1991); and *Expresionismus a české umění 1905–1927*, texts by Michal Bregant and others (Prague: Národní galerie, 1994).

15. Brod, "Jaro v Praze," first published in *Die Gegenwart* (1907), excerpted in Lamač, *Osma a Skupina*, 32.

16. Arnošt Procházka, "Poznámky výstavní a jiné," first published in *Moderní revue* (1908), excerpted in Lamač, *Osma a Skupina*, 34.

17. See *Katalog výstavy děl sochaře Augusta Rodina v Praze* (Prague: SVU Mánes, 1902); *Edvard Munch: XX. výstava spolku výtvarných umělců "Mánes" v Praze* (Prague:

SVU Mánes, 1905). On the impact of these exhibitions see, apart from references cited in note 14 to this chapter, *Pocta Rodinovi 1902–1992*, exhibition catalogue, text Marie Halířová (Prague: Národní galerie, 1992); and Emil Filla, "Eduard Munch a naše generace," in his *O výtvarném umění* (Prague: Karel Brož, 1948), 66–76.

18. *Francouzští impressionisté: katalog 23. výstavy SVU Mánes v Praze 1907*, text by F. X. Šalda (Prague: SVU Mánes, 1907); *Les Indépendants: XXXI. výstava SVU Mánes v Praze*, text by Antonín Matějček (Prague: SVU Mánes, 1910).

19. Emil Filla in conversation with V. Závada, originally published in *Rozpravy Aventina* (1932), excerpted in Lamač, *Osma a Skupina*, 36.

20. *Moderní umění, soubor sestaven A. Mercereauem v Paříži: 45. výstava SVU Mánes v Praze*, text by Alexander Mercereau (Prague: SVU Mánes, 1914).

21. S. K. Neumann, "Otevřená okna," originally published in *Lidové noviny* (1913), reprinted in Padrta, *Osma a Skupina*, 138–40.

22. Míka, *Dějiny Prahy v datech*, 234.

23. Jaroslav Hašek, *The Good Soldier Švejk*, trans. Cecil Parrott (London: Penguin, 1973), 215 (Epilogue to Part I, which is a defense of his use of spoken Czech and its customary vulgarities).

24. Ibid., 214–16.

25. Karel Čapek, "Josef Mánes," *Musaion* (Spring 1920), reprinted in his *Spisy*, vol. 18, *O umění a kultuře II* (Prague: Československý spisovatel, 1985), 158–59. He also points out that while Mánes was illustrating Hanka's *Rukopisy*, Manet was painting his "Déjeuner sur l'herbe."

26. Peroutka, *Jací jsme*, 122–23.

27. Letter of 1904, quoted in Jiří Mucha, *Alphonse Maria Mucha*, 197.

28. Letter of 2 December 1909, quoted in Jiří Mucha, *Alphonse Maria Mucha*, 239.

29. Quoted in ibid., 181–83.

30. Miroslav Buchvaldek et al., *Dějiny Československa v datech* (Prague: Svoboda, 1968), 464.

31. V. V. Š[tech], "Poštovní známky," *Umění*, vol. 1 (1918–21), 265. Dissatisfaction with Mucha's stamps was so universal that the Ministry of Posts and Telegraphs organized a competition for new ones. One winner was Max Švabinský with his portrait of the president of the republic for the thousand-*heller* stamp. This note by Štech concludes: "It will represent us well abroad."

32. Respectively, from Mucha's memoirs and letter to his wife of 1909, as quoted in Jiří Mucha, *Alphonse Maria Mucha*, 237.

33. Jednota umělců výtvarných was founded in 1898 largely by professors in Prague art schools. From 1903 it published the magazine *Dílo* (*The Work*). It organized 167 exhibitions before it was dissolved by the communists, along with other Czech artists' societies, in 1952; the first, in 1899, was devoted to Luděk Marold. This latter information from *Soupis výstav Jednoty umělců výtvarných*, no author, no date, unpublished typescript in archives of Národní galerie, oddělení vědeckých informací, Prague. An earlier society had been founded under the same name in 1849 by Josef Mánes and others, but it broke up in 1856.

34. These are pictured in František Žákavec, *Max Švabinský*, vol. 1 (Prague: Jan Štenc, 1933), 240–41. On the building more generally, see Milan Kreuzzieger et al., *Obecní dům v Praze: historie a rekonstrukce* (Prague: Enigma, 1997).

35. See references to Czech cubism cited earlier in this chapter, note 14, especially

the two catalogues entitled *Český kubismus*. The best overall study of Prague modernist architecture in the first half of the century is Rostislav Švácha's richly illustrated *Od moderny k funkcionalismu: proměny pražské architektury první poloviny dvacátého století* (Prague: Victoria Publishing, 1995); see also the (bilingual) guidebook by Michal Bregant et al., *Kubistická Praha/Cubist Prague 1909–1925* (Prague: Středoevropské nakladatelství, 1995). Josef Pechar and Petr Urlich, eds., *Programy české architektury* (Prague: Odeon, 1981) reproduces texts by architects and critics from 1900 to 1956; among those represented are Jan Kotěra, Vlastislav Hofman, Pavel Janák, Josef Chochol, Vít Obrtel, and Karel Teige, as well as editorial statements of architectural magazines (e.g., *Styl*, *Stavba*, *Stavitel*) and programs of groups and organizations (among them Devětsil and the Levá fronta, both of which are discussed further below). A rare study of Czech cubist architecture and design in English is Ivan Margolius, *Cubism in Architecture and the Applied Arts: Bohemia and France 1910–1914* (Newton Abbot: David and Charles, 1979); see also his *Prague: A Guide to Twentieth-Century Architecture* (London: Ellipsis, 1996).

36. Jiří Mucha, *Alphonse Maria Mucha*, 267.

37. See the extracts from a range of reviews given in ibid., 277, and the review by František Žákavec in *Umění*, vol. 2, (1929–30), 242–44..

38. *Ottův slovník naučný nové doby*, vol. I/2 (1931), 1084. Figures from 1921 census.

39. *Český svět*, vol. 16, no. 33 (22 April 1920), unpaginated. The whole issue, which is written in both Czech and English, is devoted to coverage of this relief effort.

40. Figures from Bělina, *Dějiny zemí koruny české*, vol. 2, 180–81.

41. Buchvaldek, *Dějiny Československa v datech*, 466–67.

42. Míka, *Dějiny Prahy v datech*, 364.

43. *Almanach hlavního města Prahy*, vol. 19 (1924), 17–18.

44. Buchvaldek, *Dějiny Československa v datech*, 466–67.

45. Míka, *Dějiny Prahy v datech*, 364–65.

46. Klement Gottwald, speech in parliament, 21 December 1929, in his *Spisy*, vol. 1 (Prague: Svoboda, 1950), 322–23.

47. Figures from 1921 census, rounded to nearest 1,000. Of the 354,342 people declaring Judaism as their religion, in Bohemia 37,300 declared Czechoslovak nationality, in Moravia and Silesia 6,000, in Slovakia 29,200. Of the 181,000 declaring Jewish as their nationality, the overwhelming majority were in Podkarpatská Rus and Slovakia; in the Czech lands only 30,200 people (out of 125,000 declaring the Jewish faith) did so. *Ottův slovník naučný nové doby*, vol. I/2 (1931), 1082–83.

48. Bradley, *Czechoslovakia*, 148.

49. See here in particular the Washington Declaration [Washingtonská deklarace] of 18 October 1918, in Veselý, *Dějiny českého státu v dokumentech*, 311–13.

50. *Ottův slovník naučný*, vol. I/2 (1931), 1082–83.

51. Richard Weiner, *Třásničky dějinných dnů (1918–1919)* (Prague: Elfa, 1991), 16–17.

52. Quoted (without source) in Olivier Poivre d'Arvor, "Le Grand Jeu et Tchécoslovaquie," in Suzanne Pagé et al., *Šíma/Le Grand Jeu*, exhibition catalogue (Paris: Musée d'Art Moderne de la Ville de Paris, 1992), 273.

53. Karel Janů and Erik Kafka, "Odsun Němců z ČSR," in *Československo*, vol. 1, no. 4 (1946), 61.

54. On Aleš see V. V. Štech, *Aleš a Slovensko* (Bratislava: Tvar, 1952); on Mánes the works by Matějček and Pečírka cited above, or the catalogue for the centennial exhibition *Josef Mánes 1820–1871*, text by Jiří Kotalík (Prague: Národní galerie, 1971). "Slovenská rodina" (watercolor, before 1860) is reproduced in Pečírka, *Josef Mánes*, plate 163; for other Slovak motifs in Mánes's work see plates 136, 137.

55. See Božena Němcová, *Národopisné a cestopisné obrazy ze Slovenska* (Prague: Státní nakladatelství krásné literatury, hudby a umění, 1955); Klusáček, *Národopisná výstava českoslovanská*, 184–89. Though the exhibits themselves are mostly drawn from the border region of Moravian Slovakia (referred to as Moravské Slovensko in this catalogue, but more often called Moravské Slovácko), both the influence (*vliv*) of and kinship (*příbuzenství*) with the costumes of what is here referred to as Hungarian Slovakia (Uherské Slovensko) are emphasized (184). Slovak *kroje* from Nitra, Pressburg, and elsewhere were exhibited at the Ethnographic Museum (Národopisné muzeum), which was established as a follow-up to the exhibition; see Žalud, *Národopisné museum v Praze: průvodce sbírkami*, 90–91.

56. The Czech is: "z nejznamenitějších mužův a spisovatelů českých." *Ottův slovník naučný*, vol. 24 (1906), 528; emphasis added.

57. Palacký, *Dějiny národu českého*, vol. 1, xi.

58. "Washingtonská deklarace," in Veselý, *Dějiny českého státu v dokumentech*, 311–13. This "Proclamation of Independence of the Czechoslovak Nation by Its Provisional Government" is reckoned among the foundational documents of the modern Czechoslovak state. It is not to be confused with the internal (and decisive) proclamation of independence by the Národní výbor (National Committee) in Prague ten days later, signed by František Soukup, Antonín Švehla, Alois Rašín, Vavro Šrobár, and Jiří Stříbrný—the so-called Men of 28 October; "Provolání národního výboru," in ibid., 319.

59. Pekař, *Dějiny československé*, 19.

60. *Ottův slovník naučný nové doby*, vol. I/2 (1931), 1083. By 1933 there were, as Ivan Olbracht puts it in his *Země bez jména* (Land Without a Name), "35,000 Czechs, linked with their land only by telephone and a twelve-hour express train journey"; quoted in F. X. Šalda, "Česká kolonisace na Podkarpatské Rusi," *Šaldův zápisník*, vol. 4 (1931–32), 319.

61. Figures from 1921 census. The first is given in Buchvaldek, *Dějiny Československa v datech*, 482, the rest in *Ottův slovník naučný nové doby*, vol. I/2 (1931), 1084.

62. Figures from 1921 census. *Ottův slovník naučný nové doby*, vol. I/2 (1931), 1084.

63. Buchvaldek, *Dějiny Československa v datech*, 481.

64. These figures are taken from the "Seznam míst v ČSR, čítajících přes 10.000 obyvatel," based on 1930 census returns, which is included as an unpaginated fold out between pages 1080 and 1081 of *Ottův slovník naučný nové doby*, vol. I/2 (1931). They are for the relevant conurbations [*aglomerace*] rather than the individual cities alone.

65. *Ottův slovník naučný*, vol. I/2 (1931), 714.

66. Figure from 1890 census, calculated on borders of Prague as established in 1922. Šiška, "Populační a bytové poměry," in Vojtíšek, *Praha v obnoveném státě československém*, 72.

67. Figure from 1890 census. *Ottův slovník naučný*, vol. 20 (1903), 653.

68. Legend to "Národopisná mapa uherských Slováků," in *Ottův slovník naučný*, vol. 23 (1905), between pp. 456 and 457.

69. Quoted in Buchvaldek, *Dějiny Československa v datech*, 272.

70. Quoted in *Ottův slovník naučný*, vol. 23 (1905), 418.

71. These figures for schools and population relate to the sixteen administrative districts of Hungary in which Slovaks formed the majority (9) or a substantial minority (7) of the population. There were a further 163,937 Slovaks living elsewhere in Hungary at the time. Population figures are calculated from the 1900 census; those for schools are for 1899. *Ottův slovník naučný*, vol. 23 (1905), 406, 415–17, respectively.

72. *Ottův slovník naučný nové doby*, vol. I/2 (1931), 1239.

73. Vavro Šrobár, speech in Czechoslovak parliament, 18 October 1919, in *Národní shromáždění československé v prvním roce republiky* (Prague: Předsednictvo Národního shromáždění, 1919), 198.

74. See *Ottův slovník naučný nové doby*, vol. I/2 (1931), 1239. Šrobár was already making this claim in his 1919 speech, cited in note 73, 199.

75. *Ottův slovník naučný nové doby*, vol. I/2 (1931), 1239.

76. *Ročenka československých profesorů*, vol. 10 (Prague: Ústřední spolek československých profesorů, 1931), 219.

77. *Ročenka Československé republiky*, vol. 9 (Prague, 1930), 325.

78. *Ročenka československých profesorů*, vol. 1 (1921–22), 207, 217.

79. Ibid., 208–17.

80. Unnamed enumerator's report, in Peroutka, *Budování státu*, vol. 1, 135. Peroutka's chapter "Stav Slovenska" (130–37) is an excellent brief discussion of the problems posed to the Czechoslovak state by Slovakia in 1918.

81. On this see Eva Broklová, ed., *První československá ústava: diskuse v ústavním výboru v lednu a únoru 1920* (Prague: Ústav pro soudobé dějiny České akademie věd, 1992). This reproduces not only the language law itself (216–18) but also the stenographed notes of the arguments that went on in the committee that drew up the Czechoslovak constitution, of which the law formed a part. See especially pp. 72–80. One representative (Ivan Dérer) begins by expressing the view of his party, the Slovak Club, that "the Czechoslovak language doesn't actually exist, but that there exist the Czech language and the Slovak language, and this [measure] does not express what [the party] want, namely, that the Slovak language would have equal rights with the Czech language." Antonín Švehla's reply is a gem. It reads, in part: "When a Czechoslovak nationality was created and when the word Czechoslovak was used, everybody soon got their bearings on what it was. If we created it for the nation and the state, it is quite possible for the language too" (Meeting of 15 January 1920, quoted p. 72).

82. This was signed by Masaryk with representatives of Slovak exile organizations in the United States, and confirmed by him as president of the Czechoslovak Republic on 14 November 1918. It also guaranteed that "Slovak will be the official language in schools, offices, and public life in general" in Slovakia. The text is given in Edvard Beneš, *Světová válka a naše revoluce*, vol. 3 (Prague: Orbis/ČIN, 1931), 365–66.

83. See Šrobár's speech of 18 October 1919, note 73.

84. Census figures, given in Buchvaldek, *Dějiny Československa v datech*, 484. In

1921 only 15,600 Slovaks were living in the Czech lands: *Ottův slovník naučný nové doby*, vol. I/2 (1931), 1082.

85. The 1929 figure is from *Ročenka Československé republiky*, vol. 9 (1930), 323; Hlinka's party took 358,883 votes. According to Buchvaldek (*Dějiny Československa v datech*, 466–67), this represented 5.7 percent of all votes cast in the republic as a whole. The same source gives the proportion gained by Hlinka's party in the 1935 election as 6.9 percent, i.e., over a third of Slovak votes.

86. "Koloniální systém a režim na Podkarpatské Rusi v ČSR, v jubilejním roce osvobození," *ReD*, vol. 2, no. 1 (1928), 46. Compare Šalda, "Česká kolonisace na Podkarpatské Rusi." See also, from the left, Stanislav K. Neumann, *Československá cesta II.–III.: karpatské léto, český podzim* (Prague: Borový, 1935), part 2.

87. *Ročenka Československé republiky*, vol. 9 (Prague, 1930), 322–23.

88. See, for example, the account of Masaryk's tour of Moravia and Silesia in 1924, as reported daily in *Lidové noviny*: Rudolf Těsnohlídek, ed., *President mezi svými: druhý zájezd na Moravu a návštěva Slezska v roce 1924* (Prague: Borový, 1924). Notice the *lidovost* of Edvard Milén's line drawings, as well as the photographs. Těsnohlídek was the author of the illustrated newspaper serial that inspired Leoš Janáček's opera *The Cunning Little Vixen* [*Příhody lišky Bystroušky*, 1923]. This is available in English: Rudolf Těsnohlídek, *The Cunning Little Vixen* (New York: Farrar, Straus and Giroux, 1985).

89. By Ministry of Education order 82757/20, 1921. *Ročenka československých profesorů*, vol. 1 (1921–22), 83.

90. "Marešův universitní zákon," in Karel Domin, Václav Vojtíšek, and Josef Hutter, *Karolinum statek národní*, 2d ed. (Prague: L. Mazáč, 1935), 13–15. The struggle over the inheritance of the ancient university went on into the 1930s; see Domin's essay, which opens this volume. See also Václav Vojtíšek, *Karlova universita vždy jen naše* (Brno: A. Píša, 1946).

91. These figures, for 1 January 1914, 31 December 1920, and 31 December 1937, respectively, from *Ottův slovník naučný nové doby*, vol. VI/1 (Prague: Novina, 1940), entry "Sokolstvo."

92. See *Umění*, vol. 1 (1918–21), 465. Otakar Španiel (1881–1955) was one winner of the competition organized by the Ministry of Finance in March 1920, along with the sculptor Jan Štursa and others; his designs for one-*sokol* and five-*sokol* coins are reproduced, together with commemorative medals of Jirásek, Aleš, and Josef Mánes which he did for SVU Mánes members, on the plate facing p. 470. Španiel, a pupil of Josef Myslbek's, was professor at Prague's Academy of Fine Arts from 1919 until his death, and the school's rector from 1946 to 1948. Among the coins he designed after 1945 were a silver fifty-crown piece celebrating Stalin's seventieth birthday (1949) and a silver hundred-crown piece marking the thirtieth anniversary of the founding of the Communist party of Czechoslovakia (1951). See Věra Němečková, *Československé pamětní mince a medaile 1948–1983*, exhibition catalogue (Cheb: Chebské muzeum, 1983).

93. An alliance of Czechoslovakia, Yugoslavia, and Romania, formalized by the Belgrade Treaty of May 1929.

94. Figures from *Ottův slovník naučný nové doby*, vol. VI/1 (1940), 99–100. All the interwar Sokol jamborees are commemorated in lavishly illustrated and for the most part richly informative volumes. See *Památník VII. sletu všesokolského v Praze 1920*, ed.

Jan Hiller (Prague: Československá obec sokolská, 1923)—note, inter alia, the letters of greeting from among others Alois Jirásek and Renata Tyršová (15, 16), and Max Švabinský's poster (plate X); *Památník IX. sletu všesokolského v Praze 1932*, ed. Rudolf Procházka (Prague: Československá obec sokolská, 1933)—among the exhibits here was Jan Štursa's sculpture "Genius," mounted on a column above a bust of Tyrš (plate XLVIII); and *Památník X. sletu všesokolského v Praze 1938*, ed. Rudolf Procházka (Prague: Československá obec sokolská, 1939). These last two jamborees were held in the Strahov stadium, built in 1926–32, which was at one time the largest such arena in the world, with a capacity of 200,000 spectators. Its dimensions can be appreciated from the pull-out panoramic photographs of massed gymnasts that are a prominent feature of these volumes. I have not been able to consult the official commemorative volume for the eighth (1932) jamboree. But see V. Šuman, *VIII. slet všesokolský v Praze 1926* (Prague: V. Neubert, n.d.), an album of souvenir photographs. One distinguished official visitor to this jamboree was the lord mayor of London.

95. This is reproduced in Ellridge, *Mucha*, 205.

96. Letter from Mucha to his sister Anděla, 12 December 1925, quoted in Jiří Mucha, *Alphonse Maria Mucha*, 275, where the whole episode is described.

97. Míka, *Dějiny Prahy v datech*, 359; Šiška, "Populační a bytové poměry," 72.

98. *Almanach hlavního města Prahy*, vol. 18 (1922), 5. This yearbook had been published annually from 1898 to 1914 by the city council under the title *Almanach královského hlavního města Prahy*; from 1922 to 1939 it appeared biennially. Publication ceased during the German occupation.

99. See Kovtun, *Případ Leopolda Hilsnera*.

100. Václav Vojtíšek, "Za ideou veliké Prahy," in Vojtíšek, *Praha v obnoveném státě*, 150.

101. Antonín Podlaha and Antonín Šorm, *Průvodce výstavou svatováclavskou* (Prague: Výbor svatováclavský, 1929), 9.

102. Ibid., 58.

103. Ibid., 8.

104. Josef Cibulka, "Obraz svatého Václava," *Umění*, vol. 3 (1929–30), 186. For contrasting assessments of the significance of the jubilee and the meanings of the image of Saint Václav see F. X. Šalda, "Slavnosti svatováclavské," in *Šaldův zápisník*, vol. 2 (1929–30), 85–88; and Eduard Bass, "Kníže nebo Svatý?" *Přítomnost*, vol. 6 (1929), 273–74.

105. Dušek, *Příručka pro sběratele československých známek a celin*, 77.

106. See Emanuel Poche, *Praha krok za krokem*, 2d ed. (Prague: Panorama, 1985), 86; Horáková, *České korunovační klenoty*.

107. At the time of writing this book.

108. Personal observation. The lines stretched all the way down the old castle steps, a distance of several hundred meters.

109. "České korunovační klenoty." Leaflet published for exhibition of crown jewels at Pražský hrad 29 January to 7 February 1993, text by M. Bravermanová (Prague: Odbor rozvoje Pražského hradu, 1993).

110. "Výstava korunovačních klenotů v jubilejním roce svatováclavském 1929." Leaflet, text by A. Podlaha (Prague: Státní tiskárna, 1929).

111. Attempts to set up such a society first began as early as 1844. Jungmann, Tomek, and Erben were all involved, together with several patriotic aristocrats and

priests, notably Canon Václav Michal Pešina. The society's proposed articles, however, were rejected by the city *gubernium* in 1846. The Jednota was definitively established on 22 May 1859, with Karel Vladislav Zap (see above, pp. 129–30) as one of its executive committee members. By 1863 the Jednota had 601 contributing members; it is, perhaps, worthy of note that the largest donations were given by abdicated Emperor Ferdinand V, Jan hrabě Kolovrat Krakovský, Ferdinand kníže Lobkovic, and Archbishop Bedřich kníže Schwarzenberg. See Kostílková, *Katedrála sv. Víta*, vol. 2, 15–17. This book contains a very detailed account of the whole "completion."

112. Cyril Merhout and Zdeněk Wirth, *Zmizelá Praha*, vol. 2, Malá strana a Hradčany (Prague: Václav Poláček, 1946), 104, 107; Poche, *Praha krok za krokem*, 81.

113. See Poche, *Praha krok za krokem*, 96; Mocker's original designs and artists' impressions of what the completed building would have looked like are reproduced in Kostílková, *Katedrála sv. Víta*, vol. 2, 40–43.

114. Aleš's original (1904) sketch for the mosaic is reproduced in his *Nástěnné malby*, plate 496; the spire has already been optimistically replaced by Mocker's projected neo-Gothic improvement, which, in the event, was never built. But as Aleš paints it, with the spire piercing the heavens, it would, indeed, have made a fine prospect, viewed by Libuše from Vyšehrad.

115. The latter device (a bear) was newly invented for the purpose. On the history and arguments surrounding the adoption of Czechoslovak flags and standards see Svoboda, *Československá státní a vojenská symbolika*, 31–47, and Milan Hlinomaz, "Vývoj československé státní symboliky v letech 1918–1990," *Sborník archivních prací*, vol. 42, no. 1 (1992), 81–140.

116. For details see the exhibition catalogue *Otevírání zakletého zámku: Josip Plečnik a pražský hrad/Opening the Enchanted Castle: Josip Plečnik at the Prague Castle*, text by Zdeněk Lukeš (Prague: Kancelář presidenta ČSFR/T91 magazine supplement, 1992). A larger exhibition followed in 1996. Linked with it was the publication of a hefty, scholarly, and very richly illustrated monograph: Luba Horáková and Magdalena Propperová, eds., *Josip Plečnik: architekt Pražského hradu* (Prague: Správa Pražského hradu, 1997). An English edition of this was simultaneously published under the title *Josip Plečnik: Architect of Prague Castle*. Plečnik (1872–1957), a Slovenian pupil of the great Viennese architect Otto Wagner and a close friend of the pioneer of Czech modernism, Jan Kotěra, was official Prague Castle architect from 1920 to 1936, when he was succeeded by Pavel Janák. See also Francois Burkhardt, Claude Eveno, and Boris Podrecca, eds., *Jože Plečnik Architect: 1872–1957* (Cambridge, Mass.: MIT Press, 1989).

117. See *Otevírání zakletého zámku*, where these are pictured, or (in greater detail) Horáková and Propperová, *Josip Plečnik*. Similar notes are struck in the "Foreword by Prague Castle," in Sarah Mucha, *Alphonse Mucha*, signed by Ivo Koukol, director of the Prague Castle Management Office.

118. *Ročenka československých profesorů*, vol. 1 (1921–22), 76–77.

119. Ibid., 76

120. Ibid., 236.

121. The words are: "Dějiny panství rakouského probírány buďtež se stanoviska osvobozených Čech." Ibid., 239. The rest of the quotations in this paragraph are taken from the same source, 236–39.

122. For a very detailed survey of the ceremonies, exhibitions, lectures, and pub-

lications accompanying the Mánes jubilee, see František Žákavec, "Mánesův rok," in *Umění*, vol. 1 (1918–21), 406–19. There was a suggestion, which was rejected, to exhume Mánes's remains ceremonially from Olšany and rebury them at Vyšehrad (406).

123. Max Švabinský et al., *Upomínka na oslavu Josefa Mánesa v roce 1920* (Prague: SVU Mánes, 1921).

124. *Umění*, vol. 3 (1929–30), 62–63.

125. Including the unfinished fragment *Viola*.

126. *Dějiny Národního divadla*, 6 vols. (Prague: Sbor pro zřízení druhého Národního divadla v Praze, 1933–36). Nejedlý was the author of vols. 3 and 6, on opera; the other authors were Jan Bartoš (vol. 1), Antonín Matějček (vol. 2), Otakar Fischer (vol. 4), and Václav Tille (vol. 5).

127. See, for example, František Žákavec's account of SVU Myslbek's commemorative exhibition "Výtvarná generace Národního divadla," in *Umění*, vol. 6 (1933), 54–58.

128. Information on the Smetana jubilee is taken mainly from Robert Smetana, ed., *Dějiny české hudební kultury*, Díl II: 1918–45 (Prague: Academia, 1981), 143–44.

129. *Kresby Bedřicha Smetany*, exhibition catalogue, text by Zdeněk Nejedlý (Prague: Umělecká beseda, 1925).

130. These are the authors' own categories as outlined in the report that accompanied their submission. "Průvodní zpráva k soutěžnímu návrhu na pomník Bedřicha Smetany v Praze," in Jiří Šetlík, ed., *Otto Gutfreund: zázemí tvorby* (Prague: Odeon, 1989), 249–51.

131. Josef Císařovský, *Oto Gutfreund* (Prague: Státní nakladatelství krásné literatury a umění, 1962), 84. The memorial is extensively described and Gutfreund's models for it pictured here. See also *Otto Gutfreund*, exhibition catalogue, texts by Jan Bauch et al. (Prague: Národní galerie, 1995).

132. Quoted in "Babička vulgaris II," *Nedělní Lidové noviny*, 23 July 1994, 5.

133. *Seznam děl Jubilejní výstavy Mikoláše Alše*, exhibition catalogue, 2 vols. (Prague: Sdružení výtvarných umělců Myslbek, 1932, 1933).

134. Ibid., vol. 1 (1932), 13–14.

135. "Starý Mistr," *Lidové noviny*, 22 January 1933, reprinted in Karel Čapek, *Spisy*, vol. 19, *O umění a kultuře III* (Prague: Československý spisovatel, 1986), 363–64. Bivoj was a legendary figure from the times of prehistoric Vyšehrad.

136. "Manifest českých spisovatelů," document 141 in Josef Harna et al., eds., *České a československé dějiny*, vol. 3, *Dokumenty a materiály* (Prague: Fortuna, 1992), 131–33.

137. The simile is from František Soukup's speech during Jirásek's funeral celebrations, in Dr. Kudrnáč, ed., *Jiráskův pohřeb a návrat do rodného Padolí* (Hronov: Družstvo pro postavení Jiráskova divadla v Hronově, 1930), 9.

138. "Národní přísaha představitelů českého kulturního a politického života," document 144 in Harna, *České a československé dějiny*, vol. 3, 135–36.

139. Soukup's speech, in Kudrnáč, *Jiráskův pohřeb*, 8.

140. See, for example, Arnošt Caha, ed., *Jirásek české mládeži* (Brno: Ústřední spolek učitelský na Moravě a ve Slezsku, 1921); no. 1 in a "Little Library of Selections from the Best Czech Writers for Youth."

141. *Ročenka československých profesorů*, vol. 1 (1921–22), 208–17.

142. Kudrnáč, *Jiráskův pohřeb*, provides a very detailed account of the ceremonies, based on contemporary press reports in *Lidové noviny*, *Národní politika*, and the local paper *Náchodské noviny*, which includes the texts of all the orations. It runs to seventy-nine pages, and is the main source for the description given here.

143. Quoted in Petr Mareš, "Ze století do století: 1930," in *Reflex*, 12 (1996), 59.

144. Kudrnáč, *Jiráskův pohřeb*, 14.

145. Ibid., 16.

146. Ibid., 20.

147. Ibid., 22.

148. Karel Čapek, "Kraj Jiráskův," in his *Spisy*, vol. 19, *O umění a kultuře III*, 200–201.

149. F. X. Šalda, "Slavnosti svatováclavské," in *Šaldův zápisník*, vol. 2 (1929–30), 85.

150. F. X. Šalda, "Alois Jirásek čili mythus a skutečnost," in *Šaldův zápisník*, vol. 2 (1929–30), 244.

151. Ibid., 249, 243.

152. Ibid., 252.

153. Ibid., 243–44. The last clause is difficult to render exactly in English; the Czech is: "nuže, tato mystika spotřeby státní diktuje své požadavky a skutečnost jest přebásňována a dobásňována do předepsaných rozměrů a profilů."

154. Ibid., 252.

155. Karel Čapek, "Alois Jirásek: pověsti a legendy ze staré Prahy," in his *Spisy*, vol. 19, *O umění a kultuře III*, 223–24.

156. Peroutka, *Jací jsme*, 120. See also his perceptive remarks on Mikoláš Aleš, in ibid., 49–51.

157. Josef Kroutvor, *Poselství ulice: z dějin plakátu a proměn doby* (Prague: Comet, 1991).

158. See his extremely informative memoirs: Václav M. Havel, *Mé vzpomínky* (Prague: Lidové noviny, 1993).

159. Baba houses are extensively discussed and photographed in Wojciech Lenikowski, ed., *East European Modernism: Architecture in Czechoslovakia, Poland and Hungary Between the Wars* (London: Thames and Hudson, 1996), 75–82. On Czech functionalism more generally see the exhibition catalogues *Český funkcionalismus 1920–1940: bytové zařízení*, text by Alena Adlerová (Prague: Uměleckoprůmyslové muzeum/ Brno: Moravská galerie, 1978); *Český funkcionalismus 1920–1940: užitá grafika*, text by Jan Rous (Prague: Uměleckoprůmyslové muzeum/Brno: Moravská galerie, 1978); and *Czech Functionalism 1918–1938*, introductory essay by Vladimír Šlapeta (London: Architectural Association, n.d. [after 1980]).

160. Tomáš Baťa, *Úvahy a projevy* (Prague: Institut Řízení, 1990).

161. František L. Gahura, "Budování Baťova Zlína," *Stavitel*, vol. 14 (1933–34), reproduced in Vladimír Šlapeta, ed., *Baťa: architektura a urbanismus*, exhibition catalogue (Zlín: Státní galerie, 1991), 7.

162. Apart from those mentioned in the text, the most important were Aleš in 1922 and 1926, Adolf Kosárka in 1924, a joint exhibition of Hyppolyt Soběslav Pinkas, Karel Purkyně, Viktor Barvitius, and Antonín Chittussi in 1925, Amálie Mánesová in 1934, and the 1938 exhibition "Czech Tradition in the Nineteenth Century." *Soupis výstav Spolku výtvarných umělců Mánes 1898–1950*, compiled Jitka Pušová, text

by Jiřina Mašínová (Prague: Národní galerie, oddělení vědeckých informací, n.d.). Unpublished typescript list, with index, marked "Count of exemplars: 100. For internal NG use."

163. *Výstava Poesie 1932*, exhibition catalogue, introduction by Kamil Novotný (Prague: SVU Mánes, 1932). See also Francoise Cailleová, "Výstava Poesie 1932," in Lenka Bydžovská and Karel Srp, eds., *Český surrealismus 1929–1953. Skupina surrealistů v ČSR: události, vztahy, inspirace*, exhibition catalogue (Prague: Galerie hlavního města Prahy/Argo, 1996), 48–53.

164. See *Soupis výstav Umělecké besedy 1863–1951*, unpublished typescript, no author credited (Prague: Národní galerie, oddělení vědeckých informací, n.d.). Štyrský and Toyen were exhibited in 1931, Šíma in 1932, Dufy in 1934, De Chirico in 1935.

165. *L'école de Paris: Francouzské moderní umění*, exhibition catalogue, ed. Josef Čapek (Praha, Umělecká beseda, 1931).

166. This is available in English as *R. U. R.*, ed. Harry Shefter, trans. P. Selver (New York: Washington Square Press, 1973).

167. Dr. Desiderius (Hugo Boettinger), *Výstava veselých kreseb*, exhibition catalogue, introduction by Jindřich Čadík (Prague: SČUG Hollar, 1937), plate 3.

168. This is a summary rather than a full translation, but all the ingredients are there. See Josef Čapek, *Povídání o pejskovi a kočičce, jak spolu hospodařili a ještě o všelijakých jiných věcech* (Prague: Albatros, 1992), 82–84. This has recently been translated into English by Lucy Doležalová under the title *All About Doggie and Pussycat, How They Kept House and All Sorts of Other Things As Well* (Prague: Albatros, 1996). This translation contains the chapter, which was routinely expurgated from communist editions and had not yet been restored to the Czech edition of 1992 cited here, on how Doggie and Pussycat celebrated 28 October, Independence Day. Doggie made the mistake of saying some nice things about Tomáš Masaryk. The most comprehensive single source on Josef Čapek, covering both his painting and his writing, is the excellent recently published monograph by Jaroslav Slavík and Jiří Opelík, *Josef Čapek* (Prague: Torst, 1996).

169. Otakar Štorch-Marien, *Sladko je žít* (Prague: Aventinum, 1992), 187.

170. The allusion is to Galileo's "Eppur si muove" [And yet it does move], the words that he allegedly muttered under his breath following his enforced recantation of the proposition that the earth moves around the sun in 1632. This translates into Czech as "A přece se točí." On the Tvrdošíjní see the exhibition catalogues *Tvrdošíjní*, text by Karel Srp (Prague: Galerie hlavního města Prahy, 1986), and *Tvrdošíjní a hosté: 2. část, užité umění, malba, kresba*, text by Karel Srp (Prague: Galerie hlavního města Prahy, 1987). On interwar Czech artistic modernisms in general see, apart from works cited elsewhere in this chapter, Anděl, *Czech Modernism 1900–1945*, and Jaroslav Anděl, ed., *Umění pro všechny smysly: meziválečná avantgarda v Československu*, exhibition catalogue (Valencia: Ivam Centre Julio González/Prague: Národní galerie, 1993).

171. As Štorch-Marien himself described it: *Sladko je žít*, 182.

172. This edition is famous. Karel B. Mádl, whom we have encountered before rhapsodizing over Mikoláš Aleš's birthplace, writes in the preface: "A young painter appeared who this time finished, auspiciously and beautifully beyond imagination, that which Kvido Mánes first began. Adolf Kašpar makes his debut here in *Babička* with all the freshness, flexibility, and felicity of his youthful talent. . . . Kašpar's illustrations and decoration for *Babička* are not run-of-the-mill pictures serving to break

and interrupt the typeset. The painter undertook in them a genuine artistic reconstruction of that world, people, and things, of that life in Staré bělidlo and on the Ratibořice estate in the twenties of the last century, with an art almost equaling that of the pen of Božena Němcová half a century ago. His drawings . . . build anew before our eyes a complete image of a remote and now forever extinct way of life, they are its visual evocation from buildings and woods, to the grandmother and her tribe, ending with the minutest toys of the children. And this effort bears no trace of dry labor and sober scholarship. It too is suffused with the same sincere, simple-hearted, and sweet tenor with which Božena Němcová endowed her every single line. Into this lovely work of Adolf Kašpar's the art of Božena Němcová was indeed movingly transported. Kašpar's work is a graphic reflection of it, as a good illustrative part of a literary-artistic work should be." Mádl concludes: "Though we know it, we repeat to ourselves ceaselessly, that book awakened us to new life. At the beginning of the last century there was the word and that word was made flesh. What we are now and what we will become in the future came about because of our books. Our gratitude toward the Czech book can never be immoderate, even if it were to reach the sky. And *Babička* is a Czech book in the very essence of the word. The form which we give it here wishes to be and is a homage of the present times, it is a grateful offering to the vassals of Božena Němcová." Božena Němcová, *Babička* (Prague: Unie, 1913; reprint of fiftieth jubilee edition of 1903; Mádl's preface is dated December 1902), 3.

173. Čapek's book covers are fully listed, and many of them are reproduced, in Vladimír Thiele, ed., *Josef Čapek a kniha: soupis knižní grafiky* (Prague: Nakladatelství československých výtvarných umělců, 1958).

174. For Josef Čapek's highly individual style see ibid. Czech photomontage is well exemplified in Karel Šourek's cover for E. F. Burian's *Jazz* (1928), František Muzika's for V. Raffel's *Tělové povídky* (1928), or Karel Teige's for Vladimír Lidin's *Mořský průvan* (1925); constructivism by Muzika's cover for Konstantin Biebl's *Nový Ikaros* (1929). All of these are illustrated in the superb exhibition catalogue *Aventinská mansarda: Otakar Štorch-Marien a výtvarné umění*, ed. Karel Srp (Prague: Galerie hlavního města Prahy, 1990).

175. The word *kmen* has a range of meanings not conveyable by any one English word, including (a) trunk of a tree, (b) stock (e.g., of Slavonic stock) or family, in the sense of family of nations, family of languages, (c) genus, (d) the basis, heart, or essence of something and (e) the root of a word.

176. Kmen Proclamation of 6 April 1926, in Srp, *Aventinská mansarda*, 7. Information on Aventinum is mainly taken from this source, Štorch-Marien, *Sladko je žít*, and Bohatcová, *Česká kniha*; on Kmen from *Almanach kmene*, annual volumes and spring almanacs from 1930 to 1938.

177. *Almanach kmene*, vol. 1 (1930–31), ed. F. X. Šalda, books listed on pp. 255–70.

178. This was on the cover of vol. 4, no. 7, May 1920, in which Jiří Wolker's poem "*Svatý Kopeček*" (discussed below, pp. 309–10) was first published. It is reproduced as a plate facing p. 160 in Jaromír Lang, *Neumannův Červen* (Prague: Orbis, 1957), which gives a detailed history of the magazine.

179. Pavel Eisner, *Milenky: německý básník a česká žena* (Prague: Concordia, 1992); *Chrám i tvrz: kniha o češtině* (Prague: Lidové noviny, 1992).

180. See Josef Škvorecký, "Franz Kafka, Jazz, and the *Anti-Semitic Reader*," and more generally Chapter 7 of the present book.

181. *Ottův slovník naučný nové doby*, vol. I/2 (1931), 1273.

182. *Československá vlastivěda*, vol. 7, *Písemnictví* (Prague: Sfinx, 1933). It is fair to add that Arne Novák's chapter on the history of Czech literature is almost three times as long as any of the others.

183. Jaroslava Vondráčková, *Kolem Mileny Jesenské* (Prague: Torst, 1991), 94. Apart from Buber-Neumann's very unreliable biography (some of whose factual errors are corrected in the afterword to the Czech edition: *Kafkova přítelkyně Milena* [Prague, Mladá fronta, 1992]), see Jana Černá, *Adresát Milena Jesenská* (Prague: Concordia, 1991), and Marta Marková-Kotyková, *Mýtus Milena: Milena Jesenská jinak* (Prague: Primus, 1993). Černá was Jesenská's daughter. Jesenská is also one of the subjects of Iggers, *Women of Prague*. The best biography of Jesenská to date is Alena Wagnerová, *Milena Jesenská* (Prague: Prostor, 1996), which is more detailed than the earlier German version of the same book (*Milena Jesenská* [Mannheim: Bollmann Verlag, 1994]). Several collections of Jesenská's own writings have now been published, including re-editions of her cookery book *Mileniny recepty* (Prague: Nakladatelství Franze Kafky, 1995) and of her 1926 collection of articles *Cesta k jednoduchosti* (Brno: Barrister a Principal, 1995), as well as the anthology *Zvenčí a zevnitř*, which contains her *Přítomnost* article "O umění zůstat stát" (discussed in the present book, pp. 226–27) and her obituary of Karel Čapek.

184. Vondráčková, *Kolem Mileny Jesenské*, 94.

185. "U[mělecký] S[vaz] Devětsil," *Pražské pondělí*, 6 December 1920, reprinted in Štěpán Vlašín et al. eds., *Avantgarda známá a neznámá*, 3 vols. (Prague: Svoboda, 1970–72), vol. 1, *Od proletářského umění k poetismu 1919–1924* (1971), 81–83. These three volumes together assemble a huge collection of texts documenting Prague avant-garde life from 1919 to 1931.

186. Vondráčková, *Kolem Mileny Jesenské*, 94.

187. Notably "Poetismus" (1924) and "Manifest poetismu" (1928), both in Karel Teige, *Svět stavby a básně: studie z dvacátých let*, Výbor z díla I (Prague: Československý spisovatel, 1966). This volume and its sequels, *Zápasy o smysl moderní tvorby: studie z třicátých let*, Výbor z díla II (Prague: Československý spisovatel, 1969), and *Osvobozování života a poezie: studie ze 40. let*, Výbor z díla III (Prague: Aurora/Český spisovatel, 1994), contain most of Teige's most important writings and very full commentaries. They have had a checkered political fate, which I discuss below, pp. 267–68.

188. Apart from work on Teige, Devětsil, and Czech surrealism cited elsewhere in these notes, see the large retrospective exhibition catalogue *Karel Teige 1900–1951*, texts by Karel Srp, and others (Prague: Galerie hlavního města Prahy, 1994); Vojtěch Lahoda, Karel Srp and Rumjana Dačeva, *Karel Teige: surrealistické koláže 1935–1951*, exhibition catalogue (Prague: Středoevropská galerie, 1994); and the special issue of *Umění*, vol. xliii, nos. 1–2, which contains the proceedings of the international conference "Karel Teige and the European Avant-Garde" held in Prague on 22–24 March 1994 in connection with the 1994 retrospective exhibition. I am most grateful to Patrick Keiller for providing me with a copy of the latter. See also the abundantly illustrated and very informative catalogue of the large Teige exhibition held in Trieste and Rome in 1996: *Karel Teige: architettura, poesie—Praga 1900–1951*, texts (in Italian, with English translations) by J. L. Cohen et al. (Milano: Electa, 1996).

189. Karel Teige and others, "Zásadní stanovisko k projevu 'Sedmi,'" *Tvorba*, vol. 4

(1929), reprinted in Vlašín, *Avantgarda známá a neznámá*, vol. 3, *Generační diskuse 1929–1931* (1970), 54–55. Other signatories included Vítězslav Nezval, Vladimír Clementis, Konstantin Biebl, František Halas, and Jiří Weil.

190. A somewhat fluid and uncertain category, it should be said. Apart from references cited elsewhere in this chapter, on Devětsil see the exhibition catalogues *Devětsil: česká výtvarná avantgarda dvacátých let*, texts by František Šmejkal, Rostislav Švácha, and Jan Rous (Prague: Galerie hlavního města Prahy, 1986); and *Devětsil: Czech Avant-Garde Art, Architecture and Design of the 1920s and '30s*, ed. Rostislav Švácha (Oxford: Museum of Modern Art/London: London Design Museum, 1990). The latter contains a list of Devětsil members. A slightly different list—E. E. Kisch's name is for instance omitted—based on the memories of Adolf Hoffmeister is given in *Jarmark umění*, nos. 11–12 (1996), 1. See also Teige, *Osvobozování života a poezie*, 575–81.

191. See Michal Schonberg, *Osvobozené* (Prague: Odeon, 1992), for a detailed history of this theater, written in part on the basis of interviews with Jiří Voskovec during the latter's exile in New York. This book was originally written (though not published) in English, as a Ph.D dissertation, under the supervision of Josef Škvorecký, at the University of Toronto.

192. Max Brod, *Franz Kafka: A Biography* (New York: Schocken, 1963), 224; Vondráčková, *Kolem Mileny Jesenské*, 23.

193. See Brod, *Franz Kafka*, 224; Kafka, *Letters to Milena*, xii.

194. Preparations were under way for the first Moscow purge trial, of Zinoviev, Kamenev, and others. See Artur London, *Doznání: v soukolí pražského procesu* (Prague: Československý spisovatel, 1990), 227–28. London's own few weeks' stay at the Lux in 1935 was used at the Slánský trial, in which he was one of the defendants, as "evidence" of his long-standing Trotskyism. On the Hotel Lux see also Bedřich Utitz, *Svědkové revoluce vypovídají* (Prague: Orbis, 1990), 8–9.

195. Devětsil, svaz revolučních umělců, "Velká francouzská revoluce ohlásila . . . ," Czech trans. of Russian résumé to Jaroslav Seifert and Karel Teige, eds, *Revoluční sborník Devětsil* (Prague, 1923); reprinted in Květoslav Chvatík and Zdeněk Pešat, eds., *Poetismus* (Prague: Odeon, 1967), 63.

196. This design is reproduced in the catalogue for the 1986 Devětsil exhibition at the Galerie hlavního města Prahy (along with Krejcar's sketch for the Olympic Department Store and photographs of several of his other buildings). See also Krejcar's 1936–37 sketches for the Czechoslovak pavilion at the World Exhibition in Paris, in Anděl, *Umění pro všechny smysly*, 96, 110.

197. Vondráčková, *Kolem Mileny Jesenské*, 100.

198. This is reproduced in Anděl, *Umění pro všechny smysly*, 18. For another celebrated example of the pictorial poem genre see Jindřich Štyrský's "Souvenir," reproduced on the front cover of this book.

199. This is reproduced in Švácha, *Devětsil: Czech Avant-Garde Art, Architecture and Design of the 1920s and '30s*, 53.

200. *ReD*, vol. 3, no. 1 (1929), 1.

201. Karel Teige, "Surrealismus není uměleckou školou," in *První výstava skupiny surrealistů v ČSR: Makovský, Štyrský, Toyen*, exhibition catalogue (Prague: SVU Mánes, 1935), 3–4. This catalogue also contains an article by Vítězslav Nezval in the same vein. The most comprehensive work to date on Czech surrealism is undoubtedly Byd-

žovská and Srp, *Český surrealismus*, an outstanding catalogue of a superb exhibition. This contains a very full bibliography. See also Stanislav Dvorský, Vratislav Effenberger, and Petr Král, eds., *Surrealistické východisko 1938–1968* (Prague: Československý spisovatel, 1969), and the ambitious study of Czech "imaginative art" —a category that comprehends, but also extends beyond, surrealism—from the 1890s to the 1970s by František Šmejkal, published to accompany the exhibition of the same title held at the Rudolfinum in Prague in 1997, *České imaginativní umění* (Prague: Galerie Rudolfinum, 1996).

202. Štyrský, Toyen, Nečas, *Průvodce Paříží a okolím* (Prague: Odeon, 1927), 50.

203. Advertisement in *ReD*, vol. 2, no. 9 (1929), p. 292.

204. Quoted in Ivan Pfaff, *Česká levice proti Moskvě 1936–1938* (Prague: Naše vojsko, 1993), 13.

205. Quoted in Karel Teige, *Zápasy o smysl moderní tvorby*, 665.

206. Stanislav Kostka Neumann, *Anti-Gide, neboli optimismus bez pověr a ilusí* (Prague: Svoboda, 1946), 102.

207. Ibid., 108

208. He is punning on the name of the poet František Halas here. Ibid., 117–18.

209. Ibid., 124.

210. S. K. Neumann, "Dnešní Mánes," *Tvorba*, vol. 12, no. 20 (1937), quoted in Pfaff, *Česká levice*, 107. A generous sampling of the kinds of creation of Toyen and Štyrský to which Neumann took offense can be found in Karel Srp, "Erotická revue a Edice 69," in Bydžovská and Srp, *Český surrealismus*, 53–65. Štyrský's *Emilie přichází* was first published in Edice 69.

211. Quoted in Pfaff, *Česká levice*, 106.

212. Karel Teige, "Moskevský proces," *Praha—Moskva*, no. 1 (September 1936), reprinted in his *Zápasy o smysl moderní tvorby*, 335–49.

213. "Projev Karla Teigeho na diskusním večeru Klubu Přítomnost v Praze 13. ledna 1937," reprinted in Pfaff, *Česká levice*, 78–81, and in Teige, *Zápasy o smysl moderní tvorby*, 626–31.

214. Teige, *Zápasy o smysl moderní tvorby*, 664.

215. Vítězslav Nezval, "Řeč ke studentstvu o roztržce se skupinou surrealistů 24.3.1938," *Tvorba*, vol. 13, 150, quoted in Pfaff, *Česká levice*, 130n.

216. Jaroslav Seifert, "Moskevský proces," reprinted in Pfaff, *Česká levice*, 77. Pfaff also reproduces two other poems by Seifert on the same theme, entitled "In Lenin's Mausoleum" and "Pushkin's Monument in Moscow."

217. F. X. Šalda, "Ve věku železa a ohně," in *Šaldův zápisník*, vol. 9 (1936–37), 6–7.

CHAPTER 6

1. Jan A. Baťa, *Budujme stát pro 40,000,000 lidí* (Zlín: Tisk, 1937), 10.

2. Edvard Beneš, speech at Masaryk's funeral on 21 September 1937, in Boháč, *Odkaz T. G. Masaryka*, 105.

3. See Karel Janů and Erik Kafka, "Odsun Němců z ČSR," in *Československo*, vol. 1, no. 4 (1946), 61.

4. Vítězslav Nezval, ed., *Ani labuť ani Lůna: sborník k stému výročí smrti K. H. Máchy*, reprint of first edition of 1936 (Prague: Společnost Karla Teiga/Concordia, 1995).

The contributors were Konstantin Biebl, Bohuslav Brouk, E. F. Burian, Adolf Hoff-meister, Záviš Kalandra, Vincenc Makovský, Jan Mukařovský, Vítězslav Nezval, Laco Novomeský, Jindřich Štyrský, Karel Teige, and Toyen. The poem from which this book takes its title can be found in *Dílo Karla Hynka Máchy*, vol. 1, 214. On the back-ground to the *sborník*, see Josef Vojvodík, "Četba jako deformování a permanentní zraňování textu: několik poznámek ke koncepci máchovského sborníku *Ani labuť ani Lůna* (1936)," in Bydžovská and Srp, *Český surrealismus*, 220–35.

5. *Výstava Národ svým výtvarným umělcům*, exhibition catalogue (Prague: Kulturní rada ústředí pro kulturní a školskou práci Národního souručenství, 1939).

6. These are listed at the back of ibid. Venues were Louny, Tábor, Hodonín, Hradec Králové, Olomouc, Chrudim, Pardubice, České Budějovice, Frýdek, Brno, Plzeň, Mo-ravská Ostrava, Litomyšl, Třebíč, Uherské Hradiště, Mladá Boleslav, Benešov, and Strakonice. In his speech launching the show at Obecní dům on 11 November 1939, Miloslav Hýsek, president of the Kulturní rada, commented that "the Czech country-side goes and always will go with the call of the heart of the nation, little mother [*matička*] Prague, in order that its glory will reach the stars." *Národ svým výtvarným umělcům* (Prague: Kulturní rada NS při Národní radě české, 1940), 16.

7. *Výstava Národ svým výtvarným umělcům*, unpaginated and untitled preface by Miloslav Hýsek. It ends with the words "Vlasti zdar!"

8. F. X. Šalda, "Umělecká tvorba a stát: meditace k 28. říjnu," in *Šaldův zápisník*, vol. 9 (1936–37), 37–51.

9. *Výstava Národ svým výtvarným umělcům*, Hýsek's preface.

10. This is reproduced as the frontispiece to *Národ svým výtvarným umělcům*.

11. For instance, the republication of Palacký's *Dějiny národu českého* by Kvasnička a Hampl in 1939, and of the four-volume *Dílo Františka Palackého* by Mazáč in 1941 (the latter was censored; the omissions are detailed in the brochure put out by the publishing house entitled "Censura a Dílo Františka Palackého" in 1945); the collec-tion *Co daly naše země Evropě a lidstvu* (What Our Land Gave to Europe and Human-ity), ed. Vilém Mathesius (Prague: Evropský literární klub, 1940), whose cover design was by Jindřich Štyrský; or the collections of poems by František Halas (*Naše paní Božena Němcová*) and Jaroslav Seifert (*Vějíř Boženy Němcové*). There were also "national pilgrimages" to Říp (30 April 1939), Domažlice (13 August 1939), and Hostýn (20 August 1939).

12. Erich Kulka, *Židé v československé Svobodově armádě* (Prague: Naše vojsko, 1990), 12. A more detailed discussion of numbers is given in Eva Schmidtová-Hart-mannová, "Ztráty československého židovského obyvatelstva 1938–1945," in Milena Janišová, ed., *Osud Židů v Protektorátu 1939–1945* (Prague: Trizonia/Ústav pro soudobé dějiny, 1991), 81–116. Kulka gives several graphic examples of official post-war erasure of this fact, including the refusal of the Union of Antifascist Fighters [*Svaz protifašistických bojovníků*] to allow inclusion of transportation lists, which individually named Jewish victims, in an official Czechoslovak exhibit in the Polish State Museum in Auschwitz.

The most grotesque such erasure, however, was perhaps the removal, after 1968, of the names of the 77,297 Jewish men, women, and children from the Czech lands known to have perished in the Holocaust, which had been inscribed on the walls of Prague's Pinkas Synagogue—which under the communists became part of the State Jewish Museum—after the war. The memorial owed its existence in large part to the persistence of one woman, Hana Volavková. The pretext for its disappearance was "renovation" of the medieval building occasioned by water damage. A typed notice in the museum in April 1992, written in English, read: "After more than twenty years the State Jewish Museum is opening to the public the Pinkas Synagogue in Prague. In the fifties its walls bore the names of almost 80,000 victims of the Second World War, from Bohemia and Moravia. In the course of the reconstruction, which took place from 1969 to 1989, those names were removed and the Museum intends to proceed with their renewal immediately, which cannot get along without the personal assistance of the public. The number of the account for the renewal of the names in the Pinkas synagogue is: 01–1225903/0300 Čsl. obchodní banka a.s. Na Příkopě 14." (Personal observation: I copied it down.) See further my note, which appeared anonymously under the title "Fact of the Issue," in *Journal of Historical Sociology*, vol. 5, no. 3 (1992), 291. The memorial has since been restored.

Bearing in mind why these people died, we might finally note how, by 1979, the State Jewish Museum was representing Jewish history in its guides: "The historical development of the Jewish religious communities is comprehended as the development of a religious group, forming an integral part of the population of the Czech lands, and thus not as the historical development of members of the so-called 'world Jewish nation,' which was artificially constructed by the ideologues of Zionism." Editorial collective of the State Jewish Museum, *Státní židovské muzeum v Praze* (Prague: Státní židovské muzeum, 1979), 7.

13. See Toman Brod, Miroslav Kárný, and Margita Kárná, eds., *Terezínský rodinný tábor v Osvětimi-Birkenau* (Prague: Terezínská iniciativa/Melantrich, 1994), 9.

14. Jiří Weil, *Žalozpěv za 77,297 obětí* (Prague: Československý spisovatel, 1958), 28. He dates this slaughter, erroneously, as 7 March 1943.

15. It was proclaimed thus by the International Students Council in London, and celebrated annually from 1941 as the International Day of Students.

16. On these events see "Pohřeb Jana Opletala," in František Kropáč and Vlastimil Louda, *Persekuce českého studentstva za okupace* (Prague: Ministerstvo vnitra/Orbis, 1945), 63–67; also František Buriánek, Rudolf Mertlík, Jan Pilař, and Josef Strnadel, eds., *17. listopad* (Prague: Orbis, 1945); and more recently Jakub Čermín et al., *17. listopad 1939 po 55 letech* (Brno: Doplněk, 1994); and Jozef Leikert, *A den se vrátil (co následovalo po 17. listopadu 1939)* (Bratislava: Astra, 1993), a book based on interviews with survivors.

17. The proclamation is reproduced as the "Motto" in Kropáč and Louda, *Persekuce českého studentstva*, 8. It was published in the afternoon papers of 17 November, read on the radio, and posted on placards throughout the Protectorate.

18. Kropáč and Louda, *Persekuce českého studentstva*, 105.

19. Ibid., 142–51.

20. Letter from State Secretary SS Gruppenführer Karl Hermann Frank to General Daluege in Berlin, 1 June 1942, in Čestmír Amort, ed., *Heydrichiáda: dokumenty* (Prague: Naše vojsko, 1965), 203–5. Frank (1898–1946) had been a leading representative of Henlein's Sudeten German party, and was from 1935–38 a member of the Czechoslovak parliament. He was executed in May 1946.

21. *Výstava Národ svým výtvarným umělcům v Praze 1940*, exhibition catalogue, ed. F. V. Mokrý and V. F. Vicek (Prague: Kulturní rada N.S. při Národní radě české, 1940).

22. These are reproduced in full in Josef Čapek, *Dějiny zblízka: soubor satirických kreseb* (Prague: Borový, 1949). The "Boots" series, in particular, is grimly surreal.

23. Compare the list of exhibits given in *Výstava národ svým výtvarným umělcům*, 27, which includes Filla's two paintings, with the list of artists exhibited in Prague according to *Národ svým výtvarným umělcům*, 26–29, which omits his name entirely.

24. For example, the critic Václav Černý. See his *Křik koruny české: paměti 1938–1945* (Brno: Atlantis, 1992), 357.

25. See Zuzana Švabinská-Vejrychová, "Doslov" to Ela Švabinská, *Vzpomínky z mládí* (Prague: Státní nakladatelství krásné literatury a umění, 1962), 352. Švabinský's marital circumstances were convoluted. He married Ela, née Vejrychová, in 1900. "Chudý kraj," Ela says in these memoirs, "became Švabinský's wedding picture" (180). Twenty years later he left Ela for her brother's wife Anna, who herself died in 1942. "Chudý kraj" is reproduced, inter alia, in Wittlich, *Česká secese*, 77; Wittlich, *Umění a život: doba secese*, 39, and Luboš Hlaváček et al., *Současné české a slovenské umění* (Prague: Odeon, 1985), 232—in no case are the colors well brought out. There is a small black-and-white reproduction in Wittlich, *Prague: Fin de Siècle*, 72.

26. Milena Jesenská, "Jsem především Češka?" in *Přítomnost*, vol. 16, no. 19 (1939), 283–84.

27. Milena Jesenská, "Česká maminka," in *Přítomnost*, vol. 16, no. 16 (1939), 238–39. See also her article "O té ženské emancipaci několik poznámek velice zaostalých" —which translates as "A Few Very Unprogressive Remarks on That Women's Emancipation" —in her *Cesta k jednoduchosti*, 52–57.

28. Milena Jesenská, "O umění zůstat stát," in *Přítomnost*, vol. 16, no. 14 (1939), 205–6. The dedication page to Milena's *Cesta k jednoduchosti* reads: "Drahému tátovi věnuje Milena." On Jesenská's wartime activities, see Marie Jirásková, *Stručná zpráva o troji volbě: Milena Jesenská, Joachim von Zedtwitz a Jaroslav Nachtmann v roce 1939 a v čase následujícím* (Prague: Nakladatelství Franze Kafky, 1996).

29. Livie Rothkirkenová, "Osud Židů v Čechách a na Moravě v letech 1938–1945," in Šimečka, *Osud Židů v Protektorátu*, 68. This figure differs from that of the 77,297 more usually cited in Czech sources, whose names were recorded on the walls of the Pinkas Synagogue in Prague after the war.

30. Erik Polák, "Terezín v 'konečném řešení' židovské otázky," in Brod, *Terezínský rodinný tábor*, 21, gives slightly different figures for the same period: 139,654 internees, of whom 33,430 (23.93 percent) died in Terezín itself.

31. See *František Zelenka: plakáty, architektura, divadlo*, exhibition catalogue, ed. Josef Kroutvor (Prague: Uměleckoprůmyslové muzeum, 1991). This exhibition was organized to commemorate the beginnings of Jewish deportation and the establishment of the Terezín ghetto. Zelenka was also a talented architect of the functionalist school; he designed the "Glass House" in Palackého ulice in Prague (pictured in this catalogue, 27), as well as villas in Baba, discussed above, pp. 198–99.

32. See Cara De Silva, ed., *In Memory's Kitchen: A Legacy from the Women of Terezín* (Northvale, N.J.: Jason Aronson, 1996).

33. Jiří Weil, "Epilog" to Hana Volavková, ed., *Dětské kresby na zastávce k smrti: Terezín 1942–1944* (Prague: Státní židovské muzeum, 1959), unpaginated. The Nazis defined, interned and murdered Jews on the basis of "race" rather than whether or not they adhered to Judaic dietary law. For their criteria of "Jewish race"—which differed between the Protectorate and "independent" Slovakia—see Zdeněk Tobolka, ed., *Na-*

učný slovník aktualit (Prague: L. Mazáč, 1939), 607–8, a hastily produced encyclopedia of the *neue Ordnung*. Roast pork, preferably with sauerkraut and dumplings [*vepřo-knedlo-zelo*], is a *Czech* national dish.

34. Arnošt Lustig, *Dita Saxova*, revised and expanded edition, trans. Jeanne Němcová (Evanston, Ill.: Northwestern University Press, 1993). Lustig himself left Czechoslovakia in 1968.

35. Vítězslav Nezval, *Z mého života* (Prague: Československý spisovatel, 1959), 84.

36. See Petr Nový, "Člověk: Jiří Weil," in Jiří Weil, *Moskva—hranice* (Prague: Mladá fronta, 1991), 8–13.

37. Ibid., 10.

38. Jiří Weil, *Dřevěná lžíce* (Prague: Mladá fronta, 1992).

39. Nový, "Člověk: Jiří Weil," 11.

40. Jiří Weil, *Žalozpěv za 77,297 obětí*.

41. Jiří Weil, *Život s hvězdou/Na střeše je Mendelssohn* (Prague: Československý spisovatel, 1990), Ediční poznámka.

42. Ibid., 195–99.

43. The lists are reproduced in Václav Buben, ed., *Šest let okupace Prahy* (Prague: Osvětový odbor hlavního města Prahy/Orbis, 1946), 173–207. Čestmír Amort (*Heydrichiáda*, 59) gives a slightly lower figure of 3,188 Czechs arrested and 1,357 shot between 27 May and 3 July, based on Daluege's report to Hitler of 1 September 1942.

44. In Buben, *Šest let okupace Prahy*, 165–66.

45. This last detail from ibid., 89. Other figures from Miroslav Moulis, *Lidice žijí* (Praha: Středočeské nakladatelství, 1972). Other sources give slightly different figures. The German report of 29 June 1942 itemizes 95 houses destroyed, 199 men over fifteen years old shot, 184 women deported to Ravensbrück, 88 children taken to Lodz, seven infants under one year old put in an institution in Prague, and "only three [that] it was possible after racial examination to send for Germanization to the lands of the old Reich" (in Amort, *Heydrichiáda*, 288). Amort himself says that of a total of 104 children, 9 were deemed capable of "Germanization" and given to SS families, 9 survived the camps, and 86 died in gas chambers at Chelmno (49).

46. Letter of 12 June 1942 from SS Standartenführer Horst Böhme to director of security police, in Amort, *Heydrichiáda*, 212–14.

47. Report to K. H. Frank, 7 July 1942, in Amort, *Heydrichiáda*, 304.

48. The records show 1,079, but 4 of these were in fact shot in Kobylisy. The great majority were Czech patriots, nine were German soldiers, the rest were executed for "economic transgressions" or "regular" crimes. See R. Karel, *Žaluji: Pankrácká kalvarie* (Prague: Orbis, 1946), vol. 2, 862–63. This book lists all victims by name and date of execution. It is a harrowing collection, in both its text and its photographs. The title means "I accuse." Its use again for the three-volume collection of memoirs from communist prisons in the 1950s edited by Antonín Kratochvíl (cited in Bearings, note 17) cannot be coincidental.

49. Jarmila Novotná, *Byla jsem šťastná* (Prague: Melantrich, 1991), 13.

50. Jan Masaryk, sleeve notes to Jarmila Novotná, "Songs of Czechoslovakia," RCA LP record number VIC 1383 (1969).

51. See, for instance, the shrill, early-normalization exhibition catalogue *Lidice 1942–1972* (Prague: Český svaz protifašistických bojovníků/Svaz českých výtvarných umělců, 1972). This exhibition was held at Prague's Mánes building in June and July

of 1972. The English summary to the catalogue (something extremely rare in this period) begins: "This is not an exhibition in the usual sense. It is an open letter to the present day, written on the edge of the death certificate of the victims of the razed village of Lidice. It is a reminder to those who were born a good deal later how and from what was born the evil of bloodshed, pillage, murder, hatred and feral relations between people. It is a clenched fist giving warning, after thirty years, that all this horror can be repeated at any time and perhaps in an even more terrifying form—as long as there are a ruling handful of sadists somewhere able to put the fetters of its distorted proposals on the broad masses, break disagreement down in the torture-chambers and drown resistance in blood and tears. It is a ballot paper with which the fallen and the tortured and surviving witnesses can vote for a better new world without hunger, without megalomaniac expansion, without wars of aggression and without man's exploitation of man. . . . Some of these works raise a fist against those who would like to revive these past terrors, who would like to threaten and destroy our new and better world" (21–22).

52. "Jarmila Novotná: české písně a arie/Czech Songs and Arias," Supraphon CD no. 11 1491-2201 (1992), sleeve notes by Jan Králík.

53. Jan Thon, "Městská knihovna pražská," in Buben, *Šest let okupace Prahy*, 83.

54. Emil Axman, "Národní museum za německé okupace," in Buben, *Šest let okupace Prahy*, 84–87; Sršeň, *Budova Národního muzea*, 102.

55. Milan Krejčí, *Pražské sochy a pomníky* (Prague: Galerie hlavního města Prahy, 1979), unpaginated. Alone of these, the memorial to Denis, erected in 1928 in the upper part of Malostranské náměstí, was not replaced. See Petr Pithart, "Neklidný život pražských pomníků a soch," 261, 263–64, and more generally on the unquiet life of Prague memorials, Zdeněk Hojda and Jiří Pokorný, *Pomníky a zapomníky*, 2d ed. (Prague: Paseka, 1997). The untranslatable title of this book is a pun: a *pomník* is a memorial; the verb *zapomenout*, from which the neologism *zapomník* is derived, means "to forget."

56. Pithart, "Neklidný život pražských pomníků a soch," 262.

57. A contemporary photograph of this is reproduced in Josef Tomeš, "Ze století do století: 1941," *Reflex*, no. 23 (1996), 59.

58. Vojtěch Drnec, "Zničení hrobu Neznámého vojína," in Buben, *Šest let okupace Prahy*, 25–27.

59. For a full list of changes in names of Prague streets, embankments, stations, and parks during the occupation, see *Původní názvy pražských ulic, nábřeží, nádraží a sadů podle stavu v roce 1938* (Prague: Česká obec turistická, 1945).

60. Bělina, *Dějiny zemí koruny české*, vol. 2, 243.

61. Josef Horák and Ladislav Vachulka, eds., *Smetanův jubilejní rok 1944: program oslav v Praze* (Prague: Národní rada česká, 1944), 42–43. Compare Jirásek, *Staré pověsti české*, 271.

62. Novotná, *Byla jsem šťastná*, 42.

63. Mirko Valina, "Znovudobytá frygická čapka," *Československo*, vol. 1, no. 1 (1946), 87–88. The two portraits are pictured side by side in the volume, p. 76.

64. That is, on 13 May. Míka, *Dějiny Prahy v datech*, 293. Konečná, *Soupis repertoáru Národního divadla*, vol. 2, 213, mentions two productions at the Národní divadlo immediately after liberation, on 13 and 14 May, but does not say of what works.

65. Konečná, *Soupis repertoáru Národního divadla*, vol. 2, 214. This production played 37 times, to 1948.

66. See, for example, the review in *Umění*, vol. 17 (1945–49), 144–45.

67. Míka, *Dějiny Prahy v datech*, 293.

68. Vojtíšek, *The Old Town Hall of Prague*, 40. On the damage in Prague see Wirth, *Zmizelá Praha*, vol. 5 (1948); Zdeněk Wirth, "Furor Teutonicus," in *Umění*, vol. 17 (1945–49), 3–10.

69. *Josef Čapek in Memoriam*, exhibition catalogue, texts by Václav Rabas and Emil Filla (Prague: Umělecká beseda, 1945). Untitled foreword by Jarmila Čapková.

70. *Dílo Josefa Čapka: obrazy, kresby, grafika, divadlo* (Prague: Umělecká beseda, 1946), exhibition catalogue, ed. Karel Šourek. There were 1,064 exhibits.

71. Nechvátal, *Vyšehradský hřbitov*, 37. The true circumstances are explained later in the text.

72. Personal observation.

73. Emil Filla, in *Josef Čapek in Memoriam* (unpaginated).

74. Edvard Beneš, speech to Slovak National Council, in V. Žižka, ed., *Bojující Československo 1938–1945* (Košice: Žikeš, 1945), 227, 230. This was the first book published on Czechoslovak soil after liberation. Its dedication reads: "This first book published on the liberated territory of the homeland, I dedicate to the memory of all those who at home and beyond the borders suffered, fought, and died for a new Czechoslovakia."

75. Dušek, *Specializovaná příručka pro sběratele československých poštovních známek*, 108.

76. Ibid., 105–6.

77. Zdeněk Nejedlý, "Za novou kulturu," in *Československo*, vol. 1 (1945), 36.

78. Ibid., 15.

79. "Košický vládní program," in Harna, *České a československé dějiny*, vol. 3, 170–71.

80. Letter of 3 December 1952, in Vladimír Clementis, *Nedokončená kronika* (Prague: Československý spisovatel, 1965), 182. According to Zdeněk Mlynář, Clementis's execution was followed by a fire sale of his personal effects among his erstwhile comrades. Božena Novotná, wife of future president Antonín Novotný, got the fine bed linen and Chinese porcelain dinner service she had long coveted. Zdeněk Mlynář, *Mráz přichází z Kremlu* (Prague: Mladá fronta, 1990), 76–77. Milan Kundera's *The Book of Laughter and Forgetting* (London: Faber, 1982) begins with a famous account of how Clementis's image was subsequently erased from the photograph of Klement Gottwald addressing the masses in Staroměstské náměstí from the balcony of the Kinský palace in February 1948, an account that leads up to what is probably the most quoted sentence Kundera ever wrote: "The struggle of man against power is the struggle of memory against forgetting" (3). Kundera qualifies that sentiment elsewhere with the observation: "Remembering is not the negative of forgetting. Remembering is a form of forgetting" (*Testaments Betrayed*, New York: HarperCollins, 1995, 128.) The original photograph and its doctored successor are nicely juxtaposed, along with two other such photographic makeovers, in Jiří Kolář's collage "Ale zbav nás . . . " (But deliver us . . .) in his *Týdeník 1968* (Prague: Torst, 1993), plate 22. Kolář's accompanying text reads: "Malanthios: erasing Aristratos and replacing him with a palm tree, or, three Socialist rules."

What Kundera does not tell us in *The Book of Laughter and Forgetting*—though it ably illustrates his thesis that memory is a form of forgetting—is that Clementis's image was to be resurrected in 1973, in 11,350,000 exemplars, on a sixty-*heller* postage stamp, one of a set commemorating "Fighters Against Nazism and Fascism During the Occupation." Fellow Slovak and fellow victim of the 1950s purges Gustáv Husák was by then KSČ general secretary. Two years later the National Gallery purchased a painting by Josef Šíma entitled "Sun of Other Worlds" (*Slunce jiných světů*, 1936), now on display in the permanent collection in Veletržní palác in Prague. Written on the frame are the words "Vladovi Clementisovi jeho Šíma, 1948" (To Vlado Clementis from his Šíma, 1948). (Personal observation.)

81. Figure given in Jiří Hanák, "Beranova židle," in *Lidové noviny*, 23 April 1994.

82. Figures (as percentages of all votes cast in the whole Czechoslovak Republic) were 13.7 percent in 1925, 15.0 percent in 1929, 14.3 percent in 1935. Buchvaldek, *Dějiny Československa v datech*, 467.

83. Bělina, *Dějiny zemí koruny české*, vol. 2, 249.

84. Beneš's most important decrees are given in full in Veselý, *Dějiny českého státu v dokumentech*, 375–405.

85. In *Lidová demokracie*, 24 June 1945, quoted in Václav Vaško, *Neumlčená kronika katolické církve v Československu po druhé světové válce*, vol. 1 (Prague: Zvon, 1990), 30–31.

86. Ibid.

87. This had been a prewar slogan of the Sudeten German party.

88. This speech, as reported in *Svobodné slovo*, 19 May 1945, is quoted in Vaško, *Neumlčená kronika*, 28, and reproduced in full in Prokop Drtina, *Československo můj osud*, vol. 2, book 1 (Prague: Melantrich, 1992), 63–64.

89. Quoted in Tomáš Staněk, *Odsun Němců z Československa 1945–1947* (Prague: Academia/Naše vojsko, 1991), 59.

90. Quoted in ibid., 60 (which also quotes similar sentiments from pronouncements at the time by David, Majer, Stránský, and others).

91. Quoted in ibid., 58, and in anon. authorial collective, *Komu sluší omluva: Češi a Sudetští Němci (dokumenty, fakta, svědectví)* (Prague: Erika, 1992), 97. The latter also quotes similar speeches by Vladimír Clementis.

92. Quoted in Staněk, *Odsun Němců*, 58–59.

93. On this see Vaško, *Neumlčená kronika*; Karel Kaplan, *Stát a církev v Československu 1948–1953* (Brno: Doplněk, 1993); and Marie Bulínová, Milena Janišová, and Karel Kaplan, eds., *Církevní komise ÚV KSČ 1949–1951: edice dokumentů*, vol. 1, Církevní komise ÚV KSČ ("Církevní šestka") duben 1949-březen 1950 (Brno: Doplněk, 1994).

94. See Josef Škvorecký, *The Miracle Game* (Toronto: Lester and Orpen Dennys, 1990), and the several accounts published in the Czech press in 1968 and reprinted in Kratochvil, *Žaluji*, vol. 3, 157–79.

95. Míka, *Dějiny Prahy v datech*, 362.

96. "Prohlášení Charty 77 (1. ledna 1977)," reprinted in Vilém Prečan, ed., *Charta 77, 1977–1989: od morální k demokratické revoluci—dokumentace* (Prague/Bratislava: Scheinfeld, 1990), 9.

97. Prokop Drtina, *Československo můj osud: kniha života českého demokrata 20. století*, 2 vols., each in 2 books (Prague: Melantrich, 1991–92).

98. See Bělina, *Dějiny zemí koruny české*, vol. 2, 253.

99. Ibid., 252–53.

100. Quoted in ibid., 253.

101. See Staněk, *Odsun Němců*, 365–72.

102. See Peroutka, *Budování státu*, vol. 2, 557–59.

103. Karel Kaplan, *Československo v letech 1945–1948* (Prague: Státní pedagogické nakladatelství, 1991), 23. The figure of 2,400,449 hectares (of which 1,405,070 was agricultural land) for Bohemia and Moravia alone is given in Buchvaldek, *Dějiny Československa v datech*, 363.

104. Figure given in Bělina, *Dějiny zemí koruny české*, vol. 2, 167.

105. See Buchvaldek, *Dějiny Československa v datech*, 363; Kaplan, *Československo v letech 1945–1948*, 22.

106. Kaplan, *Československo v letech 1945–1948*, 22.

107. Vladimír Koucký, "První rok míru a svobody," *Tvorba*, vol. 15, no. 1 (2 January 1946).

108. Kaplan, *Československo v letech 1945–1948*, 48.

109. Buchvaldek, *Dějiny Československa v datech*, 468; Bělina, *Dějiny zemí koruny české*, 256–57.

110. Martin Zeman, "Jan Masaryk jak ho jsme znali," special supplement to *Svět v obrazech*, March 1948, back cover.

111. For a detailed discussion of the numbers see Pěkný, *Historie Židů v Čechách a na Moravě*, 388–405. He estimates that at the end of the war there were around 24,000 Jews living in the Czech lands, of whom around one-third came from Podkarpatská Rus; that 18,000 emigrated between 1948 and 1950, and perhaps a further 6,000 in 1968–69; and that the total Jewish population of the Czech lands in 1993 was approximately 3,500 people. Immediately before the war, it was close to 120,000; see above, p. 227.

112. *Přehled obcí a částí v ČSR, jejichž názvy zanikly, byly změněny . . .* (Prague: Ústřední správa spojů, 1964).

CHAPTER 7

1. On the history of the National Gallery and its component collections, see Jiří Kotalík, ed., *Národní galerie* (Prague: Odeon, 1984), introduction; Jiří Kotalík, "Národní galerie v Praze," *Zpravodajství* (NG), no. 4 (18 March 1986) 1–8; and Vít Vlnas, ed., *200 let Národní galerie*, exhibition catalogue (Prague: Národní galerie, 1996). On the Modern Gallery see works cited in ch. 4, note 79. On the Hollar Society see František Dvořák, Josef Lhota, and Jiří Machalický, *SČUG Hollar 1917–1992: současná grafika*, exhibition catalogue (Prague: SČUG Hollar, 1992). The Society itself was finally abolished in 1970 and refounded in 1989.

2. Information on National Gallery exhibitions is taken from the following typescript listings, which are held in the archives of the Scientific Information Division of the National Gallery in Prague: "Soupis výstav Národní galerie uspořádaných v Praze v letech 1945–1990," compiled by Helena Obrová, 1990; "Soupis výstav Národní galerie v zahraničí," compiled by Jitka Pušová and Marcela Hojdová, 1991; and a listing headed simply "Regiony 1948–1985," no date, no author, which details NG

exhibitions in regional galleries. I am extremely grateful to Marcela Hojdová for providing me with copies of this material.

3. Laclotte, *Alfons Mucha 1860–1939*, 140–41.

4. This figure was supplied to me by Marcela Hojdová, from files in the Scientific Information Division of the National Gallery archives. Accurate counts of visitors were not consistently kept before the 1970s. By way of comparison (and from the same source), Josef Mánes attracted 161,071 in 1971; Aleš and Myslbek 21,000 in 1973; Švabinský 103,645 in 1974; "Classics of Czech Art" 169,007 in 1976; Trnka 113,840 in 1979; Josef Čapek 38,037 the same year; Aleš 132,486 in 1979–80; "Baroque in Bohemia" 101,608 in 1982; and an exhibition of French art, "From Courbet to Cezanne," 128,174 in 1982. Russian art generally fared abysmally, with exhibitions attracting 13,178 in 1977 and 3,499 in 1980; official Czechoslovak contemporary art (e.g., the 1976 exhibition "National Artists of the ČSSR," 4,109 visitors) did little better. In the immediate aftermath of the Velvet Revolution, Andy Warhol (1990) got 80,280 visitors, "Czech Art 1908–1968" 98,517, and "Czech Cubism" (1992; catalogue cited above), which was a superb exhibition, a disappointing 31,452. By this time entrance fees were being charged.

5. The bibliography to the 1980 Prague Mucha retrospective lists well over two hundred items in all. Jiří Mucha's works aside, only two books on Mucha published after 1948 are in Czech, and four articles, two of which deal with postage stamps. Laclotte, *Alfons Mucha 1860–1939*, 142–46.

6. Jana Brabcová, "Opožděné poselství," in Laclotte, *Alfons Mucha 1860–1939*, 94–95.

7. *Le Figaro* (Paris) 21 February 1980, quoted in Jiří Mucha, *Alphonse Maria Mucha*, 285.

8. P. Smetana, untitled afterword in *Monumentální úkol současného výtvarnictví* (Prague: SVU Mánes, 1947). Unpaginated exhibition catalogue.

9. "Žně" is in the Památník Maxe Švabinského in Kroměříž, unless, that is, it has been restored since 1993, when I saw it, to a former private owner. It measures 348 × 464 cm. It needs to be seen in color to be appreciated. There are several black-and-white reproductions of both the whole and details in Hana Frankensteinová, *Max Švabinský: dílo 1924–1948* (Prague: Orbis, 1949), 129–59. There is a good color reproduction of Švabinský's third sketch for "Žně" in Hana Volavková, *Max Švabinský* (Prague: Odeon, 1982), plate 35.

10. As well as Julius Fučík, Švabinský's postwar subjects include Petr Bezruč, Stanislav Kostka Neumann, Fráňa Šrámek, Zdeněk Nejedlý, Ivan Olbracht, Jiří Wolker, and Vítězslav Nezval, all communist cultural icons. All are reproduced in Ludvík Páleníček, *Švabinského český slavín* (Prague: Státní pedagogické nakladatelství, 1985). For the poster see Václav Formánek et al., *Deset let Československé lidově demokratické republiky ve výtvarném umění 1945–1955*, exhibition catalogue (Prague: Ministerstvo kultury, 1955). There were over 2,600 exhibits.

11. Milan Kundera, *The Joke*, trans. Michael Henry Heim (London: Penguin, 1984), 166.

12. Ferdinand Peroutka, "Případ Julia Fučíka," in his *Budeme pokračovat*, 118. The full, uncensored version of Fučík's book was published for the first time only in 1995; Julius Fučík, *Reportáž psaná na oprátce* (Prague: Torst, 1995). This edition itemizes the formerly expurgated passages.

13. Milan Kundera, *Poslední máj*, 2d rev. ed. (Prague: Československý spisovatel, 1961), 28–29. The translation here, of the last six lines of the twenty-three-page poem, does not attempt to preserve the rhyming couplets of the original. The temptation of Christ to which I refer is described most fully in the Gospel of Saint Matthew (4:1–11) and the Gospel of Saint Luke (4:1–13).

14. Antonín Matějček, "Švabinského stokorunová bankovka," *Umění*, vol. 6 (1933), 206.

15. Páleníček, *Švabinského český slavín*. For his portraits of Masaryk and other pre-war Czech personalities, see any of the pre-1948 books on Švabinský listed in the sources.

16. Thoroughly representative are the conference proceedings *Sjezd národní kultury* (Prague: Orbis, 1948) and (relating in particular to the visual arts) *Za rozkvět československého výtvarného umění: projevy z konference výtvarných umělců v Jízdárně pražského hradu* (Prague: Orbis, 1951). See also, for an early and sad capitulation to KSČ cultural norms on the part of an old-established artists' society, "Prohlášení S.V.U. Mánes," as well as the accompanying "Provolání Svazu československých výtvarných umělců," in *Volné směry*, vol. 40 (1947–48), 146–47.

17. See for example, the demagogic editorial and appended quotations from Lenin, Gottwald, Neumann, Nejedlý, and others in *Květy*, 24 April 1958, which juxtaposes reproductions of the artists on display with nineteenth-century Czech "classics." This was effectively replied to, among other things with other quotations from Neumann himself positively evaluating the Osma back in 1913–14, in "Ještě k Osmě," in *Literární noviny*, 2 May 1958. Otherwise see "Výstava moderního českého umění v Jízdárně," *Lidová demokracie*, 2 March 1958; "Výstava 'Zakladatelé moderního českého umění,'" *Rudé právo*, 4 March 1958; Prokop H. Toman, "Zakladatelé českého moderního umění," in *Svět v obrazech*, 22 March 1958, and "Zakladatelé českého moderního umění," in *Práce*, 9 March 1958; Jiří Kotalík, "České moderní umění," in *Literární noviny*, 15 March 1958. Many of these reviews, though positive, emphasize that the work on display is a "closed chapter," "unrepeatable," and on no account to be taken as "a model." Even Václav Formánek, who explicitly criticizes the catchall epithet "formalism" and baldly states that "we are afraid of our own past" concludes his article in this vein: "K výstavě Zakladatelů v Praze," *Výtvarná práce*, 8 March 1958. Miroslav Lamač discusses the background to the exhibition: "Předmluva" to Padrta, *Osma a Skupina*, 7–12.

18. Lamač, *Osma a Skupina*, was ready for the press in the early 1970s but was finally published only in 1988. Lamač fell foul of normalization. Jiří Padrta's selection of texts, also titled *Osma a Skupina*, came out only in 1992. Padrta himself died in 1978. See Lamač, "Předmluva" to latter for fuller details.

19. See Šmejkal, *Devětsil*, opening paragraphs.

20. See Jaromír Hořec, *Doba ortelů: dokumenty—vzpomínky—iluze a skutečnosti* (Brno: Scholaris, 1992).

21. František Halas, "Staré ženy," in his *Životem umřít* (Prague: Československý spisovatel, 1989), 127–34.

22. The headstone is photographed in Hořec, *Doba ortelů*, insert between pp. 80 and 81.

23. Pavel Kosatík, "Causa Záviš Kalandra," *Reflex*, no. 24 (1996), 54. Ivan Pfaff refers to the same manifesto but spent a year in Prague trying fruitlessly to track it

dǫwn; he infers its existence from the many attacks published against it by Štoll and Fučík in the KSČ press at the time. *Česká levice proti Moskvě*, 15, 47.

24. See Kundera, *Book of Laughter and Forgetting*, 66. Breton's letter, dated "Paris, 13 June 1950," is given in Czech translation, from which I quote, as "Otevřený dopis Paulu Éluardovi," *Analogon*, no. 1 (June 1969), 67. This same issue of this magazine provided a selection of extracts from Kalandra's own writings (59–66).

25. The full range of posts thus controlled by the KSČ is given in Ústřední výbor KSČ, "Kádrový pořádek Ústředního výboru Komunistické strany Československa (květen 1984)." An internal KSČ document marked "secret" and "only for the use of party organs," this was published by the Alliance antikomunistická in Prague in 1991 under the title *Rudá nomenklatura*. Karel Kaplan, ed., *Kádrová nomenklatura KSČ 1948–1956: sborník dokumentů* (Prague: Sešity Ústavu pro soudobé dějiny ČSAV, no. 2, 1992), gives similar documents from 1948 to 1956. A representative sampling of the work of Czech and Slovak "national artists" may be found in Hlaváček, *Současné české a slovenské umění*.

26. Bohatcová, *Česká kniha*, 275.

27. Ibid., 273–77.

28. F. Staněk, Z. Tobolka, "Persekuce české literatury," 6 June 1917, in *Za právo a stát*, 188.

29. See the letter from Václav Beneš Šumavský, editor of *Národní politika*, to Alois Jirásek, 18 October 1916, reproduced in Miloslav Novotný, ed., *Roky Aloisa Jiráska* (Prague: Melantrich, 1953), 352.

30. *Zlatá Praha*, vol. 36, nos. 5–6 (13 November 1918).

31. This is given in full in *Národní shromáždění československé v prvním roce republiky*, 121–3.

32. See *ReD*, vol. 3, no. 1 (1929), 4–6.

33. Quoted in Maurice Nadeau, *The History of Surrealism* (Cambridge, Mass.: Belknap Press of Harvard University Press, 1989), 25.

34. Miloslav Novotný, *Pláč kultury v ČSR 1918–1928: sborník dokumentů* (Prague: soukromý tisk, 1928), 28. This is rare, only fifty-nine numbered copies having been produced (in order precisely to get around the censorship, which did not apply to such private publications). The copy I consulted is in the library of the Ústav pro českou a světovou literaturu of the Czech Academy of Sciences, Prague.

35. Ibid., 3–5.

36. "Pokyny k provedení prověrky knižních sbírek v knihovnách všech druhů." Printed four-page leaflet, issued sometime in 1953, headed "Důvěrné!" Supplied to me (with thanks) by paní Černá of the Národní knihovna, Prague.

37. I consulted this catalogue, which was on public display, and the notebooks on which it is based, which were not, in April 1993 in the Klementinum in Prague. I am grateful to the staff of the Národní knihovna for allowing me this access.

38. Perry Anderson and *New Left Review* did much to construct the peculiar category of "Western Marxism"; Anderson's book *Considerations on Western Marxism* is on the Index too.

39. See Bohatcová, *Česká kniha*, 275.

40. See Miroslav Ivanov, *Justiční vražda aneb smrt Milady Horákové* (Prague: Betty, 1991), 273–74.

41. Eduard Goldstücker, František Kautman, and Pavel Reiman, eds., *Franz Kafka:*

Liblická konference 1963 (Prague: Československá akademie věd, 1963); Otakar Mohyla, ed., *IV. sjezd Svazu československých spisovatelů (Protokol): Praha 27.–29. června 1967* (Prague: Československý spisovatel, 1968).

42. Leader of the KSS from 1945 to 1954 and prime minister until deposed, Široký played a major role in the 1950s purges and especially in the campaign against "bourgeois Slovak nationalism."

43. This letter is reproduced in Ludvík Svoboda, *Cestami života*, vol. 2 (Prague: Prospektrum, 1992), 5.

44. For example, Karel Bartošek, *Pražské povstání 1945* (Prague, 1965); *Muži a válka: prózy z druhé světové války* (Prague: Naše vojsko, 1966); Z. Konečný and F. Mainuš, eds., *Nezapomenutelné jaro: vzpomínky sovětských vojáků na osvobození Československa* (Prague: Státní nakladatelství politické literatury, 1965); *Partyzánské hnutí v Československu za druhé světové války* (Prague: Naše vojsko, 1961); *Pražská květnová revoluce 1945: k prvnímu výročí slavného povstání pražského lidu* (Prague: Melantrich, 1946); *Slovenské národní povstání: sborník k 15. výročí* (Prague: Státní nakladatelství politické literatury, 1959); *Šest let okupace Prahy*; and many more.

45. Milan Blahynka et al., eds., *Čeští spisovatelé 20. století: slovníková příručka* (Prague: Československý spisovatel, 1985). Similar comments apply to Vladimír Forst, ed., *Slovník české literatury 1970–1981* (Prague: Československý spisovatel, 1985); and Petr Bílek, *175 autorů: Čeští prozaici, básníci a literární kritici publikující v 70. letech v nakladatelství Československý spisovatel* (Prague: Československý spisovatel, 1982). Essential counterpoints to these are Jiří Brabec et al., *Slovník zakázaných autorů 1948–1980* (Prague: Státní pedagogické nakladatelství, 1991); Blahoslav Dokoupil, et al., *Slovník českého románu 1945–1991* (Ostrava: Sfinga, 1992), and the revised and expanded version of this, same editors, *Slovník české prózy 1945–1994* (Ostrava: Sfinga, 1994); and Zdeňka Rachůnková, *Zamlčovaní překladatelé: bibliografie 1948–1989* (Prague: Ivo Železný, 1992). The best single bibliographic source on exile publications is probably Jan Čulík, *Knihy za ohradou: česká literatura v exilových nakladatelstvích 1971–1989* (Prague: Trizonia, 1993).

46. *Malá československá encyklopedie*, 6 vols. (Prague: Academia, 1984–87).

47. František Ebel et al., eds., *Deset let Československé republiky*, 3 vols. (Prague: Státní tiskárna, 1928).

48. Miloslav Novotný, ed., *Naše umění v odboji* (Prague: Evropský literární klub, 1938). On ELK's publications see *ELK 1935–1945* (Prague: ELK, 1946). This was the publishing house for which Jiří Weil briefly became editor after the war.

49. On this see Petr Pithart, "Kavalír Josef Pekař," in his *Dějiny a politika*, 71–103.

50. See the lists of positions controlled by the KSČ Central Committee in the documents cited in note 25.

51. Bohumil Hrabal, *Too Loud a Solitude*, trans. Michael Henry Heim (New York: Harcourt Brace Jovanovich, 1990), 2–3.

52. Successive editions of the textbook *Dějepis 9: pro základní školy* (Prague: Státní pedagogické nakladatelství), (1970) 237; (1975) 252.

53. Jaroslav Seifert, *Osm dní*, 2d ed. (Prague: Československý spisovatel, 1968). These poems have been translated into English: *Eight Days: An Elegy for Thomas Masaryk*, trans. Paul Jagasich and Tom O'Grady (Iowa City, Iowa: The Spirit That Moves Us Press, 1985). The fullest selection of Seifert's poetry in English is *The Selected Poetry of Jaroslav Seifert*, trans. Edward Osers (New York: Collier, 1987).

asy krásy světament>

54. Jaroslav Seifert, *Všecky krásy světa* (Prague: Československý spisovatel, 1982). The censored passages were restored in the second edition published by Československý spisovatel in 1992, whose notes give full details of the book's publication history and the censor's mutilations.

55. Originally published in the "O sobě" column in *Rozpravy Aventina*, quoted in *Reflex*, no. 39 (1992), 68.

56. Ivan Skála, "Cizí hlas," in *Tvorba*, vol. 19 (1950), 285–86.

57. Ludvík Vaculík, *Morčata* (Prague: Československý spisovatel, 1991), frontispiece. Skála's letter to Vaculík of 11 November 1970 is also reproduced here. The novel is available in English as *The Guinea Pigs* (London: Penguin, 1975). For a representative collection of Skála's own post-1968 writing, see his *Kontinuita* (Prague: Československý spisovatel, 1980). Vaculík's "Two Thousand Words" ("Dva tisíce slov") was published—in a special print run of three hundred thousand copies—in *Literární listy*, vol. 1, no. 18 (27 June 1968).

58. See Vilém Prečan, *Nezávislá literatura a samizdat v Československu 70. a 80. let* (Prague: Ústav pro soudobé dějiny ČSAV, 1992), and Václav Burian et al., *Česká a slovenská literatura v exilu a samizdatu* (Olomouc: Hanácké noviny, 1991). Apart from Vaculík himself, Petlice authors included Ivan Klíma, Eva Kantůrková, Jaroslav Seifert, Václav Černý, Jan Patočka, and Václav Havel. Petlice also published the Ceylon journey of the enormously popular travel writers Miroslav Zikmund and Jiří Hanzelka, who had also fallen foul of the authorities.

59. See Alena Nádvorníková, "Poslední rok Karla Teigeho," in Srp et al., *Karel Teige 1900–1951*, 168. The Společnost Karla Teiga (Karel Teige Society) has published, from former StB archives, the list of materials removed from Ebertová's apartment, but the comparable list for the raid on Teige's apartment is apparently missing. *Jarmark umění*, nos. 11–12 (1996), 8–11.

60. Mojmír Grygar, "Teigovština—trockistická agentura v naší kultuře," in *Tvorba*, vol. 20, nos. 42–44, October 1951.

61. For details, see chap. 5, note 187.

62. See Srp, *Karel Teige 1900–1951*.

63. See Sršeň, *Budova Národního muzea*, 102–6.

64. See Němečková, *Československé pamětní mince*; and *A Catalogue of Czechoslovak Coins* (Prague: Státní banka Československa, 1975).

65. Transcribed from "Marta Kubišová: songy a balady," Supraphon LP record album 10 0587–1311 (1990). The lyrics are by J. Brabec and P. Rada. Her version of "Hey, Jude" is on the same album.

66. T. G. Masaryk, *Cesta demokracie: soubor projevů za republiky*, vol. 1, 1918–1920 (Prague: ČIN, 1934), 10. The words he quotes from Komenský are "vláda věcí Tvých k Tobě zase se navrátí, lide český"; the words of the song "když tvá ztracená vláda věcí tvých zpět se k tobě navrátí, lide, navrátí." Havel acknowledges both Masaryk and Komenský and paraphrases as "Tvá vláda, lide, se k tobě navrátila"; Václav Havel, *Projevy leden-červen 1990* (Prague: Vyšehrad, 1990), 19.

67. Šamberger, *Celostátní výstava archivních dokumentů*, epigraph quote (from Nejedlý himself) to Nejedlý's untitled preface, 7.

68. Ibid., 197.

69. Zdeněk Nejedlý, "Komunisté, dědici velikých tradic českého národa," in his *O*

smyslu českých dějin, vol. 16 in *Spisy Zdeňka Nejedlého* (Prague: Státní nakladatelství politické literatury, 1953), 217–67.

70. *Svému osvoboditeli československý lid* (Prague: Orbis, 1955), 10. No author or editor credited.

71. Ibid., 9.

72. Ibid., 13–15.

73. Vlasta Štursová, "Pomník generalissima J. V. Stalina v Praze," in *Slovanský přehled,* vol. 41, nos. 4–5 (1955), 162. The visual possibilities this site offered for monumentalization had been realized much earlier. In 1912, the magazine *Český svět* published a design for an equally humongous memorial on Letná to—Jindřich Fügner and Miroslav Tyrš. This latter is reproduced—appropriately—in Dvorský, Effenberger, and Král, *Surrealistické východisko,* in the unpaginated set of illustrations following p. 232.

74. Quoted in Mikoláš Aleš, *Boj našeho lidu za svobodu,* folder of reproductions of his work, ed. Jaromír Neumann (Prague: Orbis, 1952), 22.

75. *Svému osvoboditeli československý lid,* 12.

76. See the amusing account by Dalibor Mácha in *Rudé právo,* 9 March 1990, under the title "Řekli mu: Stalina odstřelíš!" The order—somewhat difficult to carry out given the magnitude of the monument—was: "It must go quickly, there mustn't be much of a bang, and it must be seen by as few people as possible."

77. Konečná, *Soupis repertoáru Národního divadla,* vol. 2.

78. Information from entry on Medek in *Československo: biografie.*

79. *Malá československá encyklopedie,* vol. 4 (1986), 154. Reactionary sentiments clearly run in the family. The elder of Rudolf Medek's two sons, Ivan (b. 1925), was director of the musical publisher Supraphon from 1970 to 1977, lost his job on signing Charta 77, and was driven into exile a year later. In 1993 he became director of the domestic policy section of the Presidential Chancellery at Václav Havel's invitation. The younger, Mikuláš (1926–1974), was a leading Czech surrealist painter much influenced by Karel Teige. He is discussed in both Bydžovská and Srp, *Český surrealismus,* and Šmejkal, *České imaginativní umění.*

80. Bohuslav Lázňovský, ed., *Průvodce po Československu,* part 1, *Země česká a moravskoslezská* (Prague: Klub československých turistů/Orbis, 1930), 44.

81. *Nový průvodce po Československu,* vol. 1, part 1, *Čechy: Praha, jižní Čechy a jihozápad středních Čech* (Prague: Orbis, 1950), 147. No author or editor credited. Produced "with the cooperation of the Ministry of Information and Enlightenment."

82. Václav Hlavsa, *Praha: průvodce městem* (Prague: Sportovní a turistické nakladatelství, n.d. [probably 1956]), 282.

83. See Pavel Kovář, "Začarovaný kopec," in *Reflex,* no. 52 (1992), 54–56. This is based on the testimony of Zázvorka's grandson.

84. On Malejovský's work, which also includes the Smetana statue on Smetanovo nábřeží in Prague, see Václav Procházka, ed., *Josef Malejovský,* exhibition catalogue (Prague: Národní galerie, 1986). Both the doors and "Jaro" are illustrated here.

85. Frankensteinová, *Max Švabinský: dílo 1924–1948,* 250. Švabinský's mosaic is abundantly illustrated in this very detailed account. Captured Czechoslovak Legionnaires were executed by the Austro-Hungarian authorities as traitors on various occasions in World War I. See Rudolf Medek, *K vítězné svobodě 1914—1918—1928*

(Prague: Památník odboje, 1928), photographs on 120 (Ukraine); 372, 374, and 376 (Italy); 391 and 404–5 (Bohemia).

86. Alois Kubíček, *Betlémská kaple v Praze* (Prague: Státní tělovýchovné nakladatelství, 1953), 24. See also his longer book *Betlémská kaple* (Prague: Státní nakladatelství krásné literatury, hudby a umění, 1960).

87. Kubíček, *Betlémská kaple v Praze*, 10.

88. Kubíček, *Betlémská kaple*, 82.

89. "M. Jan Hus přátelům v Čechách," letter of 10 June 1415, in Ivan Hlaváček, ed., *Ze zpráv a kronik doby Husitské* (Prague: Svoboda, 1981), 176–78; emphasis added.

90. *A Catalogue of Czechoslovak Coins* (this is unpaginated; section headed "The Current Coins").

91. See Císařovský, *Oto Gutfreund*, numbers 240–43 in the "Katalog díla" given at the end of the book. The actual coin that went into circulation retained the motif of smoking chimneys, without the wheat, but many other coins of the time had agricultural motifs.

92. Dušek, *Příručka pro sběratele československých poštovních známek*, 114. Jirásek, *Staré pověsti české*, 13.

93. The decree of 25 October 1945 was valid as of 28 October 1945; hence the anniversary.

94. The first Spartakiáda actually took place in Prague in 1921. Originally Spartakiády were the festivals of a rival organization to Sokol, the Dělnické tělocvičné jednoty (Workers' Gymnastic Unions), founded by Social Democrats in 1897.

95. *Nový průvodce po Československsku*, vol. 1, part 1, 160.

96. Vladimír Karbusický and Jaroslav Vanický, eds., *Český revoluční zpěvník* (Prague: Státní nakladatelství krásné literatury, hudby a umění, 1953). A *budovatel* is simply a builder, but after 1948 the word came to mean a builder of socialism, and it is in its adjectival form, for which there is no simple equivalent in English—the meaning of words being given by the forms of life in which they are embedded—that the word occurs here.

97. *Malá československá encyklopedie*, vol. 4, 892.

98. As my wife Alena, who was a child in Czechoslovakia in the 1950s, well remembers.

99. On Krásná jizba see further Anděl, *Umění pro všechny smysly*.

100. I allude, of course, to the opening sentences of a famous analysis of another popular democratic revolution that turned shortly afterward into a coup d'état: Karl Marx, "The 18th Brumaire of Louis Bonaparte," in Karl Marx and Friedrich Engels, *Collected Works* (New York: International Publishers), vol. 11 (1979), 103–4.

101. *Museum Klementa Gottwalda* (Prague, n.d. [after March 1962]). No author or editor credited. Unpaginated guidebook to the standing exhibitions.

102. Leaflet entitled "Č. S. 1894–1994" (Prague: Česká spořitelna, 1994). No author credited.

103. *Museum Klementa Gottwalda*.

104. This is, of course, the opening sentence of L. P. Hartley, *The Go-Between* (London: Guild Publishing, 1978).

105. These are pictured on p. 111 of Dušek, *Příručka pro sběratele československých známek*.

106. Julius Fučík, *V zemi, kde zítra již znamená včera*, excerpts in Kateřina Blahynková and Milan Blahynka, eds., *Dobrá zvěst: z cest za poznáním SSSR ve dvacátých a třicátých letech* (Prague: Československý spisovatel, 1987).

107. In full, Státní nakladatelství krásné literatury a umění. For much of the fifties it was known as SNKLHU (Státní nakladatelství krásné literatury, hudby a umění).

108. Jacket blurb to František Ladislav Čelakovský, *Ohlas písní ruských/Ohlas písní českých* (Prague: Orbis, 1948).

109. See Zdeňka Broukalová and Saša Mouchová, *Bibliografický soupis knih vydaných SNKLU v letech 1953–1962* (Prague: Státní nakladatelství krásné literatury a umění, 1964), appendix.

110. Kundera, *Book of Laughter and Forgetting*, 158. There is a mistranslation here: Černokostelecká třída does not mean "the Avenue of the Black Church" but the avenue leading to Kostelec nad Černými lesy, a settlement outside Prague. And unless he was an unusually old husband, Tamina's father would not have been born on Černokostelecká but on Jungmannova třída, as the street had been renamed, after Josef Jungmann, from c. 1884 to 1920, when it became Fochova třída. See Čarek, *Ulicemi města Prahy*, 357.

111. Letter to Oskar Pollak, 20 December 1902, in Franz Kafka, *Letters to Friends, Family, and Editors*, trans. Richard Winston and Clara Winston (New York: Schocken, 1977). I have altered the translation: "old crone" is not an accurate rendition of either the sense or the associations of Kafka's "*Mutterlein.*" It matters, because he is directly drawing on the Czech *matička*, meaning "little mother," which is how Czechs affectionately refer to their capital city.

112. It was moved to Hvězda Castle in 1966; see Ctibor Rybár et al., *Co je co v Praze* (Prague: ČTK/Pressfoto, 1989), 351.

113. Milan Krejčí, *Pražské pomníky a sochy* (Prague: Galerie hlavního města Prahy, 1979), unpaginated.

114. Čarek, *Ulicemi města Prahy*, 337.

115. Ibid., 366.

116. The source for the following information about National Theater productions, unless otherwise stated, is Konečná, *Soupis repertoáru Národního divadla*.

117. Quoted in Šíp, *Česká opera*, 119.

118. See Ch. 1, note 23 for details of prewar stagings of Čapek plays at the Národní divadlo.

119. *Ottův slovník naučný*, vol. 25 (1906), 965.

120. Emanuel Poche et al., *Encyklopedie českého výtvarného umění* (Prague: Academia, 1975), 261.

121. See, for example, the plates in Václav Formánek, *Josef Lada* (Prague: Odeon, 1980).

122. Božena Němcová, *Babička*, 164–65.

123. The story is told in Jarmila Novotná, *Byla jsem šťastná*, 241.

124. See on this the excellent exhibition catalogue, Marie Mžyková, ed., *Navrácené poklady: restitutio in integrum* (Prague: Pragafilm, 1994).

125. Regarding Sokol see ibid., 14–15. I saw some of the majolica on display in Trojský zámek in the early 1990s. The Havels' collection of ceramics and porcelain was started by Václav Havel's maternal grandfather Hugo Vavrečka. See Jana Kybalová, *Keramická sbírka Hugo Vavrečky*, exhibition catalogue (Prague: Uměleckoprůmyslové muzeum, 1995), on its contents and history.

126. This became a major court case after 1989. The gallery won.

127. František Nečásek et al., *Výstava díla Mikoláše Alše* (Prague: Orbis, 1952), frontispiece; see also *Výstava díla Mikoláše Alše: seznam děl vystavených v Jízdárně pražského hradu* (Prague: Orbis, 1952); and V. V. Štech and Emanuel Svoboda, *M. Aleš: výstava jeho života a díla pro českou knihu a divadlo* (Prague: Národní museum, 1952). All of these are exhibition catalogues.

128. Typescript minutes of meeting of 10 January 1952, headed "Zápis ze schůze užšího výboru pro pořádání výstav M. Alše v jubilejním roce 1952," in the file on the exhibition in the archives of the Scientific Information Division of the Národní galerie in Prague. Attendance figures (which I discuss below, p. 299) are also given in another document in this same box, handwritten, entitled "Výstava M. Alše."

129. See above, p. 189.

130. František Nečásek, "V Alšově jubilejním roce," introduction to exhibition catalogue *Výstava díla Mikoláše Alše 1852–1952*, 13–14.

131. See *Seznam děl Jubilejní výstavy Mikoláše Alše*, vol. 1 (1932), 57–58; vol. 2 (1933), 59–60.

132. Nečásek, "V Alšově jubilejním roce," in *Výstava díla Mikoláše Alše 1852–1952*, 13–14.

133. Ibid., 14.

134. František Nečásek, "Rodný domek Klementa Gottwalda," in Jaroslav Jelínek et al., *Český jazyk pro třetí ročník* (Prague: Státní pedagogické nakladatelství, 1981), 155. František Nečásek (1913–68), née Vagenknecht, was a big wheel in KSČ cultural politics. From 1934 to 1938 he was an editor of *Rudé právo*, from 1941 to 1945 chief director of the Czech broadcasting service of Radio Moscow, in 1945–46 chief editor of the newspaper *Mladá fronta*, from 1948 to 1953 head of the cultural and press division of the presidential chancellery, from 1953 to 1959 chief director of Czechoslovak Radio, and from 1959 until his death in 1968 head of the flagship artistic publishing house Odeon. *Malá československá encyklopedie*, vol. 4 (1986), 449.

135. Jelínek, *Český jazyk pro třetí ročník*, 32–33.

136. These were included after the 1989 revolution: *Spisy*, volumes 20 (*Hovory s T. G. Masarykem*, 1990) and 24 (*Básnické počátky—překlady*, 1993), respectively.

137. F. X. Šalda, "Umělecká tvorba a stát," 42.

138. Reproduced in Novotný, *Roky Aloise Jiráska*, 403.

139. Ibid., 405.

140. See Broukalová and Mouchová, *Bibliografický soupis knih vydaných SNKLU*.

141. Calculated from Konečná, *Soupis repertoáru Národního divadla*.

142. See note 128.

143. The source for these figures is Marcela Hojdová of the National Gallery. See note 4.

144. There is an English edition of this: Hans Christian Andersen, *Fairy Tales* (London: Hamlyn, 1959).

145. Jan Poš, "Činorodé snění," in Jana A. Brabcová, ed., *Jiří Trnka 1912–1969*, exhibition catalogue (Prague: Národní galerie, 1992), 5.

146. Jacket blurb to Alois Jirásek, *Na ostrově* (Prague: Svoboda, 1948). No author credited.

147. Zdeněk Nejedlý, "Doslov," in Jirásek, *Na ostrově*, 210–11.

148. Interestingly, this event is not mentioned in Konečná, *Soupis repertoáru Národního divadla*. Gottwald's greeting, in the form of a letter dated 22 August 1951, is given in Novotný, *Roky Aloisa Jiráska*, 5. There is a photograph, which forms the basis of my description here, in the same book, p. 408.

149. Reproduced in Novotný, *Roky Aloisa Jiráska*, 5.

150. The plaque is pictured in ibid., 419.

151. Rybár, *Co je co v Praze*, 300.

152. Zdeněk Nejedlý, "Litomyšl," in *Ottův slovník naučný*, vol. 16 (1900), 174–75.

153. F. X. Šalda, "Osobnost Zdeňka Nejedlého," in Bedřich Bělohlávek, ed., *Padesát let Zdeňka Nejedlého* (Prague: Bedřich Bělohlávek, 1928). Unfortunately, from the point of view of giving accurate references, this rather thick book is unpaginated; hence, no page references are given here on throughout my subsequent discussion for quotations from this article, or from this Festschrift.

154. In his untitled contribution to Bělohlávek, *Padesát let Zdeňka Nejedlého*.

155. In her untitled contribution to Bělohlávek, *Padesát let Zdeňka Nejedlého*.

156. "Osobnost Zdeňka Nejedlého," in Bělohlávek, *Padesát let Zdeňka Nejedlého*.

157. Václav Novotný, "Zdeněk Nejedlý: historik," in Bělohlávek, *Padesát let Zdeňka Nejedlého*.

158. *Ottův slovník naučný*, vol. 22 (1904), 586. Figures from 1900 census, for the village of Samotišky, above which the church is situated.

159. "Svatý Kopeček," in Antonín Dokoupil, ed., *Čtení z Jiřího Wolkera* (Prague: Václav Petr, 1925), 87–94.

160. Ibid., introduction, 8.

161. The epigraph is given as the frontispiece to ibid. Actually, Wolker was not yet twenty-four. He was born on 29 March 1900 and died (of tuberculosis) on 3 January 1924.

162. Josef Hora, speech at Karel Čapek's funeral, in Opelík, *Karel Čapek ve fotografii*, 170.

163. Ústřední výbor KSČ, "Všemu pracujícímu lidu Československa," in *Lidová tvořivost*, vol. 4, no. 5 (May 1953), 144.

164. See Josef Křivánek and Jaromír Vítek, *Pražské metro* (Prague: Nakladatelství dopravy a spojů, 1987), 50. On the semiotics of the Prague subway more generally see the excellent chapter "Metro" in Macura, *Šťastný věk*, 88–95.

165. Kundera, *Book of Laughter and Forgetting*, 65–67.

166. Kundera, *Unbearable Lightness of Being*, 3.

167. Kundera, *Art of the Novel*, 135.

168. Milan Kundera, *Life is Elsewhere*, trans. Peter Kussi, with a new preface by the author (London: Penguin, 1986), 270–71.

169. Ibid., 169.

170. Preface to ibid., vi.

171. *Life Is Elsewhere*, 262.

172. Ibid., 264.

173. As Kundera acknowledges. See his preface to ibid.

174. *Life Is Elsewhere*, 167.

175. See Kundera, preface to ibid., vi.

176. Kundera, *Book of Laughter and Forgetting*, 67–8. The poem of Éluard that

Kundera quotes here is "Le Visage de la Paix" (The Face of Peace), which may be found in French and in English translation in Paul Éluard, *Selected Poems*, ed. and trans. Gilbert Bowen (London: Calder/New York: Riverrun Press, 1987), 134–41.

177. Kundera, *Book of Laughter and Forgetting*, 65–6.

178. Viktor Dyk, "Země mluví," in Novotný, *Naše umění v odboji*, 105–6.

179. Milan Kundera, "Vánoce," originally published in the collection *Člověk zahrada širá* (Prague: Československý spisovatel, 1953), 25, quoted here as reprinted in Macura, *Šťastný věk*, 38.

180. Ian McEwan, "An Interview with Milan Kundera," *Granta*, 11 (1984), 23.

181. Kundera, *Art of the Novel*, 126.

182. Ibid., 44.

183. Zdeněk Pluhař, *Opustíš-li mne*, 7th ed. (Prague: Československý spisovatel, 1985), 465–66.

184. I am grateful to both my father-in-law, Ladislav Borůvka, and my friend Marie Voráčková for supplying me with their own *kádrové spisy* of various dates. These particular questions were asked on the forms for years following the 1968 invasion. I have given only a selection of information required on these reports here, not the whole catechism.

185. The indictments are reproduced, together with sections of the transcript of the trial, in Bedřich Utitz, *Neuzavřená kapitola: politické procesy padesátých let* (Prague: Dokořán, 1991), 16–17. The phrase is "*židovského původu*." Of the other three, Frank and Šváb are described as "Czech," Clementis as "Slovak." Class origin is also given, so that Jewishness and wealth, wherever possible, are inextricably associated.

SOURCES

THIS BIBLIOGRAPHY lists only sources directly pertaining to Czech history and culture. Details of all other works cited in this book are provided in the footnotes. I have given host volumes (anthologies, newspapers, periodicals, edited collections, etc.) here rather than the individual items cited from them; again, full details of the latter may be found in the notes.

UNPUBLISHED SOURCES (LISTED BY INSTITUTIONAL LOCATION)

In Oddělení vědeckých informací, Národní galerie, Prague

Výstavy Umělecké besedy [Exhibitions of Umělecká beseda, 1863–1951]. Typescript, compilers not credited, n.d.

Soupis výstav Spolku výtvarných umělců Mánes 1898–1950 [List of exhibitions of SVU Mánes 1898–1950]. Typescript, compiled by Jitka Pušová and Jiřina Mašínová, n.d.

Soupis výstav Jednoty umělců výtvarných [List of exhibitions of Jednota umělců výtvarných, 1899–1952]. Typescript, compilers not credited, n.d.

Soupis výstav Sdružení českých umělců Hollar 1918–1956 [List of exhibitions of SČUG Hollar 1918–1956]. Typescript, compiled by Jitka Pušová and Jiřina Mašínová, 1987.

Soupis výstav Národní galerie uspořádaných v Praze v letech 1945–1990 [List of exhibitions of the National Gallery arranged in Prague in the years 1945–1990]. Typescript, compiled by Helena Obrová, 1990.

Soupis výstav Národní galerie v zahraničí [List of exhibitions of the National Gallery abroad, 1945–1989]. Typescript, compiled by Jitka Pušová and Marcela Hojdová, 1991.

Regiony 1948–1985 [The regions, 1948–1985]. Typescript list of NG exhibitions staged in Czechoslovak regional galleries. Compilers not credited, n.d.

"Zápis ze schůze užšího výboru pro pořádaní výstav M. Alše v jubilejním roce 1952 . . ." [Minutes of a meeting of the steering committee for organizing the Mikoláš Aleš exhibitions in the jubilee year 1952 . . .]. Typescript, dated 10 January 1952. Filed with catalogues for the 1952 Aleš exhibitions.

"Výstava M. Alše," handwritten chart listing daily numbers of visitors to the 1952 Aleš exhibition at Jízdárna pražského hradu. Filed with catalogues for the 1952 Aleš exhibitions.

In Národní knihovna, Prague

Handwritten notebooks, untitled, listing books banned during the communist period; see above, pp. 259–60, for fuller discussion.

"Pokyny k provedení prověrky knižních sbírek v knihovnách všech druhů" [Instructions for carrying out the screening of book collections in libraries of all types]. Printed memo, marked "Confidential," undated, but issued in 1953.

Prozatímní katalog bývalé prohibiti literatury [Provisional catalogue of formerly prohibited literature].

Other Sources

"An die vaterländischen Freunde der Wissenschaften" [To the Patriotic Friends of Science]. Printed proclamation by Oberstburggraf Franz Graf von Kolowrat, dated 15 April 1818.

Pláč kultury v ČSR 1918–1928: sborník dokumentů [The cry of culture in the Czechoslovak Republic 1918–1928: a miscellany of documents]. Ed. Miloslav Novotný. Prague: soukromý tisk, 1928. Only fifty-nine numbered copies were produced of this private publication; consulted in library of Ústav pro českou a světovou literaturu Československé akademie věd, Prague.

"Kádrový spis" [Cadre File]. Contains, inter alia, printed questionnaire [Dotazník] and required brief autobiography [Životopis]. 1950 and 1974 exemplars, supplied to me, with thanks, by Ladislav Borůvka and Marie Voráčková, respectively.

NEWSPAPERS, MAGAZINES, AND YEARBOOKS (*LISTED ALPHABETICALLY BY TITLE*)

Acta Musei pragensis

Almanach Kmene [Kmen Almanac]

Almanach královského hlavního města Prahy (from 1922 *Almanach hlavního města Prahy*) [Almanac of the Royal Capital City Prague]

Almanach Národní besedy [Almanac of Národní beseda]

Analagon

Cross Currents

Československo [Czechoslovakia]

Český svět [The Czech World]

Jarmark umění [The Fleamarket of Art]

Květy [Blossoms]

Lidová demokracie [People's Democracy]

Lidová tvořivost [Folk Art]

Lidové noviny [People's News]

Literární listy [Literary Pages]

Literární noviny [Literary News]

Národní divadlo [The National Theater]

Národní shromáždění československé v prvním roce republiky [The Czechoslovak National Assembly in the First Year of the Republic]. Prague: Předsednictvo Národního shromáždění, 1919.

Naše Slovensko [Our Slovakia]

Pestrý týden [Weekly Variety]

Práce [Work]

Přítomnost [The Present]

ReD (Revue Devětsilu) [Devětsil Review]

Reflex

Revolver review

Revoluční sborník Devětsil [Revolutionary Miscellany Devětsil]. Ed. Jaroslav Seifert and Karel Teige. Prague: 1922.

Ročenka Československé republiky [Yearbook of the Czechoslovak Republic]

Ročenka československých profesorů [Yearbook of Czechoslovak Gymnasium Teachers]

Rudé právo [Red Right]
Sborník archivních prací [Miscellany of Archival Research]
Slovanský přehled [Slav Survey]
Statistika královského hlavního města Prahy [Statistics of the Royal Capital City of Prague]. Ed. Josef Erben. Prague: Obecní statistická komisse královského hlavního města Prahy, 1871.
Svět v obrazech [The World in Pictures]
Světozor [Worldwatch]
Šaldův zápisník [Šalda's Notebook]
Tvorba [Creativity]
Umění [Art]
Umění a řemesla [Arts and Crafts]
Volné směry [Free Directions]
Výtvarná práce [Creative Work]
Zlatá Praha [Golden Prague]
Zpravodajství (Národní galerie) [National Gallery press releases]
Ženské listy [The Women's Paper]
Život II [Life II]

PUBLISHED DOCUMENTS AND ANTHOLOGIES OF CONTEMPORARY TEXTS
(LISTED CHRONOLOGICALLY BY DATE OF THE RELEVANT DOCUMENTS)

Dějiny českého státu v dokumentech [History of the Czech state in documents]. Ed. Zdeněk Veselý. Prague: Victoria Publishing, 1994.
České a slovenské dějiny [Czech and Slovak history]. Vol. 3, *Dokumenty a materiály*. Ed. Josef Harna et al., Historický ústav Československé akademie věd. Prague: Fortuna, 1992.
Město vidím veliké . . . cizinci o Praze [I see a great city . . . foreigners on Prague]. Ed. V. Schwartz. Prague: Borový, 1940.
Husitské manifesty [Hussite manifestos]. Ed. Amadeo Molnár. Prague: Odeon, 1986.
The Jews of Bohemia and Moravia: A Historical Reader. Ed. Wilma Abeles Iggers. Detroit: Wayne State University Press, 1992.
Popis obyvatelstva hlavního města Prahy z roku 1770 [Description of the population of the capital city Prague in 1770]. Ed. Eduard Šebesta and Adolf L. Krejčík. Prague: Rodopisná společnost československá, 1933.
Obrození národa: svědectví a dokumenty [The rebirth of the nation: testimonies and documents]. Ed. Jan Novotný. Prague: Melantrich, 1979.
Za právo a stát: sborník dokladů o československé vůli k svobodě 1848–1919 [For right and state: a collection of documents on the Czechoslovak will to freedom 1848–1919]. No editor credited; published for tenth anniversary of Czechoslovak independence. Prague: Státní nakladatelství, 1928.
Prahl, Roman, and Lenka Bydžovská. *Volné směry: časopis secese a moderny* [Free Directions: a magazine of the secession and modernism]. Prague: Torst, 1993 (a history, with documents).
Programy české architektury [Programs of Czech architecture]. Ed. Josef Pechar and Petr Urlich. Prague: Odeon, 1981.

Osma a Skupina výtvarných umělců 1907–1917: teorie, kritika, polemika [The Eight and the Group of Fine Artists: theory, criticism, polemic]. Ed. Jiří Padrta. Prague: Odeon, 1992.

Naše umění v odboji [Our art in the resistance]. Ed. Miloslav Novotný. Prague: Evropský literární klub, 1938.

Beneš, Edvard, ed., *Světová válka a naše revoluce* [The World War and our revolution]. Vol. 3. Prague: Orbis/ČIN, 1931.

Weiner, Richard. *Třásničky dějinných dnů (1918–1919)* [The edgings of historic days (1918–1919)]. Prague: ELFA, 1991.

První československá ústava: diskuse v ústavním výboru v lednu a únoru 1920 [The first Czechoslovak constitution: discussions in the constitutional committee in January and February 1920]. Ed. Eva Broklová. Prague: Ústav pro soudobé dějiny, Česká akademie věd, 1992.

The Tradition of Constructivism. Ed. Stephen Bann. New York: Viking Press 1974; reprinted as a Da Capo paperback, 1990.

Avantgarda známá a neznámá [The avant-garde known and unknown]. 3 vols. Ed. Štěpán Vlašín. Vol. 1, *Od proletářského umění k poetismu 1920–1924* [From proletarian art to poetism 1920–1924]. Vol. 2, *Vrchol a krize poetismu 1925–1928* [The pinnacle and crisis of poetism 1925–1928]. Vol. 3, *Generační diskuse 1929–1931* [Generational discussion 1929–1931]. Prague: Svoboda, 1969–72.

Poetismus [Poetism]. Ed. Květoslav Chvatík and Zdeněk Pešat. Prague: Odeon, 1967.

Dobrá zvěst: z cest za poznáním SSSR ve dvacátých a třicátých letech [Good tidings: from journeys in pursuit of knowledge of the USSR in the 1920s and 1930s]. Ed. Kateřina Blahynková and Milan Blahynka. Prague: Československý spisovatel, 1987.

President mezi svými: druhý zájezd na Moravu a návštěva Slezska v roce 1924—články a zprávy Lidových novin [The president among his own: the second journey to Moravia and visit to Silesia in 1924—articles and reports in *Lidové noviny*]. Ed. Rudolf Těsnohlídek. Prague: Borový, 1924.

Ani labuť ani Lůna: sborník k stému výročí K. H. Máchy [Neither the swan nor the Moon; a miscellany for the hundredth anniversary of Karel Hynek Mácha]. Ed. Vítězslav Nezval. Reprint of first edition of 1936. Prague: Společnost Karla Teiga/ Concordia, 1995.

Odkaz T. G. Masaryka [The legacy of T. G. Masaryk]. Ed. Jasoň Boháč. Prague: Práce, 1990 (reprint of articles, photographs, and documents from *Právo lidu*, 14–22 September 1937).

Surrealistické východisko 1938–1968 [The surrealist point of departure, 1938–1968]. Ed. Stanislav Dvorský, Vratislav Effenberger, and Petr Král. Prague: Československý spisovatel, 1969.

Heydrichiáda: dokumenty [The Heydrich affair: documents]. Ed. Čestmír Amort. Prague: Naše vojsko, 1965 (documents and commentary).

Bojující Československo 1938–1945 [Czechoslovakia fighting 1938–1945]. Ed. V. Žižka. Košice: Žikeš, 1945.

Komu sluší omluva? Češi a sudetští Němci—dokumenty, fakta, svědectví [Who is to apologize? Czechs and Sudeten Germans—documents, facts, testimonies]. Anonymous authorial collective. Prague: Erika, 1992.

Sjezd národní kultury 1948: sbírka dokumentů [Congress of the national culture 1948: a collection of documents]. Ed. Miroslav Kouřil. Prague: Orbis, 1948.

Církevní komise ÚV KSČ 1949–1951: edice dokumentů [Church Commission of the Central Committee of the KSČ 1949–1951: an edition of documents]. Vol. 1, ed. Marie Bulínová, Milena Janišová, and Karel Kaplan. Prague: Ústav pro soudobé dějiny/Brno: Doplněk, 1994.

Za rozkvět československého výtvarného umění: projevy z konference výtvarných umělců v Jízdárně pražského hradu [For a flowering of Czechoslovak creative art: speeches from the conference of creative artists at the Riding School of Prague Castle]. Ed. Lubor Kára. Prague: Orbis, 1951.

Jaromír Hořec, *Doba ortelů: dokumenty, vzpomínky, iluze a skutečnosti* [The time of verdicts: documents, memories, illusions and realities]. Prague: Scholaris, 1992 (documents and commentary).

Bedřich Utitz, *Neuzavřená kapitola: politické procesy padesátých let* [An unclosed chapter: the political trials of the 1950s]. Prague: Lidové nakladatelství, 1990 (documents and commentary).

Kádrová nomenklatura KSČ 1948–1956: sborník dokumentů [The cadre nomenklatura of the KSČ 1948–1956: a collection of documents]. Ed. Karel Kaplan. Prague: Sešity ústavu pro soudobé dějiny, Československá akademie věd, 1992.

Franz Kafka: Liblická konference 1963 [Franz Kafka: the Liblice Conference 1963]. Ed. Eduard Goldstücker, František Kautman, and Pavel Reiman. Prague: Československá akademie věd, 1963.

III. sjezd Svazu československých spisovatelů Prague 22.–24. května 1963: protokol [3d congress of the Union of Czechoslovak Writers . . .]. Ed. Nora Krausová, Otakar Mohyla, and Marta Staňková. Prague: Československý spisovatel, 1963.

IV. sjezd Svazu československých spisovatelů (Protokol): Prague 27.–29. června 1967 [4th congress of the Union of Czechoslovak Writers . . .]. Ed. Otakar Mohyla. Prague: Československý spisovatel, 1968.

Charta 77, 1977–1989: od morální k demokratické revoluci—dokumentace [Charter 77, 1977–1989: from moral to democratic revolution—documents]. Ed. Vilém Prečan. Prague/Bratislava: Scheinfeld, 1990.

Rudá nomenklatura: kádrový pořádek Ústředního výboru Komunistické strany Československa [The red nomenklatura: cadre order of the Central Committee of the Communist Party of Czechoslovakia (May 1984)]. Introduction by Jiří Pavlis. Prague: Antikomunistická aliance/GMA 91, 1992.

Blahoslavená Anežka Česká: sborník ke svatořečení [The Blessed Agnes of Bohemia: a collection for her canonization]. Ed. Bohumil Svoboda. Prague: Česká katolická Charita, 1989.

ESSAYS AND COLLECTIONS OF WORKS BY INDIVIDUAL AUTHORS (*LISTED ALPHABETICALLY BY AUTHOR*)

Baťa, Jan. *Budujme stát pro 40,000,000 lidí* [Let us build a state for 40,000,000 people]. Zlín: Tisk, 1937.

Baťa, Tomáš. *Úvahy a projevy* [Essays and speeches]. Prague: Institut řízení, 1990 (originally Zlín: Tisk, 1932).

Čapek, Karel. *Spisy Karla Čapka* [Writings of Karel Čapek]. Vols. 17–19, *O umění a kultuře* [On art and culture] 1–3. Prague: Československý spisovatel, 1984, 1985, 1986.

Eisner, Pavel. *Chrám i tvrz: kniha o češtině* [A cathedral as well as a fortress: a book about Czech]. Prague: Lidové noviny, 1992 (photoreprint of 1946 ed.).

———. *Milenky: německý básník a česká žena* [Lovers: the German poet and the Czech woman]. Prague: Concordia, 1992.

Filla, Emil. *O výtvarném umění* [On fine art]. Prague: Karel Brož, 1948.

Goll, Jaroslav. *Jaroslava Golla vybrané spisy drobné* [Selected minor writings of Jaroslav Goll]. 2 vols. Prague: Historický klub, 1928–29.

Gottwald, Klement. *Spisy Klementa Gottwalda* [Writings of Klement Gottwald]. Vol. 1. Prague: Svoboda, 1950.

Havel, Václav. *Projevy leden–červen 1990* [Speeches January–June 1990]. Prague: Vyšehrad, 1990.

———. *Open Letters: Selected Writings 1965–1990.* Ed. Paul Wilson; trans. Paul Wilson, A. G. Brain, Erazim Kohák, Roger Scruton, and George Theiner. New York: Knopf, 1991.

Janáček, Leoš. *Janáček's Uncollected Essays on Music.* Ed. and trans. Mirka Zemanová. New York: Marion Boyars, 1989 (Janáček's newspaper feuilletons 1886–1928).

Jesenská, Milena. *Cesta k jednoduchosti* [The road to simplicity]. Reprint of first edition of 1926. Brno: Barrister a Principal, 1995.

———. *Zvenčí a zevnitř* [From without and from within]. Prague: Nakladatelství Franze Kafky, 1996.

Jungmann, Josef. *Josefa Jungmanna vybrané spisy* [Selected writings of Josef Jungmann]. Prague: Otto, 1918.

Kisch, Egon Erwin. *Vždycky na levém křídle: výbor z díla* [Always on the left wing: a selection from his work]. Prague: Naše vojsko, 1953.

Kundera, Milan. *The Art of the Novel.* Trans. Linda Asher. New York: Grove, 1988.

———. *Testaments Betrayed.* Trans. Linda Asher. New York: HarperCollins, 1995.

Marx, Karl, and Friedrich Engels. *Collected Works.* Vol. 8. New York: International Publishers, 1977.

Masaryk, Tomáš Garrigue. *Karel Havlíček.* 3d ed. Prague: Jan Laichter, 1920.

———. *Cesta demokracie: soubor projevů za republiky* [The journey of democracy: a collection of speeches during the Republic]. 2 vols. Prague: ČIN, 1933–34.

———. *Česká otázka* [The Czech question]. Prague: Svoboda, 1990.

———. *Jan Hus: naše obrození a naše reformace* [Jan Hus: our rebirth and our Reformation]. Prague: JK, 1990.

Nejedlý, Zdeněk. *Spisy Zdeňka Nejedlého* [Writings of Zdeněk Nejedlý]. Vol. 16, *O smyslu českých dějin* [On the meaning of Czech history]. Prague: Státní nakladatelství politické literatury, 1953.

———. Vol. 35, *Za kulturu lidovou a národní* [For a popular and national culture]. Prague: Státní nakladatelství politické literatury, 1953.

Neruda, Jan. *Studie krátké a kratší* [Studies short and shorter]. Prague: L. Mazáč, 1928.

Neumann, Stanislav Kostka. *Anti-Gide, neboli optimismus bez pověr a ilusí* [Anti-Gide, or optimism without superstitions and illusions]. Prague: Svoboda, 1946.

Palacký, František. *Dílo Františka Palackého* [The work of František Palacký]. 4 vols. Prague: L. Mazáč, 1941 (with supplement, 1945, which restores passages censored out by the German occupation authorities).

———. *Úvahy a projevy z české literatury, historie a politiky* [Essays and speeches from Czech literature, history and politics]. Prague: Melantrich, 1977.

Pekař, Josef. *O smyslu českých dějin* [On the meaning of Czech history]. Prague: Rozmluvy, 1990.

————. *Postavy a problémy českých dějin* [Figures and problems in Czech history]. Prague: Vyšehrad, 1990.

Peroutka, Ferdinand. *Budeme pokračovat* [We shall go on]. Toronto: Sixty-Eight Publishers, 1984.

————. *Jací jsme/Demokratický manifest* [What we are like/Democratic manifesto]. Prague: Středočeské nakladatelství, 1991.

Pithart, Petr. *Dějiny a politika: eseje a úvahy z let 1977–1989* [History and politics: essays and studies 1977–1989]. Prague: Prostor, 1990.

Šalda, František Xaver. *Soubor díla F. X. Šaldy* [Collected works of F. X. Šalda]. Vol. 11, *Kritické projevy 2—1894–1895* [Critical pieces 2]. Prague: Melantrich, 1950.

Skála, Ivan. *Kontinuita* [Continuity]. Prague: Československý spisovatel, 1980.

Škvorecký, Josef. *Talkin' Moscow Blues: Essays About Literature, Politics, Movies, and Jazz*. Ed. Sam Solecki, various translators. Toronto: Lester and Orpen Dennys, 1988.

Štyrský, Jindřich. *Každý z nás stopuje svoji ropuchu: texty 1923–1940* [Every one of us tracks his toad: texts 1923–1940]. Prague: Thyrsus, 1996.

Teige, Karel. *Výbor z díla* [Selection from his work]. Ed. Jiří Brabec, Vratislav Effenberger, Květoslav Chvatík, and Robert Kalivoda. Vol. 1, *Svět stavby a básně: studie z dvacátých let* [The world of building and poetry: studies from the 1920s]. Vol. 2, *Zápasy o smysl moderní tvorby: studie z 30. let* [Struggles over the meaning of modern creativity: studies from the 1930s]. Vol. 3, *Osvobozování života a poesie: studie z 40. let* [Liberating life and poetry: studies from the 1940s]. Prague: Československý spisovatel, 1966, 1969, and Aurora/Český spisovatel, 1994, respectively.

MEMOIRS, DIARIES, CORRESPONDENCE, AND INTERVIEWS (*LISTED ALPHABETICALLY BY AUTHOR*)

Brod, Max. *Pražský kruh* [The Prague circle]. Prague: Akropolis, 1993.

————. *Život plný bojů* [A life full of struggles]. Prague: Nakladatelství Franze Kafky, 1994.

Čapek, Karel. *Spisy Karla Čapka* [Writings of Karel Čapek].
  Vols 22 & 23, *Korespondence* [Correspondence], 1 and 2. Prague: Český spisovatel, 1993.
  Vol. 20, *Hovory s T. G. Masarykem* [Conversations with T. G. Masaryk]. Prague: Československý spisovatel, 1990.

Černý, Václav. *Paměti* [Memoirs]. Vol. 1, *Paměti 1921–1938*. Vol. 2, *Křik koruny české, paměti 1938–1945* [Cry of the Czech crown, memoirs 1938–1945]. Vol. 3, *Paměti 1945–1972*. Brno: Atlantis, 1994, 1992, 1992, respectively.

Clementis, Vladimír. *Nedokončená kronika* [Unfinished chronicle]. Prague: Československý spisovatel, 1965.

Drtina, Prokop. *Československo můj osud: kniha života českého demokrata 20. století* [Czechoslovakia my fate: a book of the life of a twentieth-century Czech democrat]. 2 volumes, each in 2 parts. Prague: Melantrich, 1991–92.

Fučík, Julius. *Reportáž psaná na oprátce* [Report from the gallows]. Prague: Československý spisovatel, 1972.

————. *Reportáž psaná na oprátce*. First full, uncensored edition. Prague: Torst, 1995.

Gutfreund, Otto. *Zázemí tvorby* [The hinterland of creativity]. Ed. Jiří Šetlík. Prague: Odeon, 1989.

Havel, Václav M. *Mé vzpomínky* [My memoirs]. Prague: Lidové noviny, 1993.

Iggers, Wilma A. *Women of Prague: Ethnic Diversity and Social Change from the Eighteenth Century to the Present.* Oxford: Berghahn Books, 1995 [a study of twelve Bohemian women, among them M. D. Rettigová, Božena Němcová, and Milena Jesenská, related largely in their own words].

Janouch, Gustav. *Conversations with Kafka: Notes and Reminiscences.* London: Derek Verschoyle, 1953.

Jirásek, Alois. *Z mých pamětí* [From my memories]. Prague: Mladá fronta, 1980.

Kafka, Franz. *The Diaries of Franz Kafka 1910–1923.* Ed. Max Brod; trans. Joseph Kresh (Diaries 1910–13) and Martin Greenberg and Hannah Arendt (Diaries 1914–23). London: Penguin, 1964.

————. *Letters to Friends, Family and Editors.* Ed. Beverly Colman, Nahum N. Glatzer, Christopher J. Kuppig, and Wolfgang Sauerlander; trans. Richard Winston and Clara Winston. New York: Schocken, 1977.

————. *Letters to Ottla and the Family.* Ed. N. N. Glatzer; trans. Richard Winston and Clara Winston. New York: Schocken, 1982.

————. *Briefe an Milena.* Ed. Jürgen Born and Michael Müller. Frankfurt: Fischer Verlag, 1986.

————. *Letters to Milena.* Ed. and trans. Philip Boehm. New York: Schocken, 1990.

Karel, R., and Vladimír Thiele, eds., *Žaluji: pankrácká kalvarie* [I accuse: Pankrác Calvary]. 2 vols. Prague: Orbis, 1946.

Krásnohorská, Eliška. *Ze vzpomínek Elišky Krásnohorské* [From the memoirs of Eliška Krásnohorská]. Prague: Československý spisovatel, 1950.

Kratochvil, Antonín, ed., *Žaluji* [I accuse]. Vol. 1, *Stalinská justice v Československu* [Stalinist justice in Czechoslovakia]. Vol. 2, *Vrátit slovo umlčeným* [Returning the word to the silenced]. Vol. 3, *Cesta k Sionu* [Journey to Zion]. Prague: Dolmen, 1990.

Kundera, Milan. Interview by Ian McEwan, *Granta*, no. 11, 1984.

Leikert, Jozef. *A den se vrátil (co následovalo po 17. listopadu 1939)* [And day returned (what followed after 17 November 1939)]. Bratislava: Astra, 1993.

London, Artur. *Doznání: v soukolí pražského procesu* [The confession: in the gearwheels of the Prague trial]. 2d ed. Prague: Československý spisovatel, 1990.

Mánes, Josef. *Dopisy Josefa Mánesa* [Letters of Josef Mánes]. Ed. Jan Kühndel. Prague: Odeon, 1968.

Masaryková, Alice. *Dětství a mládí: vzpomínky a myšlenky* [Childhood and youth: reminiscences and thoughts]. Prague: Ústav T. G. Masaryka, 1994.

Mlynář, Zdeněk. *Mráz přichází z Kremlu* [Frost arrives from the Kremlin]. Prague: Mladá fronta, 1990.

Mucha, Jiří. *Podivné lásky* [Peculiar loves]. Prague: Mladá fronta, 1958.

Němcová, Božena. *Z dopisů Boženy Němcové* [From the letters of Božena Němcová]. Prague: Státní nakladatelství dětské knihy, 1962.

————. *Lamentace: dopisy mužům* [Lamentations: letters to men]. Prague: Český spisovatel, 1995.

Nezval, Vítězslav. *Z mého života* [From my life]. Prague: Československý spisovatel, 1959.

Novotná, Jarmila. *Byla jsem šťastná* [I was happy]. Prague: Melantrich, 1991.

Putík, Jaroslav. *Odysea po česku* [A Czech-style odyssey]. Prague: Prostor, 1992.

Seifert, Jaroslav. *Všecky krásy světa* [All the beauties of the world]. Prague: Československý spisovatel, 1982.

——. 2d domestic (and first uncensored domestic) edition. Prague: Československý spisovatel, 1992.

Škvorecký, Josef, and Zdena Salivarová. *Samožerbuch* [A book of self-congratulation]. Prague: Panorama, 1991 (originally Toronto: Sixty-Eight Publishers, 1977).

Štorch-Marien, Otakar. *Paměti nakladatele* [Memoirs of a publisher]. Vol. 1, *Sladko je žít* [Sweet it is to live]. Vol. 2, *Ohňostroj* [Fireworks]. Vol. 3, *Tma a co bylo potom* [The dark and what came after]. Prague: Aventinum 1992 (2d ed.) and Československý spisovatel 1969, 1972 respectively.

Švabinská, Ela. *Vzpomínky z mládí* [Reminiscences from youth]. Prague: Státní nakladatelství krásné literatury a umění, 1962.

Svoboda, Ludvík. *Cestami života* [Through life's journeys]. Vol. 2. Prague: Prospektum, 1992.

Tyršová, Renata. *Miroslav Tyrš: jeho osobnost a dílo; podle zápisků, korespondence, rukopisné pozůstalosti a mých vzpomínek* [Miroslav Tyrš: his personality and work; according to records, correspondence, his literary estate and my memories]. Prague: Český čtenář, 1932–34.

Utitz, Bedřich. *Svědkové revoluce: někdejší spolupracovníci Lenina a Stalina vypovídají* [Witnesses of revolution: onetime co-workers of Lenin and Stalin tell their stories]. Prague: Orbis, 1990. (Interviews on Westdeutscher Rundfunk, Cologne, 1983–84.)

EXHIBITION CATALOGUES AND GUIDES TO PERMANENT COLLECTIONS (*LISTED CHRONOLOGICALLY*)

Všeobecná zemská výstava v Praze . . . Hlavní katalog [Universal Land Exhibition in Prague . . . main catalogue]. Ed. Josef Fořt. Prague: 1891.

Sto let práce: zpráva o všeobecné zemské výstavě v Praze 1891 [One hundred years of work: report on the Universal Land Exhibition in Prague 1891]. Josef Kafka et al., 3 vols., vol. 3 in two parts. Prague: 1892–95.

Jubilejní výstava zemská království českého v Praze 1891 [The Jubilee Land Exhibition of the Czech Kingdom in Prague 1891]. No editor credited. Prague: Šimáček, 1894.

Národopisná výstava českoslovanská v Praze 1895 [The Czechoslavic Ethnographic Exhibition in Prague 1895]. K. Klusáček et al. Prague: Otto, 1895.

Národopisná výstava českoslovanská v Praze 1895: hlavní katalog a průvodce [The Czechoslavic Ethnographic Exhibition in Prague 1895: main catalogue and guide]. Ed. Josef Kafka. Prague: 1895.

Katalog výstavy děl sochaře Augusta Rodina v Praze [Catalogue of the exhibition of the works of the sculptor August Rodin in Prague]. Texts by F. X. Šalda and Stanislav Sucharda. Prague: SVU Mánes, 1902.

Edvard Munch: XX. výstava spolku výtvarných umělců "Mánes" v Praze [Eduard Munch: 20th exhibition of SVU Mánes in Prague]. Introduction by K. Svoboda. Prague: SVU Mánes, 1905.

Moderní galerie království českého v Praze [The Modern Gallery of the Czech Kingdom in Prague]. No author credited. Prague: Unie, 1907.

Francouzští impressionisté: katalog 23. výstavy SVU Mánes v Praze 1907 [French impressionists: catalogue of the 23rd exhibition of SVU Mánes in Prague]. Introduction by F. X. Šalda. Prague: SVU Mánes, 1907.

Les Indépendants: XXXI. výstava SVU Mánes v Praze [The Independents: 31st exhibition of SVU Mánes in Prague]. Introduction by Antonín Matějček. Prague: SVU Mánes, 1910.

Národopisné museum v Praze: průvodce sbírkami [The Ethnographic Museum in Prague: guide to the collections]. 3d ed. Ed. August Žalud. Prague: Společnost Národopisného muzea českoslovanského, 1913.

Moderní umění, soubor sestaven A. Mercereauem v Paříži: 45. výstava SVU Mánes v Praze [Modern Art, a collection assembled by A. Mercereau in Paris: 45th exhibition of SVU Mánes in Prague]. Introduction by Alexandre Mercereau. Prague: SVU Mánes, 1914.

Kresby Bedřicha Smetany [Drawings of Bedřich Smetana]. Introduction by Zdeněk Nejedlý. Prague: Umělecká beseda, 1925.

Průvodce výstavou svatováclavskou [Guide to the Saint Václav exhibition]. Antonín Podlaha and Antonín Šorm. Prague: Výbor svatováclavský, 1929.

"Výstava korunovačních klenotů v jubilejním roce svatováclavském 1929" [The exhibition of the crown jewels in the Saint Václav jubilee year 1929]. Leaflet, text by Antonín Podlaha. Prague: Státní tiskárna, 1929.

L'école de Paris: francouzské moderní umění [The Paris school: French modern art]. Ed. Josef Čapek. Prague: Umělecká beseda, 1931.

Výstava Poesie 1932 [Exhibition Poesie 1932]. Introduction Kamil Novotný. Prague: SVU Mánes, 1932.

Seznam děl Jubilejní výstavy Mikoláše Alše [Lists of works at the jubilee exhibition of Mikoláš Aleš]. 2 vols. Text by V. V. Štech and others. Prague: Sdružení výtvarných umělců "Myslbek," 1932, 1933.

První výstava skupiny surrealistů v ČSR: Makovský, Štyrský, Toyen [The first exhibition of the group of surrealists in the Czechoslovak Republic: Makovský, Štyrský, Toyen]. Karel Teige and Vítězslav Nezval. Prague: SVU Mánes, 1935.

Dr. Desiderius (Hugo Boettinger): výstava veselých kreseb [an exhibition of humorous drawings]. Introduction by Jindřich Čadík. Prague: SČUG Hollar, 1937.

Výstava Národ svým výtvarným umělcům [The exhibition "The nation to its creative artists"]. Preface by Miloslav Hýsek. Prague: Kulturní rada ústředí pro kulturní a školskou práci Národního souručenství, 1939.

Národ svým výtvarným umělcům [The nation to its creative artists]. Contains texts of speeches opening the exhibition on 11 November 1939 by Miloslav Hýsek, Jan Kapras, Josef Nebeský, and T. F. Šimon. Prague: Kulturní rada Národního souručenství při Národní radě české, 1940.

Výstava Národ svým výtvarným umělcům v Praze 1940 [The exhibition "The nation to its creative artists" in Prague 1940]. Ed. F. V. Mokrý and V. F. Vicek. Prague: Kulturní rada Národního souručenství při Národní radě české, 1940.

Josef Čapek in Memoriam. Texts by Václav Rabas and Emil Filla; foreword by Jarmila Čapková. Prague: Umělecká beseda, 1945.

Dílo Josefa Čapka: obrazy, kresby, grafika, divadlo [The work of Josef Čapek: pictures, drawings, graphic art, theater]. Ed. Karel Šourek. Prague: Umělecká beseda, 1946.

Monumentální úkol současného umění [The monumental task of contemporary art]. Text by P. Smetana. Prague: SVU Mánes, 1947.

Monumentální Mikoláš Aleš [The monumental Mikoláš Aleš]. Karel Šourek. Prague: Umělecká beseda, 1947.

Výstava díla Mikoláše Alše [Exhibition of the work of Mikoláš Aleš]. Texts by František Nečásek, Emanuel Svoboda, Miroslav Míčko, and V. V. Štech. Prague: Orbis, 1952.

Výstava díla Mikoláše Alše: seznam děl vystavených v Jízdárně pražského hradu [Exhibition of the work of Mikoláš Aleš: list of works exhibited at the Riding School of Prague Castle]. Emanuel Svoboda and František Dvořák. Prague: Orbis, 1952.

M. Aleš: výstava jeho života a díla pro českou knihu a divadlo [M. Aleš: an exhibition of his life and work for the Czech book and theater]. V. V. Štech and Emanuel Svoboda. Prague: Národní museum, 1952.

Deset let Československé lidově demokratické republiky ve výtvarném umění [Ten years of the popular democratic Czechoslovak Republic in creative art]. Václav Formánek et al. Prague: Ministerstvo kultury, 1955.

Zakladatelé moderního českého umění [Founders of modern Czech art]. Miroslav Lamač, Jiří Padrta, Jan Tomeš. Brno: Dům umění, 1957.

Celostátní výstava archivních dokumentů: od hrdinné minulosti k vítězství socialismu [All-state exhibition of archival documents: from the heroic past toward the victory of socialism]. Zdeněk Šamberger et al. Prague: Ministerstvo vnitra, 1958.

Museum Klementa Gottwalda [The Klement Gottwald Museum]. No author credited. Prague: Museum Klementa Gottwalda, n.d. [after March 1962].

Dada, Surrealism and Their Heritage. William S. Rubin. New York: Museum of Modern Art, 1968.

Josef Mánes 1820–1871. Ed. Jiří Kotalík. Prague: Národní galerie, 1971.

Lidice 1942–1972. Includes English résumé by Vladimír Brehovszký. Prague: Český svaz protifašistických bojovníků/Svaz českých výtvarných umělců, 1972.

Český funkcionalismus 1920–1940: bytové zařízení [Czech functionalism 1920–1940: interior furnishings]. Alena Adlerová. Prague: Uměleckoprůmyslové muzeum/Brno: Moravská galerie, 1978.

Český funkcionalismus 1920–1940: užitá grafika [Czech functionalism 1920–1940: applied graphic art]. Jan Rous. Prague: Uměleckoprůmyslové muzeum/Brno: Moravská galerie, 1978.

Almanach Akademie výtvarných umění v Praze k 180. výročí založení (1799–1979) [Almanac of the Academy of Fine Arts in Prague: for the 180th anniversary of its foundation (1799–1979)]. Jiří Kotalík et al. Prague: Akademie výtvarných umění/Národní galerie, 1979.

Státní židovské muzeum v Praze [The State Jewish Museum in Prague]. Unnamed authorial collective. Prague: Státní židovské muzeum, 1979.

Alfons Mucha 1860–1939. Michel Laclotte et al. Prague: Národní galerie, 1980.

The Precious Legacy: Judaic Treasures from the Czechoslovak State Collections. Ed. David Altshuler. New York: Summit Books, 1983.

Československé pamětní mince a medaile 1948–1983 [Czechoslovak commemorative coins and medals 1948–1983]. Věra Němečková. Cheb: Chebské muzeum, 1983.

Josef Malejovský. Ed. Václav Procházka. Prague: Národní galerie, 1986.

Devětsil: česká výtvarná avantgarda dvacátých let [Devětsil: the Czech artistic avant-garde of the 1920s]. František Šmejkal, Rostislav Švácha, and Jan Rous. Prague: Galerie hlavního města Prahy, 1986.

Czech Functionalism 1918–1938. Introductory essay by Vladimír Šlapeta. London: Architectural Association, n.d. [after 1986].

Tvrdošíjní [The Obstinates]. Karel Srp. Prague: Galerie hlavního města Prahy, 1986.

Tvrdošíjní a hosté: 2. část, užité umění, malba, kresba [The Obstinates and guests: 2d part, applied art, painting, drawing]. Karel Srp. Prague: Galerie hlavního města Prahy, 1987.

Umělecká beseda: k 125. výročí založení [Umělecká beseda: for the 125th anniversary of its founding]. Jiří Kotalík. Prague: Národní galerie, 1988.

Czech Modernism 1900–1945. Jaroslav Anděl et al. Houston: Museum of Fine Arts/ Bullfinch Press, 1989.

Devětsil: Czech avant-garde art, architecture and design of the 1920s and '30s. Ed. Rostislav Švácha. Oxford: Museum of Modern Art/London: London Design Museum, 1990.

Aventinská mansarda: Otakar Štorch-Marien a výtvarné umění [The Aventinum Loft: Otakar Štorch-Marien and fine art]. Ed. Karel Srp. Prague: Galerie hlavního města Prahy, 1990.

Nerealizované návrhy československých papírových platidel 1918–1988 [Unrealized designs for Czechoslovak banknotes 1918–1988]. Věra Němečková, Jiří Pekárek and Jaroslav Šůla. Hradec Králové: Muzeum východních Čech, 1991.

Český kubismus: architektura a design 1910–1925 [Czech cubism: architecture and design 1910–1925]. Texts by Petr Wittlich, Josef Kroutvor, and others. Weil am Rhein: Vitra Design Museum, 1991.

Le cubisme à Prague [Cubism in Prague]. Claude Pétry et al. Paris: Jacques London, 1991.

František Zelenka: plakáty, architektura, divadlo [František Zelenka: posters, architecture, theater]. Ed. Josef Kroutvor. Prague: Uměleckoprůmyslové muzeum, 1991.

Grafika české avantgardy 1907–1918 [Graphic art of the Czech avant-garde 1907–1918]. Ed. Jana Wittlichová. Prague: Národní galerie, 1991.

Český kubismus 1909–1925: malířství, sochařství, umělecké řemeslo, architektura [Czech cubism 1909–1925: painting, sculpture, applied arts, architecture]. Ed. Jiří Švestka and Tomáš Vlček. Prague: Národní galerie/Stuttgart: Gerd Hatje, 1991.

Baťa: architektura a urbanismus [Baťa: architecture and urbanism]. Ed. Vladimír Šlapeta. Zlín: Státní galerie, 1991.

Štyrský, Toyen, artificialismus: 1926–1931 [Štyrský, Toyen, artificialism: 1926–1931]. Lenka Bydžovská and Karel Srp. Prague: Středočeská galerie, 1992.

Šíma/Le grand jeu. Texts by Suzanne Pagé et al. Paris: Musée d'Art Moderne de la Ville de Paris, 1992.

Moderní galerie tenkrát 1902–1942 [The Modern Gallery then, 1902–1942]. R. Musil et al. Prague: Národní galerie, 1992.

Pocta Rodinovi 1902–1992 [Homage to Rodin 1902–1992]. Marie Halířová. Prague: Národní galerie, 1992.

Jiří Trnka 1912–1969. Ed. Jana Brabcová. Prague: Národní galerie, 1992.

SČUG Hollar 1917–1992: současná grafika [The Hollar Graphic Art Society 1917–1992: contemporary graphic art]. František Dvořák, Josef Lhota, and Jiří Machalický. Prague: SČUG Hollar, 1992.

Otevírání zakletého zámku: Josip Plečnik a pražský hrad/Opening the Enchanted Castle: Josip Plečnik and the Prague Castle. Zdeněk Lukeš. Prague: Kancelář presidenta ČSFR/T91 magazine supplement, 1992.

"České korunovační klenoty" [The Czech crown jewels]. Leaflet, text by M. Bravermanová, published for exhibition at Prague Castle 29 Jan.–7 Feb. 1993. Prague: Odbor rozvoje pražského hradu, 1993.

Umění pro všechny smysly: meziválečná avantgarda v Československu [Art for all the senses: the interwar avant-garde in Czechoslovakia]. Ed. Jaroslav Anděl. Valencia: Ivam Centre Julio González/Prague: Národní galerie, 1993.

Karel Teige 1900–1951. Karel Srp and others. Prague: Galerie hlavního města Prahy, 1994.

Karel Teige: surrealistické koláže 1935–1951 [Karel Teige: surrealist collages 1935–1951]. Vojtěch Lahoda, Karel Srp, and Rumjana Dačeva. Prague: Středoevropská galerie, 1994.

Alphonse Mucha: Pastels, Posters, Drawings and Photographs—An Exhibition at the Imperial Stables, Prague Castle. Ed. Sarah Mucha. London: Mucha Foundation, 1994.

Navrácené poklady: restitutio in integrum [Returned treasures: restitutio in integrum]. Ed. Marie Mžyková. Prague: Pragafilm, 1994.

Na křižovatce Evropy: Karel Čapek a Penklub [At the crossroads of Europe: Karel Čapek and PEN]. Eva Wolfová et al. Prague: Památník Národního písemnictví, 1994.

Expresionismus a české umění 1905–1927 [Expressionism and Czech art 1905–1927]. Michal Bregant et al. Prague: Národní galerie, 1994.

Mezery v historii 1890–1938: polemický duch Střední Evropy—Němci, Židé, Češi [Gaps in history 1890–1938: the polemical spirit of Central Europe—Germans, Jews, Czechs]. Ed. Hana Rousová. Prague: Galerie hlavního města Prahy, 1994.

Czech Modern Art 1900–1960. Ed. Lenka Zapletalová. Guide to the permanent exhibition of the National Gallery's collection of modern Czech art in Veletržní palác. Prague: Národní galerie, 1995.

Otto Gutfreund. Texts by Jan Bauch et al. Prague: Národní galerie, 1995.

Keramická sbírka Hugo Vavrečky [The ceramics collection of Hugo Vavrečka]. Jana Kybalová. Prague: Uměleckoprůmyslové muzeum, 1995.

200 let Národní galerie [Two hundred years of the National Gallery]. Ed. Vít Vlnas. Prague: Národní galerie, 1996.

Obrazárna v Čechách [The picture-gallery in Bohemia]. Ed. Vít Vlnas. Prague: Národní galerie, 1996.

Dějiny v obrazech: historické náměty v umění 19. století v Čechách [History in pictures: historical subjects in nineteenth-century art in Bohemia]. Naděžda Blažíčková. Prague: Národní galerie, 1996.

Český surrealismus 1929–1953. Skupina surrealistů v ČSR: události, vztahy, inspirace [Czech surrealism 1929–1952. The Group of Surrealists in the Czechoslovak Republic: events, links, inspiration]. Ed. Lenka Bydžovská and Karel Srp. Prague: Galerie hlavního města Prahy/Argo, 1996.

Karel Teige: architettura, poesie—Praga 1900–1951. Texts (in Italian and English) by J. L. Cohen et al. Milan: Electa, 1996.

České imaginativní umění. František Šmejkal. Prague: Galerie Rudolfinum, 1996.

Slovanská epopej—historie Slovanstva v obrazech—Alfons Mucha [The Slav Epic—a history of Slavdom in pictures—Alfons Mucha]. Guide to the standing exhibition at the château in Moravský Krumlov. No author credited. Moravský Krumlov: Městské středisko v Moravském Krumlově, n.d.

OFFICIAL HISTORIES, FESTSCHRIFTEN AND COMMEMORATIVE LITERATURE
(*LISTED CHRONOLOGICALLY*)

Šubert, František Adolf. *Národní divadlo v Praze: dějiny jeho i stavba dokončená* [The National Theater in Prague: its history as well as its completed building]. Prague: Otto, 1881–83.

Müller, Josef, and Ferdinand Tallowitz, eds., *Památník vydaný na oslavu dvacetiletého trvání tělocvičné jednoty Sokola Pražského* [Memorial published in celebration of the gymnastic union Prague Sokol lasting twenty years]. Prague: Sokol, 1883.

Schwartz, František V., ed. *Památník Besedy měšťanské v Praze na oslavu padesátileté činnosti spolku 1845-6—1895-6* [Memorial of the Prague Burghers' Club in celebration of fifty years of the activity of the society 1845-6—1895-6]. Prague: Měšťanská beseda, 1896.

Pamětní list . . . k slavnosti položení základního kamene k Husovu pomníku [Memorial publication . . . for the celebration of the laying of the foundation stone for the Hus monument]. Texts by Svatopluk Čech, Josef Pekař, and others. Prague: Spolek pro zbudování "Husova pomníku," 1903.

Scheiner, Josef, ed. *Pátý slet všesokolský pořádaný v Praze . . . 1907* [The 5th all-Sokol festival in Prague . . . 1907]. Prague: Česká obec sokolská, 1907.

Jelínek, H., ed. *Padesát let Umělecké besedy* [Fifty years of Umělecká beseda]. Prague: Umělecká beseda, 1913.

Upomínka na oslavu Josefa Mánesa v roce 1920 [Souvenir of the celebration of Josef Mánes in the year 1920]. Includes texts of speeches by Max Švabinský and others. Prague: SVU Mánes, 1921.

Hýsek, Miloslav, and Karel B. Mádl, eds. *Alois Jirásek: sborník studií a vzpomínek na počest jeho sedmdesátých narozenin* [Alois Jirásek: a collection of studies and memoirs in honor of his seventieth birthday]. Prague: Otto, 1921.

Hiller, Jan, ed. *Památník VII. sletu všesokolského v Praze 1920* [Memorial of the 7th all-Sokol festival in Prague 1920]. Prague: Československá obec sokolská, 1923.

Šuman, V. *VIII. slet všesokolský v Praze 1926* [The 8th all-Sokol festival in Prague 1926]. Prague: V. Neubert, n.d.

Ebel, František, et al., eds. *Deset let Československé republiky* [Ten years of the Czechoslovak Republic]. 3 vols. Prague: Státní tiskárna, 1928.

Medek, Rudolf, ed. *K vítězné svobodě 1914—1918—1928* [Toward victorious liberty 1914—1918—1928]. Prague: Památník odboje, 1928.

Bělohlávek, Bedřich, ed. *Padesát let Zdeňka Nejedlého* [Fifty years of Zdeněk Nejedlý]. Prague: Bedřich Bělohlávek, 1928.

Dr. Kudrnáč, ed. *Jiráskův pohřeb a návrat do rodného Padolí* [Jirásek's funeral and return to his native Padolí]. Hronov: Družstvo pro postavení Jiráskova divadla v Hronově, 1930.

Honzáková, Albina, ed. *Československé studentky let 1890–1930* [Czechoslovak female students 1890–1930]. Prague: Ženská národní rada and Spolek "Minerva," 1930.

Procházka, Rudolf, ed. *Památník IX. sletu všesokolského v Praze 1932* [Memorial of the 9th all-Sokol festival in Prague 1932]. Prague: Československá obec sokolská, 1933.

Skácelík, F., ed. *Sedmdesát let Umělecké besedy* [Seventy years of Umělecká beseda]. Prague: Umělecká beseda, 1933.

Dějiny Národního divadla [History of the National Theater]. Vol. 1 (The building and its architects) by Jan Bartoš. Vol. 2 (The theater's artistic decorations) by Antonín Matějček. Vols. 3 and 6 (Opera to 1900 and 1900–18, respectively) by Zdeněk Nejedlý. Vol. 4 (Plays to 1900) by Otakar Fischer. Vol. 5 (Plays 1900–1918) by Václav Tille. Prague: Sbor pro zřízení druhého Národního divadla v Praze, 1933–36.

Domin, Karel, Václav Vojtíšek, and Josef Hutter. *Karolinum statek národní* [The Karolinum, a national property]. 2d ed. Prague: L. Mazáč, 1935.

Vojtíšek, Václav, ed. *Praha v obnoveném státě československém* [Prague in the renewed Czechoslovak state]. Prague: Rada hlavního města Prahy, 1936.

Procházka, Rudolf, ed. *Památník X. sletu všesokolského v Praze 1938* [Memorial of the 10th all-Sokol festival in Prague 1938]. Prague: Československá obec sokolská, 1939.

Mathesius, Vilém, ed. *Co daly naše země Evropě a lidstvu* [What our land gave to Europe and humanity]. Prague: Evropský literární klub, 1940.

Fröhlichová, Zdenka. *Kronika rynečku na Starém městě pražském* [Chronicle of the little square (Malé náměstí) in Prague's Old Town]. Prague: Rott, 1940.

Horák, Josef, and Ladislav Vachulka, eds. *Smetanův jubilejní rok 1944: program oslav v Praze* [The Smetana jubilee year 1944: program of celebrations in Prague]. Prague: Národní rada česká, 1944.

ELK 1935–1945 [European Literary Club 1935–1945]. Prague: Evropský literární klub, 1946. No editor credited.

Vojtíšek, Václav. *Karlova universita vždy jen naše* [Charles University, always only ours]. Brno: A. Píša, 1946.

Hájek, Karel. *Poslední cesta TGM* [Tomáš Garrigue Masaryk's last journey]. Prague: Orbis, 1947.

Svému osvoboditeli československý lid [The Czechoslovak people to its liberator]. No author credited. Prague: Orbis, 1955.

Wichterle, Otto, et al. *Sto let České akademie věd a umění* [One hundred years of the Czech Academy of Sciences and Arts]. Prague: Československá akademie věd, 1991.

Horáková, Ljuba, ed. *České korunovační klenoty: pamětní vydání ke vzniku České republiky MCMXCIII* [The Czech crown jewels: memorial publication for the foundation of the Czech Republic 1993]. Prague: Kancelář presidenta České republiky, 1993.

Katedrála sv. Víta: pamětní vydání k 650. výročí založení svatovítské katedrály [Saint Vitus's Cathedral: memorial publication for the 650th anniversary of the foundation of Saint Vitus's Cathedral]. Vol. 1, Ivo Hlobil, Petr Chotěbor, and Zdeněk Mahler, *Stavba* [Construction]. Vol. 2, Marie Kostílková, *Dostavba* [Completion]. Prague: Správa Pražského hradu, 1994.

Kreuzzieger, Milan, et al. *Obecní dům v Praze: historie a rekonstrukce* [Obecní dům in Prague: history and reconstruction]. Prague: Enigma, 1997.

ENCYCLOPEDIAS, BIOGRAPHICAL DICTIONARIES, DIRECTORIES, AND OTHER
WORKS OF REFERENCE (*LISTED CHRONOLOGICALLY*)

[Riegrův] *Slovník naučný* [(Rieger's) Encyclopedia]. 11 vols. Prague: Kober, 1860–74.

Ottův slovník naučný [Otto's Encyclopedia]. 27 vols. plus 1 supp. vol. Prague: Jan Otto, 1888–1909.

Národní album: sbírka podobizen a životopisů českých lidí [The national album: a collection of portraits and biographies of Czech people]. J. J. Benešovský-Veselý et al. Prague: Josef Vilímek, n.d. [1900].

Kronika královské Prahy a obcí sousedních [Chronicle of royal Prague and neighboring communities]. František Ruth. 3 vols. Prague: Pavel Körber, 1903.

Malý Ottův slovník naučný [Otto's Smaller Encyclopedia]. 2 vols. Prague: Otto, 1905–6.

Československá vlastivěda [Czechoslovak homeland-science]. 10 vols. in 13 parts. Prague: Sfinx, 1929–36.

Ottův slovník naučný nové doby [Otto's Contemporary Encyclopedia]. Uncompleted: 12 vols (A–Užok). Prague: Otto, from 1936 Novina, 1930–1943.

Kulturní adresář ČSR: biografický slovník žijících kulturních pracovníků a pracovnic [Cultural directory of the Czechoslovak Republic: a biographical dictionary of living men and women working in the cultural sphere]. Ed. Antonín Dolenský. Prague: Josef Zeibrdlich, 1934.

Atlas Republiky československé [Atlas of the Czechoslovak Republic]. Prague: Česká akademie věd a umění, 1935.

Přehledné dějiny literatury české od nejstarších dob po naše dny [Historical survey of Czech literature from the earliest times up to our own days]. Jan V. Novák and Arne Novák, 4th ed. Olomouc: R. Promberger, 1936–39.

Československo biografie [Czechoslovakia biography]. 2 vols. Prague: Státní tiskárna, 1939.

Naučný slovník aktualit 1939 [Dictionary of current affairs 1939]. Ed. Zdeněk Tobolka. Prague: L. Mazáč, 1939.

Původní názvy pražských ulic, nábřeží, nádraží a sadů podle stavu v r. 1938 [Original names of Prague streets, embankments, stations and parks as they were in 1938]. Prague: Česká obec turistická, 1945.

Seznam ulic, náměstí atd. hlavního města Prahy (stav k 1. květnu 1948) [List of streets, squares etc. of the capital city Prague (as of 1 May 1948)]. Prague: Dopravní podniky hl. m. Prahy, 1948.

Nový slovník československých výtvarných umělců [New dictionary of Czechoslovak creative artists]. Prokop Toman. Unchanged photoreprint of 3d edition of 1947–50. Ostrava: Chagall, 1993–94.

Dodatky ke slovníku československých výtvarných umělců [Supplement to the Dictionary of Czechoslovak creative artists]. Prokop Toman and Prokop H. Toman. Unchanged photoreprint of 1st ed. of 1955. Ostrava: Chagall, 1994.

Ulicemi města Prahy od 14. století do dneška [Through the streets of Prague from the 14th century to the present]. Jiří Čarek, Václav Hlavsa, Josef Janáček, and Václav Lím. Prague: Orbis, 1958.

Bibliografický soupis knih vydaných SNKLU v letech 1953–1962 [Bibliographic listing of books published by the State Publishing House for Belles-Lettres and Art 1953–

1962]. Zdenka Broukalová and Saša Mouchová. Prague: Státní nakladatelství krásné literatury a umění, 1964.

Přehled obcí a částí v ČSR, jejichž názvy zanikly, byly změněny. . . . [Directory of communities and (their) parts in the Czechoslovak Socialist Republic whose names became extinct, (or) were changed . . .]. Prague: Ústřední správa spojů, 1964.

Slovník českých spisovatelů [Dictionary of Czech writers]. Ed. Rudolf Havel and Jiří Opelík. Prague: Československý spisovatel, 1964.

Kulturně historické pamětní desky v Praze [Culturally historic commemorative plaques in Prague]. Maximilian Neutzler. Prague: Pražské středisko státní památkové péče a ochrany přírody, 1973.

Encyklopedie českého výtvarného umění [Encyclopedia of Czech fine art]. Emanuel Poche et al. Ústav teorie a dějin umění Československé akademie věd. Prague: Academia, 1975.

A Catalogue of Czechoslovak Coins. No author credited. Prague: Státní banka československá, 1975.

Pražské sochy a pomníky [Prague statues and memorials]. Milan Krejčí. Prague: Galerie hlavního města Prahy, 1979.

175 autorů: čeští prozaici, básníci a literární kritici publikující v 70. letech v nakladatelství Československý spisovatel [175 authors: Czech prose writers, poets and literary critics publishing with Československý spisovatel in the 1970s]. Ed. Petr Bílek. Prague: Československý spisovatel, 1982.

Česká opera a její tvůrci [Czech opera and its creators]. Ladislav Šíp. Prague: Supraphon, 1983.

Soupis repertoáru Národního divadla v Praze 1881–1983. Ed. Hana Konečná. 3 vols. Prague: Národní divadlo, 1983.

Opera on Record. Vol. 2, ed. Alan Blyth. London: Hutchinson, 1983.

Malá československá encyklopedie [Smaller Czechoslovak Encyclopedia]. Bohumil Kvasil, et al., eds. Encyklopedický institut Československé akademie věd. 6 vols. Prague: Academia, 1984–87.

Čeští spisovatelé 20. století: slovníková příručka [Czech writers of the twentieth century: a dictionary handbook]. Milan Blahynka et al. Prague: Československý spisovatel, 1985.

Slovník české literatury 1970–1981 [Dictionary of Czech literature 1970–1981]. Ed. Vladimír Forst. Ústav pro českou a světovou literaturu Československé akademie věd. Prague: Československý spisovatel, 1985.

Pražské metro [The Prague subway]. Josef Křivánek and Jaromír Vítek. Prague: Nakladatelství dopravy a spojů, 1987.

Specializovaná příručka pro sběratele československých poštovních známek a celin [Specialized handbook for collectors of Czechoslovak postage stamps and entires]. Alois Dušek et al. Prague: Svaz československých filatelistů, 1988.

Členové České akademie věd a umění [Members of the Czech Academy of Sciences and Arts]. Alena Šlechtová and Josef Levora. *Práce z dějin Československé akademie věd,* vol. 3, series B. Prague: Ústřední archiv Československé akademie věd, 1989.

Nemovité kulturní památky hlavního města Prahy: operativní seznam [Fixed cultural monuments of the capital city Prague: operational list]. 2 vols. Prague: Ústav státní památkové péče a ochrany přírody, 1990.

Slovník zakázaných autorů 1948–1980 [Dictionary of banned authors 1948–1980]. Jiří Brabec, Jiří Gruša, Igor Hájek, Petr Kabeš, and Jan Lopatka. Prague: Státní pedagogické nakladatelství, 1991. First published in samizdat, Edice Petlice, 1978, reprinted Toronto: Sixty-Eight Publishers, 1981.

Slovník českého románu 1945–1991 [Dictionary of the Czech novel 1945–1991]. Blahoslav Dokoupil *et al.* Ostrava: Sfinga, 1991.

Katalog Sixty-Eight Publishers. Prague: Společnost Josefa Škvoreckého, 1991.

Co je nového v Praze: nové názvy ulic, náměstí, nábřeží, sadů, mostů a stanic metra [What is new in Prague: new names of streets, squares, embankments, parks, bridges and subway stations]. No author credited. Prague: Gabriel, 1991.

Československá státní a vojenská symbolika [Czechoslovak state and military symbolics]. Zbyšek Svoboda. Prague: Federální ministerstvo obrany, 1991.

Česká a Slovenská literatura v exilu a samizdatu [Czech and Slovak literature in exile and samizdat]. Václav Burian et al. Olomouc: Hanácké noviny, 1991.

Československý biografický slovník [Czechoslovak biographical dictionary]. Josef Tomeš et al. Encyklopedický institut Československé akademie věd. Prague: Academia, 1992.

Nezávislá literatura a samizdat v Československu 70. a 80. let [Independent literature and samizdat in Czechoslovakia in the 1970s and 1980s]. Vilém Prečan. Prague: Ústav pro soudobé dějiny, 1992.

Zamlčovaní překladatelé: bibliografie 1948–1989 [Incognito translators: bibliography 1948–1989]. Zdeňka Rakůnková. Prague: Obec překladatelů/Ivo Železný, 1992.

Kdo byl kdo v našich dějinách do roku 1918 [Who was who in our history up to 1918]. Pavel Augusta et al. Prachatice: Rovina, 1992.

Knihy za ohradou: česká literatura v exilových nakladatelstvích 1971–1989 [Books beyond the pale: Czech literature in émigré publishing houses 1971–1989]. Jan Čulík. Prague: Trizonia, n.d. [1993].

Slovník české prózy 1945–1994 [Dictionary of Czech prose 1945–1994]. Blahoslav Dokoupil et al. Ostrava: Sfinga, 1994 (revised and expanded edition of their 1991 *Slovník českého románu*).

Československé mince 1918–1993/Mince České a Slovenské Republiky 1993–1994 [Czechoslovak coins 1918–1993/Coins of the Czech and Slovak Republics 1993–1994]. Vlastislav Novotný and Vlastimír Šimek. Hodonín: OB a ZP servis, 1994.

Nová encyklopedie českého výtvarného umění [New encyclopedia of Czech fine art]. Ed. Anděla Horová. 2 vols. Prague: Academia, 1995.

GUIDEBOOKS AND PHOTOGRAPHIC ALBUMS (*LISTED CHRONOLOGICALLY*)

Zap, Karel Vladislav. *Popsání hlavního města království českého* [A description of the capital city of the Czech kingdom]. Revised and enlarged edition. Prague: I. L. Kober, 1868.

Štyrský, Toyen, Nečas. *Průvodce Paříží a okolím* [Guide to Paris and its surrounds]. Prague: Odeon, 1927.

Lázňovský, Bohuslav, ed. *Průvodce po Československu* [Guide to Czechoslovakia]. Part 1, *Země česká a moravskoslezská* [The Bohemian and Moravian-Silesian land]. Prague: Klub československých turistů/Orbis, 1930.

Vojtíšek, Václav. *The Old Town Hall of Prague.* Prague: Corporation of Prague, 1936.

Wirth, Zdeněk. *Stará Praha: obraz města a jeho veřejného života v 2. polovici XIX. století podle původních fotografií* [Old Prague: a picture of the city and its public life in the second half of the nineteenth century according to original photographs]. Prague: Otto, 1942.

Zmizelá Praha [Vanished Prague]. Vol. 1, V. V. Štech, Zdeněk Wirth, and Václav Vojtíšek, *Staré a Nové město s Podskalím* [Old and New Towns, Podskalí]. Vol. 2, Cyril Merhout and Zdeněk Wirth, *Malá strana a Hradčany*. Vol. 3, Hana Volavková, *Židovské město pražské* [The Prague Jewish town]. Vol. 4, Emanuel Poche and Zdeněk Wirth, *Vyšehrad a zevní okresy Prahy* [Vyšehrad and outer districts of Prague]. Vol. 5, Zdeněk Wirth, *Opevnění, Vltava a ztráty na památkách 1945* [Fortifications, the Vltava, and damage to historic monuments in 1945]. Vol. 6, Antonín Novotný, *Grafické pohledy 1493–1850* [Views in graphic art 1493–1850]. Prague: Václav Poláček, 1945–48.

Nový průvodce po Československu [New guide to Czechoslovakia]. Vol. 1, part 1, *Čechy: Praha, jižní Čechy a jihozápad středních Čech* [Bohemia: Prague, Southern Bohemia and South-Western Central Bohemia]. No author or editor credited. Prague: Orbis, 1950.

Kubíček, Alois. *Betlémská kaple v Praze* [The Bethlehem Chapel in Prague]. Prague: Státní tělovýchovné nakladatelství, 1953.

Hlavsa, Václav. *Praha: průvodce městem* [Prague: a guide to the city]. Prague: Sportovní a turistické nakladatelství, n.d. [c. 1956].

Scheufler, Pavel. *Praha 1848–1914: čtení nad dobovými fotografiemi* [Prague 1848–1914: readings on contemporary photographs]. Prague: Panorama, 1984.

———. *Fotografické album Čech 1830–1914* [Photographic album of Bohemia 1830–1914]. Prague: Odeon, 1989.

Emanuel Poche, *Praha krok za krokem* [Prague step by step]. 2d ed. Prague: Panorama, 1985.

Všetečka, Jiří, and Petr Klučina. *Praha husitská* [Hussite Prague]. Prague: Naše vojsko, 1986.

Rybár, Ctibor, et al. *Co je co v Praze* [What's what in Prague]. Prague: ČTK/Pressfoto, 1989.

Sršeň, Lubomír. *Budova Národního muzea v Praze 1891–1991: architektura, umělecká výzdoba a původní uměleckořemeslné vybavení* [The National Museum building in Prague 1891–1991: architecture, artistic decoration and original craftwork]. Prague: Národní muzeum, 1991.

Tryml, Michal. *Staroměstské náměstí*. Prague: Oswald, 1991.

Nechvátal, Bořivoj. *Vyšehradský hřbitov* [Vyšehrad cemetery]. Prague: Národní kulturní památka Vyšehrad, 1991.

Rybár, Ctibor, et al. *Židovská Praha: glosy k dějinám a kultuře; průvodce památkami* [Jewish Prague: glosses on history and culture; guide to monuments]. Prague: TV Spektrum/Akropolis, 1991.

James, Hilary A. and Jiří P. Musil. *Prague, My Love: An Unusual Guide Book to the Hidden Corners of Prague*. Prague: Crossroads of Prague, 1992.

Bregant, Michal, et al. *Kubistická Praha/Cubist Prague 1909–1925*. Prague: Středoevropské nakladatelství, 1995.

Margolius, Ivan. *Prague: A Guide to Twentieth-Century Architecture*. London: Ellipsis, 1996.

LITERARY WORKS (*LISTED ALPHABETICALLY BY AUTHOR*)

Andersen, Hans Christian. *Fairy Tales*. Illustrated by Jiří Trnka. London: Hamlyn, 1959.

Apollinaire, Guillaume. *Alcools: Poems by Guillaume Apollinaire*. Trans. Donald Revell. Hanover, N.H., and London: Wesleyan University Press, 1995.

Bezruč, Petr. *Slezské písně* [Silesian songs]. Brno: Nový lid, 1928.

Borovský, Karel Havlíček. *Stokrát plivni do moře* [Spit a hundred times into the sea]. Prague: Československý spisovatel, 1990.

Brousek, Antonín, ed. *Podivuhodní kouzelníci: čítanka českého stalinismu v řeči vázané z let 1945–1955* [Marvelous magicians: a reader of Czech Stalinism in verse from the years 1945–1955]. London: Rozmluvy, 1987.

Čapek, Josef. *Povídání o pejskovi a kočičce, jak spolu hospodařili a ještě o všelijakých jiných věcech* [Stories about Doggie and Pussycat, how they kept house together and about all sorts of other things as well]. Prague: Albatros, 1992.

———. *All About Doggie and Pussycat, How They Kept House and All Sorts of Other Things as Well*. Trans. Lucy Doležalová. Prague: Albatros, 1996.

Čapek, Karel. *Spisy* [Writings]. Vol. 24, *Básnické počátky—překlady* [Poetic beginnings—translations]. Prague: Český spisovatel, 1993.

———. *Dashenka, or, the Life of a Puppy*. Trans. M. and R. Weatherall. London: Allen and Unwin, 1933.

———. *The Mother*. Trans. Paul Selver. London: Allen and Unwin, 1939.

———. *R. U. R*. Trans. Paul Selver. New York: Washington Square Press, 1973.

———. *War with the Newts*. Trans. Ewald Osers. London: Unwin, 1985.

Čech, Svatopluk. *Adamité* [The Adamites]. Prague: Šimáček, 1897.

Čelakovský, František Ladislav. *Ohlas písní ruských/Ohlas písní českých* [An echo of Russian songs/An echo of Czech songs]. Prague: Orbis, 1948.

Éluard, Paul. *Selected Poems*. Trans. Gilbert Bowen. London: Calder, 1987.

Erben, Karel Jaromír. *Prostonárodní písně a říkadla* [Folk songs and rhymes]. Prague: Evropský literární klub, 1937.

Halas, František. *Životem umřít* [To die by living]. Prague: Československý spisovatel, 1989.

Hanka, Václav. *Polyglotta králodvorského rukopisu* [Multilingual edition of the Dvůr Králové manuscript]. Prague: F. Řivnáč, 1876.

Hašek, Jaroslav. *The Good Soldier Švejk*. Trans. Cecil Parrott. London: Penguin, 1973.

Hrabal, Bohumil. *Too Loud a Solitude*. Trans. Michael Henry Heim. New York: Harcourt Brace Jovanovich, 1990.

Jirásek, Alois. *Na ostrově* [On the island]. Prague: Svoboda, 1948.

———. *Psohlavci* [The Dogheads]. Prague: Československý spisovatel, 1980.

———. *Staré pověsti české* [Old Czech legends]. Prague: Papyrus, 1992.

———. *Old Czech Legends*. Trans. Marie K. Holeček. London and Boston: UNESCO/ Forest Books, 1992.

Klíma, Ivan. *Love and Garbage*. Trans. Ewald Osers. London: Penguin, 1991.

Komenský [Comenius], Jan Amos. *The Labyrinth of the World and the Paradise of the Heart*. Trans. Count Lützow. New York: Dutton, 1901; reprinted New York: Arno Press, 1971.

Kundera, Milan. *Člověk zahrada širá* [Man the expansive garden]. Prague: Československý spisovatel, 1953.

————. *Poslední máj* [The last May]. 2d rev. ed. Prague: Československý spisovatel, 1961.

————. *The Book of Laughter and Forgetting*. Trans. Henry Michael Heim. London: Faber, 1982.

————. *The Joke*. Trans. Henry Michael Heim. London: Penguin, 1984.

————. *The Unbearable Lightness of Being*. Trans. Michael Henry Heim. New York: Harper, 1985.

————. *Life is Elsewhere*. Trans. Peter Kussi. London: Penguin, 1986.

Lustig, Arnošt. *The Street of Lost Brothers*. Trans. Vera Borkovec, Jeanne Němcová, and Josef Lustig. Evanston, Ill.: Northwestern University Press, 1990.

————. *Dita Saxova*. Revised and expanded edition. Trans. Jeanne Němcová. Evanston, Ill.: Northwestern University Press, 1993.

Mácha, Karel Hynek. *Dílo Karla Hynka Máchy* [Work of Karel Hynek Mácha]. 2 vols. Prague: Československý spisovatel, 1986.

Němcová, Božena. *Babička* [Grandma]. Prague: Unie, 1913 (reprint of jubilee edition of 1903).

————. *Národopisné a cestopisné obrazy ze Slovenska* [Ethnographic and travel pictures from Slovakia]. Prague: Státní nakladatelství krásné literatury, hudby a umění, 1955.

Neruda, Jan. *Prague Tales*. Trans. Michael Henry Heim; intro. Ivan Klíma. London: Chatto and Windus, 1993.

Neumann, Stanislav Kostka. *Československá cesta II.-III.: karpatské léto, český podzim* [Czechoslovakian journey II–III: Carpathian summer, Bohemian autumn]. Prague: Borový, 1935.

Nezval, Vítězslav. *Abeceda* [Alphabet]. Dance composition by Milča Mayerová, typography and photomontage by Karel Teige. Photoreprint of first edition of 1926. Prague: Torst, 1993.

Pluhař, Zdeněk. *Opustíš-li mne* [If you leave me]. Prague: Československý spisovatel, 1985.

Rukopis královédvorský a Rukopis zelenohorský [The Dvůr Králové and Zelená Hora manuscripts]. Ed. J. Karlík and V. Seykora. Prague: Rukopisný fond vědecký, 1936.

Seifert, Jaroslav. *Osm dní* [Eight days]. 2d ed. Prague: Československý spisovatel, 1968.

————. *Eight Days: An Elegy for Thomas Masaryk*. Trans. Paul Jagasich and Tom O'Grady. Iowa City, Iowa: The Spirit That Moves Us Press, 1985.

————. *The Selected Poetry of Jaroslav Seifert*. Trans. Edward Osers. New York: Collier, 1987.

Škvorecký, Josef. *The Miracle Game*. Trans. Paul Wilson. Toronto: Lester and Orpen Dennys, 1990.

Těsnohlídek, Rudolf. *The Cunning Little Vixen*. Trans. Tatiana Firkusny, Maritza Morgan, and Robert T. Jones. New York: Farrar, Straus and Giroux, 1985.

Vaculík, Ludvík. *Morčata* [The guinea pigs]. Prague: Československý spisovatel, 1991.

Weil, Jiří. *Žalozpěv na 77,297 obětí* [Elegy for 77,297 victims]. Prague: Československý spisovatel, 1958.

————. *Život s hvězdou/Na střeše je Mendelssohn* [Life with a star/Mendelssohn is on the roof]. Prague: Československý spisovatel, 1990.

————. *Moskva—hranice* [Moscow—the border]. Prague: Mladá fronta, 1991.

————. *Dřevěná lžíce* [The wooden spoon]. Prague: Mladá fronta, 1992.

Wolker, Jiří. *Čtení z Jiřího Wolkera* [Readings from Jiří Wolker]. Ed. Antonín Dokoupil. Prague: Václav Petr, 1925.

SCHOOL TEXTBOOKS AND READERS (*LISTED CHRONOLOGICALLY*)

Caha, Arnošt, ed. *Jirásek české mládeži* [Jirásek to Czech youth]. Brno: Ústřední spolek učitelský na Moravě a ve Slezsku, 1921.

Pekař, Josef. *Dějiny československé* [Czechoslovak history]. Prague: Akropolis, 1991 (first published 1921).

Dohnal, Miloň, and Leoš Stolařík. *Dějepis: pro 9. ročník základní devítileté školy* [History: for ninth grade in elementary school]. Prague: Státní pedagogické nakladatelství, 1970.

Dohnal, Miloň. *Dějepis: pro 9. ročník základní devítileté školy* [History: for ninth grade in elementary school]. Prague: Státní pedagogické nakladatelství, 1975.

Jelínek, Jaroslav, et al. *Český jazyk pro třetí ročník* [Czech for grade 3]. Prague: Státní pedagogické nakladatelství, 1979.

Dějiny zemí koruny české [History of the lands of the Czech crown]. Vol. 1, *Od příchodu Slovanů do roku 1740* [From the arrival of the Slavs to 1740], ed. Petr Čornej. Vol. 2, *Od nástupu osvícenství po naši dobu* [From the ascent of the Enlightenment to our time], ed. Pavel Bělina and Jiří Pokorný. Prague: Paseka, 1992.

MAPS, ALBUMS OF REPRODUCTIONS, SONGBOOKS, COOKBOOKS, RECORD ALBUMS, AND OTHER MISCELLANEA (*LISTED CHRONOLOGICALLY*)

"Bohemia Newly described by John Speed. Anno dom: 1626. Are to be sold in popshead Alley by G. Humble." William C. Wonders Map Collection, University of Alberta.

Rettigová, Magdaléna Dobromila. *Domácí kuchařka* [Home cookery]. Reprint of 4th edition of 1844. Prague: Odeon, 1986.

Album Františka Kupky [František Kupka album]. Ed. Karl Eugen Schmidt. Prague: B. Kočí, n.d. [1904?].

Peřin, František J., ed. *Národní zpěvník* [National songbook]. Prague: B. Stýblo, n.d. [c. 1918–20].

Jesenská, Milena. *Mileniny recepty* [Milena's recipes]. Prague: Nakladatelství Franze Kafky, 1995.

Čapek, Josef. *Dějiny zblízka: soubor satirických kreseb* [History close up: a miscellany of satirical drawings]. Prague: Borový, 1949.

Aleš, Mikoláš. *Špalíček národních písní a říkadel* [A bundle of national songs and rhymes]. Prague: Orbis, 1950.

————. *Boj našeho lidu za svobodu* [The struggle of our people for freedom]. Folder of reproductions, ed. Jaromír Neumann. Prague: Orbis, 1952.

Karbusický, Vladimír, and Jaroslav Vanický, eds., *Český revoluční zpěvník* [Czech revolutionary songbook]. Prague: Státní nakladatelství krásné literatury, hudby a umění, 1953.

Volavková, Hana, ed. *Dětské kresby na zastávce k smrti: Terezín 1942–1944* [Children's drawings on the way station to death: Terezín 1942–1944]. Prague: Státní židovské muzeum, 1959.

Songs of Czechoslovakia. RCA record album VIC 1383 (1969). Sleeve notes by Jan Masaryk.

Drawings of Mucha. No editor credited. New York: Dover, 1978.

Červinková-Riegrová, Marie. Libretto to Antonín Dvořák, *Jakobín*, with Supraphon record album set 1112 2481/3 (1980).

Páleníček, Ludvík, ed. *Švabinského český slavín* [Švabinský's Czech pantheon]. Prague: Státní pedagogické nakladatelství, 1985.

Kytice písní společenských/Czech Revival Male Choruses. Supraphon record album 1112 4095G (1987). Sleeve notes.

Marta Kubišová: songy a balady. Supraphon record album 10 0587–1311 (1990). Lyrics of song "Modlitba pro Martu," by J. Brabec and P. Rada.

Jarmila Novotná: české písně a arie/Czech Songs and Arias. Supraphon compact disk 11 1491–2201 (1992). Sleeve notes by Jan Králík.

Dehner, Jan, ed. *Antonín Dvořák: Jakobín*, theater program, Národní divadlo. Prague: 1993.

Kolář, Jiří. *Týdeník 1968* [Weekly 1968]. Prague: Torst, 1993.

Jiří Suchý, *Jen pro pány: pojednání o zadních partiích žen, slečen, dívek a holek* [For gentlemen only: a treatise on the hinder parts of women, misses, young ladies and girls]. Prague: Klokočí, 1994.

Č.S. 1894–1994. Illustrated brochure, no author credited. Prague: Česká spořitelna, 1994.

De Silva, Cara, ed. *In Memory's Kitchen: A Legacy from the Women of Terezín.* Northvale, N.J.: Jason Aronson, 1996.

Various inscriptions on buildings, gravestones, and monuments, as in the notes.

BIOGRAPHICAL LITERATURE *(LISTED ALPHABETICALLY BY AUTHOR)*

Brod, Max. *Franz Kafka: A Biography.* New York: Schocken, 1963.

Buber-Neumann, Margarete. *Mistress to Kafka: The Life and Death of Milena.* London: Secker and Warburg, 1966.

———. *Kafkova přítelkyně Milena.* Prague: Mladá fronta, 1992.

Černá, Jana. *Adresát Milena Jesenská* [Addressee Milena Jesenská]. Prague: Concordia, 1991.

Dvořáková, Zora. *Miroslav Tyrš: prohry a vítězství* [Miroslav Tyrš: defeats and victories]. Prague: Olympia, 1989.

Jirásková, Marie. *Stručná zpráva o trojí volbě: Milena Jesenská, Joachim von Zedtwitz a Jaroslav Nachtmann v roce 1939 a v čase následujícím* [A short report on three choices: Milena Jesenská, Joachim von Zedtwitz and Jaroslav Nachtmann in 1939 and in the time that came after]. Prague: Nakladatelství Franze Kafky, 1996.

Karl, Frederick. *Franz Kafka: Representative Man. Prague, Germans, Jews and the Crisis of Modernism.* New York: Ticknor and Fields, 1991.

Kosatík, Pavel. *Osm žen z hradu* [Eight women from the Castle]. Prague: Mladá fronta, 1993.

Mádl, Karel B. *Mikoláš Aleš.* Prague: SVU Mánes, 1911.

Marková-Kotyková, Marta. *Mýtus Milena: Milena Jesenská jinak* [The myth Milena: Milena Jesenská otherwise]. Prague: Primus, 1993.

Morava, Jiří. *C. k. disident Karel Havlíček* [Imperial-Royal Dissident Karel Havlíček]. Prague: Panorama, 1991.

Mucha, Jiří. *Kankán se svatozáří: život a dílo Alfonse Muchy* [Can-can with a halo: the life and work of Alfons Mucha]. Prague: Obelisk, 1969.

———. *Alphonse Maria Mucha: His Life and Art*. New York: Rizzoli, 1989.

———. *Alfons Mucha*. Prague: Mladá fronta, 1994.

Nejedlý, Zdeněk. *Bedřich Smetana*. In his *Spisy Zdeňka Nejedlého* [Writings of Zdeněk Nejedlý], vols. 21–27. Prague: Orbis, 1950–54.

Novotný, Miloslav, ed. *Roky Aloisa Jiráska* [The years of Alois Jirásek]. Prague: Melantrich, 1953.

Opelík, Jiří. *Karel Čapek ve fotografii* [Karel Čapek in photographs]. Prague: Středočeské nakladatelství, 1991.

Páleníček, Ludvík. *Max Švabinský: život a dílo na přelomu epoch* [Max Švabinský: life and work at the turn of epochs]. Prague: Melantrich, 1984.

Ravik, Slavomír. *K. H. Borovský: portrét bojovníka* [Karel Havlíček Borovský: portrait of a fighter]. Prague: Pražská imaginace, 1991.

———. *Karel Sabina (portrét konfidenta)* [Karel Sabina: portrait of an informer]. Prague: Pražská imaginace, 1992.

Štech, V. V. *Aleš a Slovensko* [Aleš and Slovakia]. Bratislava: Tvar, 1952.

Tomášek, Dušan, and Robert Kvaček, *Causa Emil Hácha* [The case of Emil Hácha]. Prague: Themis, 1995.

Vaněk, Vladimír. *Jan Masaryk*. Prague: Torst, 1994.

Vlašínová, Drahomíra. *Eliška Krásnohorská*. Prague: Melantrich, 1987.

Vondráčková, Jaroslava. *Kolem Mileny Jesenské* [Around Milena Jesenská]. Prague: Torst, 1991.

Wagnerová, Alena. *Milena Jesenská*. Prague: Prostor, 1996.

CHRONICLES, HISTORIES, MONOGRAPHS, AND ARTICLES (*LISTED ALPHABETICALLY BY AUTHOR OR EDITOR*)

Althshuler, Bruce. *The Avant-Garde in Exhibition: New Art in the Twentieth Century*. New York: Abrams, 1994.

Augusta, Pavel, and František Honzák. *Sto let Jubilejní* [100 years of the Jubilee Exhibition]. Prague: Státní nakladatelství technické literatury, 1991.

Bergerová, Natalia, ed. *Na křižovatce kultur: historie československých Židů* [At the crossroads of cultures: A history of Czechoslovak Jews]. Prague: Mladá fronta, 1992.

Bláhová, Marie, ed. *Kronika tak řečeného Dalimila* [The chronicle of so-called Dalimil]. Prague: Svoboda, 1977.

———. *Kroniky doby Karla IV.* [Chronicles from the time of Charles IV]. Prague: Svoboda, 1987.

Bohatcová, Mirjam et al. *Česká kniha v proměnách staletí* [The Czech book in the metamorphoses of the centuries]. Prague: Panorama, 1990.

Borkovský, Ivan et al. *Dějiny Prahy* [History of Prague]. Prague: Nakladatelství politické literatury, 1964.

Brabcová, Jana. *Luděk Marold*. Prague: Odeon, 1988.

Bradley, J. F. N. *Czechoslovakia: A Short History*. Edinburgh: Edinburgh University Press, 1971.

Brock, Peter, and H. Gordon Skilling, eds. *The Czech Renascence of the Nineteenth Century*. Toronto: University of Toronto Press, 1970.

Brod, Toman, Miroslav Kárný, and Margita Kárná, eds. *Terezínský rodinný tábor v Osvětimi-Birkenau* [The Terezín family camp in Auschwitz-Birkenau]. Prague: Terezínská iniciativa/Melantrich, 1994.

Buben, Václav, ed. *Šest let okupace Prahy* [Six years of occupation of Prague]. Prague: Osvětový odbor hlavního města Prahy/Orbis, 1946.

Buchner, Alexandr. *Opera v Praze* [Opera in Prague]. Prague: Panton, 1985.

Buchvaldek, Miroslav et al. *Dějiny Československa v datech* [History of Czechoslovakia in dates]. Prague: Svoboda, 1968.

Buriánek, František et al., eds. *17. listopad* [17 November]. Prague: Orbis, 1945.

Burkhardt, Francois, Claude Eveno, and Boris Podrecca, eds. *Jože Plečnik Architect: 1872–1957*. Cambridge, Mass.: MIT Press, 1989.

Čermín, Jakub et al. *17. listopad 1939 po 55 letech* [17 November 1939 after 55 years]. Brno: Doplněk, 1994.

Černý, František, general editor. *Dějiny českého divadla* [History of the Czech theater]. 4 vols, 1. Beginnings. 2. National revival. 3. Plays 1848–1918. 4. The Czechoslovak Republic and the Nazi occupation. Prague: Academia, 1965–83.

Císařovský, Josef. *Oto Gutfreund*. Prague: SNKLU, 1962.

Cohen, Gary B. *The Politics of Ethnic Survival: Germans in Prague: 1861–1914*. Princeton, N.J.: Princeton University Press, 1981.

Denis, Arnošt [Ernest]. *Čechy po Bílé hoře* [Bohemia after the White Mountain]. 2 vols. Prague: Bursík a Kohout, 1905.

Dobrovský, Josef. *Dějiny české řeči a literatury* [History of Czech language and literature]. Trans. from first German edition of 1792. Prague: Československý spisovatel, 1951.

Ellridge, Arthur. *Mucha: The Triumph of Art Nouveau*. Paris: Terrail, 1992.

Formánek, Václav. *Josef Lada*. Prague: Odeon, 1980.

Frankensteinová, Hana. *Max Švabinský: dílo 1924–1948* [Max Švabinský: work 1924–1948]. Prague: Orbis, 1949.

French, Alfred. *The Poets of Prague*. Oxford: Oxford University Press, 1969.

Galík, Josef et al. *Panorama české literatury: literární dějiny od počátku do současnosti* [A panorama of Czech literature: a literary history from the beginning to the present]. Olomouc: Rubico, 1994.

Hanak, Harry, Robert R. Pynsent, and Stanley B. Winters, eds. *T. G. Masaryk (1850–1937)*. 3 vols. London: Macmillan, 1990.

Hanuš, Josef. *Národní museum a naše obrození* [The National Museum and our rebirth]. Prague: Národní museum, 1921.

Haubelt, Josef. *České osvícenství* [The Czech Enlightenment]. Prague: Svoboda, 1986.

Heller, Servác. *Jubileum velké doby: obraz našeho národního rozmachu před padesáti lety* [A jubilee of a great time: a portrait of our national upsurge fifty years ago]. Prague: Pražská akciová tiskárna, 1918.

Hilmera, Jiří. *Stavovské národu! O tom, jak se Stavovské divadlo stalo součástí divadla Národního* [The Estates to the nation! On how the Estates Theater became a part of the National Theater]. Prague: Stavovské divadlo, 1991.

Hlaváček, Ivan, ed. *Ze zpráv a kronik doby Husitské* [From reports and chronicles of the Hussite period]. Prague: Svoboda, 1981.

Hlaváček, Luboš et al. *Současné české a slovenské umění* [Contemporary Czech and Slovak art]. Prague: Odeon/Bratislava: Tatran, 1985.

Hlavačka, Milan. *Jubilejní výstava 1891* [The Jubilee Exhibition of 1891]. Prague: Techkom, 1991.

Hojda, Zdeněk, and Jiří Pokorný. *Pomníky a zapomníky* [Memorials and forgetorials (sic)]. 2d edition. Prague: Paseka, 1997.

Horáková, Luba, and Magdalena Propperová, eds. *Josip Plečnik: architekt Pražského hradu* [Josip Plečnik: architect of Prague Castle]. Prague: Správa Pražského hradu, 1997.

Horská, Pavla. *Prague—Paris*. Prague: Orbis, 1990.

Horský, Zdeněk. *Pražský orloj* [The Prague horologe]. Prague: Panorama, 1988.

Ivanov, Miroslav. *Justiční vražda aneb smrt Milady Horákové* [Judicial murder or the death of Milada Horáková]. Prague: Betty, 1991.

Janišová, Milena, ed. *Osud Židů v Protektorátu 1939–1945* [The fate of Jews in the Protectorate 1949–1945]. Prague: Trizonia/Ústav pro soudobé dějiny, 1991.

Kaplan, Karel. *Československo v letech 1945–1948* [Czechoslovakia in the years 1945–1948]. Prague: Státní pedagogické nakladatelství, 1991.

———. *Stát a církev v Československu 1948–1953* [State and church in Czechoslovakia 1948–1953]. Brno: Doplněk, 1993.

Kárný, Miroslav. *"Konečné řešení": genocida českých Židů v německé protektorátní politice* [The "final solution": the genocide of Czech Jews in German Protectorate politics]. Prague: Academia, 1991.

Kárný, Miroslav, and Vojtěch Blodig, eds. *Terezín v konečném řešení židovské otázky* [Terezín in the final solution of the Jewish question]. Prague: Logos, 1992.

Kieval, Hillel J. *The Making of Czech Jewry: National Conflict and Jewish Society in Bohemia 1870–1918*. New York: Oxford University Press, 1988.

Kop, František. *Národní museum: památník našeho kulturního obrození* [The National Museum: monument of our cultural rebirth]. Prague: Družstvo vlast, 1941.

———. *Založení University Karlovy v Praze* [The founding of Charles University in Prague]. Prague: Atlas, 1945.

Kosmas. *Kosmova kronika česká* [Kosmas's Czech chronicle]. Ed. Marie Bláhová and Zdeněk Fiala. Prague: Svoboda, 1972.

Kotalík, Jiří, ed. *Národní galerie* [The National Gallery]. Prague: Odeon, 1984.

Kovtun, Jiří. *Tajuplná vražda: případ Leopolda Hilsnera* [A murder full of mysteries: the case of Leopold Hilsner]. Prague: Sefer, 1994.

Kropáč, František, and Vlastimil Louda. *Persekuce českého studentstva za okupace* [Persecution of Czech students during the occupation]. Prague: Ministerstvo vnitra/Orbis, 1945.

Kroutvor, Josef. *Poselství ulice: z dějin plakátu a proměn doby* [The message of the street: a history of the poster and changing times]. Prague: Comet, 1991.

Kubíšek, Alois. *Betlémská kaple* [The Bethlehem Chapel]. Prague: Státní nakladatelství krásné literatury, hudby a umění, 1960.

Kulka, Erich. *Židé v československé Svobodově armádě* [The Jews in Svoboda's Czechoslovak army]. Prague: Naše vojsko, 1990.

Kusák, Dalibor, and Marta Kadlečíková. *Mucha*. Prague: BB/Art, 1992.

Lamač, Miroslav. *František Kupka*. Prague: Odeon, 1984.

————. *Osma a Skupina výtvarných umělců 1907–1917* [The Eight and the Group of Creative Artists 1907–1917]. Prague: Odeon, 1988.

Lang, Jaromír. *Neumannův Červen* [Neumann's *Červen*]. Prague: Orbis, 1957.

Lass, Andrew. "Presencing, Historicity and the Shifting Voice of Written Relics in 18th-Century Bohemia." *Bohemica*, vol. 28, no. 1 (1987).

————. "Romantic Documents and Political Monuments: The Meaning-fulfillment of History in 19th-century Czech Nationalism." *American Ethnologist*, vol. 15, no. 3 (1988).

————. "What Keeps the Czech Folk 'Alive'?" *Dialectical Anthropology*, vol. 14, no. 1 (1989).

Lenikowski, Wojciech, ed. *East European Modernism: Architecture in Czechoslovakia, Hungary and Poland Between the Wars*. London: Thames and Hudson, 1996.

Loriš, Jan. *Mánesův orloj* [Mánes's horologe]. Prague: Orbis, 1952.

Macura, Vladimír. *Šťastný věk: symboly, emblémy a mýty 1948–1989* [The happy age: symbols, emblems and myths 1948–1989]. Prague: Pražská imaginace, 1992.

Margolius, Ivan. *Cubism in Architecture and the Applied Arts: Bohemia and France 1910–1914*. Newton Abbot: David and Charles, 1979.

Matějček, Antonín, and František Žákavec. *Dílo Josefa Mánesa* [The work of Josef Mánes]. Vol. 1 (Antonín Matějček), *Národní písně* [National songs]. Vol. 2 (František Žákavec), *Lid československý* [The Czechoslovak people]. Vol. 3 (Antonín Matějček), *Rukopis Královédvorský* [The Dvůr Králové manuscript]. Prague: Jan Štenc, 1928 (2d ed.), 1923, 1927, respectively.

Maur, Eduard. *Kozina a Lomikar* [Kozina and Lomikar]. Prague: Melantrich, 1989.

Míčko, Miroslav. *Výtvarné dědictví rukopisů* [The artistic heritage of the manuscripts]. Prague: Vyšehrad, 1940.

Míčko, Miroslav, and Emanuel Svoboda. *Dílo Mikoláše Alše* [The work of Mikoláš Aleš]. Vol. 3, *Nástěnné malby* [Murals]. Prague: Státní nakladatelství krásné literatury a umění, 1964.

Míka, Zdeněk et al. *Dějiny Prahy v datech* [History of Prague in dates]. Prague: Panorama, 1988.

Moulis, Miroslav. *Lidice žijí* [Lidice lives]. Prague: Středočeské nakladatelství, 1972.

Mráz, Bohumír, and Marcela Mrázová. *Secese* [The Secession]. Prague: Obelisk, 1971.

Nadeau, Maurice. *The History of Surrealism*. Cambridge, Mass.: Belknap Press of Harvard University Press, 1989.

Nejedlý, Zdeněk. *Dějiny husitského zpěvu* [History of Hussite song]. Vol. 1, *Zpěv předhusitský* [Pre-Hussite song]. In *Spisy Zdeňka Nejedlého* [Writings of Zdeněk Nejedlý], vol. 40. Prague: Československá akademie věd, 1954.

Novák, Arne. *Czech Literature*. Ed. and with a supplement by William E. Harkins; trans. Peter Kussi. Ann Arbor: Michigan Slavic Publications, 1976 [translation of Novák's chapter in *Československá vlastivěda*, vol. 7, 1933, as updated by Antonín Grund in 1946].

Obrazová, Pavla, and Jan Vlk. *Maior gloria: svatý kníže Václav* [Maior gloria: the holy prince Václav]. Prague: Paseka, 1994.

Otruba, Mojmír, ed. *Rukopisy královédvorský a zelenohorský: dnešní stav poznání* [The Dvůr Králové and Zelená Hora manuscripts: the state of knowledge today]. *Sborník Národního muzea*, Řada C, vol. 13, nos 1–5. Prague: Národní muzeum/Academia, 1969.

Palacký, František. *Dějiny národu českého v Čechách a v Moravě* [History of the Czech nation in Bohemia and Moravia]. 6 vols. Prague: Kvasnička a Hampl, 1939.

Pečírka, Jaromír. *Josef Mánes: živý pramen národní tradice* [Josef Mánes: a living source of the national tradition]. Prague: SVU Mánes/Melantrich, 1939.

Pekař, Josef. *Žižka a jeho doba* [Žižka and his time]. Prague: Odeon, 1992.

Pěkný, Tomáš. *Historie Židů v Čechách a na Moravě* [History of the Jews in Bohemia and Moravia]. Prague: Sefer, 1993.

Peroutka, Ferdinand. *Budování státu* [The building of a state]. 4 vols. Prague: Lidové noviny, 1991.

Petráň, Josef. *Staroměstská exekuce* [The Old Town execution]. Prague: Mladá fronta, 1971.

Pfaff, Ivan. *Česká levice proti Moskvě 1936–1938* [The Czech left against Moscow 1936–1938]. Prague: Naše vojsko, 1993.

Poche, Emanuel et al. *Čtvero knih o Praze* [A quartet of books on Prague]. Vol. 1, *Praha středověká* [Medieval Prague]. Vol. 2, *Praha na úsvitu nových dějin* [Prague at the dawn of modern history]. Vol. 3, *Praha národního probuzení* [Prague in the national awakening]. Vol. 4, *Praha našeho věku* [Prague in our time]. Prague: Panorama, 1978–88.

Podiven [pseudonym for Petr Pithart, Petr Příhoda, and Milan Otáhal]. *Češi v dějinách nové doby (pokus o zrcadlo)* [The Czechs in modern history: an attempt at a mirror]. Prague: Rozmluvy, 1991.

Poggio-Bracciolini [i.e., Bracciolini, Poggio], *Mistr Jan Hus na Koncilu kostnickém, Jeho výslech, odsouzení a upálení dne 6. července 1415* [Master Jan Hus at the Council of Konstanz: his interrogation, sentencing and immolation on 6 July 1415]. Illustrations by Jan Dědina and Alfons Mucha. Prague: Otto, 1902.

Půlpán, Karel. *Nástin českých a československých hospodářských dějin do roku 1990* [An outline of Czech and Czechoslovak economic history to 1990]. 2 vols. Prague: Univerzita Karlova, 1993.

Rennert, Jack, and Alain Weill. *Alphonse Mucha: The Complete Posters and Panels*. Boston: G. K. Hall, 1984.

Sayer, Derek (Anonymous) note on the Pinkas synagogue, Prague, under title "Fact of the Issue," in *Journal of Historical Sociology*, vol. 5, no. 3 (1992).

———. "Prague as a Vantage-Point on Modern European History." *METU Studies in Development*, vol. 22, no. 3 (1995).

———. "The Language of Nationality and the Nationality of Language: Prague 1780–1920." *Past and Present*, no. 151 (1996).

———. "Contemporaneities." Forthcoming in *Common Knowledge*.

Schonberg, Michal. *Osvobozené* [Liberated]. Prague: Odeon, 1992.

Seton-Watson, R. W. *A History of the Czechs and Slovaks*. New York: Hutchinson, 1943.

Škvorecký, Josef. "Bohemia of the Soul." *Daedalus*, vol. 119, no. 1, 1990.

Slavík, Jaroslav, and Jiří Opelík. *Josef Čapek*. Prague: Torst, 1996.

Smetana, Robert, ed. *Dějiny české hudební kultury* [History of Czech musical culture]. Vol. 2, 1918–1945. Prague: Academia, 1981.

Smetana, Vladimír. "František Palacký: průkopník českého naučného slovníku" [František Palacký: pioneer of a Czech encyclopedia]. *Malá řada Encyklopedického institutu ČSAV*. Prague: Československá akademie věd, 1969.

Staněk, Tomáš. *Odsun Němců z Československa 1945–1947* [The expulsion of the Germans from Czechoslovakia 1945–1947]. Prague: Academia/Naše vojsko, 1991.

Švácha, Rostislav. *Od moderny k funkcionalismu: proměny pražské architektury první poloviny dvacátého století* [From modernism to functionalism: transformations in Prague architecture in the first half of the twentieth century]. Prague: Victoria Publishing, 1995.

Taylor, A. J. P. *The Habsburg Monarchy, 1809–1918*. London: Penguin, 1990.

Thiele, Vladimír, ed. *Josef Čapek a kniha: soupis knižní grafiky* [Josef Čapek and the book: a listing of his graphic art for books]. Prague: Nakladatelství československých výtvarných umělců, 1958.

Tomek, Václav Vladivoj. *Dějepis města Prahy* [History of the city of Prague]. 12 vols., various editions. Prague: František Řivnáč, 1879–1905.

———. *Jan Žižka*. Prague: V ráji, 1993 (photoreprint of Otto edition of 1879).

Vachtová, Ludmila. *František Kupka*. Prague: Odeon, 1968.

Vaško, Václav. *Neumlčená kronika katolické církve v Československu po druhé světové válce* [Unsilenced chronicle of the Catholic Church in Czechoslovakia after World War II]. 2 vols. Prague: Zvon, 1990.

Vlček, Tomáš. *Praha 1900: studie k dějinám kultury a umění Prahy v letech 1890–1914* [Prague 1900: a study in the history of the culture and art of Prague in the years 1890–1914]. Prague: Panorama, 1986.

Volavková, Hana. *Dílo Mikoláše Alše* [The work of Mikoláš Aleš]. Vol. 11, *Ilustrace české poezie a prózy* [Illustration of Czech poetry and prose]. Prague: Státní nakladatelství krásné literatury a umění, 1964.

———. *Josef Mánes: malíř vzorků a ornamentu* [Josef Mánes: painter of designs and decoration]. Prague: Odeon, 1981.

———. *Max Švabinský*. Prague: Odeon, 1982.

Petr Wittlich, *Česká secese* [The Czech Secession]. Prague: Odeon, 1985.

———. *Umění a život—doba secese* [Life and art—the time of the Secession]. Prague: Artia, 1987.

———. *Prague: fin de siècle*. Paris: Flammarion, 1992.

Žákavec, František. *Max Švabinský*. Prague: Jan Štenc, 1933.

Zap, Karel Vladislav. *Česko-Moravská kronika* [Czech-Moravian chronicle]. Prague: I. L. Kober, 1862.

Žemla, Josef. *Historie sloupu Mariánského na Staroměstském náměstí* [History of the Mary column in the Old Town Square]. Pamphlet, Knihovna 28. října. Prague: V. Rytíř, 12 Nov. 1918.

INDEX

Page numbers in italics refer to illustrations.

About the Author

Derek Sayer is Professor of Sociology at the University of Alberta in Edmonton. He is the author of several books, including (with Philip Corrigan) *The Great Arch: English State Formation as Cultural Revolution*.